The Complete MEDITERRANEAN DIET COOKBOOK for Beginners 2022

1000+ Quick and Health Recipes to Increase Longevity and Lose Weight | 28 Day Kickstart Meal Plan to Change your Eating Lifestyle

Alicia Travis

Author Bio

Alicia Travis is a cook and expert in Mediterranean cuisine, she began her career in Lousiana attending several cooking courses, in 2007 she decided to change and improve herself moving for a few months to Europe, where she lived working in several restaurants, before in Greece and then in Italy where she developed her love for Mediterranean cuisine. Today she runs two restaurants in Dubai and this book collects all the best recipes she has experimented and tried over many years of studying and learning.

Table of Contents

Chapter 2: Sides, Salads, and Soups
..................................**42**

Chapter 5 Fish and Seafood.......... 133

Chapter 6 Fruits and Desserts 157

Chapter 9 Dinner 230

INTRODUCTION

THE MEDITERRANEAN DIET: A LIFESTYLE

It has been object of many studies and one of the most exported (and copied) intangible assets of the Mediterranean: we are talking about the Mediterranean diet!
This diet is not just a set of ingredients and recommended food, but a real lifestyle based on good habits derived from the food tradition of the countries overlooking the Mediterranean Sea, including Italy, Spain and Greece.
Nowadays, bringing unrefined cereals, vegetables, and fruit to the table for our meals seems normal, but it results from long years of spreading the Mediterranean diet.
This is how the Mediterranean diet, the most popular in the world, was born
What if we told you that the Mediterranean diet was actually studied and systematized by an American scholar? Yes, at the beginning of the 1950's, the American biologist and physiologist Ancel Keys carefully analyzed the diet of the populations of the Mediterranean Basin, comparing it with other countries' diets.
The famous Seven Countries Study, conducted by Keys, was based on the observation of the eating habits and lifestyles of seven countries (United States, Finland, Holland, Italy, Greece, Japan and former Yugoslavia), with the objective of understanding their effects on the well-being of those populations, with a particular focus on the incidence of cardiovascular diseases. The research lasted for decades and allowed for a detailed and careful comparison of the seven different diets, highlighting that:
- in the countries of northern Europe the most common foods were milk, potatoes, animal fats and sweets;
- the United States were characterized by a high consumption of meat, fruit and sweets;

- in Italy, the extensive use of cereals (especially in the form of bread and pasta) and wine was evident; - in former Yugoslavia the most common foods were bread, vegetables and fish;
- in Greece, the consumption of olive oil and fruit was prevalent;
- in Japan people mainly ate fish, rice and products derived from soy.

Keys' research showed that a diet based on the consumption of cereals, vegetables, fruit, fish and olive oil was by far a better alternative to the typical American and Northern European diets, too rich in fats, animal proteins and sugars.
In 2013 the Mediterranean diet became part of the Unesco World Heritage as an intangible asset of humanity. Its principles are summarized in a food pyramid that illustrates the quantity and frequency of how food should be consumed throughout the day.
At the base of the pyramid that summarizes the Mediterranean diet, we find the food to be consumed a lot of times a day, while at the top we find the food that should be eaten less often during the week.

The characteristics of the Mediterranean diet
The Mediterranean diet is characterized by a series of elements to be consumed daily in well-defined proportions, in order to obtain a balanced diet that includes all the macronutrients, distributed approximately in the following proportion: 60% carbohydrates, 25-30% fats, 10-15% proteins.
The foods to be eaten daily are 3 portions of unrefined cereals, such as pasta, rice and bread, but also spelt or oat, 3 portions of fruit, 6 portions of vegetables.
Yogurt and milk can be consumed every day, while cheese shouldn't be eaten more than twice a week.

Vegetable proteins, such as the ones contained in legumes, are by far preferable to the animal ones. The consumption of meat, with a preference for the white one, should be limited to once or twice a week, while it is recommended to eat fish from 3 to 4 times a week.

As for fats, in the Mediterranean diet, up to a maximum of 3 servings per day are allowed, with a preference for fats containing mono-unsaturated acids, above all olive oil.

In particular, the Mediterranean diet involves eating:

- Vegetables, herbs and spices;
- Fruit;
- Nuts and seeds;
- Legumes;
- Potatoes;
- Whole-grain food, bread;
- Fish, seafood;
- Extra virgin olive oil in abundance;
- Poultry, eggs;
- Fish;
- Cheese;
- Milk and yogurt (once a day, alternately);
- Red meat, rarely (maximum once/twice a week).

Within this book, you will learn over 1000 easy-to-prepare Mediterranean recipes, which are divided into:

-Breakfast and Snacks Recipes, for starting your day in the right way with a fantastic, tasty, and healthy meal every day;

-Sides, Salads, and Soups, so that you will always know what to cook to complement your main dishes, and enrich them with excellent side dishes or salads;

-Vegetable Recipes, so that you will discover many different ways to prepare and cook your greens, based on the Italian, Greek, Spanish, and French cuisine;

-Poultry and Meat Recipes, so that you will have plenty of choices when it comes to deciding what to have as a main dish in your meal;

-Fish and Seafood Recipes, that you will easily be able to replicate at home to enjoy one of the healthiest foods ever cooked in many different ways;

-A 28-Day Kick-Start Meal Plan designed for different calories needs, to promote a healthy and lasting weight loss - forget forever all the frustrating yo-yo diet cycles.

— CHAPTER 1 —

BREAKFAST

ALICIA TRAVIS

Warm Bulgur Breakfast Bowls with Fruits

Preparation time: 10 minutes |
Cooking time: 15 minutes | **Servings:** 6
Ingredients:
2 cups unsweetened almond milk
1½ cups uncooked bulgur
2 cups water
½ teaspoon ground cinnamon
2 cups frozen (or fresh, pitted) dark sweet cherries
8 dried (or fresh) figs, chopped
½ cup chopped almonds
¼ cup loosely packed fresh mint, chopped
Directions:
Combine the milk, bulgur, water, and cinnamon in a medium saucepan, stirring, and bring just to a boil. Low the heat to medium-low and allow to simmer for 10 minutes, or until the liquid is absorbed. Lower the heat and stir in the frozen cherries (no need to thaw), figs, and almonds. Cover and let the hot bulgur thaw the cherries and partially hydrate the figs, for about 1 minute. Fold in the mint and stir to combine, then serve.
Nutrition facts (per serving)
calories: 207 | fat: 6.0g | protein: 8.0g | carbs: 32.0g | fiber: 4.0g | sodium: 82mg

Marinara Poached Eggs

Preparation time: 4 minutes | **Cooking time:** 15 minutes | **Servings:** 6
Ingredients:
1 tablespoon extra-virgin olive oil
1 cup chopped onion
2 garlic cloves, minced
(14.5-ounce / 411-g) cans no-salt-added Italian diced tomatoes, undrained
6 large eggs
½ cup chopped fresh flat-leaf parsley
Directions:
Preheat the oil in a skillet over medium-high heat. Add the onion and sauté for 6 minutes, stirring occasionally. Add garlic and cook for 2-3 mins more. Pour the tomatoes with their juices over the onion mixture and cook for 2 to 3 minutes until bubbling. Reduce the heat to medium and use a large spoon to make six indentations in the tomato mixture. Crack the eggs into each indentation. Cook for 7/9 minutes, or until the eggs are cooked to your preference. Serve with the parsley sprinkled on top.
Nutrition facts (per serving)
calories: 89 | fat: 6.0g | protein: 4.0g | carbs: 4.0g | fiber: 1.0g | sodium: 77mg

Spinach Cheese Pie

Preparation time: 10 minutes |

Cooking time: 30 minutes | **Servings:** 8
Ingredients:
2 tablespoons extra-virgin olive oil
1 onion, chopped
1 pound (454 g) frozen spinach, thawed
¼ teaspoon ground nutmeg
¼ teaspoon garlic salt
¼ teaspoon freshly ground black pepper
4 large eggs, divided
1 cup grated Parmesan cheese, divided
2 puff pastry doughs, at room temperature
4 hard-boiled eggs, halved
Nonstick cooking spray
Directions:
Preheat the oven to 360°F (170 °C). Spritz a baking sheet with nonstick cooking spray and set aside. Heat a large skillet over medium-high heat. Add the oil and onion and sauté for about 5 minutes, stirring occasionally, or until translucent. Squeeze the excess water from the spinach. Add to the skillet and cook, uncovered, so that any excess water from the spinach can evaporate. Season with the nutmeg, garlic salt, and black pepper. Remove from heat and set to cool. Beat 3 eggs in a small bowl. Add the beaten eggs and ½ cup Parmesan cheese to the spinach mixture, stirring well. Roll out the pastry dough on the prepared baking sheet. Layer the spinach mixture on the top of the dough, leaving 2 inches around each edge. Once the spinach is spread onto the pastry dough, evenly place the hard-boiled egg halves throughout the pie, then cover with the second pastry dough. Pinch the edges closed. Beat the remaining 1 egg in the bowl. Brush the egg wash over the pastry dough. Bake in the preheated oven for 15 to 20 minutes until golden brown. Sprinkle with the remaining ½ cup Parmesan cheese. Cool for 3-6 minutes before cutting and serving.
Nutrition facts (per serving)
calories: 417 | fat: 28.0g | protein: 17.0g | carbs: 25.0g | fiber: 3.0g | sodium: 490mg

Baked Ricotta with Honey Pears

Preparation time: 5 minutes | **Cooking time:** 22 to 25 minutes | **Servings:** 4
Ingredients:
1 (1-pound / 454-g) container whole-milk ricotta cheese
2 large eggs
¼ cup whole-wheat pastry flour
1 tablespoon sugar
1 teaspoon vanilla extract
¼ teaspoon ground nutmeg
1 pear, cored and diced
2 tablespoons water
1 tablespoon honey
Nonstick cooking spray
Directions:
Heat the oven to 390°F (195°C). Spray four ramekins with nonstick cooking spray. Beat together the ricotta,

eggs, flour, sugar, vanilla, and nutmeg in a large bowl until combined. Spoon the mixture into the ramekins. Bake in the oven for 20 to 24 minutes, or until the ricotta is just set. Meanwhile, in a medium-small saucepan over medium-high heat, simmer the pear in the water for 10 minutes, or until slightly softened. Take off from the heat and stir in the honey. Remove the ramekins from the oven and cool slightly on a wire rack. Top the ricotta ramekins with the pear and serve.

Nutrition facts (per serving)
calories: 329 | fat: 19.0g | protein: 17.0g | carbs: 23.0g | fiber: 3.0g | sodium: 109mg

›Cinnamon Pistachio Smoothie

Preparation time: 5 minutes |
Cooking time: 0 minutes | **Servings:** 1
Ingredients:
½ cup unsweetened almond milk
½ cup plain Greek yogurt
Zest and juice of ½ orange
1 tablespoon extra-virgin olive oil
1 tablespoon shelled pistachios, coarsely chopped
¼ to ½ teaspoon ground allspice
¼ teaspoon vanilla extract
¼ teaspoon ground cinnamon
Directions:
In a blender, combine ½ cup almond milk, yogurt, orange zest and juice, olive oil, pistachios, allspice, vanilla, and cinnamon. It must be creamy and smooth, add almond milk to achieve your desired consistency. Serve chilled.

Nutrition facts (per serving)
calories: 264 | fat: 22.0g | protein: 6.0g | carbs: 12.0g | fiber: 2.0g | sodium: 127mg

›Breakfast Pancakes with Berry Sauce

Preparation time: 3 minutes |
Cooking time: 15 minutes | **Servings:** 4
Ingredients:
Pancakes:
1 cup almond flour
1 teaspoon baking powder
¼ teaspoon salt
6 tablespoon extra-virgin olive oil, divided
3 large eggs, beaten
Zest and juice of 1 lemon
½ teaspoon vanilla extract
Berry Sauce:
1 cup frozen mixed berries
1 tablespoon water, plus more as needed
½ teaspoon vanilla extract
Directions:
Pancakes
In a medium-large bowl, combine the almond flour, baking powder, and salt and stir to break up any clumps. Add 4 tablespoons olive oil, beaten eggs, lemon zest and juice, and vanilla extract and stir until well mixed. Heat 1 and a half tablespoon of olive oil

in a skillet. Spoon about 2 and a half tablespoons of batter for each pancake. Cook until bubbles begin to form, 5 to 6 minutes. Flip and cook for another 2 to 3 minutes. Repeat with the remaining 1 and half tablespoon of olive oil and batter.
Make the Berry Sauce
Combine the frozen berries, water, and vanilla extract in a small saucepan and heat over medium-high heat for 3 to 4 minutes until bubbly, adding more water as needed. Using the back of a spoon or fork, mash the berries and whisk until smooth.
Serve the pancakes with the berry sauce.

Nutrition facts (per serving)
calories: 275 | fat: 26.0g | protein: 4.0g | carbs: 8.0g | fiber: 2.0g | sodium: 271mg

›Banana Corn Fritters

Preparation time: 5 minutes |
Cooking time: 12 minutes | **Servings:** 2
Ingredients:
½ cup yellow cornmeal
¼ cup flour
2 small ripe bananas, peeled and mashed
2 tablespoons unsweetened almond milk
1 large egg, beaten
½ teaspoon baking powder
¼ to ½ teaspoon ground chipotle chili
¼ teaspoon ground cinnamon
¼ teaspoon sea salt
1 tablespoon olive oil
Directions:
Stir the ingredients except for the olive oil in a large bowl until smooth. Heat a nonstick skillet over medium-high heat. Add the olive oil and drop about 2 tablespoons of batter for each fritter. Cook for 2 to 3 minutes until the bottoms are golden brown, then flip. Cook for 2 minutes more, until cooked through. Repeat with the remaining batter. Serve warm.

Nutrition facts (per serving)
calories: 396 | fat: 10.6g | protein: 7.3g | carbs: 68.0g | fiber: 4.8g | sodium: 307mg

›Apple-Tahini Toast

Preparation time: 5 minutes |
Cooking time: 0 minutes | **Servings:** 1
Ingredients:
2 slices whole-wheat bread, toasted
2 tablespoons tahini
1 small apple of your choice, cored and thinly sliced
1 teaspoon honey
Directions:
Spread the tahini on the toasted bread. Place the apple slices on the bread and drizzle with the honey. Serve immediately.

Nutrition facts (per serving)
calories: 458 | fat: 17.8g | protein: 11.0g | carbs: 63.5g | fiber: 10.5g | sodium: 285mg

Avocado Smoothie

Preparation time: 5 minutes |
Cooking time: 0 minutes | **Servings:** 2
Ingredients:
1 large avocado
1½ cups unsweetened coconut milk
2 tablespoons honey
Directions:
All the ingredients must go in a blender and blend until smooth and creamy. Serve immediately.
Nutrition facts (per serving)
calories: 686 | fat: 57.6g | protein: 6.2g | carbs: 35.8g | fiber: 10.7g | sodium: 35mg

Savory Breakfast Oatmeal

Preparation time: 10 minutes |
Cooking time: 10 minutes | **Servings:** 2
Ingredients:
½ cup steel-cut oats
1 cup water
1 medium cucumber, chopped
1 large tomato, chopped
1 tablespoon olive oil
Pinch freshly grated Parmesan cheese
Sea salt and freshly ground pepper
Flat-leaf parsley or mint, chopped, for garnish
Directions:
Combine the water and sauce in a medium saucepan and bring to a boil over high heat, stirring continuously, or until the water is absorbed, about 15 minutes. Divide the oatmeal between 2 bowls and scatter the tomato and cucumber on top. Add the olive oil and sprinkle with the Parmesan cheese. Season with salt and pepper to taste. Serve garnished with the parsley.
Nutrition facts (per serving)
calories: 197| fat: 8.9g | protein: 6.3g | carbs: 23.1g | fiber: 6.4g | sodium: 27mg

Feta and Olive Scrambled Eggs

Preparation time: 5 minutes |
Cooking time: 5 minutes | **Servings:** 2
Ingredients:
4 large eggs
1 tablespoon unsweetened almond milk
Sea salt and freshly ground pepper
1 tablespoon olive oil
¼ cup crumbled feta cheese
10 Kalamata olives, pitted and sliced
Small bunch fresh mint, chopped, for garnish
Directions:
Combine the eggs in a bowl. Add the milk and a pinch of sea salt and whisk well. Heat a medium non-stick skillet over medium heat and add the olive oil. Use a egg mixture and stir constantly, or until they just begin to curd and firm up, about 2 minutes. Add the feta cheese and olive slices and stir until evenly combined. Season to taste with salt and pepper. Split the

mixture between 2 plates and serve garnished with the fresh chopped mint.
Nutrition facts (per serving)
calories: 244 | fat: 21.9g | protein: 8.4g | carbs:3.5g | fiber: 0.6g | sodium: 339mg

Cheesy Breakfast Muffins

Preparation Time: 15 minutes |
Cooking Time: 12 minutes | **Servings:** 6
Ingredients:
4 tablespoons melted butter
3/4 tablespoons baking powder
1 cup almond flour
2 large eggs
2 ounces cream cheese
2 tablespoons heavy whipping cream
A handful of shredded Mexican blend cheese
Directions:
Preheat the oven to 400°F. Grease 6 muffin tin cups with melted butter and set aside. Combine the baking powder and almond flour in a bowl. Stir well and set aside.Stir together four tablespoons melted butter, eggs, shredded cheese, and cream cheese in a separate bowl. The egg and the dry mixture must be combined using a hand mixer to beat until it is creamy and well blended. The mixture must be scooped into the greased muffin cups evenly. Baking time: 12 minutes
Nutrition facts:
Calories: 214
Fat: 15.6g
Fiber: 3.1g
Carbohydrates: 5.1 g
Protein: 9.5 g

Spinach, Mushroom, and Goat Cheese Frittata

Preparation Time: 15 minutes
Cooking Time: 20 minutes
Servings: 5
Ingredients:
2 tablespoons olive oil
1 cup fresh mushrooms, sliced
6 bacon slices, cooked and chopped
1 cup spinach, shredded
10 large eggs, beaten
1/2 cup goat cheese, crumbled
Pepper and salt
Directions:
Preheat the oven to 350°F. Heat oil and add the mushrooms and fry for 3 minutes until they start to brown, stirring frequently. Fold in the bacon and spinach and cook for about 1 to 2 minutes, or until the spinach is wilted. Slowly pour in the beaten eggs and cook for 3 to 4 minutes. Making use of a spatula, lift the edges for allowing uncooked egg to flow underneath.
Top with the goat cheese, then sprinkle the salt and pepper to season. Bake in the preheated oven for about 15 minutes until lightly golden brown around

the edges.
Nutrition facts:
Calories: 265
Fat: 11.6g
Fiber: 8.6g
Carbohydrates: 5.1 g
Protein: 12.9g

➤Yogurt Waffles

Preparation Time: 15 minutes
Cooking Time: 25 minutes
Servings: 5
Ingredients:
1/2 cup golden flax seeds meal
3 tablespoons almond flour
1 and 1/2 tablespoons granulated Erythritol
1 tablespoon unsweetened vanilla whey protein powder
1/4 teaspoon baking soda
1/2 teaspoon organic baking powder
1/4 teaspoon xanthan gum
Salt, as required
1 large organic egg, white and yolk separated
1 organic whole egg
2 tablespoons unsweetened almond milk
11/2 tablespoons unsalted butter
3 ounces plain Greek yogurt
Directions:
Pre-heat the waffle iron and then grease it. In a large bowl, add the flour, Erythritol, protein powder, baking soda, baking powder, xanthan gum, salt, and mix until well combined.In another bowl or container, put in the egg white and beat until stiff peaks form.
In a third bowl, add two egg yolks, whole egg, almond milk, butter, yogurt, and beat until well combined. Place egg mixture into the bowl of the flour mixture and mix until well combined. Gently, fold in the beaten egg whites. Place 1/5 cup of the mixture in preheated waffle iron and cook for about 4–5 minutes or until golden brown. Repeat with the remaining mixture. Serve warm.
Nutrition facts:
Calories: 265
Fat: 11.5g
Fiber: 9.5g
Carbohydrates: 5.2g
Protein: 7.5g

➤Green Vegetable Quiche

Preparation Time: 20 minutes
Cooking Time: 20 minutes
Servings: 4
Ingredients:
6 organic eggs
1/2 cup unsweetened almond milk
Salt and ground black pepper, as required
2 cups fresh baby spinach, chopped
Half a cup green bell pepper, seeded and chopped

1 scallion, chopped
1/4 cup fresh cilantro, chopped
1 tablespoon fresh chives, minced
3 tablespoons mozzarella cheese, grated
Directions:
Preheat your oven to 400°F. Lightly grease a pie dish. In a bowl, add eggs, almond milk, salt, and black pepper, and beat until well combined. Set aside. In another bowl, add the vegetables and herbs and mix well. At the bottom of the prepared pie dish, place the veggie mixture evenly and top with the egg mixture.Let bake for about 20 min. Remove the quiche from the oven and immediately sprinkle with the Parmesan cheese. Set aside for about 5 minutes before slicing. Cut into desired sized wedges and serve warm.
Nutrition facts:
Calories: 298
Fat: 10.4g
Fiber: 5.9g
Carbohydrates: 4.1 g
Protein: 7.9g

➤Cheesy Broccoli Muffins

Preparation Time: 15 minutes
Cooking Time: 20 minutes
Servings: 6
Ingredients:
2 tablespoons unsalted butter
6 large organic eggs
1/2 cup heavy whipping cream
1/2 cup Parmesan cheese, grated
Salt and ground black pepper, as required
11/4 cups broccoli, chopped
2 tablespoons fresh parsley, chopped
1/2 cup Swiss cheese, grated
Directions:
Grease a 12-cup muffin tin. In a bowl or container, put in the cream, eggs, Parmesan cheese, salt, and black pepper, and beat until well combined. Divide the broccoli and parsley in the bottom of each prepared muffin cup evenly. Top with the egg mixture, followed by the Swiss cheese. Let the muffins bake for about 19 minutes, rotating the pan once halfway through. Carefully, invert the muffins onto a serving platter and serve warm.
Nutrition facts:
Calories: 241
Fat: 11.5g
Fiber: 8.5g
Carbohydrates: 4.1 g
Protein: 11.1g

➤Berry Chocolate Breakfast Bowl

Preparation Time: 10 minutes
Cooking Time: 0 minutes
Servings: 2
Ingredients:
1/2 cup strawberries, fresh or frozen

1/2 cup blueberries, fresh or frozen
1 cup unsweetened almond milk
Sugar-free maple syrup to taste
2 tbsp. unsweetened cocoa powder
1 tbsp. cashew nuts for topping

Directions:

The berries must be divided into four bowls, pour on the almond milk. Drizzle with the maple syrup and sprinkle the cocoa powder on top, a tablespoon per bowl. Top with the cashew nuts and enjoy immediately.

Nutrition facts:

Calories: 287
Fat: 5.9g
Fiber: 11.4g
Carbohydrates: 3.1 g
Protein: 4.2g

›Goat Cheese Frittata

Preparation Time: 15 minutes
Cooking Time: 15 minutes
Servings: 4
Ingredients:
1 tbsp. avocado oil for frying
2 oz. (56 g) bacon slices, chopped
1 red bell pepper
1 small yellow onion, chopped
2 scallions, chopped
1 tbsp. chopped fresh chives
Salt and black pepper to taste
8 eggs, beaten
1 tbsp. unsweetened almond milk
1 tbsp. chopped fresh parsley
3 1/2 oz. (100 g) goat cheese, divided 3/4 oz. (20 g) grated Parmesan cheese

Directions:

Let the oven preheat to 350°F/175°C. Heat the avocado oil in a medium cast-iron pan and cook the bacon for 5 minutes or golden brown. Stir in the bell pepper, onion, scallions, and chives. Cook for 3 to 4 minutes or until the vegetables soften. Season with salt and black pepper.

In a bowl or container, the eggs must be beaten with the almond milk and parsley. Pour the mixture over the vegetables, stirring to spread out nicely. Share half of the goat cheese on top. Once the eggs start to set, divide the remaining goat cheese on top, season with salt, black pepper, and place the pan in the oven— Bake for 5 to 6 minutes or until the eggs set all around. Take out the pan, scatter the Parmesan cheese on top, slice, and serve warm.

Nutrition facts:

Calories: 412
Fat: 15.4g
Fiber: 11.2g
Carbohydrates: 4.9 g
Protein: 10.5g

›Fluffy Chocolate Pancakes

Preparation Time: 15 minutes
Cooking Time: 12 minutes
Servings: 4
Ingredients:
2 cups (250 g) almond flour
2 tsp. baking powder
2 tbsp. Erythritol
3/4 tsp. salt
2 eggs
1 1/3 cups (320 ml) almond milk
2 tbsp. butter + more for frying Topping:
2 tbsp. unsweetened chocolate buttons
Sugar-free maple syrup
4 tbsp. semi-salted butter

Directions:

In a bowl or container, mix the almond flour, baking powder, Erythritol, and salt. Whisk the eggs, almond milk, and butter in another bowl. Combine in the dry ingredients and mix well. Melt about 1 1/2 tablespoon of butter in a non-stick skillet, pour in portions of the batter to make small circles, about two pieces per batch (approximately 1/4 cup of batter each). Sprinkle some chocolate buttons on top and cook for 1 to 2 minutes or until set beneath. Turn the pancakes and cook for one more minute or until set. Remove the pancakes onto a plate and make more with the remaining ingredients. Work with more butter and reduce the heat as needed to prevent sticking and burning. Drizzle the pancakes with some maple syrup, top with more butter (as desired), and enjoy!

Nutrition facts:

Calories: 384
Fat: 12.9g
Fiber: 5.4g
Carbohydrates: 7.5 g

›Almond Banana Bread

Preparation time: 10 minutes
Cooking time: 4 hours
Servings: 2
Ingredients:
1 egg
2 tablespoons butter, melted
½ cup sugar
1 cup flour
½ teaspoon baking powder
¼ teaspoon baking soda
A pinch of cinnamon powder
A pinch of nutmeg, ground
2 bananas, mashed
¼ cup almonds, sliced
Cooking spray

Directions:

In a bowl, mix sugar with flour, baking powder, baking soda, cinnamon and nutmeg and stir. Add egg, butter, almonds and bananas and stir really well. Grease your slow cooker with cooking spray, pour bread mix, cover and cook on Low for 4 hours. Slice bread and serve for breakfast. Enjoy!

Nutrition facts:
Calories 211,
Fat 3,
Fiber 6,
Carbs 12, Protein 5

›Sage Potato Casserole

Preparation time: 10 minutes
Cooking time: 3 hours and 30 minutes
Servings: 2
Ingredients:
1 teaspoon onion powder
2 eggs, whisked
½ teaspoon garlic powder
½ teaspoon sage, dried
Salt and black pepper to taste
½ yellow onion, chopped
1 tablespoons parsley, chopped
2 garlic cloves, minced
A pinch of red pepper flakes
½ tablespoon olive oil
2 red potatoes, cubed

Directions:
Grease your slow cooker with the oil, add potatoes, onion, garlic, parsley and pepper flakes and toss a bit. In a bowl, mix eggs with onion powder, garlic powder, sage, salt and pepper, whisk well and pour over potatoes. Cover, cook on High for 3 hours and 30 minutes, divide into 2 plates and serve for breakfast. Enjoy!

Nutrition facts:
Calories 218,
Fat 6,
Fiber 6,
Carbs 14, Protein 5

›APPLE AND MILLET MUFFINS

Preparation time: 10 minutes
Cooking time: 50 minutes
Servings: 2
Ingredients:
2 Fuji apples, cored and grated
1 C. sunflower seeds
½ tsp. fresh lemon zest, grated finely
¾ C. fresh apple juice
1 C. uncooked millet
¾ C. raisins
2 tbsp. fresh lemon juice
Directions:
Preheat the oven to 350 °F. Grease a 12 cups muffin pan. In a bowl, add ingredients except apple juice and mix until well combined. Put the mixture into prepared muffin cups. Drizzle each muffin cup with 1 tbsp. of apple juice. With foil pieces, cover the muffin cups and bake for about 30 minutes. Remove the foil pieces and bake for about 20 minutes more. Remove the

muffin pan from the oven and place onto a wire rack to for about 10 minutes. Invert the muffins onto wire rack and serve warm.
Enjoy!
Nutrition facts:
Calories 145,
Fat 4,
Fiber 7,
Carbs 27,
Protein 10

›Cream Cheese Banana Breakfast

Preparation time: 10 minutes
Cooking time: 4 hours
Servings: 2
Ingredients:
½ French baguette, sliced
2 bananas, sliced
2 ounces cream cheese
1 tablespoon brown sugar
¼ cup walnuts, chopped
1 egg, whisked
3 tablespoons skim milk
2 tablespoons honey
½ teaspoon cinnamon powder
A pinch of nutmeg, ground
¼ teaspoon vanilla extract
1 tablespoon butter
Cooking spray
Directions:
Spread cream cheese on all bread slices and grease your slow cooker with cooking spray. Arrange bread slices in your slow cooker, layer banana slices, brown sugar and walnuts. In a bowl, mix eggs with skim milk, honey, cinnamon, nutmeg and vanilla extract, and whisk and add over bread slices. Add butter, cover, cook on Low for 4 hours, divide between plates and serve for breakfast. Enjoy!
Nutrition facts:
Calories 251,
Fat 5,
Fiber 7,
Carbs 12, Protein 4

›CHERRY PANCAKES

Preparation time: 10 minutes
Cooking time: 20 minutes
Servings: 2
Ingredients:
1 tsp. unsalted margarine
1/8 tsp. ground cinnamon
3 eggs
1 tbsp. unsalted margarine, melted
2 C. fresh sweet cherries, pitted and halved
½ C. whole-wheat pastry flour
Pinch of salt
½ C. fat-free milk
1 tsp. organic vanilla extract
¼ C. unsalted almonds, chopped

Directions:
Preheat the oven to 450 °F. In a 10-inch ovenproof skillet, add 1 tsp. of margarine and place the skillet into oven while preheating. In a bowl, mix flour, cinnamon and salt. In another bowl, add eggs, milk, melted margarine and vanilla and beat. Add egg mixture and mix until well combined. Remove the skillet from oven and tilt to spread the melted margarine evenly. Place cherries in the bottom of skillet in a single layer. Place the flour mixture over cherries evenly and top with almonds. Bake about 20 and set aside to cool for at least 5 minutes before slicing. Cut into 4 equal-sized wedges and serve. Enjoy!

Nutrition facts:
Calories 222,
Fat 5,
Fiber 6,
Carbs 9,
Protein 11

›Chocolate Toast

Preparation time: 15 minutes
Cooking time: 40 minutes
Servings: 4
Ingredients:
4 white bread slices
1 tablespoon vanilla extract
2 tablespoons Novella
1 banana, mashed
1 tablespoon coconut oil
¼ cup full-fat milk
Directions:
Mix vanilla extract, Novella, mashed banana, coconut oil, and milk. Pour the mixture in the slow cooker and cook on High for 40 minutes. Make a quick pressure release and cool the chocolate mixture. Spread the toasts with cooked mixture.

Nutrition facts:
148 calories,
2g protein,
18.2 g carbohydrates,
7.1g fat,
1.5g fiber,
2mg cholesterol,
73mg sodium,
182mg potassium.

›Sweet potato breakfast pie

Preparation time: 10 minutes
Cooking time: 7 hours
Servings: 6
Ingredients:
1 shredded sweet potato (peeled)
1 pound turkey bacon
9 eggs
1 small diced sweet onion
1 tsp. cinnamon
1 tsp. dried basil

Salt and pepper
Directions:
Grease your slow cooker as you would a baking dish. Shred the sweet potato and get all ingredients ready. Cut the bacon into small pieces. Then whisk the eggs and add all the ingredients into the slow cooker. Cook on low temperature for 7 to 8 hours. You can serve it as a pie, by cutting slices or like a cake cutting squares.
Nutrition:
245 Cal,
11.5 g total fat (4.6 g sat. fat), 152 mg chop. 189 mg sodium,
7.5 g carb.
3.9g fiber,
9.6. G protein.

›Fried Apple Slices

Preparation time: 10 minutes
Cooking time: 6 hours
Servings: 6
Ingredients:
1 teaspoon ground cinnamon
3 tablespoons cornstarch
3 pounds Granny Smith apples
¼ teaspoon nutmeg, freshly grated
1 cup sugar, granulated
2 tablespoons butter
Directions:
Put the apple slices in the crock pot and stir in nutmeg, cinnamon, sugar and cornstarch. Top with butter and cover the lid. Cook on LOW for about 6 hours, stirring about halfway. Dish out to serve hot.
Nutrition facts:
Calories: 234
Fat: 4.1g
Carbohydrates: 52.7g

›Banana & Blueberry Oats

Preparation time: 10 minutes
Cooking time: 6 hours
Servings: 2
Ingredients:
1/2 cup steel cut oats
¼ cup quinoa
½ cup blueberries 1 banana, mashed
A pinch of cinnamon powder
2 tablespoons maple syrup
2 cups water
Cooking spray ½ cup coconut milk
Directions:
Grease your slow cooker with cooking spray, add oats, quinoa, blueberries, banana, cinnamon, maple syrup, water and coconut milk, stir, cover and cook on Low for 6 hours. Divide into 2 bowls and serve for breakfast. Enjoy!
Nutrition facts:
Calories 200,

Fat 4
Fiber 5
Carbs 8
Protein 5

➤Pear and Maple Oatmeal

Preparation time: 10 minutes
Cooking time: 7 hours
Servings: 2
Ingredients:
1 and ½ cups milk
½ cup steel cut oats
½ teaspoon vanilla extract
1 pear, chopped
½ teaspoon maple extract
1 tablespoon sugar
Directions:
In your slow cooker, combine milk with oats, vanilla, pear, maple extract and sugar, stir, cover and cook on Low for 7 hours. Divide into bowls and serve for breakfast. Enjoy!
Nutrition facts:
Calories 200,
Fat 5,
Fiber 7,
Carbs 14,
Protein 4

➤Almond & Strawberry Oatmeal

Preparation time: 10 minutes
Cooking time: 6 hours
Servings: 2
Ingredients:
2 cup steel cut oats
3 cups water
1 cup almond milk
1 cup strawberries, chopped
½ cup Greek yogurt
½ teaspoon cinnamon powder ½ teaspoon vanilla extract
Directions:
In your slow cooker, mix oats with water, milk, strawberries, yogurt, cinnamon and vanilla, toss, cover and cook on Low for 6 hours. Stir your oatmeal one more time, divide into bowls and serve for breakfast. Enjoy!
Nutrition:
Calories 201,
Fat 3,
Fiber 6,
Carbs 12,
Protein 6

➤Coconut Raisins Oatmeal

Preparation time: 10 minutes
Cooking time: 8 hours
Servings: 2

Ingredients:
½ cup water
½ cup coconut milk
½ cup steel cut oats
½ cup carrots, grated
¼ cup raisins
A pinch of cinnamon powder
A pinch of ginger, ground
A pinch of nutmeg, ground
¼ cup coconut flakes, shredded
1 tablespoon orange zest, grated
½ teaspoon vanilla extract
½ tablespoon maple syrup
2 tablespoons walnuts, chopped
Directions:
In your slow cooker, mix water with coconut milk, oats, carrots, raisins, cinnamon, ginger, nutmeg, coconut flakes, orange zest, vanilla extract and maple syrup, stir, cover and cook on Low for 8 hours. Add walnuts, stir, divide into 2 bowls and serve for breakfast. Enjoy!
Nutrition:
Calories 200,
Fat 4,
Fiber 6,
Carbs 8,
Protein 8

➤Cauliflower with Eggs

Preparation time: 10 minutes
Cooking time: 7 hours
Servings: 2
Ingredients:
Cooking spray
4 eggs, whisked
A pinch of salt and black pepper
¼ teaspoon thyme, dried
½ teaspoon turmeric powder
1 cup cauliflower florets
½ small yellow onion, chopped
3 ounces breakfast sausages, sliced
½ cup cheddar cheese, shredded
Directions:
Grease your slow cooker with cooking spray and spread the cauliflower florets on the bottom of the pot.
Add the eggs mixed with salt, pepper and the other ingredients and toss. Put the lid on, cook on Low for 7 hours, divide between plates and serve for breakfast.
Nutrition:
Calories 261,
Fat 6,
Fiber 7,
Carbs 22, Protein 6

➤Caramel Pecan Sticky Buns

Preparation time: 40 minutes
Cooking time: 2 hours

Servings: 4
Ingredients:
¾ cup packed brown sugar
15 ounces refrigerated biscuits
1 teaspoon ground cinnamon
6 tablespoons melted butter ¼ cup pecans, finely chopped
Directions:
Mix together brown sugar, cinnamon and chopped nuts in a bowl. Dip refrigerator biscuits in melted butter to coat, then in the brown sugar mixture. Grease a crockpot and layer the biscuits in the crock pot.
Top with the remaining brown sugar mixture and cover the lid. Cook on HIGH for about 2 hours and dish out to serve.
Nutrition facts:
Calories: 583
Fat: 23.5g
Carbohydrates: 86.2g

➤Vegetables Omelet

Preparation time: 10 minutes
Cooking time: 2 hours
Servings: 2
Ingredients
6 eggs
½ cup milk
¼ teaspoon salt
Black pepper, to taste
1/8 teaspoon garlic powder
1/8 teaspoon chili powder
2 cup broccoli florets
1 red bell pepper, thinly sliced
1 small yellow onion, finely chopped
1 garlic clove, minced
For Garnishing
Chopped tomatoes
Fresh parsley
Shredded cheddar cheese
Chopped onions
Directions:
Mix together eggs, milk, garlic powder, chili powder, salt and black pepper in a large mixing bowl. Grease a crockpot and add garlic, onions, broccoli florets and sliced peppers. Stir in the egg mixture and cover the lid.
Cook on HIGH for about 2 hours. Top with cheese and allow it to stand for about 3 minutes. Dish out the omelet into a serving plate and garnish with chopped onions, chopped tomatoes and fresh parsley.
Nutrition facts:
Calories: 136
Fat: 7.4g
Carbohydrates: 7.8g

➤Chia Oatmeal

Preparation time: 10 minutes
Cooking time: 8 hours

Servings: 2
Ingredients:
2 cups almond milk
1 cup steel cut oats
2 tablespoons butter, soft
½ teaspoon almond extract
2 tablespoons chia seeds
Directions:
In your slow cooker, mix the oats with the chia seeds and the other ingredients, toss, put the lid on and cook on Low for 8 hours. Stir the oatmeal one more time, divide into 2 bowls and serve.
Nutrition:
Calories 812,
Fat 71.4,
Fiber 9.4,
Carbs 41.1,
Protein 11

➤Vanilla Pumpkin Bread

Preparation time: 10 minutes
Cooking time: 2 hours
Servings: 2
Ingredients:
Cooking spray
½ cup white flour
½ cup whole wheat flour
½ teaspoon baking soda
A pinch of cinnamon powder
2 tablespoons olive oil
2 tablespoons maple syrup
1 egg
½ tablespoon milk
½ teaspoon vanilla extract
½ cup pumpkin puree
2 tablespoons walnuts, chopped
2 tablespoons chocolate chips
Directions:
In a bowl, mix white flour with whole wheat flour, baking soda and cinnamon and stir. Add maple syrup, olive oil, egg, milk, vanilla extract, pumpkin puree, walnuts and chocolate chips and stir well. Grease a loaf pan that fits your slow cooker with cooking spray, pour pumpkin bread, transfer to your cooker and cook on High for 2 hours. Slice bread, divide between plates and serve. Enjoy!
Nutrition facts calories 200,
fat 3,
fiber 5,
Carbs 8,
Protein 4

➤Blueberry Fat Bombs

Preparation Time: 10 minutes
Cooking Time: 0 minutes
Servings: 12
Ingredients:
1/2 cup blueberries, mashed

1 1/2 cup coconut oil, at room temperature
1/2 cup cream cheese, at room temperature
1 pinch nutmeg
6 drops liquid stevia

Directions:
Line the 12-cup muffin tin with 12 paper liners. Put all the ingredients and process until it has a thick and mousse-like consistency. Pour the mixture into the 12 cups of the muffin tin. Put the muffin tin into the refrigerate to chill for 1 to 3 hours.

Nutrition facts:
Calories: 120
Fat: 12.5g
Fiber: 1.4g
Carbohydrates:2.1 g
Protein:3.1 g

›Cheesy Zucchini Triangles with Garlic Mayo Dip

Preparation Time:20 minutes
Cooking Time: 30 minutes
Servings: 4
Ingredients:
Garlic Mayo Dip:
1 cup crème Fraiche
1/3 cup mayonnaise
1/4 tsp. sugar-free maple syrup
1 garlic clove, pressed
1/2 tsp. vinegar
Salt and black pepper to taste
Cheesy Zucchini Triangles:
2 large zucchinis, grated
1 egg
1/4 cup almond flour
1/4 tsp. paprika powder
3/4 tsp. dried mixed herbs
1/4 tsp. swerve sugar
1/2 cup grated mozzarella cheese

Directions:
Start by making the dip; in a medium bowl, mix the crème Fraiche, mayonnaise, maple syrup, garlic, vinegar, salt, and black pepper. Cover the bowl with a new plastic wrap and refrigerate while you make the zucchinis. Let the oven preheat at 400F. Line a baking tray with greaseproof paper. Set aside. Put the zucchinis in a cheesecloth and press out as much liquid as possible. Pour the zucchinis in a bowl. Add the egg, almond flour, paprika, dried mixed herbs, and swerve sugar. Mix well and spread the mixture on the baking tray into a round pizza-like piece with 1-inch thickness. Let it bake for 25 minutes. Reduce the oven's heat to 350°F/175°C, take out the tray, and sprinkle the zucchini with the mozzarella cheese. Let it melt in the oven. Remove afterward, set aside to cool for 5 minutes, and then slice the snacks into triangles. Serve immediately with the garlic mayo dip.

Nutrition facts:
Calories: 286
Fat: 11.4g

Fiber: 8.4g
Carbohydrates:4.3 g
Protein: 10.1g

›Herbed Cheese Chips

Preparation Time: 15 minutes
Cooking Time: 15 minutes
Servings: 8
Ingredients:
3 tbsp. coconut flour
1/2 C. strong cheddar cheese, grated and divided
1/4 C. Parmesan cheese, grated
2 tbsp. butter, melted
1 organic egg
1 tsp. fresh thyme leaves, minced

Directions:
Preheat the oven to 3500 F. Line a large baking sheet with parchment paper. In a bowl, place the coconut flour, 1/4 C. of grated cheddar, Parmesan, butter, and egg and mix until well combined. Make eight equal-sized balls from the mixture. Arrange the balls onto a prepared baking sheet in a single layer about 2-inch apart. Form into flat discs. Sprinkle each disc with the remaining cheddar, followed by thyme. Bake for around 15 minutes.

Nutrition facts:
Calories: 101
Fat: 6.5g
Fiber: 1.4g
Carbohydrates: 1.2g
Protein: 3.1g

›Cauliflower Poppers

Preparation Time: 20 minutes
Cooking Time: 30 minutes
Servings: 4
Ingredients:
4 C. cauliflower florets
2 tsp. olive oil
1/4 tsp. chili powder
Pepper and salt

Directions:
Preheat the oven to 4500 F. Grease a roasting pan. In a bowl, add all ingredients and toss to coat well. Transfer the cauliflower mixture into a prepared roasting pan and spread in an even layer. Roast for about 25-30 minutes. Serve warm.

Nutrition facts:
Calories: 102
Fat: 8.5g
Fiber: 4.7g
Carbohydrates:2.1 g
Protein: 4.2g

›Crispy Parmesan Chips

Preparation Time: 10 minutes
Cooking Time: 5 minutes

Servings: 8
Ingredients:
1 teaspoon butter
8 ounces full-fat Parmesan cheese, shredded or freshly grated
Directions:
Preheat the oven to 400°F. The Parmesan cheese must be spooned onto the baking sheet in mounds, spread evenly apart. Spread out the mounds with the back of a spoon until they are flat. Bake the crackers until the edges are browned, and the centers are still pale about 5 minutes.
Nutrition facts:
Calories: 101
Fat: 9.4g
Fiber: 3.1g
Carbohydrates:2.5 g
Protein: 1.2g

›Apple Crepes

Preparation Time: 15 minutes
Cooking Time: 24 minutes
Servings: 4
Ingredients:
1½ C. whole-wheat flour
Pinch of salt
1½ C. fat-free milk
2 apples, peeled, cored and sliced thinly
½ tsp. powdered stevia
3 large eggs, beaten
2 tbsp. unsalted margarine, melted and cooled
Directions:
In a bowl, sift together flour, stevia and salt. Make a well in n the center of flour mixture. Add beaten egg in the well and mix until well combined. Slowly add milk and mix until well combined. Add margarine and mix until well combined. Cover the bowl and set aside about 1-2 hours. Heat a non-stick skillet over medium-low heat. Add about ¼ C. of the mixture and tilt the pan to spread evenly in the bottom of the skillet. Place about 6-8 apple slices over the crepe mixture evenly. Cook for about 2 minutes. Carefully flip the side and cook for about 2 minutes. Repeat with remaining mixture. Serve warm.
Nutrition facts:
Calories: 367
Fat: 12.1g
Carbohydrates:56 g

›Sweet Onion Dip

Preparation Time: 15 minutes
Cooking Time: 25-30 minutes
Servings: 4
Ingredients:
3 cup sweet onion chopped
1 tsp. pepper sauce
2 cups Swiss cheese shredded
Ground black pepper
2 cups mayonnaise

1/4 cup horseradish
Directions:
Take a bowl, add sweet onion, horseradish, pepper sauce, mayonnaise, and Swiss cheese, mix them well and transfer into the pie plate. Preheat oven at 375. Now put the plate into the oven and bake for 25 to 30 minutes until edges turn golden brown. Sprinkle pepper to taste and serve with crackers.
Nutrition facts:
Calories: 278
Fat: 11.4g
Fiber: 4.1g
Carbohydrates:2.9 g
Protein: 6.9g

›Keto Trail Mix

Preparation Time: 5 minutes
Cooking Time: 0 minutes
Servings: 3
Ingredients:
1/2 cup salted pumpkin seeds
1/2 cup slivered almonds
3/4 cup roasted pecan halves
3/4 cup unsweetened cranberries
1 cup toasted coconut flakes
Directions:
In a skillet, place almonds and pecans. Heat for 2-3 minutes and let cool. Once cooled, in a large resealable plastic bag, combine all ingredients. Seal and shake vigorously to mix. Evenly divide into suggested Servings: and store in airtight meal prep containers.
Nutrition facts:
Calories: 98
Fat: 1.2g
Fiber: 4.1g
Carbohydrates:1.1 g
Protein: 3.2g

›Keto Bread

Preparation Time: 5 minutes
Cooking Time: 25 minutes
Servings: 4
Ingredients:
5 tablespoons butter, at room temperature, divided
6 large eggs, lightly beaten
11/2 cups almond flour
3 teaspoons baking powder
1 tbsp. coconut oil
Pinch pink Himalayan salt
Directions:
Preheat the oven to 390°F. In a container, mix the eggs, almond flour, remaining four tablespoons of butter, baking powder, oil, and pink Himalayan salt until thoroughly blended. Pour into the prepared pan. Bake for around 25 minutes. Slice and serve.
Nutrition facts:
Calories: 121
Fat: 4.3g

Fiber: 2.1g
Carbohydrates:0.1 g
Protein: 2.3g

>Cold Cuts and Cheese Pinwheels

Preparation Time: 20 minutes
Cooking Time: 0 minutes
Servings: 2
Ingredients:
8 ounces cream cheese, at room temperature
1/4-pound salami, thinly sliced
2 tablespoons sliced pepperoncini
Directions:
Layout a sheet of plastic wrap on a large cutting board or counter. Place the cream cheese in the center of the plastic wrap, and then add another layer of plastic wrap on top. Using a rolling pin, roll the cream cheese until it is even and about 1/4 inch thick. Try to make the shape somewhat resemble a rectangle. Pull off the top layer of plastic wrap. Place the salami slices so they overlap to cover the cream-cheese layer completely. On top of the salami Place piece of plastic wrap layer to flip over your cream cheese–salami rectangle. Flip the layer, so the cream cheese side is up. Remove the plastic wrap and add the sliced pepperoncini in a layer on top. Roll the layered ingredients into a tight log, pressing the meat and cream cheese together. (You want it as tight as possible.) Then wrap the roll with plastic wrap and refrigerate for at least 6 hours so it will set. Slice and serve.
Nutrition facts:
Calories: 141
Fat: 4.9g
Fiber: 2.1g
Carbohydrates:0.3 g
Protein: 8.5g

>Zucchini Balls with Capers and Bacon

Preparation Time: 3 hrs.
Cooking Time: 20 minutes
Servings: 10
Ingredients:
2 zucchinis, shredded
2 bacon slices, chopped
1 1/2 cup cream cheese, at room temperature
1 cup fontina cheese
1/4 cup capers
1 clove garlic, crushed
1/2 cup grated Parmesan cheese
1/2 tsp. poppy seeds
1/4 tsp. dried dill weed
1/2 tsp. onion powder
Salt and black pepper, to taste
1 cup crushed pork rinds
Directions:
Preheat oven to 360 F. Thoroughly mix zucchinis, capers, 1/2 of Parmesan cheese, garlic, cream cheese, bacon, and fontina cheese until well combined.

Shape the mixture into balls. Refrigerate for 3 hours. In a mixing bowl, mix the remaining Parmesan cheese, crushed pork rinds, dill, black pepper, onion powder, poppy seeds, and salt. Roll cheese ball in Parmesan mixture to coat. Arrange in a greased baking dish in a single layer and bake in the oven for 15-20 minutes, shaking once.
Nutrition facts:
Calories: 227
Fat: 12.5g
Fiber: 9.4g
Carbohydrates:4.3 g
Protein: 14.5g

>Strawberry Fat Bombs

Preparation Time: 30 minutes
Cooking Time: 0 minutes
Servings: 6
Ingredients:
100 g strawberries
100 g cream cheese
50 g butter
2 tbsp. erythritol powder
1/2 teaspoon vanilla extract
Directions:
Put the cream cheese and butter (cut into small pieces) in a mixing bowl. Let rest for 30 to 60 minutes at room temperature. Wash the strawberries and remove the green. Pour into a bowl and process into a puree with a serving of oil or a mixer. Add erythritol powder and vanilla extract and mix well. Mix the strawberries with the other ingredients and make sure that they have reached room temperature. Put butter and the cream cheese into a container. Mix with a hand mixer or a food processor to a homogeneous mass.
Pour the mixture into small silicone muffin molds. Freeze.
Nutrition facts:
Calories: 95
Fat: 9.1g
Fiber: 4.1g
Carbohydrates:0.9 g
Protein: 2.1g

>Kale Chips

Preparation Time: 5 minutes
Cooking Time: 25 minutes
Servings: 6
Ingredients:
400 g of kale
1 to 2 teaspoons of salt
2 tbsp. butter
50 g bacon fat

Directions:
Remove the stems and coarse ribs from the kale and tear the leaves into 5 cm pieces. Wash the kale leaves thoroughly and dry them in a salad spinner. Put the

butter in a pan with the bacon fat and warm it up over low heat. Add salt and stir well. Set aside and let cool. Pack the kale in a zippered bag and pour the cooled, liquid mixture of bacon fat and butter into it. Close the zippered bag and gently shake the kale leaves with the butter mixture. The leaves should take on a glossy color due to an even film of fat.

Serve with salt as desired. Bake it for 25 minutes or until the leaves turn brown and crispy. Let cool, divide into the recommended portions, and store in an airtight container.

Nutrition facts:
Calories: 59
Fat: 2.1g
Fiber: 4.5g
Carbohydrates:0.9 g
Protein: 0.4g

>Cheese Bites with Pickle

Preparation time: 20 minutes |
Cooking time: 0 minutes | **Servings:** 10
Ingredients:
10 ounces (283 g) Swiss cheese, shredded
10 ounces (283 g) cottage cheese
¼ cup sour cream
1 tablespoon pickle, minced
Sea salt and ground black pepper
1 teaspoon granulated garlic
¾ cup pecans, finely chopped
Directions
Beat the Swiss cheese, cottage cheese, sour cream, minced pickles, and seasonings until everything is well incorporated. Place the mixture for 2 hours in your refrigerator. Form the mixture into bite-sized balls using your hands and a spoon. Roll the cheese balls over the chopped pecans to coat them evenly. Bon appétit!
Nutrition facts:
calories: 200 | fat: 15.6g | protein: 11.4g | carbs: 4.8g | net carbs: 3.8g | fiber: 1.0g

>Cheese and Shrimp-Stuffed Celery

Preparation time: 10 minutes
Cooking time: 5 minutes
Servings: 6
Ingredients:
5 ounces (142 g) shrimp
10 ounces (283 g) cottage cheese, at room temperature
4 ounces (113 g) Coby cheese, shredded
2 scallions, chopped
1 teaspoon yellow mustard
Sea salt, to taste
½ teaspoon oregano
6 stalks celery, cut into halves
Directions:
Cook the shrimp in a lightly greased skillet over medium-high heat for 2 minutes; turn them over and

cook for 2 minutes. Chop the shrimp, then transfer to a bowl. Add in the cheese, scallions, mustard, and spices. Mix to combine well. Divide the shrimp mixture between the celery stalks and serve. Bon appétit!
Nutrition facts:
calories: 127
fat: 6.1g
protein: 13.4g
carbs: 4.2g
net carbs: 3.7g
fiber: 0.5g

>Meaty Jalapeños

Preparation time: 15 minutes
Cooking time: 40 minutes
Servings: 10
Ingredients:
2 ounces (57 g) bacon, chopped
½ pound (227 g) ground pork
½ pound (227 g) ground beef
½ cup red onion, chopped
2 garlic cloves, minced
1 teaspoon taco seasoning mix
Sea salt and ground black pepper
½ cup tomato purée
1 teaspoon stone-ground mustard
20 jalapeño peppers, deveined and halved lengthwise
4 ounces (113 g) Parmesan cheese, preferably freshly grated
Directions:
Preheat a nonstick skillet over medium-high heat. Now, cook the bacon, pork, and beef for about 4 minutes until no longer pink. Add the garlic, onion and cook 2 and half minutes until they are tender. Sprinkle with the taco seasoning mix, salt, and black pepper. Fold in the tomato purée and mustard. Cook medium-low heat for 4 minutes more. Spoon the mixture into jalapeño peppers. Put in the preheated oven at 390°F (199°C) for about 20 minutes.
Top with Parmesan and bake an additional 6 minutes or until cheese is golden on the top. Bon appétit!
Nutrition facts :
calories: 190 | fat: 13.3g | protein: 12.6g | carbs: 4.8g | net carbs: 3.6g | fiber: 1.2g

>Pork Skewers with Greek Dipping Sauce

Preparation time: 15 minutes
Cooking time: 10 minutes
Servings: 2
½ pound (227 g) pork loin, cut into bite-sized pieces
2 garlic cloves, pressed
1 scallion stalk, chopped
¼ cup dry red wine
1 thyme sprig
1 rosemary sprig
1 tablespoon lemon juice

1 teaspoon stone ground mustard
1 tablespoon olive oil
Dipping Sauce:
½ cup Greek yogurt
½ teaspoon dill, ground
½ Lebanese cucumber, grated
1 teaspoon garlic, minced
Sea salt, to taste
½ teaspoon ground black pepper
2 tablespoons cilantro leaves, roughly chopped
Directions:
Place the pork loin in a ceramic dish; add in the garlic, scallions, wine, thyme, rosemary, lemon juice, mustard, and olive oil. Let them marinate in your refrigerator for 2 to 3 hours Thread the pork pieces onto bamboo skewers. Grill for 7 minutes per side. Meanwhile, whisk the remaining ingredients until well mixed. Serve the pork skewers with the sauce for dipping and enjoy!
Nutrition facts:
calories: 313 | fat: 20.0g | protein: 29.2g | carbs: 2.2g | net carbs: 1.6g | fiber: 0.6g

›BLT Cups

Preparation time: 5 minutes
Cooking time: 20 minutes
Servings: 10
5 ounces (142 g) bacon, chopped
5 tablespoons Parmigiano-Reggiano cheese, grated
1 teaspoon adobo sauce
2 tablespoons mayonnaise
Sea salt and ground black pepper
2 1/2 tablespoons green onions, minced
10 pieces lettuce
10 tomatoes cherry tomatoes, discard the insides
Directions:
Preheat a frying pan over moderate heat. Now cook bacon in the frying pan and make it crisp, about 7 minutes, reserve. In a mixing bowl, thoroughly combine the cheese, adobo sauce, mayo, salt, black pepper, and green onions.
Divide the mayo mixture between the cherry tomatoes. Divide the cooked bacon between the cherry tomatoes. Top with the lettuce and serve immediately. Bon appétit!
Nutrition facts:
calories: 93 | fat: 8.2g | protein: 2.6g | carbs: 1.5g | net carbs: 1.1g | fiber: 0.4g

›Turkey-Stuffed Mini Peppers

Preparation time: 5 minutes
Cooking time: 20minutes
Servings: 5
2 teaspoons olive oil
1 teaspoon mustard seeds
5 ounces (142 g) ground turkey
Salt and ground black pepper, to taste
8 mini bell peppers, cut lengthwise, stems and seeds removed

2 ounces (57 g) garlic and herb seasoned chevre goat cheese, crumbled
Directions:
Heat the oil .Once hot, cook mustard seeds with ground turkey until the turkey is no longer pink. Crumble with a fork. Season with salt and black pepper. Lay the pepper halves cut-side-up on a parchment-lined baking sheet. Put meat mixture into the center of each pepper half. Top each pepper with cheese. Put in the oven at 390ºF (190ºC) for 10 minutes. Bon appétit!
Nutrition facts:
calories: 200 | fat: 17.1g | protein: 7.8g | carbs: 2.9g | net carbs: 2.0g | fiber: 0.9g

›Bacon-Wrapped Poblano Poppers

Preparation time: 10 minutes
Cooking time: 35 minutes
Servings: 16
10 ounces (283 g) cottage cheese, at room temperature
6 ounces (170 g) Swiss cheese, shredded
Sea salt and ground black pepper
½ teaspoon shallot powder
½ teaspoon cumin powder
⅓ teaspoon mustard seeds
16 poblano peppers, deveined and halved
16 thin slices bacon, sliced lengthwise
Directions
Mix the cheese, salt, black pepper, shallot powder, cumin, and mustard seeds until well combined. Divide the mixture between the pepper halves. Wrap each pepper with 3 slices of bacon: secure with toothpicks. Arrange the stuffed peppers on the rack in the baking sheet. Bake in the preheated oven at 380ºF (190ºC) for about 30 minutes until the bacon is sizzling and browned. Bon appétit!
Nutrition facts:
calories: 184 | fat: 14.1g | protein: 8.9g | carbs: 5.8g | net carbs: 5.0g | fiber: 0.8g

›Cocktail Meatballs

Preparation time: 5 minutes
Cooking time: 15 minutes
Servings: 2
¼ pound (113 g) ground turkey
¼ pound (113 g) ground pork
1 ounce (28 g) bacon, chopped
¼ cup flaxseed meal
½ teaspoon garlic, pressed
1 egg, beaten
½ cup Cheddar cheese, shredded
Sea salt, to season
¼ teaspoon ground black pepper
¼ teaspoon cayenne pepper
¼ teaspoon marjoram
Directions:
Preheat your oven to 390ºF (190ºC). Thoroughly com-

bine all ingredients in a mixing bowl. Now, form the mixture into meatballs. Place your meatballs in a parchment-lined baking sheet. Bake in the preheated oven for about 18 minutes, rotating the pan halfway through. Serve with toothpicks and enjoy!

Nutrition facts:
calories: 570 | fat: 42.3g | protein: 40.2g | carbs: 6.4g | net carbs: 0.8g | fiber: 5.6g

›Caribbean Baked Wings

Preparation time: 15 minutes
Cooking time: 45 minutes
Servings: 2
4 chicken wings
1 tablespoon coconut aminos
2 tablespoons rum
2 tablespoons butter
1 tablespoon onion powder1 tablespoon garlic powder
½ teaspoon salt
¼ teaspoon freshly ground black pepper
½ teaspoon red pepper flakes
¼ teaspoon dried dill
2 tablespoons sesame seeds

Directions:
Pat dries the chicken wings. Toss the chicken wings with the remaining ingredients until well coated. Arrange the chicken wings on a parchment-lined baking sheet. Put in the preheated oven at 410°F (210°C) for 45 minutes until golden brown. Serve with your favorite sauce for dipping. Bon appétit!

Nutrition facts:
calories: 287 | fat: 18.6g | protein: 15.5g | carbs: 5.1g | net carbs: 3.3g | fiber: 1.8g

›Wrapped Asparagus with Ham

Preparation time: 10 minutes
Cooking time: 15 minutes
Servings: 6
1½ pounds (680 g) asparagus spears, trimmed
1 teaspoon shallot powder
½ teaspoon granulated garlic
½ teaspoon paprika
Kosher salt and ground black pepper
1 tablespoon sesame oil
10 slices ham

Directions:
Toss the asparagus spears with the shallot powder, garlic, paprika, salt, and black pepper. Drizzle sesame oil all over the asparagus spears. Working one at a time, wrap a ham slice on each asparagus spear; try to cover the entire length of the asparagus spear. Place the wrapped asparagus spears on a parchment-lined roasting pan. Bake in the preheated oven at 380°F (190°C) for about 18 minutes or until thoroughly cooked. Bon appétit!

Nutrition facts:
calories: 120 | fat: 6.5g | protein: 10.1g | carbs: 6.2g

| net carbs: 3.2g | fiber: 3.0g

›Kale Chips

Preparation time: 15 minutes
Cooking time: 15 minutes
Servings: 2
Ingredients:
2 cups kale, torn into pieces
1 tablespoons olive oil
Sea salt, to taste
¼ teaspoon pepper
½ teaspoon onion powder ½ teaspoon garlic powder
½ teaspoon fresh dill, minced
½ tablespoon fresh parsley, minced

Directions:
Preheat your oven to 310°F (155°C). Toss the kale leaves with all other ingredients until well coated. Bake for 15 to 20 minutes. Store the chips in an airtight container. Bon appétit!

Nutrition facts:
calories: 69 | fat: 6.5g | protein: 0.5g | carbs: 1.5g | net carbs: 1.0g | fiber: 0.5g

›Bacon Fat Bombs

Preparation time: 20 minutes
Cooking time: 0 minutes
Servings: 8
Ingredients:
½ stick butter, at room temperature
8 ounces (227 g) cottage cheese, at room temperature
8 ounces (227 g) Mozzarella cheese, crumbled
1 teaspoon shallot powder
1 teaspoon Italian seasoning blend
2 ounces (57 g) bacon bits

Directions:
Mix the butter, cheese, shallot powder, and Italian seasoning blend until well combined. Place the mixture in your refrigerator for 60 minutes. Shape the mixture into 18 balls. Roll each ball in the bacon bits until coated on all sides. Enjoy!

Nutrition facts:
calories: 150 | fat: 9.4g | protein: 13.0g | carbs: 2.1g | net carbs: 1.6g | fiber: 0.5g

›Almond Milk Quinoa

Cooking time: 20 minutes
Servings: 1
Ingredients:
½ cup quinoa
¾ cup almond milk, canned
2 bananas, sliced
1 teaspoon cinnamon
2 tablespoons peanut butter
1 teaspoon vanilla
1 nutmeg, crushed
Directions

Add cinnamon, quinoa, almond milk, vanilla, and nutmeg to a pan and bring to a boil. Low the heat and cook for 21 minutes, covered. When cooked, fluff with a fork. Transfer the quinoa to a bowl. Serve topped with bananas and peanut butter.

›Quinoa and Sweet Potatoes

Cooking time: 40 minutes
Servings: 2
Ingredients:
½ cup quinoa
2 sweet potatoes, sliced red beet
2 tablespoons raw walnuts, chopped
2 tablespoons coconut oil, melted
1 tablespoon olive oil
1 teaspoon balsamic vinegar
lemon juice
Lemon zest
Pepper, salt, to taste
Directions:
Preheat the oven to 375 F(196g). Place the sweet potatoes and beets. Drizzle with coconut oil and sprinkle with pepper and salt. Bake for 40 minutes. Cook the quinoa as the package directions. After the beets and potatoes are baked, transfer them to a bowl to cool. Slice the beets into tiny pieces. Combine together and serve

›Honey Buckwheat Coconut

Cooking time: 15 minutes
Servings: 2
Ingredients:
¼ cup buckwheat, toasted, ground
1 tablespoon coconut, shredded
2 tablespoons pecans, chopped
½ cup + 2 tablespoons coconut milk
1 tablespoon raw honey
¾ teaspoon vanilla
¾ cup of water
2 tablespoons currants
1 drizzle coconut syrup
Directions:
Put the water, coconut milk, vanilla, honey and in a saucepan. Stir in the ground buckwheat, at this point reduce the heat to low. Cook for 7/8 minutes, keeping covered. Add water during cooking. Put everything in a bowl and grate over the coconut, and add the pecans, currants and a drizzle of coconut syrup.

›Potato Tempeh

Cooking time: 20 minutes
Servings: 4
Ingredients:
1 package (8 oz) tempeh, finely diced
4 red potatoes
6 leaves lacinato kale, stemmed, chopped
2 tablespoons olive oil
1 medium onion, chopped

1 medium green bell pepper, diced
1 teaspoon smoked paprika
1 teaspoon seasoning, salt-free
Ground pepper, salt, to taste
Directions:
Microwave the potatoes until done. Finely chop them when cool. Mix all the ingredients and cook medium high heat till the mixture is browned. Add salt and pepper then serve

›Breakfast Toast

Cooking time: 6 minutes
Servings: 1
Ingredients:
2 slices bread, gluten-free
2 teaspoons cinnamon
2 tablespoons flaxseed, ground
6 oz. soy milk
2 teaspoons vanilla extract
Directions:
Mix soy milk, vanilla extract, cinnamon, flaxseed, in a baking dish. At this point, put the slices of bread in the mixture. Preheat a skillet over medium heat and toast the bread 2 minutes per side.

›Pumpkin Pancakes

Cooking time: 10 minutes
Servings: 12
Ingredients:
1-cup all-purpose flour
2 teaspoons baking powder
½ cup pumpkin puree
1 egg
3 tablespoons chia seeds
3 tablespoons coconut oil, melted, slightly cooled
1 cup almond milk
2 teaspoons vanilla extract
1 tablespoon white vinegar
1 tablespoon maple syrup
1 teaspoon pumpkin pie spice
½ teaspoon kosher salt
Directions:
Mix vinegar and almond milk in a bowl. Let rest for 5 minutes. Mix eggs into the almond milk, then stir in maple syrup and pumpkin puree Mix togheter wet and dry ingredients. Heat at medium high. Take 1/3 of the dough and pour it into the pan. Cook for 1 1/2 minutes, then flip and cook until golden brown.Mix flour, baking soda powder, pumpkin pie spice, chia seeds, and salt.

›Blueberry Bars

Cooking time: 5 minutes
Servings: 15
Ingredients:
½ cup dried blueberries
1 ½ cups rolled oats

¾ cup whole almonds
1/3 cup ground flaxseed
1/3 cup walnuts
¼ cup sunflower seeds
½ cup pistachios
1/3 cup pepitas
¼ cup apple sauce
1/3 cup maple syrup
1 cup almond butter

Directions:
In a bowl, mix together the blueberries, flax seeds, oatmeal, almonds, sunflower seeds, walnuts, pistachios, and pepitas. Mix the almond butter well, then pour the mixture into a baking tray with parchment paper. Roll out the dough evenly. Mix the applesauce and maple syrup. After that remove from the freezer and lift the batter out of the pan. Divide the dough into 15 bars and serve.

›Chickpea Scramble Breakfast Bowl

Cooking time: 10 minutes
Servings: 2
Ingredients:
For chickpea scramble:
1 can (15 oz.) chickpeas
A drizzle olive oil
¼ white onion, diced
2 garlic cloves, minced
½ teaspoon turmeric
½ teaspoon pepper
½ teaspoon salt
For breakfast bowl:
1 avocado, wedged
Greens, combined
Handful parsley, minced
Handful cilantro, minced

Directions:
Put chickpeas and water in a container. Mash part of the chickpeas with the help of a fork. Mix pepper, salt and turmeric. Fry the onions with the olive oil, at which point put a little bit of garlic for 1 minute. Add the chickpeas and sauté for 6 minutes. Get 2 breakfast bowls.
Put combined greens in the bottom of the bowl. Top with chickpea scramble, parsley, and cilantro. Enjoy with avocado wedges.

›Quinoa, Oats, Hazelnut and Blueberry Salad

Cooking time: 35 minutes
Servings: 8
Ingredients:
1 cup golden quinoa, dry
1 cup oats, cut into pieces
2 cups blueberries
2 cups hazelnuts, roughly chopped, toasted
½ cup dry millet
2 large lemons, zested, juiced
3 tablespoons olive oil, divided

½ cup maple syrup
1 cup Greek yogurt
1 (1-inch) piece fresh ginger, peeled, cut
¼ teaspoon nutmeg

Directions:
Combine quinoa, oats and millet in a large bowl. Rinse, drain and set aside. Add one tablespoon olive oil into a saucepan and place over medium-high heat. Cook the rinsed grains in it for 3 minutes. Add 4 ½ cups water and salt. Add the zest of 1 lemon and ginger. When the mixture boils, cover the pot and cook in reduced heat for 20 minutes. Remove from heat. Let rest for 5 minutes. Uncover and fluff with a fork. Discard the ginger and layer the grains on a large baking sheet. Let cool for 30 minutes. Transfer the grains into a large bowl and mix in the remaining lemon zest. Combine the juice of both lemons with the remaining olive oil in a separate bowl. Stir in the yogurt, maple syrup, and nutmeg. Pour the mixture into the grains and stir. Mix in the blueberries and hazelnuts. Refrigerate overnight, then serve.

›Buttered Overnight Oats

Cooking time: 5 minutes
Servings: 1
Ingredients:
¾ cup rolled oats
½ teaspoon cinnamon
2 tablespoons chia seeds
1 ripe banana, mashed
2 tablespoons peanut butter
½ cup + 1 tbsp. water
1 cup vanilla almond milk, unsweetened
2 tablespoons maple syrup
1 pinch salt

Directions:
Get a mason jar and add oats, cinnamon, chia seeds and salt to it. Combine properly. Stir in almond milk, mashed banana, and ½ cup water. Mix peanut butter and 1 tablespoon water in a bowl then add into the jar and stir. Stir in the maple syrup and refrigerate overnight. Serve.

›Protein Breakfast Burrito

Cooking time: 30 minutes
Servings: 4
Ingredients:
For tofu:
1 package (12 oz.) firm tofu
¼ cup parsley, minced
1 tablespoon hummus
1 teaspoon oil
1 teaspoon nutritional yeast
½ teaspoon cumin
½ teaspoon chili powder
¼ teaspoon salt
3 garlic cloves
For vegetables:
5 baby potatoes, sliced into pieces

2 cups kale, chopped
1 tablespoon water
1 medium red bell pepper, sliced thin
½ teaspoon ground cumin
½ teaspoon chili powder
1 pinch salt
For assembling:
4 large tortillas
1 medium avocado, ripe, chopped
Hot sauce
Cilantro
Directions:
Preheat the oven to 400 F. Squeeze out excess moisture from tofu by wrapping it in a towel and placing a heavy object on top. Crumble into fine pieces and set aside. Place potatoes and red pepper onto a parchment paper lined baking sheet, then sprinkle with water, cumin, chili powder and salt. Toss and bake for 22 minutes. In the 17 minutes' mark, add kale, toss and bake for extra 5 minutes. Preheat a skillet over medium heat. Add tofu and oil once skillet is hot, then sauté for 8 minutes, stirring frequently. Meanwhile, mix hummus, yeast, chili powder, cumin and salt in a bowl, then add 2 tablespoons water. Stir in parsley. Pour the mixture into the tofu and cook until slightly browned. Place aside. Roll out each tortilla and scoop a large portion of potato mixture, tofu mixture, avocado, cilantro and a bit of hot sauce into the middle of each tortilla. Roll up and seal the seam, then serve immediately.

›Hummus Toast

Cooking time: 5 minutes
Servings: 1
Ingredients:
2 slices wheat bread, sprouted, toasted
¼ cup hummus
1 tablespoon sunflower seeds, unsalted, roasted
1 tablespoon hemp seeds
Directions:
Top the toasted breads with hummus, sunflower seeds and hemp seeds. Enjoy!

›Almond Milk Banana Smoothie

Cooking time: 5 minutes
Servings: 1
Ingredients:
2 bananas, frozen
¾ cup almond milk
2 tablespoons peanut butter
2 tablespoons cacao powder
For topping:
½ banana, sliced
Chocolate granola
Directions:
Blend bananas, almond milk, peanut butter and cacao powder in a blender until smooth. Transfer to a bowl and cover with sliced banana and granola. Enjoy!

›Nutritious Toasted Chickpeas

Cooking time: 30 minutes
Servings: 2
Ingredients:
2 cup chickpeas, cooked
6 bread slices, toasted
2 large tomatoes, skinned, chopped
2 tablespoons olive oil
3 small shallots, diced
½ teaspoon cinnamon
¼ teaspoon smoked paprika
½ teaspoon sweet paprika
2 large garlic cloves, diced
½ teaspoon sugar
Black pepper, to taste
½ teaspoon salt
Directions:
Heat olive oil in a frying pan. Sauté shallots, stirring frequently until almost translucent. Add garlic then sauté until garlic is softened. Add the spices into the pan. Cook for 1 minute, stirring frequently. Add the tomatoes into the pan. Add some water, then cook on medium-low heat until a thick sauce forms. Stir in the chickpeas and cook for 3 minutes, then sprinkle with black pepper, sugar and salt. Top toasted bread with the chickpeas mixture and serve.

›Ricotta cloud Pancakes

Cooking time: 20 minutes
Servings: 1
Ingredients:
1 cup almond flour
1 tsp baking powder
2 ½ tbsp erythritol
⅓ tsp salt
1 ¼ cups ricotta cheese
⅓ cup coconut milk
2 large eggs
1 cup heavy whipping cream
Directions:
In a bowl, whisk the almond flour, baking powder, erythritol, and salt. Crack the eggs into the blender and process for 30 seconds. Add the ricotta cheese, continue processing it while gradually pour the coconut milk for about 90 seconds. The mixture will be creamy and smooth. Pour it into the dry ingredients and whisk to combine. Set a skillet over medium heat and heat for a minute. Then, fetch a soup spoonful of mixture into the skillet and cook for 1 minute.
Flip the pancake and cook further for 1 minute. Remove onto a plate and repeat the cooking process until the batter is exhausted. Serve the pancakes with whipping cream. Enjoy!

›Tomato Tofu Breakfast Tacos

Servings: 3
Cooking time: 20 minutes
Ingredients:

10 small corn tortillas, warmed
3 Roma tomatoes
1 block (16 oz.) firm tofu
lime juice
½ tablespoon olive oil
1 tablespoon paprika, smoked
½ medium red onions, diced
1 poblano pepper, cored, diced
1 red bell pepper, roasted, chopped
¾ teaspoon salt + ¼ tsp. to taste
1 tablespoon chili powder
1 ripe avocado

Directions:
Heat oil over medium heat in a medium-high frying pan. Sauté the red onion and poblano pepper for 5 minutes. In the meantime, blend the Roma tomatoes until properly chopped, but not thoroughly blended. Set aside. To the frying pan, add smoked paprika, chili powder, red pepper and salt. Sauté for 1 minute. Add the Roma tomatoes and stir. Stir in the crumbled tofu, then cook for 10 minutes, stirring infrequently. Add the lime juice and cook for 1 minute. Remove from heat and season with ¼ teaspoon salt.
Top each tortilla with the tofu mixture and mashed avocado then enjoy.

›Peanut Butter Oats

Cooking time: 10 minutes
Servings: 2
Ingredients:
1 cup rolled oats
2 tablespoons peanut butter
1 ½ cups almond milk
1 scoop vanilla protein powder
Directions:
In a bowl, stir the oats, almond milk, peanut butter, and protein powder together. Cover and refrigerate for 2 hours. Serve afterward.

›Protein Pancakes

Cooking time: 15 minutes
Servings: 6
Ingredients:
1 cup all-purpose flour
¼ cup brown rice protein powder
1 tablespoon baking powder
2 tablespoons maple syrup
1 cup of water
½ teaspoon salt
Directions:
In a bowl, combine all dry ingredients. Mix in maple syrup and water, plus more water if necessary. Preheat a non-stick frying pan over medium heat. Scoop a portion of the mixture into the pan and cook until bubbles form in the center of the pancake.
Flip and cook for several more minutes.
Do this with the remaining pancakes batter and enjoy!

›Savory Vegan Omelet

Cooking time: 25 minutes
Servings: 1
Ingredients:
For the Omelet:
¾ cup (5 oz.) firm tofu, drained, patted dry
1 teaspoon cornstarch
2 tablespoons nutritional yeast
Olive oil
2 garlic cloves, minced
¼ teaspoon paprika
Black pepper and salt
For the filling:
1 cup veggies (tomato, spinach, etc.), sliced
Directions:
Preheat the oven to 375 F. Heat an oven-safe skillet over medium heat then add olive oil and garlic. Cook garlic for 2 minutes. Add garlic and the remaining ingredients (except for the vegetables) to a food processor and mix until smooth and combined. Add 1 ½ tablespoons water. Set aside. Add more olive oil to the skillet. Add the vegetables and sprinkle with pepper and salt. Cook until done, then set aside.
Turn off the heat. Ensure the skillet is coated with enough oil. Add ¼ of the vegetables and add the tofu mixture on top. Spread the tofu mixture across the entire skillet using a spoon but don't create gaps in it. Place on the stove and cook over medium heat for 5 minutes. Bake in the oven for 15 minutes. In the 13 minutes' mark, add the remaining vegetables on top the omelet and cook for extra 2 minutes. Remove from the oven. Fold over with a spatula and serve.

›Protein Patties

Cooking time: 15 minutes
Servings: 5
Ingredients:
1 can (15 oz.) chickpeas
1 teaspoon fennel seeds
1 teaspoon caraway seeds
1 tablespoon ground flax seeds
1 tablespoon tamari
2 tablespoons water
2 garlic cloves, peeled, chopped
1 teaspoon turmeric
1 teaspoon dried sage
Pepper, salt, to taste
Directions:
Preheat the oven to 300 F. Pulse all the ingredients til smooth. Set aside. Brush the skillet with vegetable oil and place over medium heat. Spoon the mixture into the skillet. Shape into a patty using the back of the spoon, then season with salt, pepper, and paprika. Cook both side bake for 15 minutes in a baking sheet. Serve warm.

›Vegan Chickpea Pancake

Cooking time: 10 minutes

Servings: 2
Ingredients:
½ cup chickpea flour
¼ teaspoon baking powder
½ cup + 2 tablespoons water
1 green onion, finely chopped
¼ cup red pepper, finely chopped
1/8 teaspoon ground black pepper
¼ teaspoon garlic powder
¼ teaspoon salt
Directions:
Preheat a skillet over medium heat. Mix the chickpea flour, baking powder, garlic powder, pepper, and salt in a bowl. Stir in the water. Mix for 15 seconds, then stir in onions and pepper. Spray the skillet with non-stick cooking spray. Pour in the batter and spread it. Cook for 6 minutes flip carefully to the other side and cook for 5 minutes. Serve with the desired toppings.

›Protein Pudding

Cooking time: 5 minutes
Servings: 1
Ingredients:
¼ cup quinoa, cooked
2 tablespoons chia seeds
2 tablespoons hemp hearts
¾ cup cashew milk
2 tablespoons maple syrup
¼ teaspoon vanilla powder
1 pinch cinnamon
Directions:
Combine all the ingredients in a jar. Close the lid and refrigerate for 1 hour and a half. Remove from the fridge and serve.

›Gluten-Free Tofu Quiche

Cooking time: 90 minutes
Servings: 8
Ingredients:
For the crust:
3 potatoes, grated
2 tablespoons vegan butter, melted
¼ teaspoon of sea salt
¼ teaspoon pepper
For the filling:
12 oz. extra-firm silken tofu, patted dry
1 cup broccoli, chopped
¾ cup cherry tomatoes halved
3 tablespoons hummus
2 tablespoons nutritional yeast
1 medium onion, diced
3 garlic cloves, chopped
Black pepper, salt, to taste
Directions:
Bring the oven to 450 F. (220D) Remove the moisture from 3 grated potatoes by squeezing them with a towel. Put them in the pan. Spread with butter and put pepper and salt. Compress it creating an even layer. bake for 30 minutes in the oven. Remove the

crust and set aside. Bring the oven temperature to 400 F (200D). Add the garlic and vegetables to the pan. 2 tablespoons of olive oil, salt and pepper. Bake for another 35. Set the oven to 380F. (190). Mix the hummus, tofu, nutritional yeast, black pepper and salt. Move the vegetables from the oven into a mixing bowl to coat and then place it on the potato crust Cook for 45 minutes at 370 F. Serve hot.

›Pumpkin Oatmeal

Cooking time: 5 minutes
Servings: 2
Ingredients:
½ cup rolled oats
¼ cup pumpkin puree
½ cup almond milk
¼ teaspoon vanilla extract
3 tablespoon PB2
¼ teaspoon instant coffee granules
½ cup water + more if needed
½ teaspoon pumpkin pie spice
Pinch of salt
Directions:
Put ½ cup of milk and ½ cup of water in a pot and bring to a boil, after which add the oats and cook for 2 minutes. Put the pumpkin puree and cook a few more minutes. Meanwhile, water is added to the PB2 and mixed until the consistency is excellent. Once this is done, add the coffee and gradually the vanilla, the spices for the pumpkin pie and a teaspoon of salt. At this point you can serve.

›Berry Quinoa

Cooking time: 20 minutes
Servings: 4
Ingredients:
1 cup quinoa, rinsed
2 cups fresh blackberries
1/3 cup pecans, chopped, toasted
4 teaspoons organic agave nectar
1 cup low-fat milk
1 cup of water½ teaspoon ground cinnamon
Directions:
Bring the oven to 350 F by placing the pecans for 6 minutes.
put the water, milk and quinoa over high heat. then you have to lower the temperature, cover and cook for 15/17 minutes. After that turn off and let it rest for 20 minutes. Put the cinnamon and blackberries. Put the quinoa and serve with pecans and a drizzle of agave nectar.

›Lime Dressing Lentil Bean Salad

Cooking time: 20 minutes
Servings: 5
Ingredients:
1 cup green lentils, uncooked
15 oz. can black beans, rinsed, drained
2 Roma tomatoes, finely diced

2/3 cup cilantro, stemmed, roughly chopped
½ small red onion, finely diced
1 red bell pepper, finely diced
For the dressing:
1 lime, juiced
1 teaspoon Dijon mustard
2 garlic cloves, minced
½ teaspoon oregano
1 teaspoon cumin
1/8 teaspoon salt

Directions:
Cook lentils according to package instructions. Drain. Mix all dressing in a bowl and set aside. Add the black beans, lentils, tomatoes, bell pepper and onions into a bowl. Sprinkle the dressing on top and toss to coat. Add the cilantro and toss lightly. Enjoy!

➤Cheddar Sausage Potatoes

Preparation time: 10 minutes
Cooking time: 4 hours
Servings: 2
Ingredients:
1 potato, chopped
½ red bell pepper, chopped
½ green bell pepper, chopped
½ yellow onion, chopped
4 ounces smoked Andouille sausage, sliced
1 cup cheddar cheese, shredded
¼ cup sour cream
pinch of oregano, dried
¼ teaspoon basil, dried
4 ounces chicken cream
Salt and black pepper to the taste
1 tablespoon parsley, chopped

Directions:
Put the potato in your slow cooker, add red bell pepper, green bell pepper, onion, sausage, cheese, sour cream, oregano, basil, salt, pepper and chicken cream, cover and cook on Low for 4 hours. Add parsley, toss, divide between plates and serve for breakfast. Enjoy!

Nutrition facts:
Calories 355,
Fat 14,
Fiber 4,
Carbs 20,
Protein 22

➤Frittatas for Breakfast

Preparation time: 5 minutes
Cooking time: 2 hours
Servings: 6
Ingredients:
Black pepper-1/2 tbsp.
Sausages-1
Eggs-8 Spinach-3/4 cup Sea salt-1 tsp.
Bell pepper-1 ½ cups
Onions-1/4 cup
Directions:

Mix together all the ingredients. Put them in the slow cooker and let it cook for 2-3 hours. Serve hot.
Nutrition facts:
Calories: 590,
Total fat: 47g,
Cholesterol: 45 mg,
Sodium: 610 mg,
Carbohydrate: 16g,
Dietary fiber: 1g, Protein: 12g

➤Easy Buttery Oatmeal

Preparation time: 10 minutes
Cooking time: 3 hours
Servings: 2
Ingredients:
Cooking spray
2 cups coconut milk
1 cup old fashioned oats
1 pear, cubed
1 apple, cored and cubed
2 tablespoons butter, melted
Directions:
Grease your slow cooker with the cooking spray, add the milk, oats and the other ingredients, toss, put the lid on and cook on High for 3 hours. Divide the mix into bowls and serve for breakfast.
Nutrition facts:
Calories 1002,
Fat 74,
Fiber 18,
Carbs 93,
Protein 16.2

➤Egg Casserole

Preparation time: 10 minutes
Cooking time: 6 hours
Servings: 4
Ingredients:
¾ cup milk
½ teaspoon salt
8 large eggs
½ teaspoon dry mustard
¼ teaspoon black pepper
4 cups hash brown potatoes, partially thawed
½ cup green bell pepper, chopped
4 green onions, chopped
12 ounces ham, diced
½ cup red bell pepper, chopped
1½ cups cheddar cheese, shredded
Directions:
Whisk together eggs, dry mustard, milk, salt and black pepper in a large bowl. Grease the crockpot and put 1/3 of the hash brown potatoes, salt and black pepper. Layer with 1/3 of the diced ham, red bell peppers, green bell peppers, green onions and cheese. Repeat the layers twice, ending with the cheese and top with the egg mixture. Cover and cook on LOW for about 6 hours. Serve this delicious casserole for breakfast.

Nutrition facts:
Calories: 453
Fat: 26g
Carbohydrates: 32.6g

➤Delish Carrots Oatmeal

Preparation time: 10 minutes
Cooking time: 8 hours
Servings: 2
Ingredients:
½ cup old fashioned oats
1ccup almond milk
2 carrots, peeled and grated
½ teaspoon cinnamon powder
2 tablespoons brown sugar
¼ cup walnuts, chopped
Cooking spray
Directions:
Grease your slow cooker with cooking spray, add the oats, milk, carrots and the other ingredients, toss, put the lid on and cook on Low for 8 hours. Divide the oatmeal into 2 bowls and serve.
Nutrition facts:
Calories 590,
Fat 40.7,
Fiber 9.1,
Carbs 49.9
Protein 12

➤Cheesy Breakfast Potatoes

Preparation time: 20 minutes
Cooking time: 5 hours
Servings: 6
Ingredients:
1 green bell pepper, diced
1½ cups cheddar cheese, shredded
1 can cream of mushroom soup
4 medium russet potatoes, peeled and diced
1 small yellow onion, diced
4 Andouille sausages, diced
¼ cup sour cream
1/3 cup water
1 teaspoon salt
¼ cup fresh parsley, chopped
1 teaspoon black pepper
1 teaspoon garlic powder
Directions:
Mix together soup, sour cream, water, black pepper, season salt and garlic powder in a one pot crock pot until completely combined. Top with cheddar cheese and diced vegetables and stir well. Cover and cook on LOW for about 5 hours. Dish out and season with more salt and pepper if desired.
Nutrition facts:
Calories: 479
Fat: 29.6g
Carbohydrates: 32g

➤Apple with Chia Mix

Preparation time: 10 minutes
Cooking time: 8 hours
Servings: 2
Ingredients:
¼ cup chia seeds
2 apples, cored and roughly cubed
1 cup almond milk
2 tablespoons maple syrup
1 teaspoon vanilla extract
½ tablespoon cinnamon powder
Cooking spray
Directions:
Grease your slow cooker with the cooking spray, add the chia seeds, milk and the other ingredients, toss, put the lid on and cook on Low for 8 hours.
Divide the mix into bowls and serve for breakfast.
Nutrition facts:
Calories 453,
Fat 29.3,
Fiber 8,
Carbs 51.1
Protein 3.4

➤Pumpkin pie with sorghum

Preparation time: 10 minutes
Cooking time: 8 hours
Servings: 4
Ingredients:
Pumpkin pie spice-1 tbsp.
Maple syrup-2 tbsp. s.
Vanilla extract-1 tsp.
Almond milk (unsweetened) - 1 cup
Sorghum-1 cup
Pumpkin puree-3/4 cup
Directions:
In a slow cooker combine all the above ingredients and mix well. Add two cups of water to it and mix again. Let the mixture cook for 8 hours so that the sorghum gets tender and the liquid gets dissolved. Serve hot.
Nutrition facts:
Calories: 221,
Total fat: 3g,
Cholesterol: 0mg,
Sodium: 52 mg,
Carbohydrate: 27g,
Dietary fiber: 5g
Protein: 6g

➤Colorful breakfast dish

Preparation time: 15 minutes
Cooking time: 8 hours
Servings: 12 Ingredients:
1/2 pound bulk crumbled Italian sausage 2 green onions
2 minced cloves garlic

1 chopped red bell pepper
18 eggs
1 cup almond milk
1 tsp. garlic powder 1 tsp. dried oregano
Black pepper
Directions:
Make sure to grease the slow cooker well before starting to use it. Cook the Italian sausage first, with the green onions and garlic in a separate skillet for about 10-12 minutes. Drain the meat fat. In the slow cooker, add the sausage, onions and garlic as well as the bell peppers. In a separate bowl, combine the eggs, coconut milk, and all seasonings. Cover the slow cooker and cook for about 6-8 hours. Serve warm.
Nutrition facts:
255 Cal,
11.5 g total fat (3.6 g sat. fat)
172 mg chop.
119 mg sodium
4.5 g carb.
4g fiber,
11.2g protein.

‣Sugary German Oatmeal

Preparation time: 10 minutes
Cooking time: 8 hours
Servings: 2
Ingredients:
Cooking spray
1 cup steel cut oats
3 cups water
6 ounces coconut milk
2 tablespoons cocoa powder
1 tablespoon brown sugar
1 tablespoon coconut, shredded
Directions:
Grease your slow cooker with cooking spray, add oats, water, milk, cocoa powder, sugar and shredded coconut, stir, cover and cook on Low for 8 hours. Stir oatmeal one more time, divide into 2 bowls and serve for breakfast. Enjoy!
Nutrition facts:
Calories 200,
Fat 4,
Fiber 5,
Carbs 17
Protein 5

‣Cranberry Apple Oats

Preparation time: 10 minutes
Cooking time: 3 hours
Servings: 2
Ingredients:
Cooking spray
2 cups water
1 cup old fashioned oats
¼ cup cranberries, dried
1 apple, chopped

1 tablespoon butter, melted
½ teaspoon cinnamon powder
Directions:
Grease your slow cooker with cooking spray, add water, oats, cranberries, apple, butter and cinnamon, stir well, cover and cook on Low for 3 hours. Stir oatmeal again, divide into bowls and serve for breakfast. Enjoy!
Nutrition facts:
Calories 182,
Fat 4,
Fiber 6,
Carbs 8,
Protein 10

‣Sausage and Potato Mix

Preparation time: 10 minutes
Cooking time: 6 hours
Servings: 2
Ingredients:
2 sweet potatoes, peeled and roughly cubed
1 green bell pepper, minced
½ yellow onion, chopped
4 ounces smoked Andouille sausage, sliced
1 cup cheddar cheese, shredded
¼ cup Greek yogurt
¼ teaspoon basil, dried
1 cup chicken stock
Salt and black pepper to the taste
1 tablespoon parsley, chopped
Directions:
In your slow cooker, combine the potatoes with the bell pepper, sausage and the other ingredients, toss, put the lid on and cook on Low for 6 hours. Divide between plates and serve for breakfast.
Nutrition facts:
Calories 623,
Fat 35.7,
Fiber 7.6,
Carbs 53.1,
Protein 24.8

‣Apple pie oatmeal

Preparation time: 20 minutes
Cooking time: 9 hours
Servings: 4
Ingredients:
Apples (peeled & diced) – 2
Old fashioned oats – 1 cup
Protein powder – ½ cup
Cinnamon – 1 teaspoon
Apple pie spice – ½ teaspoon
Salt – ½ teaspoon
Unsweetened applesauce – ½ cup
Unsweetened almond milk – ½ cup
Low-sugar maple syrup – 2 tablespoon Sweetener of choice – ¼ cup
Directions:

Combine all the ingredients in a slow cooker.
Cook covered for 6-9 hours on low. Stir well.
Nutrition facts:
225 Cal, 4 g
Total fat (0 g sat. fat)
35 g carb.
8g fiber,
13 g protein.

›Carrots and Zucchini Oatmeal

Preparation time: 10 minutes
Cooking time: 8 hours
Servings: 2
Ingredients:
½ cup steel cut oats
1 cup coconut milk
1 carrot, grated
¼ zucchini, grated
A pinch of nutmeg, ground
A pinch of cloves, ground
½ teaspoon cinnamon powder
2 tablespoons brown sugar
¼ cup pecans, chopped
Cooking spray
Directions:
Grease your slow cooker with cooking spray, add
oats, milk, carrot, zucchini, nutmeg, cloves, cinnamon
and sugar, toss, cover and cook on Low for 8 hours.
Divide into 2 bowls, sprinkle pecans on top and serve.
Enjoy!
Nutrition facts:
Calories 200,
Fat 4,
Fiber 8,
Carbs 11
Protein 5

›Quinoa Spinach Casserole

Preparation time: 10 minutes
Cooking time: 4 hours
Servings: 2
Ingredients:
¼ cup quinoa
1 cup milk
2 eggs
A pinch of salt and black pepper
¼ cup spinach, chopped
¼ cup cherry tomatoes, halved
2 tablespoons cheddar cheese, shredded
2 tablespoons parmesan, shredded
Cooking spray
Directions:
In a bowl, mix eggs with quinoa, milk, salt, pepper, tomatoes, spinach and cheddar cheese and whisk well.
Grease your slow cooker with cooking spray, add
eggs and quinoa mix, spread parmesan all over,
cover and cook on High for 4 hours.
Divide between plates and serve.
Enjoy!

Nutrition facts:
Calories 251,
Fat 5,
Fiber 7,
Carbs 19,
Protein 11

›Coconut Quinoa Mix

Preparation time: 10 minutes
Cooking time: 8 hours
Servings: 2
Ingredients:
½ cupquinoa
1 cup water
½ cup coconut milk
1 tablespoon maple syrup
A pinch of salt
1 tablespoon berries
Directions:
In your slow cooker, mix quinoa with water, coconut
milk, maple syrup and salt, stir well, cover and cook on
Low for 8 hours. Divide into 2 bowls, sprinkle berries on
top and serve for breakfast. Enjoy!
Nutrition facts:
Calories 261,
Fat 5,
Fiber 7,
Carbs 12
Protein 5

›Milky Apple Oatmeal

Preparation time: 10 minutes
Cooking time: 8 hours
Servings: 2
Ingredients:
½ cup steel cut oats
1 apple, chopped 1 cup apple juice
1 cup milk
2 tablespoons maple syrup
1 teaspoon vanilla extract
½ tablespoon cinnamon powder
A pinch of nutmeg, ground
Cooking spray
Directions:
Grease your slow cooker with the cooking spray, add
oats, apple, apple juice, milk, maple syrup, vanilla
extract, cinnamon and nutmeg, stir, cover and cook
on Low for 8 hours. Stir oatmeal one more time, divide
into bowls and serve. Enjoy!
Nutrition facts:
Calories 221,
Fat 4,
Fiber 6,
Carbs 8,
Protein 10

›Veggie Hash Brown Mix

Cooking time: 6 hours and 5 minutes
Servings: 2
Ingredients:
1 tablespoon olive oil
½ cup white mushrooms, chopped
½ yellow onion, chopped
¼ teaspoon garlic powder ¼ teaspoon onion powder
¼ cup sour cream
10 ounces hash browns
¼ cup cheddar cheese, shredded
Salt and black pepper to the taste
½ tablespoon parsley, chopped
Directions:
Heat up a pan with the oil over medium heat, add the onion and mushrooms, stir and cook for 5 minutes. Transfer this to the slow cooker, add hash browns and the other ingredients, toss, put the lid on and cook on Low for 6 hours. Divide between plates and for breakfast.
Nutrition facts:
Calories 571,
Fat 35.6,
Fiber 5.4,
Carbs 54.9
Protein 9.7

›Banana oatmeal

Preparation time: 5 minutes
Cooking time: 8 hours
Servings: 4
Ingredients:
Steel cut oats – 1 cup
Mashed ripe banana – 1
Chopped walnuts – ¼ cup
Skim milk – 2 cups
Water – 2 cups
Flax seed meal – 2 tablespoon
Cinnamon – 2 teaspoon
Vanilla – 1 teaspoon
Nutmeg – ½ teaspoon
Salt – ½ teaspoon
Banana slices – for garnish
Chopped walnuts – for garnish
Directions:
Combine all the ingredients in a slow cooker except the banana slices and walnuts. Cook covered for 8 hours on low. Stir well. Serve topped with walnuts and banana slices.
Nutrition facts:
290 Cal,
8 g total fat (7 g sat. fat),
2 mg cholesterol
366 mg sodium
42 g carb.
6.6g fiber,
11 g protein.

›Cheesy Tater Tot Casserole

Preparation time: 10 minutes
Cooking time: 4 hours
Servings: 2
Ingredients:
Cooking spray
10 ounces tater tots, frozen
2 eggs, whisked
½ pound turkey sausage, ground
1 tablespoon heavy cream
¼ teaspoon thyme, dried
¼ teaspoon garlic powder
A pinch of salt and black pepper
½ cup Colby jack cheese, shredded
Directions:
Grease your slow cooker with cooking spray, spread tater tots on the bottom, add sausage, thyme, garlic powder, salt, pepper and whisked eggs. Add cheese, cover pot and cook on Low for 4 hours. Divide between plates and serve for breakfast. Enjoy!
Nutrition facts:
Calories 231,
Fat 5,
Fiber 9,
Carbs 15
Protein 11

›Cheddar & Bacon Casserole

Preparation time: 10 minutes
Cooking time: 3 hours
Servings: 2
Ingredients:
5 ounces hash browns, shredded
2 bacon slices, cooked and chopped
2 ounces cheddar cheese, shredded
3 eggs, whisked
1 green onion, chopped
¼ cup milk
Cooking spray
A pinch of salt and black pepper
Directions:
Grease your slow cooker with cooking spray and add hash browns, bacon and cheese.
In a bowl, mix eggs with green onion, milk, salt and pepper, whisk well and add to slow cooker. Cover, cook on High for 3 hours, divide between plates and serve. Enjoy!
Nutrition facts:
Calories 281,
Fat 4,
Fiber 6,
Carbs 12,
Protein 11

›Breakfast turkey meatloaf

Preparation time: 10 minutes
Cooking time: 4 hours
Servings: 6
Ingredients:

2 pounds ground turkey
1 chopped small red onion
2 minced cloves garlic
1 tsp. garlic powder 1 tsp. dried oregano
1 tsp. dried basil
¼ cup coconut flour
Salt and pepper
2 eggs
Coconut oil

Directions:
Heat some coconut oil in a skillet, cook the garlic and onion for 5 minutes. Set aside. Add the ground turkey in a bowl with the garlic, onions, and all spices. Use your hands to mix thoroughly. Shape the meat as a loaf and place it in the bottom of the slow cooker. Cook for about 3.5 hours. Serve with your favorite homemade ketchup.

Nutrition facts:
195 Cal,
7.5 g total fat (1.6 g sat. fat),
102 mg cholesterol
119 mg sodium,
5.5 g carb.
5g fiber
9.2g protein.

›Broccoli Casserole

Preparation time: 10 minutes
Cooking time: 6 hours
Servings: 2
Ingredients:
2 eggs, whisked
1 cup broccoli florets
2 cups hash browns
½ teaspoon coriander, ground
½ teaspoon rosemary, dried
½ teaspoon turmeric powder
½ teaspoon mustard powder
A pinch of salt and black pepper
1 small red onion, chopped ½ red bell pepper, chopped
1 ounce cheddar cheese, shredded
Cooking spray

Directions:
Grease your slow cooker with the cooking spray, and spread hash browns, broccoli, bell pepper and the onion on the bottom of the pan. In a bowl, mix the eggs with the coriander and the other ingredients, whisk and pour over the broccoli mix in the pot. Put the lid on, cook on Low for 6 hours, divide between plates and serve for breakfast.

Nutrition facts:
Calories 261,
Fat 7,
Fiber 8,
Carbs 20,
Protein 11

›Pumpkin Oatmeal

Preparation time: 10 minutes
Cooking time: 7 hours
Servings: 2
Ingredients:
Cooking spray
½ cup steel cut oats
1 cup water
1 cup almond milk
1 and ½ tablespoon maple syrup
½ teaspoon vanilla extract
½ teaspoon pumpkin pie spice
½ cup pumpkin, chopped
¼ teaspoon cinnamon powder

Directions:
Grease your slow cooker with cooking spray, add steel cut oats, water, almond milk, maple syrup, vanilla, pumpkin spice, pumpkin and cinnamon, stir, cover and cook on Low for 7 hours. Stir one more time, divide into bowls and serve. Enjoy!

Nutrition facts:
Calories 242
fat 3
fiber 8
carbs 20
protein 7

›Smooth apple butter

Preparation time: 10 minutes
Cooking time: 7 hours
Servings: 4
Ingredients:
16-20 dates - cut into halves
4 diced apples, peeled and cored
1 cup apple cider
½ cup molasses
2 Tbsp. ground cinnamon
½ Tsp. nutmeg

Directions:
Simply place all ingredients in your slow cooker and mix well. Cook for about 7 hours. The apples should be very tender, so you can easily blend them in your food processor. Put actually everything from the slow cooker in the food processor and activate until the texture is every smooth. Spread on whatever your heart desires!

Nutrition facts:
79 Cal,
1.9 g total fat (0.2 g sat. fat)
0 mg chop. 27 mg sodium,
12.5 g carb.
4g fiber,
7.2g protein.

— CHAPTER 2 —

SIDES, SALADS AND SOUPS

ALICIA TRAVIS

➤Artichoke and Arugula Salad

Preparation time: 10 minutes
Cooking time: 0 minutes
Servings: 6
Salad:
6 canned oil-packed artichoke hearts, sliced
6 cups baby arugula leaves
6 fresh olives, pitted and chopped
1 cup cherry tomatoes, sliced in half
Dressing:
1 teaspoon Dijon mustard
2 tablespoons balsamic vinegar
1 clove garlic, minced
2 tablespoons extra-virgin olive oil
For Garnish:
 fresh basil leaves, thinly sliced
Directions:
Mix ingredients for the salad in a large salad bowl, then toss to combine well. Mix ingredients for the dressing in a small bowl, then stir to mix well. Dress the salad, then serve with basil leaves on top.
Nutrition facts:
calories: 134 | fat: 12.1g | protein: 1.6g | carbs: 6.2g | fiber: 3.0g | sodium: 65mg

➤Baby Potato and Olive Salad

Preparation time: 10 minutes
Cooking time: 20 minutes
Servings: 6
2 pounds (907 g) baby potatoes, cut into 1-inch cubes
1 tablespoon low-sodium olive brine
3 tablespoons lemon juice
¼ teaspoon kosher salt
3 tablespoons extra-virgin olive oil
½ cup sliced olives
2 tablespoons torn fresh mint
1 cup sliced celery (about 2 stalks)
2 tablespoons chopped fresh oregano
Directions:
Put the tomatoes in a saucepan, then pour in enough water to submerge the tomatoes about 1 inch. Bring to a boil. Simmer for 14 minutes or until the potatoes are soft. Meanwhile, combine the olive brine, lemon juice, salt, and olive oil in a small bow. Stir to mix well. Transfer the cooked tomatoes in a colander, then rinse with running cold water. Pat dry with paper towels. Transfer the tomatoes in a large salad bowl, then drizzle with olive brine mixture. Spread with remaining ingredients and toss to combine well. Serve immediately.
Nutrition facts:
calories: 220 | fat: 6.1g | protein: 4.3g | carbs: 39.2g | fiber: 5.0g | sodium: 231mg

➤Barley, Parsley, and Pea Salad

Preparation time: 10 minutes
Cooking time: 10 minutes
 Servings: 4
2 cups water
1 cup quick-cooking barley
1small bunch flat-leaf parsley, chopped (about 1 to

1½ cups)
2 cups sugar snap pea pods
Juice of 1 lemon
½ small red onion, diced
2 tablespoons extra-virgin olive oil
Sea salt and freshly ground pepper
Directions:
Pour the water in a saucepan. Bring to a boil. Add the barley to the saucepan, then put the lid on. Reduce the heat to low. Simmer the barley for 10 minutes or until the liquid is absorbed, then let sit for 5 minutes. Open the lid, then transfer the barley in a colander and rinse under cold running water. Pour the barley in a large salad bowl and add the remaining ingredients. Toss to combine well. Serve immediately.
Nutrition facts:
calories: 152 | fat: 7.4g | protein: 3.7g | carbs: 19.3g | fiber: 4.7g | sodium: 20mg

➤Cheesy Peach and Walnut Salad

Preparation time: 10 minutes
Cooking time: 0 minutes
Servings: 1
1 ripe peach, pitted and sliced
¼ cup chopped walnuts, toasted
¼ cup shredded Parmesan cheese
1 teaspoon raw honey
Zest of 1 lemon
1 tablespoon chopped fresh mint
Directions:
Combine the peach, walnut, and cheese in a medium bowl, then drizzle with honey. Spread the lemon zest and mint on top. Toss to combine everything well. Serve immediately.
Nutrition facts :
calories: 373 | fat: 26.4g | protein: 12.9g | carbs: 27.0g | fiber: 4.7g | sodium: 453mg

➤Greek Chicken, Tomato, and Olive Salad

Preparation time: 10 minutes
Cooking time: 0 minutes
Servings: 2
Salad:
2 grilled boneless, skinless chicken breasts, sliced (about 1 cup)
10 cherry tomatoes, halved
8 pitted Kalamata olives, halved
½ cup thinly sliced red onion
Dressing:
¼ cup balsamic vinegar
1 teaspoon freshly squeezed lemon juice
¼ teaspoon sea salt
¼ teaspoon freshly ground black pepper
1 teaspoons extra-virgin olive oil for servings
2 cups roughly chopped romaine lettuce
½ cup crumbled feta cheese
Directions:
Mix ingredients for the salad in a large-medium bowl. Toss to combine well. Combine the ingredients for the dressing in another bowl. Stir to mix well.

43

Pour the dressing the bowl of salad, then toss to coat well. Refrigerate for at least 120 minutes. Remove the bowl from the refrigerator. Spread the lettuce on a large plate, then top with marinated salad. Scatter the salad with feta cheese and serve immediately.

Nutrition facts:
calories: 328 | fat: 16.9g | protein: 27.6g | carbs: 15.9g | fiber: 3.1g | sodium: 1102mg

➤Ritzy Summer Fruit Salad

Preparation time: 10 minutes
Cooking time: 0 minutes
Servings: 8
Salad:
1cup fresh blueberries
1cups cubed cantaloupe
2 cups red seedless grapes
1cup sliced fresh strawberries
1cups cubed honeydew melon
Zest of 1 large lime
½ cup unsweetened toasted coconut flakes
Dressing:
¼ cup raw honey
Juice of 1 large lime
¼ teaspoon sea salt
½ cup extra-virgin olive oil
Directions:
Mix ingredients for the salad in a large salad bowl, then toss to combine well. Mix ingredients for the dressing in a small bowl, then stir to mix well. Dress the salad and serve immediately.

Nutrition facts (per serving)
calories: 242 | fat: 15.5g | protein: 1.3g | carbs: 28.0g | fiber: 2.4g | sodium: 90mg

➤Roasted Broccoli and Tomato Panzanella

Preparation time: 10 minutes
Cooking time: 20 minutes
Servings: 4
pound (454 g) broccoli (about 3 medium stalks), trimmed, cut into 1-inch florets and ½inch stem slices
2tablespoons extra-virgin olive oil, divided
1½ cups cherry tomatoes
1½ teaspoons honey, divided
2cups cubed whole-grain crusty bread
1 tablespoon balsamic vinegar
¼ teaspoon kosher salt
½ teaspoon freshly ground black pepper
Directions:
Preheat the oven to 450°F (236°C). Toss the broccoli with 1 tablespoon of olive oil in a large bowl to coat well. Arrange the broccoli on a baking sheet, then add the tomatoes to the same bowl and toss with the remaining olive oil. Add 1 teaspoon of honey and toss again to coat well. Transfer the tomatoes on the baking sheet beside the broccoli. Place the baking sheet in the hoven and roast for 14 minutes, then add the bread cubes and flip the vegetables. Roast for an additional 3 minutes or until the broccoli is lightly charred and the bread cubes are golden brown.

Mix remaining ingredients, except for the Parmesan and oregano, in a small bowl. Stir to mix well. Transfer the roasted vegetables and bread cubes to the large salad bowl, then dress them and spread with Parmesan and oregano leaves. Toss and serve immediately.

Nutrition facts:
calories: 162 | fat: 6.8g | protein: 8.2g | carbs: 18.9g | fiber: 6.0g | sodium: 397mg

➤Sumptuous Greek Vegetable Salad

Preparation time: 20 minutes
Cooking time: 0 minutes
Servings: 6
Salad:
1 (15-ounce / 427-g) can chickpeas, drained and rinsed
1 (14-ounce / 397-g) can artichoke hearts, drained and halved
1 head Bibb lettuce, chopped (about 2½ cups)
1 cucumber, peeled deseeded, and chopped (about 1½ cups)
1½ cups grape tomatoes, halved
¼ cup chopped basil leaves
½ cup sliced black olives
½ cup cubed feta cheese
Dressing:
1 tbsp. freshly squeezed lemon juice (from about ½ small lemon)
¼ teaspoon freshly ground black pepper
1 tablespoon chopped fresh oregano
1 tablespoon extra-virgin olive oil
1 tablespoon red wine vinegar
1 teaspoon honey
Directions:
Mix ingredients for the salad in a large salad bowl, then toss to combine well. Mix ingredients for the dressing in a small bowl, then stir to mix well. Dress the salad and serve immediately.
Nutrition facts:
calories: 165 | fat: 8.1g | protein: 7.2g | carbs: 17.9g | fiber: 7.0g | sodium: 337mg

➤Brussels Sprout and Apple Slaw

Preparation time: 15 minutes
Cooking time: 0 minutes
Servings: 4
Salad:
1 pound (454 g) Brussels sprouts, stem ends removed and sliced thinly
1 apple, cored and sliced thinly
½ red onion, sliced thinly
Dressing:
1 teaspoon Dijon mustard
2 teaspoons apple cider vinegar
1 tablespoon raw honey
1 cup plain coconut yogurt
1 teaspoon sea salt
For Garnish:
½ cup pomegranate seeds
½ cup chopped toasted hazelnuts
Directions:

Mix ingredients for the salad in a large salad bowl, then toss to combine well. Mix ingredients for the dressing in a small-medium bowl, then stir to mix well. Dress the salad let sit for 10 minutes. Serve with pomegranate seeds and toasted hazelnuts on top.

Nutrition facts:
calories: 248 | fat: 11.2g | protein: 12.7g | carbs: 29.9g | fiber: 8.0g | sodium: 645mg

➤Butternut Squash and Cauliflower Soup

Preparation time: 15 minutes
Cooking time: 4 hours
Servings: 4 to 6
Ingredients:
1 pound (454 g) butternut squash, peeled and cut into 1-inch cubes
1 small head cauliflower, cut into 1,5-inch pieces
1 onion, sliced
2 tablespoons coconut oil
1 tablespoon currypowder
½ cup no-added-sugar apple juice
4 cups low-sodium vegetable soup
2 tablespoons coconut oil
1 teaspoon sea salt
¼ teaspoon freshly ground white pepper
¼ cup chopped fresh cilantro, divided

Directions:
Mix the ingredients, except for the cilantro, in the slow cooker. Stir to mix well. Cook on medium-high heat for 4 and a half hours or until the vegetables are tender. Pour the soup in a food processor, then pulse until creamy and smooth. Pour the puréed soup in a large serving bowl and garnish with cilantro before serving.

Nutrition facts (per serving)
calories: 415 | fat: 30.8g | protein: 10.1g | carbs: 29.9g | fiber: 7.0g | sodium: 1386mg

➤Cherry, Plum, Artichoke, and Cheese Board

Preparation time: 15 minutes
Cooking time: 0 minutes
Servings: 4
2 cups rinsed cherries
2 cups rinsed and sliced plums
2 cups rinsed carrots, cut into sticks
1 cup canned low-sodium artichoke hearts, rinsed and drained
1 cup cubed feta cheese

Directions:
Arrange all the ingredients in separated portions on a clean board or a large tray, then serve with spoons, knife, and forks.

Nutrition facts:
calories: 417 | fat: 13.8g | protein: 20.1g | carbs: 56.2g | fiber: 3.0g | sodium: 715mg

➤Cucumber Gazpacho

Preparation time: 10 minutes

Cooking time: 0 minutes
Servings: 4
2 cucumbers, peeled, deseeded, and cut into chunks
½ cup mint, finely chopped
2 cups plain Greek yogurt
2 garlic cloves, minced
2 cups low-sodium vegetable soup
1 tablespoon no-salt-added tomato paste
3 teaspoons fresh dill
Sea salt and freshly ground pepper

Directions:
Put the cucumber, mint, yogurt, and garlic in a food processor, then pulse until creamy and smooth. Transfer the puréed mixture in a large serving bowl, then add the vegetable soup, tomato paste, dill, salt, and ground black pepper. Stir to mix well.
Keep the soup in the refrigerator for at least 2 hours, then serve chilled.

Nutrition facts:
calories: 133 | fat: 1.5g | protein: 14.2g | carbs: 16.5g | fiber: 2.9g | sodium: 331mg

➤Veggie Slaw

Preparation time: 20 minutes
Cooking time: 0 minutes
Servings: 4 to 6
Salad:
2 large broccoli stems, peeled and shredded
½ celery root bulb, peeled and shredded
¼ cup chopped fresh Italian parsley
1 large beet, peeled and shredded
1 carrots, peeled and shredded
1 small red onion, sliced thin
1 zucchini, shredded
Dressing:
1 teaspoon Dijon mustard
½ cup apple cider vinegar
1 tablespoon raw honey
1 teaspoon sea salt
¼ teaspoon freshly ground black pepper
2 tablespoons extra-virgin olive oil
Topping:
½ cup crumbled feta cheese
Directions:
Mix ingredients for the salad in a medium-large salad bowl, then toss to combine well. Mix ingredients for the dressing in a small-medium bowl, then stir to mix well. Dress the salad, then serve with feta cheese on top.

Nutrition facts:
calories: 387 | fat: 30.2g | protein: 8.1g | carbs: 25.9g | fiber: 6.0g | sodium: 980mg

➤Grilled Bell Pepper and Anchovy Antipasto

Preparation time: 15 minutes
Cooking time: 8 minutes
Servings: 4
2 tablespoons extra-virgin olive oil, divided
4 medium red bell peppers, quartered, stem and seeds removed
6 ounces (170 g) anchovies in oil, chopped

2 tablespoons capers, rinsed and drained
1 cup Kalamata olives, pitted
1 small shallot, chopped
Sea salt and freshly ground pepper

Directions:
Heat the grill to medium-high heat. Grease the grill grates with 1 tablespoon of olive oil. Arrange the red bell peppers on the preheated grill grates, then grill for 8 minutes or until charred. Turn off the grill and allow the pepper to cool for 10 minutes. Transfer the charred pepper in a colander. Rinse and peel the peppers under running cold water, then pat dry with paper towels. Cut the peppers into chunks and combine with remaining ingredients in a large bowl. Toss to mix well. Serve immediately.

Nutrition facts :
calories: 227 | fat: 14.9g | protein: 13.9g | carbs: 9.9g | fiber: 3.8g | sodium: 1913mg

>Marinated Mushrooms and Olives

Preparation time: 1 hour 10 minutes
Cooking time: 0 minutes
Servings: 8
1 pound (454 g) white button mushrooms, rinsed and drained
1 pound (454 g) fresh olives
½ tablespoon crushed fennel seeds
1 tablespoon white wine vinegar
2 tablespoons fresh thyme leaves
Pinch chili flakes
Sea salt and freshly ground pepper
2 tablespoons extra-virgin olive oil

Directions:
Combine the ingredients in a large bowl. Toss to mix well. Refrigerate at least 60 minutes to marinate. Remove the bowl from the refrigerate and let sit under room temperature for 10 minutes, then serve.

Nutrition facts:
calories: 111 | fat: 9.7g | protein: 2.4g | carbs: 5.9g | fiber: 2.7g | sodium: 449mg

>Root Vegetable Roast

Preparation time: 15 minutes
Cooking time: 25 minutes
Servings: 4 to 6
1bunch beets, peeled and cut into 1-inch cubes
2small sweet potatoes, peeled and cut into 1,5-inch cubes
3parsnips, peeled and cut into 1-inch rounds
4carrots, peeled and cut into 1-inch rounds
1 tablespoon raw honey
1 teaspoon sea salt
½ teaspoon freshly ground black pepper
tablespoon extra-virgin olive oil
tablespoons coconut oil, melted

Directions:
Heat the oven to 405°F (205°C). Line a baking sheet with parchment paper. Mix ingredients in a large bowl. Toss to coat the vegetables well. Pour the mixture in the baking sheet, then place the sheet in the preheated oven. Roast for 25 minutes or until the vegetables are lightly browned and soft. Take off vege-

tables from the oven and allow to cool before serving.
Nutrition facts (per serving)
calories: 461 | fat: 18.1g | protein: 5.9g | carbs: 74.2g | fiber: 14.0g | sodium: 759mg

>Sardines with Lemony Tomato Sauce

Preparation time: 10 minutes
Cooking time: 40 minutes | Servings: 4
2 tablespoons olive oil, divided
4 Roma tomatoes, peeled and chopped, reserve the juice
1 small onion, sliced thinly
Zest of 1 orange
Sea salt and freshly ground pepper
1 pound (454 g) fresh sardines, rinsed, spine removed, butterflied
½ cup white wine
2 tablespoons whole-wheat breadcrumbs

Directions:
Preheat the oven to 426°F (220°C). Grease a baking dish with 1 tablespoon of olive oil. Heath the remaining olive oil in a nonstick skillet over medium-low heat until shimmering. Add the tomatoes with juice, onion, orange zest, salt, and ground pepper to the skillet and simmer for 18-20 minutes or until it thickens. Pour half of the mixture on the bottom of the baking dish, then top with the butterflied sardines. Pour the remaining mixture and white wine over the sardines. Spread the breadcrumbs on top, then place the baking dish in the preheated oven. Bake for 20 minutes or until the fish is opaque. Remove the baking sheet and serve the sardines warm.

Nutrition facts:
calories: 363 | fat: 20.2g | protein: 29.7g | carbs: 9.7g | fiber: 2.0g | sodium: 381mg

>Greens, Fennel, and Pear Soup with Cashews

Preparation time: 15 minutes
Cooking time: 15 minutes
Servings: 4 to 6
2 tablespoons olive oil
1 fennel bulb, cut into ¼-inch-thick slices
2 leeks, white part only, sliced
2 pears, peeled, cored, and cut into ½-inch cubes
1 teaspoon sea salt
¼ teaspoon freshly ground black pepper
½ cup cashews
2 cups packed blanched spinach
3 cups low-sodium vegetable soup

Directions:
Preheat the olive oil in a stockpot over high heat until shimmering. Add the fennel and leeks, then sauté for 5 minutes or until tender. Add the pears and sprinkle with salt and pepper, then sauté for another 3 minutes or until the pears are soft. Add the cashews, spinach, and vegetable soup. Bring to a boil. Reduce the heat to low. Cover and simmer for 5 minutes. Pour the soup in a food processor, then pulse until creamy and smooth. Pour the soup back to the pot and heat over low heat until heated through. Transfer the soup to a

medium-large serving bowl and serve immediately.

Nutrition facts:
calories: 266 | fat: 15.1g | protein: 5.2g | carbs: 32.9g | fiber: 7.0g | sodium: 628mg

›Moroccan Lentil, Tomato, and Cauliflower Soup

Preparation time: 15 minutes
Cooking time: 4 hours
Servings: 6
1 cup chopped carrots
1 cup chopped onions
3 cloves garlic, minced
½ teaspoon ground coriander
1 teaspoon ground cumin
1 teaspoon ground turmeric
¼ teaspoon ground cinnamon
¼ teaspoon freshly ground black pepper
1 cup dry lentils
28 ounces (794 g) tomatoes, diced, reserve the juice
1½ cups chopped cauliflower
4 cups low-sodium vegetable soup
1 tablespoon no-salt-added tomato paste
1 teaspoon extra-virgin olive oil
1 cup chopped fresh spinach
¼ cup chopped fresh cilantro
1 tablespoon red wine vinegar (optional)
Directions:
Put onions and carrott in the slow cooker, then sprinkle with minced garlic, coriander, cumin, turmeric, cinnamon, and black pepper. Stir to combine well.
Add the lentils, tomatoes, and cauliflower, then pour in the vegetable soup and tomato paste. Drizzle with olive oil. Stir to combine well. Cook high for 4 hours or until the vegetables are tender. In the last 30 minutes during the cooking time, open the lid and stir the soup, then fold in the spinach. Pour the cooked soup in a large serving bowl, then spread with cilantro and drizzle with vinegar. Serve immediately.

Nutrition facts:
calories: 131 | fat: 2.1g | protein: 5.6g | carbs: 25.0g | fiber: 5.5g | sodium: 364mg

›Mushroom and Soba Noodle Soup

Preparation time: 15 minutes
Cooking time: 10 minutes
Servings: 4
2 tablespoons coconut oil
8 ounces (227 g) shiitake mushrooms, stemmed and sliced thin
1 tablespoon minced fresh ginger
4 scallions, sliced thin
1 garlic clove, minced
1 teaspoon sea salt
4 cups low-sodium vegetable broth
3 cups water
3 ounces (113 g) soba noodles
1 bunch spinach, blanched, rinsed and cut into strips
1 tablespoon freshly squeezed lemon juice
Directions:
Preheat the coconut oil in a stockpot over medium,

heat until melted.
Add the mushrooms, ginger, scallions, garlic, and salt. Sauté for 5 minutes or until fragrant and the mushrooms are tender. Pour in the vegetable broth and water. boil, then put the soba noodles and cook for 6 minutes or until al dente. Turn off the heat and add the spinach and lemon juice. Stir to mix well. Pour the soup in a large bowl and serve immediately.

Nutrition facts:
calories: 254 | fat: 9.2g | protein: 13.1g | carbs: 33.9g | fiber: 4.0g | sodium: 1773mg

›Pumpkin Soup with Crispy Sage Leaves

Preparation time: 15 minutes
Cooking time: 10 minutes
Servings: 4
1 tablespoon olive oil
2 garlic cloves, cut into ⅛-inch-thick slices
1 onion, chopped
2 cups freshly puréed pumpkin
4 cups low-sodium vegetable soup
2 teaspoons chipotle powder
1 teaspoon sea salt
½ teaspoon freshly ground black pepper
½ cup vegetable oil
12 sage leaves, stemmed
Directions:
Preheat the olive oil in a stockpot over high heat until shimmering. Add the garlic and onion, then sauté for 5 minutes or until the onion is translucent. Pour in the puréed pumpkin and vegetable soup in the pot, then sprinkle with chipotle powder, salt, and ground black pepper. Stir to mix well. Bring to a boil. Low the heat and simmer for 4-5 minutes. Meanwhile, heat the vegetable oil in a nonstick skillet over high heat.
Add the sage leaf to the skillet and sauté for a minute or until crispy. Transfer the sage on paper towels to soak the excess oil. Gently pour the soup in three serving bowls, then divide the crispy sage leaves in bowls for garnish. Serve immediately.

Nutrition facts:
calories: 380 | fat: 20.1g | protein: 8.9g | carbs: 45.2g | fiber: 18.0g | sodium: 1364mg

›Rich Chicken and Small Pasta Broth

Preparation time: 10 minutes
Cooking time: 4 hours
Servings: 6
6 boneless, skinless chicken thighs
4 stalks celery, cut into ½-inch pieces
4 carrots, cut into 1-inch pieces
1 medium yellow onion, halved
2 garlic cloves, minced
2 bay leaves
Sea salt and freshly ground black pepper
6 cups low-sodium chicken stock
½ cup stelline pasta
¼ cup chopped fresh flat-leaf parsley
Directions:
Combine the chicken thighs, celery, carrots, onion,

and garlic in the slow cooker. Spread with bay leaves and sprinkle with salt and pepper. Toss to mix well. Pour in the chicken stock. Cook high for 4 and a half hours. In the last 20 minutes of the cooking, remove the chicken from the slow cooker and transfer to a bowl to cool. Discard the bay leaves and add the pasta to the slow cooker. Put the lid on and cook for 13-15 minutes or until al dente. Meanwhile, slice the chicken, then put the chicken and parsley in the slow cooker and cook for 5 minutes or until well combined. Pour the soup in a large bowl and serve immediately.

Nutrition facts:
calories: 285 | fat: 10.8g | protein: 27.4g | carbs: 18.8g | fiber: 2.6g | sodium: 815mg

➤Roasted Root Vegetable Soup

Preparation time: 10 minutes
Cooking time: 35 minutes
Servings: 6
2 parsnips, peeled and sliced
2 carrots, peeled and sliced
2 sweet potatoes, peeled and sliced
1 teaspoon chopped fresh rosemary
1 teaspoon chopped fresh thyme
1 teaspoon sea salt
½ teaspoon freshly ground black pepper
1 tablespoon extra-virgin olive oil
4 cups low-sodium vegetable soup
½ cup grated Parmesan cheese, for garnish (optional)
Directions:
Heat the oven to 405°F (205°C). Line a baking sheet with aluminum foil. Combine the parsnips, carrots, and sweet potatoes in a large bowl, then sprinkle with rosemary, thyme, salt and pepper. Toss to coat the vegetables well. put vegetables on the baking sheet, then roast in the preheated oven for 30 minutes or until lightly browned and soft. Flip the vegetables halfway through the roasting. Pour the roasted vegetables with vegetable broth in a food processor, then pulse until creamy and smooth. Pour the puréed vegetables in a saucepan, then warm over low heat until heated through. Spoon the soup in a large serving bowl, then scatter with Parmesan cheese. Serve immediately.

Nutrition facts:
calories: 192 | fat: 5.7g | protein: 4.8g | carbs: 31.5g | fiber: 5.7g | sodium: 797mg

➤Super Mushroom and Red Wine Soup

Preparation time: 40 minutes
Cooking time: 35 minutes
Servings: 6
2 ounces (57 g) dried morels
2 ounces (57 g) dried porcini
1 tablespoon extra-virgin olive oil
8 ounces (227 g) button mushrooms, chopped
8 ounces (227 g) portobello mushrooms, chopped
3 shallots, finely chopped
2 cloves garlic, minced
1 teaspoon finely chopped fresh thyme
Sea salt and freshly ground pepper
⅓ cup dry red wine
4 cups low-sodium chicken broth

½ cup heavy cream
1 small bunch flat-leaf parsley, chopped
Directions:
Put the dried mushrooms in a medium-large bowl and pour in enough water to submerge the mushrooms. Soak for 30 minutes and drain.
Preheat the olive oil in a stockpot over medium-high heat until shimmering. Add the mushrooms and shallots to the pot and sauté for 10 minutes or until the mushrooms are tender. Add the garlic and sauté for 60 seconds or until fragrant. Sprinkle with thyme, salt, and pepper. Pour in the dry red wine and chicken broth. Bring to a boil over high heat. Reduce the heat to low. Simmer for 20 minutes. After simmering, pour half of the soup in a food processor, then pulse until creamy and smooth. Pour the puréed soup back to the pot, then mix in the cream and heat over low heat until heated through. Pour the soup in a medium-large serving bowl and spread with chopped parsley before serving.

Nutrition facts:
calories: 139 | fat: 7.4g | protein: 7.1g | carbs: 14.4g | fiber: 2.8g | sodium: 94mg

➤Cheesy Roasted Broccolini

Preparation time: 5 minutes
Cooking time: 10 minutes
Servings: 2
1 bunch broccolini (about 5 ounces / 142 g)
1 tablespoon olive oil
½ teaspoon garlic powder
¼ teaspoon salt
1 tablespoon grated Romano cheese
Directions:
Heat the oven to 395°F (205°C). Line a sheet pan with parchment paper. Slice the tough ends off the broccolini and put in a medium bowl. Add the olive oil, garlic powder, and salt and toss to coat well. Arrange the broccolini on the prepared sheet pan. Roast in the preheated oven for 7 minutes, flipping halfway through the cooking time. Remove the pan and sprinkle the cheese over the broccolini. Using tongs, carefully flip the broccolini over to coat all sides. Return to the oven and cook for other 3-4 minutes, or until the cheese melts and starts to turn golden. Serve warm.

Nutrition facts:
calories: 114 | fat: 9.0g | protein: 4.0g | carbs: 5.0g | fiber: 2.0g | sodium: 400mg

➤Orange-Honey Glazed Carrots

Preparation time: 10 minutes
Cooking time: 15 to 20 minutes
Servings: 2
½ pound (227 g) rainbow carrots, peeled
2 tablespoons fresh orange juice
1 tablespoon honey
½ teaspoon coriander
Pinch salt
Directions:
Heat the oven to 396°F (205°C). Cut the carrots

lengthwise into slices of even thickness and place in a large bowl. Stir together the orange juice, honey, coriander, and salt in a small bowl. Pour the orange juice mixture over the carrots and toss until well coated. Spread the carrots in a baking dish in a single layer. Roast for 15 to 20 minutes until fork tender. Let cool for 5 minutes before serving.

Nutrition facts (per serving)
calories: 85 | fat: 0g | protein: 1.0g | carbs: 21.0g | fiber: 3.0g | sodium: 156mg

➤Roasted Cauliflower

Preparation time: 10 minutes
Cooking time: 20 minutes
Servings: 2
½ large head cauliflower, stemmed and broken into florets (about 3 cups)
1 tablespoon olive oil
2 tablespoons freshly squeezed lemon juice
2 tablespoons tahini
1 teaspoon harissa paste
Pinch salt
Directions:
Heat the oven to 396°F (200°C). Line a sheet pan with parchment paper. Toss the cauliflower florets with the olive oil in a large bowl and transfer to the sheet pan. Roast in the oven for 13-15 minutes, flipping the cauliflower once or twice, or until it starts to become golden. Mix the lemon juice in a different bowl, tahini, harissa, and salt and stir to mix well. Remove the pan and toss the cauliflower with the lemon tahini sauce. Return to the oven and roast for another 5 minutes. Serve hot.

Nutrition facts:
calories: 205 | fat: 15.0g | protein: 4.0g | carbs: 15.0g | fiber: 7.0g | sodium: 161mg

➤Sautéed White Beans with Rosemary

Preparation time: 10 minutes
Cooking time: 12 minutes | **Servings:** 2
1 tablespoon olive oil
2 garlic cloves, minced
1 (15-ounce / 425-g) can white cannellini beans, drained and rinsed
1 teaspoon minced fresh rosemary plus 1 whole fresh rosemary sprig
¼ teaspoon dried sage
½ cup low-sodium chicken stock
Salt, to taste
Directions:
Preheat the olive oil in a saucepan over medium-high heat.
Add the garlic and sauté for 30 seconds until fragrant. Add the beans, minced and whole rosemary, sage, and chicken stock and bring the mixture to a boil. Low the heat to medium-low and allow to simmer for 10 minutes, or until most of the liquid is evaporated. Mash part of the beans to thicken them.
Season with salt to taste. Remove the rosemary sprig before serving.

Nutrition facts:
calories: 155 | fat: 7.0g | protein: 6.0g | carbs: 17.0g | fiber: 8.0g | sodium: 153mg

➤Moroccan Spiced Couscous

Preparation time: 10 minutes
Cooking time: 8 minutes | **Servings:** 2
1 tablespoon olive oil
¾ cup couscous
¼ teaspoon cinnamon
¼ teaspoon garlic powder
¼ teaspoon salt, plus more as needed
1 cup water
2 tablespoons minced dried apricots
2 tablespoons raisins
2 teaspoons minced fresh parsley
Directions:
Preheat the olive oil in a saucepan over medium-high heat until it shimmers.
Add the couscous, cinnamon, garlic powder, and salt. Stir for 1 minute to toast the couscous and spices.
Add the water, apricots, and raisins and bring the mixture to a boil.
Cover and turn off the heat. Allow the couscous to sit for 4 to 5 minutes and then fluff it with a fork. Sprinkle with the fresh parsley. Season with more salt as needed and serve.

Nutrition facts:
calories: 338 | fat: 8.0g | protein: 9.0g | carbs: 59.0g | fiber: 4.0g | sodium: 299mg

➤Lemon-Tahini Hummus

Preparation time: 15 minutes
Cooking time: 0 minutes | **Servings:** 6
1 and a half (15-ounce / 425-g) can chickpeas, drained and rinsed
4 tablespoons extra-virgin olive oil, divided
4 to 5 tablespoons tahini (sesame seed paste)
2 lemons, juiced
1 lemon, zested, divided
1 tablespoon minced garlic
Pinch salt
Directions:
In a food processor, mix the chickpeas, 2 tablespoons of olive oil, tahini, lemon juice, half of the lemon zest, and garlic and pulse for up to 1 minute, scraping down the sides of the food processor bowl.
Taste and add salt as needed. Feel free to add 1 teaspoon of water at a time to thin the hummus to a better consistency.
Transfer the hummus to a serving bowl. Serve drizzled with the remaining 2 tablespoons of olive oil and remaining half of the lemon zest.
Nutrition facts:
calories: 216 | fat: 15.0g | protein: 5.0g | carbs: 17.0g | fiber: 5.0g | sodium: 12mg

Lemon and Spinach Orzo

Preparation time: 5 minutes
Cooking time: 10 minutes
1 cup dry orzo
1 (6-ounce / 170-g) bag baby spinach
1 cup halved grape tomatoes
2 tablespoons extra-virgin olive oil
¼ teaspoon salt
Freshly ground black pepper
¾ cup crumbled feta cheese
1 lemon, juiced and zested
Directions:
Boil the water. Stir in the orzo and cook uncovered for 8 minutes. Drain the water, then return the orzo to medium heat. Add the spinach and tomatoes and cook. Sprinkle with salt, olive oil, and pepper and mix well. Top with the feta cheese, lemon juice and zest, then toss one or two more times and serve.
Nutrition facts:
calories: 610 | fat: 27.0g | protein: 21.0g | carbs: 74.0g | fiber: 6.0g | sodium: 990mg

Zesty Spanish Potato Salad

Preparation time: 10 minutes |
Cooking time: 5 to 7 minutes | **Servings:** 6 to 8
4 russet potatoes, peeled and chopped
3 large, hard-boiled eggs, chopped
1 cup frozen mixed vegetables, thawed
½ cup plain, unsweetened, full-fat Greek yogurt
5 tablespoons pitted Spanish olives
½ teaspoon freshly ground black pepper
½ teaspoon dried mustard seed
½ tablespoon freshly squeezed lemon juice
½ teaspoon dried dill
Salt, to taste
Directions:
Place the potatoes in a medium-large pot of water and boil for 5 to 7 minutes, until just fork tender, checking periodically for doneness. You don't have to overcook them.Mix the eggs, vegetables, yogurt, olives, pepper, mustard, lemon juice, and dill. Season with salt to taste. Once the potatoes are cooled somewhat, add them to the large bowl, then toss well and serve.
Nutrition facts:
calories: 192 | fat: 5.0g | protein: 9.0g | carbs: 30.0g | fiber: 2.0g | sodium: 59mg

Greek Salad with Dressing

Preparation time: 10 minutes
Cooking time: 0 minutes
Servings: 4 to 6
1 head iceberg lettuce
2 cups cherry tomatoes
1 large cucumber
1 medium onion
¼ cup lemon juice
½ cup extra-virgin olive oil
1 teaspoon salt
1 clove garlic, minced
1 cup Kalamata olives, pitted
1 (6-ounce / 170-g) package feta cheese, crumbled
Directions:
Cut the lettuce into 1-inch pieces and put them in a large salad bowl.
Cut the tomatoes in half and add them to the salad bowl. Slice the cucumber into bite-sized pieces and add them to the salad bowl. Thinly slice the onion and add it to the salad bowl. In bowl, whisk together the oil, lemon juice, salt, and garlic. Pour the dressing over the salad and gently toss to evenly coat. Complete the salad with the Kalamata olives and feta cheese and serve.
Nutrition facts:
calories: 539 | fat: 50.0g | protein: 9.0g | carbs: 18.0g | fiber: 4.0g | sodium: 1758mg

Tricolor Summer Salad

Preparation time: 10 minutes
Cooking time: 0 minutes | **Servings:** 3 to 4
¼ cup while balsamic vinegar
2 tablespoons Dijon mustard
1 tablespoon sugar
½ teaspoon garlic salt
½ teaspoon freshly ground black pepper
¼ cup extra-virgin olive oil
1½ cups chopped orange, yellow, and red tomatoes
½ cucumber, peeled and diced
1 small red onion, thinly sliced
¼ cup crumbled feta (optional)
Directions:
In a small-medium bowl, whisk the vinegar, mustard, sugar, pepper, and garlic salt. Then slowly whisk in the olive oil. In a medium-large bowl, add the tomatoes, cucumber, and red onion. Add the dressing. Toss once or twice and serve with the feta crumbles (if desired) sprinkled on top.
Nutrition facts:
calories: 246 | fat: 18.0g | protein: 1.0g | carbs: 19.0g | fiber: 2.0g | sodium: 483mg

Chicken and Small Pasta Soup

Preparation time: 5 minutes
Cooking time: 20 minutes | **Servings:** 6
1 tablespoon extra-virgin olive oil
2 garlic cloves, minced
3 cups packed chopped kale center ribs removed
1 cup minced carrots
8 cups no-salt-added chicken or vegetable broth
¼ teaspoon kosher or sea salt
¼ teaspoon freshly ground black pepper
¾ cup uncooked acini de pepe or small pasta
2 cups shredded cooked chicken (about 12 ounces / 340 g)
3 tablespoons grated Parmesan cheese
Directions:
Heat the oil. Add the garlic and cook for 35-50seconds, stirring frequently. Add the kale and carrots

and cook for 5 minutes, stirring occasionally. Add the broth, salt, and pepper, and turn the heat to high. Put the broth to a boil and add the pasta. Bring the heat to medium for 10 minutes, or until the pasta is cooked through. Add the chicken and cook for another 2 minutes to warm through. Ladle the soup into six bowls. Top each with ½ tablespoon of cheese and serve.

Nutrition facts:
calories: 275 | fat: 19.0g | protein: 16.0g | carbs: 11.0g | fiber: 2.0g | sodium: 298mg

›Mushroom Barley Soup

Preparation time: 5 minutes
Cooking time: 20 to 23 minutes | **Servings:** 6
2 tablespoons extra-virgin olive oil
1 cup chopped carrots
1 cup chopped onion
5½ cups chopped mushrooms
6 cups no-salt-added vegetable broth
1 cup uncooked pearled barley
¼ cup red wine
1 tablespoons tomato paste
4 sprigs fresh thyme or ½ teaspoon dried thyme
1 dried bay leaf
6 tablespoons grated Parmesan cheese
Directions:
In a medium-large stockpot over medium heat, heat the oil. Add the onion and the carrots and cook for 5 minutes, stirring frequently. Turn up the heat to medium-high and add the mushrooms. Cook for 3 minutes, stirring frequently. Add the broth, barley, wine, tomato paste, thyme, and bay leaf. Bring the soup to a boil. Once it's boiling, stir a few times, reduce the heat to medium-low, cover, and cook for another 12 to 15 minutes, until the barley is cooked through. Remove the bay leaf and serve the soup in bowls with 1 tablespoon of cheese sprinkled on top of each.

Nutrition facts:
calories: 195 | fat: 4.0g | protein: 7.0g | carbs: 34.0g | fiber: 6.0g | sodium: 173mg

›Paella Soup

Preparation time: 6 minutes
Cooking time: 24 minutes | **Servings:** 6
2 tablespoons extra-virgin olive oil
1 cup chopped onion
1½ cups coarsely chopped green bell pepper
1½ cups coarsely chopped red bell pepper
2 garlic cloves, chopped
1 teaspoon ground turmeric
1 teaspoon dried thyme
2 teaspoons smoked paprika
2½ cups uncooked instant brown rice
2 cups low-sodium or no-salt-added chicken broth
2½ cups water
1 cup frozen green peas, thawed
1 (28-ounce / 794-g) can low-sodium or no-salt-added crushed tomatoes
1 pound (454 g) fresh raw medium shrimp, shells and tails removed

Directions:
In a medium-large stockpot over medium-high heat, heat the oil. Add the onion, bell peppers, and garlic. Cook for 8 minutes, stirring occasionally. Add the turmeric, thyme, and smoked paprika, and cook for 2 minutes more, stirring often. Stir in the rice, broth, and water. Bring to a boil over high heat. Reduce the heat to medium 10 minutes. Stir the peas, tomatoes, and shrimp into the soup. Cook for 4 minutes, until the shrimp is cooked, turning from gray to pink and white. The soup will be very thick, when ready to serve. Ladle the soup into bowls and serve hot.

Nutrition facts:
calories: 431 | fat: 5.7g | protein: 26.0g | carbs: 69.1g | fiber: 7.4g | sodium: 203mg

›Bell Pepper, Cabbage and Arugula Coleslaw

Preparation Time: 15 minutes
Cooking Time: 0 minutes
Servings: 4
Ingredients:
Sea salt and ground black pepper
2 teaspoons balsamic vinegar
1 teaspoon fresh garlic, minced
2 tablespoons tahini (sesame paste)
1 tablespoon yellow mustard
¼ teaspoon paprika
1 red bell pepper, deveined and sliced
1 green bell pepper, deveined and sliced
½ pound (227 g) Napa cabbage, shredded
2 cups arugula, torn into pieces
1 Spanish onion, thinly sliced into rings
4 tablespoons sesame seeds, lightly toasted
Directions:
Combine the bell peppers, cabbage, arugula, and Spanish onion. Dress Make a dressing by whisking the balsamic vinegar, garlic, tahini, mustard, salt, black pepper, and paprika. Salad and toss until everything is well incorporated. Garnish with sesame seeds just before serving. Serve well chilled and enjoy!

Nutrition facts:
Calories: 123
Protein: 27g
Carbohydrate: 2,8g
Fat: 10 g

›Blueberry Cantaloupe Avocado Salad

Preparation Time: 5 minutes
Cooking Time: 0 minutes
Servings: 2
Ingredients:
1 diced cantaloupe
2–3 chopped avocados
1 package of blueberries
¼ cup olive oil
1/8 cup balsamic vinegar
Directions:
Mix all ingredients.

Nutrition facts:
Calories: 406
Protein: 9g
Carbohydrate: 32g
Fat: 5 g

➤Beet Salad

Preparation Time: 5 minutes
Cooking Time: 0 minutes
Servings: 2
Ingredients:
2–3 fresh, raw beets grated or shredded in food processor
3 tablespoons olive oil
2 tablespoons balsamic vinegar
¼ teaspoon salt
1/3 teaspoon cumin
Dash stevia powder or liquid
Dash pepper
Directions:
Mix all ingredients together for the best raw beet salad.
Nutrition facts:
Calories: 156
Protein: 8g
Carbohydrate: 40g
Fat: 5 g

➤Broccoli Salad

Preparation Time: 5 minutes
Cooking Time: 0 minutes
Servings: 2
Ingredients:
1 head broccoli, chopped
2–3 slices of fried bacon, crumbled
1 diced green onion
½ cup raisins or craisins
½–1 cup of chopped pecans
¾ cup sunflower seeds
½ cup of pomegranate
Dressing:
1 cup organic mayonnaise
¼ cup baking stevia
2 teaspoons white vinegar
Directions:
Mix all ingredients together. Mix dressing and fold into salad.
Nutrition facts:
Calories: 239
Protein: 10g
Carbohydrate: 33g
Fat: 2 g

➤Roasted Garlic Potatoes

Preparation Time: 5 minutes
Cooking Time: 30 minutes
Servings: 2
Ingredients:
5 red new potatoes, chopped

¼ cup olive oil
2–3 cloves of minced garlic
1 tablespoon rosemary
Directions:
Preheat oven to 425 degrees.
Stir all ingredients together in a bowl.
Pour into a baking sheet and bake for 30 minutes.
Nutrition facts:
Calories: 176
Protein: 5g
Carbohydrate: 30g
Fat: 2 g

➤Sweet and Sour Cabbage

Preparation Time: 5 minutes
Cooking Time: 15 minutes
Servings: 2
Ingredients:
1 tablespoon honey or maple syrup
1 teaspoon baking stevia
2 tablespoons water
1 tablespoon olive oil
¼ teaspoon caraway seeds
¼ teaspoon salt
1/8 teaspoon pepper
2 cups chopped red cabbage
1 diced apple
Directions:
Cook all the ingredients in a covered saucepan on the stove for 13-15 minutes.
Nutrition facts:
Calories: 170
Protein: 17g
Carbohydrate: 20g
Fat: 8 g

➤Barley and Lentil Salad

Preparation Time: 5 minutes
Cooking Time: 0 minutes
Servings: 2
Ingredients:
1 head romaine lettuce
¾ cup cooked barley
2 cups cooked lentils
1 diced carrot
¼ chopped red onion
¼ cup olives
½ chopped cucumber
3 tablespoons olive oil
2 tablespoons fresh lemon juice
Directions:
Mix all ingredients together. Add kosher salt and black pepper.
Nutrition facts:
Calories: 213
Protein: 21g
Carbohydrate: 6g
Fat: 9 g

›Taste of Normandy Salad

Preparation Time: 25 minutes
Cooking Time: 5 minutes
Servings: 4 to 6
Ingredients:
For the walnuts:
2 tablespoons butter
¼ cup sugar or honey
1 cup walnut pieces
½ teaspoon kosher salt
For the dressing
3 tablespoons extra-virgin olive oil
1½ tablespoons champagne vinegar
1½ tablespoons Dijon mustard
¼ teaspoon kosher salt
For the salad:
1 head red leaf lettuce, torn into pieces
3 apples, cored and cut into thin wedges
4 heads endive
1 (8-ounce) Camembert wheel, cut into thin wedges
Directions:
To make the walnuts. Melt the tbsp. butter. Stir in the sugar and cook until it dissolves. Add the walnuts and cook for 4-6 minutes, stirring, until toasty. Season with salt and transfer to a plate to cool. To make the dressing. In a medium/large bowl, whisk the oil, vinegar, mustard, and salt until combined. To make the salad Add the lettuce and endive to the bowl with the dressing and toss to coat. Transfer to a serving platter. Decoratively arrange the apple and Camembert wedges over the lettuce and scatter the walnuts on top. Serve immediately.
Nutrition facts:
Calories: 699;
Total fat: 52g;
Total carbs: 44g;
Cholesterol: 60mg;
Fiber: 17g;
Protein: 23g;
Sodium: 1170mg

›Norwegian Niçoise Salad: Smoked Salmon, Cucumber, Egg, and Asparagus

Preparation Time: 20 minutes
Cooking Time: 5 minutes
Servings: 4
Ingredients:
For the vinaigrette
3 tablespoons walnut oil
2 tablespoons champagne vinegar
1 tablespoon chopped fresh dill
½ teaspoon kosher salt
¼ teaspoon ground mustard
Freshly ground black pepper
For the salad:
Handful green beans, trimmed
1 (3- to 4-ounce) package spring greens
12 spears pickled asparagus
4 large soft-boiled eggs, halved

8 ounces smoked salmon, thinly sliced
1 cucumber, thinly sliced
1 lemon, quartered
Directions:
To make the dressing
In a small/medium bowl, mix the oil, vinegar, dill, salt, ground mustard, and a few grinds of pepper until emulsified. Set aside.
To make the salad
Start by blanching the green beans: Bring a pot of salted water to a boil. Drop in the beans. Cook or 1 to 2 minutes until they turn bright green, then immediately drain and rinse under cold water. Set aside. Divide the spring greens among 4 plates. Toss each serving with dressing to taste. Arrange 3 asparagus spears, 1 egg, 2 ounces of salmon, one-fourth of the cucumber slices, and a lemon wedge on each plate. Serve immediately.
Nutrition facts:
Calories: 257;
Total fat: 18g;
Total carbs: 6g;
Cholesterol: 199mg;
Fiber: 2g;
Protein: 19g;
Sodium: 603mg

›Caesar Salad Crunchy Chickpeas

Cooking Time: 20 minutes
Preparation Time: 5 minutes
Servings: 6
Ingredients:
2 tablespoons extra-virgin olive oil
2 (15-ounce) cans chickpeas, drained and rinsed
1 teaspoon garlic powder
1 teaspoon kosher salt
1 teaspoon dried oregano
1 teaspoon onion powder
2 tablespoons grated Parmesan cheese
½ cup mayonnaise
1 clove garlic, peeled and smashed
2 tablespoons freshly squeezed lemon juice
½ tablespoon Worcestershire sauce
1 teaspoon Dijon mustard
3 heads romaine lettuce
½ tablespoon anchovy paste
Directions:
To make the chickpeas:
Preheat the oven to 450°F. Line a baking sheet with parchment paper. In a medium/large bowl, mix chickpeas, garlic powder, oil, salt, oregano, onion powder. Scatter the coated chickpeas on the prepared baking sheet. Roast for about 20 minutes, tossing occasionally, until the chickpeas are golden and have a bit of crunch.
To make the dressing:
Whisk the mayonnaise, garlic, Parmesan, lemon juice, Worcestershire sauce, mustard, and anchovy paste until combined.
To make the salad:
In a medium/large bowl, combine the lettuce and dressing. Toss to coat. Top with the roasted chickpeas

and serve.

Nutrition facts:
Calories: 367;
Total fat: 22g;
Total carbs: 35g;
Cholesterol: 9mg;
Fiber: 13g;
Protein: 12g;
Sodium: 407mg

➤Summertime Slaw

Preparation Time: 20 minutes
Cooking Time: 30 minutes
Servings: 10-12 servings
Ingredients:
One-third cup of canola oil
Three-quarter cups each of
White vinegar
Sugar
One teaspoon. each of
Pepper
Salt
One tablespoon. of water
Half a teaspoon. of red pepper flakes (crushed and optional)
Two tomatoes (medium-sized, seeded, peeled, and chopped)
One pack of coleslaw mix (fourteen oz.)
One sweet red pepper (small-sized, chopped)
One green pepper (small-sized, chopped)
One onion (large-sized, chopped)
Half a cup of sweet pickle relish
Directions:
Take a saucepan of large size and in it, combine water, sugar, oil, vinegar, pepper, salt, and if you want, then red pepper flakes too. Cook them over medium heat by continuously stirring the mixture. Comes to a boil. Cook for another two minutes or so and make sure that all the sugar has dissolved. Once done, cool the mixture to room temperature by stirring it.
Take a salad bowl of large size and in it, combine the pickle relish, coleslaw mix, peppers, onion, and tomatoes. On top of the mixture, add the dressing and toss the mixture to coat it properly. Cover the mixture and put it in the refrigerator for a night.
Nutrition Facts: Calories: 138 Protein: 1g Fat: 6g Carbs: 21g Fiber: 2g

➤Romaine Lettuce and Radicchios Mix

Preparation Time: 6 minutes
Cooking Time: 0 minutes
Servings: 4
Ingredients:
2 tablespoons olive oil
A pinch of salt and black pepper
2 spring onions, chopped
3 tablespoons Dijon mustard
Juice of 1 lime
½ cup basil, chopped
4 cups romaine lettuce heads, chopped
3 radicchios, sliced

Directions:
In a bowl, combine the lettuce with the spring onions and the other ingredients, toss and serve.
Nutrition facts:
Calories: 87,
Fats: 2 g,
Fiber: 1 g,
Carbs: 1 g,
Protein: 2 g

➤Greek Salad

Preparation Time: 15 Minutes
Cooking Time: 15 Minutes
Servings: 5
Ingredients:
For Dressing:
½ teaspoon black pepper
¼ teaspoon salt
½ teaspoon oregano
1 tablespoon garlic powder
2 tablespoons Balsamic
1/3 cup olive oil
For Salad:
½ cup sliced black olives
½ cup chopped parsley, fresh
1 small red onion, thin sliced
1 cup cherry tomatoes, sliced
1 bell pepper, yellow, chunked
1 cucumber, peeled, quarter and slice
4 cups chopped romaine lettuce
½ teaspoon salt
2 tablespoons olive oil
Directions:
In a small bowl, blend all the ingredients for the dressing and let this set in the refrigerator. To assemble the salad, mix all the ingredients in a large-sized bowl and toss the veggies gently but thoroughly to mix. Serve the salad with the dressing in amounts as desired
Nutrition facts:
Calories: 234,
Fat: 16.1 g,
Protein: 5 g,
Carbs: 48 g

➤Salmon Asparagus Salad

Cooking Time: 10 minutes
Preparation Time: 16 minutes
Servings: 8
Ingredients:
1 lb. fresh asparagus
2 heads red leaf lettuce, rinsed and torn
1/2 cup pecans,
1/2 cup frozen green peas, thawed
1/4 lb. smoked salmon, cut into 1-inch chunks
2 tablespoons. lemon juice
1/4 cup olive oil
1 teaspoon Dijon mustard
1/2 teaspoon salt
1/4 teaspoon pepper
Directions:
Boil a pot of water. Stir in asparagus and cook for 5

minutes until tender. Let it drain; set aside. In a skillet, cook the pecans over medium heat for 5 minutes, stirring constantly until lightly toasted. Combine the asparagus, toasted pecans, salmon, peas, and red leaf lettuce and toss in a large bowl. In another bowl, combine lemon juice, pepper, Dijon mustard, salt, and olive oil. You can coat the salad with the dressing or serve it on its side.

Nutrition facts:
Calories: 159
Total Carbohydrate: 7 g
Cholesterol: 3 mg
Total Fat: 12.9 g
Protein: 6 g
Sodium: 304 mg

›Shrimp Cobb Salad

Preparation Time: 25 minutes
Cooking Time: 10 minutes
Servings: 2
Ingredients:
2 1/2 tablespoons. Fresh lemon juice
1 (10 oz.) package romaine lettuce hearts
4 slices center-cut bacon
1 lb. large shrimp, peeled and deveined
1/2 teaspoon ground paprika
1/2 teaspoon whole grain Dijon mustard
1/4 teaspoon ground black pepper
1 1/2 tablespoons. Extra-virgin olive oil
1/4 teaspoon salt, divided
2 cups cherry tomatoes, quartered
1 ripe avocado, cut into wedges
1 cup shredded carrots
Directions:
In a medium/large skillet over medium heat, cook the bacon for 4 minutes on each side till crispy. Take away from the skillet and place on paper towels; let cool for 5 minutes. Break the bacon into bits. Pour out the bacon fat, leaving behind only 1 tablespoon. in the skillet. Bring the skillet back to medium-high heat. Add black pepper and paprika to the shrimp for seasoning. Cook the shrimp around 2 minutes each side until it is opaque. Sprinkle with 1/8 teaspoon of salt for seasoning. Combine the remaining 1/8 teaspoon of salt, mustard, olive oil and lemon juice together in a small bowl. Stir in the romaine hearts. On each serving plate, place on 1 and 1/2 cups of romaine lettuce. Add on top the same amounts of avocado, carrots, tomatoes, shrimp and bacon.

Nutrition facts:
Calories: 528
Total Carbohydrate: 22.7 g
Cholesterol: 365 mg
Total Fat: 28.7 g
Protein: 48.9 g
Sodium: 1166 mg

›Toast with Herbed Cream Cheese, Smoked Salmon, greens

Cooking time: 5 minutes

Preparation time: 10 minutes
Servings: 2
Ingredients:
½ teaspoon garlic powder
¼ teaspoon kosher salt
¼ cup cream cheese,
2 tablespoons chopped fresh flat-leaf parsley
2 tablespoons chopped fresh chives or sliced scallion
2 slices bread
4 ounces smoked salmon
Small handful microgreens or sprouts
1 tablespoon capers, drained and rinsed
¼ small red onion, very thinly sliced
Directions:
To make the herbed cream cheese. In a medium/large bowl, combine the cream cheese, parsley, chives, garlic powder, and salt. Using a fork, mix until combined. Chill until ready to use. To make the toast Toast the bread. Spread the cheese over each toast, then put salmon. Garnish with the microgreens, red onion, capers.

Nutrition facts:
Calories: 194;
Total fat: 8g;
Cholesterol: 26mg;
Fiber: 2g;
Protein: 12g;
Sodium: 227mg

›Crab Melt with Avocado and Egg

Cooking Time: 15 minutes
Preparation Time: 15 minutes
Servings: 2
Ingredients:
3 tablespoons butter, divided
2 English muffins, split
1 (4-ounce) can lump crabmeat
2 tomatoes, cut into slices
4 large eggs
6 ounces sliced or shredded cheddar cheese
Kosher salt
Microgreens, for garnish
2 large avocados, halved, pitted, and cut into slices
Directions:
Preheat the broiler. Toast the English muffin halves. Place the toasted halves, cut side up, on a baking sheet. Spread 1½ teaspoons of butter evenly over each half, allowing the butter to melt into the crevices. Top each with tomato slices, then divide the crab over each, and finish with the cheese. Broil the cheese melts. Meanwhile, in a medium/large skillet over medium heat, melt the remaining 1 tablespoon of butter, swirling to coat the bottom of the skillet. Crack the eggs into the skillet, giving ample space for each. Sprinkle with salt. Cook for about 3 minutes. Flip the eggs and cook the other side until the yolks are set to your liking. Place 1 egg on each muffin half. Top with avocado slices and microgreens.

Nutrition facts:
Calories: 1221;
Total fat: 84g;
Cholesterol: 94mg;

Fiber: 2g;
Protein: 12g;
Sodium: 888mg

➤Parsley Zucchini and Radishes

Preparation time: 5 minutes
Cooking time: 15 minutes
Servings: 4
Ingredients:
1-pound zucchinis, cubed
1 cup radishes, halved
1 tablespoon olive oil
1 tablespoon balsamic vinegar
2 tomatoes, cubed
3 tablespoons parsley, chopped
Salt and black pepper to taste
Directions:
In a pan, mix the zucchinis with the radishes, oil and the other ingredients, toss, introduce in the fryer and cook at 350 degrees F for 15 minutes. Divide between plates and serve.
Nutrition facts: Cal: 170, Fat 6, Fiber 2, Carbs 5, Protein 6

➤Cherry Tomatoes Sauté

Preparation time: 5 minutes
Cooking time: 15 minutes
Servings: 4
Ingredients:
1 tablespoon olive oil
1 pound cherry tomatoes, halved
Juice of 1 lime
2 tablespoons parsley, chopped
A pinch of salt and black pepper
Directions
In a pan, mix the tomatoes with the oil and the other ingredients, toss, introduce the pan in the machine and cook at 360 degrees F for 15 minutes.
Divide between plates and serve.
Nutrition facts: Calories 141, Fat 6, Fiber 2, Carbs 4, Protein 7

➤Creamy Eggplant

Preparation time: 5 minutes
Cooking time: 20 minutes
Servings: 4
Ingredients
2 pounds eggplants, roughly cubed
1 cup heavy cream
2 tablespoons butter, melted
Salt and black pepper to taste
½ teaspoon chili powder
½ teaspoon turmeric powder
Directions
In a pan, mix the eggplants with the cream, butter and the other ingredients, toss, introduce in the machine and cook at 370 degrees F for 20 minutes.

Divide between plates and serve.
Nutrition facts: Cal: 151, Fat 3, Fiber 2, Carbs 4, Protein 6

➤Eggplant and Carrots Mix

Preparation time: 5 minutes
Cooking time: 25 minutes
Servings: 4
Ingredients
1-pound eggplants, roughly cubed
1 pound baby carrots
1 cup heavy cream
½ teaspoon chili powder
1 teaspoon garlic powder
1 tablespoon chives, chopped
A pinch of salt and black pepper
Directions:
In a pan, mix the eggplants with the carrots, cream and the other ingredients, toss, introduce in the air fryer and cook at 376 degrees F for 25 minutes. Divide between plates and serve.
Nutrition facts: Cal: 129, Fat 6, Fiber 2, Carbs 5, Protein 8

➤Parmesan Eggplants

Preparation time: 5 minutes
Cooking time: 20 minutes
Servings: 4
Ingredients
1-pound eggplants, roughly cubed
1 tablespoon olive oil
1 teaspoon garlic powder
1 cup parmesan, grated
A pinch of salt and black pepper
Cooking spray
Directions
In the air fryer's pan, mix the eggplants with the oil and the other ingredients except the parmesan and toss. Sprinkle the parmesan on top, put the pan in the machine and cook at 370 degrees F for 20 minutes. Divide between plates and serve.
Nutrition facts: cal: 183, fat 6, fiber 2, carbs 3, protein 8

➤Kale Sauté

Preparation time: 5 minutes
Cooking time: 15 minutes
Servings: 4
Ingredients
1 tablespoon avocado oil
1 pound baby kale
½ cup heavy cream
Salt and black pepper to taste
¼ teaspoon chili powder
1 tablespoon dill, chopped
¼ cup walnuts, chopped
Directions
In a pan, mix the kale with the oil, cream and the other ingredients, toss, introduce the pan in the machine

and cook at 360 degrees F for 15 minutes. Divide between plates and serve.
Nutrition facts: Cal: 160, Fat 7, Fiber 2, Carbs 4, Protein 5

›Carrots Sauté

Preparation time: 5 minutes
Cooking time: 20 minutes
Servings: 4
Ingredients
2 pounds baby carrots, peeled
1 tablespoon balsamic vinegar
2 tablespoons olive oil
Salt and black pepper to taste
1 tablespoon lemon juice
1/3 cup almonds, chopped
½ cup walnuts, chopped
Directions
In a pan, mix the carrots with the vinegar, oil and the other ingredients, toss, introduce the pan in the machine and cook at 380 degrees F for 20 minutes. Divide between plates and serve.
Nutrition facts: Cal: 121, Fat 9, Fiber 2, Carbs 4, Protein 5

›Beans and Sprouts

Preparation time: 5 minutes
Cooking time: 20 minutes
Servings: 4
Ingredients
1 tablespoon avocado oil
1 pound Brussels sprouts, trimmed and halved
Beans
1 tablespoon balsamic vinegar
A pinch of salt and black pepper
1 tablespoon dill, chopped
Directions
In a pan, mix the sprouts with the beans and the other ingredients, toss, put in the air fryer and cook at 380 degrees F for 20 minutes. Divide between plates and serve.
Nutrition facts: Cal: 141, Fat 3, Fiber 2, Carbs 4, Protein 3

› Balsamic Radishes

Preparation time: 10 minutes
Cooking time: 20 minutes
Servings: 4
Ingredients
1-pound radishes, halved
1 tablespoon balsamic vinegar
1 teaspoon chili powder
1 tablespoon avocado oil
Salt and black pepper to taste
Directions
In a pan that fits the air fryer, combine the radishes with the vinegar and the other ingredients, toss, introduce the pan in the air fryer and cook at 380 degrees

F for 20 minutes. Divide between plates and serve.
Nutrition facts: Cal: 151, Fat 2, Fiber 3, Carbs 5, Protein 5

›Spaghetti Squash Casserole

Preparation time: 10 minutes
Cooking time: 20 minutes
Servings: 4
Ingredients
12 oz spaghetti squash
1 teaspoon ground cinnamon
½ teaspoon salt
1 sweet potato, grated
1 tablespoon almond flour
2 eggs
1 tablespoon olive oil
1 onion, diced
¼ teaspoon thyme
Directions
Peel the spaghetti squash and chop it into the ½ inch chunks.
Then place the squash in the air fryer basket.
Add salt and ground cinnamon. Cook the sweet potatoes for 5 minutes at 380 F. After this, make the layer of the grated potato over the sweet potato.
Beat the eggs in the bowl. Add almond flour and stir the mixture. Then add olive oil, diced onion, and thyme. Stir the mixture. Pour it over the grated potato.
Cook the casserole for 15 minutes at 365 F.
When the time is over, and casserole is cooked – let it chill little and serve!
Nutrition facts: Calories 166, Fat 9.8, Fiber 2.6, Carbs 16.5, Protein 5.7

›Cinnamon Baby Carrot

Preparation time: 8 minutes
Cooking time: 15 minutes
Servings: 4
Ingredients
1-pound baby carrot
1 tablespoon ground cinnamon
1 teaspoon ground ginger
¼ cup almond milk
1 tablespoon olive oil
Directions
Wash the baby carrot carefully and sprinkle with the ground cinnamon, ground ginger, and olive oil.
Stir the vegetables and transfer them to the air fryer basket. Cook the baby carrot for 10 minutes at 380 F.
Then stir the baby carrots and add almond milk.
Stir the vegetables again and cook for 5 minutes more at the same temperature.
Let the cooked carrot chill little and serve it!
Nutrition facts: Calories 110, Fat 7.3, Fiber 4.6, Carbs 11.9, Protein 1.2

›Eggplant Tongues

Preparation time: 10 minutes

Cooking time: 14 minutes
Servings: 2
Ingredients
2 eggplants
1 teaspoon minced garlic
1 teaspoon olive oil
¼ teaspoon ground black pepper
Directions
Wash the eggplants carefully and slice them. Rub every eggplant slice with the minced garlic, olive oil, and ground black pepper. Place the eggplants in the air fryer and cook for 7 minutes from each side at 375 F. When the eggplant tongues are cooked – serve them immediately!
Nutrition facts: Calories 160, Fat 3.3, Fiber 19.4, Carbs 32.9, Protein 5.5

›Super Tasty Onion Petals

Preparation time: 10 minutes
Cooking time: 15 minutes
Servings: 4
Ingredients
13 oz onion, peeled
1 teaspoon basil, dried
1 teaspoon ground coriander
1 tablespoon olive oil
¼ teaspoon ground nutmeg
¾ teaspoon turmeric
Directions
Cut the onion into the petals and sprinkle with the basil, ground coriander, olive oil, ground nutmeg, and turmeric. Mix the onion petals and transfer them to the air fryer basket. Cook the petals for 15 minutes at 375 F. Stir the petals every 3 minutes. When the onion petals are cooked – they will have a soft texture. Serve the side dish immediately!
Nutrition facts: Calories 69, Fat 3.7, Fiber 2.1, Carbs 9, Protein 1.

›Eggplant Garlic Salad with Tomatoes

Preparation time: 10 minutes
Cooking time: 15 minutes
Servings: 6
Ingredients
3 tomatoes, chopped
2 eggplants, chopped
1 tablespoon olive oil
1 teaspoon avocado oil
1 tablespoon vinegar
½ teaspoon ground black pepper
½ teaspoon dried basil
2 garlic cloves, chopped
Directions
Place the chopped eggplants in the air fryer. Sprinkle the eggplants with the olive oil, ground black pepper, and dried basil. Stir the eggplants and cook for 15 minutes at 390 F. Stir the vegetables every 5 minutes. Then place the tomatoes in the bowl. Add cooked eggplants, vinegar, and chopped garlic. Then sprinkle

the salad with the avocado oil and stir it. Serve the cooked salad or keep it in the fridge!
Nutrition facts: Calories 80, Fat 2.9, Fiber 7.3, Carbs 13.6, Protein 2.4

›Curry Eggplants

Preparation time: 10 minutes
Cooking time: 14 minutes
Servings: 2
Ingredients
2 eggplants
1 teaspoon vinegar
1 tablespoon olive oil
1 teaspoon curry powder
1 garlic clove
3 tablespoons chicken stock
Directions
Peel the eggplants and cut them into the cubes. Sprinkle the eggplants with the curry powder and chicken stock. Put the vegetables in the air fryer and cook for 14 minutes at 390 F. Stir the eggplants every 5 minutes. When the eggplants are cooked – let them chill till the room temperature. Sprinkle the vegetables with the olive oil and vinegar. Stir and serve!
Nutrition facts: Calories 204, Fat 8.2, Fiber 19.7, Carbs 33.4, Protein 5.7

›Sauteed Asparagus

Preparation time: 10 minutes
Cooking time: 8 minutes
Servings: 2
Ingredients
1 onion, chopped
½ lemon
14 oz asparagus
1 teaspoon ghee
1 teaspoon salt
Directions
Place the onion, salt, and ghee in the air fryer basket. Cook it at 400 F for 2 minutes. Meanwhile, chop the asparagus roughly. Place the chopped asparagus in the air fryer basket. Squeeze the lemon juice over the asparagus. Cook the side dish for 6 minutes at 395 F. Stir it every 3 minutes of cooking. Let the cooked asparagus chill little. Enjoy!
Nutrition facts: Calories 86, Fat 2.5, Fiber 5.9, Carbs 14.8, Protein 5.2

›Roasted Apple with Bacon

Preparation time: 20 minutes
Cooking time: 10 minutes
Servings: 8
Ingredients
6 apples
7 oz bacon, chopped
½ teaspoon salt
½ teaspoon paprika
½ teaspoon ground black pepper

1 tablespoon avocado oil

Directions

Make the medium holes in the apples. Combine the chopped bacon, salt, paprika, ground black pepper, and avocado oil. Stir the mixture. Fill the apple holes with the bacon mixture. Put the apples in the air fryer basket. Cook the apples for 10 minutes at 380 F. When the time is over and the apples are cooked – chill them for 6 minutes and serve!

Nutrition facts: Calories 224, Fat 10.9, Fiber 4.2, Carbs 23.7, Protein 9.7

›Fennel Slices

Preparation time: 10 minutes
Cooking time: 10 minutes
Servings: 2
Ingredients
12 oz fennel bulb
1 teaspoon paprika
½ teaspoon chili flakes
1 tablespoon olive oil
1 teaspoon cilantro, dried

Directions

Slice the fennel bulb and sprinkle it with the paprika, chili flakes, and dried cilantro on each side. Then sprinkle the fennel with the olive oil and transfer the vegetables to the air fryer basket. Cook the fennel slices for 10 minutes at 380 F. Flip the fennel slices into another side after 5 minutes of cooking. Enjoy the cooked side dish!

Nutrition facts: Calories 116, Fat 7.5, Fiber 5.7, Carbs 13, Protein 2.3

›Butternut Squash Rice

Preparation time: 10 minutes
Cooking time: 20 minutes
Servings: 4
Ingredients
1-pound butternut squash
1 tablespoon ghee
1 onion, diced
1 teaspoon salt
1 oz fresh parsley, chopped
1 tablespoon olive oil

Directions

Chop the butternut squash into the rice pieces. Put the ghee in the air fryer basket and add diced onion. Sprinkle the onion with the salt and olive oil. Cook it at 400 F for 2 minutes. Then stir the onion and add the butternut squash rice. Stir it and cook the meal for 18 minutes at 380 F. Stir the squash every 4 minutes. When the meal is cooked – sprinkle it with the chopped parsley and stir. Serve it immediately!

Nutrition facts: Calories 123, Fat 6.9, Fiber 3.1, Carbs 16.3, Protein 1.7

›Eggplant Lasagna

Preparation time: 20 minutes

Cooking time: 30 minutes
Servings: 3
Ingredients
1 eggplant
2 tomatoes
1 tablespoon olive oil
1 onion, diced
1 garlic clove, chopped
1 teaspoon dried basil
1 teaspoon ground black pepper
½ teaspoon turmeric
1 teaspoon cumin
½ cup chicken stock
1 tablespoon fresh dill, chopped
4 oz mushrooms, chopped

Directions

Slice the eggplants. Slice the tomatoes. Combine together the diced onion, olive oil, chopped garlic, dried basil, ground black pepper, turmeric, cumin, and fresh dill in the bowl. Stir the mixture. Then make the layer of the sliced eggplants in the air fryer basket. Sprinkle it with the spice mixture. Put the tomatoes over the eggplants and add mushrooms. Sprinkle the vegetables with the spice mixture and repeat all the steps till you finish all the ingredients. Add chicken stock and cook lasagna for 30 minutes at 365 F. Let the cooked lasagna chill little and serve it!

Nutrition facts: Calories 127, Fat 5.6, Fiber 8, Carbs 18.9, Protein 4.4

›Stuffed Eggplants with Cherry Tomatoes

Preparation time: 15 minutes
Cooking time: 25 minutes
Servings: 2
Ingredients
1 eggplant
5 oz cherry tomatoes
1 shallot, chopped
½ teaspoon salt
¾ teaspoon nutmeg
¾ teaspoon chili pepper
1 tablespoon olive oil

Directions

Cut the eggplant into the halves. Remove the meat from the eggplants. Chop the cherry tomatoes and combine them together with the salt, shallot, nutmeg, chili pepper, and olive oil. Stir the mixture. Fill the eggplants with the vegetables. Put the stuffed vegetables in the air fryer basket and cook for 25 minutes at 370 F. Then chill the cooked eggplants little. Serve!

Nutrition facts: Calories 136, Fat 7.9, Fiber 9.2, Carbs 16.9, Protein 3

›Eggplant Satay

Preparation time: 15 minutes
Cooking time: 18 minutes
Servings: 3

Ingredients

3 eggplants
1 tablespoon vinegar
1 tablespoon olive oil
1 teaspoon sesame seeds
1 teaspoon dried dill
½ teaspoon dried parsley
½ teaspoon ground nutmeg

Directions

Cut the eggplants into the cubes. Then skew the eggplant onto the skewers. Sprinkle the eggplants with the olive oil, vinegar, sesame seeds, dried dill, dried parsley, and ground nutmeg. Place the eggplant satay in the air fryer basket and cook it for 18 minutes at 375 F. When the eggplants are soft – the meal is cooked. Let it chill little and serve!

Nutrition facts: Calories 187, Fat 6.3, Fiber 19.6, Carbs 32.9, Protein 5.7

›Lentil Bolognese

Preparation time: 20 minutes
Cooking time: 40 minutes
Servings: 4
Ingredients
Two boxes of penne pasta
One onion (medium-sized, finely chopped)
One red bell pepper (finely chopped)
Two tablespoons. of olive oil
Two carrots (large-sized, sliced)
Four cloves of garlic (large ones, minced)
One tablespoon. of miso
One teaspoon. each of
Pepper
Salt
Four cups of water
One can of tomato paste (measuring five and a half ounces)
One cup each of
Brown lentils (dried)
Cherry tomatoes (halved)

Directions

Take a large-sized skillet and start by heating the oil in it on medium flame. Then, add the chopped onions. In about five minutes, they will soften and appear to be translucent. Then, add the red pepper, carrots, sugar, and sea salt to the skillet and keep cooking. Stir the mixture from time to time. In fifteen minutes, everything will be well caramelized. Then, add the tomato paste and the garlic and let the mixture cook for three minutes or until you get a caramelized fragrance from the paste. Then, add the lentils, miso, and water to the skillet and bring the mixture to a boil. When the mixture is boiling, keep the skillet uncovered while the lentils are cooking. This will take about twenty-five to thirty minutes. Keep stirring the lentils from time to time, and in case they look dry, add some water. After that, add the cherry tomatoes and keep stirring. While you are cooking the lentils, take a large pot and fill it with water. Add generous amounts of salt and bring the water to a boil. Then, add the chickpea pasta into the water and cook it for about five to six minutes or until al dente. Don't overcook it. Once done, drain the water.

Nutrition facts: Calories 486, Fat 4, Fiber 9.7, Carbs 86.5, Protein 2.8

›Thyme Mushrooms and Carrot Bowl

Preparation time: 10 minutes
Cooking time: 20 minutes
Servings: 4
Ingredients
1 cup baby carrot
8 oz mushrooms, sliced
1 teaspoon thyme
1 teaspoon salt
1 cup chicken stock
1 teaspoon chili flakes
1 teaspoon coconut oil

Directions

Place the baby carrot in the air fryer basket. Add thyme, salt, and chili flakes. Cook the baby carrot for 10 minutes at 380 F. Then add the sliced mushrooms and coconut oil. Stir it well and cook the vegetables for 10 minutes more at 370 F. Stir the vegetables after 5 minutes of cooking. Chill the cooked side dish and enjoy!

Nutrition facts: Calories 25, Fat 1.5, Fiber 0.7, Carbs 2.2, Protein 2

›Sesame Mushroom Slices

Preparation time: 10 minutes
Cooking time: 6 minutes
Servings: 3
Ingredients
1 tablespoon sesame seeds
1 tablespoon avocado oil
14 oz mushrooms, sliced
1 teaspoon chili flakes
¼ teaspoon ground paprika

Directions

Put the sliced mushrooms in the air fryer basket. Add chili flakes and ground paprika. Then add avocado oil and stir the mushrooms. Cook the mushrooms for 4 minutes at 400 F. Stir the mushrooms after 2 minutes of cooking. Sprinkle the mushrooms with the sesame seeds and stir well. Cook the mushrooms for 2 minutes more at the same temperature. Serve the mushrooms immediately!

Nutrition facts: Calories 52, Fat 2.5, Fiber 2, Carbs 5.4, Protein 4.8

›Beef and Spinach Salad

Preparation time: 15 minutes
Cooking time: 20 minutes | **Servings:** 4
3 tablespoons olive oil
½ pound (227 g) beef rump steak, cut into strips
Salt and black pepper, to taste
1 teaspoon cumin
A pinch of dried thyme
2 garlic cloves, minced

4 ounces (113 g) Feta cheese, crumbled
½ cup pecans, toasted
2 cups spinach
1½ tablespoons lemon juice
¼ cup fresh mint, chopped

Directions

Season the beef with salt, 1 tablespoon of olive oil, garlic, thyme, pepper, and cumin. Place on a pre-heated to medium heat grill, and cook for 10 minutes, flip once. Remove the grilled beef to a cutting board, leave to cool, and slice into strips. Sprinkle the pecans on a lined baking sheet, place in the oven at 350°F (180°C), and toast for 10 minutes.

In a bowl, combine the spinach with black pepper, mint, remaining olive oil, salt, lemon juice, Feta cheese, and pecans, and toss well to coat. Top with the beef slices and enjoy.

Nutrition facts

calories: 435 | fat: 43.1g | protein: 17.1g | carbs: 5.3g | net carbs: 3.4g | fiber: 1.9g

➤Marinated Pork and Veg Salad

Preparation time: 15 minutes
Cooking time: 15 minutes | **Servings:** 6
¼ cup rice vinegar
¼ cup rice wine
¼ cup coconut aminos
1 tablespoon brown mustard
1 jalapeño pepper, chopped
2 garlic cloves, pressed
2 tablespoons olive oil
2 pounds (907 g) pork rib chops
Flaky sea salt and ground black pepper
½ teaspoon celery seeds
6 cups lettuce, torn into small pieces
1 bell pepper, deseeded and sliced
1 cucumber, sliced
1 tomato, sliced
4 scallions, chopped
½ lemon, juiced
½ cup sour cream, for garnish

Directions

Place the vinegar, wine, coconut aminos, mustard, jalapeño pepper, garlic, and pork in a ceramic dish. Cover and let it marinate for 2 and a half hours in your refrigerator. Heat the olive oil in an oven-safe pan over a medium-high flame. Discard the marinade and cook the pork rib chops for 3 to 5 minutes. Flip them overusing a pair of tongs. Cook for 4 minutes or until a good crust is formed. Sprinkle with salt, black pepper, and celery seeds. Then, bake the pork rib chops in the preheated oven for 10 minutes until an instant read thermometer reads 145°F (63°C). Shred the pork rib chops and reserve. Add the lettuce, bell pepper, cucumber, tomato, and scallions to a salad bowl. Top with the shredded pork, drizzle lemon juice over everything and garnish with sour cream. Enjoy!

Nutrition facts

calories: 297 | fat: 14.1g | protein: 35.2g | carbs: 6.0g | net carbs: 4.5g | fiber: 1.5g

➤Spanish Chicken and Pepper Salad

Preparation time: 10 minutes
Cooking time: 15 minutes | **Servings:** 6
1½ pounds (680 g) chicken breasts
½ cup dry white wine
1 onion, chopped
2 Spanish peppers, deveined and chopped
1 Spanish Naga chili pepper, chopped
2 garlic cloves, minced
2 cups arugula
¼ cup mayonnaise
1 tablespoon balsamic vinegar
1 tablespoon stone-ground mustard
Sea salt and freshly ground black pepper

Directions

Place the chicken breasts in a saucepan. Add the wine to the saucepan and cover the chicken with water. Bring to a boil over medium-high heat. Cook for 15 minutes (an instant-read thermometer should register 165°F (74°C)). Transfer the chicken into a cutting board; cut into bite-sized pieces and transfer to a salad bowl. Add the ingredients to the salad bowl and gently stir to combine. Serve well chilled.

Nutrition facts:

calories: 280 | fat: 16.2g | protein: 27.2g | carbs: 4.9g | net carbs: 4.0g | fiber: 0.9g

➤Chicken Thigh Green Salad

Preparation time: 10 minutes
Cooking time: 15 minutes | **Servings:** 2
2 chicken thighs, skinless
Sea salt and cayenne pepper, to season
½ teaspoon Dijon mustard
1 tablespoon red wine vinegar
¼ cup mayonnaise
1 small-sized celery stalk, chopped
2 spring onion stalks, chopped
½ head Romaine lettuce, torn into pieces
½ cucumber, sliced

Directions

Fry the chicken thighs until thoroughly heated and crunchy on the outside; an instant-read thermometer should read about 165°F (74°C). Discard the bones and chop the meat. Place the other ingredients in a serving bowl and stir until everything is well incorporated. Layer the chopped chicken thighs over the salad. Serve well chilled and enjoy!

Nutrition facts (per serving)

calories: 455 | fat: 29.1g | protein: 40.2g | carbs: 6.6g | net carbs: 2.8g | fiber: 3.8g

➤Kale and Smoked Salmon Salad

Preparation time: 15 minutes
Cooking time: 0 minutes | **Servings:** 4
¼ cup extra virgin olive oil
1 tablespoon lemon juice

½ teaspoon garlic powder
½ teaspoon sea salt
¼ teaspoon black pepper
6 ounces (170 g) chopped and dribbled kale (from 8 to 10 ounces / 227 to 283 g untrimmed)
¼ cup salted roasted sunflower seeds
8 ounces (227 g) smoked salmon, cut into pieces

Directions

In a medium/large bowl, whisk together the olive oil, lemon juice, garlic powder, sea salt, and black pepper. Add the chopped kale. Use the hands to massage the kale with the dressing mixture. Grab a bunch, squeeze with the dressing, release, and repeat.
Do this for a couple of minutes, until the kale starts to soften. Add the sunflower seeds and smoked salmon. Toss together.

Nutrition facts (per serving)

calories: 258 | fat: 20.0g | protein: 14.0g | carbs: 6.0g | net carbs: 6.0g | fiber: 0g

➤Grilled Chicken and Cucumber Salad

Preparation time: 10 minutes
Cooking time: 15 minutes | **Servings:** 2
2 chicken breasts
2 tablespoons extra-virgin olive oil
4 tablespoons apple cider vinegar
1 cup grape tomatoes, halved
1 Lebanese cucumber, thinly sliced

Directions

Preheat your grill to medium-high temperature. Now, grill the chicken breasts for 5 to 7 minutes on each side. Slice the chicken into strips and transfer them to a nice salad bowl. Toss with the olive oil, vinegar, grape tomatoes, and cucumber. Garnish with fresh snipped chives if desired. Bon appétit!

Nutrition facts (per serving)

calories: 402 | fat: 18.1g | protein: 51.5g | carbs: 5.2g | net carbs: 3.7g | fiber: 1.5g

➤Berries e Spinach Salad

Preparation time: 15 minutes
Cooking time: 0 minutes | **Servings:** 2
Salad
8 cups fresh baby spinach
¾ cup fresh strawberries, hulled and sliced
¾ cup fresh blueberries
¼ cup onion, sliced
¼ cup almond, sliced
¼ cup feta cheese, crumbled
Dressing
1/3 cup olive oil
2 tablespoons fresh lemon juice
¼ teaspoon liquid stevia
1/8 teaspoon garlic powder
Salt, to taste

Directions

For salad: In a bowl, add the spinach, berries, onion, and almonds, and mix. For dressing: In another small bowl, add all the ingredients and beat until well com-

bined. Place the dressing over salad and gently, toss to coat well.

Nutrition facts (per serving)

calories: 190 | fat: 17.9g | protein: 20.9g | carbs: 8.0g | net carbs: 2.9g | fiber: 5.1g

➤Caprese Salad

Preparation time: 15 minutes
Cooking time: 0 minutes | **Servings:** 5
2 medium/large tomatoes, each cut into 5 slices
Coarse salt to taste
6 ounces (170 g) fresh Mozzarella, cut into 10 slices
2 avocados, cut into 30 thin slices
3 to 4 large basil leaves, chopped, plus additional leaves for garnish
¼ cup extra-virgin olive oil or avocado oil
1 lime, halved
Ground black pepper
Italian seasoning (optional)

Directions

Lay the tomato slices on a serving plate and sprinkle with salt. On top of each tomato, stack a Mozzarella slice, 3 avocado slices, and some chopped basil. Drizzle with the oil and squeeze some lime juice over the top. Sprinkle with pepper and Italian seasoning, if using. Garnish each stack with a basil leaf, if desired.

Nutrition facts (per serving)

calories: 284 | fat: 25.7g | protein: 7.5g | carbs: 8.0g | net carbs: 3.5g | fiber: 4.5g

➤Egg and Avocado Salad in Lettuce Cups

Preparation time: 15 minutes
Cooking time: 15 minutes | **Servings:** 2
4 large eggs
1 avocado, halved
Pink Himalayan salt
Freshly ground black pepper
½ teaspoon freshly squeezed lemon juice
4 butter lettuce cups, washed and patted dry with paper towels or a clean dish towel
2 radishes, thinly sliced

Directions

In a medium/large saucepan, cover the eggs with water. Place over high heat and bring the water to a boil. Then, turn off the heat and cover about 10/12 minutes. Remove the eggs and run them under cold water for 1 minute or submerge them in an ice bath. Then gently tap the shells and peel. Run cold water over your hands as you remove the shells. In a medium bowl, chop the hardboiled eggs. Add in the avocado to the bowl and mash the flesh with a fork. Season with pink Himalayan salt and pepper, add the lemon juice, and stir to combine. Place the 4 lettuce cups on two plates. Top the lettuce cups with the egg salad and the slices of radish and serve.

Nutrition facts (per serving)

calories: 259 | fat: 20.1g | protein: 15.1g | carbs: 8.0g

| net carbs: 2.9g | fiber: 5.1g

›Greek Caper Salad

Preparation time: 10 minutes
Cooking time: 0 minutes | **Servings:** 4
5 tomatoes, chopped
1 large cucumber, chopped
1 green bell pepper, chopped
1 small red onion, chopped
16 Kalamata olives, chopped
4 tablespoons capers
7 ounces (198 g) Feta cheese, chopped
1 teaspoon oregano, dried
4 tablespoons olive oil Salt to taste
Directions:
Place tomatoes, pepper, cucumber, onion, Feta and olives in a bowl. Mix to combine. Season with salt. Combine the capers, olive oil and oregano in a small bowl. Drizzle the dressing over the salad.
Nutrition facts (per serving)
calories: 324 | fat: 27.8g | protein: 9.4g | carbs: 11.9g | net carbs: 8.0g | fiber: 3.9g

›Spicy Leek and Green Cabbage Salad

Preparation time: 15 minutes
Cooking time: 40 minutes | **Servings:** 4
4 tablespoons extra-virgin olive oil
1 medium-sized leek, chopped
½ pound (227 g) green cabbage, shredded
½ teaspoon caraway seeds
Sea salt, to taste
4-5 black peppercorns
1 garlic clove, minced
1 teaspoon yellow mustard
1 tablespoon balsamic vinegar
½ teaspoon Sriracha sauce
Directions
Drizzle 3 tbsp. of the olive oil over the leek and cabbage; sprinkle with caraway seeds, salt, black peppercorns. Roast in the preheated oven at 420°F (216°C) for 37 to 40 minutes. Place the roasted mixture in a salad bowl. Toss with the remaining tbsp. of olive oil garlic, mustard, vinegar, and Sriracha sauce.
Serve immediately and enjoy
Nutrition facts (per serving)
calories: 116 | fat: 10.1g | protein: 1.0g | carbs: 6.5g | net carbs: 4.7g | fiber: 1.8g

›Chicken and Sunflower Seed Salad

Preparation time: 15 minutes
Cooking time: 15 minutes | **Servings:** 3
1 chicken breast, skinless
¼ mayonnaise
¼ cup sour cream
2 tablespoons Cottage cheese, room temperature
Salt and black pepper, to taste

¼ cup sunflower seeds, hulled and roasted
½ avocado, peeled and cubed
½ teaspoon fresh garlic, minced
2 tablespoons scallions, chopped
Directions:
Boil a pot of salted water. Add the chicken to the boiling water; now, turn off the heat, cover, and let the chicken stand in the hot water for 15 minutes. Then, drain the water; chop the chicken into bite-sized pieces. Add the remaining ingredients and mix well. Place in the refrigerator for one and half hour. Serve well chilled. Enjoy!
Nutrition facts (per serving)
calories: 401 | fat: 35.2g | protein: 16.2g | carbs: 5.7g | net carbs: 2.9g | fiber: 2.8g

›Arugula and Avocado Salad

Preparation time: 15 minutes
Cooking time: 0 minutes | **Servings:** 4
Salad:
6 cups baby arugula
1 avocado, diced
½ cup cherry tomatoes, halved
⅓ cup shaved Parmesan cheese
¼ cup thinly sliced red onions
¼ cup pili nuts or pine nuts
Dressing:
3 tablespoons extra-virgin olive oil
1 tablespoon red wine vinegar
1 small clove garlic, pressed or minced
Salt and pepper, to taste
Directions:
Put the salad ingredients in a bowl and gently toss.
In a small bowl, stir together the dressing ingredients. Toss the salad with the dressing.
Nutrition facts (per serving)
calories: 274 | fat: 23.9g | protein: 8.7g | carbs: 9.0g | net carbs: 4.0g | fiber: 5.0g

›Asparagus and Mozzarella Caprese Salad

Preparation time: 15 minutes
Cooking time: 0 minutes | **Servings:** 2
1 teaspoon fresh lime juice
1 tablespoon hot Hungarian paprika infused oil
½ teaspoon kosher salt
¼ teaspoon red pepper flakes
½ pound (227 g) asparagus spears, trimmed
1 cup grape tomatoes, halved
2 tablespoons red wine vinegar
1 garlic clove, pressed 1-2 drops liquid stevia
1 tablespoon fresh basil
1 tablespoon fresh chives
½ cup Mozzarella, grated
Directions
Heat your grill to the hottest setting. Toss your asparagus with the lime juice, hot Hungarian paprika infused oil, salt, and red pepper flakes. Place the asparagus

spears on the hot grill. Grill until one side chars; then, grill your asparagus on the other side. Cut the asparagus spears in pieces and transfer to a salad bowl. Add the grape tomatoes, red wine, garlic, stevia, basil, and chives; toss to combine well. Top with freshly grated Mozzarella cheese and serve immediately.

Nutrition facts (per serving)
calories: 190 | fat: 13.2g | protein: 9.6g | carbs: 7.5g | net carbs: 4.2g | fiber: 3.3g

›Spinach and Bacon Salad

8 cups baby spinach
4 slices bacon, pan-fried and chopped
3 large eggs, hard-boiled and sliced
10 grape tomatoes, halved
2 avocados, sliced or cubed
½ medium red onion, thinly sliced
½ cup sliced white mushrooms
⅓ cup chopped pecans
Ground black pepper
¾ cup ranch or blue cheese dressing

Directions
In a big bowl, toss the spinach, bacon, hard-boiled eggs, tomatoes, avocados, onion, mushrooms, and pecans. Season with pepper to taste. Top with the dressing just before serving.

Nutrition facts (per serving)
calories: 402 | fat: 34.6g | protein: 12.9g | carbs: 11.1g | net carbs: 7.4g | fiber: 3.7g

›Mediterranean Tomato and Zucchini Salad

Preparation time: 15 minutes
Cooking time: 10 minutes | **Servings:** 4
½ pound (227 g) Roma tomatoes, sliced
½ pound (227 g) zucchini, sliced
1 Lebanese cucumber, sliced
1 cup arugula
½ teaspoon oregano
½ teaspoon basil
½ teaspoon rosemary
½ teaspoon ground black pepper
Sea salt, to season
4 tablespoons extra-virgin olive oil
2 tablespoons fresh lemon juice
½ cup Kalamata olives, pitted and sliced
4 ounces (113 g) Feta cheese, cubed

Directions
Arrange the Roma tomatoes and zucchini slices on a roasting pan; spritz cooking oil over your vegetables. Bake in the oven at 360°F (190°C) for 6 to 7 minutes. Let them cool slightly, then, transfer to a salad bowl. Add in the cucumber, arugula, herbs, and spices. Sprinkle olive oil and lemon juice over your veggies; toss to combine well. Top with Kalamata olives and Feta cheese. Serve at room temperature and enjoy!

Nutrition facts (per serving)
calories: 242 | fat: 22.1g | protein: 6.4g | carbs: 6.9g

| net carbs: 5.1g | fiber: 1.8g

›Roasted Asparagus Salad

Preparation time: 15 minutes
Cooking time: 15 minutes | **Servings:** 5
14 ounces (397 g) asparagus spears, trimmed
2 tablespoons olive oil
½ teaspoon oregano
½ teaspoon rosemary
Sea salt and freshly ground black pepper
5 tablespoons mayonnaise
3 tablespoons sour cream
1 tablespoon wine vinegar
1 teaspoon fresh garlic, minced
1 cup cherry tomatoes, halved

Directions
In a lightly greased roasting pan, toss the asparagus with the olive oil, oregano, rosemary, salt, and black pepper. Roast in the preheated oven at 430°F (225°C) for 13 to 15 minutes until just tender. Meanwhile, in a mixing bowl, thoroughly combine the mayonnaise, sour cream, vinegar, and garlic; dress the salad and top with the cherry tomato halves. Serve at room temperature. Bon appétit!

Nutrition facts (per serving)
calories: 180 | fat: 17.6g | protein: 2.6g | carbs: 4.5g | net carbs: 2.5g | fiber: 2.0gRoasted

›Asparagus and Cherry Tomato Salad

Preparation time: 15 minutes
Cooking time: 20 minutes | **Servings:** 3
1 pound (454 g) asparagus, trimmed
¼ teaspoon ground black pepper
Flaky salt, to season
3 tablespoons sesame seeds
1 tablespoon Dijon mustard
½ lime, freshly squeezed
3 tablespoons extra-virgin olive oil
2 garlic cloves, minced
1 tablespoon fresh tarragon, snipped
1 cup cherry tomatoes, sliced

Directions
Heat your oven to 410°F (210°C). Spritz a roasting pan with nonstick cooking spray. Roast the asparagus for about 13 minutes, turning the spears over once or twice. Sprinkle with salt, pepper, and sesame seeds; roast an additional 3 to 4 minutes. To make the dressing, whisk the tbsp. of Dijon mustard, lime juice, olive oil, and minced garlic. Chop the asparagus spears into bite-sized pieces and place them in a nice salad bowl. Add the tarragon and tomatoes to the bowl; gently toss to combine. Dress your salad and serve at room temperature. Enjoy!

Nutrition facts (per serving)
calories: 160 | fat: 12.4g | protein: 5.7g | carbs: 6.2g | net carbs: 2.2g | fiber: 4.0g

›Charred Broccoli and Sardine Salad

Preparation time: 5 minutes
Cooking time: 5 minutes | **Servings:** 4
1 pound (454 g) broccoli florets
½ white onion, thinly sliced
2 (4-ounce / 113-g) cans sardines in oil, drained
2 tablespoons fresh lime juice
1 teaspoon stone-ground mustard

Directions
Heat a lightly greased cast-iron skillet over medium-high heat. Cook the broccoli florets for 5 to 6 minutes until charred; work in batches. In salad bowls, place the charred broccoli with onion and sardines. Toss with the lime juice and mustard. Serve at room temperature. Bon appétit!

Nutrition facts (per serving)
calories: 160 | fat: 7.2g | protein: 17.6g | carbs: 5.6g | net carbs: 2.6g | fiber: 3.0g

›Zucchini and Bell Pepper Slaw

Preparation time: 15 minutes |
Cooking time: 0 minutes | **Servings:** 3
1 zucchini, shredded
1 yellow bell pepper, sliced
1 red onion, thinly sliced
2 tablespoons extra-virgin olive oil
1 tablespoon balsamic vinegar
1 teaspoon Dijon mustard
¼ teaspoon cumin seeds
¼ teaspoon ground black pepper
Sea salt, to taste

Directions
Thoroughly combine all ingredients in a salad bowl. Refrigerate for 1 hour before serving or serve right away. Enjoy!

Nutrition facts (per serving)
calories: 97 | fat: 9.5g | protein: 0.8g | carbs: 2.7g | net carbs: 2.4g | fiber: 0.3g

›Herbed Chicken Salad

Preparation time: 15 minutes
Cooking time: 15 minutes | **Servings:** 4
Poached Chicken:
2 chicken breasts, skinless and boneless
½ teaspoon salt
2 bay laurels
1 thyme sprig
1 rosemary sprig
Salad:
4 scallions, trimmed and thinly sliced
1 tablespoon fresh coriander, chopped
1 teaspoon Dijon mustard
2 teaspoons freshly squeezed lemon juice
1 cup mayonnaise, preferably homemade
Directions
Place all ingredients for the poached chicken in a

stockpot; cover with water and bring to a rolling boil. Reduce the heat and simmer until a meat thermometer reads 165°F (74°C). Let the poached chicken cool to room temperature. Cut into strips and transfer to a nice salad bowl. Toss the poached chicken with the salad ingredients; serve well chilled and enjoy!

Nutrition facts (per serving)
calories: 540 | fat: 48.9g | protein: 18.9g | carbs: 3.2g | net carbs: 2.8g | fiber: 0.4g

›Tomato, Mozzarella Salad

Preparation time: 15 minutes
Cooking time: 0 minutes | **Servings:** 4
Dressing
½ cup fresh basil leaves
2 garlic cloves, peeled
4 tablespoons olive oil
2 tablespoon balsamic vinegar
Salt and ground black pepper, to taste
Salad
2 cups cherry tomatoes
3 ounces mozzarella cheese balls
5 cups fresh arugula
3 cherry tomatoes
3 ounces mozzarella
5 cups arugula

Directions:
For filling: In a small blender, add all the ingredients and pulse until smooth. For salad: In a large bowl, add all the ingredients and mix. Place the dressing over salad and toss to coat well. Serve well chilled and enjoy!

Nutrition facts (per serving)
calories: 123 | fat: 9.2g | protein: 4.6g | carbs: 5.8g | net carbs: 2.8g | fiber: 3.0g

›Feta Cucumber Salad

Preparation time: 15 minutes
Cooking time: 0 minutes | **Servings:** 5
2 medium-large cucumbers
½ cup thinly sliced red onions
4 ounces (113 g) Feta cheese, crumbled
Salt and pepper to taste
Dressing:
¼ cup extra-virgin olive oil
1 tablespoon red wine vinegar
1 tablespoon Swerve confectioners-style sweetener
½ teaspoon dried ground oregano
Directions
Peel the cucumbers as desired and cut lengthwise, then slice. In a medium-sized bowl, toss the cucumbers with the onions. Add the Feta and toss to combine.
Make the dressing:
Place the ingredients in a small/medium bowl and whisk to combine. Gently toss the salad with the dressing and season to taste with salt and pepper.

Nutrition facts (per serving)
calories: 172 | fat: 15.2g | protein: 4.5g | carbs: 6.5g | net carbs: 3.7g | fiber: 2.8g

➤Keto Red Curry

Servings: 6-8
Preparation Time: About 40 minutes
Ingredients:
cup broccoli florets
large handful of fresh spinach
Tbsp. coconut oil
¼ medium onion
tsp. garlic, minced
tsp. fresh ginger, peeled and minced
tsp. soy sauce
Tbsp. red curry paste
½ cup coconut cream
Directions:
Add half the coconut oil to a saucepan and heat over medium-high heat. When the oil is hot, add the onion to the pan and sauté for 3-4 minutes, until it is semi-translucent.
Add in the garlic to the pan and sauté, stirring, just until fragrant, about 30 seconds. Lower the heat to medium-low and add broccoli florets. Sauté, stirring, for about 1-2 minutes. Put the vegetables to the side of the pan and add the red curry paste. Sauté until the paste is fragrant, then mix everything together. Add the spinach on top of the vegetable mixture. Then add the coconut cream and stir. Add the rest of the coconut oil, the soy sauce, and the minced ginger. Bring to a simmer for 5-10 minutes. Serve hot.
Nutrition facts:
Total Fat: 41 g
Carbs: 8 g
Protein: 4 g

➤Kale Soup

Servings: 6-8
Preparation Time: About 40 minutes
Ingredients:
4 cups fresh kale, chopped
½ cup canned white beans
2 cloves garlic, minced
½ onion, diced
½ cup celery, diced
¼ tsp. freshly ground black pepper
Salt to taste
1 cup of water
Directions:
Place all ingredients into a heavy stockpot.
Bring to a low/medium simmer and cook until fragrant, about 30 minutes. Add water if necessary, during cooking. Transfer the soup to serving bowls.
Nutrition facts:
Total Fat: 15 g
Carbs: 15 g
Protein: 9 g

➤Creamy Jalapeño Soup

Servings: 8-10
Preparation Time: About 45 minutes
Ingredients:
3 Tbsp. butter
2 cloves garlic, minced
½ onion, chopped
½ bell pepper, chopped
2 jalapeño peppers, seeded and chopped
3 cups vegetable stock
½ cup heavy cream
¼ tsp. paprika
1 tsp. cumin
1 tsp. salt
½ tsp. freshly ground black pepper
Directions:
Heat butter in a heavy stockpot over medium-high heat. When the butter is melted, add onion, bell pepper, and jalapeños and sauté until the onion is soft about 5 minutes. Bring to a low/medium simmer and cook until the chicken is thoroughly cooked and the vegetables are tender about 30 minutes. Add water if necessary, during cooking. Stir in the cream, stirring to combine. Transfer to serving bowls and serve hot.
Nutrition facts:
Total Fat: 40 g
Carbs: 4 g
Protein: 41 g

➤Chili Mediterranean Soup

Servings: 8-10
Preparation Time: About 40 minutes
Ingredients:
¼ cup sesame oil
6 dried red Thai chilis
5 cloves garlic, crushed
2 Tbsp. fresh ginger, peeled and sliced
3 cups vegetable stock
¼ cup of soy sauce
¼ cup dry sherry
Salt to taste
¼ cup fresh Thai basil, chopped
Directions:
Heat the sesame oil in a heavy stockpot over medium-high heat. Add the garlic, chilis, and ginger to the pot and sauté just until fragrant, about a minute. Lower the heat and add the rest, excluding the basil, to the pot. Bring to a low/medium simmer and cook until the soup is fragrant about 30 minutes. Add water if necessary, during cooking. Bring the soup to a boil and combine the basil, stirring until the basil is fragrant and wilted. Transfer to serving bowls and serve hot.
Nutrition facts:
Total Fat: 15 g
Carbs: 7 g
Protein: 31 g

➤Mushroom Soup

Servings: 8-10
Preparation Time: About 40 minutes
Ingredients:
1 onion, chopped
3 cloves garlic, minced
2 cups fresh button mushrooms, chopped
1 medium yellow summer squash, chopped
3 cups vegetable stock
Salt and pepper to taste

1 tsp. poultry seasoning
Directions:
Add all ingredients to a heavy stockpot.
Bring to a low/medium simmer and cook until the soup is fragrant about 30 minutes. Add water if necessary, during cooking. Transfer soup to serving bowls and serve.
Nutrition facts:
Total Fat: 15 g
Carbs: 9 g
Protein: 30 g

›Vegetable Soup

Servings: 6-8
Preparation Time: About 40 minutes
Ingredients:
1 onion, diced
2 Tbsp. tomato paste
2 whole star anise
1 Tbsp. fresh ginger, peeled and minced
3 cloves garlic, minced
6 cups of water
1 tsp. ground pepper
½ tsp. curry powder
2 carrots, peeled and sliced
Directions:
Place all ingredients in a heavy stockpot.
Bring to a low/medium simmer and cook until the soup is fragrant about 30 minutes. Add water if necessary, during cooking. Serve the stew hot.
Nutrition facts:
Total Fat: 9 g
Carbs: 8 g
Protein: 15 g

›Green Chili Soup

Servings: 6-8
Preparation Time: About 2 hours
Ingredients:
½ cup dry navy beans, soaked for an hour in hot water
1 onion diced
3 New Mexico green chili peppers, chopped
5 cloves garlic, minced
1 cup cauliflower, diced
4 cups vegetable stock
¼ cup fresh cilantro, chopped
1 tsp. ground coriander
1 tsp. ground cumin
1 tsp. salt
Directions:
Put the ingredients, into a medium/large, heavy stockpot.
Bring to a low/medium simmer and cook until the beans are tender about 60 minutes.
Add water if necessary, during cooking.
Using an immersion blender, blend the soup.
Return the soup to a simmer.
Transfer the soup to serving bowls.
Nutrition facts:

Total Fat: 5 g
Carbs: 13 g
Protein: 22 g

›Vegetarian Red Chili

Servings: 6-8
Preparation Time: About 35 minutes
Ingredients:
3 tsp. chili powder
2 tsp. ground cumin
2 tsp. salt
1 tsp. dried oregano
1 Tbsp. olive oil
1 onion, chopped
2 cloves garlic, minced
1 cup canned diced tomatoes
1 Tbsp. canned chipotle chilis, chopped
2 corn tortillas, torn into small pieces
½ cup of water
Directions:
In a bowl, mix chili powder, cumin, salt, and oregano. In a blender blend tomatoes, chilis, and tortilla pieces until smooth. Heat the Tbsp. of olive oil in a stockpot over high heat. When the oil is hot, sauté the onions until they're softened, about 3 minutes. Put on garlic and sauté for about a minute more. Stir in the spice mixture and sauté until fragrant, about 30 seconds. Add the tomato/tortilla mixture to the pot, along with 2 cups water. Bring to a low/medium simmer and cook until fragrant about 20 minutes. Add water if necessary, during cooking. Transfer the chili to serving bowls and serve hot.
Nutrition facts:
Total Fat:24g
Carbs: 12 g
Protein: 30 g

›Vegetarian Green Chili

Servings: 6-8
Preparation Time: About 30 minutes
Ingredients:
3 tomatillos, sliced
3 jalapeño peppers, seeded and chopped
2 New Mexico green chili peppers, seeded and chopped
6 cloves garlic, minced
1 tomato, chopped
3 cups vegetable stock
2 tsp. cumin
Salt and pepper to taste
Directions:
Put the tomatillos, jalapeños, New Mexico chilis, garlic, chicken stock, and tomato into a heavy stockpot.
Add the cumin, salt, and pepper on top of the meat.
Bring to a low/medium simmer and cook until fragrant, about 20 minutes. Add water if necessary, during cooking. Using an immersion blender, blend the sauce.
Transfer the chili to serving bowls and serve hot, garnished with chopped fresh cilantro.
Nutrition facts:
Total Fat: 4 g

Carbs: 4 g
Protein: 26 g

➤Tortilla Soup

Servings: 6-8
Preparation Time: About 30 minutes
Ingredients:
2 corn tortillas, torn into pieces
½ onion, chopped
1 cup tomatoes, chopped
2 cloves garlic
1 Tbsp. canned chipotle chili in adobo sauce, chopped
½ jalapeño pepper
¼ cup fresh cilantro, chopped
1 tsp. salt
1 Tbsp. olive oil
4 cups of water
Directions:
In a blender, combine onion, tomatoes, garlic, chipotle, jalapeño, and cilantro. Blend until the mixture is smooth. Heat the tbsp. olive oil in a heavy stockpot over low/medium heat. When the oil is hot, add the blended mixture to the pot. Cook, stirring, until fragrant, about 1-2 minutes. Add in the tortillas, chicken, and water to the pot. Bring to a low/medium simmer and cook until fragrant, about 20 minutes. Add water if necessary, during cooking. Transfer to serving bowls and serve hot.
Nutrition facts:
Total Fat: 5 g
Carbs: 5 g
Protein: 12 g

➤Keto Vegetable Soup

Servings: 6-8
Preparation Time: About 45 minutes
Ingredients:
1 turnip, cut into bite-size pieces
1 onion, chopped
6 stalks celery, diced
1 carrot, sliced
15 oz. pumpkin puree
1 lb. green beans frozen or fresh
8 cups chicken stock
2 cups of water
1 Tbsp. fresh basil, chopped
¼ tsp. thyme leaves
1/8 tsp. rubbed sage
Salt to taste
1 lb. fresh spinach, chopped
Directions:
Put all the ingredients, excluding the spinach, into a heavy stockpot. Bring to a low/medium simmer and cook until the vegetables are tender about 30 minutes. Add water if necessary, during cooking.
Add the fresh spinach and stir until it's wilted about 5 minutes. Transfer to serving bowls and serve hot.
Nutrition facts:
Total Fat: 0 g
 Carbs: 10 g

Protein: 3 g

➤Keto Cabbage Soup

Servings: 6-8
Preparation Time: About 45 minutes
Ingredients:
¼ cup onion, diced
1 clove garlic, minced
1 tsp. cumin
1 head cabbage, chopped
1 ¼ cup canned diced tomatoes
5 oz. canned green chilis
4 cups vegetable stock
Salt and pepper to taste
Directions:
Heat a heavy stockpot over medium-high heat. When the oil is hot, add the cup of onions and sauté for 5- 7 minutes more. Put on the garlic and sauté for 2 minutes. Bring to a low/medium simmer and cook until the vegetables are tender about 30 minutes. Add water if necessary, during cooking. Transfer to serving bowls and serve hot.
Nutrition facts:
Total Fat: 18 g
Carbs: 6 g
Protein: 17 g

➤Vegetarian Black Soup

Ingredients (4 servings)
2 15-ounce cans of black beans (undrained)
16-ounce of vegetable broth
½ cup of sauce
Shredded cheese (optional)
Sour cream (optional)
Chopped onion (optional)
Fresh chopped cilantro (optional)
Directions:
Mash the black beans(undrained) with a potato masher or make use of the food processor as a substitute. If using a food processor, add more water until they are mostly smooth. Pour the cans of beans into a medium-sized saucepan. Add sauce, vegetable broth and chili powder to the saucepan. Boil all the ingredients. As soon as all the ingredients are boiled, it is ready to serve. Depending on your preference, the vegetarian black soup can go with shredded cheese, sour cream, onion, and cilantro. Instead of this, you can make use of cheese and sour cream as an alternative. Serve and enjoy!
Nutrition facts
Calories: 157
Carbs: 30g.
Protein: 7g
Fat: 1g
Fiber: 9g

➤Vegetarian Bean and Barley Vegetable Soup

Ingredients (6 servings)

½ of a large onion (diced)
to 3 cloves of garlic (minced)
tablespoons of oil/margarine
ribs of celery (diced)
medium of sized carrots (diced)
Any other vegetables of your choice (about ½ cup each)
cups of water
cup of pearled barley (uncooked)
cup of pinto beans
1/3 cup of tomato paste
¼ teaspoon of salt
½ teaspoon of barley
¼ teaspoon of celery (optional)
½ teaspoon of pepper
½ teaspoon of thyme
½ teaspoon of oregano
teaspoon of onion powder
large bay of leaves
Salt and pepper

Directions

Sauté the onions and garlic in the tablespoons of oil/ margarine, in a large soup or stockpot for two minutes Add celery, carrots and other vegetables of your choice and allow to cook between 3 and 5 minutes Add vegetable broth and other vegetables. Let it simmer. Mix the remaining ingredients. Once it is simmering, bring the heat to medium-low and cover pot Let it simmer for up to 30 minutes or an hour. Stir occasionally until barley is soft and fluffy. Remove bay leaves before serving food. Before serving the soup, taste and add more spices, pepper and salt if necessary. Serve soup and enjoy!

Nutrition facts
Calories: 116
Carbs: 19g.
Protein: 5g.
Fat: 3g
Fiber: 6g

›Vegetarian Curried Corn Soup

Ingredients (3 servings)
tablespoon of vegetable oil
½ cup of green bell pepper (well chopped)
½ cup of red bell pepper (well chopped)
¼ cup of shallots (minced)
tablespoon of curry powder
½ tablespoon of salt
cups of fresh corn or as alternative 16-ounce bag frozen corn (3 cups)
½ tablespoon of freshly ground pepper
cups plain of soymilk or any non-diary milk
cup of vegetable stock
½ cup of shredded cheddar cheese

Directions
Heat the tbs. of vegetable oil in a large saucepan with medium-high heat. After heating oil, add ball peppers and cook for about four minutes. While cooking stir occasionally until the bell peppers are tender. Add shallots in the last one minute and stir until it is browned. Add curry powder and stir and stair

for another minute. Add the corn, pepper, pepper, vegetable stock and boil. Reduce heat and cook until vegetable is tender in 5 minutes. Add 2 cups of corn mixture to a food processor or a blender. Add a cup of soymilk. Blend until the mixture is almost smooth. After boiling, pour the mixture into the saucepan. Add and stir the remaining soymilk under medium heat. Cook for about 5 minutes. Sprinkle each serving with two tablespoons cheese. Serve and enjoy!

Nutrition facts
Calories: 100
Carbs: 20g
Protein:3g
Fat: 3g
Fiber: 7g

›Vegetarian Coconut Vegetable Soup

Ingredients (4 servings)
onion (diced)
bell peppers (red, diced)
¼ teaspoon of cayenne
½ tablespoon of coriander
½ tablespoon of cumin
tablespoons of olive oil
can of chickpeas
carrot (sliced)
cloves of garlic
½ cup of basil or cilantro (fresh chopped)
teaspoon of salt
limes (freshly squeezed juice)
½ cup of vegetable broth
cup of coconut milk
cup of peanut butter
2½ cups of tomatoes (finely diced)

Directions
Sauté onions, garlic and pepper in oil in a large pot. Make ingredients to be soft for at least 3 to 5 minutes Leaving out basil, add the rest of the ingredients and allow it to simmer. Cook over low heat for an hour Add half of it to the food processor, allow it to be very smooth and return to the pot. Add either of basil or cilantro, and your coconut food is ready. Before serving the soup, taste and add more seasoning if necessary. Serve, and enjoy!

Nutrition facts
Calories: 120
Carbs: 44g
Protein: 10g
Fat: 10g
Fiber: 2g

›Vegetarian Minestrone Soup

Ingredients (6 servings)
Pepper (to taste)
bay leaf
Salt (to taste)
cloves of garlic (minced)
Optional: 1 cup green of beans (chopped)
½ onions (chopped)

stalks of celery (chopped)
carrots (chopped)
tablespoon of oregano
tablespoon of basil (chopped)
cups of tomatoes (diced)
cups of vegetable broth
Zucchini (chopped)
1½ cups of macaroni pasta

Directions

In a large pot, put vegetable broth then add diced tomatoes, basils, oregano, carrots, celery, onion, zucchini, green beans, garlic and bay leaves. Slowly cook the soup to a low simmer and allow the soup to cook over very low heat for 45/60 minutes, which could also extend to one hour. Cook until the vegetables are tender. Note that you should stir the soup occasionally while it is cooking. Add salt and pepper and the macaroni pasta to the soup. Then bring the heat up a little to a medium-low level. Once this is done, allow the soup to simmer for another 10 or 20 minutes, or allow soup to simmer up until the pasta is done cooking Before serving the soup, taste and add more spices, pepper, and salt if necessary. Remove the bay leaf from the soup. Serve and enjoy!

Nutrition facts
Calories: 120
Carbs: 44g.
Protein: 10g
Fat: 10g
Fiber: 2g

➤Fat-Free Cabbage Soup Recipe

Ingredients (4 servings)
pound of cabbage (chopped)
cups of vegetable broth
Dash salt (to taste)
Dash pepper (to taste)
onions (chopped)
Dash Tabasco or hot sauce (to taste)
¼ cup of cilantro (chopped)
cloves of garlic (minced)

Directions

In a large saucepan, add chopped onions, minced garlic, vegetable broth, Tabasco or hot sauce together with a bit of salt with pepper. Once all these ingredients are combined, cover saucepan and allow it to simmer in medium-low heat for 20 minutes or more. Note that you should stir the soup occasionally while it is cooking. After about 20 minutes of cooking, carefully pour half of the soup into a blender or food processor. Process or blend the soup together until it is smooth. As a substitute to this, note that you can make use of an immersion blender to process the soup until it is blended halfway. You can decide to process the soup as you prefer and how you like the soup. If you used the non-emersion blender method, return the blended portion of the soup to the saucepan and reheat it when needed Add fresh chopped cilantro, add more pepper, and hot sauce how you want it. Serve and enjoy!

Nutrition facts
Calories: 72
Carbs: 12G
Protein: 3g.
Fat: 3g
Fiber: 4g

➤Easy Vegetarian Pumpkin Soup

Ingredients (4 servings)
tablespoon of margarine
onion (diced)
16-ounce can of pumpkin puree
1/3 cups of vegetable broth
½ tablespoon of nutmeg
½ tablespoon of sugar
Salt (to taste)
Pepper (to taste)
cups of soymilk or any milk as a substitute

Directions

Using a large saucepan, add onion to margarine and cook it between 3 and 5 minutes until the onion is clear. Add pumpkin puree, vegetable broth, sugar, pepper, and other ingredients and stir to combine. Cook in medium heat for between 10 and fifteen minutes. Before serving the soup, taste and add more spices, pepper, and salt if necessary. Serve soup and enjoy!

Nutrition facts
Calories: 118
Carbs: 16g
Protein: 2G
Fat: 6g
Fiber: 3g

➤Gazpacho Soup

Ingredients (3 servings)
1 large cucumber (to be sliced into chunks)
4 big ripe tomatoes (coarsely chopped)
½ bell pepper (any color)
2 cloves of garlic (minced)
1 celery rib (chopped)
1 tablespoon of lemon juice
¼ tablespoon of celery pepper
1 tablespoon of fresh basil (chopped)
1 tablespoon of fresh parsley (chopped)
Dash black pepper
½ tablespoon salt
3 tablespoons of red wine (vinegar/balsamic vinegar)
½ sweet onions (quartered)

Directions

To make the gazpacho place the cucumber chunks, chopped tomatoes, bell pepper, garlic, celery, lemon juice, and onion in the food processor or blender. You may choose to blend or process in batches if needed Add the vinegar (red/balsamic), salt, pepper to the blender or food processor and blend or process together until it is smooth or nearly smooth (the texture depends on you). The next step is to pour soup into a serving bowl and stir in the fresh chopped parsley and basil. Cover the serving bowl with plastic wrap or foil or cover it with a plastic wrap and put the bowl inside the refrigerator for about 30 minutes or until when you are set to serve the gazpacho soup. You can decide to add some extra fresh herbs to the soup for presentation as well as some avocado slices or crusty croutons. Serve gazpacho soup with the following: green salad some artisanal or homemade bread as a substitute, balsamic vinegar, and olive oil for dipping for a light but complete meal. Serve and enjoy!

Nutrition facts
Calories: 87
Carbs: 18g
Protein: 3g
Fat: 1g
Fiber: 2g

➤Crockpot Vegetarian Split Pea Soup

Ingredients (8 servings)
2 cups of split pea soup (uncooked)
8 cups of vegetable broth (or water)
2 potatoes (chopped)
2 cubes of bouillon (vegetarian)
Optional: 2 ribs of celery (chopped)
1 onion (diced)
2 cloves of garlic (minced)
2 carrots (sliced)
1 teaspoon of dry mustard
1 teaspoon of sage
1 teaspoon of thyme
1 teaspoon of cumin

Directions
Add peas, vegetable broth, and bouillon cubes in crock- pot or slow cooker. Stir it and break up the bouillon cubes a bit. Add chopped potatoes, onions, celery, carrot and garlic. Add mustard, cumin, sage, thyme, and bay leaves, and stir. Season soup lightly with salt and pepper. Cook for about 4 hours/till peas split. Taste and check seasoning. Serve, and enjoy!

Nutrition facts
Calories: 198
Fat: 5g
Carbs: 21g
Fiber: 7g
Protein: 18g

— CHAPTER 3 —

VEGETABLE RECIPES

ALICIA TRAVIS

Zoodles with Walnut Pesto

Preparation time: 10 minutes
Cooking time: 10 minutes | **Servings:** 4
4 medium zucchinis, spiralized
¼ cup extra-virgin olive oil, divided
1 teaspoon minced garlic, divided
½ teaspoon crushed red pepper
¼ teaspoon freshly ground black pepper, divided
¼ teaspoon kosher salt, divided
2 tablespoons grated Parmesan cheese, divided
1 cup packed fresh basil leaves
¾ cup walnut pieces, divided

Directions

In a large bowl, stir together the zoodles, 1 tablespoon of the olive oil, ½ teaspoon of the minced garlic, red pepper, ⅛ teaspoon of the black pepper and ⅛ teaspoon of the salt. Set aside. Heat ½ tablespoon of the oil in a large skillet over medium-high heat. Add half of the zoodles to the skillet and cook for 5 minutes, stirring constantly. Transfer the cooked zoodles into a bowl. Repeat with another half tablespoon of the oil and the remaining zoodles. When done, add the cooked zoodles to the bowl.
Make the pesto:
In a food processor, mix well the remaining ½ teaspoon of the minced garlic, ⅛ teaspoon of the black pepper and ⅛ teaspoon of the salt, 1 tablespoon of the Parmesan, basil leaves and ¼ cup of the walnuts. Pulse until smooth and then slowly drizzle the remaining 2 tablespoons of the oil into the pesto. Pulse again until well combined. Add the pesto to the zoodles and the Parmesan and the remaining ½ cup of the walnuts. Toss to coat well. Serve immediately.

Nutrition facts (per serving)
calories: 166 | fat: 16.0g | protein: 4.0g | carbs: 3.0g | fiber: 2.0g | sodium: 307mg

Cheesy Sweet Potato Burgers

Preparation time: 10 minutes | **Cooking time:** 19 to 20 minutes | **Servings:** 4
1 large sweet potato (about 8 ounces / 227 g)
2 tablespoons extra-virgin olive oil, divided
1 cup chopped onion
1 large egg
1 garlic clove
1 cup old-fashioned rolled oats
1 tablespoon dried oregano
1 tablespoon balsamic vinegar
¼ teaspoon kosher salt
½ cup crumbled Gorgonzola cheese

Put potatoes until softened in the center in the microwave on high for 4 to 5 minutes. Cool slightly before slicing in half. Meanwhile, in a medium-large skillet over medium-high heat, heat 1 tablespoon of the olive oil. Add the onion and sauté for 5 minutes. Add the cooked onion, egg, garlic, oats, oregano, vinegar and salt. Pulse until smooth. Add the cheese and pulse four times to barely combine. Form the mixture into four burgers. Place the burgers on a plate and press to flatten each to about ¾-inch thick. Heat one tablespoon of the oil over medium-high heat for about 2 minutes. Add the burgers to the hot oil, then reduce the heat to medium. Cook the burgers for 3/5 minutes per side. Enjoy

Nutrition facts (per serving)
calories: 290 | fat: 12.0g | protein: 12.0g | carbs: 43.0g | fiber: 8.0g | sodium: 566mg

Eggplant and Zucchini Gratin

Preparation time: 10 minutes
Cooking time: 19 minutes | **Servings:** 6
2 large zucchinis, finely chopped
1 large eggplant, finely chopped
¼ teaspoon kosher salt
¼ teaspoon freshly ground black pepper
3 tablespoons extra-virgin olive oil, divided
¾ cup unsweetened almond milk
1 tablespoon all-purpose flour
⅓ cup plus 2 tablespoons grated Parmesan cheese
1 cup chopped tomato
1 cup diced fresh Mozzarella
¼ cup fresh basil leaves

Preheat the oven to 420/425°F (220°C). In a large bowl, toss together the zucchini, eggplant, salt and pepper. Heat a tbs of oil. Put half of the vegetable mixture into the pan. Stir and cook for 5 minutes, stirring. Place the cooked vegetables in a medium roasting pan. Add the veggies to the baking dish. Place a medium saucepan over medium heat. Add the remaining 1 tbsp of the oil and flour to the saucepan. Whisk together until well blended. Slowly pour the warm milk into the saucepan, whisking the entire time. Continue to whisk frequently until the mixture thickens a bit. Add ⅓ cup of the Parmesan cheese and whisk until melted. Pour the cheese sauce over the vegetables in the baking dish and mix well. Fold in the tomatoes and Mozzarella cheese. Roast in the oven until the gratin is almost set and not runny, or for 10 minutes. Top with the fresh basil leaves and the remaining 2 tablespoons of the Parmesan cheese before serving.

Nutrition facts (per serving)
calories: 122 | fat: 5.0g | protein: 10.0g | carbs: 11.0g | fiber: 4.0g | sodium: 364mg

Veggie-Stuffed Portobello Mushrooms

Preparation time: 5 minutes | **Cooking time:** 24 to 25 minutes | **Servings:** 6
3 tablespoons extra-virgin olive oil, divided
1 cup diced onion
2 garlic cloves, minced
1 large zucchini, diced
3 cups chopped mushrooms
1 cup chopped tomato
1 teaspoon dried oregano
¼ teaspoon kosher salt
¼ teaspoon crushed red pepper
6 large portobello mushrooms, stems and gills re-

moved
Cooking spray
4 ounces (113 g) fresh mozzarella cheese, shredded

In a medium skillet over medium heat, heat 2 tablespoons of the oil. Add onion and sauté for 4/5 minutes. Stir in the garlic and sauté for 1 minute. Stir in the zucchini, mushrooms, tomato, oregano, salt and red pepper. Cook for 10 minutes, stirring constantly. Remove from the heat. Meanwhile, heat a grill pan over medium/high heat. Brush the remaining 1 tablespoon of the oil over the portobello mushroom caps. Place the mushrooms, bottom-side down, on the grill pan. Cover with an aluminum sheet foil sprayed with nonstick cooking spray. Cook for 5 minutes. Flip the mushroom caps over, and spoon about ½ cup of the cooked vegetable mixture into each cap. Top each with about 2 and a half tablespoons of the Mozzarella. Cover and grill for 4 to 5 minutes, or until the cheese is melted. Using a spatula, transfer the portobello mushrooms to a plate. Let cool for about 5 minutes before serving.

Nutrition facts (per serving)
calories: 111 | fat: 4.0g | protein: 11.0g | carbs: 11.0g | fiber: 4.0g | sodium: 314mg

➤Brussels Sprouts Linguine

Preparation time: 5 minutes
Cooking time: 25 minutes | **Servings:** 4
8 ounces (227 g) whole-wheat linguine
⅓ cup plus 2 tbsps extra-virgin olive oil, divided
1 medium sweet onion, diced
2 to 3 garlic cloves, smashed
8 ounces (227 g) Brussels sprouts, chopped
½ cup chicken stock
⅓ cup dry white wine
½ cup shredded Parmesan cheese
1 lemon, quartered

Cook pasta in the boiled water for about 5 minutes. Drain the pasta and reserve 1 and a half cup of the pasta water. Mix the cooked pasta with 2 tablespoons of the olive oil. Set aside. In a large skillet, heat the remaining ⅓ cup of olive oil over medium heat. Put the onion in the skillet and sauté for about 4 minutes, or until tender. Add the smashed garlic cloves and sauté for 1 minute, or until fragrant. Add the Brussels sprouts, mix and cook covered for 10 minutes. Pour in the chicken stock to prevent burning. Once the Brussels sprouts have wilted and are fork-tender, add white wine and cook for about 5 minutes, or until reduced. Add the pasta to the skillet and add the pasta water as needed. Top with the Parmesan cheese and squeeze the lemon over the dish right before eating.

Nutrition facts (per serving)
calories: 502 | fat: 31.0g | protein: 15.0g | carbs: 50.0g | fiber: 9.0g | sodium: 246mg

➤Beet and Watercress Salad

Preparation time: 15 minutes
Cooking time: 8 minutes | **Servings:** 4

2 pounds (907 g) beets, scrubbed, trimmed and cut into ¾-inch pieces
½ cup water
1 teaspoon caraway seeds
½ teaspoon table salt, plus more for seasoning
1 cup plain Greek yogurt
1 small garlic clove, minced
5 ounces (142 g) watercress, torn into bite-size pieces
1 tbsps extra-virgin olive oil, plus more for drizzling
2 tablespoon white wine vinegar, divided
Black pepper, to taste
1 teaspoon grated orange zest
2 tablespoons orange juice
¼ cup coarsely chopped fresh dill
¼ cup hazelnuts, toasted, skinned and chopped
Coarse sea salt, to taste

Combine the beets, water, caraway seeds and table salt in the Instant Pot. Set the lid in place. Cook for 8 minutes on High Pressure. Carefully open the lid. Bring beets to a plate. Set aside to cool slightly. In a bowl, mix the yogurt, garlic and 3 tablespoons of the beet cooking liquid. In a medium-large bowl, toss the watercress with 2 teaspoons of the oil and 1 teaspoon of the vinegar. Season with table salt and pepper. Spread the yogurt mixture over a serving dish. Arrange the watercress on top of the yogurt mixture, leaving a 1-inch border of the yogurt mixture. Add the beets to the now-empty large bowl and toss with the orange zest and juice, the remaining 2 teaspoons of the vinegar and the remaining 1 teaspoon of the oil. Season with table salt and pepper. Arrange the beets on top of the watercress mixture. Drizzle with the olive oil and sprinkle with the dill, hazelnuts and sea salt. Serve immediately.

Nutrition facts (per serving)
calories: 240 | fat: 15.0g | protein: 9.0g | carbs: 19.0g | fiber: 5.0g | sodium: 440mg

➤Garlicky Broccoli Rabe

Preparation time: 10 minutes
Cooking time: 5 to 6 minutes | **Servings:** 4
14 ounces (397 g) broccoli rabe, trimmed and cut into 1-inch pieces
2 teaspoons salt, plus more for seasoning
Black pepper, to taste
2 tablespoons extra-virgin olive oil
3 garlic cloves, minced
¼ teaspoon red pepper flakes

Bring 3 and a half quarts of water to a boil in a large saucepan. Add the broccoli rabe and 2 teaspoons of the salt to the boiling water and cook until wilted and tender, or for 2 to 3 minutes. Drain the broccoli rabe. Put into ice water and let sit until chilled. Drain and pat dry. In a skillet over medium heat, heat the oil and add the garlic and red pepper flakes. Sauté for about 2-3 minutes, or until the garlic begins to sizzle. Increase the heat to medium-high. Stir the broccoli rabe and cook until heated through, or for about 1 minute, stirring constantly. Season with salt and pepper.

Serve immediately.
Nutrition facts (per serving)
calories: 87 | fat: 7.3g | protein: 3.4g | carbs: 4.0g |
fiber: 2.9g | sodium: 1196mg

›Sautéed Cabbage with Parsley

Preparation time: 10 minutes
Cooking time: 12 to 14 minutes |
Servings: 4 to 6
1 small head green cabbage (about 1¼ pounds / 567
g), cored and sliced thin
2 tablespoons extra-virgin olive oil, divided
1 onion, halved and sliced thin
¾ teaspoon salt, divided
¼ teaspoon black pepper
¼ cup chopped fresh parsley
1½ teaspoons lemon juice

Place the cabbage in a medium-large bowl with
cold water. Let sit for 3 minutes. Drain well. Preheat
1 tbsp of the extra-virgin olive oil in a skillet over medium-high heat until shimmering. Add the onion and
¼ teaspoon of the salt and cook for 5 to 7 minutes, or
until softened and lightly browned. Transfer to a bowl.
Heat the oil in the now-empty skillet with medium-high
heat until shimmering. Add the cabbage and sprinkle with the remaining ½ teaspoon of salt and black
pepper. Cover and cook for about 3 minutes, without
stirring, or until cabbage is wilted and lightly browned
on the bottom. Stir and continue to cook for about
2-4 minutes, uncovered, or until the cabbage is ten-
der-crisp and lightly browned in places, stirring once
halfway through cooking. Off heat, stir in the cooked
onion, parsley and lemon juice. Transfer to a plate
and serve.
Nutrition facts (per serving)
calories: 117 | fat: 7.0g | protein: 2.7g | carbs: 13.4g
| fiber: 5.1g | sodium: 472mg

›Braised Cauliflower with White Wine

Preparation time: 10 minutes
Cooking time: 12 to 16 minutes
Servings: 4 to 6
3 tbsp + 1 teaspoon extra-virgin olive oil, divided
3 garlic cloves, minced
⅛ teaspoon red pepper flakes
1 head cauliflower (2 pounds / 907 g), cored and cut
into 1½-inch florets
¼ teaspoon salt, plus more for seasoning
Black pepper, to taste
⅓ cup vegetable broth
⅓ cup dry white wine
2 tablespoons minced fresh parsley

Combine 1 teaspoon of the oil, garlic and pepper
flakes in a small bowl. Heat the remaining 3 tablespoons of the oil in a skillet over medium-high heat until
shimmering. Add the cauliflower and ¼ teaspoon of
the salt and cook for 7 to 9 minutes, stirring occasio-

nally, or until florets are golden brown. Push the cauliflower towards the sides of the skillet. Add in the garlic
mixture to the center of the skillet. Cook for about 40
seconds. Stir the garlic mixture into the cauliflower. Boil
with wine and broth. Reduce the heat to medium-low.
Cook while covered for 5-7 minutes, or until the cauliflower is crisp-tender. Stop heating, stir in the parsley
and season with salt and pepper. Serve immediately.
Nutrition facts (per serving)
calories: 143 | fat: 11.7g | protein: 3.1g | carbs: 8.7g
| fiber: 3.1g | sodium: 263mg

›Cauliflower Steaks with Arugula

Preparation time: 5 minutes
Cooking time: 20 minutes | **Servings:** 4
Cauliflower:
1 head cauliflower
Cooking spray
½ teaspoon garlic powder
4 cups arugula
Dressing:
1½ tablespoons extra-virgin olive oil
1½ tablespoons honey mustard 1 teaspoon freshly
squeezed lemon juice

Preheat the oven to 420/425°F (220°C). Remove the
leaves head and cut it in half lengthwise. Cut 1½inch-
thick steaks from each half. Spritz both sides of each
steak with cooking spray and season both sides with
garlic powder. Put the steaks on a baking sheet, cover
with foil, and roast in the oven for 8-10 minutes.
Remove the baking sheet and gently pull back the
foil to avoid the steam. Flip the steaks, then roast uncovered for 10 minutes more. Meanwhile, prepare the
dressing: mix the olive oil, honey mustard and lemon
juice in a small bowl. When the cauliflower steaks are
done, divide them into four equal portions. Top each
portion with one-quarter of the arugula and dressing.
Serve immediately.
Nutrition facts (per serving)
calories: 115 | fat: 6.0g | protein: 5.0g | carbs: 14.0g
| fiber: 4.0g | sodium: 97mg

›Parmesan-Stuffed Zucchini Boats

Preparation time: 5 minutes
Cooking time: 15 minutes | **Servings:** 4
1 cup canned low-sodium chickpeas, drained and
rinsed
1 cup no-sugar-added spaghetti sauce
2 zucchinis
¼ cup shredded Parmesan cheese

Preheat the oven to 420/425°F (220°C). In a medium
bowl, stir together the chickpeas and spaghetti sauce.
Just cut zucchini in half and scrape a spoon gently
down the length of each half to remove the seeds.
Fill each zucchini half with the chickpea sauce and
top with one-quarter of the Parmesan cheese.
Now put zucchini halves on a baking sheet and roast
in the oven for 15 minutes. Transfer to a plate. Let rest

for 5 minutes before serving.
Nutrition facts (per serving)
calories: 139 | fat: 4.0g | protein: 8.0g | carbs: 20.0g | fiber: 5.0g | sodium: 344mg

‣Baby Kale and Cabbage Salad

Preparation time: 10 minutes
Cooking time: 0 minutes | **Servings:** 6
2 bunches of baby kale, thinly sliced
½ head green savoy cabbage
1 medium red bell pepper, thinly sliced
1 garlic clove, thinly sliced
1 cup toasted peanuts
Dressing:
Juice of 1 lemon
¼ cup apple cider vinegar
1 teaspoon ground cumin
¼ teaspoon smoked paprika

In a medium-large mixing bowl, toss together the kale and cabbage. Make the dressing: whisk the lemon juice, vinegar, cumin, and paprika together in a small bowl. Put the dressing on the greens and massage with your hands. Add the pepper, garlic and peanuts to the mixing bowl. Toss to combine. Serve immediately.
Nutrition facts (per serving)
calories: 199 | fat: 12.0g | protein: 10.0g | carbs: 17.0g | fiber: 5.0g | sodium: 46mg

‣Grilled Romaine Lettuce

Preparation time: 5 minutes
Cooking time: 3 to 5 minutes | **Servings:** 4
Romaine:
2 heads romaine lettuce, halved lengthwise
2 tablespoons extra-virgin olive oil
Dressing:
½ cup unsweetened almond milk
1 tablespoon extra-virgin olive oil
¼ bunch fresh chives, thinly chopped
1 garlic clove, pressed
1 pinch red pepper flakes

Heat a grill pan over medium heat. Brush each lettuce half with olive oil. Place the lettuce halves, flat-side down, on the grill. Grill for 3-5 minutes, or until the lettuce slightly wilts and develops light grill marks. Meanwhile, whisk together all the ingredients for the dressing in a small bowl. Drizzle 2 tbsps of the dressing over each romaine half and serve.
Nutrition facts (per serving)
calories: 126 | fat: 11.0g | protein: 2.0g | carbs: 7.0g | fiber: 1.0g | sodium: 41mg

‣Mini Crustless Spinach Quiches

Preparation time: 10 minutes
Cooking time: 20 minutes | **Servings:** 6
2 tablespoons extra-virgin olive oil
1 onion, finely chopped
2 cups baby spinach
2 garlic cloves, minced
8 large eggs, beaten
¼ cup unsweetened almond milk
½ teaspoon sea salt
¼ teaspoon freshly ground black pepper
1 cup shredded Swiss cheese
Cooking spray

Preheat the oven to 370/375°F (190°C). Spritz a 6-cup muffin tin with cooking spray. Set aside. Heat the olive oil in a medium-large skillet over medium-high heat, until shimmering. Add the onion and cook for about 4 minutes, or until soft. Add the spinach and cook for about 1-2 minutes, stirring constantly, or until the spinach softens. Add the garlic and sauté for about 30 seconds. Remove from the heat and let cool. Whisk together the eggs, milk, salt and pepper in a medium bowl. Stir the cooled vegetables and the cheese into the egg mixture. Spoon the mixture into the prepared muffin tins. Bake for about 15 minutes or until the eggs are set. Let rest for 5 minutes before serving.
Nutrition facts (per serving)
calories: 218 | fat: 17.0g | protein: 14.0g | carbs: 4.0g | fiber: 1.0g | sodium: 237mg

‣Butternut Noodles with Mushrooms

Preparation time: 10 minutes
Cooking time: 12 minutes | **Servings:** 4
¼ cup extra-virgin olive oil
1 pound (454 g) cremini mushrooms, sliced
½ red onion, finely chopped
1 teaspoon dried thyme
½ teaspoon sea salt
3 garlic cloves, minced
½ cup dry white wine
Pinch of red pepper flakes
4 cups butternut noodles
4 ounces (113 g) grated Parmesan cheese

Heat the olive oil medium-high heat until shimmering. Add the mushrooms, onion, thyme, and salt to the skillet. Cook for about 4-7 minutes, stirring occasionally, or until the mushrooms start to brown. Add the garlic and sauté for 30 about seconds. Stir in the white wine and red pepper flakes. Fold in the noodles. Cook for about 5 minutes, stirring occasionally, or until the noodles are tender. Serve topped with the grated Parmesan.
Nutrition facts (per serving)
calories: 244 | fat: 14.0g | protein: 4.0g | carbs: 22.0g | fiber: 4.0g | sodium: 159mg

‣Potato Tortilla with Leeks and Mushrooms

Preparation time: 30 minutes
Cooking time: 50 minutes | **Servings:** 2
1 tablespoon olive oil

1 and a half cup thinly sliced leeks
5 ounces (113 g) baby bell (cremini) mushrooms, sliced
1 medium/small potato, peeled and sliced ¼-inch thick
½ cup unsweetened almond milk
5 large eggs, beaten
1 teaspoon Dijon mustard
½ teaspoon salt
½ teaspoon dried thyme
Pinch black pepper
3 ounces (85 g) Gruyere cheese, shredded

Preheat the oven to 340/350ºF (180ºC).
Heat the olive oil in a large sauté pan over medium-high heat. Add the leeks, mushrooms, and potato and sauté for about 10 minutes, or until the potato starts browning. Low the heat to medium-low, cover, and cook for an additional 10 minutes, or until the potato begins to soften. Add 1-2 tbsps of water to prevent sticking to the bottom of the pan, if needed. Meanwhile, whisk together the milk, beaten eggs, mustard, salt, thyme, black pepper, and cheese in a medium bowl until combined. Once the potatoes are fork-tender, turn off the heat. Transfer the cooked vegetables to an oiled nonstick ovenproof pan and put them in a nice layer along the bottom and slightly up the sides of the pan. Pour the milk mixture evenly over the vegetables. Bake in the oven for 26 to 30 minutes, or until the eggs are completely set and the top is golden and puffed.Take out of the oven and cool for 4-5 minutes before cutting and serving.

Nutrition facts:
cal: 541 | fat: 33.1g | protein: 32.8g | carbs: 31.0g | fiber: 4.0g | sodium: 912mg

›Mushrooms Ragu with Cheesy Polenta

Preparation time: 20 minutes
Cooking time: 30 minutes | **Servings:** 2
½ ounce (14 g) dried porcini mushrooms
1 pound (454 g) baby bell (cremini) mushrooms, quartered
2 tablespoons olive oil
1 garlic clove, minced
1 large shallot, minced
1 tablespoon flour
2 teaspoons tomato paste
½ cup red wine
1 cup mushroom stock (or reserved liquid from soaking the porcini mushrooms, if using)
1 fresh rosemary sprig
½ teaspoon dried thyme
1½ cups water
½ teaspoon salt, plus more as needed
⅓ cup instant polenta
2 tablespoons grated Parmesan cheese

Soak the dried porcini mushrooms in 1 cup of hot water for about 15 minutes to soften them. When they are ready, scoop them out of the water, reserving the soaking liquid. Mince the porcini mushrooms.

Heat the olive oil in a medium-large sauté pan over medium-high heat. Add the mushrooms, garlic, and shallot and sauté for 10 minutes, or until the vegetables begin to caramelize. Add the flour and tomato paste and cook for an additional 30 seconds. Add the red wine, mushroom stock, rosemary, and thyme. Bring the mixture to a boil, while stirring, or until it has thickened. Reduce the heat and allow to simmer for 10 minutes. Meanwhile, bring the water to a boil in a saucepan, then sprinkle it with salt. Add the instant polenta and quickly stir while it thickens. Scatter with the grated Parmesan cheese. Season with more salt as needed.

Nutrition facts (per serving)
calories: 450 | fat: 16.0g | protein: 14.1g | carbs: 57.8g | fiber: 5.0g | sodium: 165mg

›Veggie Rice Bowls with Pesto Sauce

Preparation time: 15 minutes
Cooking time: 1 minute | **Servings:** 2
2 cups water
1 cup arborio rice, rinsed
Salt and ground black pepper, to taste
2 eggs
1 cup broccoli florets
½ pound (227 g) Brussels sprouts
1 carrot, peeled and chopped
1 small beet, peeled and cubed
¼ cup pesto sauce
Lemon wedges, for serving

Put the water, rice, salt, and pepper in the Instant Pot. Insert a trivet over rice and place a steamer basket on top. Add the eggs, broccoli, Brussels sprouts, carrots, beet cubes, salt, and pepper to the steamer basket. Lock the lid. Select the Manual mode and set the cooking time to 1 minute at High Pressure. When the timer beeps, perform a natural pressure release for 10 minutes, then release any remaining pressure. Carefully open the lid. Remove the steamer basket and trivet from the pot and transfer the eggs to a bowl with ice water. Peel and halve the eggs. Use a fork to fluff the rice. Divide the rice, broccoli, Brussels sprouts, carrot, beet cubes, and eggs into two bowls. Top with a dollop of pesto sauce and serve with lemon wedges.

Nutrition facts (per serving)
calories: 590 | fat: 34.1g | protein: 21.9g | carbs: 50.0g | fiber: 19.6g | sodium: 670mg

›Roasted Cauliflower and Carrots

Preparation time: 10 minutes
Cooking time: 30 minutes | **Servings:** 2
4 cups cauliflower florets (about ½ small head)
2 medium carrots, peeled, halved, and sliced into quarters lengthwise
2 tablespoons olive oil, divided
½ teaspoon salt, divided
½ teaspoon garlic powder, divided
2 teaspoons za'atar spice mix, divided
1 (15-ounce / 425-g) can chickpeas, drained, rinsed,

and patted dry
¾ cup plain Greek yogurt
1 teaspoon harissa spice paste, plus additional as needed

Preheat the oven to 390/400°F (205°C). Line a sheet pan with foil or parchment paper. Put the cauliflower and carrots in a medium-large bowl. Drizzle with 1 tablespoon of olive oil and sprinkle with ¼ teaspoon of salt, ¼ teaspoon of garlic powder, and 1 teaspoon of za'atar. Toss to combine well. Put the vegetables on one half of the prepared sheet pan in a single layer. Put the chickpeas in the same bowl and season with the remaining 1 tablespoon of olive oil, ¼ teaspoon of salt, ¼ teaspoon of garlic powder, and the remaining 1 teaspoon of za'atar. Toss to combine well. Put the chickpeas on the other half of the sheet pan. Roast in the preheated oven for 30 minutes, or until the vegetables are crisp-tender. Flip the vegetables halfway through and stir the chickpeas, so they cook evenly. Meanwhile, whisk the yogurt and harissa together in a small bowl. Taste and add additional harissa as needed. Serve the vegetables and chickpeas with the yogurt mixture on the side.

Nutrition facts (per serving)
calories: 468 | fat: 23.0g | protein: 18.1g | carbs: 54.1g | fiber: 13.8g | sodium: 631mg

›Sauté ed Spinach and Leeks

Preparation time: 5 minutes
Cooking time: 8 minutes | **Servings:** 2
3 tablespoons olive oil
2 garlic cloves, crushed
2 leeks, chopped
2 red onions, chopped
9 ounces (255 g) fresh spinach
1 teaspoon kosher salt
½ cup crumbled goat cheese

Coat the bottom of the Instant Pot with olive oil. Add the garlic, leek, and onions and stir-fry for about 5 minutes, on Sauté mode. Put in the spinach. Sprinkle with the salt and sauté for an additional 3 minutes, stirring constantly. Transfer to a plate and scatter with the goat cheese before serving.

Nutrition facts (per serving)
calories: 447 | fat: 31.2g | protein: 14.6g | carbs: 28.7g | fiber: 6.3g | sodium: 937mg

›Zoodles with Beet Pesto

Preparation time: 10 minutes
Cooking time: 50 minutes | **Servings:** 2
1 medium red beet, peeled, chopped
½ cup walnut pieces
½ cup crumbled goat cheese
3 garlic cloves
2 tablespoons freshly squeezed lemon juice
2 tbsps plus 2 teaspoons extra-virgin olive oil, divided
¼ teaspoon salt
4 small zucchinis, spiralized

Preheat the oven to 370/375°F (190°C). Wrap the chopped beet in a piece of aluminum foil and seal well. Roast in the preheated oven for 30 to 40 minutes until tender. Meanwhile, heat a skillet over medium-high heat until hot. Add the walnuts and toast for 5 to 7 minutes, or until fragrant and lightly browned. Remove the cooked beets and place them in a food processor. Add the toasted walnuts, goat cheese, garlic, lemon juice, 2 tablespoons of olive oil, and salt. Pulse until smoothly blended. Set aside. Heat the remaining 2 tsps of extra-virgin olive oil in a large skillet over medium heat. Add in the zucchini and toss to coat in the oil. Cook for 2-3 minutes, stirring gently, or until the zucchini is softened. Transfer the zucchinis to a serving plate and toss with the beet pesto, then serve.

Nutrition facts (per serving)
calories: 423 | fat: 38.8g | protein: 8.0g | carbs: 17.1g | fiber: 6.0g | sodium: 338mg

›Sweet Potato Chickpea Buddha Bowl

Preparation time: 10 minutes
Cooking time: 10 to 15 minutes
Servings: 2
Sauce:
1 tablespoon tahini
2 tablespoons plain Greek yogurt
2 tablespoons hemp seeds
1 garlic clove, minced
Pinch salt
Freshly ground black pepper, to taste
Bowl:
1 small, sweet potato, peeled and diced
1 teaspoon extra-virgin olive oil
1 cup from 1 (15-ounce / 425-g) can low-sodium chickpeas, drained and rinsed2 cups baby kale

Make the Sauce
Whisk together the tahini and yogurt in a small bowl. Stir in the hemp seeds and minced garlic. Season with salt pepper. Add 2 to 3 tablespoons of water in order to create a creamy yet pourable consistency and set aside.
Make the Bowl
Preheat the oven to 420/425°F (220°C). Line a baking sheet with parchment paper. Place the sweet potato on the prepared baking sheet and drizzle with olive oil. Toss well. Roast in the preheated oven for 14 to 15 minutes, stirring once during cooking, or until fork-tender and browned. In each of the 2 bowls, place ½ cup of chickpeas, 1 cup of baby kale, and half of the cooked sweet potato. Serve drizzled with half of the prepared sauce.

Nutrition facts (per serving)
calories: 323 | fat: 14.1g | protein: 17.0g | carbs: 36.0 g | fiber: 7.9g | sodium: 304mg

›Zucchini Patties

Preparation time: 15 minutes
Cooking time: 5 minutes | **Servings:** 2

2 medium zucchinis, shredded
1 teaspoon salt, divided
2 eggs
2 tablespoons chickpea flour
1 tablespoon chopped fresh mint
1 scallion, chopped
2 tablespoons extra-virgin olive oil

Put the shredded zucchini in a fine-mesh strainer and season with ½ teaspoon of salt. Set aside. Beat together the eggs, chickpea flour, mint, scallion, and remaining ½ teaspoon of salt in a medium bowl. Squeeze the zucchinis to drain as much liquid as possible. Add the zucchini to the egg mixture and stir until well incorporated. Heat the extra-virgin olive oil in a medium-large skillet over medium-high heat. Drop the zucchini mixture by spoonfuls into the skillet. Gently flatten the zucchini with the back of a spatula. Cook until golden brown for 2 to 3 minutes. Flip and cook for an additional 2 minutes. Remove from the heat and serve.

Nutrition facts (per serving)
calories: 264 | fat: 20.0g | protein: 9.8g | carbs: 16.1g | fiber: 4.0g | sodium: 1780mg

›Zucchini Crisp

Preparation time: 10 minutes
Cooking time: 20 minutes | **Servings:** 2
4 zucchinis, sliced into ½-inch rounds
½ cup unsweetened almond milk
1 teaspoon fresh lemon juice
1 teaspoon arrowroot powder
½ teaspoon salt, divided
½ cup whole wheat breadcrumbs
¼ cup nutritional yeast
¼ cup hemp seeds
½ teaspoon garlic powder
¼ teaspoon crushed red pepper
¼ teaspoon black pepper

Preheat the oven to 370/375°F (190°C). Line two baking sheets with parchment paper and set them aside. Put the zucchini in a medium bowl with the almond milk, lemon juice, arrowroot powder, and ¼ teaspoon of salt. Stir to mix well. In a large bowl with a lid, thoroughly combine the breadcrumbs, nutritional yeast, hemp seeds, garlic powder, crushed red pepper and black pepper. Add the zucchini in batches and shake until the slices are evenly coated. Arrange the zucchini on the baking sheets in a single layer. Bake in the preheated oven for about 20 minutes, or until the zucchini slices are golden brown. Season with the remaining ¼ teaspoon of salt before serving.

Nutrition facts (per serving)
calories: 255 | fat: 11.3g | protein: 8.6g | carbs: 31.9g | fiber: 3.8g | sodium: 826mg

›Creamy Sweet Potatoes and Collards

Preparation time: 20 minutes
Cooking time: 35 minutes | **Servings:** 2

1 tablespoon avocado oil
3 garlic cloves, chopped
1 yellow onion, diced
½ teaspoon crushed red pepper flakes
1 large, sweet potato, peeled and diced
2 bunches collard greens (about 2 pounds/907 g), stemmed, leaves chopped into 1-inch squares
1 (14.5-ounce / 411-g) can diced tomatoes with juice
1 (15-ounce / 425-g) can red kidney beans or chickpeas, drained and rinsed
1½ cups water
½ cup unsweetened coconut milk Salt and black pepper, to taste

Melt the avocado oil in a large, deep skillet over medium-high heat. Add the garlic, onion, and red pepper flakes and cook for 3 minutes. Stir in the sweet potato and collards. Add the tomatoes with their juice, beans, water, and coconut milk and mix well. Bring the mixture just to a boil. Low the heat to medium-low, cover, and simmer for about 30 minutes, or until softened. Season to taste with salt and pepper.

›Vegetarian Chili with Avocado Cream

Preparation Time: 15 minutes
Cooking Time: 25 minutes
Servings: 8
Ingredients:
2 tablespoons olive oil
1/2 onion, finely chopped
1 tablespoon minced garlic
2 jalapeño peppers, chopped
1 red bell pepper, diced
1 teaspoon ground cumin
2 tablespoons chili powder
2 cups pecans, chopped
4 cups canned diced tomatoes and their juice *Topping:*
1 cup sour cream
1 avocado, diced
2 tablespoons fresh cilantro, chopped
Directions:
Heat olive oil. Toss in the onion, garlic, jalapeño peppers, and red bell pepper, then sauté for about 4 minutes until tender. Place the chili powder and cumin and stir for 30 seconds. Fold in the pecans, tomatoes, and their juice, then bring to a boil. Simmer uncovered for about 20 minutes to infuse the flavors, stirring occasionally. Remove from the heat to eight bowls. Evenly top each bowl of chili with the sour cream, diced avocado, and fresh cilantro.
Nutrition facts:
Calories: 318
Fat: 14.4g
Fiber: 17.5g
Carbohydrates: 9.5 g
Protein: 14g

Cherry Tomato Gratin

Preparation Time: 15 minutes
Cooking Time: 20 minutes
Servings: 4
Ingredients:
2 tablespoons olive oil,
1/2 cup cherry tomatoes halved
1/2 cup mayonnaise, Keto-friendly
1/2 cup vegan Mozzarella cheese, cut into pieces
1 ounce (28 g) vegan Parmesan cheese, shredded
1 tablespoon basil pesto
Pepper and salt
1 cup watercress
Directions:
Let the oven heat up to 400F. Grease a baking pan with olive oil. Combine the cherry tomatoes, mayo, vegan Mozzarella cheese, 1/2 ounce (14 g) of Parmesan cheese, basil pesto, salt, and black pepper baking pan. Scatter with the remaining Parmesan. Baking time: 20 minutes. Take them out of the oven and divide them among four plates. Top with watercress and olive oil, and slice to serve.
Nutrition facts:
Calories: 254
Fat: 12.1g
Fiber: 9.3g
Carbohydrates: 11.1g
Protein: 9.5g

Stuffed Zucchini

Preparation Time: 20 minutes
Cooking Time: 20 minutes
Servings: 4
Ingredients:
4 medium zucchinis, halved lengthwise
1 cup red bell pepper, seeded and minced
1/2 cup Kalamata olives, pitted and minced
1/2 cup fresh tomatoes, minced
1 teaspoon garlic, minced
1 tablespoon dried oregano, crushed
Salt and ground black pepper, as required
1/2 cup feta cheese, crumbled
Directions:
Grease a large baking sheet. Scoop out the flesh of each zucchini half using a melon baller. Discard the flesh. Mix the bell pepper, olives, tomatoes, garlic, oregano, salt, and black pepper in a bowl.
Stuff each zucchini half with the veggie mixture evenly. Arrange zucchini halves onto the prepared baking sheet and bake for about 15 minutes. Now, set the oven to broiler on high. Top each zucchini half with feta cheese and broil for about 3 minutes. Serve hot.
Nutrition facts:
Calories: 314
Fat: 12.4g
Fiber: 9.4g
Carbohydrates:.4.1 g
Protein: 7.4g

Creamy Zoodles

Preparation Time: 15 minutes
Cooking Time: 10 minutes
Servings: 4
Ingredients:
11/4 cups heavy whipping cream
1/4 cup mayonnaise
Salt and ground black pepper, as required
30 ounces zucchini, spiralized with blade C
3 ounces Parmesan cheese, grated
2 tablespoons fresh mint leaves
2 tablespoons butter, melted
Directions:
The heavy cream must be added to a pan then brought to a boil. Lower the heat to low and cook until reduced in half. Put in the pepper, mayo, and salt; cook until mixture is warm enough. Add the zucchini noodles and gently stir to combine. Stir in the Parmesan cheese. Divide the zucchini noodles onto four serving plates and immediately drizzle with the melted butter. Serve immediately.
Nutrition facts:
Calories: 241
Fat: 11.4g
Fiber: 7.5g
Carbohydrates:3.1 g
Protein: 5.1g

Black Bean Veggie Burger

Preparation Time: 15 minutes
Cooking Time: 20 minutes
Servings: 2
Ingredients:
1/2 onion (chopped small)
1 (14-ounce) can of black beans (well-drained)
2 slices of bread (crumbled)
1/2 teaspoon of seasoned salt
1 teaspoon of garlic powder
1 teaspoon of onion powder
1/2 cup of almond flour
Dash salt (to taste)
Dash pepper (to taste)
Oil for frying (divide)
Directions:
Combine onions and sauté and pour it into the small frying pan. Fry them until they are soft. This process usually takes between 4 and 5 minutes. Get a large bowl. Mash the black beans inside it. Ensure that the beans are almost smooth. Sauté your onions and crumble the bread. Add the sautéed onions, mashed black beans, crumbled bread, seasoned salt, garlic powder, and onion powder in the bowl. Ensure you mix to combine well. Add some flour to the ingredients by adding a teaspoon per time. Stir everything together until it is well combined. While mixing, make sure that it is very thick. To achieve this, you may want to use your hand to work your flour well. Make the

mixed black beans into patties. Ensure that each of the patties is approximately 1/2 inch thick. The best way to do this is to make a ball with the black beans. After doing this, flatten the ball gently. Place your frying pan on medium-low heat. Add some oil.

Fry your black bean patties in the frying pan until they are slightly firm and lightly browned on each side. This usually takes about 3 minutes. Ensure you adjust the head well because if the pan is too hot, the bean burgers will be brown in the middle and will not be well cooked in the middle. To serve, assemble your veggie burgers and enjoy them with all the fixings. You can also serve get a plate, serve them with a little ketchup or hot sauce. To increase the nutrition of the meal, you can add a nice green salad.

Nutrition facts:
Calories: 376
Fat: 15.1g
Fiber: 12.9g
Carbohydrates:9.4 g
Protein: 11.6g

➤Keto Red Curry

Preparation Time: 20 minutes
Cooking Time: 15-20 minutes
Servings: 6
Ingredients:
1 cup broccoli florets
1 large handful of fresh spinach
4 tbsp. coconut oil
1/4 medium onion
1 tsp. garlic, minced
1 tsp. fresh ginger, peeled and minced
2 tsp. soy sauce
1 Tbsp. red curry paste
1/2 cup coconut cream

Directions:
Add half the coconut oil to a saucepan and heat over medium-high heat. When the oil is hot, put the onion into the pan and sauté for 3-4 minutes, until it is semitranslucent. Sauté garlic, stirring, just until fragrant, about 30 seconds. Lower the heat to medium-low and add broccoli florets. Sauté, stirring, for about 1-2 minutes. Now, add the red curry paste. Sauté until the paste is fragrant, then mix everything. Add the spinach on top of the vegetable mixture. When the spinach begins wilting, add the coconut cream and stir. Add the rest of the coconut oil, the soy sauce, and the minced ginger. Bring to a simmer for 5-10 minutes. Serve hot.

Nutrition facts:
Calories: 265
Fat: 7.1g
Fiber: 6.9g
Carbohydrates:2.1 g
Protein: 4.4g

➤Sweet-And-Sour Tempeh

Preparation Time: 10 minutes
Cooking Time: 25 minutes
Servings: 4
Ingredients:
Tempeh
1 package of tempeh
3/4 cup of vegetable broth
2 tablespoons of soy sauce
2 tablespoons olive oil
Sauce
1 can of pineapple juice
2 tablespoons of brown sugar
1/4 cup of white vinegar
1 tablespoon of cornstarch
1 red bell pepper
1 chopped white onion

Directions:
Place a skillet on high heat. Pour in the vegetable roth and tempeh in it. Add the soy sauce to the tempeh. Let it cook until it softens. This usually takes 10 minutes. When it is well cooked, remove the tempeh and keep the liquid. We are going to use it for the sauce. Put the tempeh in another skillet placed on medium heat. Sauté it with olive oil and cook until the tempeh is browned. This should take 3 minutes. Place a pot of the reserved liquid from the cooked tempeh on medium heat. Add the pineapple juice, vinegar, brown sugar, and cornstarch. Stir everything together until it's well combined. Let it simmer for 5 minutes. Add the onion and pepper to the sauce. Stir in until the sauce is thick. Reduce the heat, add the cooked tempeh and pineapple chunks to the sauce. Leave it to simmer together. Remove from heat and serve with any grain food of your choice.

Nutrition facts:
Calories: 312
Fat: 10g
Fiber: 4.1g
Carbohydrates:2.1 g
Protein: 5.2g

➤Casserole with Black Beans

Preparation Time: 20 minutes
Cooking Time: 20 minutes
Servings: 6
Ingredients:
2 cups of minced garlic cloves
2 cups of Monterey Jack and cheddar
3/4 cup of sauce
1 1/2 cups chopped red pepper
2 teaspoons ground cumin
2 cans of black beans
12 corn tortillas
3 chopped tomatoes
1/2 cup of sliced black olives
2 cups of chopped onion

Directions:
Let the oven heat to 350F. Place a large pot over medium heat. Pour the onion, garlic, pepper, cumin,

sauce, and black beans in the pot — Cook the ingredients for 3 minutes, stirring frequently. Arrange the tortillas in the baking dish. Ensure they are well spaced and even overlapping the dish if necessary. Spread half of the bean mixture on the tortillas. Sprinkle with the cheddar.

Repeat the process across the tortillas until everything is well stuffed. Cover the baking dish with foil paper and place it in the oven. Bake it for 15 minutes. Remove from the oven to cool down a bit. Garnish the casserole with olives and tomatoes

Nutrition facts:
Calories: 325
Fat: 9.4g
Fiber: 11.2g
Carbohydrates:3.1 g
Protein: 12.6g

›Baked Zucchini Gratin

Preparation Time: 25 minutes
Cooking Time: 30 minutes
Servings: 2
Ingredients:
1 large zucchini, cut into 1/3-inch-thick slices
Pink Himalayan salt
1-ounce Brie cheese, rind trimmed off
1 tablespoon butter
Freshly ground black pepper
1/3 cup shredded Gruyere cheese
1/4 cup crushed pork rinds
Directions:
Preheat the oven to 400°F. When the zucchini has been "weeping" for about 30 minutes, in a small saucepan over medium-low heat, heat the Brie and butter, occasionally stirring, until the cheese has melted. The mixture is thoroughly combined for about 2 minutes. Arrange the zucchini in an 8-inch baking dish, so the zucchini slices overlap a bit. Season with pepper. Pour the Brie mixture over the zucchini, and top with the shredded Gruyere cheese. Sprinkle the crushed pork rinds over the top. Bake for about 25 minutes, until the dish is bubbling and the top is nicely browned, and serve.

Nutrition facts:
Calories: 324
Fat: 11.5g
Fiber: 5.1g
Carbohydrates:2.2 g
Protein: 5.1g

›Veggie Greek Moussaka

Preparation Time: 20 minutes
Cooking Time: 30 minutes
Servings: 6
Ingredients:
2 large eggplants, cut into strips
1 cup diced celery
1 cup diced carrots

1 small white onion, chopped
2 eggs
1 tsp. olive oil
3 cups grated Parmesan
1 cup ricotta cheese
3 cloves garlic, minced
2 tsp. Italian seasoning blend
Salt to taste Sauce:
1 1/2 cups heavy cream
1/4 cup butter, melted
1 cup grated mozzarella cheese
2 tsp. Italian seasoning
3/4 cup almond flour
Directions:
Preheat the oven to 350ºF. Lay the eggplant strips, sprinkle with salt, and let sit there to exude liquid. Heat olive oil heat and sauté the onion, celery, garlic, and carrots for 5 minutes. Mix the eggs, 1 cup of Parmesan cheese, ricotta cheese, and salt in a bowl; set aside. Pour the heavy cream into a pot and bring to heat over a medium fire while continually stirring.

Stir in the remaining Parmesan cheese and one teaspoon of Italian seasoning. Turn the heat off and set it aside. To lay the moussaka, spread a small amount of the sauce at the bottom of the baking dish.

Pat dry the eggplant strips and make a single layer on the sauce. A layer of ricotta cheese must be spread on the eggplants, sprinkle some veggies on it, and repeat everything. Evenly mix the melted butter, almond flour, and one teaspoon of Italian seasoning in a small bowl. Spread the top of the moussaka layers with it and sprinkle the top with mozzarella cheese. Bake for 23-25 minutes until the cheese is slightly burned. Slice the moussaka and serve warm.

Nutrition facts:
Calories: 398
Fat: 15.1g
Fiber: 11.3g
Carbohydrates:3.1 g
Protein: 5.9g

›Gouda Cauliflower Casserole

Preparation Time: 15 minutes
Cooking Time: 15 minutes
Servings: 4
Ingredients:
2 heads cauliflower, cut into florets
1/3 cup butter, cubed
2 tbsp. melted butter
1 white onion, chopped
Salt and black pepper to taste
1/4 almond milk
1/2 cup almond flour
1 1/2 cups grated gouda cheese
Directions:
Preheat the oven to 350ºF and put the cauliflower florets in a large microwave-safe bowl. Sprinkle with a bit of water, and steam in the microwave for 4 to 5 minutes. Melt the 1/3 cup of butter in a saucepan over

medium heat and sauté the onion for 3 minutes. Add the cauliflower, season with salt and black pepper, and mix in almond milk. Simmer for 3 minutes. Mix the remaining melted butter with almond flour. Stir into the cauliflower as well as half of the cheese. Sprinkle the top with the remaining cheese and bake for 10 minutes until the cheese has melted and golden brown. Plate the bake and serve with salad.

Nutrition facts:
Calories: 349
Fat: 9.4g
Fiber: 12.1g
Carbohydrates:4.1 g
Protein: 10g

›Spinach and Zucchini Lasagna

Preparation Time: 15 minutes
Cooking Time: 30 minutes
Servings: 4
Ingredients:
2 zucchinis, sliced
Salt and black pepper to taste
2 cups ricotta cheese
2 cups shredded mozzarella cheese
3 cups tomato sauce
1 cup baby spinach
Directions:
Let the oven heat to 375 and grease a baking dish with cooking spray. Put the zucchini slices in a colander and sprinkle with salt. Let sit and drain liquid for 5 minutes and pat dry with paper towels. Mix the ricotta, mozzarella cheese, salt, and black pepper to evenly combine and spread 1/4 cup of the mixture in the bottom of the baking dish. Layer 1/3 of the zucchini slices on top, spread 1 cup of tomato sauce over and scatter a 1/3 cup of spinach on top. Repeat process. Grease one end of foil with cooking spray and cover the baking dish with the foil. Let it bake for about 35 minutes. And bake further for 5 to 10 minutes or until the cheese has a nice golden-brown color. Remove the dish, sit for 5 minutes, make slices of the lasagna, and serve warm.

Nutrition facts:
Calories: 376
Fat: 14.1g
Fiber: 11.3g
Carbohydrates:2.1 g
Protein: 9.5g

›Lemon Cauliflower "Couscous" with Halloumi

Preparation Time: 5 minutes
Cooking Time: 5 minutes
Servings: 2
Ingredients:
4 oz halloumi, sliced
1 cauliflower head, cut into small florets
1/4 cup chopped cilantro

1/4 cup chopped parsley
1/4 cup chopped mint
1/2 lemon juiced
Salt and black pepper to taste
Sliced avocado to garnish
Directions:
Heat the pan and add oil
Add the halloumi and fry it on both sides until golden brown, set aside. Turn the heat off. Next, pour the cauliflower florets in a food processor and pulse until it crumbles and resembles couscous. Transfer to a bowl and steam in the microwave for 2 minutes. They should be slightly cooked but crunchy. Stir in the cilantro, parsley, mint, lemon juice, salt, and black pepper. Garnish the couscous with avocado slices and serve with grilled halloumi and vegetable sauce.

Nutrition facts:
Calories: 312
Fat: 9.4g
Fiber: 11.9g
Carbohydrates:1.2 g
Protein: 8.5g

›Spicy Cauliflower Steaks with Steamed Green Beans

Preparation Time: 15 minutes
Cooking Time: 20 minutes
Servings: 4
Ingredients:
2 heads cauliflower, sliced lengthwise into 'steaks.'
1/4 cup olive oil
1/4 cup chili sauce
2 tsp. erythritol
Salt and black pepper to taste
2 shallots, diced
1 bunch green beans, trimmed
2 tbsp. fresh lemon juice
1 cup of water Dried parsley to garnish
Directions:
In a bowl or container, mix the olive oil, chili sauce, and erythritol. Brush the cauliflower with the mixture. Grill for 6 minutes. Flip the cauliflower, cook further for 6 minutes. Let the water boil, place the green beans in a sieve, and set over the steam from the boiling water. Cover with a clean napkin to keep the steam trapped in the sieve. Cook for 6 minutes. After, remove to a bowl and toss with lemon juice. Remove the grilled caulis to a plate, sprinkle with salt, pepper, shallots, and parsley. Serve with the steamed green beans.

Nutrition facts:
Calories: 329
Fat: 10.4g
Fiber: 3.1g
Carbohydrates:4.2 g
Protein: 8.4g

›Cheesy Cauliflower Falafel

Preparation Time: 20 minutes
Cooking Time: 15 minutes
Servings: 4
Ingredients:
1 head cauliflower, cut into florets
1/3 cup silvered ground almonds
2 tbsp. cheddar cheese, shredded
1/2 tsp. mixed spice
Salt and chili pepper to taste
3 tbsp. coconut flour
3 fresh eggs
4 tbsp. ghee
Directions:
Blend the florets in a blender until a grain meal consistency is formed. Pour the rice in a bowl, add the ground almonds, mixed spice, salt, cheddar cheese, chili pepper, coconut flour, and mix until evenly combined. Beat the eggs in a bowl until creamy in color and mix with the cauliflower mixture. Shape 1/4 cup each into patties. Melt ghee and fry the patties for 5 minutes on each side to be firm and browned. Remove onto a wire rack to cool, share into serving plates, and top with tahini sauce.
Nutrition facts:
Calories: 287
Fat: 9.2g
Fiber: 4.1g
Carbohydrates:3.2 g
Protein: 13.2g

>Tofu Sesame Skewers with Warm Kale Salad

Preparation Time: 2 hrs.
Cooking Time: 25 minutes
Servings: 4
Ingredients:
14 oz Firm tofu
4 tsp. sesame oil
1 lemon, juiced
5 tbsp. sugar-free soy sauce
3tsp. garlic powder
4 tbsp. coconut flour
1/2 cup sesame seeds
Warm Kale Salad:
4 cups chopped kale
2 tsp. + 2 tsp. olive oil
1 white onion, thinly sliced
3 cloves garlic, minced
1 cup sliced white mushrooms
1 tsp. chopped rosemary
Salt and black pepper to season
1 tbsp. balsamic vinegar
Directions:
Mix sesame oil, lemon juice, soy sauce, garlic powder, and coconut flour in a bowl. Wrap the tofu in a paper towel, squeeze out as much liquid from it, and cut it into strips. Stick on the skewers, height-wise. Place onto a plate, pour the soy sauce mixture over, and turn in the sauce to be adequately coated. Heat the griddle pan over high heat. Pour the sesame seeds into a plate and roll the tofu skewers in the seeds for a generous coat. Grill the tofu in the griddle pan to be golden brown on both sides, about 12 minutes.
Heat 2 tbsps. of olive oil in a skillet over low/medium heat and sauté onion to begin browning for 10 minutes with continuous stirring.
Add the remaining olive oil and mushrooms. Continue cooking for 10 minutes. Add garlic, rosemary, salt, pepper, and balsamic vinegar. Cook for 1 minute. Put the kale in a salad bowl; when the onion mixture is ready, pour it on the kale and toss well. Serve the tofu skewers with the warm kale salad and a peanut butter dipping sauce.
Nutrition facts:
Calories: 276
Fat: 11.9g
Fiber: 9.4g
Carbohydrates:21 g
Protein: 10.3g

>Eggplant Pizza with Tofu

Preparation Time: 15 minutes
Cooking Time: 45 minutes
Servings: 2
Ingredients:
2 eggplants, sliced
1/3 cup butter, melted
2 garlic cloves, minced
1 red onion
12 oz tofu, chopped
7 oz tomato sauce
Salt and black pepper to taste
1/2 tsp. cinnamon powder
1 cup Parmesan cheese, shredded
1/4 cup dried oregano
Directions:
Let the oven heat to 400F. Arrange the eggplant slices on a baking sheet and brush with some butter. Bake in the oven until lightly browned, about 20 minutes. Heat the remaining butter in a skillet; sauté garlic and onion until fragrant and soft, about 3 minutes. Stir in the tofu and cook for 3-4 minutes. Add the tomato sauce, salt and black pepper. Simmer for 10 minutes. Sprinkle with Parmesan cheese and oregano. Bake for 10 minutes.
Nutrition facts:
Calories: 321
Fat: 11.3g
Fiber: 8.4g
Carbohydrates:4.3 g
Protein: 10.1g

>Brussel Sprouts with Spiced Halloumi

Preparation Time: 20 minutes
Cooking Time: 30 minutes
Servings: 2
Ingredients:
10 oz halloumi cheese, sliced

1 tbsp. coconut oil
1/2 cup unsweetened coconut, shredded
1 tsp. chili powder
1/2 tsp. onion powder
1/2 pound Brussels sprouts, shredded
4 oz butter
Salt and black pepper to taste
Lemon wedges for serving

Directions:
Mix the shredded coconut, chili powder, salt, coconut oil, and onion powder in a bowl. Then, toss the halloumi slices in the spice mixture. The grill pan must be heated, then cook the coated halloumi cheese for 2-3 minutes. Transfer to a plate to keep warm.
The half butter must be melted in a pan, add, and sauté the Brussels sprouts until slightly caramelized. Then, season with salt and black pepper. Dish the Brussels sprouts into serving plates with the halloumi cheese and lemon wedges. Melt left butter and drizzle over the Brussels sprouts and halloumi cheese. Serve.

Nutrition facts:
Calories: 276
Fat: 9.5g
Fiber: 9.1g
Carbohydrates:4.1 g
Protein: 5.4g

›Cauliflower Rice-Stuffed Bell Peppers

Preparation time: 15 minutes
Cooking time: 45 minutes | **Servings:** 6
2 tablespoons vegetable oil
2 tablespoons yellow onion, chopped
1 teaspoon fresh garlic, crushed
½ pound (227 g) ground pork
½ pound (227 g) ground turkey
1 cup cauliflower rice
½ teaspoon sea salt
¼ teaspoon red pepper flakes, crushed
½ teaspoon ground black pepper
1 teaspoon dried parsley flakes
6 medium-sized bell peppers, deveined and cleaned
½ cup tomato sauce
½ cup Cheddar cheese, shredded

Directions
Preheat the oil in a pan over medium flame. When it becomes hot, sauté the onion and garlic for 2 to 3 minutes. Add the ground meat and cook for 5-6 minutes longer or until it is nicely browned. Add cauliflower rice and seasoning. Continue to cook for 3-4 minutes. Divide the filling among the prepared bell peppers. Cover with foil. Place the peppers in a baking pan; Then add tomato sauce. Bake in the preheated oven at 380ºF (193ºC) for 20 minutes. Uncover, then top with cheese, and bake for 10 minutes more. Enjoy!

Nutrition facts (per serving)
calories: 245 | fat: 12.8g | protein: 16.6g | carbs: 3.3g | net carbs: 2.3g | fiber: 1.0g

›Vegetable Patties

Preparation Time: 15 minutes
Cooking Time: 20 minutes
Servings: 4
Ingredients:
1 tbsp. olive oil
1 onion, chopped
1 garlic clove, minced
1/2 head cauliflower, grated
1 carrot, shredded
3 tbsp. coconut flour
1/2 cup Gruyere cheese, shredded
1/2 cup Parmesan cheese, grated
2 eggs, beaten
1/2 tsp. dried rosemary
Salt and black pepper, to taste

Directions:
Cook onion and garlic in warm olive oil over medium heat, until soft, for about 3 minutes. Stir in grated cauliflower and carrot and cook for a minute; allow cooling and set aside. Add the other ingredients to the cooled vegetables, form balls from the mixture, and then press each ball to form a burger patty.
Set oven to 400 F and bake the burgers for 20 minutes. Flip and bake for another 10 minutes or until the top becomes golden brown.

Nutrition facts:
Calories: 315
Fat: 12.1g
Fiber: 8.6g
Carbohydrates:3.3 g
Protein: 5.8g

›Vegan Sandwich with Tofu & Lettuce Slaw

Preparation Time: 15 minutes
Cooking Time: 15minutes
Servings: 2
Ingredients:
1/4 pound firm tofu, sliced
2 low carb buns
1 tbsp. olive oil
Marinade
2 tbsp. olive oil
Salt and black pepper to taste
1 tsp. allspice
1/2 tbsp. xylitol
1 tsp. thyme, chopped
1 habanero pepper, seeded and minced
2 green onions, thinly sliced
1 garlic clove
Lettuce slaw
1/2 small iceberg lettuce, shredded
1/2 carrot, grated
1/2 red onion, grated
2 tsp. liquid stevia
1 tbsp. lemon juice

85

2 tbsp. olive oil
1/2 tsp. Dijon mustard
Salt and black pepper to taste
Directions:
Put the tofu slices in a bowl. Blend the marinade ingredients for a minute. Cover the tofu with this mixture and place it in the fridge to marinate for 1 hour. Combine the lemon juice, stevia, olive oil, Dijon mustard, salt, and pepper in a container. Stir in the lettuce, carrot, and onion; set aside. Heat oil, cook the tofu on both sides for 6 minutes in total. Remove to a plate. In the buns, add the tofu and top with the slaw. Close the buns and serve.
Nutrition facts:
Calories: 315
Fat: 10.4g
Fiber: 15.1g
Carbohydrates:9.4 g
Protein: 8.4g

➤Herbed Eggplant

Preparation time: 15 minutes
Cooking time: 20 minutes | **Servings:** 2
1 teaspoon basil
½ teaspoon oregano
½ teaspoon rosemary
½ teaspoon coarse sea salt
1 large-sized eggplant, cut into slices lengthwise
2 tablespoons coconut aminos
1 teaspoon balsamic vinegar
1 tablespoon olive oil
½ teaspoon Sriracha sauce
¼ cup fresh chives, chopped
Directions:
Toss your eggplant with basil, oregano, rosemary, and salt. Place the eggplant on a parchment-lined roasting pan. Roast in the preheated oven at 420°F (216°C) for approximately 15 minutes. Meanwhile, mix the coconut aminos, vinegar, oil, and Sriracha sauce. Drizzle the Sriracha mixture over the eggplant slices. Place under the preheated broil for 3 to 5 minutes. Garnish with fresh chives and serve warm.
Nutrition facts (per serving)
calories: 102 | fat: 7.0g | protein: 1.6g | carbs: 8.0g | net carbs: 3.3g | fiber: 4.7g

➤Pizza Bianca

Preparation Time: 10 minutes
Cooking Time: 10 minutes
Servings: 2
Ingredients:
2 tbsp. olive oil
4 eggs
2 tbsp. water
1 jalapeño pepper, diced
1/4 cup mozzarella cheese, shredded
2 chives, chopped
2 cups egg Alfredo sauce
1/2 tsp. oregano

1/2 cup mushrooms, sliced
Directions:
Preheat oven to 360 F. In a bowl, whisk eggs, water, and oregano. Heat the olive oil in a medium/large skillet. The egg mixture must be poured in, then let it cook until set, flipping once. Remove and spread the alfredo sauce and jalapeño pepper all over. Top with mozzarella cheese, mushrooms and chives. Let it bake for 10 minutes
Nutrition facts:
Calories: 314
Fat: 15.6g
Fiber: 10.3g
Carbohydrates:5.9 g
Protein: 10.4g

➤Romano Zucchini Cups

Preparation time: 10 minutes
Cooking time: 15 minutes | **Servings:** 4
1 teaspoon sea salt
1 (½-pound / 227-g) zucchini, grated
½ cup almond flour
2 eggs, beaten
1 cup Romano cheese, grated
Directions:
Place the salt and grated zucchini in a bowl; let it sit for 15 minutes, squeeze using a cheesecloth and discard the liquid. Now, stir in the almond flour, eggs, and Romano cheese. Spritz a 12cup mini-muffin pan with cooking spray. Bake in the preheated oven until the surface is no longer wet to the touch, or for 15 minutes. Let them cool for 5 minutes to set up.
Bon appétit!
Nutrition facts (per serving)
calories: 225 | fat: 18.0g | protein: 13.4g | carbs: 3.0g | net carbs: 1.5g | fiber: 1.5g

➤Pumpkin and Cauliflower Curry

Preparation time: 15 minutes
Cooking time: 7 to 8 hours
Servings: 6
1 tablespoon extra-virgin olive oil
4 cups coconut milk
1 cup diced pumpkin
1 cup cauliflower florets
1 red bell pepper, diced
1 zucchini, diced
1 sweet onion, chopped
2 teaspoons grated fresh ginger
2 teaspoons minced garlic
1 tablespoon curry powder
2 cups shredded spinach
1 avocado, diced, for garnish
Directions:
Lightly grease the insert of the slow cooker with olive oil. Add the coconut milk, pumpkin, cauliflower, bell pepper, zucchini, onion, ginger, garlic, and curry powder. Cover and cook on low for 6 and a half to 7 hours. Stir in the spinach. Garnish each bowl with a

spoonful of avocado and serve.

Nutrition facts (per serving)
calories: 501 | fat: 44.0g | protein: 7.0g | carbs: 19.0g | net carbs: 9.0g | fiber: 10.0g

›Popcorn Mushrooms

Preparation time: 10 minutes
Cooking time: 10 minutes
Servings: 4
Ingredients
16 oz mushrooms
2 tablespoons almond flour
2 tablespoons water
½ teaspoon minced garlic
1 tablespoon olive oil
¼ teaspoon chili flakes
Directions
Mix up together the almond flour, water, minced garlic, and chili flakes in the bowl. Stir the mixture. Coat the mushrooms with the almond flour mixture. Spray the olive oil inside the air fryer basket. Put the mushrooms and cook them for 10 minutes at 365 F. Stir the mushrooms every 2 minutes. Serve the cooked popcorn mushrooms only hot!
Nutrition facts: Calories 135, Fat 10.8, Fiber 2.6, Carbs 6.9, Protein 6.6

›Leek Sauté

Preparation time: 10 minutes
Cooking time: 15 minutes
Servings: 2
Ingredients
10 oz leek, chopped
8 oz mushrooms, chopped
1 shallot, chopped
2 teaspoons olive oil
¼ teaspoon salt
½ teaspoon chili flakes
Directions
Put the chopped mushrooms in the air fryer basket. Add olive oil and salt. Then sprinkle the mushrooms with the chili flakes and stir well. Cook the mushrooms for 5 minutes at 365 F. Stir the mushrooms and add chopped shallot and leek. Stir the vegetables. Continue to cook the vegetables for 10 minutes more at 360 F. Stir the vegetable from time to time. When all the ingredients are soft – the meal is cooked.
Nutrition facts: Calories 151, Fat 5.4, Fiber 3.7, Carbs 23.9, Protein 5.7

›Sweet Potato Hasselback

Preparation time: 15 minutes
Cooking time: 35 minutes
Servings: 4
Ingredients
4 sweet potatoes
4 garlic cloves, peeled

½ teaspoon thyme
1 tablespoon olive oil
1 teaspoon dried basil
½ teaspoon dried oregano
1 teaspoon chili flakes
3 tablespoons water
Directions
Peel the potatoes and cut them into the shape of the Hasselback. Put the sweet potatoes in the air fryer basket and cook them at 360 F for 20 minutes. Meanwhile, mix the thyme, olive oil, dried basil, dried oregano, chili flakes, and water. Chop the garlic and add it to the mixture too. Stir the spices. Brush the Hasselback sweet potatoes with the spice mixture generously. Cook the meal for 15 minutes more. When the meal is cooked, let it chill a little. Enjoy!
Nutrition facts: Calories 36, Fat 3.6, Fiber 0.2, Carbs 1.3, Protein 0.2

›Stuffed Tomatoes

Preparation time: 20 minutes
Cooking time: 15 minutes
Servings: 2
Ingredients
7 oz mushrooms, chopped
1 teaspoon minced garlic
1 tablespoon fresh dill, chopped
1 onion diced
2 tomatoes
1 tablespoon olive oil
½ teaspoon chili flakes
Directions
Remove the meat from the tomatoes to make the tomato cups. Combine the chopped mushrooms, minced garlic, fresh dill, diced onion, olive oil, and chili flakes. Stir the mixture well. Fill the tomato cups with the mushroom mixture and put them in the air fryer. Cook the side dish for 15 minutes at 360 F. When the tomatoes are cooked – let them rest for 5 minutes and serve!
Nutrition facts: Calories 132, Fat 7.7, Fiber 3.9, Carbs 14.5, Protein 5.2

›Ratatouille Kebabs

Preparation time: 10 minutes
Cooking time: 20 minutes
Servings: 4
Ingredients
1 eggplant
1 sweet pepper
1 zucchini
1 onion, peeled
1 tomato
1 tablespoon olive oil
½ teaspoon chili flakes
½ teaspoon ground coriander
½ teaspoon salt
Directions

Slice the eggplant, zucchini, and onion. Cut the sweet pepper and tomato into the squares. Skew the vegetables on the skewers. Then sprinkle the vegetables with olive oil, chili flakes, ground coriander, and salt. Put the kebabs in the air fryer basket and cook for 20 minutes at 360 F. Then transfer the cooked kebabs to the serving plate gently. Enjoy!
Nutrition facts: Calories 90, Fat 3.9, Fiber 5.8, Carbs 13.8, Protein 2.5

➤Parmesan Sweet Potato Casserole

Preparation Time: 15 minutes
Cooking Time: 35 minutes
Servings: 2
Ingredients:
2 sweet potatoes, peeled
½ yellow onion, sliced
½ cup cream
¼ cup spinach
2 oz. Parmesan cheese, shredded
½ teaspoon salt
1 tomato
1 teaspoon olive oil
Directions:
Chop the sweet potatoes. Chop the tomato. Chop the spinach. Spray the air fryer tray with olive oil, then place on the layer of the chopped sweet potato. Add the layer of the sliced onion. Afterwards, sprinkle the sliced onion with the chopped spinach and tomatoes. Sprinkle the casserole with salt and shredded cheese. Pour cream. Preheat the air fryer to 390 F. Cover the air fryer tray with foil. Cook the casserole for 35 minutes. When the casserole is cooked, you can serve it. Enjoy!
Nutrition facts: Calories: 93Fat: 1.8g Fiber: 3.4gCarbs: 20.3gProtein: 1.8g

➤Spicy Zucchini Slices

Preparation Time: 10 minutes
Cooking Time: 6 minutes
Servings: 2
Ingredients:
1 teaspoon cornstarch
1 zucchini
½ teaspoon chili flakes
1 tablespoon flour
1 egg
¼ teaspoon salt
Directions:
Slice the zucchini and sprinkle with chili flakes and salt. Crack the egg and whisk it. Dip the zucchini slices in the whisked egg. Combine cornstarch with flour. Stir it. Coat the zucchini slices with the cornstarch mixture. Preheat the air fryer to 400 F. Place the zucchini slices in the air fryer tray. Cook the zucchini slices for 4 minutes. Afterwards, flip the slices to another side and cook for 2 minutes more. Serve the zucchini slices hot. Enjoy!

Nutrition facts: Calories: 67Fat: 2.4gFiber: 1.2gCarbs: 7.7gProtein: 4.4g

➤Cheddar Potato Gratin

Preparation Time: 15 minutes
Cooking Time: 20 minutes
Servings: 2
Ingredients:
2 potatoes
1/3 cup half and half
1 tablespoon oatmeal flour
¼ teaspoon ground black pepper
1 egg
2 oz. Cheddar cheese
Directions:
Clean the potatoes and slice them into thin pieces. Preheat the air fryer to 365 F. Put the potato slices in the air fryer and cook them for 10 minutes. Meanwhile, combine the half and half, oatmeal flour and ground black pepper. Crack the egg into the liquid and whisk it carefully. Shred Cheddar cheese. When the potato is cooked – take 2 ramekins and place the potatoes on them. Pour the half and half mixture. Sprinkle the gratin with shredded Cheddar cheese. Cook the gratin for 10 minutes at 360 F. Serve the meal immediately. Enjoy!
Nutrition facts: Calories: 353Fat: 16.6gFiber: 5.4gCarbs: 37.2g Protein: 15g

➤Salty Lemon Artichokes

Preparation Time: 15 minutes
Cooking Time: 45 minutes
Servings: 2
Ingredients:
1 lemon
2 artichokes
1 teaspoon kosher salt
1 garlic head
2 teaspoons olive oil
Directions:
Cut off the edges of the artichokes. Cut the lemon into the halves. Peel the garlic head and chop the garlic cloves roughly. Then place the chopped garlic in the artichokes. Sprinkle the artichokes with olive oil and kosher salt. Then squeeze the lemon juice into the artichokes. Wrap the artichokes in the foil. Preheat the air fryer to 330 F. Place the wrapped artichokes in the air fryer and cook for 45 minutes. When the artichokes are cooked – discard the foil and serve. Enjoy!
Nutrition facts: Calories: 133Fat: 5gFiber: 9.7gCarbs: 21.7gProtein: 6g

➤Asparagus & Parmesan

Preparation Time: 10 minutes
Cooking Time: 6 minutes
Servings: 2
Ingredients:

1 teaspoon sesame oil
11 oz. asparagus
1 teaspoon chicken stock
½ teaspoon ground white pepper
3 oz. Parmesan

Directions:
Wash the asparagus and chop it roughly. Sprinkle the chopped asparagus with the chicken stock and ground white pepper. Then sprinkle the vegetables with the sesame oil and shake them. Place the asparagus in the air fryer basket. Cook the vegetables for 4 minutes at 400 F. Meanwhile, shred Parmesan cheese. When the time is over – shake the asparagus gently and sprinkle with the shredded cheese. Cook the asparagus for 2 minutes more at 400 F. After this, transfer the cooked asparagus to the serving plates. Serve and taste it!

Nutrition facts: Calories: 189Fat: 11.6gFiber: 3.4gCarbs: 7.9gProtein: 17.2g

➤Carrot Lentil Burgers

Preparation Time: 10 minutes
Cooking Time: 12 minutes
Servings: 2
Ingredients:
6 oz. lentils, cooked
1 egg
2 oz. carrot, grated
1 teaspoon semolina
½ teaspoon salt
1 teaspoon turmeric
1 tablespoon butter

Directions:
Crack the egg and whisk it. Add the cooked lentils and mash the mixture using a fork. Then sprinkle the mixture with the grated carrot, semolina, salt, and turmeric. Mix it up and make the medium burgers. Put the butter into the lentil burgers. It will make them juicy. Preheat the air fryer to 360 F. Put the lentil burgers in the air fryer and cook for 12 minutes. Flip the burgers to the other side after 6 minutes of cooking. Chill the cooked lentil burgers and serve them. Enjoy!

Nutrition facts: Calories: 404Fat: 9gFiber: 26.9gCarbs: 56gProtein: 25.3g

➤Corn on Cobs

Preparation Time: 10 minutes
Cooking Time: 10 minutes
Servings: 2
Ingredients:
2 fresh corns on cobs
2 teaspoons butter
1 teaspoon salt
1 teaspoon paprika
¼ teaspoon olive oil

Directions:
Preheat the air fryer to 400 F. Rub the corn on cobs with salt and paprika. Then sprinkle the corn on cobs with olive oil. Place the corn on cobs in the air fryer basket. Cook the corn on cobs for 10 minutes. When the time is over, transfer the corn on cobs in the serving plates and gently rub the butter. Serve the meal immediately. Enjoy!

Nutrition facts: Calories: 122Fat: 5.5gFiber: 2.4gCarbs: 17.6gProtein: 3.2g

➤Sugary Carrot Strips

Preparation Time: 10 minutes
Cooking Time: 10 minutes
Servings: 2
Ingredients:
2 carrots
1 teaspoon brown sugar
1 teaspoon olive oil
1 tablespoon soy sauce
1 teaspoon honey
½ teaspoon ground black pepper

Directions:
Peel the carrot and cut it into strips. Then put the carrot strips in the bowl. Sprinkle the carrot strips with olive oil, soy sauce, honey, and ground black pepper. Shake the mixture gently. Preheat the air fryer to 360 F. Cook the carrot for 10 minutes. After this, shake the carrot strips well. Enjoy!

Nutrition facts: Calories: 67Fat: 2.4gFiber: 1.7gCarbs: 11.3gProtein: 1.1g

➤Onion Green Beans

Preparation Time: 10 minutes
Cooking Time: 12 minutes
Servings: 2
Ingredients:
11 oz. green beans
1 tablespoon onion powder
1 tablespoon olive oil
½ teaspoon salt
¼ teaspoon chili flakes

Directions:
Wash the green beans carefully and place them in the bowl. Sprinkle the green beans with onion powder, salt, chili flakes, and olive oil. Shake the green beans carefully. Preheat the air fryer to 400 F. Put the green beans in the air fryer and cook for 8 minutes. After this, shake the green beans and cook them for 4 minutes more at 400 F. When the time is over – shake the green beans. Serve the side dish and enjoy!

Nutrition facts: Calories: 1205Fat: 7.2gFiber: 5.5gCarbs: 13.9gProtein: 3.2g

➤Mozzarella Radish Salad

Preparation Time: 10 minutes
Cooking Time: 20 minutes
Servings: 2
Ingredients:
8 oz. radish

4 oz. Mozzarella
1 teaspoon balsamic vinegar
½ teaspoon salt
1 tablespoon olive oil
1 teaspoon dried oregano
Directions:
Wash the radish carefully and cut it into halves. Preheat the air fryer to 360 F. Put the radish halves in the air fryer basket. Sprinkle the radish with salt and olive oil. Cook the radish for 20 minutes. Shake the radish after 10 minutes of cooking. When the time is over – transfer the radish to the serving plate. Chop Mozzarella roughly. Sprinkle the radish with Mozzarella, balsamic vinegar, and dried oregano. Stir it gently with the help of 2 forks. Serve it immediately.
Nutrition facts: Calories: 241Fat: 17.2gFiber: 2.1gCarbs: 6.4gProtein: 16.9g

›Cremini Mushroom Satay

Preparation Time: 10 minutes
Cooking Time: 6 minutes
Servings: 2
Ingredients:
7 oz. cremini mushrooms
2 tablespoon coconut milk
1 tablespoon butter
1 teaspoon chili flakes
½ teaspoon balsamic vinegar
½ teaspoon curry powder
½ teaspoon white pepper
Directions:
Wash the mushrooms carefully. Then sprinkle the mushrooms with the chili flakes, curry powder, and white pepper. Preheat the air fryer to 400 F. Add the butter in the air fryer basket and melt it. Place the mushrooms in the air fryer and cook for 2 minutes. Shake the mushrooms well and sprinkle with coconut milk and balsamic vinegar. Cook the mushrooms for 4 minutes more at 400°F. Skewer the mushrooms on the wooden sticks and serve. Enjoy!
Nutrition facts: Calories 116Fat: 9.5gFiber: 1.3gCarbs: 5.6gProtein: 3g

›Eggplant Ratatouille

Preparation Time: 15 minutes
Cooking Time: 15 minutes
Servings: 2
Ingredients:
1 eggplant
1 sweet yellow pepper
3 cherry tomatoes
1/3 white onion, chopped
½ teaspoon garlic clove, sliced
1 teaspoon olive oil
½ teaspoon ground black pepper
½ teaspoon Italian seasoning
Directions:
Preheat the air fryer to 360 F. Peel the eggplants and chop them. Put the chopped eggplants in the air fryer basket. Chop the tomatoes and add them to the air fryer basket.
Then add chopped onion, sliced garlic clove, olive oil, ground black pepper, and Italian seasoning. Chop the sweet yellow pepper roughly and add it to the air fryer basket. Shake the vegetables gently and cook for 15 minutes. Stir the meal after 8 minutes of cooking. Transfer the cooked ratatouille in the serving plates. Enjoy!
Nutrition facts: Calories: 149Fat: 3.7gFiber: 11.7gCarbs: 28.9gProtein: 5.1g

›Cheddar Portobello Mushrooms

Preparation Time: 15 minutes
Cooking Time: 6 minutes
Servings: 2
Ingredients:
2 Portobello mushroom hats
2 slices Cheddar cheese
¼ cup panko breadcrumbs
½ teaspoon salt
½ teaspoon ground black pepper
1 egg
1 teaspoon oatmeal
2 oz. bacon, chopped cooked
Directions:
Crack the egg and whisk it. Mix the oatmeal, breadcrumbs, pepper and salt in a bowl. Dip the mushroom hats in the beaten egg. Then you need to bread the mushroom hats with breadcrumbs. Bring the air fryer to 400 F (220 D.) Cook the mushrooms for 3 minutes. Then, place the cheese and the chopped bacon on the mushroom hats and cook for 4 minutes. When the meal is ready, let it cool. Enjoy!
Nutrition facts: Calories: 376Fat: 24.1gFiber: 1.8gCarbs: 14.6gProtein: 25.2g

›Salty Fagiolini

Preparation Time: 15 minutes
Cooking Time: 6 minutes
Servings: 2
Ingredients:
1 cup of fagiolini, inside a shell
The salt, for taste
Directions:
Over a medium-low heat, place a large saucepan. Add 2 quarts of fagiolini and water. Cover and simmer for about 5-8 minutes, until tender. Drain and add salt to sprinkle.
Nutrition facts: Calories: 376Fat: 24.1gFiber: 1.8gCarbs: 14.6gProtein: 25.2g

›Brussels Sprouts and Rhubarb Mix

Preparation time: 5 minutes
Cooking time: 20 minutes
Servings: 4

Ingredients
1 pound Brussels sprouts, trimmed and halved
½ pound rhubarb, sliced
2 tablespoons avocado oil
Juice of 1 lemon
A pinch of salt and black pepper
1 tablespoon chives, chopped
1 teaspoon chili paste
Directions
In a pan, mix the sprouts with the rhubarb and the other ingredients, toss, put the pan in the fryer and cook at 390 degrees F for 20 minutes. Divide between plates and serve.
Nutrition facts: Cal: 200, Fat 9, Fiber 2, Carbs 6, Protein 9

›Creamy Cauliflower

Preparation time: 5 minutes
Cooking time: 20 minutes
Servings: 4
Ingredients
1 pound cauliflower florets
1 cup cream cheese, soft
½ cup mozzarella, shredded
½ cup coconut cream
4 bacon strips, cooked and chopped
Salt and black pepper to taste
Directions
In the air fryer's pan, mix the cauliflower with the cream cheese and the other ingredients, toss, introduce the pan in the machine and cook at 400 degrees F for 20 minutes. Divide between plates and serve.
Nutrition facts: Cal: 203, Fat 13, Fiber 2, Carbs 5, Protein 9

›Cumin Cauliflower

Preparation time: 5 minutes
Cooking time: 20 minutes
Servings: 4
Ingredients
1 pound cauliflower florets
1 teaspoon cumin, ground
Juice of 1 lime
1 tablespoon butter, melted
A pinch of salt and black pepper
1 tablespoon chives, chopped
¼ teaspoon cloves, ground
Directions
In the air fryer, mix the cauliflower with the cumin, lime juice and the other ingredients, toss and cook at 390 degrees F for 20 minutes. Divide between plates and serve.
Nutrition facts: Cal: 182, Fat 8, Fiber 2, Carbs 4, Protein 8

›Kale Mash

Preparation time: 5 minutes
Cooking time: 20 minutes
Servings: 4
Ingredients
2 tablespoons butter, melted
1 pound kale, torn
1 cup heavy cream
4 garlic cloves, minced
2 spring onions, chopped
A pinch of salt and black pepper
1 tablespoon chives, chopped
Directions
In a pan, mix the kale with the butter, cream and the other ingredients, stir, put the pan in the machine and cook at 380F for 22 minutes. Blend the mix using an immersion blender, divide between plates and serve.
Nutrition facts: Calories 198, Fat 9, Fiber 2, Carbs 6, Protein 8

— CHAPTER 4 —

POULTRY AND MEATS

ALICIA TRAVIS

›Beef, Tomato, and Lentils Stew

Preparation time: 10 minutes
Cooking time: 10 minutes | **Servings:** 4
1 tablespoon extra-virgin olive oil
1 pound (454 g) extra-lean ground beef
1 onion, chopped
1 (14-ounce / 397-g) can chopped tomatoes with garlic and basil, drained
1 (14-ounce / 397-g) can lentils, drained
½ teaspoon sea salt
⅛ teaspoon freshly ground black pepper

Heat the olive oil until shimmering. Add the beef and onion to the pot and sauté for 5 minutes or until the beef is lightly browned. Add the remaining ingredients. Bring to a boil. Low the heat and cook for 4 more minutes or until the lentils are tender. Keep stirring during the cooking. Pour them in a large serving bowl and serve immediately.

Nutrition facts (per serving)
calories: 460 | fat: 14.8g | protein: 44.2g | carbs: 36.9g | fiber: 17.0g | sodium: 320mg

›Ground Beef, Tomato, and Kidney Bean Chili

Preparation time: 10 minutes
Cooking time: 15 minutes | **Servings:** 4
1 tablespoon extra-virgin olive oil
1 pound (454 g) extra-lean ground beef
1 onion, chopped
2 (14-ounce / 397-g) cans kidney beans
2 (28-ounce / 794-g) cans chopped tomatoes, juice reserved
Chili Spice:
1 teaspoon garlic powder
1 tablespoon chili powder
½ teaspoon sea salt

Heat oil in until shimmering. Add the beef and onion to the pot and sauté for 5 minutes or until the onion is translucent and the beef is lightly browned. Add the remaining ingredients. Bring to a boil. Low the heat and cook for 10 more minutes. Keep stirring during the cooking. Pour them in a large serving bowl and serve immediately.

Nutrition facts (per serving)
calories: 891 | fat: 20.1g | protein: 116.3g | carbs: 62.9g | fiber: 17.0g | sodium: 561mg

›Lamb Tagine with Couscous and Almonds

Preparation time: 15 minutes
Cooking time: 7 hours 7 minutes | **Servings:** 6
2 tablespoons almond flour
Juice and zest of 1 navel orange
2 tablespoons extra-virgin olive oil
2 pounds (907 g) boneless lamb leg, fat trimmed and cut into 1½-inch cubes

½ cup low-sodium chicken stock
2 large white onions, chopped
1 teaspoon pumpkin pie spice
¼ teaspoon crushed saffron threads
1 teaspoon ground cumin
¼ teaspoon ground red pepper flakes
½ teaspoon sea salt
2 tablespoons raw honey
1 cup pitted dates
3 cups cooked couscous, for serving
2 tablespoons toasted slivered almonds, for serving

Combine the almond flour with orange juice in a large bowl. Stir until smooth, then mix in the orange zest. Heat the olive oil medium-high heat until shimmering. Add the lamb cubes and sauté for 7 minutes or until lightly browned. Pour in the flour mixture and chicken stock, then add the onions, pumpkin pie spice, saffron, cumin, ground red pepper flakes, and salt. Stir to mix well. Pour them in the slow cooker. Cover and cook on low for 6 and a half hours or until the internal temperature of the lamb reaches at least 145°F (63°C). When the cooking is complete, mix in the honey and dates, then cook for another an hour.
Put the couscous in a tagine bowl or a large bowl, then top with lamb mixture. Scatter with slivered almonds and serve immediately.

Nutrition facts (per serving)
calories: 447 | fat: 10.2g | protein: 36.3g | carbs: 53.5g | fiber: 4.9g | sodium: 329mg

›Potato Lamb and Olive Stew

Preparation time: 20 minutes
Cooking time: 3 hours 42 minutes | **Servings:** 10
4 tablespoons almond flour
¾ cup low-sodium chicken stock
1¼ pounds (567 g) small potatoes, halved
3 cloves garlic, minced
4 large shallots, cut into ½-inch wedges
3 sprigs fresh rosemary
1 tablespoon lemon zest
Coarse sea salt and black pepper
3½ pounds (1.6 kg) lamb shanks, fat trimmed and cut crosswise into 1½-inch pieces
2 tablespoons extra-virgin olive oil
½ cup dry white wine
1 cup pitted green olives, halved
2 tablespoons lemon juice

Combine 1 tablespoon of almond flour with chicken stock in a bowl. Stir to mix well. Put the flour mixture, potatoes, garlic, shallots, rosemary, and lemon zest in the slow cooker. Sprinkle with salt and black pepper. Stir to mix well. Set aside. Combine the remaining almond flour with salt and black pepper in a large bowl, then dunk the lamb shanks in the flour and toss to coat. Heat the olive oil medium-high heat until shimmering. Add the well-coated lamb and cook for 10 minutes or until golden brown. Flip the lamb pieces halfway through the cooking time. Transfer the cooked lamb to the slow cooker. Pour the wine in the same skillet, then cook for 2 minutes or until it reduces in half. Pour the wine in the slow cooker. Cook on high for 3 hrs and 25 mins slow cooker or until the lamb is very tender. In the last 18-20 minutes of the cooking, open the lid and fold in the olive halves to cook. Pour the stew on a large plate, let them sit for 5 minutes, then skim any fat remains over the face of the liquid. Drizzle with lemon juice and sprinkle with salt and pepper. Serve warm.

Nutrition facts (per serving)
calories: 309 | fat: 10.3g | protein: 36.9g | carbs: 16.1g | fiber: 2.2g | sodium: 239mg

➤Slow Cook Lamb Shanks with Cannellini Beans Stew

Preparation time: 20 minutes
Cooking time: 10 hours 15 minutes | **Servings:** 12
1 (19-ounce / 539-g) can cannellini beans, rinsed and drained
1 large yellow onion, chopped
2 medium-sized carrots, diced
1 large stalk celery, chopped
2 cloves garlic, thinly sliced
4 (1½-pound / 680-g) lamb shanks, fat trimmed
2 teaspoons tarragon
½ teaspoon sea salt
¼ teaspoon ground black pepper
1 (28-ounce / 794-g) can diced tomatoes, with the juice

Combine the beans, onion, carrots, celery, and garlic in the slow cooker. Stir to mix well. Add the lamb shanks and sprinkle with tarragon, salt, and ground black pepper. Pour in the tomatoes with juice, then cover the lid and cook on high for an hour.
Low the heat and cook for 9 hours or until the lamb is super tender. Transfer the lamb on a plate, then pour the bean mixture in a colander over a separate bowl to reserve the liquid. Let the liquid sit for 5 minutes until set, then skim the fat from the surface of the liquid. Pour the bean mixture back to the liquid. Remove the bones from the lamb heat and discard the bones. Put the lamb meat and bean mixture back to the slow cooker. Cover and cook to reheat for 15 minutes or until heated through. Pour them on a large serving plate and serve immediately.

Nutrition facts (per serving)
calories: 317 | fat: 9.7g | protein: 52.1g | carbs: 7.0g | fiber: 2.1g | sodium: 375mg

➤Herbed-Mustard-Coated Pork Tenderloin

Preparation time: 10 minutes
Cooking time: 15 minutes | **Servings:** 4
3 tablespoons fresh rosemary leaves
¼ cup Dijon mustard
½ cup fresh parsley leaves
6 garlic cloves
½ teaspoon sea salt
¼ teaspoon freshly ground black pepper
1 tablespoon extra-virgin olive oil
1 (1½-pound / 680-g) pork tenderloin

Preheat oven to 410°F (210°C). Mix all in a food processor, except for the pork tenderloin. Pulse until it has a thick consistency. Put the pork on a baking sheet, then rub with the mixture to coat well. Bake the sheet for 15 minutes or until the internal temperature of the pork reaches at least 165°F (74°C). Flip the tenderloin halfway through the cooking time. Transfer the cooked pork tenderloin to a large plate and allow to cool for 5 minutes before serving.

Nutrition facts (per serving)
calories: 363 | fat: 18.1g | protein: 2.2g | carbs: 4.9g | fiber: 2.0g | sodium: 514mg

➤Macadamia Pork

Preparation time: 10 minutes
Cooking time: 10 minutes | **Servings:** 4
1 (1-pound / 454-g) pork tenderloin, cut into ½-inch slices and pounded thin
1 teaspoon sea salt, divided
¼ teaspoon freshly ground black pepper, divided
½ cup macadamia nuts
1 cup unsweetened coconut milk
1 tablespoon extra-virgin olive oil
Preheat the oven to 390/400°F (205°C).

On a surface, rub the pork with ½ teaspoon of the salt and ⅛ teaspoon of the ground black pepper. Set aside. Take the macadamia nuts in a food processor, then combine with remaining salt and black pepper in a bowl. Stir to mix well and set aside. Combine the coconut milk and olive oil in a separate bowl. Stir to mix well. Dredge the pork chops into the bowl of coconut milk mixture, then dunk into the bowl of macadamia nut mixture to coat well. Shake the excess off.
Put the well-coated pork chops on a baking sheet, then bake for 10 minutes or until the internal temperature of the pork reaches 168/170°F (74°C). Transfer the pork chops to a serving plate and serve immediately.

Nutrition facts (per serving)
calories: 436 | fat: 32.8g | protein: 33.1g | carbs: 5.9g | fiber: 3.0g | sodium: 310mg

➤Grilled Chicken and Zucchini Kebabs

Preparation time: 10 minutes
Cooking time: 20 minutes | **Servings:** 4
¼ cup extra-virgin olive oil
2 tablespoons balsamic vinegar
1 teaspoon dried oregano, crushed between your fingers
1 pound (453.5 g) boneless, skinless chicken breasts, cut into 1½-inch pieces
2 medium zucchinis, cut into 1-inch pieces
½ cup Kalamata olives, pitted and halved
2 tablespoons olive brine
¼ cup torn fresh basil leaves
Nonstick cooking spray
Special Equipment:
14 to 15 (12-inch) wooden skewers, soaked for at least 30 minutes

Preheat the grill to medium-high heat. In a bowl, mix

together the olive oil, vinegar, and oregano. Divide the marinade between two large plastic zip-top bags. Put chicken to one bag and the zucchini to another. Seal and massage the marinade into both the chicken and zucchini. Thread the chicken onto 6 wooden skewers. Thread the zucchini onto 8 or 9 wooden skewers. Cook the kebabs in batches on the grill for 5 minutes, flip, and grill for 5 minutes more, or until any chicken juices run clear. Remove the chicken and zucchini from the skewers to a large serving bowl. Toss with the olives, olive brine, and basil and serve.

Nutrition facts (per serving)
calories: 283 | fat: 15.0g | protein: 11.0g | carbs: 26.0g | fiber: 3.0g | sodium: 575mg

►Almond-Crusted Chicken Tenders with Honey

Preparation time: 10 minutes
Cooking time: 20 minutes | **Servings:** 4
1 tablespoon honey
1 tablespoon whole-grain or Dijon mustard
¼ teaspoon freshly ground black pepper
¼ teaspoon kosher or sea salt
1 pound (453,5 g) boneless, skinless chicken breast tenders or tenderloins
1 cup almonds, roughly chopped
Nonstick cooking spray

Preheat the oven to 420/425°F (220°C).. Place a wire cooling rack on the parchment-lined baking sheet and spray the rack well with nonstick cooking spray. In a medium-large bowl, combine the honey, mustard, pepper, and salt. Add the chicken to coat. Set aside. Dump the almonds onto a large sheet of parchment paper and spread them out. Press the coated chicken tenders into the nuts until evenly coated on all sides. Place the chicken on the rack. Bake in the oven for 13 to 22 minutes, or until the internal temperature of the chicken measures 165°F (74°C) on a meat thermometer and any juices run clear. Cool for 5 minutes before serving.

Nutrition facts (per serving)
calories: 222 | fat: 7.0g | protein: 11.0g | carbs: 29.0g | fiber: 2.0g | sodium: 448mg

►Parsley-Dijon Chicken and Potatoes

Preparation time: 5 minutes
Cooking time: 22 minutes | **Servings:** 6
1 tablespoon extra-virgin olive oil
1½ pounds (681 g) boneless, skinless chicken thighs, cut into 1-inch cubes, patted dry
1½ pounds (680 g) Yukon Gold potatoes, unpeeled, cut into ½-inch cubes
2 garlic cloves, minced
¼ cup dry white wine
1 cup low-sodium or no-salt-added chicken broth
1 tablespoon Dijon mustard
¼ teaspoon freshly ground black pepper
¼ teaspoon kosher or sea salt

1 cup chopped fresh flat-leaf (Italian) parsley, including stems
1 tablespoon freshly squeezed lemon juice
In a medium-large skillet over medium-high heat, heat the oil. Add the chicken and cook for 4-7 minutes, stirring only after the chicken has browned on one side. Remove the chicken. Cook the potatoes for 5 minutes adding to the skillet, stirring only after the potatoes have become golden and crispy on one side. Push the potatoes to the side of the skillet, add the garlic, and cook, stirring constantly, for 1 minute. Add the wine and cook for 1 and a half minute, until nearly evaporated. Add the chicken broth, mustard, salt, pepper, and reserved chicken. Boil. Cook for 9 to 11 minutes, until the internal temperature of the chicken measures 170/175°F (74°C) on a meat thermometer and any juices run clear. Stir in the parsley during the last minute of cooking. Stir in the lemon juice.

Nutrition facts (per serving)
calories: 324 | fat: 9.0g | protein: 16.0g | carbs: 45.0g | fiber: 5.0g | sodium: 560mg

►Gyro Burgers with Tahini Sauce

Preparation time: 15 minutes
Cooking time: 10 minutes | **Servings:** 4
2 tablespoons extra-virgin olive oil
1 tablespoon dried oregano
1¼ teaspoons garlic powder, divided
1 teaspoon ground cumin
½ teaspoon freshly ground black pepper
¼ teaspoon kosher or sea salt
1 pound (454 g) beef flank steak, top round steak, or lamb leg steak, center cut, about 1 inch thick
1 medium-large green bell pepper, halved and seeded
2 tablespoons tahini or peanut butter
1 tablespoon hot water (optional)
½ cup plain Greek yogurt
1 tablespoon freshly squeezed lemon juice
1 cup thinly sliced red onion
4 (6-inch) whole-wheat pita breads, warmed
Nonstick cooking spray

Set an oven rack about 3-4 inches below the broiler element. Preheat the oven broiler to high. Line a medium/large, rimmed baking sheet with aluminum foil. Place a wire cooling rack on the foil and spray the rack with nonstick cooking spray. Set aside. Mix the olive oil, oregano, 1 teaspoon of garlic powder, cumin, pepper, and salt. Rub the oil mixture on all sides of the steak, reserving 1 teaspoon of the mixture. Place the steak on the prepared rack. Rub the remaining oil mixture on the bell pepper, and place on the rack, cut side down. Press the pepper with the heel of your hand to flatten. Broil for 5 minutes. Flip the steak and the pepper pieces, and broil for 2 to 5 minutes more, until the pepper is charred and the internal temperature of the meat measures 145°F (63°C) on a meat thermometer. Put the pepper and steak on a cutting board to rest for 5 minutes. Meanwhile, in a small-medium bowl, whisk the tahini until smooth (adding 1 tablespoon of hot water if your tahini is sticky). Add

the remaining ¼ teaspoon of garlic powder and the yogurt and lemon juice and whisk thoroughly.
Slice the steak crosswise into ¼-inch-thick strips. Slice the bell pepper into strips. Divide the steak, bell pepper, and onion among the warm pita breads. Drizzle with tahini sauce and serve.

Nutrition facts (per serving)
calories: 348 | fat: 15.0g | protein: 33.0g | carbs: 20.0g | fiber: 3.0g | sodium: 530mg

➤Beef Kebabs with Onion and Pepper

Preparation time: 15 minutes
Cooking time: 10 minutes | **Servings:** 6
2 pounds (907 g) beef fillet
1½ teaspoons salt
1 teaspoon freshly ground black pepper
½ teaspoon ground nutmeg
½ teaspoon ground allspice
⅓ cup extra-virgin olive oil
1 large onion, cut into 8 quarters
1 medium-large red bell pepper, cut into 1-inch cubes

Preheat the grill to high heat. Cut the beef into 1-inch cubes and put them in a large bowl. In a small-medium bowl, mix the salt, black pepper, allspice, and nutmeg. Pour the olive oil over the beef and toss to coat. Evenly sprinkle the seasoning over the beef and toss to coat all pieces. Skewer the beef, alternating every 1 or 2 pieces with a piece of onion or bell pepper. Put the skewers, every 2 to 3 minutes flip until all sides have cooked to desired doneness, 6 minutes for medium-rare, 8 minutes for well done. Serve hot.

Nutrition facts (per serving)
calories: 485 | fat: 36.0g | protein: 35.0g | carbs: 4.0g | fiber: 1.0g | sodium: 1453mg

➤Grilled Pork Chops

Preparation time: 20 minutes
Cooking time: 10 minutes | **Servings:** 4
¼ cup extra-virgin olive oil
2 tablespoons fresh thyme leaves
1 teaspoon smoked paprika
1 teaspoon salt
4 pork loin chops, ½-inch-thick

Mix the olive oil, thyme, paprika, and salt. Put the pork chops in a plastic zip-top bag or a bowl and coat them with the spice mix. Let them marinate for 15 minutes. Preheat the grill to high heat. Cook the pork chops for 3 to 5 minutes on each side until cooked through. Serve warm.

Nutrition facts (per serving)
calories: 282 | fat: 23.0g | protein: 21.0g | carbs: 1.0g | fiber: 0g | sodium: 832mg

➤Greek-Style Lamb Burgers

Preparation time: 10 minutes
Cooking time: 10 minutes | **Servings:** 4

1 pound (454 g) ground lamb
½ teaspoon salt
½ teaspoon freshly ground black pepper
4 tablespoons crumbled feta cheese
Buns, toppings, and tzatziki, for serving (optional)

Preheat the grill to high heat. In a medium-large bowl, using your hands, combine well the lamb with the salt and pepper. Divide the meat into 4 portions. Divide each portion in half to make a top and a bottom. Flatten each half into a 3-inch circle. Make a dent in the center of one of the halves and place 1 tablespoon of the feta cheese in the center. Place the second half of the patty on top of the feta cheese and press down to close the 2 halves together, making it resemble a round burger. Grill each side for 3 minutes, for medium-well. Serve on a bun with your favorite toppings and tzatziki sauce, if desired.

Nutrition facts (per serving)
calories: 345 | fat: 29.0g | protein: 20.0g | carbs: 1.0g | fiber: 0g | sodium: 462mg

➤Chicken Bruschetta Burgers

Preparation time: 10 minutes
Cooking time: 16 minutes | **Servings:** 2
1 tablespoon olive oil
2 garlic cloves, minced
3 tablespoons finely minced onion
1 teaspoon dried basil
3 tablespoons minced sun-dried tomatoes packed in olive oil
8 ounces (227 g) ground chicken breast
¼ teaspoon salt
3 pieces small Mozzarella balls, minced

Heat the olive oil , then put the garlic and onion and sauté for 6 minutes til tender. Stir in the basil. Remove from the skillet to a medium bowl. Add the tomatoes, ground chicken, and salt and stir until incorporated. Mix in the Mozzarella balls. Make two burgers, each about ¾-inch thick. Heat the same skillet over medium-high heat and add the burgers. Cook each side, until they reach an internal temperature of 165°F (74°C) or for 4-6 minutes. Serve warm.

Nutrition facts (per serving)
calories: 300 | fat: 17.0g | protein: 32.2g | carbs: 6.0g | fiber: 1.1g | sodium: 724mg

➤Chicken Cacciatore

Preparation time: 15 minutes
Cooking time: 1 hour and 30 minutes
Servings: 2
1½ pounds (680 g) bone-in chicken thighs, skin removed and patted dry
Salt, to taste
2 tablespoons olive oil
½ large onion, thinly sliced
4 ounces (113 g) baby bells mushrooms, sliced
1 red sweet pepper, cut into 2-inch pieces
1 (15-ounce / 425-g) can crushed fire-roasted toma-

toes
1 fresh rosemary sprig
½ cup dry red wine
1 teaspoon Italian herb seasoning
½ teaspoon garlic powder
3 tablespoons flour

Season the chicken thighs with salt. Heat the olive oil in a Dutch oven over medium-high heat. Add the chicken and brown for 4-5 minutes per side. Add the onion, mushrooms, and sweet pepper to the Dutch oven and sauté for another 5 minutes. Add the tomatoes, rosemary, wine, Italian seasoning, garlic powder, and salt, stirring well. Bring the mixture to a boil, then low the heat. Allow to simmer slowly for at least 1 hour, stirring occasionally, or until the chicken is tender. Measure out 1 cup of the sauce from the pot and put it into a bowl. Add the flour and whisk well. Increase the heat to medium-high and slowly whisk the slurry into the pot. Stir until it comes to a boil and cook until the sauce is thickened. Remove the chicken from the bones and shred it, and add it back to the sauce before serving, if desired.

Nutrition facts (per serving)
calories: 520 | fat: 23.1g | protein: 31.8g | carbs: 37.0g | fiber: 6.0g | sodium: 484mg

▸Chicken Gyros with Tzatziki Sauce

Preparation time: 15 minutes
Cooking time: 10 minutes | **Servings:** 2
2 tablespoons freshly squeezed lemon juice
2 tablespoons olive oil, divided
1 teaspoon minced fresh oregano
½ teaspoon garlic powder
Salt, to taste
8 ounces (227 g) chicken tenders
1 small eggplant, cut into 1-inch strips lengthwise
1 small zucchini, cut into ½-inch strips lengthwise
½ red pepper, seeded and cut in half
½ English cucumber, peeled and minced
¾ cup plain Greek yogurt
1 tablespoon minced fresh dill
2 (8-inch) pita breads

Combine the lemon juice, 1 tablespoon of olive oil, oregano, garlic powder, and salt in a medium bowl. Add the chicken and let marinate for 28-30 minutes. Place the eggplant, zucchini, and red pepper in a large mixing bowl and sprinkle with the remaining 1 tablespoon of olive oil and salt. Toss well to coat. Let the vegetables rest while the chicken is marinating. Make the tzatziki sauce: Combine the cucumber, yogurt, salt, and dill in a medium bowl. Stir well to incorporate and set aside in the refrigerator. When ready, preheat the grill to medium-high heat and oil the grill grates. Drain any liquid from the vegetables and put them on the grill. Remove the chicken tenders from the marinade and put them on the grill. Grill the chicken and vegetables for 3 minutes per side, or until the chicken is no longer pink inside. Remove the vegetables and chicken from the grill. On the grill, heat the pitas for about 30 seconds, flipping them frequently.

Divide the chicken tenders and vegetables between the pitas and top each with ¼ cup of the prepared sauce. Roll the pitas up like a cone and serve.
Nutrition facts (per serving)
calories: 586 | fat: 21.9g | protein: 39.0g | carbs: 62.0g | fiber: 11.8g | sodium: 955mg

▸Crispy Pesto Chicken

Preparation time: 15 minutes
Cooking time: 50 minutes | **Servings:** 2
12 ounces (340 g) small red potatoes (3 or 4 potatoes), scrubbed and diced into 1-inch pieces 1 tablespoon olive oil
½ teaspoon garlic powder
¼ teaspoon salt
1 (8-ounce / 227-g) boneless, skinless chicken breast
3 tablespoons prepared pesto

Preheat the oven to 420/425°F (220°C). Line a baking sheet with parchment paper. Combine the potatoes, olive oil, garlic powder, and salt in a medium bowl. Toss well to coat. Arrange the potatoes on the parchment paper and roast for 10 minutes. Flip the potatoes and roast for an additional 10 minutes. Meanwhile, put the chicken in the same bowl and toss with the pesto, coating the chicken evenly. Check the potatoes to make sure they are golden brown on the top and bottom. Toss them again and add the chicken breast to the pan. Turn the heat down to 340/350°F (180°C) and roast the chicken and potatoes for 30 minutes. Check to make sure the chicken reaches an internal temperature of 165°F (74°C) and the potatoes are fork-tender. Let cool for 5 minutes before serving.
Nutrition facts (per serving) calories: 378 | fat: 16.0g | protein: 29.8g | carbs: 30.1g | fiber: 4.0g | sodium: 425mg

▸Beef Stew with Beans and Zucchini

Preparation time: 20 minutes
Cooking time: 6 to 8 hours | **Servings:** 2
1 (15-ounce / 425-g) can diced or crushed tomatoes with basil
1 teaspoon beef base
2 tablespoons olive oil, divided
8 ounces (227 g) baby bell (cremini) mushrooms, quartered
2 garlic cloves, minced
½ large onion, diced
1 pound (454 g) cubed beef stew meat
3 tablespoons flour
¼ teaspoon salt
Pinch freshly ground black pepper
¾ cup dry red wine
¼ cup minced brined olives
1 fresh rosemary sprig
1 (15-ounce / 425-g) can white cannellini beans, rinsed
1 medium/large zucchini, cut in half lengthwise and

then cut into 1-inch pieces.

Place the tomatoes into a slow cooker and set it to low heat. Add the beef base and stir to incorporate. Heat 1 tablespoon of olive oil in a medium/large sauté pan over medium heat. Add the mushrooms and onion and sauté for 10 minutes, stirring occasionally, or until they're golden. Add the garlic and cook for 30-35 seconds more. Transfer the vegetables to the slow cooker. In a plastic food storage bag, combine well the stew meat with the flour, salt, and pepper. Seal the bag and shake to combine. Heat the remaining 1 tablespoon of olive oil in the sauté pan over high heat. Add the floured meat and sear to get a crust on the outside edges. Deglaze the pan by adding about half of the red wine and scraping up any browned bits on the bottom. Stir so the wine thickens a bit and transfer to the slow cooker along with any remaining wine. Stir the stew to incorporate the ingredients. Stir in the olives and rosemary, cover, and cook for 6 to 8 hours on Low. About 28/30 minutes before the stew is finished, add the beans and zucchini to let them warm through. Serve warm.

Nutrition facts (per serving)
calories: 389 | fat: 15.1g | protein: 30.8g | carbs: 25.0g | fiber: 8.0g | sodium: 582mg

➤Greek Beef Kebabs

Preparation time: 15 minutes
Cooking time: 20 minutes | **Servings:** 2
6 ounces (170 g) beef sirloin tip, trimmed of fat and cut into 2-inch pieces
3 cups of any mixture of vegetables: mushrooms, summer squash, zucchini, onions, red peppers, cherry tomatoes
½ cup olive oil
¼ cup freshly squeezed lemon juice
2 tablespoons balsamic vinegar
2 teaspoons dried oregano
1 teaspoon garlic powder
1 teaspoon salt
1 teaspoon minced fresh rosemary
Cooking spray

Put the beef in a plastic freezer bag. Slice the vegetables into similar-size pieces and put them in a second freezer bag. Make the marinade: Mix the olive oil, lemon juice, balsamic vinegar, oregano, garlic powder, salt, and rosemary in a measuring cup. Whisk well to combine. Pour half of the marinade over the vegetables, and the other half over the beef. Put the beef and vegetables in the refrigerator to marinate for 4 hours. Preheat the grill to medium/high heat and spray the grill grates with cooking spray. Thread the meat onto skewers and the vegetables onto separate skewers. Grill the meat for 3-5 minutes per side. They should only take 9 to 12 minutes to cook, depending on the thickness of the meat. Grill the vegetables for about 3 minutes per side, or until they have grill marks and are softened. Serve hot.

Nutrition facts (per serving)
calories: 284 | fat: 18.2g | protein: 21.0g | carbs: 9.0g

| fiber: 3.9g | sodium: 122mg

➤Chermoula Roasted Pork Tenderloin

Preparation time: 15 minutes
Cooking time: 20 minutes | **Servings:** 2
½ cup fresh cilantro
½ cup fresh parsley
6 small garlic cloves
3 tablespoons olive oil, divided
3 tablespoons freshly squeezed lemon juice
2 teaspoons cumin
1 teaspoon smoked paprika
½ teaspoon salt, divided
Pinch freshly ground black pepper
1 (8-ounce / 227-g) pork tenderloin

Preheat the oven to 420/425°F (220°C). In a food processor, combine the cilantro, parsley, garlic, 2 tablespoons of olive oil, lemon juice, cumin, paprika, and ¼ teaspoon of salt. Pulse 16 to 20 times, or until the mixture is fairly smooth. Scrape the sides down as needed to incorporate all the ingredients. Transfer the sauce to a small/medium bowl and set aside. Season the pork tenderloin on all sides with the remaining ¼ teaspoon of salt and a generous pinch of black pepper. Heat the remaining tbsp of olive oil in a sauté pan. Sear the pork for 3 minutes, turning often, until golden brown on all sides. Transfer the pork to a baking dish and roast in the preheated oven for 15 minutes, or until the internal temperature registers 140/145°F (63°C). Cool for 5 minutes before serving.

Nutrition facts (per serving)
calories: 169 | fat: 13.1g | protein: 11.0g | carbs: 2.9g | fiber: 1.0g | sodium: 332mg

➤Lamb Kofta (Spiced Meatballs)

Preparation time: 15 minutes
Cooking time: 30 minutes | **Servings:** 2
¼ cup walnuts
1 garlic clove
½ small onion
1 roasted piquillo pepper
2 tablespoons fresh mint
2 tablespoons fresh parsley
¼ teaspoon cumin
¼ teaspoon allspice
¼ teaspoon salt
Pinch cayenne pepper
8 ounces (227 g) lean ground lamb

Preheat the oven to 340/350°F (180°C). Line a baking sheet with aluminum foil. In a food processor, combine well the garlic, walnuts, onion, roasted pepper, mint, parsley, cumin, allspice, salt, and cayenne pepper. Pulse about 10 times to combine everything. Transfer the spice mixture to a medium/large bowl and add the ground lamb. With your hands or a spatula, mix the spices into the lamb. Roll the lamb into 1½-inch balls (about the size of golf balls). Arrange the meatballs on the prepared baking sheet and bake for

30 minutes, or until cooked to an internal temperature of 160/165°F (74°C).

➤Country-Style Chicken Stew

Preparation Time: 20 minutes
Cooking Time: 1 hour
Servings: 6
Ingredients:
1 pound chicken thighs
2 tablespoons butter, room temperature
1/2 pound carrots, chopped
1 bell pepper, chopped
1 chili pepper, deveined and minced
1 cup tomato puree
Kosher salt and ground black pepper
1/2 teaspoon smoked paprika
1 onion, finely chopped
1 teaspoon garlic, sliced
4 cups vegetable broth
1 teaspoon dried basil
1 celery, chopped
Introductions:
Melt the butter in a stockpot over medium/high flame. Sweat the onion and garlic until just tender and fragrant. Reduce the heat to medium-low. Stir in the broth, chicken thighs, and basil; bring to a rolling boil. Add in the remaining Ingredients. Partially cover and let it simmer for 45 to 50 minutes. Shred the meat, discarding the bones; add the chicken back to the pot.
Nutrition facts:
280 Calories
14.7g Fat
2.5g Carbs
25.6g Protein
2.5g Fiber

➤Autumn Chicken Soup with Root Vegetables

Preparation Time: 10 minutes
Cooking Time: 25 minutes
Servings: 4
Ingredients:
4 cups chicken broth
1 cup full-fat milk
1 cup double cream
1/2 cup turnip, chopped
2 chicken drumsticks, boneless and cut into small pieces
Salt and pepper, to taste
1 tablespoon butter
1 teaspoon garlic, finely minced
1 carrot, chopped
1/2 parsnip, chopped
1/2 celery
1 whole egg
Directions:
Melt the butter in a heavy-bottomed pot over medium-high heat; sauté the garlic until aromatic or about 1 minute. Add in the vegetables and cook until they've softened. Add in the chicken and cook until it

is no longer pink for about 4 minutes. Season with salt and pepper. Pour in the chicken broth, milk, and heavy cream and bring it to a boil.
Reduce the heat to. Partially cover and continue to simmer for 20 to 25 minutes longer. Afterwards, fold the beaten egg and stir until it is well incorporated.
Nutrition facts:
342 Calories
22.4g Fat
6.3g Carbs
25.2g Protein
1.3g Fiber

➤Panna Cotta with Chicken and Bleu d' Auvergne

Preparation Time: 10 minutes
Cooking Time: 20 minutes
Servings:
Ingredients:
2 chicken legs, boneless and skinless
1 tablespoon avocado oil
2 teaspoons granular erythritol
3 tablespoons water
1 cup Bleu d' Auvergne, crumbled
2 gelatin sheets
3/4 cup double cream
Salt and cayenne pepper, to your liking
Directions:
Preheat the oil in a frying pan over medium/high heat; fry the chicken for about 10 minutes.
Soak the gelatin sheets in cold water. Cook with the cream, erythritol, water, and Bleu d' Auvergne.
Season with pepper and salt and let it simmer over the low heat, stirring for about 3 minutes. Spoon the mixture into four ramekins.
Nutrition facts:
306 Calories
18.3g Fat
4.7g Carbs
29.5g Protein
0g Fiber

➤Breaded Chicken Fillets

Preparation Time: 15 minutes
Cooking Time: 30 minutes
Servings: 4
Ingredients:
1 pound chicken fillets
3 bell peppers, quartered lengthwise
1/3 cup Romano cheese
2 teaspoons olive oil
1 garlic clove, minced
Kosher salt and ground black pepper
1/3 cup crushed pork rinds
Directions:
Start by preheating your oven to 400/410 degrees F. Mix the crushed pork rinds, Romano cheese, olive oil and minced garlic. Dredge the chicken into this mixture. Place the chicken in a lightly greased baking dish. Season with salt and black pepper. Scatter the pep-

pers around the chicken and bake in the preheated oven for 20 to 25 minutes or until thoroughly cooked.

Nutrition facts:
367 Calories
16.9g Fat
6g Carbs
43g Protein
0.7g Fiber

›Chicken Drumsticks with Broccoli and Cheese

Preparation Time: 40 minutes
Cooking Time: 1 hour 15 minutes
Servings: 4
Ingredients:
1 pound chicken drumsticks
1 pound broccoli, broken into florets
2 cups cheddar cheese, shredded
1/2 teaspoon dried oregano
1/2 teaspoon dried basil
3 tablespoons olive oil
1 celery, sliced
1 cup green onions, chopped
1 teaspoon minced green garlic
Directions:
Roast the chicken drumsticks in the preheated oven at 380 degrees F for 30 to 35 minutes. Add in the broccoli, celery, green onions, and green garlic.
Add in the oregano, basil and olive oil; roast an additional 15 minutes.
Nutrition facts:
533 Calories
40.2g Fat
5.4g Carbs
35.1g Protein
3.5g Fiber

›Turkey Ham and Mozzarella Pâté

Preparation Time: 5 minutes
Cooking Time: 10 minutes
Servings: 6
Ingredients:
4 ounces turkey ham, chopped
2 tablespoons fresh parsley, roughly chopped
2 tablespoons flaxseed meal
4 ounces mozzarella cheese, crumbled
2 tablespoons sunflower seeds
Directions:
Thoroughly combine the ingredients, except for the sunflower seeds, in your food processor.
Spoon the mixture into a serving bowl and scatter the sunflower seeds over the top.
Nutrition facts:
212 Calories
18.8g Fat
2g Carbs
10.6g Protein
1.6g Fiber

›Chicken with Avocado Sauce

Preparation Time: 10 minutes
Cooking Time: 20 minutes
Servings: 4
Ingredients:
8 chicken wings, boneless, cut into bite-size chunks
2 tablespoons olive oil
Sea salt and pepper, to your liking
2 eggs
1 teaspoon onion powder
1 teaspoon hot paprika
1/3 teaspoon mustard seeds
1/3 cup almond meal
For the Sauce:
1/2 cup mayonnaise
1/2 medium avocado
1/2 teaspoon sea salt
1 teaspoon green garlic, minced
Directions:
Pat dry the chicken with a paper towel.
Thoroughly combine the almond meal, salt, pepper, onion powder, paprika, and mustard seeds.
Whisk the eggs in a separate dish. Dredge the chicken chunks into the whisked eggs, then in the almond meal mixture. In a frying pan, heat the oil over a moderate heat; once hot, fry the chicken for about 10 minutes, stirring continuously to ensure even cooking. Make the sauce by whisking all the sauce Ingredients.
Nutrition facts:
370 Calories
25g Fat
4.1g Carbs
31.4g Protein
2.6g Fiber

›Duck and Eggplant Casserole

Preparation Time: 10 minutes
Cooking Time: 45 minutes
Servings: 4
Ingredients:
1 pound ground duck meat
1 ½ tablespoons ghee, melted
1/3 cup double cream
1/2 pound eggplant, peeled and sliced
1 ½ cups almond flour
Salt and black pepper, to taste
1/2 teaspoon fennel seeds
1/2 teaspoon oregano, dried
8 eggs
Directions:
Mix the almond flour with salt, black, fennel seeds, and oregano. Fold in one egg and the melted ghee and whisk to combine well. Press the crust into the bottom of a lightly oiled pie pan. Cook the ground duck until no longer pink for about 3 minutes, stirring continuously. Whisk the remaining eggs and double cream. Fold in the browned meat and stir until everything is well incorporated. Pour the mixture into the prepared crust. Top with the eggplant slices.
Bake for about 40 minutes. Cut into four pieces.

Nutrition facts:
562 Calories
49.5g Fat
6.7g Carbs
22.5g Protein
2.1g Fiber

➤Boozy Glazed Chicken

Preparation Time: 40 minutes
Cooking Time: 1 hour + marinating time
Servings: 4
Ingredients:
2 pounds chicken drumettes
2 tablespoons ghee, at room temperature
Sea salt and ground black pepper
1 teaspoon Mediterranean seasoning mix
2 vine-ripened tomatoes, pureed
3/4 cup rum
3 tablespoons coconut aminos
A few drops of liquid Stevia
1 teaspoon chili peppers, minced
1 tablespoon minced fresh ginger
1 teaspoon ground cardamom
2 tablespoons fresh lemon juice
Directions:
Toss the chicken with the melted ghee, salt, black pepper, and Mediterranean seasoning mix until well coated on all sides. In another bowl, thoroughly combine the pureed tomato puree, rum, coconut aminos, Stevia, chili peppers, ginger, cardamom, and lemon juice. Pour the tomato mixture over the chicken drumettes; let it marinate for 2 hours. Bake in the preheated oven at 410 degrees F for about 45 minutes. Add in the reserved marinade and place under the preheated broiler for 10 minutes.
Nutrition facts:
307 Calories
12.1g Fat
2.7g Carbs
33.6g Protein
1.5g Fiber

➤Herbed Chicken Breasts

Preparation Time: 10 minutes
Cooking Time: 40 minutes
Servings: 8
Ingredients:
4 chicken breasts, skinless and boneless
1 Italian pepper, deveined and thinly sliced
10 black olives, pitted
1 ½ cups vegetable broth
2 garlic cloves, pressed
2 tablespoons olive oil
1 tablespoon Old Sub Sailor
Salt, to taste
Directions:
Rub the chicken with the garlic and Old Sub Sailor; salt to taste. Heat the oil in a frying pan over a moderately high heat.

Sear the chicken for about 4-5 minutes or until it is browned on all sides.
Add in the pepper, olives, and vegetable broth and bring it to boil. Low the heat simmer and continue to cook, partially covered, for 30 to 35 minutes.
Nutrition facts:
306 Calories
17.8g Fat
3.1g Carbs
31.7g Protein
0.2g Fiber

➤Cheese and Ham Chicken Roulade

Preparation Time: 15 minutes
Cooking Time: 35 minutes
Servings: 2
Ingredients:
1/2 cup Ricotta cheese
4 slices of ham
1 pound chicken fillet
1 tablespoon fresh coriander, chopped
Salt and ground black pepper, to taste pepper
1 teaspoon cayenne pepper
Directions:
Season the chicken fillet with salt and pepper. Spread the Ricotta cheese over the chicken fillet, sprinkle with the fresh coriander. Roll up and cut into 4 pieces. Wrap each piece with 1 slice of ham: secure with a kitchen twine. Place the wrapped chicken in a parchment-lined baking pan. Now, bake in the preheated oven at 385 degrees F for about 30 minutes.
Nutrition facts:
499 Calories
18.9g Fat
5.7g Carbs
41.6g Protein
0.6g Fiber

➤Greek-Style Saucy Chicken Drumettes

Preparation Time: 25 minutes
Cooking Time: 50 minutes
Servings: 6
Ingredients:
1 ½ pounds chicken drumettes
1/2 cup port wine
1/2 cup onions, chopped
2 garlic cloves, minced
1 teaspoon tzatziki spice mix
1 cup double cream
2 tablespoons butter
Sea salt and crushed mixed peppercorns, to season
Directions:
Melt the butter in an oven-proof skillet over a moderate heat; then, cook the chicken for about 8 minutes. Add in the onions, garlic, wine, tzatziki spice mix, double cream, salt, and pepper. Bake in the preheated oven at 380/390 degrees F for 35 to 40 minutes (a meat thermometer should register 165 degrees F).

Nutrition facts:
333 Calories
20.2g Fat
2g Carbs
33.5g Protein
0.2g Fiber

➤Old-Fashioned Turkey Chowder

Preparation Time: 15 minutes
Cooking Time: 35 minutes
Servings: 4
Ingredients:
2 tablespoons olive oil
2 tablespoons yellow onions, chopped
2 cloves garlic, roughly chopped
1/2 pound leftover roast turkey, shredded and skin removed
1 teaspoon Mediterranean spice mix
3 cups chicken bone broth
1 ½ cups milk
1/2 cup double cream
1 egg, lightly beaten
2 tablespoons dry sherry
Directions:
Preheat the olive oil in a heavy-bottomed pot over a moderate flame. Sauté the onion and garlic until they've softened. Stir in the leftover roast turkey, Mediterranean spice mix, and chicken bone broth; bring to a rapid boil. Partially cover and continue to cook for 20-25 minutes. Turn the heat to simmer. Pour in the milk and double cream and continue to cook until it has reduced slightly. Fold in the egg and dry sherry; continue to simmer, stirring frequently, for a further 2 minutes.
Nutrition facts:
350 Calories
25.8g Fat
5.5g Carbs
20g Protein
0.1g Fiber

➤Festive Turkey Rouladen

Preparation Time: 15 minutes
Cooking Time: 30 minutes
Servings: 5
Ingredients:
2 pounds turkey fillet, marinated and cut into 10 pieces
10 strips ham
1/2 teaspoon chili powder
1 teaspoon marjoram
1 sprig rosemary, finely chopped
2 tablespoons dry white wine
1 teaspoon garlic, finely minced
1 ½ tablespoons butter, room temperature
1 tablespoon Dijon mustard
Sea salt and freshly ground black pepper
Directions:
Start by preheating your oven to 430 degrees F.
Pat the turkey dry and cook in hot butter for about 3

minutes per side. Add in the mustard, chili powder, marjoram, rosemary, wine, and garlic.
Continue to cook for 2 minutes more. Wrap each turkey piece into one ham strip and secure with toothpicks.
Roast in the preheated oven for about 28-30 minutes.
Nutrition facts:
286 Calories
9.7g Fat
6.9g Carbs
39.9g Protein
0.3g Fiber

➤Pan-Fried Chorizo Sausage

Preparation Time: 10 minutes
Cooking Time: 20 minutes
Servings: 4
Ingredients:
16 ounces smoked turkey chorizo
1 ½ cups Asiago cheese, grated
1 teaspoon oregano
1 teaspoon basil
1 cup tomato puree
4 scallion stalks, chopped
1 teaspoon garlic paste
Sea salt and ground black pepper
1 tablespoon dry sherry
1 tablespoon extra-virgin olive oil
2 tablespoons fresh coriander, roughly chopped
Directions:
Preheat the oil in a frying pan over moderately high heat. Now, brown the turkey chorizo, crumbling with a fork for about 5 minutes. Add in the other Ingredients, except for cheese; continue to cook for 10 minutes more or until cooked through.
Nutrition facts:
330 Calories
17.2g Fat
4.5g Carbs
34.4g Protein
1.6g Fiber

➤Turkey Soup

Preparation Time: 15 minutes
Cooking Time: 40 minutes
Servings: 8
Ingredients:
2 pounds turkey carcass
1 tablespoon olive oil
1/2 cup leeks, chopped
1 celery rib, chopped
2 carrots, sliced
6 cups turkey stock
Himalayan salt and black pepper, to taste
Directions:
In a heavy-bottomed pot, preheat the olive oil until sizzling. Once hot, sauté the celery, carrots, leek for about 6 minutes. Add the salt, pepper, turkey, and stock; bring to a boil. Turn the heat to simmer. Continue to cook, partially covered, for about 35 minutes.

Nutrition facts:
211 Calories
11.8g Fat
3.1g Carbs
23.7g Protein
0.9g Fiber

➤Herby Chicken Meatloaf

Preparation Time: 20 minutes
Cooking Time: 30 minutes
Servings: 6
Ingredients:
2 ½ lb ground chicken
3 tbsp flaxseed meal
2 large eggs
2 tbsp olive oil
1 lemon, 1 tbsp juiced
¼ cup chopped parsley
¼ cup chopped oregano
4 garlic cloves, minced
Lemon slices to garnish
Directions:
Preheat oven to 400 F. In a bowl, combine ground chicken and flaxseed meal; set aside. In a small/medium bowl, whisk the eggs with olive oil, lemon juice, parsley, oregano, and garlic.
Pour the mixture onto the chicken mixture and mix well. Spoon into a greased loaf pan and press to fit. Bake for 40 minutes.
Remove the pan, drain the liquid, and let cool a bit. Slice, garnish with lemon slices, and serve.
Nutrition facts:
Cal 362
Net Carbs 1.3g
Fat 24g
Protein 35g

➤Lovely Pulled Chicken Egg Bites

Preparation Time: 15 minutes
Cooking Time: 30 minutes
Servings: 4
Ingredients:
2 tbsp butter
1 chicken breast
2 tbsp chopped green onions
½ tsp red chili flakes
12 eggs
¼ cup grated Monterey Jack
Directions:
Preheat oven to 400 F. Line a 12-hole muffin tin with cupcake liners. Melt butter in a skillet over medium heat and cook the chicken until brown on each side, 10 minutes.
Transfer to a plate and shred with 2 forks. Divide between muffin holes along with green onions and red chili flakes.
Into each muffin hole crack an egg and scatter the cheese on top. Bake for 15 minutes until eggs set. Serve.
Nutrition facts:

Cal 393
Net Carbs 0.5g
Fat 27g
Protein 34g

➤Creamy Mustard Chicken with Shirataki

Preparation Time: 20 minutes
Cooking Time: 30 minutes
Servings: 4
Ingredients:
2 (8 oz) packs angel hair shirataki
4 chicken breasts, cut into strips
1 cup chopped mustard greens
1 yellow bell pepper, sliced
1 tbsp olive oil
1 yellow onion, finely sliced
1 garlic clove, minced
1 tbsp wholegrain mustard
5 tbsp heavy cream
1 tbsp chopped parsley
Directions:
Boil 2 cups of water in a medium-large pot.
Strain the shirataki pasta and rinse well under hot running water. Allow proper draining and pour the shirataki pasta into the boiling water.
Cook for 3 minutes and strain again. Place a dry skillet and stir-fry the shirataki pasta until visibly dry, 1-2 minutes; set aside.
Preheat olive oil in a skillet, season the chicken with salt and pepper and cook for 8-10 minutes; set aside. Stir in bell pepper, onion and garlic and cook until softened, 5 minutes.
Mix in mustard and heavy cream; simmer for 2 minutes and mix in the chicken and mustard greens for 2 minutes. Stir in shirataki pasta, garnish with parsley and serve.
Nutrition facts:
Cal 692
Net Carbs 15g
Fats 38g
Protein 65g

➤Parsnip & Bacon Chicken Bake

Preparation Time: 10 minutes
Cooking Time: 50 minutes
Servings: 4
Ingredients:
6 bacon slices, chopped
2 tbsp butter
½ lb parsnips, diced
2 tbsp olive oil
1 lb ground chicken
2 tbsp butter
1 cup heavy cream
2 oz cream cheese, softened
1 ¼ cups grated Pepper Jack
¼ cup chopped scallions
Directions:
Preheat oven to 300 F. Put the bacon in a pot and

fry it until brown and crispy, 6 minutes; set aside. Melt butter in a skillet and sauté parsnips until softened and lightly browned. Transfer to a greased baking sheet. Preheat olive oil in the same pan and cook the chicken until no longer pink, 8 minutes. Spoon onto a plate and set aside too. Add heavy cream, cream cheese, and two-thirds of the Pepper Jack cheese to the pot. Melt the ingredients over medium heat, frequently stirring, 7 minutes. Spread the parsnips on the baking dish, top with chicken, pour the heavy cream mixture over, and scatter bacon and scallions. Sprinkle the remaining cheese and bake until the cheese melts and is golden, 30 minutes. Serve warm.

Nutrition facts:
Cal 757
Net Carbs 5.5g
Fat 66g
Protein 29g

>Chicken Bake with Onion & Parsnip

Preparation Time: 15 minutes
Cooking Time: 30 minutes
Servings:
Ingredients:
3 parsnips, sliced
1 onion, sliced
4 garlic cloves, crushed
2 tbsp olive oil
2 lb chicken breasts
½ cup chicken broth
¼ cup white wine
Salt and black pepper to taste
Directions:
Preheat oven to 360 F. Warm oil in a skillet over medium heat and brown chicken for 1-2 minutes, and transfer to a baking dish. Arrange the vegetables around the chicken and add in wine and chicken broth. Bake for 25 minutes, stirring once. Serve warm.
Nutrition facts:
Cal 278
Net Carbs 5.1g
Fat 8.7g
Protein 35g

>Cucumber-Turkey Canapes

Preparation Time: 10 minutes
Cooking Time: 5 minutes
Servings: 6
Ingredients:
2 cucumbers, sliced
2 cups dices leftover turkey
¼ jalapeño pepper, minced
1 tbsp Dijon mustard
¼ cup mayonnaise
Salt and black pepper to taste
Directions:
Cut mid-level holes in cucumber slices with a knife and set aside. Mix turkey, jalapeño pepper, mustard, mayonnaise, salt, and black pepper in a bowl. Carefully fill cucumber holes with turkey mixture and

serve.
Nutrition facts:
Cal 170
Net Carbs 1.3g
Fat 14g
Protein 10g

>Baked Chicken Skewers with Rutabaga Fries

Preparation Time: 20 minutes
Cooking Time: 45 minutes
Servings: 6
Ingredients:
2 chicken breasts, halved
Salt and black pepper to taste
4 tbsp olive oil
¼ cup chicken broth
1 lb rutabaga
2 tbsp olive oil
Directions:
Set oven to 400 F. Grease and line a baking sheet. In a bowl, mix 2 tbsp of the olive oil, salt, and pepper and add in the chicken; toss to coat. Set in the fridge for 20 minutes. Peel and chop rutabaga to form fry shapes and place into a separate bowl. Coat with the remaining olive oil and season with salt and pepper. Arrange the rutabaga shapes on the baking sheet and bake for 10 minutes. Take the chicken from the refrigerator and thread onto the skewers. Place over the rutabaga, pour in the chicken broth, and bake for 30 minutes. Serve immediately.
Nutrition facts:
Cal: 579
Net Carbs: 6g
Fat: 53g
Protein: 39g

>Louisiana Chicken Fettuccine

Preparation Time: 10 minutes
Cooking Time: 45 minutes
Servings: 4
Ingredients:
1 medium-large red bell pepper, deseeded and thinly sliced
1 medium green bell pepper, deseeded and thinly sliced
2 cups grated mozzarella
½ cup grated Parmesan
1 cup shredded mozzarella
1 egg yolk
2 tbsp olive oil
4 chicken breasts, cubed
1 yellow onion, thinly sliced
4 garlic cloves, minced
4 tsp Cajun seasoning
1 cup Alfredo sauce
½ cup marinara sauce
2 tbsp chopped fresh parsley
Directions:
Microwave mozzarella cheese for 2 minutes. Take out

the bowl and allow cooling for 1 minute. Mix in egg yolk until well-combined. Lay a parchment paper on a flat surface, pour the cheese mixture on top and cover with another parchment paper. Flatten the dough into 1/8-inch thickness. Take off the parchment paper and cut the dough into thick fettuccine strands. Place in a bowl and refrigerate overnight. Bring 2 cups water to a boil. Then add fettuccine. Cook for 1 minute and drain; set aside. Preheat oven to 340/350 F. Heat olive oil in a skillet and cook chicken for 6 minutes. Transfer to a plate. Add garlic, onion and bell peppers to the skillet and cook for 5 minutes. Return the chicken to the pot and stir in Cajun seasoning, Alfredo sauce, and marinara sauce. Cook for 3 minutes. Stir in fettuccine and transfer to a greased baking dish. Cover with the mozzarella and Parmesan cheese and bake for 15 minutes. Garnish with parsley and serve.

Nutrition facts:
Cal 778
Net Carbs 4g
Fats 38g
Protein 93g

›Chicken Wraps in Bacon with Spinach

Preparation Time: 12 minutes
Cooking Time: 30 minutes
Servings: 5
Ingredients:
4 chicken breasts
8 slices bacon
Salt and black pepper to taste
2 tbsp olive oil
For the buttered spinach:
2 tbsp butter
1 lb spinach
4 garlic cloves, minced
Directions:
Preheat oven to 450 F. Wrap each chicken breast with 2 bacon slices, season with salt and pepper, and place on a baking sheet. Drizzle with olive oil and bake for 15 minutes until the bacon browns and chicken cooks within. Melt butter in a skillet and sauté spinach and garlic until the leaves wilt, 5 minutes. Season with salt and pepper. Serve with buttered spinach.

Nutrition facts:
Cal 856
Net Carbs 2.4g
Fat 60g
Protein 71g

›Pork Cutlets with Juniper Berries

Preparation time: 10 minutes
Cooking time: 20 minutes | **Servings:** 2
1 tablespoon lard, softened at room temperature
2 pork cutlets, 2-inch-thick
⅓ cup dry red wine
2 garlic cloves, sliced
½ teaspoon whole black peppercorns
4 tablespoons flaky salt
1 teaspoon juniper berries

½ teaspoon cayenne pepper
Directions:
Melt the lard in a nonstick skillet over a moderate flame. Now, brown the pork cutlets for about 8 minutes, turning them over to ensure even cooking; reserve. Add a splash of wine. Stir the remaining ingredients and continue to cook until fragrant or for a minute or so. Return the pork cutlets to the skillet, continue to cook until the sauce has thickened, and everything is heated through about 10 minutes. Serve warm. Bon appétit!
Nutrition facts (per serving)
calories: 370 | fat: 20.5g | protein: 40.2g | carbs: 1.2g | net carbs: 1.0g | fiber: 0.2g

›Beef Shanks Braised in Red Wine Sauce

Preparation Time: 20 minutes
Cooking Time: 8 hrs.
Servings: 6
Ingredients:
2 tablespoons olive oil
2 pounds (907 g) beef shanks
2 cups dry red wine
3 cups beef stock
1 sprig of fresh rosemary
5 garlic cloves, finely chopped
1 onion, finely chopped
Pepper and salt
Directions:
Heat olive oil. Put the beef shanks into the skillet and fry for 5 to 10 minutes until well browned. the beef shanks halfway through. Set aside. The red wine must be poured into the pot and let it simmer. Add the cooked beef shanks, dry red wine, beef stock, rosemary, garlic, onion, salt, and black pepper to the slow cooker. Stir to mix well. Slow cook with the lid on for 8 hrs.
Nutrition facts:
Calories: 341
Fat: 19.6g
Fiber: 10 g
Carbohydrates:15.4 g
Protein: 21.6g

›Cheesy Bacon Squash Spaghetti

Preparation Time: 30 minutes
Cooking Time: 50 minutes
Servings: 4
Ingredients:
2 pounds spaghetti squash
2 pounds bacon
1/2 cup of butter
2 cups of shredded parmesan cheese
Salt and Black pepper
Directions:
Let the oven preheat to 375F. Trim or remove each stem of spaghetti squash, slice into rings no more than

an inch wide, and take out the seeds.

Lay the sliced rings down on the baking sheet, bake for 40-45 minutes. It is ready when the strands separate easily when a fork is used to scrape it. Let it cool. Cook sliced up bacon until crispy. Take out and let it cool. Take off the shell on each ring, separate each strand with a fork, and put them in a bowl. Heat the strands in a microwave to get them warm, then put in butter and stir around till the butter melts. Pour in parmesan cheese and bacon crumbles and add salt and pepper to your taste. Enjoy.

Nutrition facts:
Calories: 398
Fat: 12.5g
Fiber: 9.4g
Carbohydrates:4.1 g
Protein: 5.1g

➤Stuffed Onions

Preparation Time: 35 minutes
Cooking Time: 45 minutes
Servings: 5
Ingredients:
5 onions (medium-sized)
3/4 pound of ground beef
2 medium eggs
Italian seasoning to taste
2 spoons of olive oil
Salt
Black pepper
1/4 cup of ground pork
4 tablespoons parmesan cheese
Worcestershire sauce to taste
2 ounces of quartered cheddar cheese
Directions:
Preheat oven to 350°F. Take out the inner layers, so the onion is hollow and bottomless. Place it in a casserole dish. In another bowl, whisk eggs lightly. In another bowl, mix well the two kinds of cheese. In another bowl, put in the ground beef, egg mixture, olive oil, ground pork, and Worcestershire sauce, 1/4 teaspoon of salt and other seasonings to taste, and mix well. Fully stuff each onion with the mix of beef and egg. Make a space in the stuffing for cheese balls and put inside. Cover the onion with another meat layer and bake for 30-45 minutes.

Nutrition facts:
Calories: 299
Fat: 12.6g
Fiber: 5.9g
Carbohydrates:4.9 g
Protein: 16.7g

➤Kalua Pork with Cabbage

Preparation Time: 10 minutes
Cooking Time: 8 hrs.
Servings: 4
Ingredients:

1-pound boneless pork butt roast
Pink Himalayan salt
Freshly ground black pepper
1 tablespoon smoked paprika or Liquid Smoke
1/2 cup of water
1/2 head cabbage, chopped
Directions:
With the crock insert in place, preheat the slow cooker to low. Generously season the pork roast with pink Himalayan salt, pepper, and smoked paprika.
Place the pork roast in the slow cooker insert and add the water. Cover and cook on low for 6 and a half,7 hours. Transfer the cooked pork roast to a plate. Put the chopped cabbage in the slow cooker and put the pork roast back in on the cabbage.
Cover and cook the cabbage and pork roast for 1 hour. Remove the pork roast from the slow cooker and place it on a baking sheet. Use two forks to shred the pork. Serve the shredded pork hot with the cooked cabbage. Reserve the liquid from the slow cooker to remoisten the pork and cabbage when reheating leftovers.

Nutrition facts:
Calories: 451
Fat: 19.3g
Fiber: 11.2g
Carbohydrates:2.1 g
Protein: 14.3g

➤Beef Wellington

Preparation Time: 20 minutes
Cooking Time: 40 minutes
Servings: 4
Ingredients:
2 (4-ounce) grass-fed beef tenderloin steaks, halved
Salt and ground black pepper, as required
1 tablespoon butter
1 cup mozzarella cheese, shredded
1/2 cup almond flour
4 tablespoons liver pâté
Directions:
Preheat your oven to 400°F. Grease a baking sheet. Season the steaks with pepper and salt. Sear the beef steaks for about 2–3 minutes per side. In a microwave-safe bowl, add the mozzarella cheese and microwave for about 1 minute. Remove from the microwave and stir the almond flour until a dough forms. Place the dough between 2 parchment paper pieces and, with a rolling pin, roll to flatten it. Remove the upper parchment paper piece. Divide the rolled dough into four pieces. Place one tablespoon of pâté onto each dough piece and top with one steak piece. Cover each steak piece with dough completely. Arrange the covered steak pieces onto the prepared baking sheet in a single layer. Baking time: 20-30 minutes. Serve warm.
Nutrition facts:
Calories: 412
Fat: 15.6g

Fiber: 9.1g
Carbohydrates:4.9 g
Protein: 18.5g

➤Sticky Pork Ribs

Preparation Time: 25 minutes
Cooking Time: 90 minutes
Servings: 8
Ingredients:
1/4 cups granulated erythritol
1 tablespoon garlic powder
1 tablespoon paprika
1/2 teaspoon red chili powder
4 pounds pork ribs, membrane removed
Salt and ground black pepper, as required
1/2 teaspoons liquid smoke
1/2 cups sugar-free BBQ sauce
Directions:
Preheat your oven to 300°F. In a bowl, mix well erythritol, garlic powder, paprika, and chili powder. Season the ribs with pepper and salt. And then coat with the liquid smoke. Now, rub the ribs evenly with erythritol mixture. Arrange ribs onto the prepared baking sheet, meaty side down. Arrange two layers of foil on top of ribs and then roll and crimp edges tightly. Bake for about 2–2 1/2 hours or until the desired doneness. Now, set the oven to broiler. Cut the ribs into serving-sized portions and evenly coat with the barbecue sauce. Arrange the ribs onto a broiler pan, bony side up. Broil for about 1–2 minutes per side. Remove from the oven and serve hot.
Nutrition facts:
Calories: 415
Fat: 18.1g
Fiber: 12.5g
Carbohydrates:3.1 g
Protein: 18.5g

➤Creamy Pork and Celeriac Gratin

Preparation Time: 20 minutes
Cooking Time: 60 minutes
Servings: 4
Ingredients:
1/2 lb. celeriac, peeled and thinly sliced
1/3 cup almond milk
1/2 cup heavy cream
1/4 tsp. nutmeg powder
Salt and black pepper to taste
1 tbsp. olive oil
1 lb. ground pork
1/2 medium white onion
chopped 1 garlic clove, minced
1/2 tsp. unsweetened tomato paste
3 tbsp. butter for greasing
1 cup crumbled queso fresco cheese
1 tbsp. chopped fresh parsley for garnish
Directions:
Let the oven preheat to 375F. In a saucepan, add the

celeriac, almond milk, heavy cream, nutmeg powder, and salt.
Cook until the celeriac softens. Drain afterward and set aside. Heat oil and cook the pork for 5 minutes or starting to brown season with salt and black pepper. Stir in the onion, garlic, and cook for 5 minutes or until the onions soften. The tomato paste must be added and continue cooking. Grease a baking dish and lay half of the celeriac on the bottom of the dish. Spread the tomato-pork sauce on top and cover with the remaining celeriac. Finish the topping with the queso fresco cheese. Let the gratin bake for about 45 minutes or until the cheese melts and is golden brown. Remove from the oven to cool for 5 to 10 minutes, garnish with the parsley, and serve afterward.
Nutrition facts:
Calories: 486
Fat: 19.4g
Fiber: 10.3g
Carbohydrates:8.5 g
Protein:19.2 g

➤BBQ Pulled Beef

Preparation Time: 15 minutes
Cooking Time: 6 hrs.
Servings: 10
Ingredients:
3 lbs. boneless chuck roast
2 tablespoons of salt
2 tablespoon of garlic powder
1 tablespoon of onion powder
1/4 apple cider vinegar
2 tablespoons of coconut aminos
1/2 cup of bone broth
1/4 cup of melted butter
1 tablespoon of black pepper
1 tablespoon of smoked paprika
2 tablespoon of tomato paste
Directions:
Mix salt, onion, paprika, black pepper, and garlic. Next is to rub the mixture on the beef and then put the beef in a slow cooker. Use another bowl to melt butter. Then, add a tomato paste, coconut aminos, and vinegar. Pour it all over the beef. Next is to add the bone broth into the slow cooker by pouring it around the beef. Cook for about 6 hrs. After that, take out the beef and increase the temperature of the cooker so that the sauce can thicken. Tear the beef before adding it to the slow cooker and toss with the sauce
Nutrition facts:
Calories: 315
Fat: 17g
Fiber: 11.9g
Carbohydrates:4.1 g
Protein: 18.9g

➤Nut-stuffed Pork Chops

Preparation Time: 20 minutes

Cooking Time: 30 minutes
Servings: 4
Ingredients:
3 ounces goat cheese
1/2 cup chopped walnuts
1/4 cup toasted chopped almonds
1 teaspoon chopped fresh thyme
4 center-cut pork chops, butterflied
Sea salt
Freshly ground black pepper
2 tablespoons olive oil
Directions:
Preheat the oven to 400°F. In a container, stir together the goat cheese, walnuts, almonds, and thyme until well mixed. Season the pork chops inside and outside with salt and pepper. Stuff each chop, pushing the filling to the bottom of the cut section. Secure the stuffing with toothpicks through the meat. Heat oil. Pan sear the pork chops until they're browned on each side, about 10 minutes in total. Put the pork chops into a baking dish and roast the chops in the oven until cooked through about 20 minutes. Serve after removing the toothpicks.
Nutrition facts:
Calories: 425
Fat: 19.5g
Fiber: 7.9g
Carbohydrates:6.5 g
Protein: 19.4g

>Sesame Pork with Green Beans

Preparation Time: 5 minutes
Cooking Time: 10 minutes
Servings: 2
Ingredients:
2 boneless pork chops
Pink Himalayan salt
Freshly ground black pepper
2 tablespoons toasted sesame oil, divided
2 tablespoons soy sauce
1 teaspoon Sriracha sauce
1 cup fresh green beans
Directions:
On a cutting board, pat the pork chops dry with a paper towel. Slice the chops into strips and season with pink Himalayan salt and pepper. In a large skillet over medium-high heat, heat one tablespoon of sesame oil. Add the pork strips and cook for 7 minutes, stirring occasionally. In a small bowl, mix the remaining one tablespoon of sesame oil, the soy sauce, and the Sriracha sauce. Pour into the skillet with the pork. Add the green beans to the skillet, reduce the heat to medium-low, and simmer for 3 to 5 minutes. Divide the pork, green beans, and sauce between two wide, shallow bowls and serve.
Nutrition facts:
Calories: 387
Fat: 15.1g
Fiber: 10g

Carbohydrates:4.1 g
Protein:18.1 g

>Coconut and Lime Steak

Preparation Time: 25 minutes
Cooking Time: 15 minutes
Servings: 4
Ingredients:
2 pounds steak, grass-fed
1 tablespoon minced garlic
1 lime, zested
1 teaspoon ginger, grated
3/4 teaspoon sea salt
1 teaspoon red pepper flakes
2 tablespoons lime juice
1/2 cup coconut oil, melted
Directions:
Take a large bowl and add garlic, ginger, salt, red pepper flakes, lime juice, zest, pour in oil, and whisk until combined. Add the steaks, toss until well coated, and marinate at room temperature for 20 minutes. After 20 minutes, take a large skillet pan, place it over medium-high heat, and when hot, add steaks (cut steaks in half if they don't fit into the pan). Cook the steaks and then transfer them to a cutting board. Let steaks cool for 5 minutes, then slice across the grain and serve.
Nutrition facts:
Calories: 512
Fat: 17.9g
Fiber: 12.5g
Carbohydrates:4.9 g
Protein: 19.9g

>Shepherd's Pie

Preparation Time: 5 minutes
Cooking Time: 3-9 minutes
Servings: 2
Ingredients:
1/4 cup olive oil
1-pound grass-fed ground beef
1/2 cup celery, chopped
1/4 cup yellow onion, chopped
3 garlic cloves, minced
1 cup tomatoes, chopped
2 (12-ounce) packages cauliflower rice, cooked and well-drained
1 cup cheddar cheese, shredded
1/4 cup Parmesan cheese, shredded
1 cup heavy cream
1 teaspoon dried thyme
Directions:
Preheat your oven to 350°F. Heat oil heat and cook the ground beef, celery, onions, and garlic for about 8–10 minutes. Immediately stir in the tomatoes. Transfer mixture into a 10x7-inch casserole dish evenly. In a food processor, add the cauliflower, cheeses, cream, thyme, and pulse until a mashed potatoes-

like mixture is formed. Spread the cauliflower mixture over the meat in the casserole dish evenly. Bake for about 35–40 minutes. Cut into desired sized pieces and serve.

Nutrition facts:
Calories: 387
Fat: 11.5g
Fiber: 9.4g
Carbohydrates:5.5 g
Protein: 18.5g

➤Egg Roll Bowls

Preparation Time: 10minutes
Cooking Time: 30 minutes
Servings: 4
Ingredients:
1 tbsp. vegetable oil
1 clove garlic, minced
1 tbsp. minced fresh ginger
1 lb. ground pork
1 tbsp. sesame oil
1/2 onion, thinly sliced
1 c. shredded carrot
1/4 green cabbage, thinly sliced
1/4 c. soy sauce
1 tbsp. Sriracha
1 green onion, thinly sliced
1 tbsp. sesame seeds
Directions:
Heat oil. Put garlic and ginger and cook until fragrant, about 1 to 2 minutes. Cook Pork until no pink remains. Push pork to the side and add sesame oil. Put onion, carrot, and cabbage. Stir to combine with meat. Then put soy sauce and Sriracha. Stir and cook until cabbage is tender, about 6 to 8 minutes. Move and mixture to a serving dish. Garnish with sesame seeds and the green onions.
Nutrition facts:
Calories: 321
Fat: 15g
Fiber: 9.5g
Carbohydrates:5.1 g
Protein: 7.4g

➤Philly Cheese Steak Wraps

Preparation Time: 10 minutes
Cooking Time: 20 minutes
Servings: 4
Ingredients:
2 tbsp. vegetable oil, divided
1 large onion, thinly sliced
2 large bell peppers, thinly sliced
1 tsp. dried oregano
Kosher salt
Freshly ground black pepper
1 lb. skirt steak, thinly sliced
1 c. shredded provolone
8 large butterhead lettuce leaves

2tbsp. freshly chopped parsley
Directions:
Heat 1 tbsp. oil and put chopped onion and sliced bell peppers and sprinkle with oregano, salt, and pepper. Cook, often stirring, until the onion and pepper are tender, about 3-5 minutes. Transfer the cooked peppers and onions to a plate and add the remaining oil in the skillet. Put the steak in the skillet and spread a single layer, season with salt and pepper. Sear until the steak is seared on one side, about 2-3 minutes. Flip and sear on the second side until cooked through, about 2-3 minutes more for medium. Put the cooked and pepper back to skillet and mix to combine. Sprinkle the cheese over onions and steak. Cover the steak skillet with a lid and cook until the cheese has melted, turn off the heat. Lay the lettuce leaves on a serving platter. Top with steak mixture on each piece of lettuce. Garnish with parsley and serve warm.
Nutrition facts:
Calories: 375
Fat: 15.1g
Fiber: 12.9g
Carbohydrates:4.3 g
Protein: 17.5g

➤Creamy Dijon Pork Filet Mignon

Preparation time: 10 minutes
Cooking time: 10 minutes | **Servings:** 6
Ingredients:
2 teaspoons lard, at room temperature
2 pounds (907 g) pork filet mignon, cut into bite-sized chunks
Flaky salt and ground black pepper, to season
1 tablespoon Dijon mustard
1 cup double cream
Directions:
Melt the lard in a saucepan over moderate heat; now, sear the filet mignon for 2 to 3 minutes per side. Season with salt and pepper to taste. Fold in the Dijon mustard and cream. Low the heat to medium-low and continue to cook for a further 6 minutes or until the sauce has reduced slightly. Serve in individual plates, garnished with cauli rice if desired. Enjoy!
Nutrition facts (per serving)
calories: 302 | fat: 16.5g | protein: 34.1g | carbs: 2.2g | net carbs: 2.1g | fiber: 0.1g

➤Beef and Vegetable Skillet

Preparation Time: 5 minutes
Cooking Time: 15 minutes
Servings: 2
Ingredients:
3 oz spinach, chopped
1/2 pound ground beef
2 slices of bacon, diced2 oz chopped asparagus
Seasoning:
3 tbsp. coconut oil
2 tsp. dried thyme

2/3 tsp. salt
1/2 tsp. ground black pepper
Directions:
Take a skillet pan, place it over medium heat, add oil and when hot, add beef and bacon and cook for 5 to 7 minutes until slightly browned. Then add asparagus and spinach, sprinkle with thyme, stir well and cook for 7 to 10 minutes until thoroughly cooked. Season skillet with salt and black pepper and serve.
Nutrition facts:
Calories: 332
Fat: 18.4g
Fiber: 9.4g
Carbohydrates:3.8 g
Protein: 14.1g

➤Beef Taco Salad

Preparation Time: 10 minutes
Cooking Time: 10 minutes
Servings: 2
Ingredients:
1-pound ground beef (80/20)
1/4 teaspoon pink Himalayan Sea salt
1/4 teaspoon freshly ground black pepper
1/4 cup mayonnaise
2 tablespoons sugar-free ketchup
2 tablespoons yellow mustard
1 tablespoon dill relish
1 (8-ounce) bag shredded lettuce
1/2 cup sliced red onion
1/2 cup chopped ripe tomato
1 dill pickle, sliced
1/4 cup shredded cheddar cheese
Directions:
In a medium sauté pan or skillet, brown the ground beef, stirring, for 7 to 10 minutes. Season with the salt and pepper, then drain the meat, if desired.
In a small bowl, combine the mayonnaise, ketchup, mustard, and relish. Fill a large bowl with the shredded lettuce. Top with the beef, red onion, tomato, dill pickle, and cheese. Put dressing, serve.
Nutrition facts:
Calories: 398
Fat: 15.1g
Fiber: 12.9g
Carbohydrates:3.1 g
Protein: 14.8g

➤Meatballs

Preparation Time: 15 minutes
Cooking Time: 20 minutes
Servings: 4
Ingredients:
Meatballs
1-pound ground beef
1 tbsp. dried parsley
1/4 tsp. allspice
1/4 tsp. nutmeg

1/2 tsp. garlic powder
Salt and pepper, to taste
1/4 onion, diced
2 tbsp. butter
Beef Gravy
4 tbsp. butter
11/2 cups beef stock
1/2 cup heavy whipping cream
1/2 cup sour cream
2 tbsp. Worcestershire sauce
1/2 tbsp. Dijon mustard
Salt and pepper, to taste
Directions:
Combine the ground beef, dried parsley, allspice, nutmeg, garlic powder, salt, pepper, and onion in a large mixing bowl. Mix the mixture with your hands and shape into 20 even-sized balls. In a skillet, melt the butter and cook the meatball in batches. Cook the meatball on all sides until golden browned and baste with the butter, set aside. Heat the butter in a pan for the gravy, scrape up the browned bits from the bottom. Add the beef stock, whipping cream, sour cream, Worcestershire sauce, Dijon mustard, salt, and pepper in the pan, then whisk together. Mix the xanthan gum with a ladleful of sauce and Pour in the gravy, stirring continuously. Stir in the meatballs back to the gravy pan, coating the meatballs with the gravy. Simmer for another 15 minutes until cooked through. Serve mashed cauliflower.
Nutrition facts:
Calories: 378
Fat: 10.4g
Fiber: 5.3g
Carbohydrates:3.1 g
Protein: 17.5g

➤Roasted Pork Shoulder

Preparation time: 20 minutes
Cooking time: 60 minutes | **Servings:** 2
1 pound (454 g) pork shoulder
4 tablespoons red wine
1 teaspoon stone ground mustard
1 tablespoon coconut aminos
1 tablespoon lemon juice
1 tablespoon sesame oil
2 sprigs rosemary
1 teaspoon sage
1 shallot, peeled and chopped
½ celery stalk, chopped
½ head garlic, peeled and separated into cloves
Sea salt and freshly cracked black pepper

Place the pork shoulder, red wine, mustard, coconut aminos, lemon juice, sesame oil, rosemary, and sage in a ceramic dish; cover and let it marinate in your refrigerator at least 3 hours. Remove the marinade and place the pork shoulder in a lightly greased baking dish. Scatter the vegetables around the pork shoulder and sprinkle with salt and black pepper. Roast in the preheated oven at 390°F (199°C) for 15 minutes.

Now, reduce the temperature to 310°F (154°C) and continue baking an additional 40 to 45 minutes. Baste the meat with the reserved marinade once or twice. Place on cooling racks before carving and serving. Bon appétit!

Nutrition facts (per serving)
calories: 500 | fat: 35.4g | protein: 40.1g | carbs: 2.6g | net carbs: 2.1g | fiber: 0.5g

▸Spicy Pork and Spanish Onion

Preparation time: 10 minutes
Cooking time: 10 minutes | **Servings:** 2
1 tablespoon olive oil
2 pork cutlets
1 bell pepper, deveined and sliced
1 Spanish onion, chopped
2 garlic cloves, minced
½ teaspoon hot sauce
½ teaspoon mustard
½ teaspoon paprika
Coarse ground black pepper and sea salt

Preheat the olive oil in a medium-large saucepan over medium-high heat. Then, fry the pork cutlets for 3 to 4 minutes until evenly golden and crispy on both sides. Decrease the temperature to medium and add the bell pepper, Spanish onion, garlic, hot sauce, and mustard; continue cooking until the vegetables have softened, for a further 3 minutes. Sprinkle with paprika, salt, and black pepper. Serve immediately and enjoy!

Nutrition facts (per serving)
calories: 402 | fat: 24.2g | protein: 40.0g | carbs: 3.5g | net carbs: 2.7g | fiber: 0.8g

▸St. Louis Ribs

Preparation time: 10 minutes
Cooking time: 2 hours | Servings: 5
2 pounds (907 g) St. Louis-style pork ribs
1 teaspoon cayenne pepper
Flaky salt and ground black pepper, to season
4 tablespoons sesame oil
2 tablespoons Swerve
1 tablespoon coconut aminos soy sauce
1 teaspoon oyster sauce
1 cup tomato sauce, no sugar added
1 teaspoon Chinese five-spice
2 garlic cloves, pressed

Season the pork ribs with the cayenne pepper, salt, and black pepper. Arrange them on a tinfoil-lined baking pan. Cover with a piece of foil and bake in the preheated oven at 360°F (182°C) for 1 hour 30 minutes. In the meantime, thoroughly combine the remaining ingredients for the glaze; whisk to combine well and brush the glaze over the pork ribs. Continue to bake at 420°F (216°C) for 30 minutes longer. Bon appétit!

Nutrition facts (per serving)
calories: 371 | fat: 21.1g | protein: 38.7g | carbs: 4.2g | net carbs: 3.0g | fiber: 1.2g

▸Pork, Squash, and Mushroom Casserole

Preparation time: 15 minutes
Cooking time: 30 minutes | **Servings:** 4
1 pound (454 g) ground pork
1 large yellow squash, thinly sliced
Salt and black pepper to taste
1 clove garlic, minced
4 green onions, chopped
1 cup chopped cremini mushrooms
1 (15-ounce / 425-g) can diced tomatoes
½ cup pork rinds, crushed
¼ cup chopped parsley
1 cup cottage cheese
1 cup Mexican cheese blend
3 tablespoons olive oil
⅓ cup water
Directions:
Preheat the oven to 365/370°F (188°C). Preheat the olive oil in a skillet over medium-high heat, add the pork, season it with black pepper and salt, and cook for 3 minutes or until no longer pink. Stir occasionally while breaking any lumps apart. Add the garlic, mushrooms, half of the green onions, , and 2 tablespoons of pork rinds. Cook for 3 minutes. Stir in the tomatoes, half of the parsley, and water. Cook further for 3 minutes, and then turn the heat off. Mix the remaining parsley, cottage cheese, and Mexican cheese blend. Set aside. Sprinkle the bottom of a baking dish with 3 tablespoons of pork rinds: top with half of the squash and a season of salt, ⅔ of the pork mixture, and the cheese mixture. Repeat the layering process a second time to exhaust the ingredients. Cover the baking dish with foil and bake for 20 minutes. After, remove the foil and brown the top of the casserole with the broiler side of the oven for 2 minutes. Remove the dish when ready and serve warm.

Nutrition facts (per serving)
calories: 496 | fat: 29.1g | protein: 36.6g | carbs: 7.1g | net carbs: 2.6g | fiber: 4.5g

▸Beef Chili

Preparation Time: 10 minutes
Cooking Time: 50 minutes
Servings: 4
Ingredients:
½ medium green bell pepper, cored, seeded, and chopped
½ medium onion, chopped
2 tablespoons extra-virgin olive oil
1 tablespoon minced garlic
1-pound ground beef (80/20)
1 (14-ounce) can crushed tomatoes
1 cup beef broth
1 tablespoon ground cumin
1 tablespoon chili powder

2 teaspoons paprika
1 teaspoon pink Himalayan Sea salt
1/4 teaspoon cayenne pepper
Directions:
In a medium pot, combine the bell pepper, onion, and olive oil. Cook over medium heat for 8 to 10 minutes until the onion, is translucent. Add the garlic and sauté. Add the ground beef and cook for 7 to 10 minutes, until browned. Add the tomatoes, broth, cumin, chili powder, paprika, salt, and cayenne. Stir to combine. Simmer the chili for 30 minutes, until the flavors come together, then enjoy.
Nutrition facts:
Calories: 376
Fat: 18.4g
Fiber: 12g
Carbohydrates:3.2 g
Protein: 15.1g

➤Roasted Pork Loin with Brown Mustard Sauce

Preparation Time: 10 minutes
Cooking Time: 70 minutes
Servings: 8
Ingredients:
1 (2-pound) boneless pork loin roast
Sea salt
Freshly ground black pepper
3 tablespoons olive oil
11/2 cups decadent (whipping) cream
3 tablespoons grainy mustard, such as Pommery
Directions:
Preheat the oven to 370°F. Season the pork roast all over with pepper and sea salt. Heat oil then all the sides of the roast must be browned, about 5-6 minutes, and place the roast in a baking dish. When there are approximately 13-15 minutes of roasting time left, place a small/medium saucepan over medium-high heat and add the heavy cream and mustard. Stir the sauce until it simmers, then low the heat. Simmer the sauce until it is vibrant and thick, about 5 minutes. Remove the pan from the heat and set aside.
Nutrition facts:
Calories: 415
Fat: 18.4g
Fiber: 11.3g
Carbohydrates:3.1 g
Protein: 17.4g

➤Texas Chili

Preparation time: 20 minutes
Cooking time: 7 to 8 hours | **Servings:** 4
¼ cup extra-virgin olive oil
1½ pounds (680 g) beef sirloin, cut into 1-inch chunks
1 sweet onion, chopped
2 green bell peppers, chopped
1 jalapeño pepper, seeded, finely chopped
2 teaspoons minced garlic

1 (28-ounce / 794-g) can diced tomatoes
1 cup beef broth
3 tablespoons chili powder
½ teaspoon ground cumin
¼ teaspoon ground coriander
1 cup sour cream, for garnish
1 avocado, diced, for garnish
1 tablespoon cilantro, chopped, for garnish
Directions
Lightly grease the insert of the slow cooker with 1 tablespoon of the olive oil. In a medium/large skillet over medium-high heat, heat the remaining 2 tablespoons of the olive oil. Add the beef and sauté until it is cooked through, about 8 minutes. Add the onion, bell peppers, jalapeño pepper, and garlic, and sauté for an additional 4 minutes. Transfer the beef mixture to the insert and stir in the tomatoes, broth, chili powder, cumin, and coriander. Cook on low and cover for 8 hours. Serve topped with the sour cream, avocado, and cilantro.
Nutrition facts (per serving)
calories: 488 | fat: 38.1g | protein: 25.9g | carbs: 17.1g | net carbs: 10.2g | fiber: 6.9g

➤Chipotle Beef Spareribs

Preparation time: 15 minutes
Cooking time: 50 minutes | **Servings:** 4
2 tablespoons erythritol
Pink salt and black pepper to taste
1 tablespoon olive oil
3 teaspoons chipotle powder
1 teaspoon garlic powder
1 pound (454 g) beef spareribs
4 tablespoons sugar-free BBQ sauce plus extra for serving
Directions
Mix the erythritol, salt, pepper, oil, chipotle, and garlic powder. Brush on the meaty sides of the ribs and wrap in foil. Sit for 30 minutes to marinate. Preheat oven to 390/400°F (205°C), place wrapped ribs on a baking sheet, and cook for 40 minutes to be cooked through. Remove ribs and aluminum foil, brush with BBQ sauce, and brown under the broiler for 10 minutes on both sides. Slice and serve with extra BBQ sauce and lettuce tomato salad.
Nutrition facts (per serving)
calories: 396 | fat: 32.8g | protein: 20.9g | carbs: 3.7g | net carbs: 3.0g | fiber: 0.7g

➤Beef and Fennel Provençal

Preparation time: 10 minutes
Cooking time: 45 minutes | **Servings:** 4
12 ounces (340 g) beef steak racks
2 fennel bulbs, sliced
Salt and black pepper, to taste
3 tablespoons olive oil
½ cup apple cider vinegar
1 teaspoon herbs de Provence
1 tablespoon Swerve

Directions

In a bowl, mix the fennel with 2 tablespoons of oil, Swerve, and vinegar, toss to coat well, and set to a baking dish. Season with herbs de Provence, pepper and salt, and cook in the oven at 400°F (205°C) for 15 minutes. Sprinkle black pepper and salt to the beef, place into an oiled pan over medium heat, and cook for a couple of minutes. Place the beef to the baking dish with the fennel and bake for 20 minutes. Split everything among plates and enjoy.

Nutrition facts (per serving)

calories: 231 | fat: 11.4g | protein: 19.1g | carbs: 8.7g | net carbs: 5.1g | fiber: 3.6g

➤Pinwheel Beef and Spinach Steaks

Preparation time: 10 minutes
Cooking time: 35 minutes | **Servings:** 6
1½ pounds (680 g) beef flank steak
Salt and black pepper to taste
1 cup crumbled Feta cheese
½ loose cup baby spinach
1 jalapeño pepper, chopped
¼ cup chopped basil leaves ù

Directions

Preheat oven to 390/400°F (205°C) and grease a baking sheet with cooking spray. Wrap the steak in plastic wrap, place on a flat surface, and gently run a rolling pin over to flatten. Take off the wraps. Sprinkle with half of the Feta cheese, top with spinach, jalapeño, basil leaves, and the remaining cheese. Roll the steak over on the stuffing and secure with toothpicks. Place in the baking sheet and cook for 30 minutes, flipping once until nicely browned on the outside and the cheese melted within. Cool for 3 minutes, slice into pinwheels and serve with sautéed veggies.

Nutrition facts (per serving)

calories: 491 | fat: 41.0g | protein: 28.0g | carbs: 2.1g | net carbs: 2.0g | fiber: 0.1g

➤Cauliflower and Tomato Beef Curry

Preparation time: 10 minutes
Cooking time: 21 minutes | **Servings:** 6
1 tablespoon olive oil
1½ pounds (680 g) ground beef
1 tablespoon ginger-garlic paste
1 teaspoon garam masala
1 (7-ounce / 198-g) can whole tomatoes
1 head cauliflower, cut into florets
Pink salt and chili pepper to taste
¼ cup water

Directions

Heat oil in a saucepan over medium-high heat, add the beef, ginger-garlic paste and season with garam masala. Cook for 5 minutes while breaking any lumps. Stir in the tomatoes and cauliflower, season with salt and chili pepper, and cook covered for 6 minutes. Add the water and bring to a boil over medium heat for 10 minutes or until the water has reduced by half. Adjust taste with salt. Spoon the curry into serving bowls. Serve with shirataki rice.

Nutrition facts (per serving)

calories: 373 | fat: 32.8g | protein: 21.9g | carbs: 4.0g | net carbs: 2.2g | fiber: 2.8g

➤Zucchini and Beef Lasagna

Preparation time: 15 minutes
Cooking time: 45 minutes | **Servings:** 4
1 pound (454 g) ground beef
2 large zucchinis, sliced lengthwise
3 cloves garlic
1 medium white onion, finely chopped
3 tomatoes, chopped
Salt and black pepper to taste
2 teaspoons sweet paprika
1 teaspoon dried thyme
1 teaspoon dried basil
1 cup shredded Mozzarella cheese
1 tablespoon olive oil
Cooking spray

Directions

Preheat the oven to 360/370°F (188°C) and lightly grease a baking dish with cooking spray. Preheat the olive oil in a skillet and cook the beef for 4 minutes while breaking any lumps as you stir. Top with onion, garlic, tomatoes, salt, paprika, and pepper. Stir and continue cooking for 5 minutes. Then, lay ⅓ of the zucchini slices in the baking dish. Top with ⅓ of the beef mixture and repeat the layering process two more times with the same quantities. Season with basil and thyme. Sprinkle the Mozzarella cheese on top and tuck the baking dish in the oven. Bake for 35 minutes. Remove the lasagna and let it rest for 10 minutes before serving.

Nutrition facts (per serving)

calories: 346 | fat: 17.9g | protein: 40.2g | carbs: 5.5g | net carbs: 2.8g | fiber: 2.7g

➤Beef and Veggie-Stuffed Butternut Squash

Preparation time: 15 minutes
Cooking time: 60 minutes | **Servings:** 4
2 pounds (907 g) butternut squash, pricked with a fork
Salt and black pepper, to taste
3 garlic cloves, minced
1 onion, chopped
1 button mushroom, sliced
28 ounces (794 g) canned diced tomatoes
1 teaspoon dried oregano
¼ teaspoon cayenne pepper
½ teaspoon dried thyme
1 pound (454 g) ground beef
1 green bell pepper, chopped

Directions

Lay the butternut squash on a lined baking sheet, set in the oven at 400°F (205°C), and bake for 40 minutes. After, cut in half, set aside to let cool, deseed, scoop out most of the flesh and let sit. Heat a greased pan over medium-high heat, add in the garlic, mushrooms, onion, and beef, and cook until the meat browns. Stir in the green pepper, salt, thyme, tomatoes, oregano, black pepper, and cayenne, and cook for 10 minutes; stir in the flesh. Stuff the squash halves with the beef mixture and bake in the oven for 10 minutes. Split into plates and enjoy.

Nutrition facts (per serving)
calories: 405 | fat: 14.5g | protein: 33.8g | carbs: 20.7g | net carbs: 12.3g | fiber: 8.4g

›Beef and Broccoli Casserole

Preparation time: 15 minutes
Cooking time: 4 hours | **Servings:** 6
1 tablespoon olive oil
2 pounds (907 g) ground beef
1 head broccoli, cut into florets
Salt and black pepper, to taste
2 teaspoons mustard
2 teaspoons Worcestershire sauce
28 ounces (794 g) canned diced tomatoes
2 cups Mozzarella cheese, grated
16 ounces (454 g) tomato sauce
2 tablespoons fresh parsley, chopped
1 teaspoon dried oregano
Directions
Apply black pepper and salt to the broccoli florets, set them into a bowl, drizzle over the olive oil, and toss well to coat completely. In a separate bowl, combine the beef with Worcestershire sauce, salt, mustard, and black pepper, and stir well. Press on the slow cooker's bottom. Scatter in the broccoli, add the tomatoes, parsley, Mozzarella, oregano, and tomato sauce. Cook for 4 hours on low; covered. Split the casserole among bowls and enjoy while hot.

Nutrition facts (per serving)
calories: 435 | fat: 21.1g | protein: 50.9g | carbs: 13.5g | net carbs: 5.5g | fiber: 8.0g

›Beef and Dill Pickle Gratin

Preparation time: 15 minutes
Cooking time: 40 minutes | **Servings:** 5
2 teaspoons onion flakes
2 pounds (907 g) ground beef
2 garlic cloves, minced
Salt and black pepper, to taste
1 cup Mozzarella cheese, shredded
2 cups Fontina cheese, shredded
1 cup Russian dressing
2 tablespoons sesame seeds, toasted
20 dill pickle slices
1 iceberg lettuce head, torn
Directions
Set a pan over medium heat, place in beef, garlic, salt, onion flakes, and pepper, and cook for 5 minutes. Remove to a baking dish, stir in Russian dressing, Mozzarella, and spread 1 cup of the Fontina cheese. Lay the pickle slices on top, spread over the remaining Fontina cheese and sesame seeds, place in the oven at 340/350°F (180°C), and bake for 20 minutes.

Arrange the lettuce on a serving platter and top with the gratin.
Nutrition facts (per serving)
calories: 585 | fat: 48.1g | protein: 40.9g | carbs: 8.5g | net carbs: 5.2g | fiber: 3.3g

›Onion Sauced Beef Meatballs

Preparation time: 15 minutes
Cooking time: 30 minutes | **Servings:** 5
2 pounds (907 g) ground beef
Salt and black pepper, to taste
½ teaspoon garlic powder
1¼ tablespoons coconut aminos
1 cup beef stock
¾ cup almond flour
1 tablespoon fresh parsley, chopped
1 tablespoon dried onion flakes
1 onion, sliced
2 tablespoons butter
¼ cup sour cream
Directions
In a bowl, combine the beef with salt, garlic powder, almond flour, onion flakes, parsley, 1 tablespoon coconut aminos, black pepper, ¼ cup of beef stock. Form 6 patties, place them on a baking sheet, put in the oven at 370°F (188°C), and bake for 18 minutes. Set a pan with the butter over medium heat, stir in the onion, and cook for 3 minutes. Stir in the remaining beef stock, sour cream, and remaining coconut aminos, and bring to a simmer. Remove from heat, adjust the seasonings. Serve the meatballs topped with onion sauce.
Nutrition facts (per serving)
calories: 434 | fat: 22.9g | protein: 32.1g | carbs: 6.9g | net carbs: 6.1g | fiber: 0.8g

›Lemony Beef Rib Roast

Preparation time: 15 minutes
Cooking time: 35 minutes | **Servings:** 6
5 pounds (2.3 kg) beef rib roast, on the bone
3 heads garlic, cut in half
3 tablespoons olive oil
6 shallots, peeled and halved
2 lemons, zested and juiced
3 tablespoons mustard seeds
3 tablespoons Swerve
Salt and black pepper to taste
3 tablespoons thyme leaves
Directions
Preheat oven to 450°F (235°C). Place garlic heads and shallots in a roasting dish, toss with olive oil, and bake for 15 minutes. Pour lemon juice on them. Score shallow crisscrosses patterns on the meat and set aside. Mix Swerve, mustard seeds, thyme, salt, pepper, and lemon zest to make a rub; and apply it all over the beef. Place the beef on the shallots and garlic; cook in the oven for 15 minutes. Reduce the heat to 400°F (205°C), cover the dish with foil, and continue cooking

for 5 minutes. Once ready, remove the dish, and let sit covered for 15 minutes before slicing.

Nutrition facts (per serving)
calories: 555 | fat: 38.5g | protein: 58.3g | carbs: 7.7g | net carbs: 2.4g | fiber: 5.3g

‣Beef and Tomato Chili

Preparation time: 20 minutes
Cooking time: 40 minutes | **Servings:** 4
1 onion, chopped
1 tablespoons olive oil
2 pounds (907 g) ground beef
15 ounces (425 g) canned tomatoes with green chilies, chopped
3 ounces (85 g) tomato paste
½ cup pickled jalapeños, chopped
1 teaspoon chipotle chili paste
4 tablespoons garlic, minced
3 celery stalks, chopped
2 tablespoons coconut aminos
Salt and black pepper, to taste
A pinch of cayenne pepper
2 tablespoons cumin
1 teaspoon onion powder
1 teaspoon garlic powder
1 bay leaf
1 teaspoon chopped cilantro
Directions
Heat oil in a pan over medium-high heat, add in the onion, celery, garlic, beef, black pepper, and salt; cook until the meat browns. Stir in jalapeños, tomato paste, canned tomatoes with green chilies, salt, garlic powder, bay leaf, onion powder, cayenne, coconut aminos, chipotle chili paste, and cumin, and cook for 30 minutes while covered. Remove and discard bay leaf. Serve in bowls sprinkled with cilantro.
Nutrition facts (per serving)
calories: 435 | fat: 25.9g | protein: 16.9g | carbs: 7.9g | net carbs: 5.1g | fiber: 2.8g

‣Beef, Pancetta, and Mushroom Bourguignon

Preparation time: 15 minutes
Cooking time: 60 minutes | **Servings:** 4
3 tablespoons coconut oil
1 tablespoon dried parsley flakes
1 cup red wine
1 teaspoon dried thyme
Salt and black pepper, to taste
1 bay leaf
⅓ cup coconut flour
2 pounds (907 g) beef, cubed
12 small white onions
4 pancetta slices, chopped
2 garlic cloves, minced
½ pound (227 g) mushrooms, chopped
Directions
In a bowl, combine the wine with bay leaf, olive oil,

thyme, pepper, parsley, salt, and the beef cubes; set aside for 3 hours. Drain the meat and reserve the marinade. Toss the flour over the meat to coat. Heat a pan over medium heat, stir in the pancetta, and cook until slightly browned. Place in the onions and garlic and cook for 3 minutes. Stir-fry in the meat and mushrooms for 4-5 minutes. Pour in the marinade and 1 cup of water; cover and cook for 50 minutes. Season to taste and serve.
Nutrition facts (per serving)
calories: 434 | fat: 25.9g | protein: 44.8g | carbs: 11.5g | net carbs: 6.9g | fiber: 4.6g

‣Herbed Veggie and Beef Stew

Preparation time: 10 minutes
Cooking time: 25 minutes | **Servings:** 4
1 pound (454 g) ground beef
2 tablespoons olive oil
1 onion, chopped
2 garlic cloves, minced
14 ounces (397 g) canned diced tomatoes
1 tablespoon dried rosemary
1 tablespoon dried sage
1 tablespoon dried oregano
1 tablespoon dried basil
1 tablespoon dried marjoram
Salt and black pepper, to taste
2 carrots, sliced
2 celery stalks, chopped
1 cup vegetable broth
Directions
Set a pan over medium-high heat, add in the olive oil, onion, celery, and garlic, and sauté for 5 minutes. Place in the beef and cook for 6 minutes. Stir in the tomatoes, carrots, broth, black pepper, oregano, marjoram, basil, rosemary, salt, and sage, and simmer for 15 minutes. Serve and enjoy!
Nutrition facts (per serving)
calories: 254 | fat: 13.1g | protein: 29.9g | carbs: 10.1g | net carbs: 5.1g | fiber: 5.0g

‣Butternut Squash and Beef Stew

Preparation time: 15 minutes
Cooking time: 35 minutes | **Servings:** 4
3 teaspoons olive oil
1 pound (454 g) ground beef
1 cup beef stock
14 ounces (397 g) canned tomatoes with juice
1 tablespoon stevia
1 pound (454 g) butternut squash, chopped
1 tablespoon Worcestershire sauce
2 bay leaves
Salt and black pepper, to taste
1 onion, chopped
1 teaspoon dried sage
1 tablespoon garlic, minced
Directions
Set a pan over medium heat and heat olive oil, stir in

the onion, garlic, and beef, and cook for 10 minutes. Add in butternut squash, Worcestershire sauce, bay leaves, stevia, beef stock, canned tomatoes, and sage, and bring to a boil. Reduce heat, and simmer for 30 minutes. Remove and discard the bay leaves and adjust the seasonings. Split into bowls and enjoy.

Nutrition facts (per serving)
calories: 342 | fat: 17.1g | protein: 31.9g | carbs: 11.6g | net carbs: 7.4g | fiber: 4.2g

➤Veal with Ham and Sauerkraut

Preparation time: 15 minutes
Cooking time: 55 minutes | **Servings:** 4
1 pound (454 g) veal, cut into cubes
18 ounces (510 g) sauerkraut, rinsed and drained
Salt and black pepper, to taste
½ cup ham, chopped
1 onion, chopped
2 garlic cloves, minced
1 tablespoon butter
½ cup Parmesan cheese, grated
½ cup sour cream
Directions
Heat a pot with the butter over medium heat, add in the onion, and cook for 3 minutes. Stir in garlic, cook for 1-2 minute. Place in the veal and ham, cook until slightly browned. Place in the sauerkraut, and cook until the meat becomes tender, about 30 minutes. Stir in sour cream, pepper, and salt. Top with Parmesan cheese and bake for 20 minutes at 350°F (180°C).
Nutrition facts (per serving)
calories: 431 | fat: 26.9g | protein: 28.6g | carbs: 10.1g | net carbs: 5.9g | fiber: 4.2g

➤Double Cheese-Stuffed Venison

Preparation time: 10 minutes
Cooking time: 25 minutes | **Servings:** 8
2 pounds (907 g) venison tenderloin
2 garlic cloves, minced
2 tablespoons chopped almonds
½ cup Gorgonzola cheese
½ cup Feta cheese
1 teaspoon chopped onion
½ teaspoon salt
Directions
Preheat your grill to medium. Slice the tenderloin lengthwise to make a pocket for the filling. Combine the rest of the ingredients in a bowl. Stuff the tenderloin with the filling. Shut the meat with skewers and grill for as long as it takes to reach your desired density.
Nutrition facts (per serving)
calories: 196 | fat: 11.9g | protein: 25.1g | carbs: 2.1g | net carbs: 1.6g | fiber: 0.5g

➤Beef Steak with Mushrooms

Preparation time: 15 minutes

Cooking time: 25 minutes | **Servings:** 6
1 cup beef stock
4 tablespoons butter
¼ teaspoon garlic powder ¼ teaspoon onion powder
1 tablespoon coconut aminos
1½ teaspoons lemon pepper
1 pound (454 g) beef steak, cut into strips
Salt and black pepper, to taste
1 cup shiitake mushrooms, sliced
3 green onions, chopped
1 tablespoon Thai red curry paste
Directions
Melt butter in a pan over medium-high heat, add in the beef, season with garlic powder, salt, black pepper, and onion powder and cook for 4 minutes. Mix in the mushrooms and stir-fry for 5 minutes. Pour in the stock, coconut aminos, lemon pepper, and Thai curry paste and cook for 15 minutes. Serve sprinkled with the green onions.
Nutrition facts (per serving)
calories: 225 | fat: 15.1g | protein: 18.9g | carbs: 4.1g | net carbs: 2.9g | fiber: 1.2g

➤Simple Beef Burgers

Preparation time: 15 minutes
Cooking time: 20 minutes | **Servings:** 6
2 pounds (907 g) ground beef
1 tablespoon onion flakes
¾ cup almond flour
¼ cup beef broth
1 tablespoon chopped parsley
1 tablespoon Worcestershire sauce
Directions
Combine all ingredients in a bowl. Mix well with your hands and make 6 patties out of the mixture. Arrange on a lined baking sheet. Bake at 370°F (188°C), for about 18 minutes, until nice and crispy.
Nutrition facts (per serving)
calories: 355 | fat: 28.1g | protein: 27.1g | carbs: 3.2g | net carbs: 2.6g | fiber: 0.6g

➤Beef Tripe with Onions and Tomatoes

Preparation time: 10 minutes
Cooking time: 25 minutes | **Servings:** 6
1½ pounds (680 g) beef tripe
4 cups buttermilk
Salt to taste
2 teaspoons creole seasoning
3 tablespoons olive oil
2 large onions, sliced
3 tomatoes, diced
Directions
Put the tripe in a bowl and cover with buttermilk. Refrigerate for 3 hours to extract bitterness and gamey taste. Remove from buttermilk, pat dry with a paper towel, and season with salt and creole seasoning. Preheat 2 tablespoons of oil in a skillet over medium-high heat and brown the tripe on both sides for 6 minutes in total. Set aside. Add the remaining oil and

sauté the onions for 3 minutes until soft. Include the tomatoes and cook for 10 minutes. Pour in a few tablespoons of water if necessary. Put the tripe in the sauce and cook for 3 minutes. Adjust taste with salt and serve with low carb rice.

Nutrition facts (per serving)
calories: 341 | fat: 26.9g | protein: 21.9g | carbs: 2.7g | net carbs: 1.0g | fiber: 1.7g

➤Bacon and Beef Stew

Preparation time: 15 minutes
Cooking time: 1 hour 10 minutes
Servings: 6
8 ounces (227 g) bacon, chopped
4 pounds (1.8 kg) beef meat for stew, cubed
4 garlic cloves, minced
2 brown onions, chopped
2 tablespoons olive oil
4 tablespoons red vinegar
4 cups beef stock
2 tablespoons tomato purée
2 cinnamon sticks
3 lemon peel strips
½ cup fresh parsley, chopped
4 thyme sprigs
2 tablespoons butter
Salt and black pepper, to taste

Directions
Set a saucepan over medium heat and warm oil, add in the garlic, bacon, and onion, and cook for 5 minutes. Stir in the beef, cook until slightly brown.
Pour in the vinegar, black pepper, butter, lemon peel strips, stock, salt, tomato purée, cinnamon sticks and thyme; stir for 3 minutes. Cook for 1 hour while covered. Get rid of the thyme, lemon peel, and cinnamon sticks. Split into serving bowls and sprinkle with parsley to serve.

Nutrition facts (per serving)
calories: 591 | fat: 36.1g | protein: 63.1g | carbs: 8.1g | net carbs: 5.6g | fiber: 2.5g

➤Pork Rind Crusted Beef Meatballs

Preparation time: 10 minutes
Cooking time: 40 minutes | **Servings**: 5
½ cup pork rinds, crushed
1 egg
Salt and black pepper, to taste
1½ pounds (680 g) ground beef
10 ounces (283 g) canned onion soup
1 tablespoon almond flour
¼ cup free-sugar ketchup
3 teaspoons Worcestershire sauce
½ teaspoon dry mustard
¼ cup water

Directions
In a bowl, combine ⅓ cup of the onion soup with the beef, pepper, pork rinds, egg, and salt. Heat a pan over medium heat, shape the mixture into 12 meat-

balls. Brown in the pan for 12 minutes on both sides. In a separate bowl, combine well the rest of the soup with the almond flour, dry mustard, ketchup, Worcestershire sauce, and water. Pour this over the beef meatballs, cover the pan, and cook for 20 minutes as you stir occasionally. Split among serving bowls and serve.

Nutrition facts (per serving)
calories: 333 | fat: 18.1g | protein: 24.9g | carbs: 7.4g | net carbs: 6.9g | fiber: 0.5g

➤Skirt Steak

Preparation time: 10 minutes
Cooking time: 10 minutes | **Servings**: 2
¼ cup soy sauce
½ cup olive oil
Juice of 1 lime
2 tablespoons apple cider vinegar
1 pound (454 g) skirt steak
Pink Himalayan salt
Freshly ground black pepper
2 tablespoons butter
¼ cup chimichurri sauce

Directions
In a small/medium bowl, mix the soy sauce, olive oil, lime juice, and apple cider vinegar. Pour into a large zip-top bag. Add the skirt steak. at least all day or, ideally, overnight. Dry the steak with a paper towel. Season both sides of the steak with pepper and pink Himalayan salt. In a large skillet over high heat, melt the butter. Add the steak and sear for about 4 minutes on each side, until well browned. Transfer the steak to a chopping board to rest for at least 5 minutes. Slice the skirt steak against the grain. Divide the slices between two plates, top with the chimichurri sauce, and serve.

Nutrition facts (per serving)
calories: 715 | fat: 45.8g | protein: 69.8g | carbs: 5.9g | net carbs: 4.1g | fiber: 1.8g

➤Veal, Mushroom, and Green Bean Stew

Preparation time: 15 minutes
Cooking time: 1 hour 55 minutes
Servings: 6
2 tablespoons olive oil
3 pounds (1.4 kg) veal shoulder, cubed
1 onion, chopped
1 garlic clove, minced
Salt and black pepper, to taste
1 cup water
1½ cups red wine
12 ounces (340 g) canned tomato sauce
1 carrot, chopped
1 cup mushrooms, chopped
½ cup green beans
2 teaspoons dried oregano

Directions
Set a pot over medium heat and warm the oil. Brown the veal for 5-6 minutes. Stir in garlic and onion, cook

for 3 minutes. Place in the wine, oregano, carrot, black pepper, salt, tomato sauce, water, and mushrooms, bring to a boil, reduce the heat to low. Cook for 1 hour and a half, then add in the green beans and cook for 5 minutes. Adjust the seasoning and split among serving bowls to serve.

Nutrition facts (per serving)
calories: 416 | fat: 21.1g | protein: 44.2g | carbs: 7.3g | net carbs: 5.1g | fiber: 2.2g

›Italian Veal Cutlets with Pecorino

Preparation time: 15 minutes
Cooking time: 1 hour 5 minutes
Servings: 6
6 veal cutlets
½ cup Pecorino cheese, grated
6 provolone cheese slices
Salt and black pepper, to taste
4 cups tomato sauce
A pinch of garlic salt
2 tablespoons butter
2 tablespoons coconut oil, melted
1 teaspoon Italian seasoning
Directions
Season the veal cutlets with garlic salt, black pepper, and salt. Set a pan over medium-high heat and warm oil and butter, place in the veal, and cook until browned on all sides. Spread half of the tomato sauce on the bottom of a baking dish that is coated with some cooking spray. Place in the veal cutlets then spread with Italian seasoning and sprinkle over the remaining sauce. Set in the oven at 360°F (182°C) and bake for 40 minutes. Scatter with the provolone cheese, then sprinkle with Pecorino cheese, and bake for another 5 minutes until the cheese is golden and melted. Serve.

Nutrition facts (per serving)
calories: 363 | fat: 21.1g | protein: 26.1g | carbs: 8.4g | net carbs: 5.9g | fiber: 2.5g

›Beef & Cheddar-Stuffed Eggplants

Preparation Time: 15 minutes
Cooking Time: 30 minutes
Servings: 4
Ingredients:
2 eggplants
2 tbsp olive oil
1 ½ lb ground beef
1 medium red onion, chopped
1 roasted red pepper, chopped
Pink salt and black pepper to taste
1 cup yellow cheddar cheese, grated
2 tbsp dill, chopped
Directions:
Preheat oven to 350°F. Lay the eggplants on a flat surface, trim off the ends, and cut in half lengthwise. Scoop out the pulp from each half to make shells. Chop the pulp. Heat oil in a skillet over medium heat. Add the ground beef, red onion, pimiento, and eggplant pulp and season with salt and pepper.

Cook for 6 minutes while stirring to break up lumps until beef is no longer pink. Spoon the beef into the eggplant shells and sprinkle with cheddar cheese. Place on a greased baking sheet and cook to melt the cheese for 15 minutes until eggplant is tender. Serve warm topped with dill.

Nutrition facts:
Kcal 574
Fat 27.5g
Net Carbs 9.8g
Protein 61,8g

›Sweet Chipotle Grilled Beef Ribs

Preparation Time: 10 minutes
Cooking Time: 35 minutes
Servings: 4
Ingredients:
4 tbsp sugar-free BBQ sauce + extra for serving
2 tbsp erythritol
Pink salt and black pepper to taste
2 tbsp olive oil
2 tsp chipotle powder
1 tsp garlic powder
1 lb beef spareribs
Directions:
Mix the erythritol, salt, pepper, oil, chipotle, and garlic powder. Brush on the meaty sides of the ribs and wrap in foil. Sit for 30 minutes to marinate. Preheat oven to 400°F. Place wrapped ribs on a baking sheet and cook for 40 minutes until cooked through. Remove ribs and aluminum foil, brush with BBQ sauce, and brown under the broiler for 10 minutes on both sides.
Slice and serve with extra BBQ sauce and lettuce tomato salad.
Nutrition facts:
Kcal 395
Fat 33g
Net Carbs 3g
Protein 21g

›Grilled Sirloin Steak with Sauce Diane

Preparation Time: 10 minutes
Cooking Time: 25 minutes
Servings: 6
Ingredients:
Sirloin steak
1 ½ lb sirloin steak
Salt and black pepper to taste
1 tsp olive oil
Sauce Diane
1 tbsp olive oil
1 clove garlic, minced
1 cup sliced porcini mushrooms
1 small onion, finely diced
2 tbsp butter
1 tbsp Dijon mustard
2 tbsp Worcestershire sauce
¼ cup whiskey
2 cups heavy cream
Directions:

Put a grill pan over high heat and as it heats, brush the steak with oil, sprinkle with salt and pepper, and rub the seasoning into the meat with your hands. Cook the steak in the pan for 4 minutes on each side for medium-rare and transfer to a chopping board to rest for 4 minutes before slicing. Reserve the juice. Preheat the oil in a frying pan over medium-high heat and sauté the onion for 3 minutes. Add the butter, mushrooms, and garlic, and cook for a couple of minutes. Add the Worcestershire sauce, the reserved juice, and mustard. Stir and cook for 1 minute. Pour in the whiskey and cook further 1 minute until the sauce reduces by half. Swirl the pan and add the cream. Let it simmer to thicken for about 3 minutes. Adjust the taste with salt and pepper. Spoon the sauce over the steaks slices and serve with celeriac mash.

Nutrition facts:
Kcal 434
Fat 17g
Net Carbs 2.9g
Protein 36g

›Easy Zucchini Beef Lasagna

Preparation Time: 25 minutes
Cooking Time: 1 hour
Servings: 4
Ingredients:
1 lb ground beef
2 large zucchinis, sliced lengthwise
3 cloves garlic
1 medium white onion, chopped
3 tomatoes, chopped
Salt and black pepper to taste
2 tsp sweet paprika
1 tsp dried thyme
1 tsp dried basil
1 cup mozzarella cheese, shredded
1 tbsp olive oil
Directions:
Preheat the oven to 370°F. Preheat the olive oil in a skillet over medium-high heat. Cook the beef for 4 minutes while breaking any lumps as you stir. Top with onion, garlic, tomatoes, salt, paprika, and pepper. Stir and continue cooking for 5 minutes. Lay 1/3 of the zucchini slices in the baking dish. Top with 1/3 of the beef mixture and repeat the layering process two more times with the same quantities. Season with basil and thyme. Sprinkle the mozzarella cheese on top and tuck the baking dish in the oven. Bake for 35 minutes. Remove the lasagna and let it rest for 10 minutes before serving.

Nutrition facts:
Kcal 344
Fat 17.8g
Net Carbs 2.9g
Protein 40.4g

›Rib Roast with Roasted Shallots & Garlic

Preparation Time: 15 minutes

Cooking Time: 40 minutes
Servings: 6
Ingredients:
5 lb beef rib roast, on the bone
3 heads garlic, cut in half
3 tbsp olive oil
6 shallots, peeled and halved
2 lemons, zested and juiced
3 tbsp mustard seeds
3 tbsp swerve
Salt and black pepper to taste
3 tbsp thyme leaves
Directions:
Preheat oven to 400°F. Place garlic heads and shallots in a roasting dish, toss with olive oil, and bake for 15 minutes. Pour lemon juice on them. Score shallow crisscrosses patterns on the meat and set aside. Mix swerve, mustard seeds, thyme, salt, pepper, and lemon zest to make a rub and apply it all over the beef. Place the beef on the shallots and garlic and cook in the oven for 20 minutes. Once ready, remove the dish, and let sit covered for 15 minutes before slicing. Serve.

Nutrition facts:
Calories: 222
Fat: 29.7g
Carb: 3g,
Protein: 5g

›Habanero & Beef Balls

Preparation Time: 10 minutes
Cooking Time: 45 minutes
Servings: 6
Ingredients:
3 garlic cloves, minced
2 lb ground beef
1 onion, chopped
2 habanero peppers, chopped
1 tsp dried thyme
2 tsp fresh cilantro, chopped
½ tsp allspice
1 tsp cumin
½ tsp ground cloves
Salt and black pepper to taste
2 tbsp butter
3 tbsp butter, melted
6 oz cream cheese
1 tsp turmeric
¼ tsp stevia
½ tsp baking powder
1½ cups flax meal
½ cup coconut flour
Directions:
In a blender, mix the onion with garlic, habaneros, and ½ cup water. Set a pan over medium heat, add 2 tbsp butter, and cook the beef for 3 minutes. Stir in the mixture, and cook for 2 minutes. Stir in cilantro, cloves, salt, cumin, turmeric, thyme, allspice, and pepper and cook for 3 minutes. In a bowl, combine well the coconut flour, stevia, flax meal, and baking powder and stir well. In a separate bowl, whisk the melted butter with

the cream cheese. Mix the 2 mixtures to obtain a dough. Form 12 balls from the mixture and roll them into circles. Split the beef mix on one-half of the dough circles, cover with the other half, seal edges, and lay on a lined sheet. Bake for 25 minutes in the oven at 350°F.

Nutrition facts:
Kcal 455
Fat 31g
Net Carbs 8.3g
Protein 27g

▸Warm Rump Steak Salad

Preparation Time: minutes
Cooking Time: 40 minutes
Servings: 4
Ingredients:
1 lb rump steak, excess fat trimmed
3 green onions, sliced
3 tomatoes, sliced
1 cup cooked green beans, sliced
2 kohlrabies, peeled and chopped
1 tbsp butter, softened
2 cups mixed salad greens
Salt and black pepper to taste
Salad dressing
2 tsp Dijon mustard
1 tbsp erythritol
Salt and black pepper to taste
3 tbsp olive oil
1 tbsp red wine vinegar

Directions:
Preheat oven to 400°F. Place the kohlrabi on a baking sheet, drizzle with olive oil and bake in the oven for 25 minutes. Let it cool. In a bowl, mix the mustard, erythritol, salt, pepper, vinegar, and oil; reserve. Melt the butter in a pan over high heat. Season the meat with salt and pepper. Place the steak in the pan and brown on both sides for 4 minutes each. Remove and let it rest for 4 more minutes before slicing. In a salad bowl, add green onions, tomatoes, green beans, kohlrabi, salad greens, and steak slices. Drizzle the dressing over and toss with two spoons. Serve the steak salad warm with chunks of low carb bread.

Nutrition facts:
Kcal 325
Fat 19g
Net Carbs 4g
Protein 28g

▸Mustard-Lemon Beef

Preparation Time: 15 minutes
Cooking Time: 25 minutes
Servings: 4
Ingredients:
2 tbsp olive oil
1 tbsp fresh rosemary, chopped
2 garlic cloves, minced
1 ½ lb beef rump steak, thinly sliced
Salt and black pepper to taste
1 shallot, chopped

½ cup heavy cream
½ cup beef stock
1 tbsp mustard
2 tsp Worcestershire sauce
2 tsp lemon juice
1 tsp erythritol
2 tbsp butter
1 tbsp fresh rosemary, chopped
1 tbsp fresh thyme, chopped

Directions:
In a bowl, combine 1 tbsp of oil with black pepper, garlic, rosemary, and salt. Toss in the beef to coat and set aside for some minutes. Heat a pan with the rest of the oil over medium heat, place in the beef steak, cook for 5-6 minutes, flipping halfway through. Set aside and keep warm. Melt the butter in the pan. Add in the shallot and cook for 2 to 3 minutes. Stir in the stock, Worcestershire sauce, erythritol, thyme, cream, mustard, and rosemary and cook for 8 minutes. Mix in the lemon juice, pepper, and salt. Arrange the beef slices on serving plates, sprinkle over the sauce, and enjoy!

Nutrition facts:
Kcal 435
Fat 30g
Net Carbs 5g
Protein 32g

▸Ribeye Steak with Shitake Mushrooms

Preparation Time: 10 minutes
Cooking Time: 25 minutes
Servings: 4
Ingredients:
1 lb ribeye steaks
1 tbsp butter
2 tbsp olive oil
1 cup shitake mushrooms, sliced
Salt and black pepper to taste
2 tbsp fresh parsley, chopped

Directions:
Preheat the olive oil in a pan over medium-high heat. Rub the steaks with salt and black pepper and cook about 4 minutes per side; reserve. Melt the butter in the pan and cook the shitakes for 4 minutes. Scatter the parsley over and pour the mixture over the steaks to serve.

Nutrition facts:
Calories: 406
Fat: 21g
Carb: 11g,
Protein: 10g

▸Parsley Beef Burgers

Preparation Time: 10 minutes
Cooking Time: 25 minutes
Servings: 6
Ingredients:
2 lb ground beef
1 tbsp onion flakes
¾ cup almond flour
¼ cup beef broth

2 tbsp fresh parsley, chopped
1 tbsp Worcestershire sauce

Directions:
Combine all ingredients in a bowl. Mix well with your hands and make 6 patties out of the mixture. Arrange on a lined baking sheet. Bake at 370°F for about 18 minutes, until nice and crispy. Serve.

Nutrition facts:
Kcal 354
Fat: 28g
Net Carbs: 2.5g
Protein: 27g

➤Beef Cauliflower Curry

Preparation Time: 15 minutes
Cooking Time: 26 minutes
Servings: 6
Ingredients:
1 tbsp olive oil
1 ½ lb ground beef
1 tbsp ginger paste
1 tsp garam masala
1 (7 oz) can whole tomatoes
1 head cauliflower, cut into florets
Salt to taste
2 garlic cloves, minced
½ tsp hot paprika

Directions:
Heat oil in a saucepan over medium-high heat. Add the beef, ginger, garlic, garam masala, paprika, and salt and cook for 5 minutes while breaking any lumps. Stir in the tomatoes and cauliflower. Cook covered for 6 minutes. Add ½ cup water and bring to a boil. Simmer for 10 minutes or until the water has reduced by half. Spoon the curry into serving bowls.
Serve with shirataki rice.

Nutrition facts:
Kcal 374
Fat 33g
Net Carbs 2g
Protein 22g

➤Italian Beef Ragout

Preparation Time: 40 minutes
Cooking Time: 1 hour 55 minutes
Servings: 4
Ingredients:
1 lb chuck steak, cubed
2 tbsp olive oil
Salt and black pepper to taste
2 tbsp almond flour
1 onion, diced
½ cup dry white wine
1 red bell pepper, seeded and diced
2 tsp Worcestershire sauce
4 oz tomato puree
3 tsp smoked paprika
1 cup beef broth
2 tbsp fresh thyme, chopped
Directions:

Lightly dredge the meat in the almond flour. Place a large skillet over medium heat, add the olive oil to heat and then sauté the onion and bell pepper for 2-4 minutes. Stir in paprika.
Add the beef and cook for 10 minutes in total while turning them halfway. Stir in white wine and let it reduce by half, about 3 minutes. Add in Worcestershire sauce, tomato puree, beef broth, salt, and pepper. Let the mixture boil for 2 minutes, reduce the heat, and let simmer for 1 ½ hours, stirring often.
Serve garnished with thyme.

Nutrition facts:
Calories: 129.2
Fat: 4.7g
Carb: 16.3g,
Protein: 27g

➤Beef Meatballs

Preparation Time: 23 minutes
Cooking Time: 35 minutes
Servings: 4
Ingredients:
½ cup pork rinds, crushed
1 egg
Salt and black pepper to taste
1 ½ lb ground beef
10 oz canned onion soup
1 tbsp almond flour
¼ cup free-sugar ketchup
3 tsp Worcestershire sauce
½ tsp dry mustard

Directions:
In a bowl, combine 1/3 cup of the onion soup with the beef, pepper, pork rinds, egg, and salt. Shape the mixture into 12 meatballs. Heat a greased pan over medium heat. Brown the meatballs for 12 minutes. In a separate bowl, combine well the rest of the soup with the almond flour, dry mustard, ketchup, Worcestershire sauce, and ¼ cup water. Pour this over the beef meatballs, cover the pan, and cook for 10 minutes as you stir occasionally. Split among bowls and serve.

Nutrition facts:
Kcal 332
Fat 18g
Net Carbs 7g
Protein 25g

➤Beef & Ale Pot Roast

Preparation Time: 30 minutes
Cooking Time: 2 hours 20 minutes
Servings: 6
Ingredients:
1 ½ lb brisket
2 tbsp olive oil
8 baby carrots, peeled
2 medium red onions, quartered
1 celery stalk, cut into chunks
Salt and black pepper to taste
2 bay leaves

1 ½ cups low carb beer (ale)

Directions:
Preheat oven to 370ºF. Preheat the olive oil in a medium/large skillet over medium heat. Season the brisket with salt and pepper. Brown the meat on both sides for 8 minutes. After, transfer to a deep casserole dish. In the dish, arrange the carrots, onions, celery, and bay leaves around the brisket and pour the beer all over it. Cover the pot and cook in the oven for 2 hours. When ready, remove the casserole. Transfer the beef to a chopping board and cut it into thick slices. Serve the beef and vegetables with a drizzle of the sauce.

Nutrition facts:
Calories: 302.2
Fat: 22.7g
Carb: 9.3g,
Protein: 8g

›Beef Tripe Pot

Preparation Time: 10 minutes
Cooking Time: 1 hour 30 minutes
Servings: 6
Ingredients:
1 ½ lb beef tripe, cleaned
4 cups buttermilk
Salt and black pepper to taste
3 tbsp olive oil
2 onions, sliced
4 garlic cloves, minced
3 tomatoes, diced
1 tsp paprika
2 chili peppers, minced

Directions:
Put the tripe in a bowl and cover with buttermilk. Refrigerate for 3 hours to extract bitterness and gamey taste. Remove from buttermilk, drain and rinse well under cold running water. Place in a pot over medium heat and cover with water. Bring to a boil and cook about for 1 hour until tender. Remove the tripe with a perforated spoon and let cool. Strain the broth and reserve. Chop the cooled tripe. Heat the oil over medium-high heat. Sauté the onions, garlic, and chili peppers for 3 minutes until soft. Stir in the paprika and add in the tripe. Cook for 5-6 minutes. Include the tomatoes and 4 cups of the reserved tripe broth and cook for 10 minutes. Adjust the seasoning with salt and pepper. Serve.

Nutrition facts:
Kcal 248
Fat 12.8g
Net Carbs 4g
Protein 8g

›Beef Stovies

Preparation Time: 12 minutes
Cooking Time: 45 minutes
Servings: 4
Ingredients:
1 lb ground beef

1 large onion, chopped
2 parsnips, peeled and chopped
1 large carrot, chopped
2 tbsp olive oil
2 garlic cloves, minced
Salt and black pepper to taste
1 cup chicken broth
¼ tsp allspice
2 tsp fresh rosemary, chopped
1 tbsp Worcestershire sauce
½ small cabbage, shredded

Directions:
Preheat the olive oil in a skillet over medium-high heat and cook the beef for 4 minutes. Season with salt and pepper, stirring occasionally while breaking the lumps in it. Add in onion, garlic, carrot, rosemary, and parsnips. Stir and cook for a minute, and pour in the chicken broth, allspice, and Worcestershire sauce. Low the heat and cook for 18-20 minutes. Stir in the cabbage, season with salt and black pepper, and cook further for 15 minutes. Turn the heat off, plate the stovies, and serve warm.

Nutrition facts:
Kcal 316
Fat 18g
Net Carbs 3g
Protein 14g

›Cauli Rice & Chicken Collard Wraps

Cooking Time: 30 minutes
Preparation Time: 10 minutes
Servings: 4
Ingredients:
2 tbsp avocado oil
2 garlic cloves, minced
1 large yellow onion, chopped
1 jalapeño pepper, chopped
Salt and black pepper to taste
1 cup cauliflower rice
1 ½ lb chicken breasts, cubed
8 collard leaves
¼ cup crème fraiche
2 tsp hot sauce

Directions:
Heat avocado oil in a deep skillet and sauté onion and garlic until softened, 3 minutes. Stir in jalapeño pepper salt, and pepper. Mix in chicken and cook until no longer pink on all sides, 10 minutes. Add in cauliflower rice and hot sauce. Sauté until the cauliflower slightly softens, 3 minutes. Lay out the collards on a clean flat surface and spoon the curried mixture onto the middle part of the leaves, about 3 tbsp per leaf. Spoon crème fraiche on top, wrap the leaves, and serve immediately.

Nutrition facts:
Cal 437
Net Carbs 1.8g
Fat 28g
Protein 38g

›Stuffed Peppers with Chicken & Broccoli

Preparation Time: 35 minutes
Cooking Time: 2 hours
Servings: 6
Ingredients:
6 yellow bell peppers, halved
1 ½ tbsp olive oil
3 tbsp butter
3 garlic cloves, minced
½ white onion, chopped
2 lb ground chicken
3 tsp taco seasoning
1 cup broccoli rice
¼ cup grated cheddar cheese
Crème fraiche for serving
Directions:
Preheat oven to 400 F. Drizzle bell peppers with olive oil. Melt butter in a skillet and sauté garlic and onion for 3 minutes. Stir in chicken and taco seasoning. Cook for 8 minutes. Mix in broccoli. Top with cheddar cheese, and place in a greased baking dish. Bake for 29-32 minutes, or until the cheese melts. Top with the crème fraiche and serve.
Nutrition facts:
Cal 386
Net Carbs 11g
Fat 24g
Protein 30g

›Grilled Chicken Kebabs with Curry & Yogurt

Preparation Time: 10 minutes
Cooking Time: 15 minutes
Servings: 4
Ingredients:
1 ½ lb boneless chicken thighs
½ cup Greek yogurt
Salt and black pepper to taste
2 tbsp curry powder
1 tbsp olive oil
Directions:
Preheat oven to 380 F. In a bowl, combine Greek yogurt, salt, pepper, curry, and olive oil. Mix in chicken, cover the bowl with a plastic wrap and marinate for 20 minutes. Remove the wrap and thread the chicken onto skewers. Grill in the middle for 4 minutes on each side or until fully cooked. Remove the chicken skewers and serve with cauliflower rice or steamed green beans.
Nutrition facts:
Cal 440
Net Carbs 0.5g
Fat 29g
Protein 41g

›Chicken with Tomato and Zucchini

Preparation Time: 10 minutes

Cooking Time: 45 minutes
Ingredients:
Servings: 4
2 tbsp ghee
1 lb chicken thighs
2 cloves garlic, minced
1 (14 oz) can whole tomatoes
1 zucchini, diced
10 fresh basil leaves, chopped
Directions:
Melt ghee in a saucepan and fry chicken for 4 minutes on each side. Remove to a plate. Sauté garlic in the same saucepan for 2 minutes, pour in tomatoes, and cook for 8 minutes. Add in zucchini and cook for 4 minutes. Stir and add the chicken. Coat with sauce and simmer for 3 minutes. Serve chicken with sauce garnished with basil.
Nutrition facts:
Cal 468
Net Carbs 2g
Fat 39g
Protein 26g

›Cream Cheese & Turkey Pastrami Rolls

Preparation Time: 20 minutes
Cooking Time: 2 hours 40 minutes
Servings: 4
Ingredients:
10 canned pepperoncini peppers, sliced and drained
8 oz softened cream cheese
10 oz turkey pastrami, sliced
Directions:
Lay a plastic wrap on a flat surface and arrange the pastrami all over, slightly overlapping each other. Spread the cheese on top of the salami and arrange the pepperoncini on top. Hold 2 opposite ends of the plastic wrap and roll the pastrami. Twist both ends to tighten and refrigerate for 2 hours. Slice into 2-inch pinwheels. Serve.
Nutrition facts:
Cal 266
Net Carbs 1g
Fat 24g
Protein 13g

›Almond Crusted Chicken Zucchini Stacks

Preparation Time: 20 minutes
Cooking Time: 30 minutes
Servings: 4
Ingredients:
1 ½ lb chicken thighs, skinless and boneless, cut into strips
3 tbsp almond flour
Salt and black pepper to taste
2 large zucchinis, sliced
4 tbsp olive oil
2 tsp Italian mixed herb blend

½ cup chicken broth

Directions:
Preheat oven to 400 F. In a zipper bag, add almond flour, salt, and pepper. Mix and add the chicken strips. Seal the bag and shake to coat.
Arrange the zucchinis on a greased baking sheet. Put salt, pepper and 2 tbsp of olive oil.
Remove the chicken from the almond flour mixture, shake off, and put 2-3 chicken strips on each zucchini. Season with herb blend and drizzle again with the remaining olive oil. Bake for 8 minutes; then pour in broth. Bake further for 10 minutes.
Serve warm.

Nutrition facts:
Cal 512
Net Carbs 1.2g
Fat 42g
Protein 29g

›Paleo Coconut Flour Chicken Nuggets

Preparation Time: 10 minutes
Cooking Time: 30 minutes
Servings: 2
Ingredients:
½ cup coconut flour
1 egg
2 tbsp garlic powder
2 chicken breasts, cubed
Salt and black pepper, to taste
½ cup butter

Directions:
In a bowl, combine salt, garlic powder, flour, and pepper and stir. In a separate bowl, beat the egg.
Add the chicken in egg mixture, then in the flour mixture. Set a pan over medium-high heat and warm butter. Add in chicken nuggets, and cook for 6 minutes on each side. Remove to paper towels, drain the excess grease, and serve.

Nutrition facts:
Cal 417
Net Carbs 4.3g
Fat 37g
Protein 35g

›Buffalo Wings

Preparation Time: 5 minutes
Cooking Time: 12 minutes
Servings: 4
Ingredients:
2 pounds (907 g) chicken wings, patted dry
1 teaspoon seasoned salt
¼ teaspoon pepper
½ teaspoon garlic powder
¼ cup buffalo sauce
3/4 cup chicken broth
1/3 cup blue cheese crumbles
¼ cup cooked bacon crumbles
2 stalks green onion, sliced
Directions:

Season the chicken wings with salt, garlic powder and pepper. Pour the buffalo sauce and broth into the Instant Pot. Stir in the chicken wings. Lock the lid cook 12 minutes at High Pressure. Once cooking is complete, do a quick pressure release. Carefully open the lid. Gently stir to coat wings with the sauce.
If you prefer crispier wings, you can broil them for 3 to 5 minutes until the skin is crispy. Remove the chicken wings from the pot to a plate. Brush them with the leftover sauce and serve topped with the blue cheese, bacon, and green onions.

Nutrition facts:
calories: 536
fat: 37.3g
protein: 47.1g
carbs: 1.0g
net carbs: 0.8g
fiber: 0.2g

›Sesame Chicken

Preparation Time: 5 minutes
Cooking Time: 24 minutes
Servings: 4
Ingredients:
1 pound (454 g) boneless, skinless chicken thighs, cut into bite-sized pieces and patted dry
Fine sea salt, to taste
2 tablespoons avocado oil or coconut oil
1 clove garlic, smashed to a paste
½ cup chicken broth
1/2 cup coconut aminos
1/3 cup Swerve
2 tablespoons toasted sesame oil
1 tablespoon lime juice
¼ teaspoon peeled and grated fresh ginger
For Garnish:
Sesame seeds
Sliced green onions
Directions:
Season all sides of chicken thighs with salt.
Set your Instant Pot to Sauté and heat the avocado oil. Add the chicken thighs and sear for about 4 minutes, or until lightly browned on all sides. Remove the chicken and set aside. Put ingredients to the Instant Pot and cook for 10 minutes, stirring occasionally, thicken the sauce. Return the chicken thighs to the pot and cook for 10 minutes, stirring occasionally, or until the chicken is cooked through. Sprinkle green onions and the sesame seeds on top for garnish and serve.

Nutrition facts:
calories: 359
fat: 29.3g
protein: 20.5g
carbs: 3.1g
net carbs: 3.0g
fiber: 1.0g

›Greek Chicken Salad

Preparation Time: 10 minutes
Cooking Time: 14 minutes

Servings: 4
Ingredients:
4 bone-in, skin-on chicken thighs
1 teaspoon fine sea salt
¾ teaspoon ground black pepper
2 tablespoons unsalted butter
2 cloves garlic, minced
¼ cup red wine vinegar
2 tablespoons lemon or lime juice
2 teaspoons Dijon mustard
½ teaspoon dried oregano leaves
½ teaspoon dried basil leaves
Greek Salad:
2 cups Greek olives, pitted
1 medium tomato, diced
1 medium cucumber, diced
¼ cup diced red onions
2 tablespoons extra-virgin olive oil
4 sprigs fresh oregano
1 cup crumbled feta cheese, for garnish
Directions:
Sprinkle the chicken thighs with the pepper and salt.
Set your Instant Pot to Sauté and melt the butter.
To the Instant Pot add the chicken thighs, skin-side down. Add the garlic and sauté for 4 minutes until golden brown. Turn the chicken thighs over and stir in the vinegar, lemon juice, mustard, oregano, and basil. Secure the lid cook 10 minutes at High Pressure. Once cooking is complete, do a quick pressure release. Carefully open the lid. Meanwhile, toss all the salad ingredients except the cheese in a large serving dish. When the chicken is finished, take ¼ cup of the liquid from the Instant Pot and stir into the salad.
Serve garnished with the cheese.
Nutrition facts:
calories: 581
fat: 44.3g
protein: 38.5g
carbs: 7.3g
net carbs: 6.0g
fiber: 1.3g

›Chicken Fajita Bowls

Preparation Time: 5 minutes
Cooking Time: 10 minutes
Servings: 3
Ingredients:
2 cups chicken broth
1 pound (454 g) chicken breasts
1 cup sauce
1 teaspoon paprika
1 teaspoon fine sea salt
1 teaspoon chili powder
½ teaspoon ground cumin
½ teaspoon ground black pepper
1 lime, halved
Directions:
Combine well all the ingredients except the lime in the Instant Pot. Lock the lid cook 10 minutes at High Pressure. When the timer beeps, perform a quick pressure release. Carefully remove the lid. Shred the chicken with two forks and return to the Instant Pot. Squeeze

the lime juice into the chicken mixture. Taste and add more salt, if needed. Give the mixture a good stir. Ladle the chicken mixture into bowls and serve.
Nutrition facts:
calories: 281
fat: 6.3g
protein: 51.5g
carbs: 5.9g
net carbs: 4.9g
fiber: 1.0g

›Ham-Wrapped Chicken

Preparation Time: 5 minutes
Cooking Time: 15 minutes
Servings: 5
Ingredients:
1½ cups water
5 chicken breast halves, butterflied
2 garlic cloves, halved
1 teaspoon marjoram
Sea salt, to taste
½ teaspoon red pepper flakes
¼ teaspoon ground black pepper
10 strips ham
Directions:
Pour the water into the Instant Pot and put the trivet. Rub the chicken breast halves with garlic. Sprinkle with marjoram, salt, red pepper flakes, and black pepper. Wrap each chicken breast into 2 ham strips and secure with toothpicks. Put the chicken on the trivet. Lock the lid. Select the Poultry mode and set the cooking time for 15 minutes at High Pressure. When the timer beeps, perform a natural pressure release for 10 minutes, then release any remaining pressure. Carefully remove the lid. Remove the toothpicks and serve warm.
Nutrition facts:
calories: 550
fat: 28.6g
protein: 68.5g
carbs: 1.0g
net carbs: 0.8g
fiber: 0.2g

›Creamy Chicken Cordon Bleu

Preparation Time: 12 minutes
Cooking Time: 15 minutes
Servings: 6
Ingredients:
4 boneless, skinless chicken breast halves, butterflied
4 (1-ounce / 28-g) slices Swiss cheese
8 (1-ounce / 28-g) slices ham
1 cup water
Chopped fresh flat-leaf parsley, for garnish
Sauce:
1½ ounces (43 g) cream cheese (3 tablespoons)
¼ cup chicken broth
1 tablespoon unsalted butter
¼ teaspoon ground black pepper
¼ teaspoon fine sea salt

Directions:

Lay the chicken breast halves on a clean work surface. Top each with a slice of Swiss cheese and 2 slices of ham. Roll the chicken around the ham and cheese, then secure with toothpicks. Set aside. Whisk together all the ingredients for the sauce in a small saucepan over medium heat, stirring. Place the chicken rolls, seam-side down, in a casserole dish. Set part of the sauce over the chicken rolls. Set the remaining sauce aside. Pour the water into the Instant Pot and insert the trivet. Place the dish on the trivet. Lock the lid cook 15 minutes at High Pressure. When the timer beeps, perform a natural pressure release for 10 minutes, then release any remaining pressure. Carefully remove the lid. Remove the chicken rolls from the Instant Pot to a plate. Put the remaining sauce over them and serve garnished with the parsley.

Nutrition facts:
calories: 314
fat: 13.6g
protein: 46.2g
carbs: 1.7g
net carbs: 1.7g
fiber: 0g

➤Cheesy Chicken Drumsticks

Preparation Time: 3 minutes
Cooking Time: 23 minutes
Servings: 5
Ingredients:
1 tablespoon olive oil
5 chicken drumsticks
½ cup chicken stock
¼ cup unsweetened coconut milk
¼ cup dry white wine
2 garlic cloves, minced
1 teaspoon shallot powder
½ teaspoon marjoram
½ teaspoon thyme
6 ounces (170 g) ricotta cheese
4 ounces (113 g) Cheddar cheese
½ teaspoon cayenne pepper
¼ teaspoon ground black pepper
Sea salt, to taste

Directions:
Heat the olive oil until sizzling. Add the chicken drumsticks and brown each side for 3 minutes. Stir in the chicken stock, milk, wine, garlic, shallot powder, marjoram, thyme. Cook 15 minutes at High Pressure. When the timer beeps, perform a natural pressure release for 10 minutes, then release any remaining pressure. Carefully remove the lid. Shred the chicken with two forks and return to the Instant Pot. Set your Instant Pot to Sauté again and add the remaining ingredients and stir well. Cook for another until the cheese is melted, or 2 minutes. Taste and add more salt, if desired. Serve immediately.

Nutrition facts:
calories: 413
fat: 24.3g

protein: 41.9g
carbs: 4.6g
net carbs: 4.0g
fiber: 0.6g

➤Curry Chicken Drumsticks

Preparation Time: 5 minutes
Cooking Time: 20 minutes
Servings: 4
Ingredients:
1½ pounds (680 g) chicken drumsticks
1 tablespoon Jamaican curry powder
1 teaspoon salt
1 cup chicken broth
½ medium onion, diced
½ teaspoon dried thyme

Directions:
Sprinkle the salt and curry powder over the chicken drumsticks. Place the chicken drumsticks into the Instant Pot, along with the remaining ingredients. Secure the lid cook 20 minutes at High Pressure. Once cooking is complete, do a quick pressure release. Carefully open the lid. Serve warm.

Nutrition facts:
calories: 290
fat: 14.6g
protein: 31.8g
carbs: 1.6g
net carbs: 1.3g
fiber: 0.3g

➤Parmesan Drumsticks

Preparation Time: 5 minutes
Cooking Time: 25 minutes
Servings: 4
Ingredients:
2 pounds (907 g) chicken drumsticks (about 8 pieces)
1 teaspoon salt
1 teaspoon dried parsley
½ teaspoon garlic powder
½ teaspoon dried oregano
¼ teaspoon pepper
1 cup water
1 stick butter
2 ounces (57 g) cream cheese, softened
½ cup grated Parmesan cheese
½ cup chicken broth
¼ cup heavy cream
1/8 teaspoon pepper

Directions:
Sprinkle the salt, parsley, garlic powder, oregano, and pepper evenly over the chicken drumsticks. Insert the trivet. Arrange the drumsticks on the trivet. Secure the lid cook 15 minutes at High Pressure. Once cooking is complete, do a quick pressure release. Carefully open the lid. Transfer the drumsticks to a foil-lined baking sheet and broil each side for 3-5 minutes, or until the skin begins to crisp. Meanwhile, pour the water out of the Instant Pot. Set your Instant

Pot to Sauté and melt the butter. Add the remaining ingredients to the Instant Pot and whisk to combine. Pour the sauce over the drumsticks and serve warm.

Nutrition facts:
calories: 788
fat: 55.8g
protein: 53.7g
carbs: 3.4g
net carbs: 3.3g
fiber: 0.1g

➤Chicken Legs with Mayo Sauce

Preparation Time: 5 minutes
Cooking Time: 20 minutes
Servings: 4
Ingredients:
4 chicken legs, bone-in, skinless
2 garlic cloves, peeled and halved
½ teaspoon coarse sea salt
½ teaspoon crushed red pepper flakes
¼ teaspoon ground black pepper
1 tablespoon olive oil
¼ cup chicken broth
Dipping Sauce:
¾ cup mayonnaise
2 tablespoons stone ground mustard
1 teaspoon fresh lemon juice
½ teaspoon Sriracha
For Garnish:
¼ cup roughly chopped fresh cilantro
Directions:
Rub the chicken legs with the garlic. Sprinkle with salt, red pepper flakes, and black pepper. Heat the olive oil. Add the chicken legs and brown for 4 to 5 minutes. Add a splash of chicken broth to deglaze the bottom of the pot. Pour the remaining chicken broth into the Instant Pot and mix well. Lock the lid cook 18 minutes at High Pressure. Whisk together the sauce ingredients in a small bowl. When the timer beeps, perform a natural pressure release for 10 minutes, then release any remaining pressure. Carefully remove the lid. Sprinkle the cilantro on top for garnish and serve with the prepared dipping sauce.
Nutrition facts:
calories: 487
fat: 42.9g
protein: 22.7g
carbs: 2.2g
net carbs: 1.5g
fiber: 0.7g

➤Chicken With Cheese Mushroom Sauce

Preparation Time: 8 minutes
Cooking Time: 14 minutes
Servings: 4
Ingredients:
2 tablespoons unsalted butter or coconut oil
2 cloves garlic, minced
¼ cup diced onions
2 cups sliced button or cremini mushrooms
4 boneless, skinless chicken breast halves
½ cup chicken broth
¼ cup heavy cream
1 teaspoon fine sea salt
1 teaspoon dried tarragon leaves
½ teaspoon dried thyme leaves
½ teaspoon ground black pepper
2 bay leaves
½ cup grated Parmesan cheese
Fresh thyme leaves, for garnish
Directions:
Melt the butter. Add the garlic, onions, and mushrooms and sauté for 4 minutes, stirring often, or until the onions are softened. Put remaining ingredients except the Parmesan and thyme leaves to the Instant Pot and stir to combine. Lock the lid, cook 10 minutes at High Pressure. When the timer beeps, perform a natural pressure release for 10 minutes, then release any remaining pressure. Carefully remove the lid. Add the Parmesan cheese to the Instant Pot with the sauce and stir until the cheese melts.
Serve garnished with the fresh thyme leaves.
Nutrition facts:
calories: 278
fat: 17.3g
protein: 27.5g
carbs: 5.1g
net carbs: 4.1g
fiber: 1.0g

➤Chicken Cacciatore

Preparation Time: 5 minutes
Cooking Time: 22 minutes
Servings: 4 to 5
Ingredients:
6 tablespoons coconut oil
5 chicken legs
1 bell pepper, diced
½ onion, chopped
1 (14-ounce / 397-g) can sugar-free or low-sugar diced tomatoes
½ teaspoon dried basil
½ teaspoon dried parsley
½ teaspoon kosher salt
½ teaspoon freshly ground black pepper
½ cup filtered water
Directions:
Press the Sauté button on the Instant Pot and melt the coconut oil. Add the chicken legs and sauté until the outside is browned. Remove the chicken and set aside. Add the bell pepper, onion, tomatoes, basil, parsley, salt, and pepper to the Instant Pot and cook for about 2 minutes. Put the chicken to the pot with water. Lock the lid and cook 18 minutes at High Pressure. Once cooking is complete, do a quick pressure release. Carefully open the lid. Serve warm.
Nutrition facts:
calories: 346
fat: 24.5g

protein: 26.8g
carbs: 5.0g
net carbs: 3.4g
fiber: 1.6g

➤Sauce Chicken Legs

Preparation Time: 5 minutes
Cooking Time: 16 minutes
Servings: 5
Ingredients:
5 chicken legs, skinless and boneless
½ teaspoon sea salt
Sauce:
1 cup puréed tomatoes
1 cup onion, chopped
1 jalapeño, chopped
2 bell peppers, deveined and chopped
2 tablespoons minced fresh cilantro
3 teaspoons lime juice
1 teaspoon granulated garlic
Directions:
Press the Sauté button to heat your Instant Pot.
Add the chicken legs and sear each side for 2 to 3 minutes until evenly browned. Season with sea salt.
Thoroughly combine all the ingredients for the sauce in a mixing bowl. Spoon the sauce mixture evenly over the browned chicken legs. Lock the lid. Select the Manual and set cook 10 minutes at High Pressure.
When the timer beeps, perform a natural pressure release for 10 minutes, then release any remaining pressure. Carefully remove the lid. Serve warm.
Nutrition facts:
calories: 357
fat: 11.6g
protein: 52.4g
carbs: 8.6g
net carbs: 7.0g
fiber: 1.6g

➤Chicken Liver Pâté

Preparation Time: 5 minutes
Cooking Time: 15 minutes
Servings: 8
Ingredients:
2 tablespoons olive oil
1 pound (454 g) chicken livers
2 garlic cloves, crushed
½ cup chopped leeks
1 tablespoon poultry seasonings
1 teaspoon dried rosemary
½ teaspoon paprika
½ teaspoon dried marjoram
½ teaspoon red pepper flakes
½ teaspoon ground black pepper
¼ teaspoon dried dill weed
Salt, to taste
1 cup water
1 tablespoon stone ground mustard
Directions:
Heat the olive oil. Add the chicken livers and sauté for

about 3 minutes until no longer pink. Add the remaining ingredients except the mustard to the Instant Pot and stir to combine. Lock the lid and cook 10 minutes at High Pressure. When the timer beeps, perform a quick pressure release. Carefully remove the lid.
Put mixture in food processor, along with the mustard. Pulse until the mixture is smooth. Serve immediately.
Nutrition facts:
calories: 112
fat: 6.9g
protein: 10.3g
carbs: 2.1g
net carbs: 1.7g
fiber: 0.4g

➤Barbecue Wings

Preparation Time: 5 minutes
Cooking Time: 12 minutes
Servings: 4
Ingredients:
1 pound (454 g) chicken wings
1 teaspoon salt
½ teaspoon pepper
¼ teaspoon garlic powder
1 cup sugar-free barbecue sauce, divided
1 cup water
Directions:
Toss the chicken wings with the salt, pepper, garlic powder, and half of barbecue sauce in a large bowl until well coated. Place the wings on the trivet.
Cook for 12 minutes at High Pressure. Once cooking is complete, do a quick pressure release. Carefully open the lid. Toss the wings with the remaining sauce. Serve immediately.
Nutrition facts:
calories: 239
fat: 15.2g
protein: 20.2g
carbs: 4.2g
net carbs: 4.1g
fiber: 0.1g

➤Curried Mustard Chicken Legs

Preparation Time: 10 minutes
Cooking Time: 20 minutes
Servings: 5
Ingredients:
5 chicken legs, boneless, skin-on
2 garlic cloves, halved
Sea salt, to taste
½ teaspoon smoked paprika
¼ teaspoon ground black pepper
2 teaspoons olive oil
1 tablespoon yellow mustard
1 teaspoon curry paste
4 strips pancetta, chopped
1 shallot, peeled and chopped
1 cup vegetable broth
Directions:
Rub the chicken legs with the garlic halves. Sprinkle

with salt, paprika, and black pepper. Set your Instant Pot to Sauté and heat the olive oil. Add the chicken legs and brown for 4 to 5 minutes. Add a splash of chicken broth to deglaze the bottom of the pot. Spread the chicken legs with mustard and curry paste. Add the pancetta strips, shallot, and remaining vegetable broth to the Instant Pot. Lock the lid. Select the Manual mode and set the cooking time for 14 minutes at High Pressure. When the timer beeps, perform a natural pressure release for 10 minutes, then release any remaining pressure. Carefully remove the lid. Serve warm.

Nutrition facts:
calories: 479
fat: 26.5g
protein: 53.1g
carbs: 4.3g
net carbs: 3.2g
fiber: 1.1g

›Lemony Mustard Pork Roast

Preparation time: 10 minutes
Cooking time: 60 minutes | **Servings:** 5
2 pounds (907 g) pork loin roast, trimmed
1½ tablespoons olive oil
1 tablespoon fresh lemon juice
1 tablespoon pork rub seasoning blend
1 tablespoon stone-ground mustard

Directions
Pat the pork loin roasts dry. Massage the pork loin roast with the olive oil. Then, sprinkle the lemon juice, pork rub seasoning blend, and mustard over all sides of the roast. Prepare a grill for indirect heat. Grill the pork loin roast over indirect heat for about 1 hour. Let the grilled pork loin stand for 10 minutes before slicing and serving. Bon appétit!

Nutrition facts (per serving)
calories: 385 | fat: 20.2g | protein: 48.0g | carbs: 0.1g | net carbs: 0g | fiber: 0.1g

›Italian Pork Sausage with Bell Peppers

Preparation time: 15 minutes
Cooking time: 20 minutes | **Servings:** 6
¼ cup olive oil
2 pounds (907 g) Italian pork sausage, chopped
1 onion, sliced
4 sun-dried tomatoes, sliced thin
Salt and black pepper, to taste
½ pound (227 g) Gruyere cheese, grated
3 yellow bell peppers, seeded and chopped
3 orange bell peppers, seeded and chopped
A pinch of red pepper flakes
½ cup fresh parsley, chopped

Directions
Set a pan over medium-high heat and warm oil, place in the sausage slices, cook each side for 2-4 minutes, remove to a bowl, and set aside. Stir in tomatoes, bell peppers, and onion, and cook for 5 minutes. Season with black pepper, pepper flakes, and salt and mix well. Cook for 1-2 minutes, remove from heat.

Lay sausage slices onto a baking dish, place the bell pepper mixture on top, scatter with the Gruyere cheese, set in the oven at 340ºF (171ºC). Bake for 10 minutes, until the cheese melts. Serve topped with parsley.

Nutrition facts (per serving)
calories: 566 | fat: 45.0g | protein: 34.0g | carbs: 9.7g | net carbs: 7.6g | fiber: 2.1g

›Chili with Meat

Preparation time: 15 minutes
Cooking time: 45 minutes | **Servings:** 4
2 ounces (57 g) bacon, diced
1 red onion, chopped
1 pound (454 g) ground pork
1 teaspoon ground cumin
2 cloves garlic, minced
1 teaspoon chipotle powder
Kosher salt and ground black pepper
½ cup beef broth
2 ripe tomatoes, crushed

Directions
Heat up a medium stockpot over a moderate flame. Cook the bacon until crisp, reserve. Cook the onion and ground pork in the bacon grease. Cook until the ground pork is no longer pink, and the onion just begins to brown. Stir in the ground cumin and garlic and continue to sauté for 30 seconds more or until aromatic. Add the chipotle powder, salt, black pepper, broth, and tomatoes to the pot. Cook, for 45 minutes and cover in part. You can add ¼ cup of water during the cooking, as needed. Serve with the reserved bacon and other favorite toppings. Enjoy!

Nutrition facts (per serving)
calories: 390 | fat: 29.8g | protein: 22.3g | carbs: 5.2g | net carbs: 3.7g | fiber: 1.5g

›Roasted Pork Loin with Collard

Preparation time: 10 minutes
Cooking time: 60 minutes | **Servings:** 4
2 tablespoons olive oil
Salt and black pepper, to taste
1½ pounds (680 g) pork loin
A pinch of dry mustard
1 teaspoon hot red pepper flakes
½ teaspoon ginger, minced
1 cup collard greens, chopped
2 garlic cloves, minced
½ lemon, sliced
¼ cup water

Directions
In a bowl, combine the ginger with salt, mustard, and black pepper. Add in the meat, toss to coat. Heat the oil. Brown the pork on all sides, for 15 minutes. Transfer to the oven and roast for 38-40 minutes at 390ºF (199ºC). To the saucepan, add collard greens, lemon slices, garlic, and water; cook for 10 minutes. Serve on a platter and sprinkle pan juices on top.

Nutrition facts (per serving)
calories: 431 | fat: 23.0g | protein: 45.0g | carbs: 3.6g

| net carbs: 3.0g | fiber: 0.6g

›Cumin Pork Chops

Preparation time: 10 minutes
Cooking time: 20 minutes | **Servings:** 4
4 pork chops
Salt and black pepper, to taste
3 tablespoons paprika
¾ cup cumin powder
1 teaspoon chili powder
Directions
In a bowl, combine the paprika with black pepper, cumin, salt, and chili. Place in the pork chops and rub them well. Heat a grill over medium temperature, add in the pork chops, cook for 5 minutes, flip, and cook for 5 minutes. Serve with steamed veggies.
Nutrition facts (per serving)
calories: 350 | fat: 18.6g | protein: 41.9g | carbs: 10.4g | net carbs: 3.9g | fiber: 6.5g

›Mediterranean Spiced Pork Roast

Preparation time: 10 minutes
Cooking time: 3 hours 50 minutes | **Servings:** 4
2 pounds (907 g) pork shoulder
2 tablespoons coconut aminos
½ cup red wine
1 tablespoon Dijon mustard
1 tablespoon Mediterranean spice mix
Directions
Place the pork shoulder, coconut aminos, wine, mustard, and Mediterranean spice mix in a ceramic dish. Cover and let it marinate in your refrigerator for 1 and a half/2 hours. Meanwhile, preheat your oven to 420°F (216°C). Place the pork shoulder on a rack set into a roasting pan. Roast for 15 to 20 minutes; reduce the heat to 330°F (166°C). Roast an additional 3 hours and 30 minutes, basting with the reserved marinade. Bon appétit!
Nutrition facts (per serving)
calories: 610 | fat: 40.2g | protein: 57.0g | carbs: 0.7g | net carbs: 0.6g | fiber: 0.1g

›Olla Podrida

Preparation time: 15 minutes
Cooking time: 40 minutes | **Servings:** 4
2 tablespoons olive oil
1½ pounds (680 g) pork ribs
1 yellow onion, chopped
2 garlic cloves, minced
2 Spanish peppers, chopped
1 Spanish Naga pepper, chopped
1 celery stalk, chopped
½ cup Marsala wine
8 ounces (227 g) button mushrooms, sliced
Sea salt and ground black pepper
1 teaspoon cayenne pepper
1 cup tomato purée

1 bay laurel
Directions:
Preheat 1 tablespoon of the olive oil in a stockpot over medium-high heat. Now, cook the pork ribs for 4 to 5 minutes per side or until brown; set aside. Then, heat the remaining tablespoon of olive oil and sauté the onion, garlic, peppers, and celery for 5 minutes more or until tender and fragrant. After that, add in a splash of red wine to scrape up the browned bits that stick to the bottom of the pot. Add the mushrooms, salt, black pepper, cayenne pepper, tomatoes, and bay laurel to the stockpot. When the mixture reaches boiling, turn the heat to a medium-low. Add the reserved pork back to the pot. Let it cook, partially covered, for 35 minutes. Serve warm and enjoy!
Nutrition facts (per serving)
calories: 360 | fat: 19.1g | protein: 38.2g | carbs: 4.9g | net carbs: 3.2g | fiber: 1.7g

›Spicy Pork Meatballs with Seeds

Preparation time: 15 minutes
Cooking time: 20 minutes | **Servings:** 2
1 tablespoon ground flax seeds
2 ounces (57 g) bacon rinds
½ pound (227 g) ground pork
1 garlic clove, minced
½ cup scallions, chopped
Sea salt and cayenne pepper, to taste
½ teaspoon smoked paprika
¼ teaspoon ground cumin
¼ teaspoon mustard seeds
½ teaspoon fennel seeds
½ teaspoon chili pepper flakes
2 tablespoons olive oil
Directions
In a mixing bowl, thoroughly combine well all ingredients, except for the olive oil, until well combined. Create balls and let them rest aside. Preheat the olive oil in a nonstick skillet and fry the meatballs for about 15 minutes or until cooked through. Serve with marinara sauce if desired. Bon appétit!
Nutrition facts (per serving)
calories: 558 | fat: 50.0g | protein: 0.6g | carbs: 2.2g | net carbs: 1.4g | fiber: 0.8g

›Pork Chops with Mushrooms

Preparation time: 10 minutes
Cooking time: 45 minutes | **Servings:** 3
8 ounces (227 g) mushrooms, sliced
1 teaspoon garlic powder
1 onion, peeled and chopped
1 cup heavy cream
3 pork chops, boneless
1 teaspoon ground nutmeg
¼ cup coconut oil
Directions
Set a pan over medium-high heat and warm the oil, add in the onion and mushrooms, and cook for

4 minutes. Stir in the pork chops, season with garlic powder, and nutmeg, and sear until browned. Put the pan in the oven at 340/350°F (180°C), and bake for 30 minutes. Remove pork chops to plates and maintain warm. Place the pan over medium heat, pour in the heavy cream over the mushroom mixture, and cook for 5 minutes; remove from heat. Sprinkle sauce over pork chops and enjoy.

Nutrition facts (per serving)
calories: 610 | fat: 40.1g | protein: 41.9g | carbs: 16.6g | net carbs: 6.7g | fiber: 9.9g

➤Pork Ragout

Preparation time: 15 minutes
Cooking time: 35 minutes | **Servings:** 2
1 teaspoon lard, melted at room temperature
¾ pound (340 g) pork butt, cut into bite-sized cubes
1 red bell pepper, deveined and chopped
1 poblano pepper, deveined and chopped
2 cloves garlic, pressed
½ cup leeks, chopped
Sea salt and ground black pepper
½ teaspoon mustard seeds
¼ teaspoon ground allspice
¼ teaspoon celery seeds
1 cup roasted vegetable broth
2 vine-ripe tomatoes, puréed
Directions
Melt the lard in a stockpot over moderate heat. Once hot, cook the pork cubes for 4 to 6 minutes, stirring occasionally to ensure even cooking. Then, stir in the vegetables and continue cooking until they are tender and fragrant. Add in the salt, black pepper, mustard seeds, allspice, celery seeds, roasted vegetable broth, and tomatoes. Reduce the heat to simmer. Let it simmer for 30 minutes longer or until everything is heated through. Ladle into individual bowls and serve hot. Bon appétit!

Nutrition facts (per serving)
calories: 390 | fat: 24.2g | protein: 33.0g | carbs: 5.3g | net carbs: 4.1g | fiber: 1.2g

➤Smoked Sausages with Peppers and Mushrooms

Preparation time: 10 minutes
Cooking time: 1 hour | **Servings:** 6
3 yellow bell peppers, seeded and chopped
2 pounds (907 g) smoked sausage, sliced
Salt and black pepper, to taste
2 pounds (907 g) portobello mushrooms, sliced
2 sweet onions, chopped
1 tablespoon Swerve
2 tablespoons olive oil
Arugula to garnish
Directions
In a baking dish, combine the sausages with Swerve, oil, black pepper, onion, bell peppers, salt, and mushrooms. Pour in 1 cup of water and toss well to ensure everything is coated, set in the oven at 320°F

(160°C) to bake for 1 hour. To serve, divide the sausages between plates and scatter over the arugula.

Nutrition facts (per serving)
calories: 524 | fat: 32.0g | protein: 28.9g | carbs: 14.4g | net carbs: 7.4g | fiber: 7.0g

➤Pork and Mixed Vegetable Stir-Fry

Preparation time: 10 minutes
Cooking time: 20 minutes | **Servings:** 4
1½ tablespoons butter
salt and chili pepper to taste
2 pounds pork loin strips
2 teaspoons ginger-garlic paste
¼ cup chicken broth
5 tablespoons peanut butter
2 cups mixed stir-fry vegetables
Directions
Melt the butter in a wok and mix the pork with salt, chili pepper, and ginger-garlic paste. Pour the pork into the wok and cook for 6 minutes until no longer pink. Mix the peanut butter with some broth until smooth, add to the pork and stir; cook for 2 minutes. Pour in the remaining broth, cook for 4 minutes, and add the mixed veggies. Simmer for 4-5 minutes. Add salt and black pepper, and spoon the stir-fry to a side of cilantro cauli rice.

Nutrition facts (per serving)
calories: 572 | fat: 49.1g | protein: 22.6g | carbs:5.3 g | net carbs: 1.1g | fiber: 4.2g

➤Double Cheese Pizza

Preparation time: 10 minutes
Cooking time: 25 minutes | **Servings:** 4
1 low carb pizza bread
Olive oil for brushing
1 cup grated Manchego cheese
1 cup crumbled goat cheese
Directions
Preheat oven to 390/400°F (205°C) and put pizza bread on a pizza pan. Brush with olive oil and sprinkle the Manchego cheese all over. Drop goat cheese on top and bake for 25 minutes until the cheese has melted. Slice the pizza with a cutter and serve.

Nutrition facts (per serving)
calories: 345 | fat: 24.1g | protein: 17.9g | carbs: 6.9g | net carbs: 6.6g | fiber: 0.3g

➤Spicy Tomato Pork Chops

Preparation time: 15 minutes
Cooking time: 36 minutes | **Servings:** 4
4 pork chops
1 tablespoon fresh oregano, chopped
2 garlic cloves, minced1 tablespoon canola oil
15 ounces (425 g) canned diced tomatoes
1 tablespoon tomato paste
Salt and black pepper, to taste
¼ cup tomato juice
1 red chili, finely chopped

Directions

Set a pan over medium-high heat and warm oil, place in the pork, season with pepper and salt, cook for 6 minutes on both sides; remove to a bowl. Add in the garlic and cook for 30 seconds. Stir in the tomato paste, tomatoes, tomato juice, and chili; bring to a boil, and reduce heat to medium-low. Place in the pork chops, cover the pan and simmer everything for 30 minutes. Remove the pork to plates and sprinkle with fresh oregano to serve.

Nutrition facts (per serving)

calories: 412 | fat: 21.0g | protein: 39.1g | carbs: 6.3g | net carbs: 3.5g | fiber: 2.8g

›Bacon Smothered Pork with Thyme

Preparation time: 10 minutes
Cooking time: 20 minutes | **Servings:** 6

7 strips bacon, chopped
6 pork chops
Pink salt and black pepper to taste
5 sprigs fresh thyme
¼ cup chicken broth
½ cup heavy cream

Directions

Cook bacon for 5 minutes medium heat. Remove with spoon onto a paper towel-lined plate to soak up excess fat. Season pork chops with black pepper and salt, and brown in the bacon fat for 4 minutes on each side. Remove to the bacon plate. Stir in the thyme, chicken broth, and heavy cream and simmer for 5 minutes. Return the chops and bacon and cook further for another 2 minutes. Serve chops and a generous ladle of sauce with cauli mash. Garnish with thyme leaves.

Nutrition facts (per serving)

calories: 434 | fat: 37.1g | protein: 22.1g | carbs: 3.1g | net carbs: 2.9g | fiber: 0.2g

— CHAPTER 5 —

FISH AND SEAFOOD

ALICIA TRAVIS

Garlic Skillet Salmon

Preparation time: 5 minutes
Cooking time: 14 to 16 minutes | **Servings:** 4
1 tablespoon extra-virgin olive oil
2 garlic cloves, minced
1 teaspoon smoked paprika
2 cups grape or cherry tomatoes
1 (12-ounce / 345-g) jar roasted red peppers, drained and chopped
2 tablespoon water
¼ teaspoon ground black pepper
¼ teaspoon kosher or sea salt
1 pound (454 g) salmon fillets, cut into 7 pieces
1 tablespoon freshly squeezed lemon juice

In a medium/large skillet over medium-high heat, heat the oil. Add the smoked paprika and garlic and cook for a min, stirring often. Add the tomatoes, water, roasted peppers, salt and black pepper. Turn up the heat to medium/high and after bring to a simmer, cook for 3-4 min, smashing and stirring the tomatoes with a spoon toward the end of the cooking time. Add the salmon to the skillet, spoon the sauce over the top, cover and cook for 11-12 min. Remove the pan with the salmon from the heat, and drizzle fresh lemon juice over the fish. Stir the sauce and serve hot.
Nutrition facts (per serving)
calories: 260 | fat: 12g | protein: 24.5g | carbs: 6g | fiber: 1.2g | sodium: 809mg

Salmon Baked in Foil

Preparation time: 5 minutes
Cooking time: 25 minutes | **Servings:** 4
2 cups cherry tomatoes
3 tablespoons extra-virgin olive oil
3 tablespoons lemon juice
3 tablespoons almond butter
1 teaspoon oregano
½ teaspoon salt
4 (5-ounce / 142-g) salmon fillets

Preheat the oven to 390/400°F (205°C). Cut the tomatoes in half and put them in a bowl. Add the olive oil, lemon juice, butter, oregano, and salt to the tomatoes and gently toss to combine. Cut 4 pieces of foil, about 12-by-12 inches each. Place the salmon fillets in the middle of each piece of foil. Divide the tomato mixture evenly over the 4 pieces of salmon. Bring the ends of the foil together and seal to form a closed pocket. Place the 4 pockets on a baking sheet. Bake in the preheated oven for 25 minutes. Remove from the oven and serve on a plate.
Nutrition facts (per serving)
calories: 410 | fat: 32.0g | protein: 30.0g | carbs: 4.0g | fiber: 1.0g | sodium: 370mg

Instant Pot Poached Salmon

Preparation time: 10 minutes
Cooking time: 3 minutes | **Servings:** 4
1 lemon, sliced ¼ inch thick
4 (6-ounce / 170-g) skinless salmon fillets, 1½ inches thick
½ teaspoon salt
¼ teaspoon pepper
½ cup water

Put the lemon slices in the bottom of the Instant Pot. Season the salmon with salt and pepper, then arrange the salmon (skin-side down) on top of the lemon slices. Pour in the water. Select the Manual mode, secure the lid and set the cooking time for 3 minutes at High Pressure. Once cooking is complete, do a quick pressure release. Carefully open the lid. Serve warm.
Nutrition facts (per serving)
calories: 350 | fat: 23.0g | protein: 35.0g | carbs: 0g | fiber: 0g | sodium: 390mg

Balsamic-Honey Glazed Salmon

Preparation time: 2 minutes
Cooking time: 8 minutes | **Servings:** 4
½ cup balsamic vinegar
1 tablespoon honey
4 (8-ounce / 227-g) salmon fillets
Sea salt and freshly ground pepper
1 tablespoon olive oil

Heat a skillet over medium-high heat. Mix the vinegar and honey in a small bowl. Season the salmon fillets with the sea salt and freshly ground pepper; brush with the honey-balsamic glaze. Add olive oil to the skillet, and the salmon fillets, cook for 3 to 4 minutes on each side until medium rare in the center and lightly browned. Let sit for 5 minutes before serving.
Nutrition facts (per serving)
calories: 454 | fat: 17.3g | protein: 65.3g | carbs: 9.7g | fiber: 0g | sodium: 246mg

Seared Salmon with Lemon Cream Sauce

Preparation time: 10 minutes
Cooking time: 20 minutes | **Servings:** 4
4 (5-ounce / 142-g) salmon fillets
Sea salt and freshly ground black pepper
1 tablespoon extra-virgin olive oil
½ cup low-sodium vegetable broth
Juice and zest of 1 lemon
1 teaspoon chopped fresh thyme
½ cup fat-free sour cream
1 teaspoon honey
1 tablespoon chopped fresh chives

Preheat the oven to 390/400°F (205°C). Season the salmon lightly on both sides with salt and pepper. Place a medium/large ovenproof skillet over medium-high heat and add the olive oil. Sear the salmon fillets on both sides until golden, about 3 minutes per side. Transfer the salmon to a baking and bake in the preheated oven until just cooked through, about 10 minutes. Meanwhile, whisk together the vegetable broth, lemon juice and zest, and thyme in a small saucepan until the liquid reduces by about one-quarter. Whisk in the sour cream and honey.

Stir in the chives and serve the sauce over the salmon.

Nutrition facts (per serving)
calories: 310 | fat: 18.0g | protein: 29.0g | carbs: 6.0g | fiber: 0g | sodium: 129mg

›Tuna and Zucchini Patties

Preparation time: 10 minutes
Cooking time: 12 minutes | **Servings:** 4
3 slices whole-wheat sandwich bread, toasted
2 (5-ounce / 142-g) cans tuna in olive oil, drained
1 large egg, lightly beaten
1 cup shredded zucchini
¼ cup diced red bell pepper
1 tbsp dried oregano
1 tsp lemon zest
¼ tsp freshly ground black pepper
¼ tsp kosher or sea salt
1 tbsp extra virgin oil
Salad greens or 4 whole-wheat rolls.

Crumble the toast into bread, crumbs with your fingers until you have 1 cup of loosely packed crumbs. Pour the crumbs into a large bowl. Add the tuna, zucchini, beaten egg, black pepper, lemon zest, oregano, bell pepper, and salt. Mix well with a fork and form the mixture into four (½cup-size) patties. Place them on a plate, press each patty flat to about ¾-inch thick. In a medium skillet over medium/high heat, heat the oil until it's very hot, about 2 min. Add the patties to the oil, then reduce the heat down to low/medium. Cook the patties for 5 min, and cook for an additional 4-5 min. Serve the patties on salad greens or whole-wheat rolls, if desired.

Nutrition facts (per serving)
calories: 757 | fat: 72.0g | protein: 5.0g | carbs: 26.0g | fiber: 4.0g | sodium: 418mg

›Mediterranean Cod Stew

Preparation time: 10 minutes
Cooking time: 20 minutes | **Servings:** 6
2 tablespoons extra-virgin olive oil
2 cups chopped onion
2 garlic cloves, minced
¾ teaspoon smoked paprika
1 (14.5-ounce / 411-g) can diced tomatoes, undrained
1 (12-ounce / 340-g) jar roasted red peppers and chopped
1 cup sliced olives, green or black
⅓ cup dry red wine
¼ teaspoon kosher or sea salt
¼ teaspoon freshly ground black pepper
1½ pounds (680 g) cod fillets, cut into 1-inch pieces
3 cups sliced mushrooms

In a medium/large stockpot over medium/hight heat, heat the oil. Add the onion and cook for about 4 minutes, stirring occasionally. Add the smoked paprika and garlic and cook for 2 min, stirring often. Mix in the tomatoes with their juices,wine, roasted peppers, pepper ,olives, and salt, and turn the heat to medium-high. Bring the mixture to a boil. Add the

cod fillets and mushrooms, and reduce the heat to medium. Cover and cook for about 8-10 minutes, stirring a few times, until the cod is cooked through and flakes easily, and serve.

Nutrition facts (per serving)
calories: 167 | fat: 5.0g | protein: 19.0g | carbs: 11.0g | fiber: 5.0g | sodium: 846mg

›Fennel Poached Cod with Tomatoes

Preparation time: 10 minutes
Cooking time: 20 minutes | **Servings:** 4
1 tablespoon olive oil
1 cup thinly sliced fennel
½ cup thinly sliced onion
1 tablespoon minced garlic
1 (15-ounce / 425-g) can diced tomatoes
2 cups chicken broth
½ cup white wine
Juice and zest of 1 orange
1 pinch red pepper flakes
1 bay leaf
1 pound (454 g) cod

Preheat the olive oil in a medium/large skillet. Add the onion and fennel and cook for 6 minutes, stirring occasionally, or until translucent. Add the garlic and cook for 45 sec/1 minute more. Add the tomatoes, chicken broth, wine, orange juice and zest, red pepper flakes, and bay leaf, and simmer for 4-6 minutes to meld the flavors. Carefully add the cod in a single layer, cover, and simmer for 6 to 7 minutes. Transfer fish to a serving dish, ladle the remaining sauce over the fish, and serve.

Nutrition facts (per serving)
calories: 336 | fat: 12.5g | protein: 45.1g | carbs:11.0g | fiber: 3.3g | sodium: 982mg

›Baked Fish with Pistachio Crust

Preparation time: 12 min
Cooking time: 18 to 20 min | **Servings:** 4
5 tablespoons extra-virgin olive oil, divided
1 pound (454 g) flaky white fish (such as cod, haddock, or halibut), skin removed
½ cup shelled finely chopped pistachios
½ cup ground flaxseed
Zest and juice of 1 lemon, divided
1 teaspoon ground cumin
1 teaspoon ground allspice
½ teaspoon salt
¼ teaspoon freshly ground black pepper

Preheat the oven to 390/400°F (205°C). Line a baking large sheet with parchment paper or aluminum foil and drizzle 2 tablespoons of olive oil over the sheet, spreading to evenly coat the bottom. Cut the fish into 4-5 equal pieces and place on the prepared baking sheet. In a bowl, combine the lemon zest, pistachios, allspice, flax seeds, cumin, salt and pepper. Pour in a drizzle of olive oil and mix well. Divide the nut mixture over the fish pieces. Pour the lemon juice and remaining 3 tablespoons olive oil over the fish and cook until cooked through, 18-20 minutes, depending on the

thickness of the fish.
Cool for 5 minutes before serving..
Nutrition facts (per serving)
calories: 510 | fat: 42.0g | protein: 27.0g | carbs: 9.0g
| fiber: 6.0g | sodium: 331mg

⟩Dill Baked Sea Bass

Preparation time: 10 min
Cooking time: 12 to 15 minutes | **Servings:** 6
¼ cup olive oil
2 pounds (907 g) sea bass
Sea salt and freshly ground pepper
1 garlic clove, minced
¼ cup dry white wine
3 teaspoons fresh dill
2 teaspoons fresh thyme

Preheat the oven to 420/430ºF (225ºC). Brush the bottom of a roasting large pan with the extra-vergine olive oil. Place the fish in the pan with extra-verigine oil. Season the fish with sea freshly pepper and salt. Combine well the remaining ingredients and pour over the fish. Bake in the preheated oven for 12 to 15 minutes, depending on the size of the fish. Serve hot.
Nutrition facts (per serving)
calories: 225 | fat: 12.0g | protein: 29.1g | carbs: 1.0g
| fiber: 0.3g | sodium: 104mg

⟩Sole Piccata with Capers

Preparation time: 10 minutes
Cooking time: 17 minutes | **Servings:** 4
1 teaspoon extra-virgin olive oil
4 (5-ounce / 142-g) sole fillets, patted dry
3 tablespoons almond butter
2 teaspoons minced garlic
2 tablespoons all-purpose flour
2 cups low-sodium chicken broth
Juice and zest of ½ lemon
2 tablespoons capers

Place a skillet over medium/high heat, add the Extra-vergine olive oil and sear the sole fillets until the fish flakes when tested with a fork (about 5 minutes on each side). Transfer the fish to a large dish next put the pan on the stove and add the almond butter. Sauté the garlic until translucent, about 3-4 min. Blend in flour to make a thick paste and bake until the mixture is golden brown (about 2-3 min). Blend chicken stock, lemon zest and juice and cook for about 5 minutes. Stir in the capers and add the sauce over the fish.
Nutrition facts (per serving)
calories: 275 | fat:13.2g | protein: 31.0g | carbs: 7.0g
| fiber: 0g | sodium: 413mg

⟩Haddock with Cucumber Sauce

Preparation time: 10 minutes
Cooking time: 10 minutes | **Servings:** 4
¼ cup plain Greek yogurt
½ scallion, white and green parts, finely chopped
½ English cucumber, grated, liquid squeezed out

2 teaspoons chopped fresh mint
1 teaspoon honey
Sea salt and freshly ground black pepper
4 (5-ounce / 142-g) haddock fillets, patted dry
Nonstick cooking spray

In a small-medium bowl, stir together the scallion, cucumber, yogurt, mint, honey, and a pinch of salt. Set aside. Season the fillets lightly with pepper and salt. Place a large skillet over medium/high heat and spray lightly with cooking spray. Cook the haddock, turning once, until it is just cooked through, about 5 minutes per side. Transfer the fish to plates. Serve topped with the cucumber sauce.
Nutrition facts (per serving)
calories: 164 | fat: 2.0g | protein: 27.0g | carbs: 4.0g
| fiber: 0g | sodium: 104mg

⟩Crispy Herb Crusted Halibut

Preparation time: 10 minutes
Cooking time: 20 minutes | **Servings:** 4
4 (5-ounce / 142-g) halibut fillets, patted dry
Extra-virgin olive oil, for brushing
½ cup coarsely ground unsalted pistachios
1 tablespoon chopped fresh parsley
1 teaspoon chopped fresh basil
1 teaspoon chopped fresh thyme
Pinch sea salt
Pinch freshly ground black pepper

Preheat the oven to 340/350ºF (180ºC). Line a baking sheet with parchment paper. Place the fillets on the baking sheet and brush them generously with olive oil. In a small bowl, stir together the pistachios, parsley, basil, thyme, salt, and pepper. Spoon the nut mixture evenly on the fish, spreading it out so the tops of the fillets are covered. Bake in the preheated oven until it flakes when pressed with a fork, about 20 minutes. Serve immediately.
Nutrition facts (per serving)
calories: 262 | fat: 11.0g | protein: 32.0g | carbs: 4.0g
| fiber: 2.0g | sodium: 77mg

⟩Breaded Shrimp

Preparation time: 10 minutes
Cooking time: 4 to 6 minutes | **Servings:** 4
2 large eggs
1 tablespoon water
2 cups seasoned Italian breadcrumbs
1 cup flour
1 teaspoon salt
Extra-virgin olive oil, as needed
1 pound (455 g) large shrimp (20 to 25), peeled and deveined

In a small/medium bowl, beat the eggs with the water, then transfer to a shallow dish. Add the breadcrumbs and salt to a separate small dish, then mix well. Place the flour in a third flat dish. Dip the shrimp in the flour, then in the beaten egg and finally in the breadcrumbs. Place on a flat plate and repeat the process with all the shrimp.

Heat a skillet over medium/high heat. Pour olive oil so that it coats the bottom of the pan. Cook shrimp for 2 to 3 minutes on each side. Pat shrimp dry on a paper towel to prevent too much oil. Serve warm.

Nutrition facts (per serving)
calories: 715 | fat: 35.0g | protein: 38.0g | carbs: 64.0g | fiber: 3.0g | sodium: 1727mg

➤Shrimp Pesto for Zoodles

Preparation time: 15 minutes
Cooking time: 10 minutes | **Servings: 4**
1 pound (454 g) fresh shrimp, peeled and deveined
½ small onion, slivered
2 tablespoons extra-virgin olive oil
8 ounces (227 g) store-bought jarred pesto
Salt and freshly ground black pepper
1 cup crumbled goat or feta cheese, plus additional for serving
¼ cup chopped flat-leaf Italian parsley, for garnish
2 large zucchinis, spiralized, for serving

In a bowl, season the shrimp with pepper and salt. In a large skillet, heat the extra-vergine olive oil over high heat. Sauté the onion until just golden, 5-6 minutes. Low the heat and add the pesto and cheese, whisking to combine and melt the cheese. Bring to a low simmer and add the shrimp. Reduce the heat back to low and cover. Cook until the shrimp is cooked through and pink, about 3 to 4 minutes.
Serve the shrimp warm over zoodles, garnishing with chopped parsley and additional crumbled cheese.

Nutrition facts (per serving)
calories: 491 | fat: 35.0g | protein: 29.0g | carbs: 15.0g | fiber: 4.0g | sodium: 870mg

➤Salt and Pepper Calamari and Scallops

Preparation time: 5 minutes
Cooking time: 10 minutes | **Servings:** 4
8 ounces (227 g) calamari steaks, cut into ½-inch-thick rings
8 ounces (227 g) sea scallops
1½ teaspoons salt, divided
1 teaspoon garlic powder
1 teaspoon freshly ground black pepper
⅓ cup extra-virgin olive oil
2 tablespoons almond butter

Place the calamari and scallops on several layers of paper towels and pat dry. Sprinkle with 1 teaspoon of salt and allow to sit for 15 minutes at room temperature. Pat dry with additional paper towels. Sprinkle with pepper and garlic powder. In a deep medium/large skillet, heat the olive oil and butter over medium/high heat. When the oil is hot , add the scallops and calamari in a single layer to the skillet and sprinkle with the remaining ½ teaspoon of salt. Cook for 2 to 4 minutes on each side, depending on the size of the scallops, until just golden but still slightly opaque in center. Using a slotted spoon, remove from the skillet and transfer to a serving platter. Allow the cooking oil to cool slightly and drizzle over the seafood before serving.

Nutrition facts (per serving)
calories: 309 | fat: 25.0g | protein: 18.0g | carbs: 3.0g | fiber: 0g | sodium: 928mg

➤Baked Cod with Vegetables

Preparation time: 15 minutes
Cooking time: 25 minutes | **Servings:** 2
1 pound (450 g) thick cod fillet, cut into 4 even portions
¼ teaspoon paprika
¼ teaspoon onion powder (optional)
3 tablespoons extra-virgin olive oil
½ cup fresh chopped basil, divided
3 tablespoons minced garlic (optional)
2 teaspoons salt
4 medium scallions
2 teaspoons freshly ground black pepper
¼ teaspoon dry marjoram (optional)
½ cup crumbled feta cheese
6 sun-dried tomato slices
1 (15-ounce / 425-g) can oil-packed artichoke hearts
½ cup dry white wine
1 cup pitted kalamata olives
4 small red potatoes, quartered
1 lemon, sliced
1 teaspoon capers (optional)

Preheat the oven to 370/385°F (195°C). Season the fish with paprika and onion powder (optional). Heat an ovenproof skillet over medium/high heat and sear the top side of the cod for about 1 minute until golden. Heat the extra-vergine olive oil in the same skillet over medium-high heat. Add the scallions, ¼ cup of basil, garlic (optional), salt, pepper, marjoram (if desired), tomato slices, and white wine and stir to combine. Bring to a boil and remove from heat. Place the the tomato basil sauce on top of cod and scatter with cheese. Place the artichokes in the pan and add the lemon slices. Scatter with the , capers (optional), olives and the remaining ¼ cup of basil. Remove from the heat and transfer to the preheated oven. Bake for 15-20 minutes, or until it flakes easily with a fork.
Place the quartered potatoes on a baking sheet or wrapped in aluminum foil. Bake in the oven for 13 to 15 minutes until fork tender. Cool for 5 minutes before serving.

Nutrition facts (per serving)
calories: 1168 | fat: 60.0g | protein: 63.8g | carbs: 94.0g | fiber: 13.0g | sodium: 4620mg

➤Slow Cooker Salmon in Foil

Preparation time: 5 minutes
Cooking time: 2 hours | **Servings:** 2
2 (6-ounce / 170-g) salmon fillets
1 tablespoon olive oil
2 cloves garlic, minced
½ tablespoon lime juice
1 teaspoon finely chopped fresh parsley
¼ teaspoon black pepper

Spread a length of foil onto a work surface and place the salmon fillets in the middle. Combine the olive oil, lime juice, parsley, garlic, and black pepper in a small bowl. Brush the mixture over the fillets. Fold over the foil and crimp the sides to form a package. Place packet in the pot over low heat, cover and cook for 2 hours and 30 minutes , or until fish flakes easily with a fork. Serve hot.

Nutrition facts (per serving)
calories: 446 | fat: 20.7g | protein: 65.4g | carbs: 1.5g | fiber: 0.2g | sodium: 240mg

▸Dill Chutney Salmon

Preparation time: 5 minutes
Cooking time: 3 minutes | **Servings:** 2
Chutney:
¼ cup fresh dill
¼ cup extra virgin olive oil
Juice from ½ lemon
Sea salt, to taste
Fish:
2 cups water
2 salmon fillets
Juice from ½ lemon
¼ teaspoon paprika
Salt and freshly ground pepper to taste

Pulse all the chutney ingredients in a food processor until creamy. Set aside. Add the water and steamer basket to the Instant Pot. Place salmon fillets, skin-side down, on the steamer basket. Drizzle the lemon juice over salmon and sprinkle with the paprika. Select the Manual mode, secure the lid and set the cooking time for 3 minutes at High Pressure. Once cooking is complete, do a quick pressure release. Carefully open the lid. Season the fillets with pepper and salt to taste. Serve topped with the dill chutney.

Nutrition facts (per serving)
calories: 636 | fat: 41.1g | protein: 65.3g | carbs: 1.9g | fiber: 0.2g | sodium: 477mg

▸Garlic-Butter Parmesan Salmon and Asparagus

Preparation time: 10 minutes
Cooking time: 15 minutes | **Servings:** 2
2 (6-ounce / 170-g) salmon fillets, skin on and patted dry
Pink Himalayan salt
Freshly ground black pepper, to taste
1 pound (454 g) fresh asparagus, ends snapped off
3 tablespoons almond butter
2 garlic cloves, minced
¼ cup grated Parmesan cheese

Preheat the oven to 390/400°F (205°C). Line a baking sheet with aluminum foil. Season both sides of the salmon fillets with pepper and salt. Put the salmon in the middle of the baking sheet and arrange the asparagus around the salmon. Heat the almond butter in a small/medium saucepan over medium heat. Add the minced garlic and cook for about 3 minu-

tes, or until the garlic just begins to brown. Drizzle the garlic-butter sauce over the salmon and asparagus and scatter the Parmesan cheese on top. Bake in the preheated oven for about 9-13 minutes, or until the salmon is cooked through and the asparagus is crisp-tender. You can switch the oven to broil at the end of cooking time for about 3 minutes to get a nice char on the asparagus. Let cool for 5 minutes before serving.

Nutrition facts (per serving)
calories: 435 | fat: 26.1g | protein: 42.3g | carbs: 10.0g | fiber: 5.0g | sodium: 503mg

▸Lemon Rosemary Roasted Branzino

Preparation time: 15 minutes
Cooking time: 30 minutes | **Servings:** 2
4 tablespoons extra-virgin olive oil, divided
2 (8-ounce / 227-g) branzino fillets, preferably at least 1 inch thick
1 garlic clove, minced
1 bunch scallions (white part only), thinly sliced
10 to 12 small cherry tomatoes, halved
1 large carrot, cut into ¼-inch rounds
2 ½ cup dry white wine
2 tablespoons paprika
2 teaspoons kosher salt
½ tablespoon ground chili pepper
1 rosemary sprigs or 1 tablespoon dried rosemary
1 small lemon, thinly sliced
½ cup sliced pitted kalamata olives

Heat a medium/large ovenproof skillet over high heat until hot, about 2 minutes. Add 1 tablespoon of olive oil and heat for 10 to 15 seconds until it shimmers. Add the branzino fillets, skin-side up, and sear for 2 minutes. Flip the fillets and cook for an additional 2 minutes. Set aside. Swirl 2 tablespoons of olive oil around the skillet to coat evenly. Add the garlic, scallions, tomatoes, and carrot, and sauté for 5 minutes, or until softened. Add the wine, stirring until all ingredients are well combined. Carefully place the fish over the sauce. Preheat the oven to 440/450°F (235°C). Brush the fillets with the remaining 1 tablespoon of olive oil and season with paprika, salt, and chili pepper. Top each fillet with a rosemary sprig and lemon slices. Scatter the olives over fish and around the skillet. Roast for about 10 minutes until the lemon slices are browned. Serve hot.

Nutrition facts (per serving)
calories: 724 | fat: 43.0g | protein: 57.7g | carbs: 25.0g | fiber: 10.0g | sodium: 2950mg

▸Grilled Lemon Pesto Salmon

Preparation time: 5 minutes
Cooking time: 6 to 10 minutes | **Servings:** 2
10 ounces (283 g) salmon fillet (1 large piece or 2 smaller ones)
Salt and freshly ground black pepper
2 tablespoons prepared pesto sauce
1 large fresh lemon, sliced
Cooking spray

138

Preheat the grill to medium-high heat. Spray the grill grates with cooking spray. Season the salmon with black pepper and salt. Spread the pesto sauce on top. Make a bed of fresh lemon slices about the same size as the salmon fillet on the hot grill, and place the salmon on top of the lemon slices. Put any additional lemon slices on top of the salmon. Grill the salmon for 6 to 10 minutes, or until the fish is opaque and flakes apart easily. Serve hot.

Nutrition facts (per serving)
calories: 316 | fat: 21.1g | protein: 29.0g | carbs: 1.0g | fiber: 0g | sodium: 175mg

›Steamed Trout with Lemon Herb Crust

Preparation time: 10 minutes
Cooking time: 15 minutes | **Servings:** 2
3 tablespoons olive oil
3 garlic cloves, chopped
2 tablespoons fresh lemon juice
1 tablespoon chopped fresh mint
1 tablespoon chopped fresh parsley
¼ teaspoon dried ground thyme
1 teaspoon sea salt
1 pound (454 g) fresh trout (2 pieces)
2 cups fish stock

Stir well the olive oil, lemon juice, mint, garlic, parsley, thyme, and salt in a small bowl. Brush the marinade onto the fish. Insert a trivet in the Instant Pot. Pour in the fish stock and place the fish on the trivet. Secure the lid. Select the Steam mode and set the cooking time for 15 minutes at High Pressure. Once cooking is complete, do a quick pressure release. Carefully open the lid. Serve warm.

Nutrition facts (per serving)
calories: 477 | fat: 29.6g | protein: 51.7g | carbs: 3.6g | fiber: 0.2g | sodium: 2011mg

›Roasted Trout Stuffed with Veggies

Preparation time: 10 minutes
Cooking time: 25 minutes | **Servings:** 2
2 (8-ounce / 227-g) whole trout fillets, dressed (cleaned but with bones and skin intact)
1 tablespoon extra-virgin olive oil
¼ teaspoon salt
⅛ teaspoon freshly ground black pepper
1 small onion, thinly sliced
½ red bell pepper, seeded and thinly sliced
1 poblano pepper, seeded and thinly sliced
2 or 3 shiitake mushrooms, sliced
1 lemon, sliced
Nonstick cooking spray

Preheat the oven to 420/425°F (220°C). Spray a baking sheet with nonstick cooking spray. Rub both trout fillets, inside and out, with the olive oil. Season with salt and pepper. Mix the onion, bell pepper, poblano pepper, and mushrooms in a large bowl. Stuff half of this mixture into the cavity of each fillet. Top the mixture with 2 or 3 lemon slices inside each fillet.
Place the fish on the prepared baking sheet side by side. Roast in the preheated oven for 25 minutes, or until the fish is cooked through and the vegetables are tender. Remove from the oven and serve on a plate.

Nutrition facts (per serving)
calories: 453 | fat: 22.1g | protein: 49.0g | carbs: 13.8g | fiber: 3.0g | sodium: 356mg

›Lemony Trout with Caramelized Shallots

Preparation time: 10 minutes
Cooking time: 20 minutes | **Servings:** 2
Shallots:
1 teaspoon almond butter
2 shallots, thinly sliced
Dash salt
Trout:
1 tablespoon plus 1 teaspoon almond butter, divided
2 (4-ounce / 113-g) trout fillets
3 tablespoons capers
¼ cup freshly squeezed lemon juice
¼ teaspoon salt
Dash freshly ground black pepper
1 lemon, thinly sliced
Make the Shallots

In a medium-large skillet over medium/high heat, cook the butter, shallots, and salt for about 20 minutes, stirring every 5 minutes, or until the shallots are wilted and caramelized. Make the Trout. Meanwhile, in another large skillet over medium/high heat, heat 1 teaspoon of almond butter. Add the trout fillets and cook each side for 3 minutes, or until flaky. Transfer to a plate and set aside. In the skillet used for the trout, stir in the capers, lemon juice, salt, and pepper, then bring to a simmer. Whisk in the remaining 1 tablespoon of almond butter. Spoon the sauce over the fish. Garnish the fish with the lemon slices and caramelized shallots before serving.

Nutrition facts (per serving)
calories: 344 | fat: 18.4g | protein: 21.1g | carbs: 14.7g | fiber: 5.0g | sodium: 1090mg

›Shrimp with Garlic

Preparation Time: 10 minutes
Cooking Time: 25 minutes
Servings: 2
Ingredients:
1 lb. shrimp
¼ teaspoon baking soda
2 tablespoons oil
2 teaspoon minced garlic
¼ cup vermouth
2 tablespoons unsalted butter
1 teaspoon parsley
Directions:
In a bowl toss shrimp with baking soda and salt, let it stand for a couple of minutes. In a skillet heat olive oil and add shrimp. Add garlic, red pepper flakes and cook for 1-2 minutes. Add vermouth and cook for another 5-6 minutes. When ready remove from heat and serve
Nutrition facts:

Calories: 289
Total Carbohydrate: 2 g
Cholesterol: 3 mg
Total Fat: 17 g
Fiber: 2 g
Protein: 7 g
Sodium: 163 mg

›Sabich Sandwich

Preparation Time: 5 minutes
Cooking Time: 15 minutes
Servings: 2
Ingredients:
2 tomatoes
Olive oil
½ lb. eggplant
¼ cucumber
1 tablespoon lemon
1 tablespoon parsley
¼ head cabbage
2 tablespoons wine vinegar
2 pita breads
½ cup hummus
¼ tahini sauce
2 hard-boiled eggs
Directions:
In a skillet, fry eggplant slices until tender. In a bowl add tomatoes, cucumber, parsley, lemon juice and season salad. In another bowl toss cabbage with vinegar. In each pita pocket add hummus, eggplant and drizzle tahini sauce. Top with eggs, tahini sauce
Nutrition facts:
Calories: 269
Total Carbohydrate: 2 g
Cholesterol: 3 mg
Total Fat: 14 g
Fiber: 2 g
Protein: 7 g
Sodium: 183 mg

›Salmon with Vegetables

Preparation Time: 10 minutes
Cooking Time: 15 minutes
Servings: 4
Ingredients:
2 tablespoons olive oil
2 carrots
1 head fennel
2 squashes
¼ onion
1-inch ginger
1 cup white wine
2 cups water
2 parsley sprigs
2 tarragon sprigs
6 oz. salmon fillets
1 cup cherry tomatoes
1 scallion
Directions:
In a skillet heat olive oil, add fennel, squash, onion, ginger, carrot and cook until vegetables are soft
Add wine, water, parsley and cook for another 4-5 mi-

nutes. Season salmon fillets and place in the pan
Cook for 5 minutes per side. Transfer salmon to a bowl, spoon tomatoes and scallion around salmon and serve
Nutrition facts:
Calories: 301
Total Carbohydrate: 2 g
Cholesterol: 13 mg
Total Fat: 17 g
Fiber: 4 g
Protein: 8 g
Sodium: 201 mg

›Crispy Fish

Preparation Time: 5 minutes
Cooking Time: 15 minutes
Servings: 4
Ingredients:
Thick fish fillets
¼ cup all-purpose flour
1 egg
1 cup breadcrumbs
2 tablespoons vegetables
Lemon wedge
Directions:
In a dish add flour, egg, breadcrumbs in different dishes and set aside. Dip each fish fillet into the flour, egg and then breadcrumbs bowl. Place each fish fillet in a heated skillet and cook for 4-5 minutes per side
When ready remove from pan and serve
Nutrition facts:
Calories: 189
Total Carbohydrate: 2 g
Cholesterol: 73 mg
Total Fat: 17 g
Fiber: 0 g
Protein: 7 g
Sodium: 163 mg

›Moules Marinières

Preparation Time: 10 minutes
Cooking Time: 30 minutes
Servings: 4
Ingredients:
2 tablespoons unsalted butter
1 leek
1 shallot
2 cloves garlic
2 bay leaves
1 cup white win
2 lb. mussels
2 tablespoons mayonnaise
1 tablespoon lemon zest
2 tablespoons parsley
1 sourdough bread
Directions:
In a saucepan melt butter, add leeks, garlic, bay leaves, shallot and cook until vegetables are soft
Bring to a boil, add mussels, and cook for 1-2 minutes
Transfer mussels to a bowl and cover. Whisk in remaining butter with mayonnaise and return mussels to pot
Add lemon juice, parsley lemon zest and stir to combi-

ne
Nutrition facts:
Calories: 321
Total Carbohydrate: 2 g
Cholesterol: 13 mg
Total Fat: 17 g
Fiber: 2 g
Protein: 9 g
Sodium: 312 mg

›Steamed Mussels with Coconut-Curry

Preparation Time: 15 minutes
Cooking Time: 20 minutes
Servings: 4
Ingredients:
6 sprigs cilantro
2 cloves garlic
2 shallots
¼ teaspoon coriander seeds
¼ teaspoon red chili flakes
1 teaspoon zest
1 can coconut milk
1 tablespoon vegetable oil
1 tablespoon curry paste
1 tablespoon brown sugar
1 tablespoon fish sauce
2 lb. mussels
Directions:
In a bowl combine lime zest, cilantro stems, shallot, garlic, coriander seed, chili and salt. In a saucepan heat oil add, garlic, shallots, pounded paste and curry paste. Cook for 3-4 minutes, add coconut milk, sugar and fish sauce. Bring to a simmer and add mussels Stir in lime juice, cilantro leaves and cook for a couple of more minutes. When ready remove from heat and serve
Nutrition facts:
Calories: 209
Total Carbohydrate: 6 g
Cholesterol: 13 mg
Total Fat: 7 g
Fiber: 2 g
Protein: 17 g
Sodium: 193 mg

›Tuna Noodle Casserole

Preparation Time: 15 minutes
Cooking Time: 20 minutes
Servings: 4
Ingredients:
2 oz. egg noodles
4 oz. fraiche
1 egg
1 teaspoon cornstarch
1 tablespoon juice from 1 lemon
1 can tuna
1 cup peas
¼ cup parsley
Directions:
Place noodles in a saucepan with water and bring to a boil. In a bowl combine egg, crème fraiche and lemon juice, whisk well

When noodles are cooked add crème fraiche mixture to skillet and mix well. Add tuna, peas, parsley lemon juice and mix well. When ready remove from heat and serve
Nutrition facts:
Calories: 214
Total Carbohydrate: 2 g
Cholesterol: 73 mg
Total Fat: 7 g
Fiber: 2g
Protein: 19 g
Sodium: 308 g

›Salmon Burgers

Preparation Time: 10 minutes
Cooking Time: 15 minutes
Servings: 4
Ingredients:
1 lb. salmon fillets
1 onion
¼ dill fronds
1 tablespoon honey
1 tablespoon horseradish
1 tablespoon mustard
1 tablespoon olive oil
2 toasted split rolls
1 avocado
Directions:
Place salmon fillets in a blender and blend until smooth, transfer to a bowl, add onion, dill, honey, horseradish and mix well. Add salt and pepper and form 4 patties. In a bowl combine mustard, honey, mayonnaise and dill. In a skillet heat oil add salmon patties and cook for 2-3 minutes per side. When ready remove from heat. Divided lettuce and onion between the buns. Place salmon patty on top and spoon mustard mixture and avocado slices. Serve when ready
Nutrition facts:
Calories: 189
Total Carbohydrate: 6 g
Cholesterol: 3 mg
Total Fat: 7 g
Fiber: 4 g
Protein: 12 g
Sodium: 293 mg

›Seared Scallops

Preparation Time: 15 minutes
Cooking Time: 20 minutes
Servings: 4
Ingredients:
1 lb. sea scallops
1 tablespoon canola oil
Directions:
Season scallops and refrigerate for a couple of minutes. In a skillet heat oil, add scallops and cook for 1-2 minutes per side. When ready remove from heat and serve
Nutrition facts:
Calories: 283
Total Carbohydrate: 10 g
Cholesterol: 3 mg

Total Fat: 8 g
Fiber: 2 g
Protein: 9 g
Sodium: 271 mg

➤Black COD

Preparation Time: 15 minutes
Cooking Time: 20 minutes
Servings: 4
Ingredients:
¼ cup miso paste
¼ cup sake
1 tablespoon mirin
1 teaspoon soy sauce
1 tablespoon olive oil
4 black cod filets
Directions:
In a bowl combine miso, soy sauce, oil and sake
Rub mixture over cod fillets and let it marinade for 20-30 minutes. Adjust broiler and broil cod filets for 10-12 minutes. When fish is cook remove and serve
Nutrition facts:
Calories: 231
Total Carbohydrate: 2 g
Cholesterol: 13 mg
Total Fat: 15 g
Fiber: 2 g
Protein: 8 g
Sodium: 298 mg

➤Miso-Glazed Salmon

Preparation Time: 10 minutes
Cooking Time: 40 minutes
Servings: 4
Ingredients:
¼ cup red miso
¼ cup sake
1 tablespoon soy sauce
1 tablespoon vegetable oil
4 salmon fillets
Directions:
In a bowl combine sake, oil, soy sauce and miso. Rub mixture over salmon fillets and marinade for 20-30 minutes. Preheat a broiler. Broil salmon for 5-10 minutes When ready remove and serve
Nutrition facts:
Calories: 198
Total Carbohydrate: 5 g
Cholesterol: 12 mg
Total Fat: 10 g
Fiber: 2 g
Protein: 6 g
Sodium: 257 mg

➤Arugula and Sweet Potato Salad

Preparation Time: 10 minutes
Cooking Time: 20 minutes
Servings: 4
Ingredients:
1 lb. sweet potatoes

1 cup walnuts
1 tablespoon olive oil
1 cup water
1 tablespoon soy sauce
3 cups arugula
Directions:
Bake potatoes at 400 F until tender, remove and set aside. In a bowl drizzle, walnuts with olive oil and microwave for 2-3 minutes or until toasted. In a bowl combine well all salad ingredients and mix. Pour over soy sauce and serve
Nutrition facts:
Calories: 189
Total Carbohydrate: 2 g
Cholesterol: 13 mg
Total Fat: 7 g
Fiber: 2 g
Protein: 10 g
Sodium: 301 mg

➤Niçoise Salad

Preparation Time: 15 minutes
Cooking Time: 10 minutes
Servings: 4
Ingredients:
1 oz. red potatoes
1 package green beans
2 eggs
½ cup tomatoes
2 tablespoons wine vinegar
¼ teaspoon salt
½ teaspoon pepper
½ teaspoon thyme
¼ cup olive oil
6 oz. tuna
¼ cup Kalamata olives
Directions:
In a bowl combine all ingredients together. Add salad dressing and serve
Nutrition facts:
Calories: 189
Total Carbohydrate: 2 g
Cholesterol: 13 mg
Total Fat: 7 g
Fiber: 2 g
Protein: 15 g
Sodium: 321 mg

➤Shrimp Curry

Preparation Time: 15 minutes
Cooking Time: 20 minutes
Servings: 4
Ingredients:
2 tablespoons peanut oil
¼ onion
2 cloves garlic
1 teaspoon ginger
1 teaspoon cumin
1 teaspoon turmeric
1 teaspoon paprika
¼ red chili powder
1 can tomatoes

1 can coconut milk
1 lb. peeled shrimp
1 tablespoon cilantro
Directions:
In a medium-large skillet add onion and cook for 4-5 minutes. Add ginger, cumin, garlic, chili, paprika and cook on low heat. Pour the tomatoes, coconut milk and simmer for 10-12 minutes. Stir in shrimp, cilantro, and cook for 2-3 minutes. When ready remove and serve
Nutrition facts:
Calories: 178
Total Carbohydrate: 3 g
Cholesterol: 3 mg
Total Fat: 17 g
Fiber: g
Protein: 9 g
Sodium: 297 mg

›Salmon Pasta

Preparation Time: 10 minutes
Cooking Time: 25 minutes
Servings: 2
Ingredients:
5 tablespoons butter
¼ onion
1 tablespoon all-purpose flour
1 teaspoon garlic powder
2 cups skim milk
¼ cup Romano cheese
1 cup green peas
¼ cup canned mushrooms
8 oz. salmon
1 package penne pasta
Directions:
Bring a pot with water to a boil. Add pasta and cook for 10-12 minutes. In a skillet melt butter, add onion and sauté until tender. Stir in garlic powder, flour, milk and cheese. Add mushrooms, peas and cook on low heat for 4-5 minutes. Toss in salmon and cook for another 2-3 minutes. When ready serve with cooked pasta
Nutrition facts:
Calories: 211
Total Carbohydrate: 7 g
Cholesterol: 13 mg
Total Fat: 18 g
Fiber: 3 g
Protein: 17 g
Sodium: 289 mg

›Crab Legs

Preparation Time: 5 minutes
Cooking Time: 20 minutes
Servings: 3
Ingredients:
3 lb. crab legs
¼ cup salted butter, melted and divided
½ lemon, juiced
¼ tsp. garlic powder
Directions:
In a bowl, toss the crab legs and two tablespoons of the melted butter together. Place the crab legs in the

basket of the fryer. Cook at 400°F for fifteen minutes, giving the basket a good shake halfway through. Combine the remaining butter with the lemon juice and garlic powder. Crack open the cooked crab legs and remove the meat. Serve with the butter dip on the side and enjoy!
Nutrition facts:
Calories: 392
Fat: 10g
Protein: 18g
Sugar: 8g

›Crusty Pesto Salmon

Preparation Time: 5 minutes
Cooking Time: 15 minutes
Servings: 2
Ingredients:
¼ cup s, roughly chopped
¼ cup pesto
2 x 4-oz. salmon fillets
2 tbsp. unsalted butter, melted
Directions:
Mix the s and pesto together. Place the salmon fillets in a round baking dish, roughly six inches in diameter. Brush the fillets with butter, followed by the pesto mixture, ensuring to coat both the top and bottom. Put the baking dish inside the fryer. Cook for twelve minutes at 390°F. The salmon is ready when it flakes easily when prodded with a fork. Serve warm.
Nutrition facts:
Calories: 290
Fat: 11g
Protein: 20g
Sugar: 9g

›Buttery Cod

Preparation Time: 10 minutes
Cooking Time: 12 minutes
Servings: 2
Ingredients:
2 x 4-oz. cod fillets
2 tbsp. salted butter, melted
1 tsp. Old Bay seasoning
½ medium lemon, sliced
Directions:
Place the cod fillets in a skillet. Brush with melted butter, season with Old Bay, and top with a few lemon wedges. Wrap the fish in aluminum foil and place it in your deep fryer. Cook for eight minutes at 350 ° F. The cod is done when it is easily peeled. Serve hot ....
Nutrition facts:
Calories: 394
Fat: 5g
Protein: 12g
Sugar: 4g

›Sesame Tuna Steak

Preparation Time: 5 minutes
Cooking Time: 12 minutes
Servings: 2

Ingredients:
1 tbsp. coconut oil, melted
2 x 6-oz. tuna steaks
½ tsp. garlic powder
2 tsp. black sesame seeds
2 tsp. white sesame seeds
Directions:
Apply the coconut oil to the tuna steaks with a brunch, then season with garlic powder. Combine the black and white sesame seeds. Embed them in the tuna steaks, covering the fish all over. Place the tuna into your air fryer. Cook for eight minutes at 400°F, turning the fish halfway through. The tuna steaks are ready when they have reached a temperature of 145°F. Serve straightaway.
Nutrition facts:
Calories: 160
Fat: 6g
Protein: 26g
Sugar: 7g

›Lemon Garlic Shrimp

Preparation Time: 10 minutes
Cooking Time: 15 minutes
Servings: 2
Ingredients:
1 medium lemon
½ lb. medium shrimp, shelled and deveined
½ tsp. Old Bay seasoning
2 tbsp. unsalted butter, melted
½ tsp. minced garlic
Directions:
Grate the rind of the lemon into a bowl. Cut the lemon in half and juice it over the same bowl. Toss in the shrimp, Old Bay, and butter, mixing everything to make sure the shrimp is completely covered. Transfer to a round baking dish roughly six inches wide, then place this dish in your fryer. Cook at 400°F for six minutes. The shrimp is cooked when it turns a bright pink color. Serve hot, drizzling any leftover sauce over the shrimp.
Nutrition facts:
Calories: 490
Fat: 9g
Protein: 12g
Sugar: 11g

›Foil Packet Salmon

Preparation Time: 5 minutes
Cooking Time: 15 minutes
Servings: 2
Ingredients:
2 x 4-oz. skinless salmon fillets
2 tbsp. unsalted butter, melted
½ tsp. garlic powder
1 medium lemon
½ tsp. dried dill
Directions:
Take a sheet of aluminum foil and cut into two squares measuring roughly 5" x 5". Lay each of the salmon fillets at the center of each piece. Brush both fillets with a tablespoon of bullet and season with a quarter te-

aspoon of garlic powder. Halve the lemon and grate the skin of one half over the fish. Cut four half-slices of lemon, using two to top each fillet. Season each fillet with a quarter teaspoon of dill. Fold the tops and sides of the aluminum foil over the fish to create a kind of packet. Place each one in the fryer. Cook for twelve minutes at 400°F. Serve hot.
Nutrition facts:
Calories: 240
Fat: 13g
Protein: 21g
Sugar: 9g

›Foil Packet Lobster Tail

Preparation Time: 5 minutes
Cooking Time: 15 minutes
Servings: 2
Ingredients:
2 x 6-oz. lobster tail halves
2 tbsp. salted butter, melted
½ medium lemon, juiced
½ tsp. Old Bay seasoning
1 tsp. dried parsley
Directions:
Lay each lobster on a sheet of aluminum foil. Pour a light drizzle of melted butter and lemon juice over each one, and season with Old Bay. Fold down the sides and ends of the foil to seal the lobster. Place each one in the fryer. Cook at 375°F for twelve minutes. Just before serving, top the lobster with dried parsley.
Nutrition facts:
Calories: 510
Fat: 18g
Protein: 26g
Sugar: 12g

›Avocado Shrimp

Preparation Time: 10 minutes
Cooking Time: 20 minutes
Servings: 2
Ingredients:
½ cup onion, chopped
2 lb. shrimp
1 tbsp. seasoned salt
1 avocado
½ cup pecans, chopped
Directions:
Pre-heat the fryer at 400°F. Put the chopped onion in the basket of the fryer and spritz with some cooking spray. Leave to cook for five minutes. Add the shrimp and set the timer for a further five minutes. Sprinkle with some seasoned salt, then allow to cook for an additional five minutes. During these last five minutes, halve your avocado and remove the pit. Cube each half, then scoop out the flesh. Take care when removing the shrimp from the fryer. Place it on a dish and top with the avocado and the chopped pecans.
Nutrition facts:
Calories: 195
Fat: 14g
Protein: 36g
Sugar: 10g

›Tilapia Tacos with Cabbage Slaw

Preparation time: 10 minutes
Cooking time: 5 minutes | **Servings:** 4
1 tablespoon olive oil
1 teaspoon chili powder
2 tilapia fillets
1 teaspoon paprika
4 keto tortillas
Slaw:
½ cup red cabbage, shredded
1 tablespoon lemon juice
1 teaspoon apple cider vinegar
1 tablespoon olive oil
Directions
Season tilapia with chili powder and paprika. Heat the olive oil in a medium/small skillet over medium-high heat. Add tilapia, and cook until blackened, about 3 minutes per side. Cut into strips. Divide the tilapia between the tortillas. Combine well all the slaw ingredients in a bowl. Divide the slaw between the tortillas.
Nutrition facts (per serving)
calories: 261 | fat: 20.1g | protein: 13.9g | carbs: 5.5g | net carbs: 3.6g | fiber: 1.9g

›Tilapia and Cauliflower Rice Cabbage Tortillas

Preparation time: 10 minutes
Cooking time: 15 minutes | **Servings:** 4
1 teaspoon avocado oil
1 cup cauli rice
4 tilapia fillets, cut into cubes
¼ teaspoon taco seasoning
Sea salt and hot paprika to taste
2 whole cabbage leaves
2 tablespoons guacamole
1 tablespoon cilantro, chopped
Directions
Microwave the cauli rice in microwave safe bowl for 4 minutes. Fluff with a fork and set aside. Warm avocado oil in a skillet over medium heat, rub the tilapia with the taco seasoning, salt, and hot paprika, and fry until brown on all sides, for about 8 minutes in total. Divide the fish among the cabbage leaves, top with cauli rice, guacamole and cilantro.
Nutrition facts (per serving)
calories: 171 | fat: 6.5g | protein: 24.4g | carbs: 2.8g | net carbs: 1.5g | fiber: 1.3g

›Salmon with Radish and Arugula Salad

Preparation time: 15 minutes
Cooking time: 10 minutes | **Servings:** 4
1 pound (454 g) salmon, cut into 4 steaks each
1 cup radishes, sliced
Salt and black pepper to taste
8 green olives, pitted and chopped
1 cup arugula
2 large tomatoes, diced
3 tablespoons red wine vinegar
2 green onions, sliced
3 tablespoons olive oil
2 slices zero carb bread, cubed
¼ cup parsley, chopped
Directions
In a bowl, mix the radishes, olives, black pepper, arugula, tomatoes, wine vinegar, green onion, olive oil, bread, and parsley. Let sit for the flavors to incorporate. Season the salmon with pepper and salt, grill on both sides for 8 minutes in total. Serve the salmon on the radish salad.
Nutrition facts (per serving)
calories: 339 | fat: 21.6g | protein: 28.4g | carbs: 5.3g | net carbs: 3.0g | fiber: 2.3g

›Halibut Tacos with Cabbage Slaw

Preparation time: 15 minutes
Cooking time: 6 minutes | **Servings:** 4
1 tablespoon olive oil
1 teaspoon chili powder
4 halibut fillets, skinless, sliced
2 low carb tortillas
Slaw:
2 tablespoons red cabbage, shredded
1 tablespoon lemon juice
Salt to taste
½ tablespoon extra-virgin olive oil
½ carrot, shredded
1 tablespoon cilantro, chopped
Directions
Combine red cabbage with salt in a bowl; massage cabbage to tenderize. Add in the remaining slaw ingredient, toss to coat and set aside. Rub the halibut with olive oil, chili powder and paprika. Heat a grill pan over medium heat. Add halibut and cook until lightly charred and cooked through, about 3 minutes per side. Divide between the tortillas. Combine all slaw ingredients in a bowl. Split the slaw among the tortillas.
Nutrition facts (per serving)
calories: 386 | fat: 25.9g | protein: 23.7g | carbs: 12.6g | net carbs: 6.4g | fiber: 6.2g

›Coconut Shrimp Stew

Preparation time: 15 minutes
Cooking time: 15 minutes | **Servings:** 6
1 cup coconut milk
2 tablespoons lime juice
¼ cup diced roasted peppers
1½ pounds (680 g) shrimp, peeled and deveined
¼ cup olive oil
1 garlic clove, minced
14 ounces (397 g) diced tomatoes
2 tablespoons sriracha sauce
¼ cup onions, chopped
¼ cup cilantro, chopped
Fresh dill, chopped to garnish
Salt and black pepper to taste
Directions:
Heat the olive oil in a pot over medium-high heat. Add onions and cook for 3-4 minutes. Add the garlic

and cook until soft. Add tomatoes, shrimp, and cilantro. Cook until the shrimp becomes opaque, about 3-4 minutes. Stir in sriracha and coconut milk, and cook, for 2 more minutes. Do NOT bring to a boil. Stir in the lime juice and season with pepper and salt to taste. Spoon the stew in bowls, garnish with fresh dill, and serve warm.

Nutrition facts (per serving)
calories: 325 | fat: 20.9g | protein: 22.8g | carbs: 6.2g | net carbs: 5.1g | fiber: 1.1g

➤Asparagus and Trout Foil Packets

Preparation time: 15 minutes
Cooking time: 15 minutes | **Servings:** 4
1 pound (454 g) asparagus spears
1 tablespoon garlic purée
1 pound (454 g) deboned trout, butterflied
Salt and black pepper to taste
3 tablespoons olive oil
2 sprigs rosemary
2 sprigs thyme
2 tablespoons butter
½ medium red onion, sliced
2 lemon slices
Directions
Preheat the oven to 390/400°F (205°C). Rub the trout with garlic purée, salt and black pepper. Prepare two aluminum foil squares. Place the fish on each square. Divide the asparagus and onion between the squares, top with a pinch of pepper and salt, thyme, a sprig of rosemary and 1 tablespoon of butter. Lay the lemon slices on the fish. Close and Wrap the fish packets securely and place them on a baking sheet. Bake in the oven for 13-16 minutes and remove once ready.
Nutrition facts (per serving)
calories: 495 | fat: 39.2g | protein: 26.9g | carbs: 7.5g | net carbs: 4.9g | fiber: 2.6g

➤Pistachio Nut Salmon with Shallot Sauce

Preparation time: 15 minutes
Cooking time: 30 minutes | **Servings:** 4
4 salmon fillets
½ teaspoon pepper
1 teaspoon salt
¼ cup mayonnaise
½ cup pistachios, chopped
Sauce:
1 shallot, chopped
2 teaspoons lemon zest
1 tablespoon olive oil
A pinch of pepper
1 cup heavy cream
Directions
Preheat the oven to 370/375°F (190°C). Brush the salmon fillets with mayonnaise and season with pepper and salt. Coat with pistachios. Place in a lined large baking dish, and bake for 13-15 min. Heat the oil in a saucepan and sauté the shallots for a few minutes. Stir in the rest of the sauce ingredients. Bring to a boil and cook until thickened. Serve the salmon topped with the sauce.

Nutrition facts (per serving)
calories: 564 | fat: 47.0g | protein: 34.0g | carbs: 8.1g | net carbs: 6.0g | fiber: 2.1g

➤Spiced Jalapeño Bites with Tomato

Preparation Time: 10 minutes
Cooking Time: 0 minutes
Servings: 4
Ingredients:
1 cup turkey ham, chopped
1/4 jalapeño pepper, minced
1/4 cup mayonnaise
1/3 tablespoon Dijon mustard
4 tomatoes, sliced
Salt and black pepper, to taste
1 tablespoon parsley, chopped
Directions:
In a bowl, mix the turkey ham, jalapeño pepper, mayo, mustard, salt, and pepper. Spread out the tomato slices on four serving plates, then top each plate with a spoonful turkey ham mixture. Serve garnished with chopped parsley.
Nutrition facts:
Calories: 250
Fat: 14.1g
Fiber: 3.7g
Carbohydrates:4.1 g
Protein:18.9 g

➤Coconut Crab Cakes

Preparation Time: 20 minutes
Cooking Time: 25 minutes
Servings: 4
Ingredients:
1 tablespoon of minced garlic
2 pasteurized eggs
2 teaspoons of coconut oil
3/4 cup of coconut flakes
3/4 cup chopped of spinach
1/4 pound crabmeat
1/4 cup of chopped leek
1/2 cup extra virgin olive oil
1/2 teaspoon of pepper
1/4 onion diced
Salt
Directions:
Pour the crabmeat in a bowl, then add in the coconut flakes and mix well. Whisk eggs in a bowl, then mix in leek and spinach. Season the egg mixture with pepper, two pinches of salt, and garlic. Then, pour the eggs into the crab and stir well. Preheat a pan, heat extra virgin olive, and fry the crab evenly from each side until golden brown. Remove from pan and serve hot.
Nutrition facts:
Calories: 254
Fat: 9.5g
Fiber: 5.4g
Carbohydrates:4.1 g
Protein: 8.9g

›Tuna Cakes

Preparation Time: 15 minutes
Cooking Time: 10 minutes
Servings: 2
Ingredients:
1 (15-ounce) can water-packed tuna, drained
1/2 celery stalk, chopped
2 tablespoon fresh parsley, chopped
1 teaspoon fresh dill, chopped
2 tablespoons walnuts, chopped
2 tablespoons mayonnaise
1 organic egg, beaten
1 tablespoon butter
3 cups lettuce
Directions:
For burgers : Add ingredients (except the butter and lettuce) in a large bowl and mix until well combined. Make two equal-sized patties from the mixture.
Melt some butter and cook the patties for about 3–4 min. Carefully flip the side and cook for 3 min.
Divide the lettuce onto serving plates.
Top each plate with one burger and serve.
Nutrition facts:
Calories: 267
Fat: 12.5g
Fiber: 9.4g
Carbohydrates:3.8 g
Protein: 11.5g

›Creamed Spinach

Preparation Time: 10 minutes
Cooking Time: 15 minutes
Servings: 4
Ingredients:
2 tablespoons unsalted butter
1 small yellow onion, chopped
1 cup cream cheese, softened
2 (12-ounce) packages frozen spinach, thawed and squeezed dry
2–3 tablespoons water
Salt and ground black pepper, as required
1 teaspoon fresh lemon juice
Directions:
Melt some butter and sauté the onion for about 6–8 minutes. Add the cream cheese and cook for about 2 minutes or until melted completely. Stir in the water and spinach and cook for about 4–5 minutes.
Stir in the salt, black pepper, and lemon juice, and remove from heat. Serve immediately.
Nutrition facts:
Calories: 214
Fat: 9.5g
Fiber: 2.3g
Carbohydrates:2.1 g
Protein: 4.2g

›Tempura Zucchini with Cream Cheese Dip

Preparation Time: 15 minutes

Cooking Time: 15 minutes
Servings: 4
Ingredients:
Tempura zucchinis:
1 1/2 cups (200 g) almond flour
2 tbsp. heavy cream
1 tsp. salt
2 tbsp. olive oil + extra for frying
1 1/4 cups (300 ml) water
1/2 tbsp. sugar-free maple syrup
2 large zucchinis, cut into 1-inch-thick strips
Cream cheese dip:
8 oz cream cheese, room temperature
1/2 cup (113 g) sour cream
1 tsp. taco seasoning
1 scallion, chopped
1 green chili, deseeded and minced
Directions:
Tempura zucchinis:
In a bowl, mix the almond flour, heavy cream, salt, peanut oil, water, and maple syrup. Dredge the zucchini strips in the mixture until well-coated. Heat about four tablespoons of olive oil in a non-stick skillet. Working in batches, use tongs to remove the zucchinis (draining extra liquid) into the oil. Fry per side for 1 to 2 minutes and remove the zucchinis onto a paper towel-lined plate to drain grease. Enjoy the zucchinis.
Cream cheese dip:
In a bowl or container, the cream cheese, taco seasoning, sour cream, scallion, and green chili must be mixed, Serve the tempura zucchinis with the cream cheese dip.
Nutrition facts:
Calories: 316
Fat: 8.4g
Fiber: 9.3g
Carbohydrates:4.1 g
Protein: 5.1g

›Bacon and Feta Skewers

Preparation Time: 15 minutes
Cooking Time: 10 minutes
Servings: 4
Ingredients:
2 lb. feta cheese, cut into 8 cubes
8 bacon slices
4 bamboo skewers, soaked
1 zucchini, cut into 8 bite-size cubes
Salt and black pepper to taste
3 tbsp. almond oil for brushing
Directions:
Wrap each feta cube with a bacon slice.
Thread one wrapped feta on a skewer; add a zucchini cube, then another wrapped feta, and another zucchini. Repeat the threading process with the remaining skewers. Preheat a grill pan to medium heat, generously brush with the avocado oil and grill the skewer on both sides for 3 to 4 minutes per side or until the set is golden brown and the bacon cooked.
Serve afterward with the tomato sauce.
Nutrition facts:
Calories: 290
Fat: 15.1g

Fiber: 4.2g
Carbohydrates:4.1 g
Protein: 11.8g

›Avocado and salmon Deviled Eggs

Preparation Time: 20 minutes
Cooking Time: 10 minutes
Servings: 4
Ingredients:
4 eggs
Ice bath
4 smoked salmon slices, chopped
1 avocado, pitted and peeled
1 tbsp. mustard
1 tsp. plain vinegar
1 tbsp. heavy cream
1 tbsp. chopped fresh cilantro
Salt and black pepper to taste
1/2 cup (113 g) mayonnaise
1 tbsp. coconut cream
1/4 tsp. cayenne pepper
1 tbsp. avocado oil
1 tbsp. chopped fresh parsley
Directions:
Boil the eggs for 8 minutes. Remove the eggs into the ice bath, sit for 3 minutes, and then peel the eggs. Slice the eggs lengthwise into halves and empty the egg yolks into a bowl. Arrange the egg whites on a plate with the hole side facing upwards. While the eggs are cooked, heat a non-stick skillet over medium heat and cook the ham for 5 to 8 minutes. Remove the salmon onto a paper towel-lined plate to drain grease. Put the avocado slices to the egg yolks and mash both ingredients with a fork until smooth.
Mix in the mustard, vinegar, heavy cream, cilantro, salt, and black pepper until well-blended. Spoon the mixture into a bag and press the mixture into the egg holes until well-filled. In a bowl, whisk the mayonnaise, coconut cream, cayenne pepper, and avocado oil. On serving plates, spoon some of the mayonnaise sauce and slightly smear it in a circular movement. Top with the deviled eggs, scatter the ham on top and garnish with the parsley. Enjoy immediately.
Nutrition facts:
Calories: 365
Fat: 11.7g
Fiber: 4.1g
Carbohydrates:3.1 g
Protein:7.9 g

›Chili-Lime Tuna Salad

Preparation Time: 10 minutes
Cooking Time: 0 minutes
Servings: 2
Ingredients:
1 tablespoon of lime juice
1/3 cup of mayonnaise
1/4 teaspoon of salt
1 teaspoon of Tajin chili lime seasoning
1/8 teaspoon of pepper
1 medium stalk celery (finely chopped)
2 cups of romaine lettuce (chopped roughly) 2 table-
spoons of red onion (finely chopped) optional: chopped green onion, black pepper, lemon juice
5 oz canned tuna
Directions:
Using a bowl of medium size, mix some of the ingredients such as lime, pepper, and chili-lime. Then, add tuna and vegetables to the pot and stir. You can serve with cucumber, celery, or a bed of greens
Nutrition facts:
Calories: 259
Fat: 11.3g
Fiber: 7.4g
Carbohydrates:2.9 g
Protein: 12.9g

›Chicken Club Lettuce Wraps

Preparation Time: 15 minutes
Cooking Time: 15 minutes
Servings: 1
Ingredients:
1 head of iceberg lettuce with the core and outer leaves removed
1 tbsp. of mayonnaise
7 slices of organic chicken or turkey breast
Bacon (2 cooked strips, halved)
Tomato (just 2 slices)
Directions:
Line your working surface with a large slice of parchment paper. Layer 6-8 large leaves of lettuce in the center of the paper to make a base of around 9-10 inches. Spread the mayo in the center and lay with chicken or turkey, bacon, and tomato. Starting with the end closest to you, roll the wrap like a jelly roll with the parchment paper as your guide. Keep it tight and halfway through, roll tuck in the ends of the wrap. When it is completely wrapped, roll the rest of the parchment paper around it, and use a knife to cut it in half.
Nutrition facts:
Calories: 179
Fat: 4.1g
Fiber: 9.7g
Carbohydrates:1.3 g
Protein: 8.5g

›BLT Salad

Preparation Time: 15 minutes
Cooking Time: 0 minutes
Servings: 4
Ingredients:
2 tablespoons melted bacon fat
2 tablespoons red wine vinegar
Freshly ground black pepper
4 cups shredded lettuce
1 tomato, chopped
6 bacon slices, cooked and chopped
2 hardboiled eggs, chopped
1 tablespoon roasted unsalted sunflower seeds
1 teaspoon toasted sesame seeds
1 cooked chicken breast, sliced (optional)
Directions:
In a medium bowl, whisk together the bacon fat and

vinegar until emulsified.

Season with black pepper. Add the tomato and lettuce to the bowl and toss the vegetables with the dressing. Divide the salad between 4 plates and top each with equal amounts of bacon, egg, sunflower seeds, sesame seeds, and chicken (if using). Serve.

Nutrition facts:
Calories: 287
Fat: 9.4g
Fiber: 11g
Carbohydrates:3.8 g
Protein: 9.9g

nutes, then slice into four pieces.

In a frying pan, warm one tablespoon of oil and cook the eggs. Stir well to create large and soft curds—season with salt and pepper. Put the eggs and grilled cheese on a serving bowl. Serve alongside tomatoes and avocado, decorated with chopped pecans.

Nutrition facts:
Calories: 219
Fat: 5.1g
Fiber: 4.9g
Carbohydrates:1.5 g
Protein: 3.9g

➤Crab-stuffed Avocado

Preparation Time: 20 minutes
Cooking Time: 0 minutes
Servings: 2
Ingredients:
1 avocado, peeled, halved lengthwise, and pitted
1/2 teaspoon freshly squeezed lemon juice
41/2 ounces Dungeness crabmeat
1/2 cup cream cheese
1/4 cup chopped red bell pepper
1/4 cup chopped, peeled English cucumber
1/2 scallion, chopped
1 teaspoon chopped cilantro
Pinch sea salt
Freshly ground black pepper

Directions:
Brush the cut edges of the avocado with the lemon juice and set the halves aside on a plate. In a bowl or container, the crabmeat, cream cheese, red pepper, cucumber, scallion, cilantro, salt, and pepper must be well mixed. The crab mixture will then be divided between the avocado

Nutrition facts:
Calories: 239
Fat: 11.4g
Fiber: 8.1g
Carbohydrates:3.8 g
Protein: 5.9g

➤Grilled Halloumi Cheese with Eggs

Preparation Time: 15 minutes
Cooking Time:10 minutes
Servings: 4
Ingredients:
4 slices halloumi cheese
3 tsp. olive oil
1 tsp. dried Greek seasoning blend
1 tbsp. olive oil
6 eggs, beaten
1/2 tsp. sea salt
1/4 tsp. crushed red pepper flakes
1 1/2 cups avocado, pitted and sliced
1 cup grape tomatoes, halved
4 tbsp. pecans, chopped

Directions:
Preheat your grill to medium. Set the Halloumi in the center of a piece of heavy-duty foil. Sprinkle oil over the Halloumi and apply Greek seasoning blend. Close the foil to create a packet. Grill for about 15 mi-

➤Onion Cod Fillets

Preparation time: 10 minutes
Cooking time: 3 hours
Servings: 4
Ingredients:
1 onion, minced
4 cod fillets
1 teaspoon salt
1 teaspoon dried cilantro
½ cup of water
1 teaspoon butter, melted

Directions
Sprinkle the cod fillets with salt, dried cilantro, and butter. Then place them in the slow cooker and top with minced onion. Add water and close the lid. Cook the fish on high for 3 hours.

Nutrition facts
109 calories,
20.3g protein,
2.6g carbohydrates,
2g fat,
0.6g fiber,
58mg cholesterol,
660mg sodium,
41mg potassium

➤Lemon Scallops

Preparation time: 10 minutes
Cooking time: 1 hours
Servings: 4
Ingredients:
1-pound scallops
1 teaspoon salt
1 teaspoon ground white pepper
½ teaspoon olive oil
3 tablespoons lemon juice
1 teaspoon lemon zest, grated
1 tablespoon dried oregano
½ cup of water

Directions:
Sprinkle the scallops with salt, ground white pepper, lemon juice, and lemon zest and leave for 10-15 minutes to marinate. After this, sprinkle the scallops with olive oil and dried oregano. Put the scallops in the slow cooker and add water. Cook the seafood on High for 1 hour.

Nutrition facts
113 calories,
19.3g protein,

4.1g carbohydrates,
1.7g fat,
0.7g fiber,
37mg cholesterol,
768mg sodium,
407mg potassium

➤Nutmeg Trout

Preparation time: 10 minutes
Cooking time: 3 hours
Servings: 4
Ingredients:
1 tablespoon ground nutmeg
1 tablespoon butter, softened
1 teaspoon dried cilantro
1 teaspoon dried oregano
1 teaspoon fish sauce
4 trout fillets
½ cup of water
Directions
In the shallow bowl mix butter with cilantro, dried oregano, and fish sauce. Add ground nutmeg and whisk the mixture. Then grease the fish fillets with nutmeg mixture and put in the slow cooker. Add remaining butter mixture and water.
Cook the fish on high for 3 hours.
Nutrition facts
154 calories,
16.8g protein,
1.2g carbohydrates
8.8g fat,
0.5g fiber,
54mg cholesterol,
178mg sodium,
305mg potassium.

➤Sweet Milkfish Saute

Preparation time: 10 minutes
Cooking time: 3 hours
Servings: 4
Ingredients:
2 mangos, pitted, peeled, chopped
12 oz milkfish fillet, chopped
½ cup tomatoes, chopped
½ cup of water
1 teaspoon ground cardamom
Directions
Mix mangos with tomatoes and ground cardamom. Transfer the ingredients in the slow cooker. Then add milkfish fillet and water. Cook the saute on High for 3 hours. Carefully stir the saute before serving.
Nutrition facts
268 calories,
24g protein,
26.4g carbohydrates,
8.1g fat, 3.1g fiber,
57mg cholesterol,
82mg sodium,
660mg potassium.

➤Cod Sticks

Preparation time: 15 minutes
Cooking time: 1.5 hours
Servings: 2
Ingredients:
2 cod fillets
1 teaspoon ground black pepper
1 egg, beaten
1/3 cup breadcrumbs
1 tablespoon coconut oil
¼ cup of water
Directions
Cut the cod fillets into medium sticks and sprinkle with ground black pepper. Then dip the fish in the beaten egg and coat in the breadcrumbs. Pour water in the slow cooker. Add coconut oil and fish sticks.
Cook the meal on High for 1.5 hours.
Nutrition facts
254 calories,
25.3g protein,
13.8g carbohydrates,
11g fat,
1.1g fiber,
137mg cholesterol,
234mg sodium,
78mg potassium.

➤Cinnamon Catfish

Preparation time: 10 minutes
Cooking time: 2.5 hours
Servings: 2
Ingredients:
2 catfish fillets
1 teaspoon ground cinnamon
1 tablespoon lemon juice
½ teaspoon sesame oil
1/3 cup water
Directions
Sprinkle the fish fillets with ground cinnamon, lemon juice, and sesame oil. Put the fillets in the slow cooker in one layer. Add water and close the lid.
Cook the meal on High for 2.5 hours.
Nutrition facts
231 calories,
25g protein,
1.1g carbohydrates,
13.3g fat,
0.6g fiber,
75mg cholesterol,
88mg sodium,
528mg potassium.

➤Hot Salmon

Preparation time: 10 minutes
Cooking time: 3 hours
Servings: 4
Ingredients:
1-pound salmon fillet, sliced
2 chili peppers, chopped
1 tablespoon olive oil
1 onion, diced

½ cup cream
½ teaspoon salt
Directions
Mix salmon with salt, onion, and olive oil.
Transfer the ingredients in the slow cooker.
Add cream and onion.
Cook the salmon on high for 3 hours.
Nutrition facts
211 calories,
22.6g protein,
3.7g carbohydrates,
12.2g fat,
0.7g fiber,
56mg cholesterol,
352mg sodium,
491mg potassium.

➤Sage Shrimps

Preparation time: 10 minutes
Cooking time: 1 hours
Servings: 4
Ingredients:
1-pound shrimps, peeled
1 teaspoon dried sage
1 teaspoon minced garlic
1 teaspoon white pepper
1 cup tomatoes chopped
½ cup of water
Directions
Put all ingredients in the slow cooker and close the lid.
Cook the shrimps on High for 1 hour.
Nutrition facts
146 calories,
26.4g protein,
4.1g carbohydrates,
2.1g fat,
0.8g fiber,
239mg cholesterol,
280mg sodium,
310mg potassium.

➤Miso Cod

Preparation time: 10 minutes
Cooking time: 4 hours
Servings: 4
Ingredients:
1-pound cod fillet, sliced
1 teaspoon miso paste
½ teaspoon ground ginger
2 cups chicken stock
½ teaspoon ground nutmeg
Directions
In the mixing bowl mix chicken stock, ground nutmeg, ground ginger, and miso paste. Then pour the liquid in the slow cooker. Add cod fillet and close the lid.
Cook the fish on Low for 4 hours.
Nutrition facts
101 calories,
20.8g protein,
1.1g carbohydrates,
1.5g fat,
0.2g fiber,

56mg cholesterol,
506mg sodium,
14mg potassium.

➤Shrimp Scampi

Preparation time: 5 minutes
Cooking time: 4 hours
Servings: 4
Ingredients:
1-pound shrimps, peeled
2 tablespoons lemon juice
2 tablespoons coconut oil
1 cup of water
1 teaspoon dried parsley
½ teaspoon white pepper
Directions
Put all ingredients in the slow cooker and gently mix.
Close the lid and cook the scampi on Low for 4 hours.
Nutrition facts
196 calories,
25.9g protein,
2.1g carbohydrates,
8.8g fat,
0.1g fiber,
239mg cholesterol,
280mg sodium,
207mg potassium

➤Lemon Dill Salmon

Preparation Time: 10 minutes
Cooking Time: 2 hours
Serves: 4
Ingredients:
1 lb. salmon fillet, skin-on
2 Tbsp. fresh dill, chopped
1/2 lemon juice
1 1/2 cups vegetable stock
1 lemon, sliced
Pepper Salt
Directions:
Line a crock pot with parchment paper. Place lemon slices on the bottom of the crock pot and then place the salmon on top of the slices. Season salmon with pepper and salt. Add lemon juice and stock to the crock pot. Cover and cook on low for 2 hours.
Serve and enjoy.
Nutrition facts
Calories 162
Fat 7.7 g
Carbohydrates 2.9 g

➤Hot Calamari

Preparation time: 10 minutes
Cooking time: 1 hours
Servings: 4
Ingredients:
12 oz calamari, sliced
¼ cup of soy sauce
1 teaspoon cayenne pepper
1 garlic clove, crushed

1 teaspoon mustard
½ cup of water
1 teaspoon sesame oil
Directions
In the bowl mix slices calamari, soy sauce, cayenne pepper, garlic, mustard, and sesame oil. Leave the ingredients for 10 minutes to marinate. Then transfer the mixture in the slow cooker, add water, and close the lid. Cook the meal on high for 1 hour.
Nutrition facts
103 calories,
14.6g protein,
4.6g carbohydrates,
2.6g fat,
0.4g fiber,
198mg cholesterol,
937mg sodium,
262mg potassium.

›Curry Squid

Preparation time: 10 minutes
Cooking time: 3 hours
Servings: 5
Ingredients:
15 oz. squid, peeled, sliced
1 teaspoon curry paste ½ cup of coconut milk
¼ cup of water
1 teaspoon dried dill
1 teaspoon ground nutmeg
Directions
Mix coconut milk with water and curry paste. Then pour the liquid in the slow cooker. Add dried dill and ground nutmeg. After this, add the sliced squid and close the lid. Cook the meal on low for 3 hours.
Nutrition facts
143 calories,
13.9g protein,
4.6g carbohydrates,
7.6g fat,
0.7g fiber,
198mg cholesterol,
42mg sodium,
281mg potassium.

›Thyme Mussels

Preparation time: 10 minutes
Cooking time: 2.5 hours
Servings: 4
Ingredients:
1-pound mussels
1 teaspoon dried thyme
1 teaspoon ground black pepper
½ teaspoon salt
1 cup of water
½ cup sour cream
Directions
In the mixing bowl mix mussels, dried thyme, ground black pepper, and salt. Then pour water in the slow cooker. Add sour cream and cook the liquid on High for 1.5 hours. After this, add mussels and cook them for 1 hour on High or until the mussels are opened.
Nutrition facts

161 calories,
14.5g protein,
5.9g carbohydrates,
8.6g fat,
0.2g fiber,
44mg cholesterol,
632mg sodium
414mg potassium.

›Coconut Catfish

Preparation time: 10 minutes
Cooking time: 2.5 hours
Servings: 3
Ingredients:
3 catfish fillets
1 teaspoon coconut shred
½ cup of coconut milk
1 teaspoon sesame seeds
2 tablespoons fish sauce
1 cup of water
2 tablespoons soy sauce
Directions
Pour water in the slow cooker. Add soy sauce, fish sauce, sesame seeds, and coconut milk. Then add coconut shred and catfish fillets. Cook the fish on high for 2.5 hours.
Nutrition facts
329 calories,
27.3g protein,
3.9g carbohydrates,
22.7g fat,
1.2g fiber,
75mg cholesterol,
1621mg sodium,
682mg potassium.

›Tender Tilapia in Cream Sauce

Preparation time: 10 minutes
Cooking time: 5 hours
Servings: 4
Ingredients:
4 tilapia fillets
½ cup heavy cream
1 teaspoon garlic powder
1 teaspoon ground black pepper
½ teaspoon salt
1 teaspoon corn flour
Directions
Mix corn flour with cream until smooth. Then pour the liquid in the slow cooker. After this, sprinkle the tilapia fillets with garlic powder, ground black pepper, and salt. Place the fish fillets in the slow cooker and close the lid. Cook the fish on Low for 5 hours.
Nutrition facts
151 calories,
21.6g protein,
1.7g carbohydrates,
6.6g fat,
0.3g fiber,
76mg cholesterol,
337mg sodium
28mg potassium

›Rosemary Salmon

Preparation Time: 10 minutes
Cooking Time: 2 hours
Serves: 2
Ingredients:
8 oz. salmon
1/4 tsp. fresh rosemary, minced
2 Tbsp. fresh lemon juice
1/3 cup water
1 Tbsp. capers 1 fresh lemon, sliced
Directions:
Place salmon into a crock pot. Pour lemon juice and water over the salmon. Arrange lemon slices on top of the salmon. Sprinkle with rosemary and capers. Cover and cook on low for 2 hours. Serve and enjoy.
Nutrition facts
Calories 164
Fat 7.3 g
Carbohydrates 3.3 g

›Fish Salpicao

Preparation time: 5 minutes
Cooking time: 1 hours
Servings: 4
Ingredients:
1 teaspoon ground black pepper
1 teaspoon cayenne pepper
1 tablespoon avocado oil
1-pound cod fillet
1 teaspoon salt
1 garlic clove, diced
Directions
Put all ingredients in the slow cooker and carefully mix. Then close the lid and cook the meal on High for 1 hour.
Nutrition facts
100 calories,
20.5g protein,
1g carbohydrates,
1.6g fat,
0.4g fiber,
56mg cholesterol,
653mg sodium,
30mg potassium.

›Sea bass Ragout

Preparation time: 15 minutes
Cooking time: 3.5 hours
Servings: 4
Ingredients:
7 oz. shiitake mushrooms
1 onion, diced
1 tablespoon coconut oil
1 teaspoon ground coriander
½ teaspoon salt
1 cup of water
12 oz. sea bass fillet, chopped
Directions
Heat the coconut oil in the skillet. Add onion and

mushrooms and roast the vegetables for 5 minutes on medium heat. Then transfer the vegetables in the slow cooker and add water. Add fish fillet, salt, and ground coriander. Cook the meal on High for 3.5 hours.
Nutrition facts
241 calories,
20.4g protein,
9.4g carbohydrates,
14g fat,
2.3g fiber
0mg cholesterol,
413mg sodium,
99mg potassium.

›Cardamom Trout

Preparation time: 10 minutes
Cooking time: 2.5 hours
Servings: 4
Ingredients:
1 teaspoon ground cardamom
1-pound trout fillet
1 teaspoon butter, melted
1 tablespoon lemon juice
¼ cup of water
1.2 teaspoon salt
Directions
In the shallow bowl mix butter, lemon juice, and salt. Then sprinkle the trout fillet with ground cardamom and butter mixture. Place the fish in the slow cooker and add water. Cook the meal on High for 2.5 hours.
Nutrition facts
226 calories,
30.3g protein,
0.4g carbohydrates,
10.6g fat,
0.2g fiber,
86mg cholesterol,
782mg sodium,
536mg potassium.

›Butter Salmon

Preparation time: 10 minutes
Cooking time: 1.5 hours
Servings: 2
Ingredients:
8 oz. salmon fillet
3 tablespoons butter
1 teaspoon dried sage
¼ cup of water

Directions
Churn butter with sage and preheat the mixture until liquid. Then cut the salmon fillets into 2 servings and put in the slow cooker. Add water and melted butter mixture. Close the lid and cook the salmon on High for 1.5 hours.
Nutrition facts
304 calories,
22.2g protein,
0.2g carbohydrates,
24.3g fat,
0.1g fiber

, 96mg cholesterol,
174mg sodium
444mg potassium.

›Tuna Casserole

Preparation time: 15 minutes
Cooking time: 6 hours
Servings: 4
Ingredients:
1 cup mushrooms, sliced
½ cup corn kernels, frozen
8 oz tuna, chopped
1 teaspoon Italian seasonings
1 cup chicken stock
½ cup Cheddar cheese, shredded
1 tablespoon sesame oil
Directions
Heat the sesame oil in the skillet. Add mushrooms
and roast them for 5 minutes on medium heat. Then
transfer the mushrooms in the slow cooker and flatten
in one layer. After this, mix Italian seasonings with tuna
and put over the mushrooms. Then top the fish with
corn kernels and cheese. Add chicken stock. Cook
the casserole on Low for 7 hours.
Nutrition facts
219 calories,
19.9g protein,
4.7g carbohydrates,
13.4g fat,
0.7g fiber,
33mg cholesterol,
311mg sodium,
315mg potassium.

›Creamy Shrimp

Preparation Time: 10 minutes
Cooking Time: 2 hours 10 minutes
Serves: 4
Ingredients:
1 lb. cooked shrimp
1 cup sour cream
10.5oz. can cream of mushroom soup
1tsp. curry powder
1 onion, chopped
Directions:
Spray a medium pan with cooking spray and heat
over medium heat. Add onion to the hot pan and
sauté until onion is soft. Transfer sautéed onion to a
crock pot along with the shrimp, curry powder, and
cream of mushroom soup. Cover and cook on low for
2 hours. Stir in sour cream and serve.
Nutrition facts
Calories 302
Fat 16.2 g
Carbohydrates 9.5 g
Sugar 1.8 g
Protein 28.6 g
Cholesterol 264 mg

›Cumin Snapper

Preparation time: 15 minutes
Cooking time: 4 hours
Servings: 4
Ingredients
1-pound snapper, peeled, cleaned
1 teaspoon ground cumin
½ teaspoon salt
½ teaspoon garlic powder
1 teaspoon dried oregano
1 tablespoon sesame oil
¼ cup of water
Directions
Cut the snapper into 4 servings. After this, in the shallow bowl mix ground cumin, salt, garlic powder, and
dried oregano. Sprinkle fish with spices and sesame oil.
Arrange the snapper in the slow cooker. Add water.
Cook the fish on Low for 4 hours.
Nutrition facts
183 calories,
29.9g protein,
0.7g carbohydrates,
5.6g fat,
0.3g fiber,
54mg cholesterol,
360mg sodium,
20mg potassium.

›Sweet and Sour Shrimps

Preparation time: 10 minutes
Cooking time: 50 minutes
Servings: 2
Ingredients:
8 oz shrimps, peeled
½ cup of water
2 tablespoons lemon juice
1 tablespoon maple syrup
Directions
Pour water in the slow cooker. Add shrimps and cook
them on High for 50 minutes. Then drain water and ass
lemon juice and maple syrup. Carefully stir the shrimps
and transfer them in the serving bowls.
Nutrition facts
165 calories,
26g protein,
8.8g carbohydrates,
2.1g fat,
0.1g fiber
239mg cholesterol,
282mg sodium
232mg potassium.

›Trout Cakes

Preparation time: 10 minutes
Cooking time: 2 hours
Servings: 2
Ingredients:
7 oz. trout fillet, diced
1 tablespoon semolina
1 teaspoon dried oregano
¼ teaspoon ground black pepper
1 teaspoon corn flour
1 egg, beaten

1/3 cup water
1 teaspoon sesame oil
Directions
In the bowl mix diced trout, semolina, dried oregano, ground black pepper, and corn flour. Then add egg and carefully mix the mixture. Heat the sesame oil well. Then make the fish cakes and put them in the hot oil. Roast them for 1 minute per side and transfer in the slow cooker. Add water and cook the trout cakes for 2 hours on High.
Nutrition facts
266 calories,
30g protein,
5.6g carbohydrates,
13.1g fat,
0.7g fiber,
155mg cholesterol,
99mg sodium,
519mg potassium.

›Haddock Chowder

Preparation time: 10 minutes
Cooking time: 6 hours
Servings: 5
Ingredients:
1-pound haddock, chopped
2 bacon slices, chopped, cooked
½ cup potatoes, chopped
1 teaspoon ground coriander
½ cup heavy cream
4 cups of water
1 teaspoon salt
Directions
Put all ingredients in the slow cooker and close the lid. Cook the chowder on Low for 6 hours.
Nutrition facts
203 calories,
27.1g protein,
2.8g carbohydrates,
8.6g fat,
0.4g fiber,
97mg cholesterol,
737mg sodium,
506mg potassium

›Orange Cod

Preparation time: 10 minutes
Cooking time: 3 hours
Servings: 4
Ingredients:
1-pound cod fillet, chopped
2 oranges, chopped
1 tablespoon maple syrup
1 cup of water
1 garlic clove, diced
1 teaspoon ground black pepper
Directions
Mix cod with ground black pepper and transfer in the slow cooker. Add garlic, water, maple syrup, and oranges.
Close the lid and cook the meal on High for 3 hours
Nutrition facts

150 calories, 2
1.2g protein,
14.8g carbohydrates,
1.2g fat,
2.4g fiber,
56mg cholesterol,
73mg sodium,
187mg potassium.

›Fish Pie

Preparation time: 15 minutes
Cooking time: 7 hours
Servings: 6
Ingredients:
7 oz. yeast dough
1 tablespoon cream cheese
8 oz. salmon fillet, chopped
1 onion, diced
1 teaspoon salt
1 tablespoon fresh dill
1 teaspoon olive oil
Directions
Brush the slow cooker bottom with olive oil. Then roll up the dough and place it in the slow cooker. Flatten it in the shape of the pie crust. After this, in the mixing bowl mix cream cheese, salmon, onion, salt, and dill. Put the fish mixture over the pie crust and cover with foil. Close the lid and cook the pie on Low for 7 hours.
Nutrition facts
158 calories,
9.5g protein,
18.6g carbohydrates,
5g fat,
1.3g fiber,
19mg cholesterol,
524mg sodium,
191mg potassium.

›Lemon Trout

Preparation time: 15 minutes
Cooking time: 5 hours
Servings: 4
Ingredients:
1-pound trout, peeled, cleaned
1 lemon, sliced
1 teaspoon dried thyme
1 teaspoon ground black pepper
1 tablespoon olive oil
½ teaspoon salt
½ cup of water
Directions
Rub the fish with dried thyme, ground black pepper, and salt. Then fill the fish with sliced lemon and sprinkle with olive oil. Place the trout in the slow cooker and add water. Cook the fish on Low for 5 hours.
Nutrition facts
252 calories,
30.4g protein,
1.9g carbohydrates,
13.2g fat,
0.6g fiber,
84mg cholesterol,

368mg sodium,
554mg potassium.

▸Coconut Shrimp Curry

Preparation Time: 10 minutes
Cooking Time: 2 hours 30 minutes
Serves: 4
Ingredients:
1 lb. shrimp
1/4 cup fresh cilantro, chopped
2 tsp. lemon garlic seasoning
1 Tbsp. curry paste
15 oz. water
30 oz. coconut milk
Directions:
Add coconut milk, cilantro, lemon garlic seasoning,
curry paste, and water to a crock pot and stir well.
Cover and cook on high for 2 hours. Add shrimp,
cover and cook for 30 minutes longer. Serve and en-
joy.
Nutrition facts
Calories 200
Fat 7.7 g
Carbohydrates 4.6 g

— CHAPTER 6 —

FRUIT AND DESSERT

ALICIA TRAVIS

›Apple and Berries Ambrosia

Preparation time: 15 minutes
Cooking time: 0 minutes | **Servings:** 4
2 cups unsweetened coconut milk, chilled
2 tablespoons raw honey
1 apple, peeled, cored, and chopped
2 cups fresh raspberries
2 cups fresh blueberries
Spoon the chilled milk in a large bowl, then mix in the honey. Stir to mix well.
Then mix in the remaining ingredients. Stir to coat the fruits well and serve immediately.
Nutrition facts (per serving)
calories: 386 | fat: 21.1g | protein: 4.2g | carbs: 45.9g | fiber: 11.0g | sodium: 16mg

›Banana, Cranberry, and Oat Bars

Preparation time: 15 minutes
Cooking time: 40 minutes | **Makes** 16 bars
2 tablespoon extra-virgin olive oil
2 medium ripe bananas, mashed
½ cup almond butter
½ cup maple syrup
⅓ cup dried cranberries
1½ cups old-fashioned rolled oats
¼ cup oat flour
¼ cup ground flaxseed
¼ teaspoon ground cloves
½ cup shredded coconut
½ teaspoon ground cinnamon
1 teaspoon vanilla extract

Preheat the oven to 390/400°F (205°C). Line a 8-inch square pan with parchment paper, then grease with olive oil. Combine the mashed bananas, almond butter, and maple syrup in a bowl. Stir to mix well.
Mix all the ingredients together to make a smooth mixture. Spread the mixture evenly on the square pan with a spatula, then bake in the preheated oven for 38-41 minutes or until a toothpick inserted in the center comes out clean. Remove them from the oven and slice into 16 bars to serve.
Nutrition facts (per serving)
calories: 145 | fat: 7.2g | protein: 3.1g | carbs: 18.9g | fiber: 2.0g | sodium: 3mg

›Berry and Rhubarb Cobbler

Preparation time: 15 minutes
Cooking time: 35 minutes | **Servings:** 8
Cobbler:
1 cup fresh raspberries
2 cups fresh blueberries
1 cup sliced (½-inch) rhubarb pieces
1 tablespoon arrowroot powder
¼ cup unsweetened apple juice
2 tablespoons melted coconut oil
¼ cup raw honey
Topping:
1 cup almond flour
1 tablespoon arrowroot powder
½ cup shredded coconut

¼ cup raw honey
½ cup coconut oil

Make the Cobbler
Preheat the oven to 340/350°F (180°C). Grease a baking dish with melted coconut oil. Combine the ingredients for the cobbler in a large bowl. Stir to mix well. Spread the mixture in the single layer on the baking dish. Set aside.
Make the Topping
Combine the almond flour, arrowroot powder, and coconut in a bowl. Stir to mix well. Fold in the honey and coconut oil. Stir with a fork until the mixture crumbled. Spread the topping over the cobbler, then bake in the preheated oven for 35 minutes or until frothy and golden brown. Serve immediately.
Nutrition facts (per serving)
calories: 305 | fat: 22.1g | protein: 3.2g | carbs: 29.8g | fiber: 4.0g | sodium: 3mg

›Citrus Cranberry and Quinoa Energy Bites

Preparation time: 25 minutes
Cooking time: 0 minutes | **Makes** 12 bites
2 tablespoons almond butter
2 tablespoons maple syrup
¾ cup cooked quinoa
1 tablespoon dried cranberries
1 tablespoon chia seeds
¼ cup ground almonds
¼ cup sesame seeds, toasted
Zest of 1 orange
½ teaspoon vanilla extract

Line a baking sheet with parchment paper.
Mix well the maple syrup and butter in a bowl. Stir to mix well. Fold in the remaining ingredients and stir until the mixture holds together and smooth. Divide the mixture into 13 equal parts, then shape each part into a ball. Arrange the balls on the baking sheet, then refrigerate for at least 15 minutes. Serve chilled.
Nutrition facts (per serving) (1 bite)
calories: 110 | fat: 10.8g | protein: 3.1g | carbs: 4.9g | fiber: 3.0g | sodium: 211mg

›Chocolate, Almond, and Cherry Clusters

Preparation time: 15 minutes
Cooking time: 3 minutes | **Makes** 10 clusters
1 cup dark chocolate (70% cocoa or higher), chopped
½ cup dried cherries
1 tablespoon coconut oil
1 cup roasted salted almonds

Melt the coconut oil and the chocolate in a saucepan for 4 min. Turn off the heat and stir in the cherries and almonds. Line a baking sheet with baking paper. Place the mixture in the refrigerator to cool on a baking sheet for at least 1 hour.
Nutrition facts (per serving)

calories: 198 | fat: 13.5g | protein: 4.0g | carbs: 17.8g | fiber: 4.0g | sodium: 57mg

➤Chocolate and Avocado Mousse

Preparation time: 40 minutes
Cooking time: 5 minutes
Servings: 4 to 6
8 ounces (227 g) dark chocolate (70% cocoa or higher), chopped
¼ cup unsweetened coconut milk
2 ripe avocados, deseeded
¼ cup raw honey
2 ripe avocados, deseeded
Sea salt, to taste

Put the chocolate in a small saucepan. Pour in the coconut milk and add the coconut oil. Place the avocado in a saucepan, then add the honey and melted chocolate. Pour the mixture into a bowl and add the salt. Place in the fridge to chill for 45 minutes and serve cold.

Nutrition facts (per serving)
calories: 655 | fat: 46.5g | protein: 7.2g | carbs: 55.9g | fiber: 9.0g | sodium: 112mg

➤Coconut Blueberries with Brown Rice

Preparation time: 55 minutes
Cooking time: 10 minutes | **Servings:** 4
1 cup fresh blueberries
2 cups unsweetened coconut milk
1 teaspoon ground ginger
¼ cup maple syrup
Sea salt, to taste
2 cups cooked brown rice

Put all the ingredients, except for the brown rice, in a pot. Cook over medium/high heat until the blueberries are tender or for 7 minutes. Pour in the brown rice and cook for 4 more minute or until the rice is soft. Serve immediately.

Nutrition facts (per serving)
calories: 475 | fat: 25.8g | protein: 7.2g | carbs: 60.1g | fiber: 5.0g | sodium: 75mg

➤Blueberry and Oat Crisp

Preparation time: 15 minutes
Cooking time: 20 minutes | **Servings:** 4
2 tablespoons coconut oil, melted
4 cups fresh blueberries
Juice of ½ lemon
2 teaspoons lemon zest
¼ cup maple syrup
1 cup gluten-free rolled oats
½ cup chopped pecans
½ teaspoon ground cinnamon
Sea salt, to taste

Preheat the oven to 340/350°F (180°C). Grease a baking sheet with coconut oil. Combine zest, blueberries, lemon juice, and maple syrup in a bowl, mix until

smooth, then spread onto a baking sheet. Combine all listed ingredients in a bowl and pour new mixture over previous mixture (blueberries mixture). Bake in the heated oven until the oats are golden brown or for 20 minutes. Serve immediately with spoons.

Nutrition facts (per serving)
calories: 495 | fat: 33.9g | protein: 5.1g | carbs: 50.8g | fiber: 7.0g | sodium: 41mg

➤Glazed Pears with Hazelnuts

Preparation time: 10 minutes
Cooking time: 20 minutes | **Servings:** 4
4 pears, peeled, cored, and quartered lengthwise
1 cup apple juice
1 tablespoon grated fresh ginger
½ cup pure maple syrup
¼ cup chopped hazelnuts

Put the pears in a saucepan, then pour in the apple juice. Bring to a boil over medium/high heat, then reduce the heat to medium/low. Stir constantly. Cover and simmer for an additional 13-15 min or until the pears are tender. In a saucepan, combine the maple syrup and ginger and bring to a boil over medium-high heat. Turn off the heat and transfer the syrup to a small bowl. Place the pears in a large bowl and add the syrup. Add the hazelnuts on top of the pears and serve.

Nutrition facts (per serving)
calories: 288 | fat: 4.1g | protein: 3.2g | carbs: 66.9g | fiber: 7.0g | sodium: 8mg

➤Lemony Blackberry Granita

Preparation time: 10 minutes
Cooking time: 0 minutes | **Servings:** 4
1 pound (454 g) fresh blackberries
1 teaspoon chopped fresh thyme
¼ cup freshly squeezed lemon juice
½ cup raw honey
½ cup water

Place the ingredients in a food processor so that the mixture is smooth and homogeneous. Pour the mixture onto a baking sheet and place it in the freezer for about 3 hours. Remove the baking sheet from the refrigerator and stir the mixture to break up the frozen bits, this process will be done twice every 3 hours.
Place the pan back in the freezer one last time and leave for 5 hours, as soon as the slush is ready you can serve it.

Nutrition facts (per serving)
calories: 185 | fat: 1.1g | protein: 3.2g | carbs: 45.9g | fiber: 6.0g | sodium: 6mg

➤Lemony Tea and Chia Pudding

Preparation time: 30 minutes
Cooking time: 0 minutes | **Servings:** 3 to 4
2 teaspoons matcha green tea powder (optional)
2 tablespoons ground chia seeds
1 to 2 dates

2 cups unsweetened coconut milk
Zest and juice of 1 lime

Put the ingredients in a food processor and pulse until creamy and smooth. Pour the mixture in a bowl, then wrap in plastic. Store in the refrigerator for at least 18-20 minutes, then serve chilled.

Nutrition facts (per serving)
calories: 225 | fat: 20.1g | protein: 3.2g | carbs: 5.9g | fiber: 5.0g | sodium: 314mg

›Sweet Spiced Pumpkin Pudding

Preparation time: 2 hours 10 minutes
Cooking time: 0 minutes | **Servings:** 6
1 cup pure pumpkin purée
2 cups unsweetened coconut milk
1teaspoon ground cinnamon
¼ teaspoon ground nutmeg
½ teaspoon ground ginger
Pinch cloves
¼ cup pure maple syrup
2 tablespoons chopped pecans, for garnish

Combine the ingredients except for the chopped pe cans, in a large bowl. Wrap the bowl and refrigerate for at least 2 hours. Remove the bowl from the refrigerator . Spread the pudding with pecans and serve chilled.

Nutrition facts (per serving)
calories: 249 | fat: 21.1g | protein: 2.8g | carbs: 17.2g | fiber: 3.0g | sodium: 46mg

›Mango and Coconut Frozen Pie

Preparation time: 1 hour 10 minutes
Cooking time: 0 minutes | **Servings:** 8
Crust:
1 cup cashews
½ cup rolled oats 1
1 cup soft pitted dates
Filling:
2 large mangoes, peeled and chopped
½ cup unsweetened shredded coconut
1 cup unsweetened coconut milk
½ cup water

Combine the ingredients for the crust in a food processor. Pulse to combine well. Pour the mixture in an 8-inch springform pan, then press to coat the bottom. Set aside. Combine the ingredients for the filling in the food processor, then pulse to purée until smooth. Pour the filling over the crust, then use a spatula to spread the filling evenly. Put the pan in the freeze for 30 minutes. Remove the pan from the freezer and allow to sit for 15 minutes under room temperature before serving.

Nutrition facts (per serving) (1 slice)
calories: 426 | fat: 28.2g | protein: 8.1g | carbs: 14.9g | fiber: 6.0g | sodium: 174mg

›Mini Nuts and Fruits Crumble

Preparation time: 15 minutes
Cooking time: 15 minutes | **Servings:** 6
Topping:
¼ cup coarsely chopped hazelnuts
1 cup coarsely chopped walnuts
1 teaspoon ground cinnamon
Sea salt, to taste
1 tablespoon melted coconut oil
Filling:
6 fresh figs, quartered
2 nectarines, pitted and sliced
1 cup fresh blueberries
2 teaspoons lemon zest
½ cup raw honey
1 teaspoon vanilla extract

Make the Topping
Combine well the ingredients for the topping in a bowl. Stir to mix well. Set aside until ready to use.
Make the Filling:
Preheat the oven to 370/385ºF (195ºC). Combine the ingredients in a small bowl. Divide the filling in five ramekins, then divide and top with nut topping. Bake in the oven until the topping is lightly browned and the filling is frothy or for 15 minutes. Serve immediately.

Nutrition facts (per serving)
calories: 335 | fat: 20.0g | protein: 6.3g | carbs: 41.9g | fiber: 6.0g | sodium: 31mg

›Mint Banana Chocolate Sorbet

Preparation time: 4 hours 5 minutes
Cooking time: 0 minutes | **Servings:** 1
1 frozen banana
2 tablespoons minced fresh mint
1 tablespoon almond butter
2 to 3 tablespoons dark chocolate chips (70% cocoa or higher)
2 to 3 tablespoons goji (optional)

Place the butter, banana, and mint in a food processor to make a smooth, homogeneous mixture.
Add the chocolate and goji and blend the mixture again. Pour all the mixture into a large bowl and freeze for at least 5 hours before serving chilled.

Nutrition facts (per serving)
calories: 215 | fat: 10.0g | protein: 3.1g | carbs: 2.0g | fiber: 4.0g | sodium: 155mg

›Pecan and Carrot Cake

Preparation time: 15 minutes
Cooking time: 45 minutes | **Servings:** 12
½ cup coconut oil, at room temperature
2 teaspoons pure vanilla extract
¼ cup pure maple syrup
6 eggs
½ cup coconut flour
1 teaspoon baking powder
1 teaspoon baking soda
½ teaspoon ground nutmeg
1 teaspoon ground cinnamon

⅛ teaspoon sea salt
½ cup chopped pecans
3 cups finely grated carrots

Preheat oven to 340/360°F (185°C) and grease a baking sheet with coconut oil. Combine the maple syrup ,vanilla extract and ½ cup of the coconut oil in a bowl and stir continuously so that the mixture is smooth. Crack the eggs into a bowl and set aside after beating well. Combine the coconut flour, baking powder, nutmeg, baking soda, cinnamon and salt in a bowl. Make a hole in the center of the flour mixture and pour in the egg mixture. Add the pecans and carrots to the small bowl. Pour the mixture onto a baking sheet. Bake the cake in the oven for 48/50 Min. Remove the cake from the oven. Allow to cool for at least 13-15 minutes, then serve.
Nutrition facts (per serving)
calories: 260 | fat: 21.0g | protein: 5.1g | carbs: 12.8g | fiber: 2.0g | sodium: 202mg

➤Raspberry Yogurt Basted Cantaloupe

Preparation time: 15 minutes
Cooking time: 0 minutes | **Servings:** 6
2 cups fresh raspberries, mashed
1 cup plain coconut yogurt
½ teaspoon vanilla extract
1 cantaloupe, peeled and sliced
½ cup toasted coconut flakes

Mix the yogurt the crushed raspberries and vanilla extract in a bowl. Arrange the melon slices on a serving platter, then add the toasted coconut raspberry mixture. Serve immediately.
Nutrition facts (per serving)
calories: 80 | fat: 4.0g | protein: 1.2g | carbs: 10.9g | fiber: 6.0g | sodium: 36mg

➤Apple Compote

Preparation time: 15 minutes
Cooking time: 10 minutes | **Servings:** 4
6 apples, peeled, cored, and chopped
¼ cup raw honey
1 teaspoon ground cinnamon
¼ cup apple juice
Sea salt, to taste

Put all the ingredients in a stockpot. Stir to mix well, then cook over medium-high heat for 10 minutes or until the apples are glazed by honey and lightly saucy. Stir constantly. Serve immediately.
Nutrition facts (per serving)
calories: 245 | fat: 0.9g | protein: 2.0g | carbs: 66.3g | fiber: 9.0g | sodium: 62mg

➤Peanut Butter and Chocolate Balls

Preparation time: 45 minutes
Cooking time: 0 minutes | **Servings:** 15 balls
¾ cup creamy peanut butter
¼ cup unsweetened cocoa powder

2 tablespoons softened almond butter
½ teaspoon vanilla extract
1¾ cups maple syrup

Mix all ingredients in a small bowl. Create balls by dividing the mixture into about 14/15 parts. Place the balls on the baking sheet and refrigerate for at least 30 minutes until the mixture is firm. Serve chilled
Nutrition facts (per serving) (1 ball)
calories: 145 | fat: 8.1g | protein: 4.0g | carbs: 16.9g | fiber: 1.0g | sodium: 70mg

➤Spiced Sweet Pecans

Preparation time: 4 minutes
Cooking time: 17 minutes | **Servings:** 4
1 cup pecan halves
3 tablespoons almond butter
1 teaspoon ground cinnamon
½ teaspoon ground nutmeg
¼ cup raw honey
¼ teaspoon sea salt

Preheat the oven to 340/350°F (180°C). Line a baking sheet with parchment paper. Combine all the ingredients in a bowl, then spread the mixture on the baking sheet with a wooden spatula. Bake in the preheated oven until the pecan halves are well browned or for 15 minutes. Serve immediately.
Nutrition facts (per serving)
calories: 325 | fat: 29.8g | protein: 3.5g | carbs: 13.9g | fiber: 4.0g | sodium: 180mg

➤Greek Yogurt Affogato with Pistachios

Preparation time: 5 minutes
Cooking time: 0 minutes | **Servings:** 4
24 ounces (680 g) vanilla Greek yogurt
2 teaspoons sugar
4 shots hot espresso
4 tablespoons chopped unsalted pistachios
4 tablespoons dark chocolate chips

Spoon the yogurt into four bowls or tall glasses. Mix ½ teaspoon of sugar into each of the espresso shots. Pour one shot of the hot espresso over each bowl of yogurt. Top each bowl with 1 tbsp of the pistachios and 1 tablespoon of the chocolate chips and serve.
Nutrition facts (per serving)
calories: 190 | fat: 6.0g | protein: 20.0g | carbs: 14.0g | fiber: 1.0g | sodium: 99mg

➤Grilled Peaches with Whipped Ricotta

Preparation time: 5 minutes
Cooking time: 14 to 22 minutes | **Servings:** 4
4 peaches, halved and pitted
2 teaspoons extra-virgin olive oil
¾ cup whole-milk Ricotta cheese
1 tablespoon honey
¼ teaspoon freshly grated nutmeg
4 sprigs mint

Cooking spray

Spritz a grill pan with cooking spray. Heat the grill pan to medium heat. Place a bowl in the refrigerator to chill. Brush the peaches all over with the oil. Place half of the peaches, cut side down, on the grill pan and cook for 3-5 min, or until grill marks appear.
Using tongs, turn the peaches over. Cover the grill pan with aluminum foil and cook for 4 to 6 minutes, set aside to cool. Repeat with the remaining peaches. Remove the bowl from the refrigerator and add the Ricotta. Using an electric beater, beat the Ricotta on high for 2 minutes. Add the honey and nutmeg and beat for 1 more minute. Divide the cooled peaches among 4 serving bowls. Top with the Ricotta mixture and a sprig of mint and serve.

Nutrition facts (per serving)
calories: 176 | fat: 8.0g | protein: 8.0g | carbs: 20.0g | fiber: 3.0g | sodium: 63mg

›Rice Pudding with Roasted Orange

Preparation time: 10 minutes
Cooking time: 19 to 20 minutes | **Servings:** 6
2 medium oranges
2 teaspoons extra-virgin olive oil
⅛ teaspoon kosher salt
2 large eggs
2 cups unsweetened almond milk
1 cup orange juice
1 cup uncooked instant brown rice
¼ cup honey
½ teaspoon ground cinnamon
1 teaspoon vanilla extract
Cooking spray

Preheat the oven to 440/450°F (235°C). Spritz a large, rimmed baking sheet with cooking spray. Set aside. Slice the unpeeled oranges into ¼-inch rounds. Brush with the oil and sprinkle with salt. Place the slices on the baking sheet and roast for 4 minutes. Flip the slices and roast for 4 more minutes, or until they begin to brown. Remove from the oven and set aside.
Crack the eggs into a medium bowl. In a medium saucepan, whisk well together the orange juice, milk, rice, honey and cinnamon. Bring to a boil over medium-high heat, stirring constantly. Low the heat to medium-low and simmer for 10 minutes, stirring occasionally. Using a measuring cup, scoop out ½ cup of the hot rice mixture and whisk it into the eggs. While constantly stirring the mixture in the pan, slowly pour the egg mixture back into the saucepan. Cook on low heat until thickened, or for 1 to 2 minutes, stirring constantly. Remove from the heat and stir in the vanilla.
Let the pudding stand for a couple of min for the rice to soften. The rice will be cooked but slightly chewy. For softer rice, let stand for another half hour.
Top with the roasted oranges. Serve warm or at room temperature.

Nutrition facts (per serving)
calories: 204 | fat: 6.0g | protein: 5.0g | carbs: 34.0g | fiber: 1.0g | sodium: 148mg

›Cherry Walnut Brownies

Preparation time: 10 minutes
Cooking time: 20 minutes | **Servings:** 9
2 large eggs
½ cup 2% plain Greek yogurt
½ cup sugar
⅓ cup honey
¼ cup extra-virgin olive oil
1 teaspoon vanilla extract
½ cup whole-wheat pastry flour
⅓ cup unsweetened dark chocolate cocoa powder
¼ teaspoon baking powder
¼ teaspoon salt
⅓ cup chopped walnuts
9 fresh cherries, stemmed and pitted
Cooking spray

Preheat the oven to 370/375°F (190°C) and set the rack in the middle of the oven. Spritz a square baking pan with cooking spray. In a medium/large bowl, whisk together the eggs, yogurt, sugar, honey, oil and vanilla. In a bowl, stir together the cocoa powder, flour, salt and baking powder. Add the flour mixture to the egg mixture and whisk until all the dry ingredients are incorporated. Fold in the walnuts. Pour the batter into the prepared pan. Push the cherries into the batter, three to a row in three rows, so one will be at the center of each brownie once you cut them into squares. Bake the brownies until just set, or for 20 minutes. Remove from the oven and place on a rack to cool for 5 minutes. Cut into nine squares and serve.

Nutrition facts (per serving)
calories: 154 | fat: 6.0g | protein: 3.0g | carbs: 24.0g | fiber: 2.0g | sodium: 125mg

›Watermelon and Blueberry Salad

Preparation time: 5 minutes
Cooking time: 0 minutes
Servings: 6 to 8
1 medium watermelon
1 cup fresh blueberries
⅓ cup honey
2 tablespoons lemon juice
2 tablespoons finely chopped fresh mint leaves

Cut the watermelon into 1-inch cubes. Put them in a bowl. Evenly distribute the blueberries over the watermelon. In an another bowl, whisk well together the honey, lemon juice and mint. Drizzle the mint dressing over the watermelon and blueberries. Serve cold.

Nutrition facts (per serving)
calories: 238 | fat: 1.0g | protein: 4.0g | carbs: 61.0g | fiber: 3.0g | sodium: 11mg

›Chocolate Bars

Preparation Time: 10 minutes
Cooking Time: 20 minutes
Servings: 16
Ingredients:
15 oz cream cheese, softened
15 oz unsweetened dark chocolate

1 tsp vanilla
10 drops liquid stevia
Directions:
Grease 8-inch square dish and set aside. In a sauce-pan dissolve chocolate over low heat. Add stevia and vanilla and stir well. Remove pan from heat and set aside. Add cream cheese into the blender and blend until smooth. Add melted chocolate mixture into the cream cheese and blend until just combined. Transfer mixture into the prepared dish and spread evenly and place in the refrigerator until firm. Slice and serve.
Nutrition facts:
Calories: 230
Fat: 24 g
Carbs: 7.5 g
Sugar: 0.1 g
Protein: 6 g
Cholesterol: 29 mg

➤Blueberry Muffins

Preparation Time: 15 minutes
Cooking Time: 35 minutes
Servings: 12
Ingredients:
2 eggs
1/2 cup fresh blueberries
1 cup heavy cream
2 cups almond flour
1/4 tsp lemon zest
1/2 tsp lemon extract
1 tsp baking powder
5 drops stevia
1/4 cup butter, melted
Directions:
heat the cooker to 350 F. Line muffin tin with cupcake liners and set aside. Add eggs into the bowl and whisk until mix. Add remaining ingredients and mix to combine. Pour mixture into the prepared muffin tin and bake for 25 minutes. Serve and enjoy.
Nutrition facts: Calories: 190 Fat: 17 g Carbs: 5 g Sugar: 1 g Protein: 5 g Cholesterol: 55 mg

➤Chia Pudding

Preparation Time: 20 minutes
Cooking Time: 0 minutes
Servings: 2
Ingredients:
4 tbsp chia seeds
1 cup unsweetened coconut milk
1/2 cup raspberries
Directions:
Add raspberry and coconut milk into a blender and blend until smooth. Pour mixture into the glass jar. Add chia seeds in a jar and stir well. Seal the jar with a lid and shake well and place in the refrigerator for 3 hours. Serve chilled and enjoy.
Nutrition facts: Calories: 360 Fat: 33 g Carbs: 13 g Sugar: 5 g Protein: 6 g Cholesterol: 0 mg

➤Avocado Pudding

Preparation Time: 20 minutes
Cooking Time: 0 minutes
Servings: 8
Ingredients:
2 ripe avocados, pitted and cut into pieces
1 tbsp fresh lime juice
14 oz can coconut milk
2 tsp liquid stevia
2 tsp vanilla
Directions:
Inside the blender Add all ingredients and blend until smooth. Serve immediately and enjoy.
Nutrition facts: Calories: 317 Fat: 30 g Carbs: 9 g Sugar: 0.5 g Protein: 3 g Cholesterol: 0 mg

➤Delicious Brownie Bites

Preparation Time: 20 minutes
Cooking Time: 0 minutes
Servings: 13
Ingredients:
1/4 cup unsweetened chocolate chips
1/4 cup unsweetened cocoa powder
1 cup pecans, chopped
1/2 cup almond butter
1/2 tsp vanilla
1/4 cup monk fruit sweetener
1/8 tsp pink salt
Directions:
Add pecans, sweetener, vanilla, almond butter, cocoa powder, and salt into the food processor and process until well combined. Transfer brownie mixture into the large bowl. Add chocolate chips and fold well. Make small round shape balls from brownie mixture and place onto a baking tray. Place in the freezer for 20 minutes. Serve and enjoy.
Nutrition facts: Calories: 108 Fat: 9 g Carbs: 4 g Sugar: 1 g Protein: 2 g Cholesterol: 0 mg

➤Pumpkin Balls

Preparation Time: 15 minutes
Cooking Time: 0 minutes
Servings: 18
Ingredients:
1 cup almond butter
5 drops liquid stevia
2 tbsp coconut flour
2 tbsp pumpkin puree
1 tsp pumpkin pie spice
Directions:
Mix pumpkin puree in a large bowl, and almond butter until well combined. Add liquid stevia, pumpkin pie spice, and coconut flour and mix well. Make small balls from mixture and place onto a baking tray. Place in the freezer for 1 hour. Serve and enjoy.
Nutrition facts: Calories: 96 Fat: 8 g Carbs: 4 g Sugar: 1 g Protein: 2 g Cholesterol: 0 mg

›Smooth Peanut Butter Cream

Preparation Time: 10 minutes
Cooking Time: 0 minutes
Servings: 8
Ingredients:
1/4 cup peanut butter
4 overripe bananas, chopped
1/3 cup cocoa powder
1/4 tsp vanilla extract
1/8 tsp salt
Directions:
In the blender add all listed ingredients and blend until smooth. Serve immediately and enjoy.
Nutrition facts: Calories: 101 Fat: 5 g Carbs: 14 g Sugar: 7 g Protein: 3 g Cholesterol: 0 mg

›Vanilla Avocado Popsicles

Preparation Time: 20 minutes
Cooking Time: 0 minutes
Servings: 6
Ingredients:
2 avocadoes
1 tsp vanilla
1 cup almond milk
1 tsp liquid stevia
1/2 cup unsweetened cocoa powder
Directions:
In the blender add all listed the ingredients and blend smoothly. Pour the mixture into cake molds and place in the freezer until firm. Serve cold.
Nutrition facts: Calories: 130 Fat: 12 g Carbs: 7 g Sugar: 1 g Protein: 3 g Cholesterol: 0 mg

›Chocolate Popsicle

Preparation Time: 20 minutes
Cooking Time: 10 minutes
Servings: 6
Ingredients:
4 oz unsweetened chocolate, chopped
6 drops liquid stevia
1 1/2 cups heavy cream
Directions:
Add heavy cream into the bowl and microwave until just begins the boiling. Add chocolate into the heavy cream and set aside for 5 minutes. Add liquid stevia into the heavy cream mixture and stir until chocolate is melted. Pour mixture into the Popsicle molds and place in freezer for 4 hours or until set. Serve and enjoy.
Nutrition facts: Calories: 198 Fat: 21 g Carbs: 6 g Sugar: 0.2 g Protein: 3 g Cholesterol: 41 mg

›Raspberry Ice Cream

Preparation Time: 10 minutes
Cooking Time: 0 minutes
Servings: 2
Ingredients:
1 cup frozen raspberries
1/2 cup heavy cream

1/8 tsp stevia powder
Directions:
Blend all listed ingredients in a blender until smooth. Serve immediately and enjoy.
Nutrition facts: Calories: 144 Fat: 11 g Carbs: 10 g Sugar: 4 g Protein: 2 g Cholesterol: 41 mg

›Chocolate Frosty

Preparation Time: 20 minutes
Cooking Time: 0 minutes
Servings: 4
Ingredients:
2 tbsp unsweetened cocoa powder
1 cup heavy whipping cream
1 tbsp almond butter
5 drops liquid stevia
1 tsp vanilla
Directions:
Add cream into the medium bowl and beat using the hand mixer for 5 minutes. Add remaining ingredients and blend until thick cream form. Pour in serving bowls and place them in the freezer for 30 minutes. Serve and enjoy.
Nutrition facts: Calories: 137 Fat: 13 g Carbs: 3 g Sugar: 0.5 g Protein: 2 g Cholesterol: 41 mg

›Chocolate Almond Butter Brownie

Preparation Time: 10 minutes
Cooking Time: 16 minutes
Servings: 4
Ingredients:
1 cup bananas, overripe
1/2 cup almond butter, melted
1 scoop protein powder
2 tbsp unsweetened cocoa powder
Directions:
Preheat the air fryer to 320/325 F. Grease air fryer baking pan and set aside. Blend all listed ingredients in a blender until smooth. Pour batter into the prepared pan and place in the air fryer basket and cook for 16 minutes. Serve and enjoy.
Nutrition facts: Calories: 82 Fat: 2 g Carbs: 11 g Sugar: 5 g Protein: 7 g Cholesterol: 16 mg

›Peanut Butter Fudge

Preparation Time: 10 minutes
Cooking Time: 10 minutes
Servings: 20
Ingredients:
1/4 cup almonds, toasted and chopped
12 oz smooth peanut butter
15 drops liquid stevia
3 tbsp coconut oil
4 tbsp coconut cream
Pinch of salt
Directions:
Line baking tray with parchment paper. Melt the coconut oil in a saucepan over medium-low heat. Add peanut butter, coconut cream, stevia, and salt in a saucepan. Stir well.

Pour fudge mixture into the prepared baking tray and sprinkle chopped almonds on top. Place the tray in the refrigerator for 1 hour or until set. Slice and serve.
Nutrition facts: Calories: 131 Fat: 12 g Carbs: 4 g Sugar: 2 g Protein: 5 g Cholesterol: 0 mg

➤Almond Butter Fudge

Preparation Time: 10 minutes
Cooking Time: 10 minutes
Servings: 18
Ingredients:
3/4 cup creamy almond butter
1 1/2 cups unsweetened chocolate chips
Directions:
Line 8*4-inch pan with parchment paper and set aside. Add chocolate chips and almond butter into the double boiler and cook over medium heat until the chocolate-butter mixture is melted. Stir well. place mixture into the prepared pan and place in the freezer until set. Slice and serve.
Nutrition facts: Calories: 197 Fat: 16 g Carbs: 7 g Sugar: 1 g Protein: 4 g Cholesterol: 0 mg

➤Bounty Bars

Preparation Time: 20 minutes
Cooking Time: 0 minutes
Servings: 12
Ingredients:
1 cup coconut cream
3 cups shredded unsweetened coconut
1/4 cup extra virgin coconut oil
1/2 teaspoon vanilla powder
1/4 cup powdered erythritol
1 1/2 oz. cocoa butter
5 oz. dark chocolate
Directions:
Heat the oven at 350 °F and toast the coconut in it for 5-6 minutes. Remove from the oven once toasted and set aside to cool. Take a bowl of medium size and add coconut oil, coconut cream, vanilla, erythritol, and toasted coconut. Mix well the ingredients to prepare a smooth mixture. Make 12 bars of equal size with the help of your hands from the prepared mixture and adjust in the tray lined with parchment paper. Place the tray in the fridge for around one hour and, in the meantime, put the cocoa butter and dark chocolate in a glass bowl. Preheat a cup of water in a saucepan over low/medium heat and place the bowl over it to melt the cocoa butter and the dark chocolate. Remove from the heat once melted properly, mix well until blended and set aside to cool.
Take the coconut bars and coat them with dark chocolate mixture one by one using a wooden stick. Adjust on the tray lined with parchment paper and drizzle the remaining mixture over them. Refrigerate for around one hour before you serve the delicious bounty bars.
Nutrition facts:
Calories: 230
Fat: 25 g
Carbohydrates: 5 g
Protein: 32 g

➤Optavia Granola

Preparation Time: 5 minutes
Cooking Time: 8 minutes
Servings: 3
Ingredients:
1 package Medifast or Optavia Oatmeal
1 packet stevia
1 teaspoon vanilla extract
1/2 teaspoon apple spice or pumpkin pie spice
Directions:
Preheat the oven to 400F. In a bowl, combine all ingredients and add enough water to get the granola to stick together. Drop the granola onto a cookie sheet lined with parchment paper. Bake for 8 minutes, but make sure to give the granola a fair shake for even browning halfway through the cooking time.
Nutrition facts:
209 Cal
Protein: 5.8 g
Carbohydrates: 42 g
Fat: 3.2 g
Sugar: 6.2 g

➤Mint Yogurt

Preparation Time: 5 minutes
Cooking Time: 10 minutes
Servings: 2
Ingredients:
2 cup of water
5 cups of milk
¾ cup plain yogurt
¼ cup fresh mint
1 tbsp. maple syrup
Directions:
Add 2 cup water to the Instant Pot Pressure Cooker. Press the STEAM function button and adjust to 1 minute. Once done, add the milk, then press the YOGURT function button and allow boiling. Add yogurt and fresh mint, then stir well. Pour into a glass and add maple syrup. Enjoy.
Nutrition facts:
Calories: 25
Fat: 0.5 g
Carbs: 5 g
Protein: 2 g

➤Chocolate Fondue

Preparation Time: 5 minutes
Cooking Time: 10 minutes
Servings: 2
Ingredients:
1 cup water
½ tsp. sugar
½ cup coconut cream
¾ cup dark chocolate, chopped
Directions:
Pour the water into your Instant Pot. To a heatproof bowl, add the chocolate, sugar, and coconut cream. Place in the Instant Pot. Seal the lid, select MANUAL, and cook for 2 minutes. When ready, do a quick release and carefully open the lid. Stir well and serve

immediately.
Nutrition facts:
Calories: 216
Fat: 17 g
Carbs: 11 g
Protein: 2 g

➤Rice Pudding

Preparation Time: 5 minutes
Cooking Time: 12 minutes
Servings: 2
Ingredients:
½ cup short grain rice
¼ cup of sugar
1 cinnamon stick
1½ cup milk
1 slice lemon peel
Salt to taste
Directions:
Rinse the rice under cold water. Put the milk, cinnamon stick, sugar, salt, and lemon peel inside the Instant Pot Pressure Cooker. Close the lid, lock in place, and make sure to seal the valve. Press the PRESSURE button and cook for 10 minutes on HIGH. When the timer beeps, choose the QUICK PRESSURE release. This will take about 2 minutes. Remove the lid. Open the pressure cooker and discard the lemon peel and cinnamon stick. Spoon in a serving bowl and serve.
Nutrition facts:
Calories: 111
Fat: 6 g
Carbs: 21 g
Protein: 3 g

➤Braised Apples

Preparation Time: 5 minutes
Cooking Time: 12 minutes
Servings: 2
Ingredients:
2 cored apples
½ cup of water
½ cup red wine
3 tbsp. sugar
½ tsp. ground cinnamon
Directions:
In the bottom of Instant Pot, add the water and place apples. Pour wine on top and sprinkle with sugar and cinnamon. Close the lid carefully and cook for 10 minutes at HIGH PRESSURE. When done, do a quick pressure release. Transfer the apples onto serving plates and top with cooking liquid. Serve immediately.
Nutrition facts:
Calories: 245
Fat: 0.5 g
Carbs: 53 g
Protein: 1 g

➤Wine Figs

Preparation Time: 5 minutes
Cooking Time: 3 minutes

Servings: 2
Ingredients:
½ cup pine nuts
1 cup red wine
1 lb. figs
Sugar, as needed
Directions:
Slowly pour the wine and sugar into the Instant Pot. Arrange the trivet inside it; place the figs over it. Close the lid and lock. Ensure that you have sealed the valve to avoid leakage. Press MANUAL mode and set timer to 3 minutes. After the timer reads zero, press CANCEL and quick-release pressure. Carefully remove the lid. Divide figs into bowls, and drizzle wine from the pot over them. Top with pine nuts and enjoy.
Nutrition facts:
Calories: 95
Fat: 3 g
Carbs: 5 g
Protein: 2 g

➤Lemon Curd

Preparation Time: 10 minutes
Cooking Time: 10 minutes
Servings: 2
Ingredients:
4 tbsp. butter
1 cup sugar
2/3 cup lemon juice
3 eggs
2 tsp. lemon zest
2 cups of water
Instructions:
Beat the sugar and butter until smooth, then add 2 whole eggs and the lemon juice. Transfer the mixture into two jars. Pour 2 cup of water into the bottom of the pressure cooker and place in the steamer rack and add the jars, letting them cook for 10/12 minutes. Release the pressure naturally for 10/12 minutes and finally add the zest and put the lids back on the jars.
Nutrition facts:
Calories: 45
Fat: 1 g
Carbs: 8 g
Protein: 1 g

➤Rhubarb Dessert

Preparation Time: 4 minutes
Cooking Time: 5 minutes
Servings: 2
Ingredients:
3 cups rhubarb, chopped
1 tbsp. ghee, melted
1/3 cup water
1 tbsp. stevia
1 tsp. vanilla extract
Directions:
Put all the listed ingredients in your Instant Pot, cover, and cook on HIGH for 5 minutes. Divide into small bowls and serve cold. Enjoy!
Nutrition facts:
Calories: 83

Fat: 2 g
Carbs: 2 g
Protein: 2 g

➤Raspberry Compote

Preparation Time: 11 minutes
Cooking Time: 30 minutes
Servings: 2
Ingredients:
1 cup raspberries
½ cup Swerve
1 tsp freshly grated lemon zest
1 tsp vanilla extract
2 cups water
Directions:
Press the SAUTÉ button on your Instant Pot, then add all the listed Ingredients. Stir well and pour in a cup of water. Cook for 5 minutes, continually stirring, then pour in 1 more cup of water and press the CANCEL button. Secure the lid properly, press the MANUAL button, and set the timer to 15 minutes on LOW pressure. When the timer buzzes, press the CANCEL button and release the pressure naturally for 10minutes.
Move the pressure handle to the "venting" position to release any remaining pressure and open the lid.
Let it cool before serving.
Nutrition facts:
Calories: 48
Fat: 0.5 g
Carbs: 5 g
Protein: 1 g

➤Poached Pears

Preparation Time: 8 minutes
Cooking Time: 10 minutes
Servings: 2
Ingredients:
1 tbsp. lime juice
2 tsp. lime zest
1 cinnamon stick
2 whole pears, peeled
1 cup of water
Fresh mint leaves for garnish
Directions:
Add all the ingredients, except for the mint, leaves to the Instant Pot. Seal the Instant Pot and choose the MANUAL button. Cook on HIGH for 10 minutes. Perform a natural pressure release. Remove the pears from the pot. Serve in bowls and garnish with mint on top.
Nutrition facts:
Calories: 59
Fat: 0.1 g
Carbs: 14 g
Protein: 0.3 g

➤Salted Vanilla Caramels

Preparation time: 5 minutes
Cooking time: 15 minutes | **Makes** 24
2 tablespoons unsalted butter, at room temperature

1 cup allulose
¼ teaspoon sea salt
¼ cup heavy whipping cream
½ teaspoon vanilla extract
Directions
In a saucepan, brown the butter over medium-low heat for about 3 minutes, making sure to stir often while the butter browns. Add the allulose and stir until well combined. Simmer for about 7 minutes, until melted, then stir in the salt. Once it starts to bubble, add the heavy cream and vanilla and stir constantly, making sure it doesn't boil over. Once combined, reduce the heat and allow to gently simmer for about 3 minutes, until reduced slightly. Remove the caramel sauce from the heat and pour it evenly into the prepared baking pan. Put into the refrigerator for a couple of hours or overnight, until cool and hardened. Cut the caramel into 24 pieces and serve. To store, wrap each candy in wax paper, twisting the sides closed. Put the candies in an airtight container in the refrigerator for up to 5 days. With refrigeration, the candies will become very firm but will soften at room temperature.
Nutrition facts (per serving)
calories: 5 | fat: 0.8g | protein: 0g | carbs: 0g | net carbs: 0g | fiber: 0g

➤Chocolate Almond Bark

Preparation time: 10 minutes
Cooking time: 0 minutes | **Makes** 15 pieces
¾ cup coconut oil
¼ cup confectioners' erythritol–monk fruit blend; less sweet: 3 tablespoons
3 tablespoons dark cocoa powder
½ cup slivered almonds
¾ teaspoon almond extract
Directions
Line the baking pan with parchment paper.
In the microwave-safe bowl, melt the coconut oil in the microwave in 10-second intervals. In the medium bowl, whisk together the melted coconut oil, confectioners' erythritol–monk fruit blend, and cocoa powder until fully combined. Stir in the slivered almonds and almond extract. Pour the mixture into the prepared baking pan and spread evenly. Put the pan in the freezer for 18-20 minutes, or until the chocolate bark is solid. Once the chocolate bark is solid, break apart into 15 roughly even pieces to serve. Store the chocolate bark in an container in the freezer. Allow to slightly thaw about 5 minutes before eating. Thaw only what you will be eating.
Nutrition facts (per serving) (1 Pieces) calories: 118 | fat: 13.0g | protein: 1.0g | carbs: 1.0g | net carbs: 0g | fiber: 1.0g

➤Chocolate Truffles

Preparation time: 10 minutes
Cooking time: 5 minutes | **Makes** 16 truffles
¼ cup full-fat coconut milk
5 ounces (142 g) sugar-free dark chocolate, finely chopped
1 tablespoon solid coconut oil, at room temperature
¼ cup unsweetened cocoa powder, for coating

Directions
Line the baking sheet with parchment paper and set aside. In the saucepan, heat the coconut milk over medium heat for about 3 minutes, until hot. Stir in the chocolate and let sit in the coconut milk until beginning to melt. When most of the chocolate has softened, stir carefully with a whisk until all of the chocolate is melted and the texture is smooth and glossy. Add the coconut oil and stir gently until combined. Transfer the mixture to the medium airtight container and refrigerate until firm and set, about 30 minutes. Using a small/medium cookie scoop or spoon, scoop out the truffles, about 1 inch in diameter each, and shape lightly in your hands. Move quickly, and only lightly touch the chocolate or it will begin to melt in your hands. Roll the truffles in the cocoa powder and place on the lined baking sheet. Refrigerate for another 10 minutes to set before serving. Store leftovers in an airtight container in the freeze for up to 3 weeks or refrigerator for up to 3 days.
Nutrition facts (per serving) (1 Truffle) calories: 75 | fat: 6.0g | protein: 2.0g | carbs: 3.0g | net carbs: 1.0g | fiber: 2.0g

➤Lemon Almond Coconut Cake

Preparation Time: 20 minutes
Cooking Time: 40-45 minutes
Servings: 8
Ingredients:
250g almond
60g desiccated coconut
Pinch of salt
150g natural sugar
1 teaspoon vanilla extract
zest of 1 large lemon
3 eggs
200g butter, melted
A handful of almond flakes
Directions
Preheat oven to 180°C. In a medium bowl, take almond, coconut, salt, sugar, vanilla, and lemon zest. Mix in remaining ingredients. Pour in a cake pan. Scatter with almond flakes. Bake for approximately 40-45 minutes until lightly browned and cooked through the middle.
Nutrition facts:
Calories: 314
Fat: 12.4g
Fiber: 6.1g
Carbohydrates:3.1 g
Protein: 3.9g

➤Pecan Pralines

Preparation time: 5 minutes
Cooking time: 15 minutes | **Makes** 18 clusters
4 tablespoons (½ stick) unsalted butter, at room temperature
¼ cup granulated erythritol–monk fruit blend
1½ cups pecan halves
½ teaspoon salt
2 tablespoons heavy whipping cream

Directions
Line the baking sheet with parchment paper.
In the skillet, melt the butter over medium-high heat. Using the silicone spatula, stir in the erythritol–monk fruit blend and combine well, making sure to dissolve the sugar in the butter. Stir in the pecan halves and salt. Once the pecans are completely covered in the glaze, add the heavy cream and quickly stir. When the heavy cream bubbles and evaporates, remove from the heat immediately. Quickly spoon the clusters of 4 to 5 pecan halves each onto the prepared baking sheet and allow to fully cool and set, 15 to 20 minutes, before enjoying. Store leftovers in an airtight container on the counter or in the refrigerator for up 5 days.
Nutrition facts (per serving) (1 Cluster) calories: 86 | fat: 9.0g | protein: 1.0g | carbs: 1.0g | net carbs: 0g | fiber: 1.0g

➤Strawberries Coated with Chocolate Chips

Preparation time: 10 minutes
Cooking time: 5 minutes | **Makes** 15
5 ounces (142 g) sugar-free dark chocolate chips
1 tablespoon vegetable shortening or lard
15 medium whole strawberries, fresh or frozen
Directions
Line the baking sheet with parchment paper. In the microwave-safe bowl, combine the chocolate and shortening. Melt in the microwave in 30-40 second intervals, stirring in between. Dip the strawberries into the melted chocolate mixture and place them on the prepared baking sheet. Put the strawberries in the freezer for 10 to 15 minutes to set before serving. Store leftovers in an airtight container in the refrigerator for up to 72 hours.
Nutrition facts (per serving) (3 Strawberries) calories: 216 | fat: 18.0g | protein: 4.0g | carbs: 11.0g | net carbs: 6.0g | fiber: 5.0g

➤Almond Milk Panna Cotta

Preparation Time: 15 minutes
Cooking Time: 5 minutes
Servings: 4
Ingredients:
11/2 C. unsweetened almond milk, divided
1 tbsp. unflavored powdered gelatin
1 C. unsweetened coconut milk
1/3 C. Swerve
3 tbsp. cacao powder
2 tsp. instant coffee granules
6 drops liquid stevia
Directions:
Add 1/2 C. of almond milk in a large bowl, and sprinkle evenly with gelatin. Set aside until soaked.
In a pan, add the remaining almond milk, coconut milk, Swerve, cacao powder, coffee granules, and stevia and bring to a gentle boil, stirring continuously. Remove from the heat. In a blender, add the gelatin mixture and hot milk mixture and pulse until smooth. Transfer the mixture into serving glasses and set aside

to cool completely.
With plastic wrap, cover each glass and refrigerate for about 3-4 hours before serving.

Nutrition facts:
Calories: 190
Fat: 8.4g
Fiber: 2.5g
Carbohydrates:1.5 g
Protein: 1.6g

›Sesame Cookies

Preparation Time: 15 minutes
Cooking Time: 15 minutes
Servings: 12
Ingredients:
1/3 cup monk fruit sweetener, granulated
3/4 teaspoon baking powder
1 cup almond flour
1 egg
1 teaspoon toasted sesame oil
1/2 cup grass-fed butter
1/2 cup sesame seeds

Directions:
Let the oven heat up to 350F. The dry ingredients must be combined in a bowl. The wet ingredients must be mixed in a separate bowl. Pour the wet mixture into the bowl for the dry ingredients. Stir until the mixture has a thick consistency and forms a dough. Put the sesame seeds in a bowl. Divide and shape the dough into 16 11/2-inch balls, then dunk the balls in the bowl of sesame seeds to coat well. Bash the balls until they are 1/2 inch thick, then put them on a baking sheet lined with parchment paper. Keep a little space between each of them. Baking Time (15 minutes) Remove the cookies from the oven and allow to cool for a few minutes before serving.

Nutrition facts:
Calories: 174
Fat: 12.4g
Fiber: 12.5g
Carbohydrates:8.5 g
Protein: 6.8g

›Chocolate Fudge

Preparation time: 10 minutes
Cooking time: 5 minutes | **Makes** 24 bars
Ingredients:
9 tablespoons (1 stick) unsalted butter
4 ounces (113 g) unsweetened baking chocolate, coarsely chopped
1 cup confectioners' erythritol–monk fruit blend; less sweet: ½ cup
8 ounces (227 g) full-fat cream cheese, at room temperature
¼ cup dark cocoa powder
1 teaspoon vanilla extract
1½ teaspoons peppermint extract

Directions:
Line the baking pan with parchment paper.
In the microwave-safe bowl, melt the butter and baking chocolate in the microwave in 30-second intervals, then set aside. In the large mixing bowl, using an electric mixer on medium high, mix the confectioners' erythritol–monk fruit blend, cream cheese, cocoa powder, vanilla, and peppermint extract until well combined, stopping and scraping the bowl once or twice, as needed. Add the melted chocolate and mix until fully incorporated. Evenly spread the batter into the prepared baking pan. Put the baking pan in the freezer for about 30 minutes, or until the fudge firms. Cut the fudge into 24 squares and serve. Store the fudge in an airtight container in the refrigerator for up to 5 days or freeze for up to 3 weeks.

Nutrition facts (per serving)
calories: 100 | fat: 10.1g | protein: 0.8g | carbs: 1.9g | net carbs: 1.0g | fiber: 0.9g

›Lemon Mug Cake

Preparation Time: 5 minutes
Cooking Time: 2 minutes
Servings: 1
Ingredients:
1 egg, lightly beaten
1/2 tsp. lemon rind
1 tbsp. butter, melted
1 1/2 tbsp. fresh lemon juice
2 tbsp. erythritol
1/4 tsp. baking powder, gluten-free
1/4 cup almond flour

Directions:
In a bowl or container, mix almond flour, baking powder, and sweetener. Add egg, lemon juice, and melted butter in almond flour mixture and whisk until well combined. Pour cake mixture into the microwave-safe mug and microwave for 90 seconds. Serve and enjoy.

Nutrition facts:
Calories: 275
Fat: 5.9g
Fiber: 2.4g
Carbohydrates:1.3 g
Protein: 4.1g

›Green Tea and Macadamia Brownies

Preparation Time: 10 minutes
Cooking Time: 20 minutes
Servings: 4
Ingredients:
4 tablespoons Swerve confectioners-style sweetener
1/4 cup unsalted butter, melted
Salt, to taste
1 egg
1 tablespoon tea matcha powder
1/4 cup coconut flour
1/2 teaspoon baking powder
1/2 cup chopped macadamia nuts

Directions:
Let the oven heat up to 350F. Combine the sweetener, melted butter, and salt in a bowl. Stir to mix well. Separate the egg into the bowl, whisk to combine well. Fold in the matcha powder, coconut flour, and baking powder, then add the macadamia nuts. Stir to combine. Pour the mixture on a baking sheet Level the mixture with a spoon to make sure it coats the

bottom of the sheet evenly.
Bake for 18 minutes or until a sharp knife inserted in the center of the brownies comes out clean. Remove the brownies from the oven and slice to serve.

Nutrition facts:
Calories: 241
Fat: 15.9g
Fiber: 6.0g
Carbohydrates:12.1 g
Protein: 9.6g

➤PB& J Cups

Preparation Time: 20 minutes
Cooking Time: 5 minutes
Servings: 4
Ingredients:
1/4 cup of water
1 teaspoon gelatin
3/4 cup of coconut oil
3/4 cup raspberries
6 to 8 tablespoon Stevia
3/4 cup peanut butter
Directions:
Line a muffin pan with parchment paper. In a pan, combine the raspberries and water over medium heat. Bring to a boil and then reduce the heat and let the water dry. Mash the berries with a fork. Add in 2 to 4 tablespoons of the powdered sweetener. Add in the gelatin and set aside to cool. Now make peanut butter mixture. In the pan, put the peanut butter and coconut oil. Cook for 30 to 60 seconds, until melted. Also, add in 2 to 4 tablespoons of the powdered sweetener. Put half of the peanut butter mixture in a muffin pan and put in the freezer to firm up about 15 minutes. Divide the raspberry mixture among the muffin cups and top with the remaining peanut butter mixture. Refrigerate until firm.

Nutrition facts:
Calories: 191
Fat: 6.1g
Fiber: 2.2g
Carbohydrates:1.8 g
Protein: 3.1g

➤Chocolate Pudding

Preparation Time: 15 minutes
Cooking Time: 45 minutes
Servings: 2
Ingredients:
1/2 teaspoon stevia powder
2 tablespoons cocoa powder
2 tablespoons water
1 tablespoon gelatin
1 cup of coconut milk
2 tablespoons maple syrup
Directions:
Heat pan with the coconut milk over medium heat; add stevia and cocoa powder and mix well. In a bowl, mix gelatin with water; stir well and add to the pan. Stir well, add maple syrup, whisk again, divide into ramekins and keep in the fridge for 45 minutes. Serve cold.

Nutrition facts:
Calories: 287
Fat: 10.4g
Fiber: 9g
Carbohydrates:2.1 g
Protein: 3.1g

➤Chocolate Walnut Cookies

Preparation Time: 15 minutes
Cooking Time: 12 minutes
Servings: 6
Ingredients:
1/4 cup coconut oil
3 tbsp. sweetener
4 tbsp. unsalted butter
1 cup sugar free chocolate chips
1 cup coconut flakes
1/2 cup pecans
1/2 cup walnuts
1 tsp. vanilla extract
4 egg yolks
Sea salt
Directions:
Take a bowl and mix coconut oil, butter, sweetener, chocolate chips, vanilla extract, egg yolks, coconut, and walnuts and stir well. Use a scope to make a cookie and drop an even amount of dough on the baking pan. Sprinkle salt as per taste and bake for 12 minutes on preheated oven at 350F until golden brown.

Nutrition facts:
Calories: 231
Fat: 7.4g
Fiber: 3.1g
Carbohydrates:2.8 g
Protein: 1.3g

➤Almond Shortbread Cookies

Preparation Time: 15 minutes
Cooking Time: 12 minutes
Servings: 6
Ingredients:
1/3 cup coconut flour
1/4 cup erythritol
2/3 cup almond flour
8 drops stevia
1/2 cup butter
1 tsp. almond or vanilla extract
1/4 tbsp. baking powder
For glaze:
1/4 cup coconut butter
8 drops stevia
Directions:
In a bowl, add coconut flour, almond flour, erythritol, baking powder, and add vanilla or almond extract, stevia, and melted butter and make a soft dough. The dough must be divided into two and chill in the refrigerator for 10 minutes. Roll the dough on a sheet and cut cookies with the help of a cookie cutter. Place cookies into a baking pan and bake for 6 minutes in a preheated oven at 180C. Now let the cookies completely cool and apply the glaze.
Nutrition facts:

Calories: 245
Fat: 9.4g
Fiber: 3.1g
Carbohydrates:2.9 g
Protein: 1.8g

➤Granny Smith Apple Tart

Preparation Time: 15 minutes
Cooking Time: 25 minutes
Servings: 6
Ingredients:
6 tbsp. butter
2 cups almond flour
1 tsp. cinnamon
2 1/3 cup sweetener
Filling:
3 cups sliced Granny Smith
1/4 cup butter
1/4 cup sweetener
1/2 tsp. cinnamon
1/2 tsp. lemon juice
Topping:
1/4 tsp. cinnamon
2 tbsp. sweetener
Directions:
Preheat oven to 370°F and combine all crust ingredients in a bowl. Press this mixture into the bottom of a greased pan. Bake for 5 minutes. Meanwhile, combine the apples and lemon juice in a bowl and sit until the crust is ready. Arrange them on top of the crust. Combine remaining filling ingredients and brush this mixture over the apples. Bake for about 30 minutes. Press the apples down with a spatula, return to oven, and bake for 20 more minutes. Combine the cinnamon and sweetener in a bowl, and sprinkle over the tart.
Nutrition facts:
Calories: 276
Fat: 11g
Fiber: 10.4g
Carbohydrates:2.1 g
Protein: 3.1g

➤Strawberry Mousse

Preparation Time: 10 minutes
Cooking Time: 5 minutes
Servings: 2
Ingredients:
1 cup heavy whipping cream
1 cup fresh strawberries, chopped
2 tbsp. Swerve1 cup cream cheese
Directions:
Add heavy whipping cream in a bowl and beat until thickened using hand mixer. Add sweetener and cream cheese and beat well. Add strawberries and fold well. Pour in serving glasses and place in the refrigerator for 1-2 hours. Serve chilled and enjoy.
Nutrition facts:
Calories: 219
Fat: 8g
Fiber: 3.1g
Carbohydrates:1.9 g

Protein: 1.2g

➤Cashew and Raspberry Truffles

Preparation Time: 10 minutes
Cooking Time: 0 minutes
Servings: 4
Ingredients:
2 cups raw cashews
2 tbsp. flax seed
1 1/2 cups sugar-free raspberry preserving
3 tbsp. swerve
10 oz unsweetened chocolate chips
3 tbsp. olive oil
Directions:
Grind the cashews and flax seeds in a blender for 45 seconds until smoothly crushed; add the raspberry and 2 tbsp. of swerve. Process further for 1 minute until well combined. Form 1-inch balls of the mixture, place on the baking sheet, and freeze for 1 hour or until firmed up. Melt the chocolate chips, oil, and 1tbsp. of swerve in a microwave for 1 1/2 minute. Toss the truffles to coat in the chocolate mixture, put on the baking sheet, and freeze further for at least 2 hours
Nutrition facts:
Calories: 199
Fat: 4.1g
Fiber: 3.1g
Carbohydrates:1 g
Protein: 3.2g

➤Bacon Fudge

Preparation time: 10 minutes
Cooking time: 40 minutes | **Makes** 24 bars
½ cup granulated erythritol–monk fruit blend
6 bacon slices
7 tablespoons (1 stick) unsalted butter, at room temperature
4 ounces (113 g) unsweetened baking chocolate, coarsely chopped
1 cup confectioners' erythritol–monk fruit blend; less sweet: ½ cup
8 ounces (227 g) full-fat cream cheese, at room temperature
¼ cup dark cocoa powder
1 teaspoon vanilla extract
1 cup chopped pistachios
Directions:
Preheat the oven to 340/350°F (180°C). Line the baking sheet with aluminum foil. Line the baking pan with parchment paper. In the shallow mixing bowl, put the granulated erythritol–monk fruit blend and dip the bacon slices into it to evenly coat both sides. Place the coated bacon on the prepared baking sheet and bake for 30 to 40 minutes, or until fully cooked. Once cooled, break into smaller pieces and set aside. In the small microwave-safe bowl, melt the butter and baking chocolate in the microwave in 30-second intervals, then set aside. In the medium mixing bowl, using an electric mixer on medium high, mix the confectioners' erythritol–monk fruit blend, cream cheese, dark cocoa powder, and vanilla until well combined, stopping and scraping the bowl once or twice, as

needed. Add the melted chocolate mixture and mix. Fold in three-quarters of the candied bacon and the chopped pistachios. Spread the batter into the prepared baking pan. Put the baking pan in the freezer for about 30 minutes or until the fudge firms. Cut the fudge into 24 squares and serve. Store the fudge in the refrigerator for up to 5 days or freeze for up to 3 weeks.

Nutrition facts (per serving) (1 Piece) calories: 142 | fat: 13.0g | protein: 3.0g | carbs: 4.0g | net carbs: 2.0g | fiber: 2.0g

›Coconut Cheesecake

Preparation Time: 15 minutes
Cooking Time: 25 minutes
Servings: 12
Ingredients:
Crust:
2 egg whites
1/4 cup erythritol
3 cups desiccated coconut
1 tsp. coconut oil
1/4 cup melted butter
Filling:
3 tbsp. lemon juice
6 ounces raspberries
2 cups erythritol
1 cup whipped cream
Zest of 1 lemon
24 ounces cream cheese
Directions:
Line the pan with parchment paper. Preheat oven to 350°F and mix all crust ingredients. Pour the crust into the pan. Bake for about 25 minutes; let cool. Whisk the cream cheese in a container. Add the lemon juice, zest, and erythritol. Fold in whipped cream mixture. Fold in the raspberries gently. Spoon the filling into the crust. Place in the fridge for 4 hours.
Nutrition facts:
Calories: 214
Fat: 11.4g
Fiber: 8.4g
Carbohydrates: 5.4g
Protein: 9.1g

›Coconut Chia Pudding

Preparation Time: 10 minutes
Cooking Time: 0 minutes
Servings: 1
Ingredients:
1/4 cup chia seeds
1 1/4 cup coconut milk
2 tbsp. unsweetened coconut
1 tsp. vanilla extract
2 tbsp. maple syrup
Directions:
Soak chia seeds in water for 2 to 3 minutes. Take a bowl, add coconut milk, maple syrup, vanilla extract, and chia seeds and whisk them well. Let it aside and mix again after 5 minutes. Place it in an airtight bag and place it in the refrigerator for 1 hour.
Serve and enjoy chilled coconut chia pudding.

Nutrition facts:
Calories: 165
Fat: 1.4g
Fiber: 5.4g
Carbohydrates:1.2 g
Protein: 3.1g

›Apple, Avocado and Mango Bowls

Preparation time: 10 minutes
Cooking time: 2 hours
Servings: 2
Ingredients:
1 cup avocado, peeled, pitted and cubed
1 cup mango, peeled and cubed
1 apple, cored and cubed
2 tablespoons brown sugar
1 cup heavy cream 1 tablespoon lemon juice
Directions:
In your slow cooker, combine the avocado with the mango and the other ingredients, toss gently, put the lid on and cook on Low for 2 hours. Divide the mix into bowls and serve.
Nutrition facts
Calories 60,
Fat 1,
Fiber 2,
Carbs 20,
Protein 1

›Ricotta Cream

Preparation time: 2 hours and 10 minutes
Cooking time: 1 hour
Servings: 10
Ingredients:
½ cup hot coffee
2 cups ricotta cheese
2 and ½ teaspoons gelatin
1 teaspoon vanilla extract
1 teaspoon espresso powder
1 teaspoon sugar 1 cup whipping cream
Directions:
In a bowl, mix coffee with gelatin, stir well and leave aside until coffee is cold. In your slow cooker, mix espresso, sugar, vanilla extract and ricotta and stir. Add coffee mix and whipping cream, cover, cook on Low for 1 hour. Divide into dessert bowls and keep in the fridge for 2 hours before serving.
Nutrition facts
Calories 200,
Fat 13,
Fiber 0,
Carbs 5,
Protein 7

›Tomato Jam

Preparation time: 10 minutes
Cooking time: 3 hours
Servings: 2
Ingredients
½ pound tomatoes, chopped

1 green apple, grated
2 tablespoons red wine vinegar
4 tablespoons sugar
Directions:
In your slow cooker, mix the tomatoes with the apple and the other ingredients, whisk, put the lid on and cook on Low for 3 hours. Whisk the jam well, blend a bit using an immersion blender, divide into bowls and serve cold.
Nutrition facts
Calories 70,
Fat 1,
Fiber 1,
Carbs 18,
Protein 1

➤Green Tea Pudding

Preparation time: 10 minutes
Cooking time: 1 hour
Servings: 2
Ingredients:
½ cup coconut milk
1 and ½ cup avocado, pitted and peeled
2 tablespoons green tea powder
2 teaspoons lime zest, grated
1 tablespoon sugar
Directions:
In your slow cooker, mix coconut milk with avocado, tea powder, lime zest and sugar, stir, cover and cook on Low for 1 hour. Divide into cups and serve cold.
Nutrition facts
Calories 107,
Fat 5,
Fiber 3,
Carbs 6,
Protein 8

➤Crunchy Almond Cookies

Preparation time: 5 minutes | **Cooking time:** 5 to 7 minutes | **Servings:** 4 to 6
Ingredients
½ cup sugar
tablespoons almond butter
large egg
1½ cups all-purpose flour
cup ground almonds
Directions
Set the oven to 390/400°F (200°C). Line a baking sheet with parchment paper. Using a mixer, whisk together the sugar and butter. Add the egg and mix until combined. Alternately add the flour and ground almonds, ½ cup at a time, while the mixer is on slow. Drop 1 tbsp of the dough on the prepared baking sheet, keeping the cookies at least 2 inches apart. Place the pan in your oven and bake for about 5-7 minutes. Let cool for 5 minutes before serving.
Nutrition facts (per serving)
calories: 604 | fat: 36.0g | protein: 11.0g | carbs: 63.0g | fiber: 4.0g | sodium: 181mg

➤Walnut and Date Balls

Preparation time: **10** minutes
Cooking time: **7** to 8 minutes | **Servings:** 6 to 8
Ingredients
cup walnuts
cup unsweetened shredded coconut
medjool dates, pitted
tablespoons almond butter
Directions
Preheat the oven to 340/350°F (180°C). Put the walnuts on a baking sheet and toast in the oven for 5 minutes. Put the shredded coconut on a clean baking sheet. Toast for about 3 to 5 minutes, or until it turns golden brown. Once done, put it in a shallow bowl. In a food processor, process the toasted walnuts until they have a medium chop. Transfer the chopped walnuts into a medium bowl. Add the dates and butter to the food processor and blend until the dates become a thick paste. Pour the chopped walnuts into the food processor with the dates and pulse just until the mixture is combined, about 5 to 7 pulses. Remove the mixture from the food processor and scrape it into a large bowl. To make the balls, spoon 1 to 2 tablespoons of the date mixture into the palm of your hand and roll around between your hands until you form a ball. Put the ball on a clean, lined baking sheet. Roll each ball in the toasted coconut until the outside of the ball is coated. Put the ball back on the baking sheet and repeat. Put all the balls into the refrigerator for 20 minutes before serving.
Nutrition facts (per serving)
calories: 489 | fat: 35.0g | protein: 5.0g | carbs: 48.0g | fiber: 7.0g | sodium: 114mg

➤Honey Baked Cinnamon Apples

Preparation time: 5 minutes
Cooking time: 20 minutes | **Servings:** 2
1 teaspoon extra-virgin olive oil
4 firm apples, peeled, cored, and sliced
½ teaspoon salt
1½ teaspoons ground cinnamon, divided
2 tablespoons unsweetened almond milk
2 tablespoons honey
Directions
Preheat the oven to 370/375°F (190°C). Coat a small casserole dish with the olive oil. Toss the apple slices with the salt and ½ teaspoon of the cinnamon in a medium bowl. Spread the apples in the prepared casserole dish and bake in the preheated oven for 20 minutes. Meanwhile, in a medium/small saucepan, heat the milk, honey, and remaining 1 teaspoon of cinnamon over medium heat, stirring frequently. When it reaches a simmer, remove the pan from the heat and cover to keep warm. Divide the apple slices between 2 plates and pour the sauce over the apples. Serve warm.
Nutrition facts (per serving)
calories: 310 | fat: 3.4g | protein: 1.7g | carbs: 68.5g | fiber: 12.6g | sodium: 593mg

Strawberries with Balsamic Vinegar

Preparation time: 5 minutes
Cooking time: 0 minutes | **Servings:** 2
2 cups strawberries, hulled and sliced
2 tablespoons sugar
2 tablespoons balsamic vinegar
Directions
Place strawberries in a small bowl, add sugar and lightly drizzle with balsamic vinegar. Toss to combine well and allow to sit for about 10 minutes before serving.
Nutrition facts (per serving)
calories: 92 | fat: 0.4g | protein: 1.0g | carbs: 21.7g | fiber: 2.9g | sodium: 5mg

Frozen Mango Raspberry Delight

Preparation time: 5 minutes
Cooking time: 0 minutes | **Servings:** 2
3 cups frozen raspberries
1 mango, peeled and pitted
1 peach, peeled and pitted
1 teaspoon honey
Directions:
Place all ingredients listed in a kitchen blender, adding a little water if needed. Put in the freezer for 12 min to firm up if desired. Serve chilled or at room temperature.
Nutrition facts (per serving)
calories: 276 | fat: 2.1g | protein: 4.5g | carbs: 60.3g | fiber: 17.5g | sodium: 4mg

Grilled Stone Fruit with Honey

Preparation time: 8 minutes
Cooking time: 6 minutes | **Servings:** 2
3 apricots, halved and pitted
2 plums, halved and pitted
2 peaches, halved and pitted
½ cup low-fat ricotta cheese
2 tablespoons honey
Cooking spray
Directions
Preheat the grill to medium heat. Spray the grill grates with cooking spray. Arrange the fruit on the grill, and cook for 2 to 3 min for side, or until lightly charred and softened. Serve warm with a sprinkle of cheese and a drizzle of honey.
Nutrition facts (per serving)
calories: 298 | fat: 7.8g | protein: 11.9g | carbs: 45.2g | fiber: 4.3g | sodium: 259mg

Mascarpone Baked Pears

Preparation time: 10 minutes
Cooking time: 20 minutes | **Servings:** 2
2 ripe pears, peeled
1 tablespoon plus 2 teaspoons honey, divided
1 teaspoon vanilla, divided
¼ teaspoon ground coriander
¼ teaspoon ginger
¼ cup minced walnuts
¼ cup mascarpone cheese
Pinch salt
Cooking spray
Directions
Preheat the oven to 340/350ºF (180ºC). Spray a small baking dish with cooking spray. Slice the pears in half lengthwise. Using a spoon, scoop out the core from each piece. Put the pears, cut side up, in the baking dish. Whisk together 1 tablespoon of honey, ginger, ½ teaspoon of vanilla and coriander in a small bowl. Pour this mixture over the pear halves. Scatter the walnuts over the pear halves. Bake in the preheated oven for 18/20 min, or until the pears are golden. Meanwhile, combine the mascarpone cheese with the remaining 2 teaspoons of honey, ½ teaspoon of vanilla, and a pinch of salt. Stir to combine well.
Nutrition facts (per serving)
calories: 308 | fat: 16.0g | protein: 4.1g | carbs: 42.7g | fiber: 6.0g | sodium: 88mg

Mixed Berry Crisp

Preparation time: 15 minutes
Cooking time: 30 minutes | **Servings:** 2
1½ cups frozen mixed berries, thawed
¼ cup oats
1 tablespoon coconut sugar
1 tablespoon almond butter
¼ cup pecans
Directions
Preheat the oven to 340/350ºF (180ºC). Divide the mixed berries between 2 ramekins Place the coconut sugar, almond butter, oats, and pecans in a food processor, and pulse a few times, until the mixture resembles damp sand. Divide the crumble topping over the mixed berries. Put the ramekins on a pan and bake for 30 minutes, or until the top is golden and the berries are bubbling. Serve warm.
Nutrition facts (per serving)
calories: 268 | fat: 17.0g | protein: 4.1g | carbs: 26.8g | fiber: 6.0g | sodium: 44mg

Orange Mug Cakes

Preparation time: 10 minutes
Cooking time: 3 minutes | **Servings:** 2
6 tablespoons flour
2 tablespoons sugar
1 teaspoon orange zest
½ teaspoon baking powder
Pinch salt
1 egg
2 tablespoons olive oil
2 tablespoons unsweetened almond milk
2 tablespoons freshly squeezed orange juice
½ teaspoon orange extract
½ teaspoon vanilla extract
Directions
Combine the flour, sugar, orange zest, baking powder, and salt in a small bowl. In another bowl, whisk well together the olive oil, egg, milk, orange juice, orange extract, and vanilla extract. Add the ingredients to the wet ingredients and stir to incorporate. The batter will be thick. Divide the mixture into two small mugs. Mi-

crowave each mug separately. The small ones should take about 60 seconds, and one large mug should take about 90 seconds, but microwaves can vary. Cool for 5 minutes before serving.

Nutrition facts (per serving)
calories: 303 | fat: 16.9g | protein: 6.0g | carbs: 32.5g | fiber: 1.0g | sodium: 118mg

➤Fruit and Nut Chocolate Bark

Preparation time: 15 minutes
Cooking time: 2 minutes | **Servings:** 2
2 tablespoons chopped nuts
3 ounces (85 g) dark chocolate chips
¼ cup chopped dried fruit (blueberries, apricots, figs, prunes, or any combination of those)
Directions
Add the nuts to a skillet over medium-high heat and toast for 60 seconds, or just fragrant. Set aside to cool. Put the chocolate chips in a microwave-safe glass bowl and microwave on High for 1 minute. Stir the chocolate and allow any unmelted chips to warm and melt. If desired, heat for an additional 20 to 30 seconds. Transfer the chocolate to the prepared sheet pan. Scatter the dried fruit and toasted nuts over the chocolate evenly and gently pat in so they stick. Finally, place the pan in the refrigerator for at least 1 hour to let the chocolate harden. When ready, break into pieces and serve.
Nutrition facts (per serving)
calories: 285 | fat: 16.1g | protein: 4.0g | carbs: 38.7g | fiber: 2.0g | sodium: 2mg

➤Cozy Superfood Hot Chocolate

Preparation time: 5 minutes
Cooking time: 8 minutes | **Servings:** 2
2 cups unsweetened almond milk
1 tablespoon avocado oil
1 tablespoon collagen protein powder
2 teaspoons coconut sugar
2 tablespoons cocoa powder
1 teaspoon ground cinnamon
1 teaspoon ground ginger
1 teaspoon vanilla extract
½ teaspoon ground turmeric
Dash salt
Dash cayenne pepper (optional)
Directions
In a medium/small saucepan over medium-high heat, warm the almond milk and avocado oil for about 7 minutes, stirring frequently. Fold in the protein powder, which will only properly dissolve in a heated liquid. Stir in the cocoa powder and coconut sugar until melted and dissolved. Carefully transfer the warm liquid into a blender, along with the cinnamon, ginger, vanilla, turmeric, salt, and cayenne pepper (if desired). Blend for 15 seconds until frothy. Serve immediately.
Nutrition facts (per serving)
calories: 217 | fat: 11.0g | protein: 11.2g | carbs: 14.8g | fiber: 6.0g | sodium: 202mg

➤Apple Crisp

Preparation Time: 10 minutes
Cooking Time: 13 minutes
Servings: 2
Ingredients:
2 apples, sliced into chunks
1 tsp. cinnamon
¼ cup rolled oats
1/4 cup brown sugar
½ cup of water
Directions:
Put all the listed ingredients in the pot and mix well. Seal the pot, choose MANUAL mode, and cook at HIGH pressure for 8 minutes. Release the pressure naturally and let sit for 5 minutes or until the sauce has thickened. Serve and enjoy.
Nutrition facts:
Calories: 218
Fat: 5 mg
Carbs: 54 g

➤Tasty Banana Cake

Preparation Time: 10 minutes
Cooking Time: 30 Minutes
Servings: 4
Ingredients:
1 tbsp. butter, soft
1 egg
1/3 cup brown sugar
2 tbsp. honey
1 banana
1 cup white flour
1 tbsp. baking powder
½ tbsp. cinnamon powder
Cooking spray
Directions:
Spurt cake pan with coking spray. Mix in butter with honey, banana, sugar, cinnamon, egg, flour and baking powder in a bowl then beat. Empty mix in cake pan with cooking spray, put into air fryer and cook at 350°F for 30 minutes. Allow for cooling, slice. Serve.
Nutrition facts:
Calories: 435
Total Fat: 7g
Total carbs: 15g

➤Simple Cheesecake

Preparation Time: 10 minutes
Cooking Time: 15 Minutes
Servings: 15
Ingredients:
1 lb. cream cheese
½ tbsp. vanilla extract
2 eggs
4 tbsp. sugar
1 cup graham crackers
2 tbsp. butter
Directions:
Mix in butter with crackers in a bowl. Compress crackers blend to the bottom cake pan, put into air fryer and cook at 340/350° F for 3-4 minutes. Mix cream

cheese with sugar, egg, vanilla in a bowl and beat properly. Sprinkle filling on crackers crust and cook cheesecake in air fryer at 310° F for 15 minutes. Keep cake in fridge for 3 hours, slice. Serve.

Nutrition facts:
Calories: 257
Total Fat: 18g
Total carbs: 22g

➤Bread Pudding

Preparation Time: 10 minutes
Cooking Time: 10 Minutes
Servings: 4
Ingredients:
6 glazed doughnuts
1 cup cherries
4 egg yolks
1 and ½ cups whipping cream
½ cup raisins
¼ cup sugar
½ cup chocolate chips.
Directions:
Mix in cherries with egg and whipping cream in a bowl then turn properly. Mix in raisins with sugar, chocolate chips and doughnuts in a bowl then stir. Mix the 2 mixtures, pour into oiled pan then into air fryer and cook at 310° F for 1 hour. Cool pudding before cutting. Serve.

Nutrition facts:
Calories: 456
Total Fat: 11g
Total carbs: 6g

➤Bread Dough and Amaretto Dessert

Preparation Time: 15 minutes
Cooking Time: 8 Minutes
Servings: 12
Ingredients:
1 lb. bread dough
1 cup sugar
½ cup butter
1 cup heavy cream
12 oz. chocolate chips
2 tbsp. amaretto liqueur
Directions:
Turn dough, cut into 18 slices and cut each piece in halves. Sweep dough pieces with butter, spray sugar, put into air fryer's basket and cook them at 340/350°F for 5 minutes. Turn them, cook for 3 minutes still. Move to a platter. Melt the heavy cream in pan over medium-high heat, put chocolate chips and turn until they melt. Put in liqueur, turn and move to a bowl. Serve bread dippers with the sauce.

Nutrition facts:
Calories: 179
Total Fat: 18g
Total carbs: 17g

➤Wrapped Pears

Preparation Time: 10 minutes

Cooking Time: 10 Minutes
Servings: 4
Ingredients:
4 puff pastry sheets
14 oz. vanilla custard
2 pears
1 egg
½ tbsp. cinnamon powder
2 tbsp. sugar
Directions:
Put wisp pastry slices on flat surface, add spoonful of vanilla custard at the center of each, add pear halves and wrap. Sweep pears with egg, spray sugar and cinnamon, put into air fryer's basket and cook at 315/320°F for 15 minutes. Split parcels on plates. Serve.

Nutrition facts:
Calories: 285
Total Fat: 14g
Total carbs: 30g

➤Air fryer Bananas

Preparation Time: 5 minutes
Cooking Time: 10 Minutes
Servings: 4
Ingredients:
3 tbsp. butter
2 eggs
8 bananas
½ cup corn flour
3 tbsp. cinnamon sugar
1 cup panko
Directions:
Warm up pan with the butter over medium heat, put panko, turn and cook for 4 minutes then move to a bowl. Spin each in flour, panko, egg blend, assemble them in air fryer's basket, grime with cinnamon sugar and cook at 280° F for 10 minutes. Serve immediately.

Nutrition facts:
Calories: 337
Total Fat: 3g
Total carbs: 23g

➤Cocoa Cake

Preparation Time: 5 minutes
Cooking Time: 17 Minutes
Servings: 6
Ingredients:
oz. butter
3 eggs
3 oz. sugar
1 tbsp. cocoa powder
3 oz. flour
½ tbsp. lemon juice
Directions:
Mix in 1 tbsp. butter with cocoa powder in a bowl and beat. Mix in the rest of the butter with eggs, flour, sugar and lemon juice in another bowl, blend properly and move half into a cake pan. Put half of the cocoa blend, spread, add the rest of the butter layer and crest with remaining cocoa. Put into air fryer and cook at 360° F for 17 minutes. Allow to cool before slicing. Serve.

Nutrition facts:
Calories: 221
Total Fat: 5g
Total carbs: 12g

›Apple Bread

Preparation Time: 5 minutes
Cooking Time: 40 Minutes
Servings: 6
Ingredients:
3 cups apples
1 cup sugar
1 tbsp. vanilla
2 eggs
1 tbsp. apple pie spice
2 cups white flour
1 tbsp. baking powder
1 stick butter
1 cup water
Directions:
Mix in egg with 1 butter stick, sugar, apple pie spice and turn using mixer. Put apples and turn properly. Mix baking powder with flour in another bowl and turn. Blend the 2 mixtures, turn and move it to spring form pan. Get spring form pan into air fryer and cook at 320°F for 40 minutes. Slice. Serve.
Nutrition facts:
Calories: 401
Total Fat: 9g
Total carbs: 29g

›Banana Bread

Preparation Time: 5 minutes
Cooking Time: 40 Minutes
Servings: 6
Ingredients:
¾ cup sugar
1/3 cup butter
1 tbsp. vanilla extract
1 egg
2 bananas
1 tbsp. baking powder
1 and ½ cups flour
½ tbsp. baking soda
1/3 cup milk
1 and ½ tbsp. cream of tartar
Cooking spray
Directions:
Mix in milk with cream of tartar, vanilla, egg, sugar, bananas and butter in a bowl and turn whole.
Mix in flour with baking soda and baking powder. Blend the 2 mixtures, turn properly, move into oiled pan with cooking spray, put into air fryer and cook at 320°F for 40 minutes. Remove bread, allow to cool, slice. Serve.
Nutrition facts:
Calories: 540
Total Fat: 16g
Total carbs: 28g

›Mini Lava Cakes

Preparation Time: 5 minutes
Cooking Time: 20 Minutes
Servings: 3
Ingredients:
1 egg
4 tbsp. sugar
2 tbsp. olive oil
4 tbsp. milk
4 tbsp. flour
1 tbsp. cocoa powder
½ tbsp. baking powder
½ tbsp. orange zest
Directions:
Mix in egg with sugar, flour, salt, oil, milk, orange zest, baking powder and cocoa powder, turn properly. Move it to oiled ramekins. Put ramekins in air fryer and cook at 320°F for 20 minutes. Serve warm.
Nutrition facts:
Calories: 329
Total Fat: 8.5g
Total carbs: 12.4g

— CHAPTER 7 —

SAUCES, DIPS AND DRESSINGS

ALICIA TRAVIS

>Tzatziki

Preparation time: 15 minutes
Cooking time: 0 minutes
Servings: 4 to 6
½ English cucumber, finely chopped
1 teaspoon salt, divided
1 cup plain Greek yogurt
8 tablespoons olive oil, divided
1 garlic clove, finely minced
1 to 2 tablespoons chopped fresh dill
1 teaspoon red wine vinegar
½ teaspoon freshly ground black pepper

Puréed the cucumber. Put the cucumber on layers of towels lining the bottom of a colander and sprinkle with ½ teaspoon of salt. Drain for 10 to 15 minutes. Mix together in a bowl the cucumber, yogurt, 6 tablespoons of olive oil, garlic, dill, vinegar, remaining ½ teaspoon of salt, and pepper until very smooth. Drizzle with the remaining 2 tbsps. of olive oil. Refrigerate until ready to serve.
Nutrition facts (per serving)
calories: 286 | fat: 29.0g | protein: 3.0g | carbs: 5.0g | fiber: 0g | sodium: 615mg

>Harissa Sauce

Preparation time: 10 minutes
Cooking time: 20 minutes |
Makes 3 to 4 cups
1 large red bell pepper
1 yellow onion, cut into thick rings
4 garlic cloves, peeled
1 cup vegetable broth
2 tablespoons tomato paste
1 tablespoon tamari
1 teaspoon ground cumin
1 tablespoon Hungarian paprika

Preheat the oven to 440/450ºF (235ºC). Line a baking sheet with parchment paper.Place the bell pepper on the prepared baking sheet, flesh-side up, and space out the onion and garlic around the pepper. Roast for 20 minutes. Transfer to a blender. Add the vegetable broth, tomato paste, tamari, cumin, and paprika. Purée until smooth. Served chilled or warm.
Nutrition facts (per serving) (¼ cup)
calories: 15 | fat: 1.0g | protein: 1.0g | carbs: 3.0g | fiber: 1.0g | sodium: 201mg

>Pineapple Sauce

Preparation time: 10 minutes
Cooking time: 0 minutes
Servings: 6 to 8
1 pound (454 g) fresh or thawed frozen pineapple, finely diced, juices reserved
1 white or red onion, finely diced
1 bunch cilantro or mint, leaves only, chopped
1 jalapeño, minced (optional)

Salt, to taste

Stir together the pineapple with its juice, onion, cilantro, and jalapeño (if desired) in a medium bowl. Season with salt to taste and serve. The sauce must be refrigerated in an container for up to 2 days.
Nutrition facts (per serving)
calories: 55 | fat: 0.1g | protein: 0.9g | carbs: 12.7g | fiber: 1.8g | sodium: 20mg

>Garlic Lemon-Tahini Dressing

Preparation time: 5 minutes
Cooking time: 0 minutes | **Servings:** 8 to 10
½ cup tahini
¼ cup extra-virgin olive oil
¼ cup freshly squeezed lemon juice
1 garlic clove, finely minced
2 teaspoons salt

Combine the tahini, olive oil, lemon juice, garlic, and salt. Cover and shake well until combined and creamy. Store in the refrigerator for up to 13 days.
Nutrition facts (per serving)
calories: 121 | fat: 12.0g | protein: 2.0g | carbs: 3.0g | fiber: 1.0g | sodium: 479mg

>Creamy Grapefruit and Tarragon Dressing

Preparation time: 6 minutes
Cooking time: 0
Servings: 4 to 6
½ cup avocado oil mayonnaise
2 tablespoons Dijon mustard
1 teaspoon dried tarragon
½ teaspoon salt
Zest and juice of ½ grapefruit
¼ teaspoon freshly ground black pepper
1 to 2 tablespoons water (optional)
Directions
In a medium-large mason jar with a lid, combine the mayonnaise, Dijon, tarragon, grapefruit zest and juice, salt, and pepper and whisk well with a fork until smooth and creamy. If a thinner dressing is preferred, thin out with water. Serve immediately.
Nutrition facts (per serving)
calories: 86 | fat: 7.0g | protein: 1.0g | carbs: 6.0g | fiber: 0g | sodium: 390mg

>Vinaigrette

Preparation time: 5 minutes
Cooking time: 0 minutes | **Makes** 1 cup
½ cup extra-virgin olive oil
¼ cup red wine vinegar
1 tablespoon Dijon mustard
1 teaspoon dried rosemary
½ teaspoon salt
½ teaspoon freshly ground black pepper

Directions
In a cup or a mansion jar with a lid, combine the olive oil, vinegar, mustard, rosemary, salt, and pepper and shake until well combined. Serve chilled or at room temperature.

Nutrition facts (per serving)
calories: 124 | fat: 14.0g | protein: 0g | carbs: 1.0g | fiber: 0g | sodium: 170mg

➤Pumpkin Spice Latte

Preparation Time: 5-10 minutes
Cooking Time: 0 minutes
Servings: 1
Ingredients:
1 ounce of unsalted butter
2 tablespoons of pumpkin spice
2 tablespoons of instant coffee powder
1 cup of boiling water
Heavy whipped cream
Directions:
Put all ingredients except cream inside a blender, and blend until the foam is formed. Pour in a cup, and sprinkle cinnamon. Add a dollop of cream and enjoy hot.
Nutrition facts:
Calories: 217
Fat: 12.9
Fiber: 2.3g
Carbohydrates:3.1 g
Protein:4.1 g

➤Butter Nutmeg Coffee

Preparation Time: 5-10 minutes
Cooking Time: 0 minutes
Servings: 1
Ingredients:
1 cup of coffee
2 tablespoons of ghee
1 tablespoon of coconut oil
1/2 teaspoon of nutmeg
Directions:
Pour coffee, ghee, oil, and nutmeg in a blender, and blend until smooth. Serve hot.
Nutrition facts:
Calories: 210
Fat:10 g
Fiber: 7.5g
Carbohydrates: 3.1g
Protein: 1.9g

➤Tropical Vanilla Milkshake

Preparation Time: 15 minutes
Cooking Time: 0 minutes
Servings: 1
Ingredients:
2 tablespoons of erythritol
1 cup of coconut milk

1/4 cup of heavy cream
1 teaspoon of vanilla extract
Directions:
Pour in the vanilla extract and erythritol into the blender. Add in the coconut milk, then the heavy cream, and blend for 10 to 20 seconds. Add ice if you'd like or freeze.
Nutrition facts:
Calories: 231
Fat: 9.5g
Fiber: 3.1g
Carbohydrates:2.9 g
Protein: 4.2g

➤Creamy Cinnamon Smoothie

Preparation Time: 15 minutes
Cooking Time: 0 minutes
Servings: 2
Ingredients:
2 cups of coconut milk
1 scoop vanilla protein powder
5 drops liquid stevia
1 teaspoon ground cinnamon
1/2 teaspoon alcohol-free vanilla extract
Directions:
Put the coconut milk, protein powder, stevia, cinnamon, and vanilla in a blender and blend until smooth. Pour into two glasses and serve immediately.
Nutrition facts:
Calories: 212
Fat: 3.1g
Fiber: 5.2g
Carbohydrates:3.7 g
Protein: 4.1g

➤Blueberry Tofu Smoothie

Preparation Time: 15 minutes
Cooking Time: 0 minutes
Servings: 1
Ingredients:
6 ounces of silken tofu
1 medium banana
2/3 cups of soy milk
1 cup of frozen or fresh blueberries (divided)
1 tablespoon of honey 2-3 ice cubes (optional)
Directions:
Drain the silken tofu to remove the excess water (silken tofu as a high-water content). Peele and slice the banana. Freeze banana sliced. This process usually takes up to 13-15 minutes. This helps to make the smoothie thicker. Get a blender. Blend the banana, tofu, and soy milk. This usually takes up to 30 seconds. Put 1/2 cup of the blueberries to the banana, tofu, and soymilk. Then blend it until it is very smooth. Put the remaining blueberries. Add honey and ice cubes. Blend it until it is well combined. Serve and enjoy.
Nutrition facts:
Calories: 312
Fat: 9.5g

Fiber: 11.8g
Carbohydrates:2.7 g
Protein: 12.1g

➤Bulletproof Coffee

Preparation Time: 5 minutes
Cooking Time:0 minutes
Servings: 1
Ingredients:
11/2 cups hot coffee
2 tablespoons MCT oil powder or Bulletproof Brain Oc-
tane Oil
2 tablespoons butter or ghee
Directions:
Pour the hot coffee into the blender.
Add the oil powder and butter, and blend until tho-
roughly mixed and frothy. Pour into a large mug and
enjoy.
Nutrition facts:
Calories: 245
Fat: 9.4g
Fiber:4.2 g
Carbohydrates:1.2 g
Protein: 2.3g

➤Morning Berry-Green Smoothie

Preparation Time: 15 minutes
Cooking Time: 0 minutes
Servings: 4
Ingredients:
1 avocado, pitted and sliced
3 cups mixed blueberries and strawberries
2 cups unsweetened almond milk
6 tbsp. heavy cream
2 tsp. erythritol
1 cup of ice cubes
1/3 cup nuts and seeds mix
Directions:
Combine the avocado slices, blueberries, strawberries,
almond milk, heavy cream, erythritol, ice cubes, nuts,
and seeds in a smoothie maker; blend in high-speed
until smooth and uniform. Pour the smoothie into drin-
king glasses and serve immediately.
Nutrition facts:
Calories: 290
Fat: 5.1g
Fiber: 11g
Carbohydrates:1.4 g
Protein: 2g

➤Dark Chocolate Smoothie

Preparation Time: 10 minutes
Cooking Time: 0 minutes
Servings: 2
Ingredients:
8 pecans
3/4 cup of coconut milk

1/4 cup of water
1 1/2 cups watercress
1 tsp. vegan protein powder
1 tbsp. chia seeds
1 tbsp. unsweetened cocoa powder
4 fresh dates, pitted
Directions:
In a blender, all ingredients must be blended until
creamy and uniform. Place into two glasses and chill
before serving.
Nutrition facts:
Calories: 299
Fat: 10g
Fiber: 12.8g
Carbohydrates:2.1 g
Protein: 4.4g

➤Super Greens Smoothie

Preparation Time: 15 minutes
Cooking Time: 0 minutes
Servings: 2
Ingredients:
6 kale leaves, chopped
3 stalks celery, chopped
1 ripe avocado, skinned, pitted, sliced
1 cup of ice cubes
2 cups spinach, chopped
1 large cucumber, peeled and chopped
Chia seeds to garnish
Directions:
In a blender, add the kale, celery, avocado, and ice
cubes, and blend for 45 seconds. Add the spinach
and cucumber, and process for another 45 seconds
until smooth. Pour the smoothie into glasses, garnish
with chia seeds, and serve the drink immediately.
Nutrition facts:
Calories: 290
Fat: 9.4g
Fiber: 12.1g
Carbohydrates:3.1 g
Protein: 8.5g

➤Kiwi Coconut Smoothie

Preparation Time: 5 minutes
Cooking Time: 0 minutes
Servings: 2
Ingredients:
2 kiwis, pulp scooped
1 tbsp. xylitol
4 ice cubes
2 cups unsweetened coconut milk
1 cup of coconut yogurt
Mint leaves to garnish
Directions:
Process the kiwis, xylitol, coconut milk, yogurt, and ice
cubes in a blender, until smooth, for about 3 minutes.
Transfer to serving glasses, garnish with mint leaves,
and serve.
Nutrition facts:

Calories: 298
Fat: 1.2g
Fiber: 12.1g
Carbohydrates:1.2 g
Protein: 3.2g

›Avocado-Coconut Shake

Preparation Time: 5 minutes
Cooking Time: 0 minutes
Servings: 2
Ingredients:
3 cups coconut milk, chilled
1 avocado, pitted, peeled, sliced
2 tbsp. erythritol
Coconut cream for topping
Directions:
Combine coconut milk, avocado, and erythritol, into the smoothie maker, and blend for 1 minute to smooth. Pour the drink into serving glasses, add some coconut cream on top of them, and garnish with mint leaves. Serve immediately.
Nutrition facts:
Calories: 301
Fat: 6.4g
Fiber: 12.9g
Carbohydrates:0.4 g
Protein: 3.1g

›Creamy Vanilla Cappuccino

Preparation Time: 5 minutes
Cooking Time: 0 minutes
Servings: 2
Ingredients:
2 cups unsweetened vanilla almond milk, chilled
1 tsp. swerve sugar
1/2 tbsp. powdered coffee
1 cup cottage cheese, cold
1/2 tsp. vanilla bean paste
1/4 tsp. xanthan gum
Unsweetened chocolate shavings to garnish
Directions:
In a blender, combine the almond milk, swerve sugar, cottage cheese, coffee, vanilla bean paste, and xanthan gum and process on high speed for 1 minute until smooth. Pour into tall shake glasses, sprinkle with chocolate shavings, and serve immediately.
Nutrition facts:
Calories: 190
Fat: 4.1g
Fiber:1.1 g
Carbohydrates:0.5 g
Protein: 2g

›Golden Turmeric Latte with Nutmeg

Preparation Time: 5 minutes
Cooking Time: 5 minutes
Servings: 2

Ingredients:
2 cups almond milk
1/3 tsp. cinnamon powder
1/2 cup brewed coffee
1/4 tsp. turmeric powder
1 tsp. xylitol
Nutmeg powder to garnish
Directions:
Add the almond milk, cinnamon powder, coffee, turmeric, and xylitol in the blender. Blend the ingredients at medium speed for 50 seconds and pour the mixture into a saucepan. Over low heat, set the pan and heat through for 6 minutes, without boiling. Keep swirling the pan to prevent boiling. Turn the heat off, and serve in latte cups, topped with nutmeg powder.
Nutrition facts:
Calories: 254
Fat: 9.1g
Fiber: 5g
Carbohydrates: 1.2g
Protein: 1 g

›Almond Smoothie

Preparation Time: 5 minutes
Cooking Time: 0 minutes
Servings: 2
Ingredients:
2 cups almond milk
2 tbsp. almond butter
1/2 cup Greek yogurt
1 tsp. almond extract
1 tsp. cinnamon
4 tbsp. flax meal
30 drops of stevia
A handful of ice cubes
Directions:
Put the yogurt, almond milk, almond butter, flax meal, almond extract, collagen peptides, and stevia to the bowl of a blender. Blend until uniform and smooth, for about 30 seconds. Pour in smoothie glasses, add the ice cubes and sprinkle with cinnamon.
Nutrition facts:
Calories: 288
Fat: 6.4g
Fiber:11 g
Carbohydrates:1 g
Protein: 1.4g

›Raspberry Vanilla Shake

Preparation Time: 5 minutes
Cooking Time: 0 minutes
Servings: 2
Ingredients:
2 cups raspberries
2 tbsp. erythritol
6 raspberries to garnish
1/2 cup cold unsweetened almond milk
2/3 tsp. vanilla extract
1/2 cup heavy whipping cream

Directions:
In a large blender, process the raspberries, milk, vanilla extract, whipping cream, and erythritol for 2 minutes; work in two batches if needed. The shake should be frosty. Pour into glasses, stick in straws, garnish with raspberries, and serve.
Nutrition facts:
Calories: 298
Fat: 5.1g
Fiber: 11g
Carbohydrates:1.2 g
Protein: 1.4g

➤Banana Smoothie

Preparation Time: 10 minutes
Cooking Time: 0 minutes
Servings: 2
Ingredients:
11/2 cups unsweetened almond milk
1/2 cup heavy (whipping) cream
1 banana
2 scoops (25–28 grams) vanilla protein powder
2 tablespoons tahini
1/2 teaspoon ground cinnamon
5 ice cubes
Directions:
Blend the smoothie. Put the almond milk, cream, banana, protein powder, tahini, cinnamon, and ice in a blender and blend until smooth and creamy. Serve. Pour into two tall glasses and serve.
Nutrition facts:
Calories: 308
Fat: 4.2g
Fiber: 9.5g
Carbohydrates:2.2 g
Protein: 7.4g

➤Creamy Mocha Smoothie

Preparation Time: 5 minutes
Cooking Time: 0 minutes
Servings: 2
Ingredients:
2 cups strong-brewed coffee
1 cup unsweetened almond milk
1 cup unsweetened coconut milk
2 tablespoons chia seeds
2 tablespoons flaxseed meal
2 tablespoons coconut oil
1/8 teaspoon ground cinnamon
Monk fruit sweetener, coarse, to taste
Directions:
Make coffee ice cubes. Put the coffee in freezer for 4 hours minimum. Blend the smoothie. Put all the coffee ice cubes (2 cups worth), almond milk, coconut milk, chia seeds, flaxseed meal, coconut oil, and cinnamon in a blender and blend smooth and creamy. Add a sweetener. Serve.
Nutrition facts:
Calories: 315

Fat: 6.1g
Fiber: 12g
Carbohydrates:1.2 g
Protein: 1.4g

➤Lemony Caper Dressing

Preparation time: 5 minutes
Cooking time: 0 minutes
½ cup sugar-free mayonnaise
2 tablespoons extra-virgin olive oil
1 tablespoon capers, drained
1 tablespoon lemon juice
1 tablespoon white vinegar
1 teaspoon grated lemon zest
½ teaspoon dried dill weed
Directions
Place all the ingredients in a medium-small blender and blend for 30 seconds, until creamy and nearly entirely smooth. Leave 1 week in fridge.
Nutrition facts (per serving)
calories: 106 | fat: 13.0g | protein: 0g | carbs: 0g | net carbs: 0g | fiber: 0g

➤Cajun Seasoning

Preparation time: 5 minutes
Cooking time: 0 minutes
1 tablespoon garlic powder
1 tablespoon kosher salt
1 tablespoon paprika
2 teaspoons cayenne pepper
2 teaspoons dried oregano leaves
2 teaspoons dried thyme leaves
2 teaspoons onion powder
1 teaspoon ground black pepper
Directions:
Put in a bowl all the ingredientsa and mix well. Store for 6 months.
Nutrition facts (per serving)
calories: 5 | fat: 0g | protein: 0g | carbs: 1.0g | net carbs: 1.0g | fiber: 0g

➤Parmesan Basil Vinaigrette

Preparation time: 5 minutes
Cooking time: 0 minutes
¼ cup fresh basil leaves
¼ cup sugar-free mayonnaise
2 tablespoons extra-virgin olive oil
2 tablespoons full-fat sour cream
1 tablespoon apple cider vinegar
1 tablespoon lemon juice
1 tablespoon granulated erythritol
1 tablespoon grated Parmesan cheese
½ teaspoon kosher salt
¼ teaspoon ground black pepper
Directions:
Place all the ingredients in a medium-small blender and blend until mostly smooth. Store in fridge 1 week.

Nutrition facts (per serving)
calories: 124 | fat: 14.0g | protein: 0g | carbs: 0g | net carbs: 0g | fiber: 0g

›Raita

Preparation time: 8 minutes
Cooking time: 0 minutes
⅓ cup full-fat Greek yogurt
⅓ cup full-fat sour cream
¼ cup finely chopped cucumbers
1 tablespoon chopped fresh cilantro
1 tablespoon chopped fresh mint
1 teaspoon granulated erythritol
1 teaspoon minced red onions
¼ teaspoon ground cumin
Directions:
Place all of the ingredients in a medium-small bowl and mix well. Serve immediately or store in an airtight container in the refrigerator for up to 3 days.
Nutrition facts (per serving)
calories: 30 | fat: 2.1g | protein: 0.9g | carbs: 1.0g | net carbs: 1.0g | fiber: 0g

›Tomato and Bacon Dressing

Preparation time: 8 minutes
Cooking time: 0 minutes
¼ cup sugar-free mayonnaise
5 cherry tomatoes
3 slices bacon, cooked and chopped
1 clove garlic, peeled
2 tablespoons chopped fresh parsley
½ teaspoon granulated erythritol
¼ teaspoon kosher salt
⅛ teaspoon ground black pepper
Directions:
Place all the ingredients in a medium-small blender and blend until mostly smooth. Store in fridge 1 week.
Nutrition facts (per serving)
calories: 95 | fat: 10.0g | protein: 2.0g | carbs: 1.0g | net carbs: 1.0g | fiber: 0g

›Basil Pesto

Preparation time: 5 minutes
Cooking time: 0 minutes | **Makes ¾ cup**
1 cup fresh basil leaves
¼ cup extra-virgin olive oil
¼ cup grated Parmesan cheese
¼ cup pine nuts
1 tablespoon chopped garlic
¼ teaspoon kosher salt
⅛ teaspoon ground black pepper
Directions:
Put all the ingredients in a medium-small blender or mini food processor. Pulse until fully combined but not quite smooth. Put in fridge 1 week or in the freezer for up to 3 months.
Nutrition facts (per serving)

calories: 140 | fat: 14.0g | protein: 2.9g | carbs: 1.4g | net carbs: 1.0g | fiber: 0.4g

›Blackened Seasoning

Preparation time: 5 minutes
Cooking time: 0 minutes | **Makes** 1 cup
3 tablespoons cayenne pepper
3 tablespoons chili powder
3 tablespoons paprika
2 tablespoons ground black pepper
1 tablespoon chipotle powder
1 tablespoon dried oregano leaves
1 tablespoon dried thyme leaves
1 tablespoon garlic powder
1 tablespoon onion powder
Directions:
Place all the ingredients in a medium-small bowl and mix well. Store in an airtight container for up to 6 months.
Nutrition facts (per serving)
calories: 7 | fat: 0g | protein: 0g | carbs: 1.5g | net carbs: 1.0g | fiber: 0.5g

›Ketchup

Preparation time: 5 minutes
Cooking time: 1 hour | **Makes** 2 cups
1 (28-ounce / 794-g) can tomato purée
⅓ cup granulated erythritol
¼ teaspoon cayenne pepper
½ cup white vinegar
1½ teaspoons dehydrated onions
½ teaspoon celery salt
½ teaspoon whole cloves
1 (1-inch) piece of cinnamon stick, broken
Directions:
Combine the tomato purée, sweetener, and cayenne pepper in a medium-sized saucepan and bring to a boil over medium heat, then reduce the heat to low. Simmer until it reduces by half, about 28-30 minutes, stirring occasionally. Meanwhile, in another small saucepan, combine the vinegar, onions, celery salt, cloves, and cinnamon stick pieces. Bring to a boil, then remove from the heat. Strain out the solids. Add the flavored vinegar to the tomato mixture. Simmer for another 18-21 minutes, or until the ketchup reaches the desired consistency. Remove from the heat and let cool. Blend the cooled ketchup with an immersion blender or in a small blender until smooth. Store in a clean jar with an airtight lid for up to 1 month in the refrigerator.
Nutrition facts (per serving)
calories: 15 | fat: 0g | protein: 0g | carbs: 3.8g | net carbs: 2.8g | fiber: 1.0g

— CHAPTER 8 —

LUNCH

ALICIA TRAVIS

›Bacon Wrapped Asparagus

Preparation Time: 10 minutes
Cooking Time: 20 minutes
Servings: 2
Ingredients:
1/3 cup heavy whipping cream
2 bacon slices, precooked
4 small spears asparagus
Salt, to taste
1 tablespoon butter
Directions:
Preheat the oven to 350/360 degrees and grease a baking sheet with butter. Meanwhile, mix cream, asparagus and salt in a bowl. Wrap the asparagus in bacon slices and arrange them in the baking dish. Transfer the baking dish to the oven and bake for about 20 minutes. Remove from the oven and serve hot. Place the bacon wrapped asparagus in a dish and set aside to cool for meal prepping. Divide it in 2 containers and cover the lid. Refrigerate for about 2 days and reheat in the microwave before serving.
Nutrition facts:
Calories: 204
Carbs: 1.4g
Protein: 5.9g
Fat: 19.3g
Sugar: 0.5g

›Spinach Chicken

Preparation Time: 10 minutes
Cooking Time: 10 minutes
Servings: 2
Ingredients:
2 garlic cloves, minced
2 tablespoons unsalted butter, divided
¼ cup parmesan cheese, shredded
¾ pound chicken tenders
¼ cup heavy cream
10 ounces frozen spinach, chopped
Salt and black pepper, to taste
Directions:
Heat 1 tablespoon of butter in a medium-large skillet and add chicken, salt and black pepper. Cook for about 3 minutes on both sides and remove the chicken to a bowl. Melt remaining butter in the skillet and add garlic, cheese, heavy cream and spinach. Cook for about 2-3 minutes and add the chicken. Cook for about 4-6 minutes on low heat and dish out to immediately serve. Place chicken in a dish and set aside to cool. Divide it in 2-3 containers and cover them. Refrigerate for about 72 hours and reheat in microwave before serving.
Nutrition facts:
Calories: 288
Carbs: 3.6g
Protein: 27.7g
Fat: 18.3g
Sugar: 0.3g

›Lemongrass Prawns

Preparation Time: 10 minutes
Cooking Time: 15 minutes
Servings: 2
Ingredients:
½ red chili pepper, seeded and chopped
2 lemongrass stalks
½ pound prawns, deveined and peeled
6 tablespoons butter
¼ teaspoon smoked paprika
Directions:
Preheat the oven to 390 degrees and grease a baking dish. Mix red chili pepper, butter, smoked paprika and prawns in a bowl. Marinate for about 2 hours and then thread the prawns on the lemongrass stalks. Arrange the threaded prawns on the baking dish and transfer it in the oven. Bake for about 15 minutes and dish out to serve immediately. Place the prawns in a dish and set aside to cool for meal prepping. Divide it in 2 containers and close the lid. Refrigerate for about 4 days and reheat in microwave before serving.
Nutrition facts:
Calories: 322
Carbs: 3.8g
Protein: 34.8g
Fat: 18g
Sugar: 0.1g
Sodium: 478mg

›Stuffed Mushrooms

Preparation Time: 20 minutes
Cooking Time: 25 minutes
Ingredients:
2 ounces bacon, crumbled
½ tablespoon butter
¼ teaspoon paprika powder
2 portobello mushrooms
1 oz cream cheese
¾ tablespoon fresh chives, chopped
Salt and black pepper, to taste
Directions:
Preheat the oven to 390/400 degrees and grease a baking dish. Heat butter in a skillet and add mushrooms. Sauté for about 4 minutes and set aside. Mix together cream cheese, chives, paprika powder, salt and black pepper in a bowl. Stuff the mushrooms with this mixture and transfer on the baking dish. Place in the oven and bake for about 18-20 minutes. These mushrooms can be refrigerated for about 3 days for meal prepping and can be served with scrambled eggs.
Nutrition facts:
Calories: 570
Carbs: 4.6g
Protein: 19.9g
Fat: 52.8g
Sugar: 0.8g
Sodium: 1041mg

Honey Glazed Chicken Drumsticks

Preparation Time: 10 minutes
Cooking Time: 20 minutes
Servings: 2
Ingredients:
½ tablespoon fresh thyme, minced
1/8 cup Dijon mustard
½ tablespoon fresh rosemary, minced
½ tablespoon honey
2 chicken drumsticks
1 tablespoon olive oil
Salt and black pepper, to taste
Directions:
Preheat the oven at 320/325 degrees and grease a baking dish. Combine well all the ingredients in a bowl except the drumsticks and mix. Add drumsticks and coat with the mixture. Cover and refrigerate to marinate overnight. Place the drumsticks in the baking dish and transfer it in the oven. Cook for about 18-20 minutes and dish out to immediately serve. Place chicken drumsticks in a dish to cool for meal prepping. Divide it in 2-3 containers and cover them. Refrigerate for about 72 hours and reheat in microwave before serving.
Nutrition facts:
Calories: 301
Carbs: 6g
Fats: 19.7g
Proteins: 4.5g
Sugar: 4.5g
Sodium: 316mg

Zucchini Pizza

Preparation Time: 10 minutes
Cooking Time: 15 minutes
Servings: 2
Ingredients:
1/8 cup spaghetti sauce
½ zucchini, cut in circular slices
½ cup cream cheese
Pepperoni slices, for topping
½ cup mozzarella cheese, shredded
Directions:
Preheat the oven to 340/350 degrees and grease a baking dish. Arrange the zucchini on the baking dish and layer with spaghetti sauce. Top with pepperoni slices and mozzarella cheese. Transfer the baking dish to the oven and bake for at least 13-15 minutes. Remove from the oven and serve immediately.
Nutrition facts:
Calories: 445
Carbs: 3.6g
Protein: 12.8g
Fat: 42g
Sugar: 0.3g
Sodium: 429mg

Omega-3 Salad

Preparation Time: 10 minutes

Cooking Time: 5 minutes
Servings: 2
Ingredients:
½ pound skinless salmon fillet, cut into 4-5 steaks
¼ tablespoon fresh lime juice
1 tablespoon olive oil
4 ½ tbsps sour cream
¼ zucchini, cut into small cubes
¼ teaspoon jalapeño pepper, seeded and chopped
Black pepper and salt
¼ tablespoon fresh dill, chopped
Directions:
Put olive oil and salmon in a medium-small skillet and cook for about 4-5 minutes on both sides. Season with black pepper and salt, stirring well and dish out. Mix well the remaining ingredients in a bowl and add cooked salmon to serve.
Nutrition facts:
Cal: 291
Fat: 21.1g
Carbs: 2.5g
Protein: 23.1g
Sugar: 0.6g
Sodium: 112mg

Crab Cakes

Preparation Time: 20 minutes
Cooking Time: 10 minutes
Servings: 2
Ingredients:
½ pound lump crabmeat, drained
2 tablespoons coconut flour
1 tablespoon mayonnaise
¼ teaspoon green Tabasco sauce
3 tablespoons butter
1 small egg, beaten
¾ tablespoon fresh parsley, chopped
½ teaspoon yellow mustard
Salt and black pepper, to taste
Directions:
Mix well all the ingredients in a bowl except butter. Make patties from this mixture. Heat butter in a skillet over medium-high heat and add patties. Cook for about 9-10 minutes on each side and dish out to serve hot. You can store the raw patties in the deep-freezer for 20-21 days. Place them in a container and place parchment paper in between the patties.
Nutritions facts:
Cal: 153
Fat: 10.8g
Carbs: 6.7g
Protein: 6.4g
Sugar: 2.4
Sodium: 46mg

Salmon Burgers

Preparation Time: 17 minutes
Cooking Time: 3 minutes
Servings: 2
Ingredients:

1 tablespoon sugar-free ranch dressing
½-ounce smoked salmon, chopped roughly
½ tablespoon fresh parsley, chopped
½ tablespoon avocado oil
1 small egg
4-ounce pink salmon, drained and bones removed
1/8 cup almond flour
¼ teaspoon Cajun seasoning

Directions:
Mix well all the ingredients in a bowl and stir well. Make patties from this mixture. Preheat a skillet over medium/high heat and add patties. Cook for about 3 minutes per side and dish out to serve. You can store the raw patties in the freezer for 20-21 days for meal prep. Place them in a container and place parchment paper in between the patties to avoid stickiness.

Nutrition facts:
Cal: 59
Fat: 12.7g
Carbs: 2.4g
Protein: 6.3g
Sugar: 0.7g
Sodium: 25mg

➤Low Carb Black Beans Chili Chicken

Preparation Time: 10 minutes
Cooking Time: 25 minutes
Servings: 10
Ingredients:
1-3/4 pounds of chicken breasts, cubed (boneless skinless)
2 sweet red peppers, chopped
1 onion, chopped
3 tablespoons of olive oil
1 can of chopped green chiles
4 cloves of garlic, minced
2 tablespoons of chili powder
2 teaspoons of ground cumin
1 teaspoon of ground coriander
2 cans of black beans, rinsed
1 can of Italian stewed tomatoes, cut up
1 cup of chicken broth or beer
1/2 to 1 cup of water

Directions:
Put oil into a skillet and place over medium heat. Add in the red pepper, chicken, and onion and cook until the chicken is brown, about five minutes. Add in the garlic, chiles, chili powder, coriander, and cumin and cook for an additional minute. Next, add in the tomatoes, beans, half cup of water, and broth and cook until it boils. Decrease the heat, uncover the skillet and cook while stirring for fifteen minutes. Serve.

Nutrition facts:
Calories: 236
Fat: 6g
Protein: 22g
Carbohydrates: 21g

➤Flavorful Taco Soup

Preparation Time: 5 minutes
Cooking Time: 15
Servings: 8
Ingredients:
1 lb of Ground beef
3 tablespoons of Taco seasoning, divided
4 cup of Beef bone broth
2 14.5-oz cans of Diced tomatoes
3/4 cup of Ranch dressing

Directions:
Put the ground beef into a pot and place over medium high heat and cook until brown, about ten minutes. Add in ¾ cup of broth and two tablespoons of taco seasoning. Cook until part of the liquid has evaporated. Add in the diced tomatoes, rest of the broth, and rest of the taco seasoning. Stir to mix, then simmer for ten minutes. Remove the pot from heat, and add in the ranch dressing. Garnish with cilantro and cheddar cheese. Serve.

Nutrition facts:
Calories: 309
Fat: 24g
Protein: 13g

➤Delicious Instant Pot Buffalo Chicken Soup

Preparation Time: 10 minutes
Cooking Time: 20 minutes
Servings: 6
Ingredients:
1 tablespoon of Olive oil
1/2 Onion, diced)
1/2 cup of Celery, diced
4 cloves of Garlic, minced
1 lb of Shredded chicken, cooked
4 cup of Chicken bone broth, or any chicken broth
3 tablespoons of Buffalo sauce
6 oz of Cream cheese
1/2 cup of Half & half

Directions:
Switch the instant pot to the sauté function. Add in the chopped onion, oil, and celery. Cook about ten minutes or until the onions are brown and translucent. Add in the garlic and cook for about 1 minute, or until fragrant. Switch off the instant pot. Add in the broth, shredded chicken, and buffalo sauce. Cover the instant pot and seal. Switch the soup feature on and set time to five minutes. When cooked, release pressure naturally for five minutes and then quickly. Scoop out one cup of the soup liquid into a blender bowl, then add in the cheese and blend until smooth. Pour the puree into the instant pot, then add in the calf and half and stir to mix. Serve.

Nutrition facts:
Servings: 1 cup
Calories: 270
Protein: 27g
Fat: 16g
Carbohydrates: 4g

>Low Carb Cream of Mushroom Soup

Preparation Time: 15 minutes
Cooking Time: 15 minutes
Servings: 5
Ingredients:
1 tablespoons of Olive oil
1/2 Onion, diced
20 oz of Mushrooms, sliced
6 cloves of Garlic, minced
2 cup of Chicken broth
1 cup of Heavy cream
1 cup of Unsweetened almond milk
3/4 teaspoon of Sea salt
1/4 teaspoon of Black pepper
Directions:
Place a pot over medium-high heat and add in olive oil. Add in the onions and mushrooms and cook for about fifteen minutes, or until browned. Next, add garlic and cook for another one minute. Add in the cream, chicken broth, sea salt, almond milk, and black pepper. Cook until boil, then simmer for fifteen mins. Puree the soup using an immersion blender.
Nutrition facts:
Servings: 1 cup
Calories: 229
Fat: 21g
Protein: 5g
Carbohydrates: 8g

>Lemony Parmesan Salmon

Preparation Time: 10 minutes
Cooking Time: 25 minutes
Servings: 4
Ingredients:
Butter, melted (2 tablespoons)
Green onions, sliced thinly (2 tablespoons)
Breadcrumbs, white, fresh (3/4 cup)
Thyme leaves, dried (1/4 teaspoon)
Salmon fillet, 1 ¼-pound (1 piece)
Salt (1/4 teaspoon)
Parmesan cheese, grated (1/4 cup)
Lemon peel, grated (2 teaspoons)
Directions:
Preheat the oven at 350 degrees Fahrenheit.
Mist cooking spray onto a baking pan (shallow). Fill with pat-dried salmon. Brush salmon with butter (1 tablespoon) before sprinkling with salt. Combine the breadcrumbs with onions, thyme, lemon peel, cheese, and remaining butter (1 tablespoon). Cover salmon with the breadcrumb mixture. Air-fry for fifteen to twenty-five minutes.
Nutrition facts:
Calories 290
Fat 10 g
Protein 30 g
Carbohydrates 0 g

>Easiest Tuna Cobbler Ever

Preparation Time: 15 minutes
Cooking Time: 25 minutes
Servings: 4
Ingredients:
Water, cold (1/3 cup)
Tuna, canned, drained (10 ounces)
Sweet pickle relish (2 tablespoons)
Mixed vegetables, frozen (1 ½ cups)
Soup, cream of chicken, condensed (10 ¾ ounces)
Pimientos, sliced, drained (2 ounces)
Lemon juice (1 teaspoon)
Paprika
Directions:
Preheat the air fryer at 375 degrees Fahrenheit.
Mist cooking spray into a round casserole (1 ½ quarts). Mix the frozen vegetables with milk, soup, lemon juice, relish, pimientos, and tuna in a saucepan. Cook for 8 minutes over medium heat. Fill the casserole with the tuna mixture. Mix the biscuit mix with cold water to form a soft dough. Beat for half a minute before dropping by four spoonfuls into the casserole. Dust the dish with paprika before air-frying for twenty to twenty-five minutes.
Nutrition facts:
Calories 320
Fat 10 g
Protein 20 g
Carbohydrates 30 g

>Deliciously Homemade Pork Buns

Preparation Time: 20 minutes
Cooking Time: 25 minutes
Servings: 8
Ingredients:
Green onions, sliced thinly (3 pieces)
Egg, beaten (1 piece)
Pulled pork, diced, w/ barbecue sauce (1 cup)
Buttermilk biscuits, refrigerated (16 1/3 ounces)
Soy sauce (1 teaspoon)
Directions:
Preheat the air fryer at 325 degrees Fahrenheit.
Use parchment paper to line your baking sheet. Combine pork with green onions. Separate and press the dough to form 8 four-inch rounds. Fill each biscuit round's center with two tablespoons of pork mixture. Cover with the dough edges and seal by pinching. Arrange the buns on the sheet and brush with a mixture of soy sauce and egg. Cook in the air fryer for twenty to twenty-five minutes.
Nutrition facts:
Calories 240
Fat 0 g
Protein 0 g
Carbohydrates 20 g

Mouthwatering Tuna Melts

Preparation Time: 15 minutes
Cooking Time: 20 minutes
Servings: 8
Ingredients:
Salt (1/8 teaspoon)
Onion, chopped (1/3 cup)
Biscuits, refrigerated, flaky layers (16 1/3 ounces)
Tuna, water packed, drained (10 ounces)
Mayonnaise (1/3 cup)
Pepper (1/8 teaspoon)
Cheddar cheese, shredded (4 ounces)
Tomato, chopped
Sour cream
Lettuce, shredded
Directions:
Preheat the air fryer at 325 degrees Fahrenheit.
Mist cooking spray onto a cookie sheet. Mix tuna with
mayonnaise, pepper, salt, and onion. Separate dough
so you have 8 biscuits: press each into 5-inch rounds.
Arrange 4 biscuit rounds on the sheet. Fill at the center
with tuna mixture before topping with cheese. Cover
with the remaining biscuit rounds and press to seal.
Air-fry for fifteen to twenty minutes. Slice each sand-
wich into halves. Serve each piece topped with let-
tuce, tomato, and sour cream.
Nutrition facts:
Calories 320
Fat 10 g
Protein 10 g
Carbohydrates 20 g

Bacon Wings

Preparation Time: 15 minutes
Cooking Time: 1 hour 15 minutes
Servings: 12
Ingredients:
Bacon strips (12 pieces)
Paprika (1 teaspoon)
Black pepper (1 tablespoon)
Oregano (1 teaspoon)
Chicken wings (12 pieces)
Kosher salt (1 tablespoon)
Brown sugar (1 tablespoon)
Chili powder (1 teaspoon)
Celery sticks
Blue cheese dressing
Directions:
Preheat the air fryer at 325 degrees Fahrenheit.
Mix sugar, salt, chili powder, oregano, pepper, and
paprika. Coat chicken wings with this dry rub. Wrap
a bacon strip around each wing. Arrange wrapped
wings in the air fryer basket. Cook for thirty minutes on
each side in the air fryer. Let cool for five minutes.
Serve and enjoy with celery and blue cheese.
Nutrition facts:
Calories 100
Fat 0 g

Protein 0 g
Carbohydrates 0 g

Pepper Pesto Lamb

Preparation Time: 15 minutes
Cooking Time: 1 hour 15 minutes
Servings: 12
Ingredients:
Pesto:
Rosemary leaves, fresh (1/4 cup)
Garlic cloves (3 pieces)
Parsley, fresh, packed firmly (3/4 cup)
Mint leaves, fresh (1/4 cup)
Olive oil (2 tablespoons)
Lamb:
Red bell peppers, roasted, drained (7 ½ ounces)
Leg of lamb, boneless, rolled (5 pounds)
Seasoning, lemon pepper (2 teaspoons)
Directions:
Preheat the oven at 325 degrees Fahrenheit. Mix the
pesto ingredients in the food processor. Unroll the
lamb and cover the cut side with pesto. Top with
roasted peppers before rolling up the lamb and tying
with kitchen twine. Coat lamb with seasoning (lemon
pepper) and air-fry for one hour.
Nutrition facts:
Calories 310
Fat 10 g
Protein 40.0 g
Carbohydrates 0 g

Tuna Spinach Casserole

Preparation Time: 30 minutes
Cooking Time: 25 minutes
Servings: 8
Ingredients:
Mushroom soup, creamy (18 ounces)
Milk (1/2 cup)
White tuna, solid, in-water, drained (12 ounces)
Crescent dinner rolls, refrigerated (8 ounces)
Egg noodles, wide, uncooked (8 ounces)
Cheddar cheese, shredded (8 ounces)
Spinach, chopped, frozen, thawed, drained (9 ounc-
es)
Lemon peel grated (2 teaspoons)
Directions:
Preheat the oven at 350 degrees Fahrenheit. Mist
cooking spray onto a glass baking dish (11x7-inch).
Follow package directions in cooking and draining
the noodles. Stir the cheese (1 ½ cups) and soup to-
gether in a skillet heated on medium. Once cheese
melts, stir in your noodles, milk, spinach, tuna, and lemon peel. Once bubbling, pour into the prepped dish.
Unroll the dough and sprinkle with remaining cheese
(1/2 cup). Roll up dough and pinch at the seams to
seal. Slice into 8 portions and place over the tuna mixture. Air-fry for twenty to twenty-five minutes.
Nutrition facts:

Calories 400
Fat 10 g
Protein 20 g
Carbohydrates 30 g

›Greek-Style Mini Burger Pies

Preparation Time: 15 minutes
Cooking Time: 40 minutes
Servings: 6
Ingredients:
Burger mixture:
Onion, large, chopped (1 piece)
Red bell peppers, roasted, diced (1/2 cup)
Ground lamb, 80% lean (1 pound)
Red pepper flakes (1/4 teaspoon)
Feta cheese, crumbled (2 ounces)
Baking mixture:
Milk (1/2 cup)
Biscuit mix, classic (1/2 cup)
Eggs (2 pieces)
Directions:
Preheat oven at 350 degrees Fahrenheit. Grease 12 muffin cups using cooking spray. Cook the onion and beef in a skillet heated on medium-high. Once beef is browned and cooked through, drain and let cool for five minutes. Stir together with feta cheese, roasted red peppers, and red pepper flakes. Whisk the baking mixture ingredients together. Fill each muffin cup with baking mixture (1 tablespoon). Air-fry for twenty-five to thirty minutes. Let cool before serving.
Nutrition facts:
Calories 270
Fat 10 g
Protein 10 g
Carbohydrates 10 g

›Family Fun Pizza

Preparation Time: 30 minutes
Cooking Time: 25 minutes
Servings: 16
Ingredients:
Pizza crust:
Water, warm (1 cup)
Salt (1/2 teaspoon)
Flour, whole wheat (1 cup)
Olive oil (2 tablespoons)
Dry yeast, quick active (1 package)
Flour, all purpose (1 ½ cups)
Cornmeal
Olive oil
Filling:
Onion, chopped (1 cup)
Mushrooms, sliced, drained (4 ounces)
Garlic cloves, chopped finely (2 pieces)
Parmesan cheese, grated (1/4 cup)
Ground lamb, 80% lean (1 pound)
Italian seasoning (1 teaspoon)
Pizza sauce (8 ounces)

Mozzarella cheese, shredded (2 cups)
Directions:
Mix yeast with warm water. Combine with flours, oil (2 tablespoons), and salt by stirring and then beating vigorously for half a minute. Let the dough sit for twenty minutes. Preheat oven at 350 degrees Fahrenheit. Prep 2 square pans (8-inch) by greasing with oil before sprinkling with cornmeal. Cut the rested dough in half; place each half inside each pan. Set aside, covered, for thirty to forty-five minutes. Cook in the air fryer for twenty to twenty-two minutes. Sauté the onion, beef, garlic, and Italian seasoning until beef is completely cooked. Drain and set aside. Cover the air fryer crusts with pizza sauce before topping with beef mixture, cheeses, and mushrooms. Return to oven and cook for twenty minutes.
Nutrition facts:
Calories 215
Fat 0 g
Protein 10 g
Carbohydrates 20.0 g

›Almond Pancakes

Preparation Time: 10 minutes
Cooking Time: 13 minutes
Servings: 12
Ingredients:
6 eggs
1/4 cup almonds; toasted
2 ounces' cocoa chocolate
1 teaspoon almond extract
1/3 cup coconut; shredded
1/2 teaspoon baking powder
1/4 cup coconut oil
1/2 cup coconut flour
1/4 cup stevia
1 cup almond milk
Cooking spray
A pinch of salt
Directions:
Mix coconut flour with stevia, baking powder, salt and coconut and stir. Add coconut oil, eggs, almond milk and the almond extract and stir well again. Add chocolate and almonds and whisk well again. Heat up a pan and add cooking spray; add 2 tablespoons batter, spread into a circle, cook until its golden, flip, cook again until it's done and transfer to a pan.
Do the same for rest of the batter and serve your pancakes right away.
Nutrition facts:
Calories: 266
Fat: 13
Fiber: 8
Carbs: 10
Protein: 11

›Mouth-watering Pie

Preparation Time: 15 minutes

Cooking Time: 45 minutes
Servings: 8
Ingredients:
3/4-pound beef; ground
1/2 onion; chopped.
1 pie crust
3 tablespoons taco seasoning
1 teaspoon baking soda
Mango sauce for serving
1/2 red bell pepper; chopped.
A handful cilantro; chopped.
8 eggs
1 teaspoon coconut oil
Salt and black pepper to taste.
Directions:
Heat up a pan, add oil, beef, cook until it browns and mixes with salt, pepper and taco seasoning. Stir again, transfer to a bowl and leave aside for now. Heat up the pan again over medium heat with cooking juices from the meat, add onion and pepper; stir and cook for 4-6 minutes. Add eggs, baking soda and some salt and stir well. Add cilantro; stir again and take off heat. Spread beef mix in pie crust, add veggies mix and spread over meat, heat oven at 350 degrees F and bake for about 43-45 minutes. Leave the pie to cool down a bit, slice, divide between plates and serve with mango sauce on top.
Nutrition facts:
Calories: 198
Fat: 11
Fiber: 1
Carbs: 12
Protein: 12

➤Chicken Omelet

Preparation Time: 5 minutes
Cooking Time: 15 minutes
Servings: 1
Ingredients:
2 bacon slices; cooked and crumbled
2 eggs
1 tablespoon homemade mayonnaise
1 tomato; chopped.
1-ounce rotisserie chicken; shredded
1 teaspoon mustard
1 small avocado; pitted, peeled and chopped.
Salt and black pepper to taste.
Directions:
In a bowl, mix eggs with some salt and pepper and whisk gently. Heat up a pan over medium heat; spray with some cooking oil, add eggs and cook your omelet for 5 minutes. Add chicken, avocado, tomato, bacon, mayo and mustard on one half of the omelet. Fold omelet, cover pan and cook for 5 minutes more Transfer to a plate and serve
Nutrition facts:
Calories: 400
Fat: 32
Fiber: 6
Carbs: 4

Protein: 25

➤Pesto Zucchini Noodles

Preparation Time: 15 minutes
Cooking Time: 15 minutes
Servings: 4
Ingredients:
4 zucchinis, spiralized
1 tbsp avocado oil
2 garlic cloves, chopped
2/3 cup olive oil
1/3 cup parmesan cheese, grated
2 cups fresh basil
1/3 cup almonds
1/8 tsp black pepper
¾ tsp sea salt
Directions:
Add zucchini noodles into a colander and sprinkle with ¼ teaspoon of salt. Cover and let sit for 30 minutes. Drain zucchini noodles well and pat dry. Preheat the oven to 400 F. Place almonds on a parchment-lined baking sheet and bake for 6-8 minutes. Transfer toasted almonds into the food processor and process until coarse. Add olive oil, cheese, basil, garlic, pepper, and remaining salt in a food processor with almonds and process until pesto texture. Heat avocado oil in a medium-large pan over medium-high heat. Add zucchini noodles and cook for 4-5 minutes. Pour pesto over zucchini noodles, mix well and cook for 1 minute. Serve immediately with baked salmon.
Nutrition facts:
Calories: 525
Fat 44 g
Carbs 3 g
Sugar 8 g
Protein 16 g
Cholesterol 30 mg

➤Baked Cod & Vegetables

Preparation Time: 15 minutes
Cooking Time: 15 minutes
Servings: 4
Ingredients:
1 lb cod fillets
8 oz asparagus, chopped
3 cups broccoli, chopped
¼ cup parsley, minced
½ tsp lemon pepper seasoning
½ tsp paprika
¼ cup olive oil
¼ cup lemon juice
1 tsp salt
Directions:
Preheat oven to 390/400 F. Line a baking sheet with parchment paper and set aside. In a medium-small bowl, combine the lemon juice, paprika, olive oil, pepper spices, and salt. Place the fish fillets in the center of the greaseproof paper. Arrange the broccoli and asparagus around the fish fillets. Pour lemon juice

mixture over the fish fillets and top with parsley. Bake in preheated oven for 13-15 minutes. Serve and enjoy.

Nutrition facts:
Calories 240
Fat 11 g
Carbs 6 g
Sugar 6 g
Protein 27 g
Cholesterol 56 mg

›Parmesan Zucchini

Preparation Time: 15 minutes
Cooking Time: 15 minutes
Servings: 4
Ingredients:
4 zucchinis, quartered lengthwise
2 tbsp fresh parsley, chopped
2 tbsp olive oil
¼ tsp garlic powder
½ tsp dried basil
½ tsp dried oregano
½ tsp dried thyme
½ cup parmesan cheese, grated
Pepper
Salt
Directions:
Preheat the oven to 340/350 F. Line baking sheet with parchment paper and set aside. In a medium-small bowl, mix together parmesan cheese, garlic powder, basil, oregano, thyme, pepper, and salt. Arrange zucchini onto the prepared baking sheet and drizzle with oil and sprinkle with parmesan cheese mixture. Bake in preheated oven for 14-15 minutes then broil for 2 minutes or until lightly golden brown. Garnish with parsley and serve immediately.

Nutrition facts:
Calories 244
Fat 14 g
Carbs 7 g
Sugar 5 g
Protein 15 g
Cholesterol 30 mg

›Chicken Zucchini Noodles

Preparation Time: 20 minutes
Cooking Time: 5 minutes
Servings: 2
Ingredients:
1 large zucchini, spiralized
1 chicken breast, skinless & boneless
½ tbsp jalapeño, minced
2 garlic cloves, minced
½ tsp ginger, minced
½ tbsp fish sauce
2 tbsp coconut cream
½ tbsp honey
½ lime juice
1 tbsp peanut butter
1 carrot, chopped

2 tbsp cashews, chopped
¼ cup fresh cilantro, chopped
1 tbsp olive oil
Pepper
Salt
Directions:
Preheat oil in a pan over medium/high heat. Season chicken breast with pepper and salt. Once the oil is hot then add chicken breast into the pan and cook for 3-4 minutes per side or until cooked. Remove chicken breast from pan. Shred chicken breast with a fork and set aside. In a medium-small bowl, mix peanut butter, jalapeño, garlic, ginger, fish sauce, coconut cream, honey, and lime juice. Set aside. In a large mixing bowl, combine spiralized zucchini, carrots, cashews, cilantro, and shredded chicken. Pour peanut butter mixture over zucchini noodles and toss to combine. Serve immediately and enjoy.

Nutrition facts:
Calories 353
Fat 21 g
Carbs 20.5 g
Sugar 8 g
Protein 25 g
Cholesterol 54 mg

›Tomato Avocado Cucumber Salad

Preparation Time: 15 mins
Cooking Time: 0 mins
Servings: 4
Ingredients:
12 oz cherry tomatoes, cut in half
5 medium-small cucumbers, chopped
3 medium-small avocados, chopped
½ tsp ground black pepper
2 tbsps olive oil
2 tbsps fresh lemon juice
¼ cup fresh cilantro, chopped
1 tsp sea salt
Directions:
Add cherry tomatoes, avocados, cucumbers, and cilantro into the large mixing bowl and mix well. Mix olive oil, lemon juice, black pepper, and salt and pour over salad. Toss well and serve immediately.

Nutrition facts:
Calories 442
Fat 31 g
Carbs 30.3 g
Sugar 4 g
Protein 2 g
Cholesterol 0 mg

›Creamy Cauliflower Soup

Preparation Time: 15 minutes
Cooking Time: 15 minutes
Servings: 6
Ingredients:
5 cups cauliflower rice
8 oz cheddar cheese, grated
2 cups unsweetened almond milk

2 cups vegetable stock
2 tbsp water
1 small onion, chopped
2 garlic cloves, minced
1 tbsp olive oil
Pepper
Salt

Directions:
Heat olive oil in a medium-large stockpot over medium heat. Add onion and garlic and cook for 1-2 minutes. Add cauliflower rice and water. Cover and cook for 5-7 minutes. Now add vegetable stock and almond milk and stir well. Bring to boil. Turn heat to low and simmer for 5 minutes. Turn off the heat. Slowly add cheddar cheese and stir until smooth. Season soup with pepper and salt. Stir well and serve hot.

Nutrition facts:
Calories 214
Fat 15 g
Carbs 3 g
Sugar 3 g
Protein 16 g
Cholesterol 40 mg

➤Taco Zucchini Boats

Preparation Time: 20 minutes
Cooking Time: 55 minutes
Servings: 4
Ingredients:
4 medium zucchinis, cut in half lengthwise
¼ cup fresh cilantro, chopped
½ cup cheddar cheese, shredded
¼ cup water
4 oz tomato sauce
2 tbsp bell pepper, mined
½ small onion, minced
½ tsp oregano
1 tsp paprika
1 tsp chili powder
1 tsp cumin
1 tsp garlic powder
1 lb lean ground turkey
½ cup sauce
1 tsp kosher salt

Directions:
Preheat the oven to 400 F. Add ¼ cup of sauce in the bottom of the baking dish. Using a spoon hollow out the center of the zucchini halves. Chop the scooped-out flesh of zucchini and set aside ¾ of a cup chopped flesh. Add zucchini halves in the boiling water and cook for 1 minute. Remove zucchini halves from water. Add ground turkey in a large pan and cook until meat is no longer pink. Add spices and mix well. Add reserved zucchini flesh, water, tomato sauce, bell pepper, and onion. Stir well and cover, simmer over low heat for 20 minutes. Stuff zucchini boats with taco meat and top each with one tablespoon of shredded cheddar cheese. Place zucchini boats in baking dish. Cover dish with foil and bake in the preheated oven for 32/35 minutes. Top with remaining sauce and chopped cilantro. Serve and enjoy.

Nutrition facts:

Calories 297
Fat 17 g
Carbs 12 g
Sugar 3 g
Protein 30.2 g
Cholesterol 96 mg

➤Healthy Broccoli Salad

Preparation Time: 25 minutes
Cooking Time: 0 minutes
Servings: 6
Ingredients:
3 cups broccoli, chopped
1 tbsp apple cider vinegar
½ cup Greek yogurt
2 tbsp sunflower seeds
3 bacon slices, cooked and chopped
1/3 cup onion, sliced
¼ tsp stevia

Directions:
In a mixing bowl, mix broccoli, onion, and bacon. In a small bowl, mix vinegar, stevia, and yogurt and pour over broccoli mixture. Stir well to combine. Sprinkle sunflower seeds on top of the salad. Store salad in the refrigerator for 30-35 minutes. Serve and enjoy.

Nutrition facts:
Calories 90
Fat 9 g
Carbs 4 g
Sugar 5 g
Protein 2 g
Cholesterol 12 mg

➤Delicious Zucchini Quiche

Preparation Time: 25 minutes
Cooking Time: 1 hour
Servings: 8
Ingredients:
6 eggs
2 medium zucchinis, shredded
½ tsp dried basil
2 garlic cloves, minced
1 tbsp dry onion, minced
2 tbsp parmesan cheese, grated
2 tbsp fresh parsley, chopped
½ cup olive oil
1 cup cheddar cheese, shredded
¼ cup coconut flour
¾ cup almond flour
½ tsp salt

Directions:
Preheat oven to 340/350 F. Grease 9-inch pie pan and set aside. Squeeze excess liquid from zucchini. Add all ingredients to medium-large bowl and mix until well combined. Pour into prepared cake pan. Bake in a preheated oven for 58-60 minutes or until cooked through. Remove from the oven and let it cool completely. Slice and serve.

Nutrition facts:

Calories 288
Fat 23 g
Carbs 5 g
Sugar 6 g
Protein 11 g
Cholesterol 139 mg

›Turkey Spinach Egg Muffins

Preparation Time: 10 minutes
Cooking Time: 20 minutes
Servings: 3
Ingredients:
5 egg whites
2 eggs
¼ cup cheddar cheese, shredded
¼ cup spinach, chopped
¼ cup milk
3 lean breakfast turkey sausage
Pepper
Salt
Directions:
Preheat the oven to 340/350 F. Grease muffin tray cups and set aside. In a pan, brown the turkey sausage links over medium-high heat until sausage is brown from all the sides. Cut sausage in ½-inch pieces and set aside. In a medium-large bowl, whisk together eggs, egg whites, milk, pepper, and salt. Stir in spinach. Pour egg mixture into the prepared muffin tray. Divide sausage and cheese evenly between each muffin cup. Bake in preheated oven until muffins are set or for 20 minutes. Serve warm and enjoy.
Nutrition facts:
Calories 123
Fat 8 g
Carbs 9 g
Sugar 6 g
Protein 13 g
Cholesterol 123 mg

›Chicken Casserole

Preparation Time: 15 minutes
Cooking Time: 40 minutes
Servings: 4
Ingredients:
1 lb cooked chicken, shredded
¼ cup Greek yogurt
1 cup cheddar cheese, shredded
½ cup sauce
4 oz cream cheese, softened
4 cups cauliflower florets
1/8 tsp black pepper
½ tsp kosher salt
Directions:
Add cauliflower florets into the microwave-safe dish and cook for 10 minutes or until tender. Add cream cheese and microwave for 25-30 seconds more. Stir well. Add chicken, yogurt, cheddar cheese, sauce, pepper, and salt and stir everything well. Preheat the oven to 375 F. Bake in preheated oven for 20 minutes. Serve hot and enjoy.

Nutrition facts:
Calories 429
Fat 23 g
Carbs 6 g
Sugar 7 g
Protein 44 g
Cholesterol 149 mg

›Aloo Gobi

Preparation Time: 15 Minutes
Cooking Time: 4 To 5 Hours
Servings: 4
Ingredients:
1 large cauliflower, cut into 1-inch pieces
1 large russet potato, peeled and diced
1 medium yellow onion, peeled and diced
1 cup canned diced tomatoes, with juice
1 cup frozen peas
¼ cup water
1 (2-inch) piece fresh ginger, finely chopped and peeled
1½ teaspoons minced garlic (3 cloves)
1 jalapeño pepper, stemmed and sliced
1 tablespoon cumin seeds
1 tablespoon garam masala
1 teaspoon ground turmeric
1 heaping tablespoon fresh cilantro
Cooked rice, for serving (optional)
Directions:
Combine the cauliflower, potato, onion, diced tomatoes, peas, water, ginger, garlic, jalapeño, cumin seeds, garam masala, and turmeric in a slow cooker; mix until well combined. Cook on low and cover for at least 5 hours and a half. Garnish with the cilantro and serve over cooked rice (if using).
Nutrition facts:
Calories: 115
Total fat: 1g
Protein: 6g
Sodium: 62mg
Fiber: 6g

›Jackfruit Carnitas

Preparation Time: 15 Minutes
Cooking Time: 8 Hours
Servings: 4
Ingredients:
2 (20-ounce) cans jackfruit, drained, hard pieces discarded
¾ cup Very Easy Vegetable Broth (here) or store bought
1 tablespoon ground cumin
1 tablespoon dried oregano
1½ teaspoons ground coriander
1 teaspoon minced garlic (2 cloves)
½ teaspoon ground cinnamon
2 bay leaves
Tortillas, for serving
Optional toppings: diced onions, sliced radishes, fresh cilantro, lime wedges, Nacho Cheese (here)

Directions:
Combine the jackfruit, vegetable broth, cumin, oregano, coriander, garlic, cinnamon, and bay leaves in a slow cooker. Stir to combine. Cover and cook on medium-low for 8 hours or on high for 4 hours. Use two forks to pull the jackfruit apart into shreds. Remove the bay leaves. Serve in warmed tortillas with your taco fixings.

Nutrition facts:
Calories: 286
Total fat: 2g
Protein: 6g
Sodium: 155mg
Fiber: 5g

›Baked Beans

Preparation Time: 15 Minutes
Cooking Time: 6 Hours
Servings: 4
Ingredients:
2 (15-ounce) cans white beans, rinsed
1 (15-ounce) can tomato sauce
1 medium yellow onion, finely diced
1½ teaspoons minced garlic (3 cloves)
3 tablespoons brown sugar
2 tablespoons molasses
1 tablespoon prepared yellow mustard
1 tablespoon chili powder
1 teaspoon soy sauce
Pinch salt
Freshly ground black pepper

Directions:
Place the beans, tomato sauce, onion, garlic, brown sugar, molasses, mustard, chili powder, and soy sauce into a slow cooker; mix well. Cover and cook on medium-low for 6 hours. Season with salt and pepper before serving.

Nutrition facts:
Calories: 468
Total fat: 2g
Protein: 28g
Sodium: 714mg
Fiber: 20g

›Brussels Sprouts Curry

Preparation Time: 15 Minutes
Cooking Time: 7 To 8 Hours
Servings: 4
Ingredients:
¾ pound Brussels sprouts, bottoms cut off and sliced in half
1 can full-fat coconut milk
1 cup Very Easy Vegetable Broth (here) or store bought
1 medium onion, diced
1 medium carrot, thinly sliced
1 medium red or Yukon potato, diced
1½ teaspoons minced garlic (3 cloves)
One (1-inch) piece fresh ginger, minced and peeled
One small serrano chile, seeded and finely chopped
2 tablespoons peanut butter
1 tablespoon rice vinegar or other vinegar
1 tablespoon cane sugar or agave nectar
1 tablespoon soy sauce
1 teaspoon curry powder
1 teaspoon ground turmeric
Pinch salt
Freshly ground black pepper
Cooked rice, for serving (optional)

Directions:
Place the Brussels sprouts, coconut milk, vegetable broth, onion, carrot, potato, garlic, ginger, serrano chile, peanut butter, vinegar, cane sugar, soy sauce, curry powder, and turmeric in a slow cooker. Mix well. Cook on low and cover for about 7-8 hours or on high for 4 to 5 hours. Season with salt and pepper. Serve over rice (if using).

Nutrition facts:
Calories: 404
Total fat: 29g
Protein: 10g
Sodium: 544mg
Fiber: 8g

›Jambalaya

Preparation Time: 15 Minutes
Cooking Time: 6 To 8 Hours
Servings: 4
Ingredients:
2 cups Very Easy Vegetable Broth (here) or store bought
1 large yellow onion, diced
1 green bell pepper, seeded and chopped
2 celery stalks, chopped
1½ teaspoons minced garlic (3 cloves)
1 can dark red kidney beans, drained
2 tablespoons Cajun seasoning
1 (15-ounce) can diced tomatoes, drained
1 can black-eyed peas, drained and rinsed
2 teaspoons dried oregano
2 teaspoons dried parsley
1 teaspoon cayenne pepper
1 teaspoon smoked paprika
½ teaspoon dried thyme
Cooked rice, for serving (optional)

Directions:
Combine the vegetable broth, onion, bell pepper, celery, garlic, kidney beans, black-eyed peas, diced tomatoes, Cajun seasoning, oregano, parsley, cayenne pepper, smoked paprika, and dried thyme in a slow cooker; mix well. Cover and cook on medium-low for about 6-8 hours. Serve over rice (if using).

Nutrition facts:
Calories: 428
Total fat: 2g
Protein: 28g
Sodium: 484mg
Fiber: 19g

➤Mushroom-Kale Stroganoff

Preparation Time: 15 Minutes
Cooking Time: 6 To 8 Hours
Servings: 4
Ingredients:
1-pound mushrooms, sliced
1½ cups Very Easy Vegetable Broth (here) or store bought
1 cup stemmed and chopped kale
1 small yellow onion, diced
2 garlic cloves, minced
2 tablespoons all-purpose flour
2 tablespoons ketchup or tomato paste
2 teaspoons paprika
½ cup vegan sour cream
¼ cup chopped fresh parsley
Cooked rice, pasta, or quinoa, for serving
Directions:
Combine the mushrooms, vegetable broth, kale, onion, garlic, flour, ketchup or tomato paste, and paprika in a slow cooker. Mix thoroughly. Cover and cook on medium-low for about 6-8 hours. Stir in the sour cream and parsley just before serving. Serve over rice, pasta, or quinoa.
Nutrition facts:
Calories: 146
Total fat: 7g
Protein: 8g
Sodium: 417mg
Fiber: 3g

➤Sloppy Joe Filling

Preparation Time: 15 Minutes
Cooking Time: 6 To 8 Hours
Servings: 4
Ingredients:
3 cups textured vegetable protein
3 cups water
2 (6-ounce) cans tomato paste, or 1 cup ketchup
1 medium yellow onion, diced
½ medium green bell pepper, finely diced
2 teaspoons minced garlic (4 cloves)
4 tablespoons vegan Worcestershire sauce
3 tablespoons brown sugar
3 tablespoons apple cider vinegar
3 tablespoons prepared yellow mustard
2 tablespoons hot sauce (optional)
1 tablespoon salt
1 teaspoon chili powder
Sliced, toasted buns or cooked rice, for serving
Directions:
Combine the textured vegetable protein, water, tomato paste, onion, bell pepper, garlic, Worcestershire sauce, brown sugar, vinegar, mustard, hot sauce (if using), salt, and chili powder in a slow cooker. Mix well. Cover and cook on medium-low for about 6-8 hours or on high for 4 to 5 hours. Serve on sliced, toasted buns or over rice.
Nutrition facts:
Calories: 452
Total fat: 4g

Protein: 75g
Sodium: 2,242mg
Fiber: 11g

➤Hoppin' John

Preparation Time: 15 Minutes
Cooking Time: 4 To 6 Hours
Servings: 4
Ingredients:
3 (15-ounce) cans black-eyed peas, rinsed
1 (14.5-ounce) can Cajun-style stewed tomatoes, with juice
2 cups hot water
1 cup stemmed and chopped kale
¾ cup finely diced red bell pepper
½ cup sliced scallions
1 medium jalapeño pepper, seeded and minced
1 teaspoon minced garlic (2 cloves)
1½ teaspoons hot sauce
1 vegetable bouillon cube
Cooked rice, for serving
Directions:
Combine the black-eyed peas, tomatoes, hot water, kale, bell pepper, scallions, jalapeño, garlic, hot sauce, and bouillon cube in a slow cooker. Stir to combine. Cover and cook on medium-low for about 4-6 hours. Serve over cooked rice.
Nutrition facts:
Calories: 164
Total fat: 2g
Protein: 10g
Sodium: 250mg
Fiber: 8g

➤Ground Beef Stroganoff

Preparation Time: 10 minutes
Cooking Time: 15 minutes
Servings: 4
Ingredients:
2 tbsp. butter
1 clove minced garlic
1 pound 80% lean ground beef
Salt and pepper, to taste
10 oz(228g) sliced mushrooms
2 tbsp. water
1 cup sour cream
1 tbsp. fresh lemon juice
1 tbsp. fresh chopped parsley
Directions:
The butter must be added to a pan. When the butter has melted and stops foaming, add the minced garlic to the skillet. Cook the garlic until fragrant, then mix in the ground beef—season with salt and pepper. Cook the ground beef until no longer pink; break up the grounds with a wooden spoon. Add the water and mushrooms to the pan and cook over medium heat. Cook until the liquid has reduced halfway, and the mushrooms are tender. Set the cooked mushrooms aside. Reduce the heat, then whisk the sour cream and paprika into the skillet. Stir in the cooked beef

and mushrooms into the pan and combine. Stir in the lemon juice and parsley.

Nutrition facts:
Calories: 380
Fat: 15.1g
Fiber: 3.6g
Carbohydrates:12.3 g
Protein: 15.4g

›Herbed Grilled Lamb

Preparation Time: 15 minutes
Cooking Time: 20 minutes
Servings: 6
Ingredients:
2 pounds of lamb
5 spoons of ghee butter
3 tablespoons of Keto mustard
2 minced garlic cloves
1 1/2 tablespoon of chopped basil
1/2 tablespoon of pepper
3 tablespoons of olive oil
1/2 teaspoon of salt
Directions:
Mix butter, mustard, and basil with a pinch of salt to taste. Then, set aside. Mix garlic, salt, and pepper together. Then, add a teaspoon of oil. Season the lamb generously with this mix. Grill the lamb on medium heat until fully cooked. Take butter mix and spread generously on chops and serve hot.

Nutrition facts:
Calories: 390
Fat: 19.5 g
Fiber: 5.9g
Carbohydrates: 3.2 g
Protein: 18.6 g

›Mushroom and Pork Bake

Preparation time: 10 minutes
Cooking time: 45 minutes | **Servings:** 6
1 onion, chopped
2 (10.5-ounce / 298-g) cans mushroom soup
6 pork chops
½ cup sliced mushrooms
Salt and ground pepper, to taste
Directions
Preheat the oven to 360-370°F (180°C). Season the pork chops with salt and black pepper, and place in a baking dish. Combine the mushroom soup, mushrooms, and onion, in a bowl. Pour this mixture over the pork chops. Bake for 45 minutes.

Nutrition facts (per serving)
calories: 402 | fat: 32.5g | protein: 19.5g | carbs: 8.4g | net carbs: 7.9g | fiber: 0.5g

›Pork Chops in Blue Cheese Sauce

Preparation Time: 5 minutes
Cooking Time: 10 minutes

Servings: 2
Ingredients:
2 boneless pork chops
Pink Himalayan salt
Freshly ground black pepper
2 tablespoons butter
1/3 cup blue cheese crumbles
1/3 cup heavy (whipping) cream
1/3 cup sour cream
Directions:
Dry the pork chops and season with pink Himalayan salt and pepper. In a medium skillet over medium-high heat, melt the butter. When the butter melts and is very hot, add the pork chops and sear on each side for 3 minutes. The pork chops must be transferred to a plate and let rest for 3 to 5 minutes. In a preheated pan, melt the blue cheese crumbles, frequently stirring so they don't burn. Add the cream and the sour cream to the pan with the blue cheese. Let simmer for a few minutes, stirring occasionally. For an extra kick of flavor in the sauce, pour the pork-chop pan juice into the cheese mixture and stir. Let simmer while the pork chops are resting. Put the pork chops on two plates, pour the blue cheese sauce over the top of each, and serve.

Nutrition facts:
Calories: 434
Fat: 14.1g
Fiber: 11.3g
Carbohydrates:3.1 g
Protein: 17.5g

›Creamy Pepper Loin Steaks

Preparation time: 15 minutes
Cooking time: 10 minutes | **Servings:** 2
1 teaspoon lard, at room temperature
2 pork loin steaks
½ cup beef bone broth
2 bell peppers, deseeded and chopped
1 shallot, chopped
1 garlic clove, minced
Sea salt, to season
½ teaspoon cayenne pepper
¼ teaspoon paprika
1 teaspoon Italian seasoning mix
¼ cup Greek yogurt
Directions
Melt the lard in a cast-iron skillet over moderate heat. Once hot, cook the pork loin steaks until slightly browned or approximately 5 minutes per side; reserve. Add a splash of the beef bone broth to deglaze the pan. Now, cook the bell peppers, shallot, and garlic until tender and aromatic. Season with salt, cayenne pepper, paprika, and Italian seasoning mix. After that, decrease the temperature to medium-low, add the Greek yogurt to the skillet and let it simmer for 2 minutes more or until heated through. Serve immediately.

Nutrition facts (per serving)
calories: 450 | fat: 19.1g | protein: 62.2g | carbs: 6.0g | net carbs: 4.9g | fiber: 1.1g

›Texas Pulled Boston Butt

Preparation time: 15 minutes
Cooking time: 3 hours | **Servings:** 4
Ingredients
Kosher salt, to season
1 teaspoon paprika
½ teaspoon oregano
½ teaspoon rosemary
1 teaspoon mustard seeds
½ teaspoon chipotle powder
1 teaspoon black peppercorns, whole
3 tablespoons apple cider vinegar
1 cup tomato sauce
1½ pounds (680 g) Boston butt
Directions
Thoroughly combine all ingredients, except for the Boston butt, in a big casserole dish. Now, place Boston butt on top skin-side up. Bake in the preheated oven at 290-300°F (155°C) for about 3 hours, checking and turning every 30 minutes. Cut the skin off and shred the pork with two forks; discard any fatty bits.
Serve with coleslaw and the bowl of cooking juices on the side for dipping.
Bon appétit!
Nutrition facts (per serving)
calories: 340 | fat: 21.1g | protein: 30.7g | carbs: 4.3g | net carbs: 3.2g | fiber: 1.1g

›Pork Medallions with Onions and Bacon

Preparation time: 10 minutes
Cooking time: 25 minutes | **Servings:** 4
Ingredients
2 onions, chopped
6 bacon slices, chopped
½ cup vegetable stock
Salt and black pepper, to taste
1 pound (454 g) pork tenderloin, cut into medallions
Directions
Set a pan over medium heat, stir in the bacon, cook until crispy, and remove to a plate. Add onions, black pepper, and salt, and cook for 5 minutes; set to the same plate with bacon. Add the pork medallions to the pan, season with black pepper and salt, brown for 3 minutes on each side, turn, reduce heat to medium, and cook for 7 minutes. Stir in the stock and cook for 2 minutes. Return the bacon and onions to the pan and cook for 1 minute.
Nutrition facts (per serving)
calories: 326 | fat: 17.9g | protein: 35.9g | carbs: 7.2g | net carbs: 5.9g | fiber: 1.3g

›Lamb Chops with Tapenade

Preparation Time: 15 minutes
Cooking Time: 25 minutes
Servings: 4

Ingredients:
FOR THE TAPENADE
1 cup pitted Kalamata olive
2 tbsps chopped fresh parsley
2 tbsps extra virgin olive oil
2 tsps minced garlic
2 tsps squeezed lemon juice
FOR THE LAMB CHOPS
2 racks French-cut lamb chops (8 bones each)
Freshly ground black pepper and sea salt
1 tablespoon olive oil
Directions:
TO MAKE THE TAPENADE
Place the olives, olive oil, parsley, lemon juice, and garlic in a food processor and process until the mixture is puréed. Transfer the tapenade to a container and store it sealed in the refrigerator until needed.
TO MAKE THE LAMB CHOPS
Preheat the oven to 450°F. Season the lamb racks with pepper and salt. Heat oil. Pan sear the lamb racks on all sides for about 5 minutes in total, until browned. Arrange the racks upright in the skillet, with the bones interlaced. Roast the racks for about 18-20 minutes for medium-rare or until the internal temperature reaches 125°F.
Nutrition facts:
Calories: 387
Fat: 17.4g
Fiber: 12.1g
Carbohydrates:5.4 g
Protein: 18.9g

›Cream of Onion Pork Cutlets

Preparation time: 10 minutes
Cooking time: 10 minutes | **Servings:** 4
2 tablespoons olive oil
4 pork cutlets
¼ cup cream of onion soup
½ teaspoon paprika
Sea salt and ground black pepper
Directions
Preheat the olive oil in a sauté pan over moderate heat. Once hot, sear the pork cutlets for 5 to 6 minutes, turning once or twice to ensure even cooking. Add in the cream of onion soup, paprika, salt, and black pepper. Cook for a further 3 minutes until heated through. The meat thermometer should register 145°F (63°C). Serve in individual plates garnished with freshly snipped chives if desired. Enjoy!
Nutrition facts (per serving)
calories: 396 | fat: 24.5g | protein: 40.2g | carbs: 0.9g | net carbs: 0.7g | fiber: 0.2g

›Pickle and Ham-Stuffed Pork

Preparation time: 20 minutes
Cooking time: 35 minutes | **Servings:** 4
Zest and juice from 2 limes
2 garlic cloves, minced
¾ cup olive oil

1 cup fresh cilantro, chopped
1 cup fresh mint, chopped
1 teaspoon dried oregano
Salt and black pepper
2 teaspoons cumin
4 pork loin steaks
2 pickles, chopped
4 ham slices
6 Swiss cheese slices
2 tablespoons mustard
Salad:
1 head red cabbage, shredded
2 tablespoons vinegar
3 tablespoons olive oil
Salt to taste
Directions
In a food processor, blitz the lime zest, oil, oregano, black pepper, cumin, cilantro, lime juice, garlic, mint, and salt. Rub the steaks with the mixture and toss well to coat; set aside for some hours in the fridge. Arrange the steaks on a working surface, split the pickles, mustard, cheese, and ham on them, roll, and secure with toothpicks. Preheat a pan over medium-high heat, add in the pork rolls, cook each side for 2 minutes and remove to a baking sheet. Bake in the oven at 340/350°F (180°C) for 25 minutes. Prepare the red cabbage salad by mixing all salad ingredients and serve with the meat.
Nutrition facts (per serving)
calories: 412 | fat: 37.1g | protein: 25.8g | carbs: 8.1g | net carbs: 3.1g | fiber: 5.0g

›Tomato Sauce and Basil Pesto Fettuccine

Preparation time: 15 minutes
Cooking time: 15 minutes | **Servings:** 4
Ingredients
4 Roma tomatoes, diced
2 teaspoons no-salt-added tomato paste
1 tablespoon chopped fresh oregano
2 garlic cloves, minced
1 cup low-sodium vegetable soup
½ teaspoon sea salt
1 packed cup fresh basil leaves
¼ cup pine nuts
¼ cup grated Parmesan cheese
2 tablespoons extra-virgin olive oil
1 pound (454 g) cooked whole-grain fettuccine
Directions
Put the tomatoes, tomato paste, oregano, garlic, vegetable soup, and salt in a skillet. Stir to mix well. Cook over medium heat for 8-11 minutes or until lightly thickened. Put the remaining ingredients, except for the fettuccine, in a food processor and pulse to combine until smooth. Pour the puréed basil mixture into the tomato mixture, then add the fettuccine. Cook until heated through for a few minutes and the fettuccine is well coated. Serve immediately.
Nutrition facts (per serving)
calories: 389 | fat: 22.7g | protein: 9.7g | carbs: 40.2g | fiber: 4.8g | sodium: 616mg

›Garlic and Parsley Chickpeas

Preparation time: 10 minutes
Cooking time: 18 to 20 minutes
Servings: 4 to 6
¼ cup extra-virgin olive oil, divided
4 garlic cloves, sliced thinly
⅛ teaspoon red pepper flakes
1 onion, chopped finely
¼ teaspoon salt, plus more to taste
Black pepper, to taste
2 (15-ounce / 425-g) cans chickpeas, rinsed
1 cup vegetable broth
2 tablespoons minced fresh parsley
2 teaspoons lemon juice
Directions
Add 3 tablespoons of the olive oil, garlic, and pepper flakes to a skillet over medium heat. Cook for about 2-3 minutes, stirring constantly, or until the garlic turns golden but not brown. Stir in the onion and ¼ teaspoon salt and cook for 5 to 7 minutes, or until softened and lightly browned. Add the chickpeas and broth to the skillet and bring to a simmer. Reduce the heat to medium-low, cover, and cook for about 7 minutes, or until the chickpeas are cooked through and flavors meld. Uncover, increase the heat to high and continue to cook for about 3 minutes more, or until nearly all liquid has evaporated. Turn off the heat, stir the parsley and lemon juice. Season to taste with pepper and salt and drizzle with remaining 1 tablespoon of the olive oil. Serve warm.
Nutrition facts (per serving)
calories: 220 | fat: 11.4g | protein: 6.5g | carbs: 24.6g | fiber: 6.0g | sodium: 467mg

›Black-Eyed Peas Salad with Walnuts

Preparation time: 10 minutes
Cooking time: 0 minutes
Servings: 4 to 6
3 tablespoons extra-virgin olive oil
3 tablespoons dukkah, divided
2 tablespoons lemon juice
2 tablespoons pomegranate molasses
¼ teaspoon salt, or more to taste
⅛ teaspoon pepper, or more to taste
2 (15-ounce / 425-g) cans black-eyed peas, rinsed
½ cup pomegranate seeds
½ cup minced fresh parsley
½ cup walnuts, toasted and chopped
4 scallions, sliced thinly
Directions
In a medium/large bowl, whisk together the olive oil, 2 tablespoons of the dukkah, lemon juice, pomegranate molasses, salt and pepper. Stir in the remaining ingredients. Season with salt and pepper. Sprinkle with the remaining 1 tablespoon of the dukkah before serving.
Nutrition facts (per serving)
calories: 155 | fat: 11.5g | protein: 2.0g | carbs: 12.5g | fiber: 2.1g | sodium: 105mg

Mashed Beans with Cumin

Preparation time: 10 minutes
Cooking time: 10 to 12 minutes
Servings: 4 to 6
1 tablespoon extra-virgin olive oil
4 garlic cloves, minced
1 teaspoon ground cumin
2 (15-ounce / 425-g) cans fava beans
3 tablespoons tahini
2 tbsps. lemon juice, plus lemon wedges for serving
Salt and pepper, to taste
1 tomato, cored and cut into ½-inch pieces
1 small onion, chopped finely
2 hard-cooked large eggs, chopped
2 tablespoons minced fresh parsley

Directions
Add the olive oil, garlic and cumin to a medium saucepan over medium heat. Cook for about 2 minutes, or until fragrant. Stir in the beans with tahini and their liquid. Bring to a simmer and cook until the liquid thickens slightly, or for 8-10 minutes. Turn off the heat, mash the beans to a coarse consistency with a potato masher. Stir in the lemon juice and 1 teaspoon pepper. Season with salt and pepper. Transfer the mashed beans to a serving dish. Top with the tomato, onion, eggs and parsley. Drizzle with the extra olive oil. Serve with the lemon wedges.

Nutrition facts (per serving)
calories: 125 | fat: 8.6g | protein: 4.9g | carbs: 9.1g | fiber: 2.9g | sodium: 131mg

Turkish Canned Pinto Bean Salad

Preparation time: 10 minutes
Cooking time: 3 minutes | **Servings:** 4 to 6
¼ cup extra-virgin olive oil, divided
3 garlic cloves, lightly crushed and peeled
2 (15-ounce / 425-g) cans pinto beans, rinsed
2 cups plus 1 tablespoon water
Salt and pepper, to taste
¼ cup tahini
3 tablespoons lemon juice
1 tablespoon ground dried Aleppo pepper, plus extra for serving
8 ounces (227 g) cherry tomatoes, halved
¼ red onion, sliced thinly
½ cup fresh parsley leaves
2 hard-cooked large eggs, quartered
1 tablespoon toasted sesame seeds

Directions
Add garlic and 1 tablespoon of the olive oil to a medium saucepan over medium heat. Cook for about 2-3 minutes, stirring constantly, or until the garlic turns golden but not brown. Add the beans, 2 cups of the water and 1 teaspoon salt and bring to a simmer. Remove from the heat, let sit and cover for 20 minutes. Drain the beans and discard the garlic. In a medium-large bowl, whisk together the remaining 3 tablespoons of the oil, tahini, lemon juice, Aleppo, the remaining 1 tablespoon of the water and ¼ teaspoon salt. Stir in the beans, tomatoes, onion and parsley. Season

with pepper and salt. Transfer to a serving platter and put the eggs. Sprinkle with the sesame seeds and extra Aleppo before serving.

Nutrition facts (per serving)
calories: 402 | fat: 18.9g | protein: 16.2g | carbs: 44.4g | fiber: 11.2g | sodium: 456mg

Fava and Garbanzo Bean Ful

Preparation time: 10 minutes
Cooking time: 10 minutes | **Servings:** 6
1 (15-ounce / 425-g) can fava beans, rinsed and drained
1 (1-pound / 454-g) can garbanzo beans, rinsed and drained
3 cups water
½ cup lemon juice
3 cloves garlic, peeled and minced
1 teaspoon salt
3 tablespoons extra-virgin olive oil

Directions
In a pot over medium heat, cook water and beans for 10 minutes. Drain the beans and transfer to a bowl. Reserve 2 cup of the liquid from the cooked beans. Add the reserved liquid, lemon juice, minced garlic and salt to the bowl with the beans. Mix to combine well. Mash up about half the beans in the bowl. Give the mixture one more stir to make sure the beans are evenly mixed. Drizzle with the olive oil and serve.

Nutrition facts (per serving)
calories: 199 | fat: 9.0g | protein: 10.0g | carbs: 25.0g | fiber: 9.0g | sodium: 395mg

Triple-Green Pasta with Cheese

Preparation time: 5 minutes
Cooking time: 14 to 16 minutes | **Servings:** 4
8 ounces (227 g) uncooked penne
1 tablespoon extra-virgin olive oil
2 garlic cloves, minced
¼ teaspoon crushed red pepper
2 cups chopped fresh flat-leaf parsley, including stems
5 cups loosely packed baby spinach
¼ teaspoon ground nutmeg
¼ teaspoon kosher salt
¼ teaspoon freshly ground black pepper
⅓ cup Castelvetrano olives, pitted and sliced
⅓ cup grated Parmesan cheese

Directions
In a large stockpot of salted water, cook the pasta for about 8 to 10 minutes. Drain the pasta and reserve ¼ cup of the cooking liquid. Meanwhile, heat the olive oil in a large skillet over medium heat. Add the garlic and red pepper and cook for 30 seconds, stirring constantly. Add the parsley and cook for 1-2 minutes, stirring constantly. Add the spinach, nutmeg, salt, and pepper, and cook for 3 minutes, stirring occasionally, or until the spinach is wilted. Add the cooked pasta and the reserved ¼ cup cooking liquid to the skillet. Stir in the olives and cook for about 2 minutes, or until most of the pasta water has been absorbed. Remove from the heat and stir the cheese before ser-

ving.

Nutrition facts (per serving)
calories: 262 | fat: 4.0g | protein: 15.0g | carbs: 51.0g | fiber: 13.0g | sodium: 1180mg

›Caprese Pasta with Roasted Asparagus

Preparation time: 5 minutes
Cooking time: 25 minutes | **Servings:** 6
8 ounces (227 g) uncooked small pasta, like orecchiette (little ears) or farfalle (bow ties)
1½ pounds (680 g) fresh asparagus, ends trimmed and stalks chopped into 1-inch pieces
1½ cups grape tomatoes, halved
2 tablespoons extra-virgin olive oil
¼ teaspoon kosher salt
¼ teaspoon freshly ground black pepper
2 cups fresh Mozzarella, drained and cut into bite-size pieces (about 8 ounces / 227 g)
⅓ cup torn fresh basil leaves
2 tablespoons balsamic vinegar
Directions
Preheat the oven to 390/400°F (205°C). In a large stockpot of salted water, cook the pasta for about 8 to 10 minutes. Drain and reserve about ¼ cup of the cooking liquid. Meanwhile, in a medium-large bowl, toss together the asparagus, tomatoes, oil, salt and pepper. Spread the mixture onto a medium-large, rimmed baking sheet and bake in the oven for 15 minutes, stirring twice during cooking. Remove the vegtables from the oven and add the cooked pasta to the baking sheet. Mix with a few tablespoons of cooking liquid to help the sauce become smoother and the saucy vegetables stick to the pasta. Gently mix in the Mozzarella and basil. Drizzle with the balsamic vinegar. Serve from the baking sheet or pour the pasta into a large bowl.

Nutrition facts (per serving)
calories: 147 | fat: 3.0g | protein: 16.0g | carbs: 17.0g | fiber: 5.0g | sodium: 420mg

›Garlic Shrimp Fettuccine

Preparation time: 10 minutes
Cooking time: 15 minutes
Servings: 4 to 6
8 ounces (227 g) fettuccine pasta
¼ cup extra-virgin olive oil
3 tablespoons garlic, minced
1 pound (454 g) large shrimp, peeled and deveined
⅓ cup lemon juice
1 tablespoon lemon zest
½ teaspoon salt
½ teaspoon freshly ground black pepper
Directions
Bring a large pot of salted water to a boil. Add the fettuccine and cook for 8 minutes. Reserve ½ cup of the liquid cooking and drain the pasta. Heat the olive oil, in a medium/large saucepan over medium heat. Add the garlic and sauté for at least 1 minute. Add

the shrimp to the saucepan and cook each side for 3 minutes. Remove the shrimp from the pan. Add the remaining ingredients to the saucepan. Stir in the cooking liquid. Add the pasta and toss together to evenly coat the pasta. Serve the pasta topped with the cooked shrimp.

Nutrition facts (per serving)
calories: 615 | fat: 17.0g | protein: 33.0g | carbs: 89.0g | fiber: 4.0g | sodium: 407mg

›Pesto Pasta

Preparation time: 10 minutes
Cooking time: 8 minutes
Servings: 4 to 6
1 pound (454 g) spaghetti
4 cups fresh basil leaves, stems removed
3 cloves garlic
1 teaspoon salt
½ teaspoon freshly ground black pepper
½ cup toasted pine nuts
¼ cup lemon juice
½ cup grated Parmesan cheese
1 cup extra-virgin olive oil
Direction
Bring a large pot water to a boil and then add the salt. Add spaghetti to the pot and cook for 8 minutes. In a food processor, place the remaining ingredients, except for the olive oil, and pulse. While the processor is running, slowly drizzle the olive oil through the top opening. Process until all the olive oil has been added. Reserve ½ cup of the cooking liquid. Drain the pasta and put it into a large bowl. Add the pesto and cooking liquid to the bowl of pasta and toss everything together. Serve immediately.

Nutrition facts (per serving)
calories: 1067 | fat: 72.0g | protein: 23.0g | carbs: 91..0g | fiber: 6.0g | sodium: 817mg

›Spaghetti with Pine Nuts and Cheese

Preparation time: 10 minutes
Cooking time: 11 minutes | **Servings:** 4 to 6
8 ounces (227 g) spaghetti
4 tablespoons almond butter
1 teaspoon freshly ground black pepper
½ cup pine nuts
1 cup fresh grated Parmesan cheese, divided
Directions
Bring a medium pot water to a boil and then add the salt. Add the pasta and cook for 8 minutes. In a medium/large saucepan over medium/high heat, combine the butter, black pepper, and pine nuts. Cook for 2-3 minutes, or until the pine nuts are lightly toasted. Reserve ½ cup of the pasta water. Drain the pasta and place it into the pan with the pine nuts. Add ¾ cup of the Parmesan cheese and the reserved pasta water to the pasta and toss everything together to evenly coat the pasta. Serve the pasta and top with the remaining ¼ cup of the Parmesan cheese. Serve immediately.

Nutrition facts (per serving)

calories: 542 | fat: 32.0g | protein: 20.0g | carbs: 46.0g | fiber: 2.0g | sodium: 552mg

➤Creamy Garlic Parmesan Chicken Pasta

Preparation time: 5 minutes
Cooking time: 15 minutes | **Servings:** 4
3 tablespoons extra-virgin oil
2 boneless, skinless chicken breasts, cut into strips
One large onion, thinly sliced
3 tablespoons garlic, minced
½ teaspoons salt
1 pound (454 g) fettuccine pasta
1 cup heavy whipping cream
¾ cup freshly grated Parmesan cheese, divided
½ teaspoon freshly ground black pepper

Directions
Heat the olive oil in a medium/large skillet over medium-high heat. Add the chicken and cook for 2 to 4 minutes. Add the onion, garlic and salt to the skillet. Cook for 7 minutes, stirring occasionally. Meanwhile, bring a medium-large pot of salted water to a boil and add the pasta, then cook for 7 minutes. While the pasta is cooking, add ½ cup of Parmesan cheese, black pepper and heavy cream to the chicken. Simmer for 3 minutes. Reserve ½ cup of the pasta water. Drain the pasta and add it to the chicken cream sauce. Add the reserved pasta water to the pasta and toss together. Simmer for 2 minutes. Top with the remaining ¼ cup of the Parmesan cheese and serve warm.

Nutrition facts (per serving)
calories: 879 | fat: 42.0g | protein: 35.0g | carbs: 90.0g | fiber: 5.0g | sodium: 1336mg

➤Bulgur Pilaf with Garbanzo

Preparation time: 5 minutes
Cooking time: 20 minutes
Servings: 4 to 6
3 tablespoons extra-virgin olive oil
1 large onion, chopped
1 (1-pound / 454-g) can garbanzo beans, rinsed and drained
2 cups bulgur wheat, rinsed and drained
1½ teaspoons salt
½ teaspoon cinnamon
4 cups water

Directions
In a medium-large pot over medium heat, heat the olive oil. Add the onion and cook for about 3-5 minutes. Add the garbanzo beans and cook for an additional 5 minutes. Stir in the remaining ingredients. Reduce the heat to low. Cover and cook for 10 minutes. When done, fluff the pilaf with a fork. Cover and let sit for another 5 minutes before serving.

Nutrition facts (per serving)
calories: 462 | fat: 13.0g | protein: 15.0g | carbs: 76.0g | fiber: 19.0g | sodium: 890mg

➤Pearl Barley Risotto with Parmesan Cheese

Preparation time: 5 minutes
Cooking time: 20 minutes | **Servings:** 6
4 cups low-sodium or no-salt-added vegetable broth
1 tablespoon extra-virgin olive oil
1 cup chopped yellow onion
2 cups uncooked pearl barley
½ cup dry white wine
1 cup freshly grated Parmesan cheese, divided
¼ teaspoon kosher or sea salt
¼ teaspoon freshly ground black pepper
Fresh chopped chives and lemon wedges, for serving (optional)

Directions
Pour the broth into a medium saucepan and bring to a simmer. Heat the olive oil in a medium-large stockpot over medium-high heat. Add the onion and cook for about 4 minutes, stirring occasionally. Add the barley and cook for 2 minutes, stirring, or until the barley is toasted. Pour in the wine and cook until most of the liquid evaporates, or for about 1 minute. Add 1 cup of the warm broth into the pot and cook, stirring, until most of the liquid is absorbed, or for about 2 minutes. Add the remaining broth, 1 cup at a time, cooking until each cup is absorbed (about 2 minutes each time) before adding the next. The last addition of broth will take a bit longer to absorb, about 4 mins. Remove the pot and stir in ½ cup of the cheese, and the salt and pepper. Serve with the remaining ½ cup of the cheese on the side, along with the chives and lemon wedges (if desired).

Nutrition facts (per serving)
calories: 421 | fat: 11.0g | protein: 15.0g | carbs: 67.0g | fiber: 11.0g | sodium: 641mg

➤Israeli Couscous with Asparagus

Preparation time: 5 minutes
Cooking time: 25 minutes | **Servings:** 6
1½ pounds (680 g) asparagus spears, ends trimmed and stalks chopped into 1-inch pieces
1 garlic clove, minced
1 tablespoon extra-virgin olive oil
¼ teaspoon freshly ground black pepper
1¾ cups water
1 (8-ounce / 227-g) box uncooked whole-wheat or regular Israeli couscous (about 1⅓ cups)
¼ teaspoon kosher salt
1 cup garlic-and-herb goat cheese, at room temperature

Directions
Preheat the oven to 420-425°F (220°C). In a large bowl, stir together the asparagus, garlic, oil, and pepper. Spread the asparagus on a large, rimmed baking sheet and roast for 10 minutes, stirring a few times. Remove the pan and spoon the asparagus into a large serving bowl. Set aside. While the asparagus is roasting, bring the water to a boil in a medium saucepan. Add the couscous and season with salt, stirring well.

Reduce the heat to medium-low. Cover and cook for at least 10-12 minutes, or until the water is absorbed. Pour the hot couscous into the bowl with the asparagus. Add the goat cheese and mix thoroughly until completely melted. Serve immediately.

Nutrition facts (per serving)
calories: 103 | fat: 2.0g | protein: 6.0g | carbs: 18.0g | fiber: 5.0g | sodium: 343mg

›Freekeh Pilaf with Dates and Pistachios

Preparation time: 10 minutes
Cooking time: 10 minutes
Servings: 4 to 6
2 tablespoons extra-virgin olive oil
1 shallot, minced
1½ teaspoons grated fresh ginger
¼ teaspoon ground coriander
¼ teaspoon ground cumin
Salt and pepper, to taste
1¾ cups water
1½ cups cracked freekeh, rinsed
3 ounces (85 g) pitted dates, chopped
¼ cup shelled pistachios, toasted and coarsely chopped
1½ tablespoons lemon juice
¼ cup chopped fresh mint

Directions
Set the Instant Pot to Sauté mode and heat the olive oil until shimmering. Add the shallot, ginger, coriander, cumin, salt, and pepper to the pot and until the shallot is softened cook, or for about 2 minutes. Stir in the water and freekeh. Secure the lid. Select the Manual mode and set the cooking time for 3-4 minutes at High Pressure. Once cooking is complete, do a quick pressure release. Carefully open the lid. Add the dates, pistachios and lemon juice and gently fluff the freekeh with a fork to combine. Season to taste with pepper and salt. Sprinkle with the mint. Serve drizzled with extra olive oil.

Nutrition facts (per serving)
calories: 280 | fat: 8.0g | protein: 8.0g | carbs: 46.0g | fiber: 9.0g | sodium: 200mg

›Quinoa with Baby Potatoes and Broccoli

Preparation time: 5 minutes
Cooking time: 10 minutes | **Servings:** 4
2 tablespoons olive oil
1 cup baby potatoes, cut in half
1 cup broccoli florets
2 cups cooked quinoa
Zest of 1 lemon
Sea salt and freshly ground pepper

Directions
Preheat the olive oil in a medium-large skillet over medium heat until shimmering. Add the potatoes and cook for about 6 to 7 minutes, or until softened and golden brown. Add the broccoli and cook for about 2-3 minutes, or until tender.
Remove from the heat and add the quinoa and lemon zest. Season with salt and pepper, then serve.

Nutrition facts (per serving)
calories: 205 | fat: 8.6g | protein: 5.1g | carbs: 27.3g | fiber: 3.7g | sodium: 158mg

›Black-Eyed Peas and Vegetables Stew

Preparation time: 15 minutes
Cooking time: 40 minutes | **Servings:** 2
½ cup black-eyed peas, soaked in water overnight
2 cups water, plus more as needed
One large carrot, peeled and cut into ½-inch pieces (about ¾ cup)
1 large beet, peeled and cut into ½-inch pieces (about ¾ cup)
¼ teaspoon turmeric
¼ teaspoon cayenne pepper
¼ teaspoon ground cumin seeds, toasted
¼ cup finely chopped parsley
¼ teaspoon salt (optional)
½ teaspoon fresh lime juice

Directions
Pour the black-eyed peas and water into a large pot, then cook over medium heat for 25 minutes.
Add the carrot and beet to the pot and cook for 10 minutes more, adding more water as needed.
Add the turmeric, cayenne pepper, cumin, and parsley to the pot and cook for another 6 minutes, or until the vegetables are softened. Stir the mixture periodically. Season with salt, if desired.
Serve drizzled with the fresh lime juice.

Nutrition facts (per serving)
calories: 89 | fat: 0.7g | protein: 4.1g | carbs: 16.6g | fiber: 4.5g | sodium: 367mg

›Chickpea Salad with Tomatoes and Basil

Preparation time: 5 minutes
Cooking time: 45 minutes | **Servings:** 2
1 cup dried chickpeas, rinsed
Water, enough to cover the chickpeas by 3 to 4 inches
1½ cups halved grape tomatoes
1 cup chopped fresh basil leaves
2 to 3 tablespoons balsamic vinegar
½ teaspoon garlic powder
½ teaspoon salt, or more to taste

Directions
In your Instant Pot, combine the chickpeas and water. Secure the lid. Select the Manual mode and set the cooking time for 45 minutes at High Pressure.
Once cooking is complete, do a natural pressure release for 20 minutes, then release any remaining pressure. Open carefully the lid and drain the chickpeas. Refrigerate to cool (unless you want to serve this warm,

which is good, too). While the chickpeas cool, in a medium-large bowl, stir together the basil, tomatoes, vinegar, garlic powder, and salt. Add the beans, stir to combine, and serve.

Nutrition facts (per serving)
calories: 395 | fat: 6.0g | protein: 19.8g | carbs: 67.1g | fiber: 19.0g | sodium: 612mg

›Mediterranean Lentils

Preparation time: 7 minutes
Cooking time: 24 minutes | **Servings:** 2
1 tablespoon olive oil
1 small sweet or yellow onion, diced
1 garlic clove, diced
1 teaspoon dried oregano
½ teaspoon ground cumin
½ teaspoon dried parsley
½ teaspoon salt, plus more as needed
¼ teaspoon freshly ground black pepper
1 tomato, diced
1 cup brown or green lentils
2½ cups vegetable stock
1 bay leaf

Direction
Set your Instant Pot to Sauté and heat the oil until it shimmers. Add the onion and cook for 3 to 4 minutes until soft. Turn off the Instant Pot and add the garlic, oregano, cumin, parsley, salt, and pepper. Cook until fragrant, about 1 minute. Stir in the tomato, lentils, stock, and bay leaf. Lock the lid. Select the Manual mode and set the cooking time for 18 minutes at High Pressure. When the timer beeps, perform a natural pressure release for 8-10 minutes, then release any remaining pressure. Carefully open the lid. Remove and discard the bay leaf. Taste and season with pepper and salt. If there's too much liquid remaining, select Sauté and cook until it evaporates. Serve warm.

Nutrition facts (per serving)
calories: 426 | fat: 8.1g | protein: 26.2g | carbs: 63.8g | fiber: 31.0g | sodium: 591mg

›Mediterranean-Style Beans and Greens

Preparation time: 10 minutes
Cooking time: 15 minutes | **Servings:** 2
1 (14.5-ounce / 411-g) can diced tomatoes with juice
1 (15-ounce / 425-g) can cannellini beans, rinsed
2 tbsps. chopped green olives, plus 1-2 sliced for garnish
¼ cup vegetable broth, plus more as needed
1 teaspoon extra-virgin olive oil
2 cloves garlic, minced
4 cups arugula
¼ cup freshly squeezed lemon juice

Directions
In a medium-large saucepan, bring the chopped olives, tomatoes and beans, to a low boil, adding just enough broth to make the ingredients saucy. Low the heat and simmer for about 4-5 minutes. Meanwhile, in a medium-large skillet, heat the olive oil over medium/high heat. When the oil is hot and starts to shimmer, add garlic and sauté for about 30 seconds just until it starts to turn slightly tan.
Add the lemon juice and arugula, stirring to coat leaves with the olive oil and juice. Cover, low the heat and simmer for 3 to 5 minutes. Serve the beans over the greens and garnish with olive slices.

Nutrition facts (per serving)
calories: 262 | fat: 5.9g | protein: 13.2g | carbs: 40.4g | fiber: 9.8g | sodium: 897mg

›Broccoli and Carrot Pasta Salad

Preparation time: 5 minutes
Cooking time: 10 minutes | **Servings:** 2
8 ounces (227 g) whole-wheat pasta
2 cups broccoli florets
1 cup peeled and shredded carrots
¼ cup plain Greek yogurt
Juice of 1 lemon
1 teaspoon red pepper flakes
Sea salt and freshly ground pepper

Directions
Bring a medium-large pot of lightly salted water to a boil. Add the pasta to the boiling water and cook until al dente, about 8 to 10 minutes. Drain the pasta and let rest for a few minutes. When cooled, combine the pasta with the veggies, yogurt, lemon juice, and red pepper flakes in a large bowl, and stir to combine. Taste and season to taste with pepper and salt. Serve immediately.

Nutrition facts (per serving)
calories: 428 | fat: 2.9g | protein: 15.9g | carbs: 84.6g | fiber: 11.7g | sodium: 642mg

›Bean and Veggie Pasta

Preparation time: 10 minutes
Cooking time: 15 minutes | **Servings:** 2
16 ounces (454 g) small whole wheat pasta, such as penne, farfalle, or macaroni
5 cups water
1 (15-ounce / 425-g) can cannellini beans rinsed
1 (14.5-ounce / 411-g) can diced (with juice) or crushed tomatoes
1 yellow onion, chopped
1 red or yellow bell pepper, chopped
2 tablespoons tomato paste
1 tablespoon olive oil
3 garlic cloves, minced
¼ teaspoon crushed red pepper (optional)
1 bunch kale, stemmed and chopped
1 cup sliced basil
½ cup pitted Kalamata olives, chopped

Directions
Add the pasta, water, beans, tomatoes (with juice if using diced), onion, bell pepper, tomato paste, oil, garlic, and crushed red pepper (if desired), to a large stockpot. Bring to a boil over high heat, stirring often. Reduce the heat to medium-high, add the kale, and

cook, continuing to stir often, until the pasta is al dente, about 10 mins. Remove from the heat and let sit for about 5 minutes. Garnish with the basil and olives and serve.

Nutrition facts (per serving)
calories: 565 | fat: 17.7g | protein: 18.0g | carbs: 85.5g | fiber: 16.5g | sodium: 540mg

➤Roasted Ratatouille Pasta

Preparation time: 10 minutes
Cooking time: 30 minutes | **Servings:** 2
1 small eggplant (about 8 ounces / 227 g)
1 small zucchini
1 portobello mushroom
1 Roma tomato, halved
½ medium sweet red pepper, seeded
½ teaspoon salt, plus additional for the pasta water
1 teaspoon Italian herb seasoning
1 tablespoon olive oil
2 cups farfalle pasta (about 8 ounces / 227 g)
2 tablespoons minced sun-dried tomatoes in olive oil with herbs
2 tablespoons prepared pesto

Directions
Slice the ends off the eggplant and zucchini. Cut them lengthwise into ½-inch slices. Place the eggplant, zucchini, mushroom, tomato, and red pepper in a large bowl and sprinkle with ½ teaspoon of salt. Using your hands, toss the vegetables well so that they're covered evenly with the salt. Let them rest for about 10 minutes. While the vegetables are resting, preheat the oven to 400°F (205°C). Line a baking sheet with parchment paper. When the oven is hot, drain off any liquid from the vegetables and pat them dry with a paper towel. Add the Italian herb seasoning and olive oil to the vegetables and toss well to coat both sides. Lay the vegetables out in a single layer on the baking sheet. Roast them for 15 to 20 minutes, flipping them over after about 10 minutes or once they start to brown on the underside. When the vegetables are charred in spots, remove them from the oven. While the vegetables are roasting, fill a large saucepan with water. Add salt and cook the pasta for about 8 to 10 minutes until al dente. Drain the pasta, reserving ½ cup of the pasta water. When cool enough to handle, cut the vegetables into large chunks (about 2 inches) and add them to the hot pasta. Stir in the sun-dried tomatoes and pesto and toss everything well. Serve immediately.

Nutrition facts (per serving)
calories: 613 | fat: 16.0g | protein: 23.1g | carbs: 108.5g | fiber: 23.0g | sodium: 775mg

➤Lentil and Mushroom Pasta

Preparation time: 10 minutes
Cooking time: 50 minutes | **Servings:** 2
2 tablespoons olive oil
1 large yellow onion, finely diced
2 portobello mushrooms, trimmed and chopped finely
2 tablespoons tomato paste

3 garlic cloves, chopped
1 teaspoon oregano
2½ cups water
1 cup brown lentils
1 (28-ounce / 794-g) can diced tomatoes with basil (with juice if diced)
1 tablespoon balsamic vinegar
Salt and black pepper, to taste
Chopped basil, for garnish
8 ounces (227 g) pasta of choice, cooked

Directions
Place a large stockpot over medium heat and add the olive oil. Once the oil is hot, add the onion and mushrooms. Cover and cook for about 4-5 minutes, or until both are soft. Add the tomato paste, oregano, and garlic and cook 2 minutes, stirring constantly. Stir in the water and lentils. Bring to a boil, then reduce the heat to medium/low and cook covered for 5 minutes. Add the tomatoes and vinegar. Reduce the heat to low and cook for about 30 minutes until the lentils are tender. Remove from the heat and season with pepper and salt. Garnish with the basil and serve over the cooked pasta.

Nutrition facts (per serving)
calories: 463 | fat: 15.9g | protein: 12.5g | carbs: 70.8g | fiber: 16.9g | sodium: 155mg

➤Spicy Sesame & Edamame Noodles

Ingredients
100 g Blue Dragon Whole-wheat Noodles
100 g vegetable 'noodles'
2 tbsp. groundnut or coconut oil
2 shallots, peeled and finely sliced
2 tsp 'lazy' garlic
2 tsp ginger puree
1 red chili, sliced
3 tbsp. sesame seeds
100 g edamame beans, podded
2 tbsp. sesame oil
2 tbsp. Blue Dragon soy sauce
a handful of fresh coriander, chopped
juice of 1 lime

Directions:
Boil the noodles for 3-4 minutes, then drain and set aside. Cook the vegetable noodles according to the guidelines and add the rest of the noodles. Heat the oil in a medium-large pot or pan and add garlic, ginger, and pepper. Cook for 2 minutes and then add sesame seeds and bean sprouts. Cook for another 2 minutes, stir and stir to make sure nothing sticks to the bottom of the pot. Pour the noodles and the noodles into the pan and cook for 2 minutes. Turn off the heat, then add sesame oil, soy sauce, and lemon juice and mix. Serve with scattered coriander.

➤Quick & Easy Tomato and Herb Gigantes Beans

Ingredients
tbsp. olive oil

onion
carrot
tsp ready-chopped garlic Protein content nutrition
facts (per serving) garlic purée
Protein content nutrition facts (per serving)2 tsp paprika
400 g tin butterbeans
400 g tin chopped tomatoes
tbsp. tomato purée
tsp sugar
tsp dried oregano
handful baby spinach
handful fresh parsley
8-10 fresh mint leaves

Directions
Heat the oil in a medium-large pot or a large bowl
with oil. Chop onions and carrots and chop them
finely and add them to the bowl with garlic and paprika. Cook over medium heat for 2 minutes. Rinse and
wash the potatoes and add to the pot, then add the
greased tomatoes. Fill the empty tomato can in half
with water and add it to the bowl with tomato puree,
sugar, and oregano. Season well with salt and black
pepper, boil, then reduce at dawn, cover and cook
for 12-14 minutes. Chop the baby spinach approximately, then add them to the pot and cook for 2 minutes.
Chop the parsley and mint almost and stir just before
serving. Taste and adjust the seasoning if necessary,
then serve with crusty bread and crispy green salad.

➤Pappardelle with Cavolo Nero (black cabbage) & Walnut Sauce

Ingredients
200 g Cavolo Nero (black cabbage)
150 g walnut pieces
250 g Pappardelle pasta
1 slice bread
150 g dairy-free milk (soy, oat or nut milk)
2 tbsp. fresh parsley
optional - 2 tbsp. vegan parmesan or nutritional yeast
flakes
1 clove garlic
olive oil

Directions
Remove the kale stems and cut them into slices of
protein nutrition facts (per serving). Heat a pan, peel
the nuts (no oil needed) and bake over medium heat
for 2-3 minutes. Turn off the heat and reserve. Boil a
large pot of water and soak Cavolo Nero for 1 minute, then use a slotted spoon or tweezers to remove it
and remove it with a sieve or stain (remove the boiling
water in the pot). Add the pappardelle to the boiling
water and simmer for 8-10 minutes. Meanwhile, sprinkle nuts, bread, milk protein content in each serving
of milk, parsley, garlic, and Parmesan (if used) in a
blender or food mixer and mix until consistent. Reach
the thick sauce, beat it — season well with salt and
black pepper. Heat the pan again, add a little olive
oil, cook for 3 to 4 minutes and turn off the heat. When
the pasta is cooked, drain it and return it to the pot. Tilt
and add the walnut sauce to combine. Finally, add
cavolo Nero, overlay, and then divide between two

dishes.

➤Veggie Sausage & Sun-Dried Tomato One Pot Pasta

Ingredients
2 tbsp. olive or rapeseed oil
3 veggie sausages
1 onion, peeled and sliced
400 g pasta shells
200 g cherry tomatoes, halved
6-8 sun-dried tomatoes, roughly chopped
1-liter water
2 tsp vegetable stock powder
100 ml dairy-free cream (I used soya)
100 g fresh baby spinach

Directions
Heat the oil in a medium-large, shallow dish and fry
the sausage and onion until the sausages brown.
Carefully separate them from the pan and cut each
piece into slices into 4 parts, then return to the pot for
another 2 minutes. Add pasta, tomatoes, sun-dried
tomatoes, water, and powder to the pot. Bring to a
boil, then low to a sweet boil, cover and cook for 12-
14 mins, stirring every few mins, until the pasta is well
cooked. Add the cream and spinach to the pot, then
stir well and cook for another minute until the spinach
has vanished.

➤Chestnut Mushroom Bourguignon

Ingredients
2 tbsp. olive oil
2 shallots or 1 small onion
10 baby Protein content nutrition facts (per serving)
chantenay carrots
1 tsp ready-chopped garlic Protein content nutrition
facts (per serving) garlic puree
250 g chestnut mushrooms
100 g button mushrooms
1½ tbsp. plain flour
200 ml red wine
150 ml of boiling water
1 tsp vegetable stock powder
1 tbsp. tomato puree
handful fresh parsley

Directions
Heat the oil in a medium-large skillet or large skillet
over high heat. Chop the peels and mash and add
the garlic to the pot. Cut and halve carrot lengths
(quadruple in large size) and add to the pan.
Chop the brown mushrooms into four sections and
clean the mushrooms. Add to the pot and cook for
2-3 minutes. Stir the flour through the mushrooms, then
add the red wine. Bring to a boil for a minute, then
add water, powdered broth, and tomato puree.
Cook over medium heat to form a thick and bright
sauce, and the mushrooms are cooked inside but not
too soft. Try and add black pepper salt and pepper
if necessary. Chop the parsley approximately and
stir approximately two thirds through the bourbon,

then wash the plate and sprinkle with the remaining parsley.

›Broad Bean, Fennel & Baby Carrot Pilaf

Ingredients
1 onion
1 fennel bulb
1 tsp garlic puree Protein content nutrition facts (per serving) ready-chopped garlic
2 tbsp. olive or rapeseed oil
220 g fresh or frozen broad beans (or a combination of broad beans and peas)
100 g baby carrots
200 g basmati rice (rinsed well under cold water)
400 ml vegetable stock
1 lemon
40 g walnuts
handful fresh parsley

Directions
Peel and chop the onions, chop the fennel and chop finely and chop the garlic cloves. Heat the oil in a medium-large pot or with a pot and fry the onion, fennel and garlic for 2 minutes to soften. Chop the baby carrots and cook in half. Add them to the pot with beans and basmati rice, then store the vegetables. Bring to a boil, sauté in a sauce and cook for 12 minutes or until the rice is cooked. At the end of cooking, check the rice for a few minutes and if it looks too dry, add a little more water. Meanwhile, chop the nuts and parsley leaves and sprinkle with lemon. When the rice is cooked, pour the lemon juice and crush the nuts and parsley. Serve immediately if necessary.

›Spelt Spaghetti with Avocado Pesto

Ingredients
200 g spelt spaghetti (white or whole-wheat)
13 asparagus spears, woody ends removed and sliced into 3-4cm pieces
100 g fresh or frozen peas
1 avocado
75 g Brazil nuts
1 clove garlic, peeled and crushed
zest and juice of 1 lemon
2 tbsp. extra virgin olive oil
50 g fresh basil
salt

Directions
Bring a large pot of boiling water and add spaghetti. After 5 minutes of cooking (or 8 boxes of whole spaghetti), add the peas and asparagus and cook for 2-3 minutes until the pasta is cooked and the asparagus is cooked naturally. While preparing the spaghetti, place all remaining ingredients in the blender or meal and cook for a minute. Add 2-3 tablespoons of water and stain again and add a little water once to achieve a thick sauce. Try and add more salt if necessary. Drain the spaghetti and return them to the pot, then stir over the sauce over low heat to cool.

›Colcannon-Topped Vegan Shepherds' Pie

Ingredients
For the Pie Filling:
1 medium-large carrot
1 sweet potato
2 tbsp. rapeseed or sunflower oil
1 onion
410 g tin cannellini beans
410 g tin green or brown lentils
410 g tin chopped tomatoes
1 tsp vegetable stock powder
2 tbsps. gravy granules (check they are vegan)
For the Colcannon Mash:
620 g potatoes
65 g curly kale
4 spring onions
55 ml dairy-free milk (soya, oat or nut milk)
20 g dairy-free margarine

Directions
Heat the oven to 180 degrees Celsius.
Boil a large pot of water. Meanwhile, peel the sweet carrots and potatoes and smooth them. Simmer for 10 minutes Also, heat the oil in a large bowl or in a large bowl with the pan, then chop and chop the onion and add to the pan, fry over low heat for 3-4 minutes. Wash and wash beans and lentils and add onions with tomatoes, broth powder, and gravitational seeds. Fill the empty tomato can with water and fill approximately two-thirds of it, then add it to the pot. When the carrots and sweet potatoes are freshly cooked, remove them with a slotted spoon and add them to the cake filling (do not waste water yet!). Cook and cover and simmer for 10 minutes. Taste and season with pepper and salt. If the mixture becomes too dry, add water; It should have a thick consistency of fat. (And if it seems also climatic, cook for a few minutes with the lid on.). Stir the pot until the potatoes are peeled, cut them into cubes, then add them to the pan and cook for 10-15 minutes. Meanwhile, cut the chives stalks as much as possible. When the potatoes are ready, drain them, return to the pot, then add the cabbage, chives, milk, and margarine and cook until they are uniform. Taste and season with pepper and salt if necessary. Disinfect the stuffed leg in a large bowl, then cover with mashed potatoes. I used a plumbing bag to create a beautiful summit, but you can flatten it and use a fork to create a pattern). Bake in the oven for 28-31 minutes until it is soft, golden and full of bubbles.

›Vegan Sausage Casserole: Bangers & Borlotti Bean Stew

Ingredients
2 tbsp. olive or rapeseed oil
6 vegan sausages
1 red onion
8 baby carrots (e.g. chantenay)
1 tsp smoked paprika

1 tsp garlic puree ready-chopped garlic
410 g tin borlotti beans (drained and rinsed)
250 g passata
2 tbsp. gravy granules (check they are vegan)
handful baby spinach

Directions

Fry the oil in a large pan and fry the sausages over medium heat to brown. Peel and chop the red onion and add it to the pot, then finely chop the carrots and cut them in half or a quarter. Add to the pan and cook for about 3-4 minutes. When the onion has softened, add the paprika and garlic to the pot and stir well. Rinse and wash the Borlotti beans and add them to the pan, and then add 250 ml of water and gravitational seeds. Bring to a boil, then reduce to medium heat and cook for 7-8 minutes until the sauce thickens and the carrots are well prepared. Add some salt or black pepper if necessary and try. Chop the spinach almost and stir only one minute before the end of the cooking time and serve immediately with a baked potato, noodles, or rice.

›BBQ Black Bean & Jalapeño Burger

Ingredients

2 x 410g tins black beans, drained and rinsed
4 spring onions
12-14 slices jalapeño (from a jar)
170 g breadcrumbs (crumbs from 4 slices of bread)
Juice and zest of 1 lime
2 tsp ready chopped garlic Protein content nutrition facts (per serving) garlic puree (or 2 cloves fresh garlic, peeled and chopped)
Handful fresh coriander, finely chopped
2 tbsp. soy sauce
2 tbsp. tahini
Salt & black pepper

Directions

Put the black beans in a food processor and press several times until it is crushed but not wholly purified. (Alternatively, break them with potato sand). Pour into a large bowl. Chop the scallions and finely chop the slices. Add both to the bowl, followed by breadcrumbs, lemon zest and juice, garlic, coriander, soy sauce, and Tahini. Season with salt and pepper.
Mix the ingredients to combine well, then divide them into approximately 5-6 pieces (or for smaller burgers 7-8). Use your hamburger machine or shape hamburgers by hand, then place them on a cooked tray covered with baking paper and refrigerate for as long as necessary.

To grill:

rinse each side with a little oil and cook for 5 minutes in the oven on the clock.

For cooking:

Brush each side with oil and bake at 190 degrees Celsius at 375 degrees Fahrenheit for 5 minutes for 20 minutes.

To fry:

fry in oil for 4/5 minutes on each side. Serve with chopped avocado, tomato slices, lettuce, purple onion, a slice of cheese and dairy-free tomato sauce.

›Slow Cooker Butternut Dhal

Ingredients

1 red onion
2 tbsp. rapeseed or sunflower oil
1 tsp garlic puree Protein content nutrition facts (per serving) ready-chopped garlic
1 tsp ginger puree Protein content nutrition facts (per serving) ready-chopped ginger
1 red chili, de-seeded and sliced
4 tsp curry powder
210 g red lentils, rinsed
420 ml tin coconut milk (I use the 'light' coconut milk, but full fat will be even creamier!)
1 tsp vegetable stock powder
320 g butternut squash
To finish:
1 lemon
1 green chili
handful fresh coriander

Directions

To build a Redmond Multicooker:
Chop and chop the onion and place in a pot with oil, garlic, ginger, pepper, and powder. Cook for 5 minutes in the FRY setting, stirring occasionally. Add lentils, coconut milk, then refill the empty can with water and add this, followed by powdered broth. Peel the butternut squash and pour it into small cubes (approximately 1 cm) and add it to the mixture. Serve the season with salt and pepper. Cook slowly in the kitchen for 2 hours, occasionally stirring until the lentils soften, and the dhal has a creamy consistency. Check and adjust seasoning and then serve. Heat 2 tablespoons of oil in a medium/small pan to bake optionally. Chop the oilseeds and chop finely and add to the pot. Cook over medium-low heat until crispy. Spoon on the dial. Chop the cilantro and sprinkle on it, then finish with a little lemon juice.

To make a slow cooker:

Chop and chop the onion and sprinkle with oil, garlic, ginger, pepper and curry powder in a pan. Cook for 4/5 minutes over medium heat, stirring occasionally. Pour slowly into the oven, then add the lentils and coconut milk. Fill the empty can again with water and add this, followed by powdered broth. Peel the butternut squash and pour it into small cubes (approximately 1 cm) and add it to the mixture. Serve the season with salt and pepper. Cook for 4 hours (or less than 8 hours), until the lentils, soften and the dhal has a thick and creamy consistency. Check and adjust seasoning and then serve. Preheat 2 tablespoons of oil in a medium-small pan to bake optionally. Chop the oilseeds and chop finely and add to the pot. Cook over medium-low heat until crispy. Spoon on the dial. Chop the cilantro and sprinkle on it, then finish with a little lemon juice.

›Herby Giant Couscous with Asparagus and Lemon

Ingredients

150 g giant couscous

100 g asparagus tips
100 g frozen peas
tbsp. walnut oil
Juice and zest of 1 lemon
Handful fresh parsley
Handful of fresh mint
Handful baby spinach
tbsp. pine nuts
Directions
Bring a medium/large pot of salted water to a boil. Add giant couscous. After 5 minutes, add asparagus and peas and boil for another 4 minutes. While the couscous is cooking, cook in a mini blender (or directly in a bowl, sharp knife and elbow grease!), Walnut oil, lemon juice, parsley, and mint. Drain the couscous and immediately stir the dressing of the baby herb and spinach. Divide between two plates and crush with pine nuts and lemon lotion.

➤Air Fryer Garlic-lime Shrimp Kebabs

Cooking Time: 18 Mints
Ingredients:
 One lime
Raw shrimp: 1 cup
Salt: 1/8 teaspoon
1 clove of garlic
Freshly ground black pepper
Directions:
In water, let wooden skewers soak for 20 minutes. Let the Air fryer preheat to 350F. In a bowl, mix shrimp, minced garlic, lime juice, kosher salt, and pepper
 Add shrimp on skewers. Place skewers in the air fryer and cook for 8 minutes. Turn halfway over. Top with cilantro and your favorite dip.
Nutrition facts: Calories: 76kcal | Carbohydrates: 4g | Protein: 13g | fat 9 g

➤Air fryer Panko-crusted Fish Nuggets

Servings: 4
Cooking Time: 10 Mints
Ingredients:
Fish fillets in cubes: 2 cups(skinless)
1 egg, beaten
Flour: 5 tablespoons
Water: 5 tablespoons
Kosher salt and pepper, to taste
Breadcrumbs mix
Smoked paprika: 1 tablespoon
Whole wheat breadcrumbs: ¼ cup
Garlic powder: 1 tablespoon
Directions:
Season the fish cubes with kosher salt and pepper.In a bowl, add flour and gradually add water, mixing as you add. Then mix in the egg. And keep mixing but do not over mix. Coat the cubes in batter then in the breadcrumb mix. Coat well. Place the cubes in a baking tray and spray with oil. Let the air fryer preheat to 200 C. Place cubes in the air fryer and cook for 12 minutes or until well cooked and golden brown. Serve with salad greens.
Nutrition facts: Cal:184.2 | Protein: 19g | Total Fat:3.3 g |

Net Carb: 10g

➤Grilled Salmon with Lemon, Soy Sauce

Servings: 4
Cooking Time: 20 Mints
Ingredients:
Olive oil: 2 tablespoons
Two Salmon fillets
Lemon juice
Water: 1/3 cup
Gluten-free soy sauce: 1/3 cup
Honey: 1/3 cup
Scallion slices
Cherry tomato
Freshly ground black pepper, garlic powder, kosher salt to taste
Directions:
Season salmon with pepper and salt. In a bowl, mix honey, soy sauce, lemon juice, water, oil. Add salmon in this marinade and let it rest for least two hours.
 Let the air fryer preheat at 180°C. Place fish in the air fryer and cook for 8 minutes. Move to a dish and top with scallion slices.
Nutrition facts: Cal 211 | fat 9g | protein 15g | carbs 4.9g

➤Crab Cakes

Servings: 6
Cooking Time: 20 Mints
Ingredients:
Crab meat: 4 cups
Two eggs
Whole wheat bread crumbs: ¼ cup
Mayonnaise: 2 tablespoons
Worcestershire sauce: 1 teaspoon
Old Bay seasoning: 1 and ½ teaspoon
Dijon mustard: 1 teaspoon
Freshly ground black pepper to taste
Green onion: ¼ cup, chopped
Directions:
 In a bowl, add Dijon mustard, Old Bay, eggs, Worcestershire, and mayonnaise mix it well. Then add in the chopped green onion and mix. Fold in the crab meat to mayonnaise mix. Then add breadcrumbs, not to over mix. Chill the mix in the refrigerator for at least 60 minutes. Then shape into patties. Let the air-fryer preheat to 350F. Cook for 10 minutes. Flip the patties halfway through. Serve with lemon wedges.
Nutrition facts: Cal 218 | Fat: 13 g | Net Carbs: 5.6 g | Protein: 16.7g

➤Air Fryer Cajun Shrimp Dinner

Servings: 4
Cooking Time: 20 Mints
Ingredients:
Peeled, 24 extra-jumbo shrimp
Olive oil: 2 tablespoons
Cajun seasoning: 1 tablespoon
one zucchini, thick slices (half-moons)

Cooked Turkey: ¼ cup
Yellow squash, sliced half-moons
Kosher salt: 1/4 teaspoon
Directions:
In a bowl, mix the shrimp with Cajun seasoning.
In another bowl, add zucchini, turkey, salt, squash and coat with oil.
Let the air fryer preheat to 400F. Move the shrimp and vegetable mix to the fryer basket and cook for three minutes. Serve hot.
Nutrition facts: Calories: 284kcal | Carbohydrates: 8g | Protein: 31 | Fat: 14g

➤Roasted Salmon with Fennel Salad

Servings: 4
Cooking Time: 10 Mints
Ingredients:
Skinless and center-cut: 4 salmon fillets
Lemon juice: 1 teaspoon(fresh)
Parsley: 2 teaspoons(chopped)
Salt: 1 teaspoon, divided
Olive oil: 2 tablespoons
Chopped thyme: 1 teaspoon
Fennel heads: 4 cups (thinly sliced)
One clove of minced garlic
Fresh dill: 2 tablespoons, chopped
Orange juice: 2 tablespoons(fresh)
Greek yogurt: 2/3 cup(reduced-fat)
Directions:
In a bowl, add half teaspoon of salt, parsley, and thyme, mix well. Rub oil over salmon, and sprinkle with thyme mixture. Put salmon fillets in the air fryer basket, cook for ten minutes at 350°F. In the meantime, mix garlic, fennel, orange juice, yogurt, half tsp. of salt, dill, lemon juice in a bowl. Serve with fennel salad.
Nutrition facts: Calories 364 | Fat 30g | Protein 38g | Carbohydrate 9g

➤Healthy Air Fryer Tuna Patties

Servings: 10
Cooking Time: 10 Mints
Ingredients:
Whole wheat breadcrumbs: half cup
Fresh tuna: 4 cups, diced
Lemon zest
Lemon juice: 1 Tablespoon
1 egg
Grated parmesan cheese: 3 Tablespoons
One chopped stalk celery
Garlic powder: half teaspoon
Dried herbs: half teaspoon
Minced onion: 3 Tablespoons
Salt, to taste
Freshly ground black pepper
Directions:
In a bowl, add lemon zest, breadcrumbs, salt, pepper, celery, eggs, dried herbs, lemon juice, garlic powder, parmesan cheese, and onion. Mix everything. Then add in tuna gently. Shape into patties. If the mixture is too loose, cool in the refrigerator. Add air fryer baking paper in the air fryer basket. Spray the baking paper

with cooking spray. Spray the patties with oil.
Cook for ten minutes at 360°F. turn the patties half-way over. Serve with lemon slices and microgreens.
Nutrition facts: Cal 214 | Fat: 15g | Net Carbs: 6g | Protein: 22g

➤Air Fryer Scallops with Tomato Cream Sauce

Servings: 2
Cooking Time: 10 Mints
Ingredients:
Sea scallops eight jumbo
Tomato Paste: 1 tbsp.
Chopped fresh basil one tablespoon
3/4 cup of low-fat Whipping Cream
Kosher salt half teaspoon
Ground Freshly black pepper half teaspoon
Minced garlic 1 teaspoon
Frozen Spinach, thawed half cup
Oil Spray
Directions:
Take a seven-inch pan(heatproof) and add spinach in a single layer at the bottom. Rub olive oil on both sides of scallops, season with kosher salt and pepper. On top of the spinach, place the seasoned scallops. Put the pan in the air fryer and cook for ten minutes at 350F, until scallops are cooked completely, and internal temperature reaches 135F. Serve immediately.
Nutrition facts: Calories: 259kcal | Carbohydrates: 6g | Protein: 19g | Fat: 13g |

➤Air Fryer Sesame Seeds Fish Fillet

Servings: 2
Cooking Time: 20 Mints
Ingredients:
Plain flour: 3 tablespoons
One egg, beaten
Five frozen fish fillets
For Coating
Oil: 2 tablespoons
Sesame seeds: 1/2 cup
Rosemary herbs
5-6 biscuit's crumbs
Kosher salt& pepper, to taste
Directions:
For two-minute sauté the sesame seeds in a pan, without oil. Brown them and set it aside. In a plate, mix all coating ingredients. Place the aluminum foil on the air fryer basket and let it preheat at 200 C. First, coat the fish in flour. Then in egg, then in the coating mix. Place in the Air fryer. If fillets are frozen, cook for ten min,
Then turn the fillet and cook for another four minutes. If not frozen, then cook for eight minutes and two minutes.
Nutrition facts: Cal 250 | Fat: 8g | Net Carbs: 12.4g | Protein: 20g

➤Air Fryer Fish and Chips

Servings: 4
Cooking Time: 35 Mints

Ingredients:
4 cups of any fish fillet
flour: 1/4 cup
Whole wheat breadcrumbs: one cup
One egg
Oil: 2 tbsp.
Potatoes
Salt: 1 tsp.
Directions:
Cut the potatoes in fries. Then coat with oil and salt. Cook in the air fryer for 18-20 minutes at 400 F, toss the fries halfway through. In the meantime, coat fish in flour, then in the whisked egg, and finally in breadcrumbs mix. Place the fish in the air fryer and let it cook at 330F for 15 minutes. Flip it halfway through, if needed. Serve with tartar sauce and salad green.
Nutrition facts: Calories: 409kcal | Carbohydrates: 44g | Protein: 30g | Fat: 11g |

➤Air fryer Crumbed Fish

Servings: 2
Cooking Time: 12 Mints
Ingredients:
Four fish fillets
Olive oil: 4 tablespoons
One egg beaten
Whole wheat breadcrumbs: ¼ cup
Directions:
Let the air fryer preheat to 180 C. In a bowl, mix breadcrumbs with oil. Mix well. First, coat the fish in the egg mix (egg mix with water) then in the breadcrumb mix. Coat well. Place in the air fryer, let it cook for 10-12 minutes. Serve hot with salad green and lemon.
Nutrition facts: 254 Cal | fat 12.7g | carbohydrates10.2g | protein 15.5g.

➤Air Fryer Lemon Garlic Shrimp

Servings: 2
Cooking Time: 10 Mints
Ingredients:
Olive oil: 1 Tbsp.
Small shrimp: 4 cups, peeled, tails removed
One lemon juice and zest
Parsley: 1/4 cup sliced
Red pepper flakes(crushed): 1 pinch
Four cloves of grated garlic
Sea salt: 1/4 teaspoon
Directions:
Let air fryer heat to 400F. Mix olive oil, lemon zest, red pepper flakes, shrimp, kosher salt, and garlic in a bowl and coat the shrimp well. Place shrimps in the air fryer basket, coat with oil spray. Cook at 400 F for 8 minutes. Toss the shrimp halfway through. Serve with lemon slices and parsley.
Nutrition facts: Cal 140 | Fat: 18g | Net Carbs: 8g | Protein: 20g

➤Quick & Easy Air Fryer Salmon

Servings: 4

Cooking Time: 12 Mints
Ingredients:
Lemon pepper seasoning: 2 teaspoons
Salmon: 4 cups
Olive oil: one tablespoon
Seafood seasoning:2 teaspoons
Half lemon's juice
Garlic powder:1 teaspoon
Kosher salt to taste
Directions:
In a bowl, add one tbsp. of olive oil and half lemon's juice. Pour this mixture over salmon and rub. Leave the skin on salmon. It will come off when cooked. Rub the salmon with kosher salt and spices. Put parchment paper in the air fryer basket. Put the salmon in the air fryer. Cook at 360 F for ten minutes. Cook until inner salmon temperature reaches 140 F. Let the salmon rest five minutes before serving. Serve with salad greens and lemon wedges.
Nutrition facts: 132 Cal | total fat 7.4g | carbohydrates 12 g | protein 22.1g

➤Shrimp Spring Rolls

Servings: 4
Cooking Time: 25 Mints
Ingredients:
Deveined raw shrimp: half cup chopped(peeled)
Olive oil: 2 and 1/2 tbsp.
Matchstick carrots: 1 cup
Slices of red bell pepper: 1 cup
Red pepper: 1/4 teaspoon(crushed)
Slices of snow peas: 3/4 cup
Shredded cabbage: 2 cups
Lime juice: 1 tablespoon
Sweet chili sauce: half cup
Fish sauce: 2 teaspoons
Eight spring rolls (wrappers)
Directions:
In a skillet, add one and a half tbsp. of olive, until smoking lightly. Stir in bell pepper, cabbage, carrots, and cook for two minutes. Turn off the heat, take out in a dish and cool for five minutes. In a bowl, add shrimp, lime juice, cabbage mixture, crushed red pepper, fish sauce, and snow peas. Mix well. Lay spring roll wrappers on a plate. Add 1/4 cup of filling in the middle of each wrapper. Fold tightly with water. Brush the olive oil over folded rolls. Put spring rolls in the air fryer basket and cook for 6 to 7 minutes at 390°F until light brown and crispy. You may serve with sweet chili sauce.
Nutrition facts: Calories 180 | Fat 9g | Protein 17g | Carbohydrate 9g

➤South West Tortilla Crusted Tilapia Salad

Servings: 2
Cooking Time: 15 Mints
Ingredients:
Tilapia fillets (Tortilla Crusted)
Mixed greens: six cups
Chipotle Lime Dressing: half cup

Diced red onion: 1/3 cup
One avocado
Cherry tomatoes: one cup
Directions:
On frozen tilapia fillet, spray the olive oil. Put in the air fryer basket, cook at 390° for 15-18 minutes.
  In a bowl, add tomatoes, red onion, and half of the greens. Coat with the Chipotle Lime Dressing.
  Serve the fish with vegetables.
Nutrition facts: 260cal | total fat 19g | carbohydrates 7.6g | protein 19.2g

➤Sriracha & Honey Tossed Calamari

Servings: 2
Cooking Time: 20 Mints
Ingredients:
Club soda: 1 cup
Sriracha: 1-2 Tbsp.
Calamari tubes: 2 cups
Flour: 1 cup
Pinches of salt, freshly ground black pepper, red pepper flakes, and red pepper
Honey: 1/2 cup
Directions:
Cut the calamari tubes into rings. Submerge them with club soda. Let it rest for ten minutes. In the meantime, in a bowl, add freshly ground black pepper, flour, red pepper, and kosher salt and mix well. Drain the calamari and pat dry with a paper towel. Coat well the calamari in the flour mix and set aside. Spray oil in the air fryer basket and put calamari in one single layer.
  Cook at 375 for 11 minutes. Toss the rings twice while cooking. Meanwhile, to make sauce honey, red pepper flakes, and sriracha in a bowl, well. Take calamari out from the basket, mix with sauce cook for another two minutes more. Serve with salad green.
Nutrition facts: Cal 252 | Fat: 38g | Carbs: 3.1g | Protein: 41g

➤Air Fryer Shrimp Tacos

Servings: 4
Cooking Time: 10 Mints
Ingredients:
Flour tortillas: 12
Avocado sliced: 1 cup
Chipotle chili powder: 1 tsp
Raw jumbo shrimp: 24 pieces, deveined, peeled, without tail
Smoked paprika: 1/2 tsp
Salt: 1/4 tsp
Olive oil: 1 tbsp.
Green sauce: ½ cup
Light brown sugar: 1 and 1/2 tsp
Garlic powder: 1/2 tsp
Low-fat sour cream: 1/2 cup
Red onion: 1/2 cup diced
Directions:
Let the oven preheat to 400 F and spray the air fryer basket with oil spray. In a bowl, mix chipotle chili powder, salt, brown sugar, smoked paprika, and garlic powder, mix well. Pat dry the shrimp, put shrimp in zip lock bag and add the seasonings and toss to coat well. Place shrimp in air fryer basket in one even layer, cook for four minutes and flip them overcook for four minutes more. For the sauce, mix sour cream and green sauce. Put shrimp in a tortilla, top with sauce, shrimp, red onion, sliced avocado. Serve with lime wedges.
Nutrition facts: Cal 228 | Fat: 18 | carbs: 16 g | Protein: 20 g

➤Air Fryer Catfish with Cajun Seasoning

Servings: 4
Cooking Time: 20 Mints
Ingredients:
Cajun seasoning: 3 teaspoons
Cornmeal: 3/4 cup
Four catfish fillets
Direction:
In a zip lock bag, add Cajun seasoning and cornmeal Wash and pat Dry the catfish fillets. Add them to the zip lock bag. Coat well the fillets with seasoning. Put catfish fillets in the air fryer. And cook for about 15 minutes at 390 F, turn fillets halfway through. To get a golden color on the fillets, cook for more five mins. Serve with lemon wedges and spicy tartar sauce.
Nutrition facts: Cal 324 | Fat: 13.9g | | Carbohydrates: 15.6g | Protein: 26.3g

➤Air Fryer Parmesan Shrimp

Servings: 4
Cooking Time: 10 Mints
Ingredients:
Olive oil: 2 tablespoons
Jumbo cooked shrimp: 8 cups, peeled, deveined
Parmesan cheese: 2/3 cup(grated)
Onion powder: 1 teaspoon
Pepper: 1 teaspoon
Four cloves of minced garlic
Oregano: 1/2 teaspoon
Basil: 1 teaspoon
Lemon wedges
Directions:
Mix parmesan cheese, onion powder, oregano, olive oil, garlic, basil, and pepper in a bowl. Coat the shrimp in this mixture. Spray oil on the air fryer basket, put shrimp in it. Cook for ten minutes, at 350 F, or until browned. Drizzle the lemon on shrimps, before serving with a microgreen salad.
Nutrition facts: Cal 198 | Fat: 13 g | Carbs: 5.6 g | Protein: 12.7g

➤Air Fryer Salmon Cakes

Servings: 2
Cooking Time: 10 Mints
Ingredients:
Fresh salmon fillet 8 oz.
Egg 1
Salt 1/8 tsp
Garlic powder ¼ tsp

Sliced lemon 1
Directions:
In the bowl, chop the salmon, add the egg & spices. Form tiny cakes. Air fryers preheat to 390. On the bottom of the air fryer bowl, lay sliced lemons—place cakes on top.
Cook them for seven minutes. Based on your diet preferences, eat with your chosen dip.
Nutrition facts: Kcal: 194, Fat: 9g, Carbs: 1g, Protein: 25g

›Garlic Parmesan Crusted Salmon

Servings: 2
Cooking Time: 15 Mints
Ingredients:
Whole wheat breadcrumbs: 1/4 cup
4 cups of salmon
Butter melted: 2 tablespoons
¼ tsp of freshly ground black pepper
Parmesan cheese: 1/4 cup(grated)
Minced garlic: 2 teaspoons
Half teaspoon of Italian seasoning
Directions:
Let the air fryer preheat to 400 F, spray the oil over the air fryer basket. Pat dry the salmon. In a bowl, mix Parmesan cheese, Italian seasoning, and breadcrumbs. In another pan, mix melted butter with garlic and add to the breadcrumbs mix. Mix well. Add black pepper and kosher salt. On top of every salmon piece, add the crust mix and press gently. Let the air fryer preheat to 400 F and add salmon in it. Cook until done to your liking. Serve hot with vegetable side dishes.
Nutrition facts: Calories 330 | Fat 19g | Carbohydrates 11g | Protein 31g

›Air Fryer Lemon Cod

Servings: 1
Cooking Time: 10 Mints
Ingredients:
One cod fillet
Dried parsley
Kosher salt and pepper, to taste
Garlic salt
One lemon
Directions:
In a bowl, mix all ingredients and coat the fish fillet with spices. Slice the lemon and lay at the bottom of the air fryer basket. Put spiced fish on top. Cover the fish with lemon slices. Cook for ten minutes at 375F, the internal temperature of fish should be 145F. Serve with micro green salad.
Nutrition facts: Calories: 101kcal | Carbohydrates: 10g | Protein: 16g | Fat: 1g |

›Breaded Air fryer Shrimp with Bang Bang Sauce

Servings: 4
Cooking Time: 20 Mints
Ingredients:

Whole wheat bread crumbs: 3/4 cup
Raw shrimp: 4 cups, deveined, peeled
Flour: half cup
Paprika: one tsp
Chicken Seasoning, to taste
2 tbsp. of one egg white
Kosher salt and pepper to taste
Bang Bang Sauce
Sweet chili sauce: 1/4 cup
Plain Greek yogurt: 1/3 cup
Sriracha: 2 tbsp.
Directions:
Let the Air Fryer preheat to 400 degrees. Add the seasonings to shrimp and coat well. In three separate bowls, add flour, bread crumbs, and egg whites.
 First coat the shrimp in flour, dab lightly in egg whites, then in the bread crumbs. With cooking oil, spray the shrimp. Place the shrimps in an air fryer, cook for four minutes, turn the shrimp over, and cook for another four minutes. Serve with micro green and bang bang sauce. Bang Bang Sauce. In a medium-small bowl, mix all the ingredients. And serve.
Nutrition facts: 229 calories | total fat 10g | carbohydrates 13g | protein 22g.

›Air Fryer Salmon with Maple Soy Glaze

Servings: 4
Cooking Time: 8 Mints
Ingredients:
Pure maple syrup: 3 tbsp.
Gluten-free soy sauce: 3 tbsp.
Sriracha hot sauce: 1 tbsp.
One clove of minced garlic
Salmon: 4 fillets, skinless
Directions:
In a zip lock bag, maple syrup, mix sriracha, garlic, and soy sauce with salmon. Mix well and let it marinate for at least half an hour. Let the air fryer preheat to 400F. with oil spray the basket. Take fish out from the marinade, pat dry. Put the salmon in the air fryer, cook for 7 to 8 minutes, or longer. In the meantime, in a medium-small saucepan, add the marinade, let it simmer until reduced to half. Add glaze over salmon and serve.
Nutrition facts: Calories 292 | Carbohydrates: 12g | Protein: 35g | Fat: 11g |

›Air Fryer Southern Style Catfish with Green Beans

Servings: 2
Cooking Time: 20 Mints
Ingredients:
Catfish fillets: 2 pieces
Green beans: half cup, trimmed
Honey: 2 teaspoons
Freshly ground black pepper and salt
Crushed red pepper: half tsp.
Flour: 1/4 cup
One egg, lightly beaten

Dill pickle relish: 3/4 teaspoon
Apple cider vinegar: half tsp
1/3 cup whole-wheat breadcrumbs
Mayonnaise: 2 tablespoons
Dill
Lemon wedges

Directions:

In a bowl, add green beans, spray them cooking oil. Coat with crushed red pepper, 1/8 teaspoon of kosher salt, and half tsp. Of honey and cook in the air fryer at 400 F until soft and browned, for 12 minutes. Take out from fryer and cover with aluminum foil. In the meantime, coat catfish in flour. Then dip in egg to coat, then in breadcrumbs. Place fish in an air fryer basket and spray with cooking oil. Cook for 8 minutes, at 390/400°F, until cooked through and golden brown. Sprinkle with pepper and salt. In the meantime, mix vinegar, dill, relish, mayonnaise, and honey in a bowl. Serve the sauce with fish and green beans.

Nutrition facts: Cal 243 | fat 18 g | Carbs 18 g | Protein 33 g

➤Crab Egg Scramble

Preparation time: 15 minutes
Cooking time: 0 minutes | **Servings:** 4
1 tablespoon olive oil
8 eggs
6 ounces (170 g) crabmeat
Salt and black pepper to taste
Sauce:
¾ cup crème fraiche
½ cup chives, chopped
½ teaspoon garlic powder
Salt to taste

Direction

Whisk the eggs with a fork in a bowl, and season with black pepper and salt. Set a sauté pan over medium/low heat and warm olive oil. Add in the eggs and scramble them. Stir in crabmeat and cook until cooked thoroughly. In a mixing dish, combine crème fraiche and garlic powder. Season with salt and sprinkle with chives. Serve the eggs with the white sauce.

Nutrition facts (per serving)

calories: 406 | fat: 32.6g | protein: 23.3g | carbs: 4.3g | net carbs: 4.2g | fiber: 0.1g

➤Cream Cheese-Stuffed Mushrooms

Preparation time: 15 minutes
Cooking time: 40 minutes | **Servings:** 10
20 button mushrooms, stalks removed
6 ounces (170 g) cream cheese
¼ cup mayonnaise
¼ teaspoon mustard seeds
½ teaspoon celery seeds
Sea salt and black pepper, to taste

Directions

Adjust an oven rack to the center position. Brush your mushrooms with nonstick cooking spray and arrange them on a baking sheet. Roast your mushrooms in the preheated oven at 375°F (190°C) for 40 minutes until

the mushrooms release liquid. In the meantime, mix the remaining ingredients until well combined. Spoon the mixture into the roasted mushroom caps. Bon appétit!

Nutrition facts (per serving)

calories: 104 | fat: 9.8g | protein: 2.6g | carbs: 2.0g | net carbs: 1.5g | fiber: 0.5g

➤Zucchini Chips

Preparation time: 10 minutes
Cooking time: 20 minutes | **Servings:** 2
1 tablespoon extra-virgin olive oil
¼ teaspoon sea salt
1 teaspoon hot paprika
½ pound (227 g) zucchini, sliced into rounds
2 tablespoons Parmesan cheese, grated

Directions

Gently toss the sliced zucchini with the olive oil, salt, and paprika. Place them on a tinfoil lined baking sheet. Sprinkle the Parmesan cheese evenly over each zucchini round. Bake in the preheated oven at 400°F (205°C) for 15 to 20 minutes or until your chips turns a golden-brown color.

Nutrition facts (per serving)

calories: 53 | fat: 4.5g | protein: 1.6g | carbs: 1.5g | net carbs: 0.9g | fiber: 0.6g

➤Hot Spare Ribs

Preparation time: 20 minutes
Cooking time: 2 hours | **Servings:** 2
1 pound (454 g) spare ribs
1 teaspoon Dijon mustard
1 tablespoon rice wine
Salt and ground black pepper, to season
1 teaspoon garlic, pressed
½ shallot powder
1 teaspoon cayenne pepper
½ teaspoon ground allspice
1 tablespoon avocado oil
Hot Sauce:
1 teaspoon Sriracha sauce
1 tablespoon olive oil
1 cup tomato sauce, sugar-free
1 teaspoon garlic, minced
Salt, to season

Directions

Arrange the spare ribs on a parchment-lined baking pan. Add the remaining ingredients for the ribs and toss until well coated. Bake in the preheated oven at 360°F (182°C) for 1 hour. Rotate the pan and roast an additional 50 to 60 minutes. Baste the ribs with the cooking liquid periodically. In the meantime, whisk the sauce ingredients until well mixed. Pour the hot sauce over the ribs. Place under the broiler and broil for 7 to 9 minutes or until an internal temperature reaches 145°F (63°C). Brush the sauce onto each rib and serve warm. Bon appétit!

Nutrition facts (per serving)

calories: 471 | fat: 27.1g | protein: 48.6g | carbs: 6.6g

| net carbs: 4.6g | fiber: 2.0g

‣Chicken and Spinach Meatballs

Preparation time: 15 minutes
Cooking time: 25 minutes | **Servings:** 10
1½ pounds (680 g) ground chicken
8 ounces (227 g) Parmigiano-Reggiano cheese, grated
1 teaspoon garlic, minced
1 tablespoon Italian seasoning mix
1 egg, whisked
8 ounces (227 g) spinach, chopped
½ teaspoon mustard seeds
Sea salt and ground black pepper
½ teaspoon paprika
Directions
Mix well all the ingredients. Now, shape the meat mixture into 20 meatballs. Transfer your meatballs to a baking sheet and brush them with a nonstick cooking oil. Bake in the preheated oven at 380-390ºF (199ºC) for about 25 minutes or until golden brown. Serve with cocktail sticks and enjoy!
Nutrition facts (per serving)
calories: 210 | fat: 12.4g | protein: 19.4g | carbs: 4.5g | net carbs: 4.0g | fiber: 0.5g

‣Deviled Eggs

Preparation time: 10 minutes
Cooking time: 20 minutes | **Servings:** 6
6 eggs
1 tablespoon green tabasco
⅓ cup sugar-free mayonnaise
Directions
Place the eggs in a medium-small saucepan, and cover with salted water. Bring to a boil over medium heat. Boil for 8 mins. Place the eggs in an ice bath and let cool for 10 minutes. Peel and slice them in. Whisk together the tabasco, mayonnaise, and salt in a small bowl. Spoon this mixture on top of every egg.
Nutrition facts (per serving)
calories: 180 | fat: 17.0g | protein: 6.0g | carbs: 5.0g | net carbs: 5.0g | fiber: 0g

‣Cauliflower Bites

Preparation time: 10 minutes
Cooking time: 30 minutes | **Servings:** 2
1½ cups cauliflower florets
1 tablespoon butter, softened
1 egg, whisked
Sea salt and ground black pepper
1 teaspoon Italian seasoning mix
½ cup Asiago cheese, grated
Directions
Pulse the cauliflower in your food processor; now, heat the butter in a nonstick skillet and cook the cauliflower until golden. Add the remaining ingredients and blend together until well incorporated. Form the mixture into balls and flatten them with the palm of your hand. Ar-

range on a tinfoil-lined baking pan. Bake in the preheated oven at 390/400ºF (205ºC) for 25 to 30 minutes. Serve with homemade ketchup. Bon appétit!
Nutrition facts (per serving)
calories: 235 | fat: 19.1g | protein: 12.4g | carbs: 4.4g | net carbs: 2.9g | fiber: 1.5g

‣Romano and Asiago Cheese Crisps

Preparation time: 15 minutes
Cooking time: 30 minutes | **Servings:** 8
1¼ cups Romano cheese, grated
½ cup Asiago cheese, grated
2 ripe tomatoes, peeled
½ teaspoon sea salt
½ teaspoon chili powder
1 teaspoon dried oregano
1 teaspoon dried basil
1 teaspoon dried parsley flakes
1 teaspoon garlic powder
Directions
Mix the cheese in a bowl. Place tablespoon-sized heaps of the mixture onto parchment lined baking pans. Bake in the preheated oven at 380ºF (193ºC) approximately 7 minutes until beginning to brown around the edges. Let them stand for about 10-15 minutes until crisp. Meanwhile, purée the tomatoes in your food processor. Bring the puréed tomatoes to a simmer, add the remaining ingredients and cook for 30 minutes or until it has thickened and cooked through. Serve the cheese crisps with the spicy tomato sauce on the side. Bon appétit!
Nutrition facts (per serving)
calories: 110 | fat: 7.5g | protein: 8.4g | carbs: 2.0g | net carbs: 1.6g | fiber: 0.4g

‣Caprese Sticks

Preparation time: 10 minutes
Cooking time: 0 minutes | **Servings:** 8
2 tablespoons extra-virgin olive oil
2 tablespoons red wine vinegar
1 tablespoon Italian seasoning blend
8 pieces Ham
8 pieces Soppressata
16 grape tomatoes
8 black olives, pitted
8 ounces (227 g) Mozzarella, cubed
2 tablespoons fresh basil leaves, chopped
1 red bell pepper, sliced
1 yellow bell pepper, sliced
Coarse sea salt, to taste
Directions
In a medium-small mixing bowl, make the vinaigrette by whisking the oil, vinegar, and Italian seasoning blend. Set aside. Slide the ingredients on the prepared skewers. Arrange the sticks on serving platter. Season with salt to taste. Serve the vinaigrette on the side and enjoy!
Nutrition facts (per serving)
calories: 142 | fat: 8.3g | protein: 12.8g | carbs: 3.2g

| net carbs: 2.2g | fiber: 1.0g

‣Anchovy Fat Bombs

Preparation time: 15 minutes
Cooking time: 0 minutes | **Servings:** 10
8 ounces (227 g) Cheddar cheese, shredded
6 ounces (175 g) cream cheese, at room temperature
4 ounces (113 g) canned anchovies, chopped
½ yellow onion, minced
1 teaspoon fresh garlic, minced
Sea salt and ground black pepper
Direction
Mix all of the ingredients in a bowl. Place the mixture in your refrigerator for 1 hour. Then, shape the mixture into bite-sized balls. Serve immediately.
Nutrition facts (per serving)
calories: 123 | fat: 8.8g | protein: 7.4g | carbs: 3.3g | net carbs: 3.3g | fiber: 0g

‣Italian Sausage and Eggplant Pie

Preparation time: 15 minutes
Cooking time: 40 minutes | **Servings:** 6
6 eggs
12 ounces (340 g) raw sausage rolls 10 cherry tomatoes, halved 2 tablespoons heavy cream
2 tablespoons Parmesan cheese
Salt and black pepper to serve
2 tablespoons parsley, chopped
5 eggplant slices
Directions
Preheat your oven to 370/375°F (190°C). Grease a pie dish with cooking spray. Press the sausage roll at the bottom of a pie dish. Arrange the eggplant slices on top of the sausage. Top with cherry tomatoes.
Whisk together the eggs along with the heavy cream, salt, Parmesan cheese, and black pepper. Spoon the egg mixture over the sausage. Bake for about 40 minutes until it is browned around the edges. Serve warm, and scatter with chopped parsley.
Nutrition facts (per serving)
calories: 341 | fat: 28.0g | protein: 1.7g | carbs: 5.9g | net carbs: 3.0g | fiber: 2.9g

‣Spanish Sausage and Cheese Stuffed Mushrooms

Preparation time: 15 minutes
Cooking time: 25 minutes | **Servings:** 6
30 button mushrooms, stalks removed and cleaned
8 ounces (227 g) Chorizo sausage, crumbled
2 scallions, chopped
2 green garlic stalks, chopped
2 tablespoons fresh parsley, chopped
10 ounces (283 g) goat cheese, crumbled
Sea salt and ground black pepper
½ teaspoon red pepper flakes, crushed
Directions
Place the mushroom caps on a lightly greased bak-

ing sheet. Mix the remaining ingredients until well combined. Divide this stuffing between the mushroom caps. Bake in the preheated oven at 330-340°F (171°C) for 25 minutes or until thoroughly cooked. Serve with cocktail sticks. Bon appétit!
Nutrition facts (per serving)
calories: 325 | fat: 23.6g | protein: 23.0g | carbs: 5.0g | net carbs: 3.8g | fiber: 1.2g

‣Tamale Dip

Preparation time: 10 minutes
Cooking time: 2 hours
Servings: 8
Ingredients:
1 jalapeño, chopped
8 ounces cream cheese, cubed
¾ cup cheddar cheese, shredded
½ cup Monterey Jack cheese, shredded
2 garlic cloves, minced
15 ounces enchilada sauce
1 cup canned corn, drained
1 cup rotisserie chicken, shredded
1 tablespoon chili powder
Salt and black pepper to taste
1 tablespoon cilantro, chopped
Directions:
In your slow cooker, mix jalapeno with cream cheese, cheddar cheese, Monterey cheese, garlic, enchilada sauce, corn, chicken, chili powder, salt and pepper, stir, cover and cook on Low for 2 hours. Add cilantro, stir, divide into bowls and serve as a snack.
Nutrition facts
Calories 200,
Fat 4,
Fiber 7,
Carbs 20,
Protein 4

‣Spinach Spread

Preparation time: 10 minutes
Cooking time: 2 hours
Servings: 2
Ingredients:
4 ounces baby spinach
2 tablespoons mayonnaise
2 ounces heavy cream
½ teaspoon turmeric powder
A pinch of salt and black pepper
1 ounce Swiss cheese, shredded
Directions:
In your slow cooker, mix the spinach with the cream, mayo and the other ingredients, toss, put the lid on and cook on Low for 2 hours. Divide into bowls and serve as a party spread.
Nutrition facts
Calories 132,
Fat 4,
Fiber 3,
Carbs 10,

Protein 4

➤BBQ Chicken Dip

Preparation time: 10 minutes
Cooking time: 1 hour and 30 minutes
Servings: 10
Ingredients:
1 and ½ cups bob sauce
1 small red onion, chopped
24 ounces cream cheese, cubed
2 cups rotisserie chicken, shredded
3 bacon slices, cooked and crumbled
1 plum tomato, chopped
½ cup cheddar cheese, shredded
1 tablespoon green onions, chopped
Directions:
In your slow cooker, mix bob sauce with onion, cream cheese, rotisserie chicken, bacon, tomato, cheddar and green onions, stir, cover and cook on Low for 1 hour and 30 minutes. Divide into bowls and serve.
Nutrition facts
Calories 251,
Fat 4,
Fiber 6,
Carbs 10,
Protein 4

➤Artichoke Dip

Preparation time: 10 minutes
Cooking time: 2 hours
Servings: 2
Ingredients:
2 ounces canned artichoke hearts, drained and chopped
2 ounces heavy cream
2 tablespoons mayonnaise
¼ cup mozzarella, shredded
2 green onions, chopped
½ teaspoon gram masala
Cooking spray
Directions:
Grease your slow cooker with the cooking spray, and mix the artichokes with the cream, mayo and the other ingredients inside. Stir, cover, cook on Low for 2 hours, divide into bowls and serve as a party dip.
Nutrition facts
Calories 100,
Fat 3,
Fiber 2,
Carbs 7,
Protein 3

➤Mexican Dip

Preparation time: 10 minutes
Cooking time: 1 hour and 30 minutes
Servings: 10
Ingredients:
24 ounces cream cheese, cubed
2 cups rotisserie chicken breast, shredded
3 ounces canned green chilies, chopped
1 and ½ cups Monterey jack cheese, shredded
1 and ½ cups sauce Verde
1 tablespoon green onions, chopped
Directions:
In your slow cooker, mix cream cheese with chicken, chilies, cheese, salsa Verde and green onions, stir, cover and cook on Low for 1 hour and 30 minutes. Divide into bowls and serve.
Nutrition facts
Calories 222,
Fat 4,
Fiber 5,
Carbs 15
Protein 4

➤Crab Dip

Preparation time: 10 minutes
Cooking time: 1 hour
Servings: 2
Ingredients:
2 ounces crabmeat
1 tablespoon lime zest, grated
½ tablespoon lime juice
2 tablespoons mayonnaise
2 green onions, chopped
2 ounces cream cheese, cubed
Cooking spray
Directions:
Grease your slow cooker with the cooking spray, and mix the crabmeat with the lime zest, juice and the other ingredients inside. Put the lid on, cook on Low for 1 hour, divide into bowls and serve as a party dip.
Nutrition facts
Calories 100,
Fat 3,
Fiber 2,
Carbs 9,
Protein 4

➤Tex Mex Dip

Preparation time: 10 minutes
Cooking time: 1 hour
Servings: 6
Ingredients:
15 ounces canned chili con carne
1 cup Mexican cheese, shredded
1 yellow onion, chopped
8 ounces cream cheese, cubed
½ cup beer
A pinch of salt
12 ounces macaroni, cooked 1 tablespoons cilantro, chopped
Directions:
In your slow cooker, mix chili con carne with cheese, onion, cream cheese, beer and salt, stir, cover and cook on High for 1 hour. Add macaroni and cilantro, stir, divide into bowls and serve.

Nutrition facts
Calories 200,
Fat 4,
Fiber 6,
Carbs 17
Protein 5

>Lemon Shrimp Dip

Preparation time: 10 minutes
Cooking time: 2 hours
Servings: 2
Ingredients:
3 ounces cream cheese, soft
½ cup heavy cream
1 pound shrimp, peeled, deveined and chopped
½ tablespoon balsamic vinegar
2 tablespoons mayonnaise½ tablespoon lemon juice
A pinch of salt and black pepper
2 ounces mozzarella, shredded
1 tablespoon parsley, chopped
Directions:
In your slow cooker, mix the cream cheese with the shrimp, heavy cream and the other ingredients, whisk, put the lid on and cook on Low for 2 hours.
Divide into bowls and serve as a dip.
Nutrition facts
Calories 342,
Fat 4,
Fiber 3,
Carbs 7
Protein 10

>Squash Sauce

Preparation time: 10 minutes
Cooking time: 3 hours
Servings: 2
Ingredients:
1 cup butternut squash, peeled and cubed
1 cup cherry tomatoes, cubed
1 cup avocado, peeled, pitted and cubed
½ tablespoon balsamic vinegar
½ tablespoon lemon juice
1 tablespoon lemon zest, grated
¼ cup veggie stock
1 tablespoon chives, chopped
A pinch of rosemary, dried
A pinch of sage, dried
A pinch of salt and black pepper
Directions:
In your slow cooker, mix the squash with the tomatoes, avocado and the other ingredients, toss, put the lid on and cook on Low for 3 hours. Divide into bowls and serve as a snack.
Nutrition facts
Calories 182,
Fat 5,
Fiber 7,
Carbs 12,
Protein 5

>Taco Dip

Preparation time: 10 minutes
Cooking time: 2 hours and 30 minutes
Servings: 7
Ingredients:
1 rotisserie chicken, shredded
2 cups pepper jack, cheese, grated15 ounces canned enchilada sauce
1 jalapeno, sliced
8 ounces cream cheese, soft 1 tablespoon taco seasoning
Directions:
In your slow cooker, mix chicken with pepper jack, enchilada sauce, jalapeno, cream and taco seasoning, stir, cover and cook on High for 1 hour. Stir the dip, cover and cook on Low for 1 hour and 30 minutes more. Divide into bowls and serve as a snack.
Nutrition facts
Calories 251,
Fat 5,
Fiber 8,
Carbs 17
Protein 5

>Beans Spread

Preparation time: 10 minutes
Cooking time: 6 hours
Servings: 2
Ingredients:
1 cup canned black beans, drained
2 tablespoons tahini paste
½ teaspoon balsamic vinegar
¼ cup veggie stock ½ tablespoon olive oil
Directions:
In your slow cooker, mix the beans with the tahini paste and the other ingredients, toss, put the lid on and cook on Low for 6 hours. Transfer to your food processor, blend well, divide into bowls and serve.
Nutrition facts
Calories 221,
Fat 6,
Fiber 5,
Carbs 19
Protein 3

>Lasagna Dip

Preparation time: 10 minutes
Cooking time: 1 hour
Servings: 10
Ingredients:
8 ounces cream cheese
¾ cup parmesan, grated
1 and ½ cups ricotta
½ teaspoon red pepper flakes, crushed
2 garlic cloves, minced
3 cups marinara sauce
1 and ½ cups mozzarella, shredded

1 and ½ teaspoon oregano, chopped
Directions:
In your slow cooker, mix cream cheese with parmesan, ricotta, pepper flakes, garlic, marinara, mozzarella and oregano, stir, cover and cook on High for 1 hour. Stir, divide into bowls and serve as a dip.
Nutrition facts
Calories 231,
Fat 4,
Fiber 7,
Carbs 21
Protein 5

›Rice Snack Bowls

Preparation time: 10 minutes
Cooking time: 6 hours
Servings: 2
Ingredients:
½ cup wild rice
1 red onion, sliced
½ cup brown rice
2 cups veggie stock
½ cup baby spinach
½ cup cherry tomatoes, halved
2 tablespoons pine nuts, toasted
1 tablespoon raisins
1 tablespoon chives, chopped
1 tablespoon dill, chopped
½ tablespoon olive oil
A pinch of salt and black pepper
Directions:
In your slow cooker, mix the rice with the onion, stock and the other ingredients, toss, put the lid on and cook on Low for 6 hours. Divide in to bowls and serve as a snack.
Nutrition facts
Calories 301,
Fat 6,
Fiber 6,
Carbs 12
Protein 3

›Roasted Vegetable Panini

Preparation time: 10 minutes
Cooking time: 15 minutes | **Servings:** 4
2 tablespoons extra-virgin olive oil, divided
1½ cups diced broccoli
1 cup diced zucchini
¼ cup diced onion
¼ teaspoon dried oregano
⅛ teaspoon kosher or sea salt
⅛ teaspoon freshly ground black pepper
1 (12-ounce / 345-g) jar roasted red peppers, drained and finely chopped
2 tablespoons grated Parmesan or Asiago cheese
1 cup fresh Mozzarella (about 4 ounces / 113 g), sliced
1 (2-foot-long) whole-grain Italian loaf, cut into 4 equal lengths
Cooking spray

Directions
Place a medium-large, rimmed baking sheet in the oven. Preheat the oven to 440/450°F (235°C) with the baking sheet inside. In a medium-large bowl, stir together 1 tablespoon of the oil, broccoli, zucchini, onion, oregano, salt and pepper. Remove the baking sheet from the oven and spritz the baking sheet with cooking spray. Spread the vegetable mixture on the baking sheet and roast for 5 minutes, stirring once halfway through cooking. Remove the baking sheet from the oven. Stir in the red peppers and Parmesan cheese. In a medium-large skillet over medium-high heat, heat the remaining 1 tablespoon of the oil. Cut open each section of bread horizontally, but don't cut all the way through. Fill each with the vegetable mix (about ½ cup), and layer 1 ounce (28 g) of sliced Mozzarella cheese on top. Close the sandwiches, and place two of them on the skillet. Place a heavy object on top and grill for 3 minutes. Flip the sandwiches and grill for another 3 mins. Repeat the grilling process with the remaining two sandwiches. Serve hot.
Nutrition facts (per serving)
calories: 116 | fat: 4.0g | protein: 12.0g | carbs: 9.0g | fiber: 3.0g | sodium: 569mg

›White Pizzas with Arugula and Spinach

Preparation time: 10 minutes
Cooking time: 20 minutes | **Servings:** 4
Ingredients
1 pound (454 g) refrigerated fresh pizza dough
2 tablespoons extra-virgin olive oil, divided
½ cup thinly sliced onion
2 garlic cloves, minced
3 cups baby spinach
3 cups arugula
1 tablespoon water
¼ teaspoon freshly ground black pepper
1 tablespoon freshly squeezed lemon juice
½ cup shredded Parmesan cheese
½ cup crumbled goat cheese
Cooking spray
Directions
Preheat the oven to 490/500°F (260°C). Spritz a large, rimmed baking sheet with cooking spray. Take the pizza dough out of the refrigerator. Heat 1 tablespoon of the extra-virgin olive oil in a medium-large skillet over medium heat. Add the onion to the skillet and cook for 4 minutes, stirring constantly. Add the garlic and cook for 1-3 minutes, stirring constantly. Stir in the spinach, arugula, water and pepper. Cook for about 2-3 minutes, stirring constantly, or until all the greens are coated with oil and they start to cook down. Remove the skillet from the heat and drizzle with the lemon juice. On a lightly floured work surface, form the pizza dough into a 12-inch circle or a 10by-12-inch rectangle, using a rolling pin. Place the dough on the baking sheet. Brush the dough with the remaining tbsp of the oil. Spread the cooked greens on top of the dough to within ½ inch of the edge. Top with the Parmesan che-

ese and goat cheese. Bake in the preheated oven for 10 to 12 minutes, or until the crust starts to brown around the edges. Remove from the oven and transfer the pizza to a cutting board. Cut into eight pieces before serving.

Nutrition facts (per serving)
calories: 521 | fat: 31.0g | protein: 23.0g | carbs: 38.0g | fiber: 4.0g | sodium: 1073mg

›Za'atar Pizza

Preparation time: 10 minutes
Cooking time: 1o to 12 minutes | **Servings:** 4 to 6
Ingredients
1 sheet puff pastry
¼ cup extra-virgin olive oil
⅓ cup za'atar seasoning
Directions
Preheat the oven to 340/350°F (180°C). Line a baking sheet with parchment paper. Place the puff pastry on the baking sheet. Cut the pastry into desired slices. Brush the pastry with the olive oil. Sprinkle with the za'atar seasoning. Put the pastry in the oven and bake until edges are lightly browned and puffed up, or for 10 to 12 minutes. Serve warm.

Nutrition facts (per serving)
calories: 374 | fat: 30.0g | protein: 3.0g | carbs: 20.0g | fiber: 1.0g | sodium: 166mg

›Mediterranean Greek Salad Wraps

Preparation time: 15 minutes
Cooking time: 0 minutes | **Servings:** 4
Ingredients
1½ cups seedless cucumber, peeled and chopped
1 cup chopped tomato
½ cup finely chopped fresh mint
¼ cup diced red onion
1 (2.25-ounce / 64-g) can sliced black olives, drained
2 tablespoons extra-virgin olive oil
1 tablespoon red wine vinegar
¼ teaspoon kosher salt
¼ teaspoon freshly ground black pepper
½ cup crumbled goat cheese
4 whole-wheat flatbread wraps or soft whole-wheat tortillas
Directions
In a medium-large bowl, stir together the cucumber, tomato, mint, onion and olives. In a medium-small bowl, whisk together the oil, vinegar, salt, and pepper. Spread the dressing over the salad. Toss gently to combine. On a clean work surface, lay the wraps. Divide the goat cheese evenly among the wraps. Scoop a quarter of the salad filling down the center of each wrap. Fold up each wrap: Start by folding up the bottom, then fold one side over and fold the other side over the top. Repeat with the remaining wraps. Serve immediately.

Nutrition facts (per serving)
calories: 225 | fat: 12.0g | protein: 12.0g | carbs: 18.0g | fiber: 4.0g | sodium: 349mg

›Salmon Salad Wraps

Preparation time: 10 minutes
Cooking time: 0 minutes | **Servings:** 6
Ingredients
1 pound (454 g) salmon fillets, cooked and flaked
½ cup diced carrots
½ cup diced celery
3 tablespoons diced red onion
3 tablespoons chopped fresh dill
2 tablespoons capers
1½ tablespoons extra-virgin olive oil
1 tablespoon aged balsamic vinegar
¼ teaspoon kosher or sea salt
½ teaspoon freshly ground black pepper
4 whole-wheat flatbread wraps or soft whole-wheat tortillas
Directions
In a medium-large bowl, stir together all the ingredients, except for the wraps. On a clean work surface, lay the wraps. Divide the salmon mixture evenly among the wraps. Fold up the bottom of the wraps, then roll up the wrap. Serve immediately.

Nutrition facts (per serving)
calories: 194 | fat: 8.0g | protein: 18.0g | carbs: 13.0g | fiber: 3.0g | sodium: 536mg

›Baked Parmesan Chicken Wraps

Preparation time: 10 minutes
Cooking time: 18 minutes | **Servings:** 6
Ingredients
1 pound (451 g) boneless, skinless chicken breasts
1 large egg
¼ cup unsweetened almond milk
⅔ cup whole-wheat breadcrumbs
½ cup grated Parmesan cheese
¾ teaspoon garlic powder, divided
1 cup canned low-sodium or no-salt-added crushed tomatoes
1 teaspoon dried oregano
6 (8-inch) whole-wheat tortillas, or whole-grain spinach wraps
1 cup fresh Mozzarella cheese, sliced
1½ cups loosely packed fresh flat-leaf (Italian) parsley, chopped
Cooking spray
Directions
Preheat the oven to 425°F (225°C). Line a large, rimmed baking sheet with aluminum foil. Place a wire rack on the aluminum foil and spritz the rack with nonstick cooking spray. Set aside. Place the chicken breasts into a medium-large plastic bag. With a rolling pin, pound the chicken so it is evenly flattened, about ¼ inch thick. Slice the chicken into six portions. In a medium-large bowl, whisk together the egg and milk. In another bowl, stir together the breadcrumbs, Parmesan cheese and ½ teaspoon of the garlic powder. Dredge each chicken breast portion into the egg mixture, and then into the Parmesan crumb mixture, pressing the crumbs into the chicken so they stick. Ar-

range the chicken on the prepared wire rack. Bake in the preheated oven for 15/18 minutes, or until the internal temperature of the chicken reads 165°F (74°C) on a meat thermometer. Transfer the chicken to a cutting board and cut each portion diagonally into ½-inch pieces. In a medium-small, microwave-safe bowl, stir together the tomatoes, oregano, and the remaining ¼ teaspoon of the garlic powder. Cover the bowl with a paper towel and microwave for at least 1-2 minutes on high, until very hot. Set aside. Wrap the tortillas in a damp paper towel and microwave for 30 to 45 seconds on high, or until warmed through. Assemble the wraps: Divide the chicken slices evenly among the six tortillas and top with the sliced Mozzarella cheese. Spread 1 tbsp of the warm tomato sauce over the cheese on each tortilla, and top each with about ¼ cup of the parsley. Wrap the tortilla: Fold up the bottom of the tortilla, then fold one side over and fold the other side over the top. Serve the wraps warm with the remaining sauce for dipping.

Nutrition facts (per serving) calories: 358 | fat: 12.0g | protein: 21.0g | carbs: 41.0g | fiber: 7.0g | sodium: 755mg

›Cheesy Fig Pizzas with Garlic Oil

Preparation time: 1 day 40 minutes | **Cooking time:** 10 minutes | **Makes** 2 pizzas
Ingredients
Dough:
1cup almond flour
1½ cups whole-wheat flour
¾ teaspoon instant or rapid-rise yeast
1 teaspoon raw honey
1¼ cups ice water
2 tablespoons extra-virgin olive oil
1¾ teaspoons sea salt
Garlic Oil:
4 tablespoons extra-virgin olive oil, divided
½ teaspoon dried thyme
2 garlic cloves, minced
⅛ teaspoon sea salt
½ teaspoon freshly ground pepper
Topping:
1 cup fresh basil leaves
1 cup crumbled feta cheese
8 ounces (227 g) fresh figs, stemmed and quartered lengthwise
2 tablespoons raw honey
Directions:
Make the Dough
Combine the flours, yeast, and honey in a food processor, pulse to combine well. Gently add water while pulsing. Let the dough sit for 10 minutes. Mix the olive oil and salt in the dough and knead the dough until smooth. Wrap in plastic and refrigerate for at least 1 day.
Make the Garlic Oil
Heat the tablespoons of olive oil in a nonstick skillet over medium-low heat until shimmering. Add the thyme, garlic, salt, and pepper and sauté for 30 seconds or until fragrant. Set them aside until ready to use.
Make the Pizzas

Preheat the oven to 490/500°F (260°C). Grease two baking sheets with 2 tablespoons of olive oil. Divide the dough in half and shape into 2 balls. Press the balls into 13-inch rounds. Sprinkle the rounds with a tough of flour if they are sticky. Top the rounds with the garlic oil and basil leaves, then arrange the rounds on the baking sheets. Scatter with feta cheese and figs. Put the sheets in the preheated oven and bake for 9 minutes or until lightly browned. Rotate the pizza halfway through. Remove the pizzas from the oven, then discard the bay leaves. Drizzle with honey. Let sit for 5 minutes and serve immediately.

Nutrition facts (per serving) (1 pizza) calories: 1350 | fat: 46.5g | protein: 27.5g | carbs: 221.9g | fiber: 23.7g | sodium: 2898mg

›Mashed Grape Tomato Pizzas

Preparation time: 10 minutes
Cooking time: 20 minutes | **Servings:** 6
Ingredients
3 cups grape tomatoes, halved
1 teaspoon chopped fresh thyme leaves
2 garlic cloves, minced
¼ teaspoon kosher salt
¼ teaspoon freshly ground black pepper
1 tablespoon extra-virgin olive oil
¾ cup shredded Parmesan cheese
6 whole-wheat pita breads
Directions:
Preheat the oven to 420/425°F (220°C). Combine the tomatoes, thyme, garlic, salt, ground black pepper, and olive oil in a baking pan. Roast in the oven for 17-20 minutes. Remove the pan from the oven, mash the tomatoes with a spatula and stir to mix well halfway through the cooking time. Meanwhile, divide and spread the cheese over each pita bread, then place the bread in a separate baking pan and roast in the oven for 5 minutes or until golden brown and the cheese melts. Transfer the pita bread onto a large plate, then top with the roasted mashed tomatoes. Serve immediately.

Nutrition facts (per serving) calories: 140 | fat: 5.1g | protein: 6.2g | carbs: 16.9g | fiber: 2.0g | sodium: 466mg

›Vegetable and Cheese Lavash Pizza

Preparation time: 15 minutes
Cooking time: 11 minutes | **Servings:** 4
Ingredients
2 (12 by 9-inch) lavash breads
2 tablespoons extra-virgin olive oil
10 ounces (284 g) frozen spinach, thawed and squeezed dry
1 cup shredded fontina cheese
1 tomato, cored and cut into ½-inch pieces
½ cup pitted large green olives, chopped
¼ teaspoon red pepper flakes
3 garlic cloves, minced
¼ teaspoon sea salt
¼ teaspoon ground black pepper
½ cup grated Parmesan cheese

Directions:

Preheat oven to 475°F (246°C). Brush the lavash breads with olive oil, then place them on two baking sheet. Heat in the preheated oven for 4 minutes or until lightly browned. Flip the breads halfway through the cooking time. Meanwhile, combine the spinach, fontina cheese, tomato pieces, olives, red pepper flakes, garlic, salt, and black pepper in a large bowl. Stir to mix well. Remove the lavash bread from the oven and sit them on two large plates, spread them with the spinach mixture, then scatter with the Parmesan cheese on top.

Bake in the oven for about 5 minutes or until the cheese melts and well browned. Slice and serve warm.

Nutrition facts (per serving)

calories: 431 | fat: 21.5g | protein: 20.0g | carbs: 38.4g | fiber: 2.5g | sodium: 854mg

---

›Dulse, Avocado, and Tomato Pitas

Preparation time: 10 minutes
Cooking time: 30 minutes | **Makes** 4 pitas
Ingredients
2 teaspoons coconut oil
½ cup dulse, picked through and separated
Ground black pepper, to taste
2 avocados, sliced
2 tablespoons lime juice
¼ cup chopped cilantro
2 scallions, light green and white parts, sliced
Sea salt, to taste
4 (8-inch) whole wheat pitas, sliced in half
4 cups chopped romaine
4 plum tomatoes, sliced
Directions:

Preheat the coconut oil in a nonstick skillet over medium heat until melted. Add the dulse and sauté for 5 minutes or until crispy. Sprinkle with ground black pepper and turn off the heat. Set aside. Put the avocado, lime juice, cilantro, and scallions in a food processor and sprinkle with salt and ground black pepper. Pulse to combine well until smooth. Toast the pitas in a baking pan in the oven for 1 minute until soft. Transfer the pitas to a clean work surface and open. Spread the avocado mixture over the pitas, then top with dulse, romaine, and tomato slices. Serve immediately.

Nutrition facts (per serving) (1 pita)

calories: 412 | fat: 18.7g | protein: 9.1g | carbs: 56.1g | fiber: 12.5g | sodium: 695mg

---

›Greek Vegetable Salad Pita

Preparation time: 10 minutes
Cooking time: 0 minutes | **Servings:** 4
Ingredients
½ cup baby spinach leaves
½ small red onion, thinly sliced
½ small cucumber, deseeded and chopped
1 tomato, chopped
1 cup chopped romaine lettuce
1 tablespoon extra-virgin olive oil
½ tablespoon red wine vinegar
1 teaspoon Dijon mustard
1 tablespoon crumbled feta cheese

Sea salt and freshly ground pepper
1 whole-wheat pita
Directions:

Combine well all the ingredients, except for the pita, in a large bowl. Toss to mix well. Stuff the pita with the salad, then serve immediately.

Nutrition facts (per serving)

calories: 137 | fat: 8.1g | protein: 3.1g | carbs: 14.3g | fiber: 2.4g | sodium: 166mg

---

›Artichoke and Cucumber Hoagies

Preparation time: 10 minutes
Cooking time: 15 minutes | **Makes** 1
Ingredients
1 (12-ounce / 340-g) whole grain baguette, sliced in half horizontally
1 cup frozen and thawed artichoke hearts, roughly chopped
1 cucumber, sliced
1 tomato, sliced
1 red bell pepper, sliced
⅓ cup Kalamata olives, pitted and chopped
¼ small red onion, thinly sliced
Sea salt and ground black pepper
1 tablespoons pesto
Balsamic vinegar, to taste

Arrange the baguette halves on a clean work surface, then cut off the top third from each half. Scoop some insides of the bottom half out and reserve as breadcrumbs. Toast the baguette in a baking pan in the oven for 1 minute to brown lightly. Put the artichokes, cucumber, tomatoes, bell pepper, olives, and onion in a large bowl. Sprinkle with salt and ground black pepper. Toss to combine well. Spread the bottom half of the baguette with the vegetable mixture and drizzle with balsamic vinegar, then smear the cut side of the baguette top with pesto. Assemble the two baguette halves. Wrap the hoagies in parchment paper and let sit for at least an hour before serving.

Nutrition facts (per serving) (1 hoagies)

calories: 1263 | fat: 37.7g | protein: 56.3g | carbs: 180.1g | fiber: 37.8g | sodium: 2137mg

---

›Brown Rice and Black Bean Burgers

Preparation time: 20 minutes
Cooking time: 40 minutes | **Makes** 8 burgers
Ingredients
1 cup cooked brown rice
1 (15-ounce / 425-g) can black beans, rinsed
1 tablespoon olive oil
2 tablespoons taco or Harissa seasoning
½ yellow onion, finely diced
1 beet, peeled and grated
1 carrot, peeled and grated
2 tablespoons no-salt-added tomato paste
2 tablespoons apple cider vinegar
3 garlic cloves, minced
¼ teaspoon sea salt
Ground black pepper, to taste
8 whole-wheat hamburger buns
Toppings:

16 lettuce leaves, rinsed well
8 tomato slices, rinsed well
Whole-grain mustard, to taste

Line a baking sheet with parchment paper. Put the brown rice and black beans in a food processor and pulse until mix well. Pour the mixture in a medium-large bowl and set aside. Preheat the olive oil in a nonstick skillet over medium heat until shimmering. Add the taco seasoning and stir for 1 minute or until fragrant. Add the onion, beet, and carrot and sauté for 5 minutes or until the onion is translucent and beet and carrot are tender. Pour in the tomato paste and vinegar, then add the garlic and cook for 3 minutes or until the sauce is thickened. Sprinkle with salt and ground black pepper. Transfer the vegetable mixture to the bowl of rice mixture, then stir to mix well until smooth. Divide and shape the mixture into 8-9 patties, then arrange the patties on the baking sheet and refrigerate for at least 1 hour. Preheat the oven to 390/400°F (205°C). Remove the baking sheet from the refrigerator and allow to sit under room temperature for 10 minutes. Bake in the preheated oven for 40-42 minutes or until golden brown on both sides. Flip the patties halfway through the cooking time. Remove the patties and allow to cool for 10 minutes. Assemble the buns with patties, lettuce, and tomato slices. Top the filling with mustard and serve immediately.

Nutrition facts (per serving) (1 burger)
calories: 544 | fat: 20.0g | protein: 15.8g | carbs: 76.0g | fiber: 10.6g | sodium: 446mg

›Classic Socca

Preparation time: 10 minutes
Cooking time: 10 minutes | **Servings:** 4
Ingredients
1½ cups chickpea flour
½ teaspoon ground turmeric
½ teaspoon sea salt
½ teaspoon ground black pepper
2 tablespoons plus 3 tsps extra-virgin olive oil
1½ cups water

Combine the chickpea flour, turmeric, salt, and black pepper in a bowl. Stir to mix well, then gently mix in 2 tablespoons of olive oil and water. Stir to mix until smooth. Heat 3 teaspoons of olive oil in an 8-inch nonstick skillet over medium-high heat until shimmering. Add half cup of the mixture into the skillet and swirl the skillet so the mixture coat the bottom evenly. Cook for 4/5 minutes or until lightly browned and crispy. Flip the socca halfway through the cooking time. Repeat with the remaining mixture. Slice and serve warm.

Nutrition facts (per serving)
calories: 207 | fat: 10.2g | protein: 7.9g | carbs: 20.7g | fiber: 3.9g | sodium: 315mg

›Alfalfa Sprout and Nut Rolls

Preparation time: 40 minutes
Cooking time: 0 minutes | **Makes** 16 bite-size pieces
Ingredients
1 cup alfalfa sprouts

2 tablespoons Brazil nuts
½ cup chopped fresh cilantro
2 tablespoons flaked coconut
1 garlic clove, minced
2 tablespoons ground flaxseeds
Zest and juice of 1 lemon
Pinch cayenne pepper
Sea salt and freshly ground black pepper
1 tablespoon melted coconut oil
2 tablespoons water
2 whole-grain wraps
Combine all ingredients, except for the wraps, in a food processor, then pulse to combine well until smooth. Unfold the wraps on a clean work surface, then spread the mixture over the wraps. Roll the wraps up and refrigerate for 30 minutes until set. Remove the rolls from the refrigerator and slice into 16 bite-sized pieces, if desired, and serve.

Nutrition facts (per serving) (1 piece)
calories: 67 | fat: 7.1g | protein: 2.2g | carbs: 2.9g | fiber: 1.0g | sodium: 61mg

›Falafel Balls with Tahini Sauce

Preparation time: 2 hours 20 minutes
Cooking time: 20 minutes | **Servings:** 4
Ingredients
Tahini Sauce:
½ cup tahini
2 tablespoons lemon juice
¼ cup finely chopped flat-leaf parsley
2 cloves garlic, minced ½ cup cold water, as needed
Falafel:
1 cup dried chickpeas, soaked overnight, drained
¼ cup chopped flat-leaf parsley
¼ cup chopped cilantro
1 large onion, chopped
1 teaspoon cumin
½ teaspoon chili flakes
4 cloves garlic
1 teaspoon sea salt
5 tablespoons almond flour
1½ teaspoons baking soda, dissolved in 1 teaspoon water
1 cups peanut oil
1 medium bell pepper, chopped
1 medium tomato, chopped
4 whole-wheat pita breads

Make the Tahini Sauce
Combine well, all the ingredients for the tahini sauce in a small/medium bowl. Stir to mix well until smooth. Wrap the bowl in plastic and refrigerate until ready to serve.
Make the Falafel
Put the chickpeas, parsley, cilantro, onion, cumin, chili flakes, garlic, and salt in a food processor. Pulse to mix well but not puréed. Add the flour and baking soda to the food processor, then pulse to form a smooth and tight dough. Put the dough in a medium/large bowl and wrap in plastic. Refrigerate for at least 2 hours to let it rise. Divide and shape the dough into walnut-sized small balls. Pour the peanut oil in a large pot and heat over high heat until the temperature of the oil

224

reaches 375ºF (190ºC). Drop 6 balls into the oil each time, and fry for 5 minutes or until golden brown and crispy. Turn the balls with a strainer to make them fried evenly. Transfer the balls on paper towels with the strainer, then drain the oil from the balls. Roast the pita breads in the oven for 5 minutes or until golden brown, if needed, then stuff the pitas with falafel balls and top with bell peppers and tomatoes. Drizzle with tahini sauce and serve immediately.

Nutrition facts (per serving)
calories: 574 | fat: 27.1g | protein: 19.8g | carbs: 69.7g | fiber: 13.4g | sodium: 1246mg

›Glazed Mushroom and Vegetable Fajitas

Preparation time: 20 minutes
Cooking time: 20 minutes | **Makes** 6
Ingredients
Spicy Glazed Mushrooms:
1 teaspoon olive oil
1 (10- to 12-ounce / 284- to 340-g) package cremini mushrooms, rinsed and drained, cut into thin slices
½ to 1 teaspoon chili powder
Sea salt and freshly ground black pepper
1 teaspoon maple syrup
Fajitas:
1 teaspoons olive oil
1 onion, chopped
Sea salt, to taste
1 bell pepper, deseeded and sliced into long strips
1 zucchini, cut into large matchsticks
6 whole-grain tortilla
2 carrots, grated
3 to 4 scallions, sliced
½ cup fresh cilantro, finely chopped
Make the Spicy Glazed Mushrooms
Preheat the oil in a non-stick skillet over medium-high heat until shimmering. Add the mushrooms and sauté for 10 minutes or until tender. Sprinkle the mushrooms with chili powder, salt, and ground black pepper. Drizzle with maple syrup. Stir to mix well and cook for 4 to 7 minutes or until the mushrooms are glazed. Set aside until ready to use.
Make the Fajitas
Preheat the oil in the same skillet over medium- low heat until shimmering. Add the onion and sauté for 4/5 minutes or until translucent. Sprinkle with salt. Add the bell pepper and zucchini and sauté for 7 minutes or until tender. Meanwhile, toast the tortilla in the oven for 5 minutes or until golden brown. Allow the tortilla to cool for a 3/4 minutes until they can be handled, then assemble the tortilla with glazed mushrooms, sautéed vegetables and remaining vegetables to make the fajitas. Serve immediately.
Nutrition facts (per serving)
calories: 403 | fat: 14.8g | protein: 11.2g | carbs: 7.9g | fiber: 7.0g | sodium: 230mg

›Mini Pork and Cucumber Lettuce Wraps

Preparation time: 20 minutes

Cooking time: 0 minutes | **Makes** 12 wraps
Ingredients
8 ounces (227 g) cooked ground pork
1 cucumber, diced
1 tomato, diced
1 red onion, sliced
1 ounce (28 g) low-fat feta cheese, crumbled
Juice of 1 lemon
1 tablespoon extra-virgin olive oil
Sea salt and freshly ground pepper
12 small, intact iceberg lettuce leaves
Combine the ground pork, cucumber, tomato, and onion in a large bowl, then scatter with feta cheese. Drizzle with lemon juice and olive oil, and sprinkle with salt and pepper. Toss to mix well. Unfold the small lettuce leaves on a large plate or several small plates, then divide and top with the pork mixture.
Wrap and serve immediately.
Nutrition facts (per serving) (1 warp)
calories: 78 | fat: 5.6g | protein: 5.5g | carbs: 1.4g | fiber: 0.3g | sodium: 50mg

›Black Bean Chili with Mangoes

Preparation time: 10 minutes
Cooking time: 10 minutes | **Servings:** 4
Ingredients
2 tablespoons coconut oil
1 onion, chopped
2 (15-ounce / 420-g) cans black beans, drained and rinsed
1 tablespoon chili powder
1 teaspoon sea salt
¼ teaspoon freshly ground black pepper
1 cup water
2 ripe mangoes, sliced thinly
¼ cup chopped fresh cilantro, divided
¼ cup sliced scallions, divided

Preheat the coconut oil in a pot over high heat until melted. Put the onion in the pot and sauté for 5 minutes or until translucent. Add the black beans to the pot. Sprinkle with chili powder, salt, and ground black pepper. Pour in the water. Stir to mix well. Bring to a boil. Reduce the heat to low, then simmering for 5 minutes or until the beans are tender. Turn off the heat and mix in the mangoes, then garnish with scallions and cilantro before serving.
Nutrition facts (per serving)
calories: 430 | fat: 9.1g | protein: 20.2g | carbs: 71.9g | fiber: 22.0g | sodium: 608mg

›Israeli-Style Eggplant and Chickpea Salad

Preparation time: 5 minutes
Cooking time: 20 minutes | **Servings:** 6
Ingredients
2 tablespoons balsamic vinegar
2 tablespoons freshly squeezed lemon juice
1 teaspoon ground cumin
¼ teaspoon sea salt
2 tablespoons olive oil, divided

1 (1-pound / 454-g) medium globe eggplant, stem removed, cut into flat cubes (about ½ inch thick)
1 (15-ounce / 425-g) can chickpeas, rinsed
¼ cup chopped mint leaves
1 cup sliced sweet onion
1 garlic clove, finely minced
1 tablespoon sesame seeds, toasted

Preheat the oven to 540/550°F (288°C) or the highest level of your oven or broiler. Grease a baking sheet with 1 tbsp. of olive oil.
Combine the balsamic vinegar, lemon juice, cumin, salt, and 1 tablespoon of olive oil in a small bowl. Stir to mix well. Arrange the eggplant cubes on the baking sheet, then brush with 2 tablespoons of the balsamic vinegar mixture on both sides. Broil in the preheated oven for 8 minutes or until lightly browned. Flip the cubes halfway through the cooking time. Meanwhile, combine the chickpeas, mint, onion, garlic, and sesame seeds in a large serving bowl. Drizzle with remaining balsamic vinegar mixture. Stir to mix well. Remove the eggplant from the oven. Allow to cool for 3-5 minutes, then slice them into ½-inch strips on a clean work surface. Add the eggplant strips in the serving bowl, then toss to combine well before serving.

Nutrition facts (per serving)
calories: 125 | fat: 2.9g | protein: 5.2g | carbs: 20.9g | fiber: 6.0g | sodium: 222mg

➤Italian Sautéd Cannellini Beans

Preparation time: 10 minutes
Cooking time: 15 minutes | **Servings:** 6
Ingredients
2 teaspoons extra-virgin olive oil
½ cup minced onion
¼ cup red wine vinegar
1 (12-ounce / 340-g) can no-salt-added tomato paste
2 tablespoons raw honey
½ cup water
¼ teaspoon ground cinnamon
2 (15-ounce / 425-g) cans cannellini beans

Preheat the olive oil in a saucepan over medium-low heat until shimmering. Add the onion and sauté for about 5 minutes or until translucent. Pour in the red wine vinegar, honey, tomato paste, and water. Sprinkle with cinnamon. Stir to mix well. Reduce the heat to low, then pour all the beans into the saucepan. Cook for 10 more minutes. Stir constantly. Serve immediately.

Nutrition facts (per serving)
calories: 435 | fat: 2.1g | protein: 26.2g | carbs: 80.3g | fiber: 24.0g | sodium: 72mg

➤Lentil and Vegetable Curry Stew

Preparation time: 20 minutes
Cooking time: 4 hours 7 minutes | **Servings:** 8
Ingredients
1 tablespoon coconut oil
1 yellow onion, diced
¼ cup yellow Thai curry paste
2 cups unsweetened coconut milk

2 cups dry red lentils, rinsed well and drained
3 cups bite-sized cauliflower florets
2 golden potatoes, cut into chunks
2 carrots, peeled and diced
8 cups low-sodium vegetable soup, divided
1 bunch kale, stems removed and chopped
Sea salt, to taste
½ cup fresh cilantro, chopped
Pinch crushed red pepper flakes

Preheat the coconut oil in a non-stick skillet over medium-high heat until melted. Add the onion and sauté for about 5 minutes or until translucent. Pour in the curry paste and sauté for another 2 minutes, then fold in the coconut milk and stir to combine well. Bring to a simmer and turn off the heat. Put the lentils, cauliflower, potatoes, and carrot in the slow cooker. Pour in 6 cups of vegetable soup and the curry mixture. Stir to combine well. Cover and cook on high for 4 hours or until the lentils and vegetables are soft. Stir periodically. During the last 30 minutes, fold the kale in the slow cooker and pour in the remaining vegetable soup. Sprinkle with salt. Pour the stew in a large serving bowl and spread the cilantro and red pepper flakes on top before serving hot.

Nutrition facts (per serving)
calories: 530 | fat: 19.2g | protein: 20.3g | carbs: 75.2g | fiber: 15.5g | sodium: 562mg

➤Chickpea, Vegetable, and Fruit Stew

Preparation time: 20 minutes
Cooking time: 6 hours 4 minutes | **Servings:** 6
Ingredients
1 large bell pepper, any color, chopped
6 ounces (170 g) green beans, trimmed and cut into bite-size pieces
3 cups canned chickpeas, rinsed and drained
1 (15-ounce / 425-g) can diced tomatoes, with the juice
1 large carrot, cut into ¼-inch rounds
2 large potatoes, peeled and cubed
1 large yellow onion, chopped
1 teaspoon grated fresh ginger
2 garlic cloves, minced
1¾ cups low-sodium vegetable soup
1 teaspoon ground cumin
1 tablespoon ground coriander
¼ teaspoon ground red pepper flakes
Sea salt and ground black pepper
8 ounces (227 g) fresh baby spinach
¼ cup diced dried figs
¼ cup diced dried apricots
1 cup plain Greek yogurt

Place the bell peppers, green beans, chicken peas, tomatoes and juice, carrot, potatoes, onion, ginger, and garlic in the slow cooker. Pour in the vegetable soup and sprinkle with cumin, coriander, red pepper flakes, salt, and ground black pepper. Stir to mix well. Put the slow cooker lid on and cook on high for 6 hours or until the vegetables are soft. Stir periodically. Open the lid and fold in the spinach, figs, apricots, and yogurt. Stir to mix well. Cook until the spinach is wilted or for about 3-5 minutes. Pour them in a large serving bowl. Allow to cool for at least 18-20 minutes, then serve warm.

Nutrition facts (per serving)
calories: 611 | fat: 9.0g | protein: 30.7g | carbs: 107.4g | fiber: 20.8g | sodium: 344mg

›Quinoa and Chickpea Vegetable Bowls

Preparation time: 20 minutes
Cooking time: 15 minutes | **Servings:** 4
Ingredients
 1 cup red dry quinoa, rinsed and drained
 2 cups low-sodium vegetable soup
2 cups fresh spinach
2 cups finely shredded red cabbage
1 (15-ounce / 425-g) can chickpeas, rinsed
1 ripe avocado, thinly sliced
1 cup shredded carrots
1 red bell pepper, thinly sliced
4 tablespoons Mango Sauce ½ cup fresh cilantro, chopped
Mango Sauce:
1 mango, diced
¼ cup fresh lime juice
½ teaspoon ground turmeric
1 teaspoon finely minced fresh ginger
¼ teaspoon sea salt
Pinch of ground red pepper
1 teaspoon pure maple syrup
2 tablespoons extra-virgin olive oil

Pour the quinoa and vegetable soup in a saucepan. Bring to a boil. Low the heat. Cover and cook for 14-16 minutes or until tender. Fluffy with a fork. Meanwhile, combine the ingredients for the mango sauce in a food processor. Pulse until smooth. Divide the quinoa, spinach, and cabbage into 4 serving bowls, then top with chickpeas, avocado, carrots, and bell pepper. Dress them with the mango sauce and spread with cilantro. Serve immediately.

Nutrition facts (per serving)
calories: 366 | fat: 11.1g | protein: 15.5g | carbs: 55.6g | fiber: 17.7g | sodium: 746mg

›Ritzy Veggie Chili

Preparation time: 15 minutes
Cooking time: 5 hours | **Servings:** 4
Ingredients
1 (28-ounce / 794-g) can chopped tomatoes, with the juice
1 (15-ounce / 425-g) can black beans, rinsed
1 (15-ounce / 425-g) can red beans, drained and rinsed
1 medium green bell pepper, chopped
1 yellow onion, chopped
1 tablespoon onion powder
1 teaspoon paprika
1 teaspoon cayenne pepper
1 teaspoon garlic powder
½ teaspoon sea salt

½ teaspoon ground black pepper
1 tablespoon olive oil
1 large hass avocado, pitted, peeled, and chopped, for garnish

Combine all the ingredients, except for the avocado, in the slow cooker. Stir to mix well. Put the slow cooker lid on and cook on high for 5 hours or until the vegetables are tender and the mixture has a thick consistency. Pour the chili in a large serving bowl. Allow to cool for 30 minutes, then spread with chopped avocado and serve.

Nutrition facts (per serving)
calories: 633 | fat: 16.3g | protein: 31.7g | carbs: 97.0g | fiber: 28.9g | sodium: 792mg

›Spicy Italian Bean Balls with Marinara

Preparation time: 20 minutes
Cooking time: 30 minutes
Servings: 2 to 4
Ingredients
Bean Balls:
1 tablespoon extra virgin olive oil
½ yellow onion, minced
1 tsp fennel seeds
2 tsps dried oregano
½ tsp crushed red pepper flakes
1 tsp garlic powder
1 (15-ounce / 420-g) can white beans (cannellini or navy), drained and rinsed
½ cup whole-grain breadcrumbs
Sea salt and ground black pepper
Marinara:
1 tablespoon extra-virgin olive oil
3 garlic cloves, minced
Handful basil leaves
1 (28-ounce / 794-g) can chopped tomatoes with juice reserved
Sea salt, to taste
Make the Bean Balls
Preheat the oven to 340/350°F (180°C). Line a baking sheet with parchment paper. Heat the extra-virgin olive oil in a non-stick skillet over medium-high heat until shimmering. Add the onion and sauté until translucent or for 3-5 minutes. Sprinkle with fennel seeds, red pepper flakes, oregano, and garlic powder, then cook until aromatic or for about 1 minute. Pour the sautéed mixture in a food processor and add the bread crumbs and beans. Sprinkle with ground black pepper and salt, then pulse to combine well and the mixture holds together. Shape the mixture into balls with a 2 ounce (55-g) cookie scoop, then arrange the balls on the baking sheet. Bake in the preheated oven until browned or for 30-31 minutes. Flip the balls halfway through the cooking time.
Make the Marinara
While baking the bean balls, heat the olive oil in a saucepan over medium/high heat. Add the basil and garlic and sauté for about 2 minutes or until fragrant. Fold in the tomatoes and juice. Bring to a boil. Reduce the heat to low. Put the lid on and simmer for about 15-17 mins. Sprinkle with salt. Transfer the bean balls on a plate and baste with marinara before serving.

Nutritions facts (per serving)
calories: 350 | fat: 16.4g | protein: 11.5g | carbs: 42.9g | fiber: 10.3g | sodium: 377mg

➤Baked Rolled Oat with Pears and Pecans

Preparation time: 15 minutes
Cooking time: 30 minutes | **Servings:** 6
Ingredients
2 and a half tablespoons coconut oil, melted, plus more for greasing the pan
3 ripe pears, cored and diced
2 cups unsweetened almond milk
1 tablespoon pure vanilla extract
¼ cup pure maple syrup
2 cups gluten-free rolled oats
½ cup raisins
¾ cup chopped pecans
¼ teaspoon ground nutmeg
1 teaspoon ground cinnamon
½ teaspoon ground ginger
¼ teaspoon sea salt

Preheat the oven to 340/350°F (180°C). Grease a baking dish with melted coconut oil, then spread the pears in a single layer on the baking dish evenly. Combine the almond milk, vanilla extract, maple syrup, and coconut oil in a bowl. Stir to mix well. Combine the remaining ingredients in a separate medium-large bowl. Stir to mix well. Fold the almond milk mixture in the bowl, then pour the mixture over the pears. Place the baking dish in the oven for 30 minutes or until lightly browned and set. Serve immediately.
Nutrition facts (per serving)
calories: 479 | fat: 34.9g | protein: 8.8g | carbs: 50.1g | fiber: 10.8g | sodium: 113mg

➤Brown Rice Pilaf with Pistachios and Raisins

Preparation time: 5 minutes
Cooking time: 15 minutes | **Servings:** 6
Ingredients
1 tablespoon extra-virgin olive oil
1 cup chopped onion
½ cup shredded carrot
½ teaspoon ground cinnamon
1 teaspoon ground cumin
2 cups brown rice
1¾ cups pure orange juice
¼ cup water
½ cup shelled pistachios
1 cup golden raisins
½ cup chopped fresh chives

Heat the extra-virgin olive oil in a saucepan over medium-high heat until shimmering. Add the onion and sauté for 3-5 minutes or until translucent. Add the carrots, cinnamon, and cumin, then sauté for 1 minutes or until aromatic. Pour int the brown rice, orange juice, and water. Bring to a boil. Low the heat to medium-low and simmer for 7 minutes or until the liquid is

almost absorbed. Transfer the rice mixture in a large serving bowl, then spread with pistachios, raisins, and chives. Serve immediately.
Nutrition facts (per serving)
calories: 264 | fat: 7.1g | protein: 5.2g | carbs: 48.9g | fiber: 4.0g | sodium: 86mg

➤Cherry, Apricot, and Pecan Brown Rice Bowl

Preparation time: 15 minutes
Cooking time: 1 hour 1 minutes | **Servings:** 2
Ingredients
2 tablespoons olive oil
2 green onions, sliced
½ cup brown rice
1 cup low -sodium chicken stock
2 tablespoons dried cherries
4 dried apricots, chopped
2 tablespoons pecans, toasted and chopped
Sea salt and freshly ground pepper

Preheat the olive oil in a medium-large saucepan over medium-high heat until shimmering. Add the green onions and sauté for 1 minutes or until fragrant. Add the rice. Stir to mix well, then pour in the chicken stock. Bring to a boil. Reduce the heat to low. Cover and simmer for 48-50 minutes or until the brown rice is soft. Add the cherries, apricots, and pecans, and simmer for 10 more minutes or until the fruits are tender. Pour them in a large serving bowl. Fluff with a fork. Sprinkle with sea salt and pepper. Enjoy!
Nutrition facts (per serving)
calories: 451 | fat: 25.9g | protein: 8.2g | carbs: 50.4g | fiber: 4.6g | sodium: 122mg

➤Curry Apple Couscous with Leeks and Pecans

Preparation time: 10 minutes
Cooking time: 8 minutes | **Servings:** 4
Ingredients
2 teaspoons extra-virgin olive oil
2 leeks, white parts only, sliced
1 apple, diced
2 cups cooked couscous
2 tablespoons curry powder
½ cup chopped pecans

Preheat the olive oil in a skillet over medium-high heat until shimmering. Add the leeks and sauté for 5 minutes or until soft. Add the diced apple and cook for at least 3 more minutes until tender. Add the couscous and curry powder. Stir to combine. Transfer them in a large serving bowl, then mix in the pecans and serve.
Nutrition facts (per serving)
calories: 254 | fat: 11.9g | protein: 5.4g | carbs: 34.3g | fiber: 5.9g | sodium: 15mg

➤Lebanese Flavor Broken Thin Noodles

Preparation time: 10 minutes

Cooking time: 25 minutes | **Servings:** 6
Ingredients
1 tablespoon extra-virgin olive oil
1 (3-ounce / 85-g) cup vermicelli, broken into 1- to 1½-
inch pieces
3 cups shredded cabbage
1 cup brown rice
3 cups low-sodium vegetable soup
½ cup water
2 garlic cloves, mashed
¼ teaspoon sea salt
⅛ teaspoon crushed red pepper flakes
½ cup coarsely chopped cilantro
Fresh lemon slices, for serving

Preheat the olive oil in a saucepan over medium-high
heat until shimmering. Add the vermicelli and sauté
for 3 minutes or until toasted. Add the cabbage and
sauté for 4 minutes or until tender. Pour in the brown
rice, vegetable soup, and water. Add the garlic and
sprinkle with red pepper flakes and salt. Bring to a boil
over high heat. Reduce the heat to medium-low. Put
the lid on and simmer for additional 10 minutes. Turn
off the heat, then let sit for 5 minutes without opening
the lid. Pour them on a large serving platter and spread with cilantro. Squeeze the lemon slices over and
serve warm.
Nutrition facts (per serving)
calories: 127 | fat: 3.1g | protein: 4.2g | carbs: 22.9g
| fiber: 3.0g | sodium: 224mg

— CHAPTER 9 —

DINNER

ALICIA TRAVIS

›Zucchini Salmon Salad

Preparation Time: 5 minutes
Cooking Time: 10 minutes
Servings: 3
Ingredients:
2 salmon fillets
2 tablespoons soy sauce
2 zucchinis, sliced
Salt and pepper to taste
2 tablespoons extra virgin olive oil
2 tablespoons sesame seeds
Salt and pepper to taste
Directions:
Drizzle the salmon with soy sauce. Heat a grill pan over medium flame. Cook salmon on the grill on each side for 2-3 minutes. Season the zucchini with salt and pepper and place it on the grill as well. Cook on each side until golden. Place the zucchini, salmon and the rest of the ingredients in a bowl. Serve the salad fresh.
Nutrition facts:
Calories: 224
Fat: 19g
Protein: 18g
Carbohydrates: 0g

›Pan Fried Salmon

Preparation Time: 5 minutes
Cooking Time: 20 minutes
Servings: 4
Ingredients:
4 salmon fillets
Salt and pepper to taste
1 teaspoon dried oregano
1 teaspoon dried basil
3 tablespoons extra virgin olive oil
Directions:
Season the fish with pepper, salt,oregano and basil. Preheat the oil in a pan and place the salmon in the hot oil, with the skin facing down. Fry on each side until golden fragrant and brown for about 2 minutes. Serve the salmon warm and fresh.
Nutrition facts:
Calories: 327
Fat: 25g
Protein: 36g
Carbohydrates: 0.3g

›Grilled Salmon with Pineapple Sauce

Preparation Time: 5 minutes
Cooking Time: 30 minutes
Servings: 4
Ingredients:
4 salmon fillets
Salt and pepper to taste
2 tablespoons Cajun seasoning
1 fresh pineapple, peeled and diced
1 cup cherry tomatoes, quartered
2 tablespoons chopped cilantro
2 tablespoons chopped parsley
1 teaspoon dried mint
2 tablespoons lemon juice

2 tablespoons extra virgin olive oil
1 teaspoon honey
Salt and pepper to taste
Directions:
Add salt, pepper and Cajun seasoning to the fish. Heat a grill pan over medium flame. Cook fish on the grill on each side for 3-4 minutes. For the sauce, mix the pineapple, tomatoes, cilantro, parsley, mint, lemon juice and honey in a bowl. Season with salt and pepper. Serve the grilled salmon with the pineapple sauce.
Nutrition facts:
Calories: 332
Fat: 12g
Protein: 34g
Carbohydrates: 0g

›Chickpea Salad

Preparation Time: 5 minutes
Cooking Time: 20 minutes
Servings: 6
Ingredients:
1 can chickpeas, drained
1 fennel bulb, sliced
1 red onion, sliced
1 teaspoon dried basil
1 teaspoon dried oregano
2 tablespoons chopped parsley
4 garlic cloves, minced
2 tablespoons lemon juice
2 tablespoons extra virgin olive oil
Salt and pepper to taste
Directions:
Combine the chickpeas, fennel, red onion, herbs, garlic, lemon juice and oil in a salad bowl. Add salt and pepper and serve the salad fresh.
Nutrition facts:
Calories: 200
Fat: 9g
Protein: 4g
Carbohydrates: 28g

›Warm Chorizo Chickpea Salad

Preparation Time: 5 minutes
Cooking Time: 20 minutes
Servings: 6
Ingredients:
1 tablespoon extra virgin olive oil
4 chorizo links, sliced
1 red onion, sliced
4 roasted red bell peppers, chopped
1 can chickpeas, drained
2 cups cherry tomatoes
2 tablespoons balsamic vinegar
Salt and pepper to taste
Directions:
Preheat the oil in a skillet and add the chorizo. Cook briefly just until fragrant then add the onion, bell peppers and chickpeas and cook for 2 additional minutes. Transfer the mixture in a salad bowl then add the tomatoes, vinegar, salt and pepper. Mix well and serve the salad right away.

Nutrition facts:
Calories: 359
Fat: 18g
Protein: 15g
Carbohydrates: 21g

›Greek Roasted Fish

Preparation Time: 5 minutes
Cooking Time: 30 minutes
Servings: 4
Ingredients:
4 salmon fillets
1 tablespoon chopped oregano
1 teaspoon dried basil
1 zucchini, sliced
1 red onion, sliced
1 carrot, sliced
1 lemon, sliced
2 tablespoons extra virgin olive oil
Salt and pepper to taste
Directions:
Add all the ingredients in a deep-dish baking pan. Season with pepper and salt and cook in the preheated oven at 350F for 20 minutes. Serve the fish and vegetables warm.
Nutrition facts:
Calories: 328
Fat: 13g
Protein: 38g
Carbohydrates: 8g

›Tomato Fish Bake

Preparation Time: 5 minutes
Cooking Time: 30 minutes
Servings: 4
Ingredients:
4 cod fillets
4 tomatoes, sliced
4 garlic cloves, minced
1 shallot, sliced
1 celery stalk, sliced
1 teaspoon fennel seeds
1 cup vegetable stock
Salt and pepper to taste
Directions:
Layer the tomatoes and cod fillets in a deep-dish baking pan. Add the rest of the ingredients and add pepper and salt. Cook in the preheated oven at 340-350F for 20 minutes. Serve the dish warm or chilled.
Nutrition facts:
Calories: 299
Fat: 3g
Protein: 64g
Carbohydrates: 2g

›Garlicky Tomato Chicken Casserole

Preparation Time: 5 minutes
Cooking Time: 50 minutes
Servings: 4
Ingredients:

4 chicken breasts
2 tomatoes, sliced
1 can diced tomatoes
2 garlic cloves, chopped
1 shallot, chopped
1 bay leaf
1 thyme sprig
½ cup dry white wine
½ cup chicken stock
Salt and pepper to taste
Directions:
Combine the chicken and the rest of the ingredients in a deep dish baking pan. Adjust the taste with pepper and salt and cover the pot with a lid or aluminum foil. Cook in the preheated oven at 320-330F for 40 minutes. Serve the casserole warm.
Nutrition facts:
Calories: 313
Fat: 8g
Protein: 47g
Carbohydrates: 6g

›Chicken Cacciatore

Preparation Time: 5 minutes
Cooking Time: 45 minutes
Servings: 6
Ingredients:
2 tablespoons extra virgin olive oil
6 chicken thighs
1 sweet onion, chopped
2 garlic cloves, minced
2 red bell peppers, cored and diced
2 carrots, diced
1 rosemary sprig
1 thyme sprig
4 tomatoes, peeled and diced
½ cup tomato juice
¼ cup dry white wine
1 cup chicken stock
1 bay leaf
Salt and pepper to taste
Directions:
Heat the oil in a heavy saucepan. Cook chicken on all sides until golden. Stir in the onion and garlic and cook for about 2 minutes. Stir in the remaining ingredients and season with salt and pepper. Cook on low heat for 30 minutes. Serve the chicken cacciatore warm and fresh.
Nutrition facts:
Calories: 363
Fat: 14g
Protein: 42g
Carbohydrates: 9g

›Cauliflower Curry

Preparation Time: 5 minutes
Cooking Time: 5 hours
Servings: 4
Ingredients:
1 cauliflower head, florets separated
2 carrots, sliced
1 red onion, chopped

¾ cup coconut milk
2 garlic cloves, minced
2 tablespoons curry powder
A pinch of salt and black pepper
1 tablespoon red pepper flakes
1 teaspoon garam masala
Directions:
In your slow cooker, mix all the ingredients. Cook on high and cover, for about 5 hours, divide into bowls and serve.
Nutrition facts:
Calories 160,
Fat 11.5,
Fiber 5.4,
Carbs 14.7,
Protein 3,6

›Herbed Roasted Chicken Breasts

Preparation Time: 5 minutes
Cooking Time: 50 minutes
Servings: 4
Ingredients:
2 tablespoons extra virgin olive oil
2 tablespoons chopped parsley
2 tablespoons chopped cilantro
1 teaspoon dried oregano
1 teaspoon dried basil
2 tablespoons lemon juice
Salt and pepper to taste
4 chicken breasts
Directions:
Combine the oil, parsley, cilantro, oregano, basil, lemon juice, salt and pepper in a bowl. Spread this mixture over the chicken and rub it well into the meat. Place in a deep-dish baking pan and cover with aluminum foil. Cook in the preheated oven at 340-350F for about 20 minutes then remove the foil and cook for 25 additional minutes. Serve the chicken warm and fresh with your favorite side dish.
Nutrition facts:
Calories: 330
Fat: 15g
Protein: 40.7g
Carbohydrates: 1g

›Seafood Paella

Preparation Time: 5 minutes
Cooking Time: 45 minutes
Servings: 8
Ingredients:
2 tablespoons extra virgin olive oil
1 shallot, chopped
2 garlic cloves, chopped
1 red bell pepper, cored and diced
1 carrot, diced
2 tomatoes, peeled and diced
1 cup wild rice
1 cup tomato juice
2 cups chicken stock
1 chicken breast, cubed
Salt and pepper to taste
2 monkfish fillets, cubed

½ pound fresh shrimps, peeled and deveined
½ pound prawns
1 thyme sprig
1 rosemary sprig
Directions:
Preheat the oil in a skillet and stir in the shallot, garlic, bell pepper, carrot and tomatoes. Cook for a few minutes until softened. Stir in the rice, tomato juice, stock, chicken, salt and pepper and cook on low heat for 20 minutes. Add the rest of the ingredients and cook for 10 additional minutes. Serve the paella warm and fresh.
Nutrition facts:
Calories: 245
Fat: 8g
Protein: 27g
Carbohydrates: 20.6g

›Fennel Wild Rice Risotto

Preparation Time: 5 minutes
Cooking Time: 35 minutes
Servings: 6
Ingredients:
2 tablespoons extra virgin olive oil
1 shallot, chopped
2 garlic cloves, minced
1 fennel bulb, chopped
1 cup wild rice
¼ cup dry white wine
2 cups chicken stock
1 teaspoon grated orange zest
Salt and pepper to taste
Directions:
Heat the oil in a heavy saucepan. Add the garlic, fennel and shallot and cook for a few minutes until softened. Stir in the rice and cook for 1-3 additional minutes then add the wine, orange zest and stock, with salt and pepper to taste. Cook on low heat for 20 minutes. Serve the risotto warm and fresh.
Nutrition facts:
Calories: 162
Fat: 2g
Protein: 8g
Carbohydrates: 20g

›Wild Rice Prawn Salad

Preparation Time: 5 minutes
Cooking Time: 35 minutes
Servings: 6
Ingredients:
¾ cup wild rice
1¾ cups chicken stock
1 pound prawns
Salt and pepper to taste
2 tablespoons lemon juice
2 tablespoons extra virgin olive oil
2 cups arugula
Directions:
Combine the rice and chicken stock in a saucepan and cook until the liquid has been absorbed entirely. Transfer the rice in a salad bowl. Season the prawns with pepper and salt and drizzle them with lemon jui-

ce and oil. Heat a grill pan over medium flame. Place the prawns on the hot pan and cook on each side for 2-3 minutes. For the salad, combine the rice with arugula and prawns and mix well. Serve the salad fresh.

Nutrition facts:
Calories: 207
Fat: 4g
Protein: 20.6g
Carbohydrates: 17g

›Chicken Broccoli Salad with Avocado Dressing

Preparation Time: 5 minutes
Cooking Time: 40 minutes
Servings: 6
Ingredients:
2 chicken breasts
1 pound broccoli, cut into florets
1 avocado, peeled and pitted
½ lemon, juiced
2 garlic cloves
¼ teaspoon chili powder
¼ teaspoon cumin powder
Salt and pepper to taste
Directions:
Cook the chicken in a large pot of salty water. Drain and cut the chicken into small cubes. Place in a salad bowl. Add the broccoli and mix well. Combine the avocado, lemon juice, garlic, chili powder, cumin powder, salt and pepper in a blender. Pulse until smooth. Spoon the dressing over the salad. Serve the salad fresh.
Nutrition facts:
Calories: 195
Fat: 11g
Protein: 14g
Carbohydrates: 3g

›Marinated Chicken Breasts

Preparation Time: 5 minutes
Cooking Time: 2 hours
Servings: 4
Ingredients:
4 chicken breasts
Salt and pepper to taste
1 lemon, juiced
1 rosemary sprig
1 thyme sprig
2 garlic cloves, crushed
2 sage leaves
3 tablespoons extra virgin olive oil
½ cup buttermilk
Directions:
Boil the chicken with salt and pepper and place it in a resealable bag. Add remaining ingredients and seal bag. Refrigerate for at least 1 hour. After 1 hour, heat a roasting pan over medium heat, then place the chicken on the grill. Cook on each side for about 8-10 mins or until juices are gone. Serve the chicken warm with your favorite side dish.

Nutrition facts:
Calories: 371
Fat: 21g
Protein: 46g
Carbohydrates: 2g

›Balsamic Beef and Mushrooms Mix

Preparation Time: 5 minutes
Cooking Time: 8 hours
Servings: 4
Ingredients:
2 pounds' beef, cut into strips
¼ cup balsamic vinegar
2 cups beef stock
1 tablespoon ginger, grated
Juice of ½ lemon
1 cup brown mushrooms, sliced
A pinch of salt and black pepper
1 teaspoon ground cinnamon
Directions:
Mix all the ingredients In your slow cooker,, cover and cook on low for 8 hours. Divide everything between plates and serve.
Nutrition facts:
Calories 446,
Fat 14,
Fiber 0.6,
Carbs 2.9,
Protein 70,8

›Simple Beef Roast

Preparation Time: 10 minutes
Cooking Time: 8 hours
Servings: 8
Ingredients:
5 pounds' beef roast
2 tablespoons Italian seasoning
1 cup beef stock
1 tablespoon sweet paprika
3 tablespoons olive oil
Directions:
In your slow cooker, mix well all the ingredients, cover and cook on low for about 8 hours. Carve the roast, divide it between plates and serve.
Nutrition facts:
Calories 587,
Fat 24.1,
Fiber 0.3,
Carbs 0.9,
Protein 86.5

›Chicken Breast Soup

Preparation Time: 5 minutes
Cooking Time: 4 hours
Servings: 4
Ingredients:
3 chicken breasts, skinless, boneless, cubed
2 celery stalks, chopped
2 carrots, chopped
2 tablespoons olive oil

1 red onion, chopped
3 garlic cloves, minced
4 cups chicken stock
1 tablespoon parsley, chopped
Directions:
In your slow cooker, mix well all the ingredients except the parsley, cover and cook on High for about 4 hours. Add the parsley, stir well, ladle the soup into bowls and serve.
Nutrition facts:
Calories 445,
Fat 21.1,
Fiber 1.6,
Carbs 7.4,
Protein 54,3

➤Pork and Peppers Chili

Preparation Time: 5 minutes
Cooking Time: 8 hours 5 minutes
Servings: 4
Ingredients:
1 red onion, chopped
2 pounds' pork, ground
4 garlic cloves, minced
2 red bell peppers, chopped
1 celery stalk, chopped
25 ounces' fresh tomatoes, peeled, crushed
¼ cup green chilies, chopped
2 tablespoons fresh oregano, chopped
2 tablespoons chili powder
A pinch of salt and black pepper
A drizzle of olive oil
Directions:
Heat up a sauté pan with the oil over medium-high heat and add the garlic, onion and the meat. Mix and brown for about 5 minutes then transfer to your slow cooker. Add the rest of the ingredients, toss, cover and cook on low for 8 hours. Divide everything into bowls and serve.
Nutrition facts:
Calories 448
Fat 13
Fiber 6.6
Carbs 20.2
Protein 63g

➤Greek-Style Quesadillas

Preparation Time: 10 minutes
Cooking Time: 10 minutes
Servings: 4
Ingredients:
4 whole wheat tortillas
1 cup Mozzarella cheese, shredded
1 cup fresh spinach, chopped
2 tablespoon Greek yogurt
1 egg, beaten
¼ cup green olives, sliced
1 tablespoon olive oil
1/3 cup fresh cilantro, chopped
Directions:
In the bowl, combine Mozzarella cheese, spinach, yogurt, egg, olives, and cilantro.

Then pour olive oil in the skillet. Place one tortilla in the skillet and spread it with Mozzarella mixture. Top it with the second tortilla and spread it with cheese mixture again. Then place the third tortilla and spread it with all remaining cheese mixture. Cover it with the last tortilla and fry it for 5 minutes from each side over the medium heat.
Nutrition facts:
Calories 193
Fat 7.7
Fiber 3.2
Carbs 23.6
Protein 8.3

➤Creamy Penne

Preparation Time: 10 minutes
Cooking Time: 25 minutes
Servings: 4
Ingredients:
½ cup penne, dried
9 oz. chicken fillet
1 teaspoon Italian seasoning
1 tablespoon olive oil
1 tomato, chopped
1 cup heavy cream
1 tablespoon fresh basil, chopped
½ teaspoon salt
2 oz. Parmesan, grated
1 cup water, for cooking
Directions:
Pour water in the pan, add penne, and boil it for 15 minutes. Then drain water. Pour olive oil in the skillet and heat it up. Slice the chicken fillet and put it in the hot oil. Sprinkle chicken with Italian seasoning and roast for 2 minutes from each side. Then add fresh basil, salt, tomato, and grated cheese. Stir well. Add heavy cream and cooked penne. Cook the meal for 5 minutes more over the medium heat. Stir it from time to time.
Nutrition facts:
Calories 388
Fat 23.4
Fiber 0.2
Carbs 17.6
Protein 17.6

➤Red Lobsters Coconut Shrimp

Servings: 4
Cooking Time: 30 Mints
Ingredients:
Pork Rinds: ½ cup (Crushed)
Jumbo Shrimp:4 cups. (deveined)
Coconut Flakes preferably: ½ cup
Eggs: two
Flour of coconut: ½ cup
Any oil of your choice for frying at least half-inch in pan
Freshly ground black pepper & kosher salt to taste
Dipping sauce (Pina colada flavor):
Powdered Sugar as Substitute: 2-3 tablespoon
Mayonnaise: 3 tablespoons
Sour Cream: ½ cup

Coconut Extract or to taste: ¼ tsp
Coconut Cream: 3 tablespoons
Pineapple Flavoring as much to taste: ¼ tsp
Coconut Flakes preferably unsweetened this is optional: 3 tablespoons
Directions:
Pina Colada (Sauce)
Mix all the ingredients into a tiny bowl for the Dipping sauce (Pina colada flavor). Combine well, and put in the fridge until ready to serve. preparation of Shrimps
Whip all eggs in a deep bowl, and a small, shallow bowl, add the crushed pork rinds, coconut flour, sea salt, coconut flakes, and freshly ground black pepper. Put the shrimp one by one in the mixed eggs for dipping, then in the coconut flour blend. Put them on a clean plate or put them on your air fryer's basket.
To Make in Air Fry Oven:
Place the shrimp battered in a single layer on your air fryer basket. Spritz the shrimp with oil and cook for 8-10 minutes at 360 ° F, flipping them through halfway.
Nutrition facts: Calories 340 | Proteins 25g | Carbs 9g | Fat 16g | Fiber 7g

▶Air Fryer Garlic-lime Shrimp Kebabs

Servings: 2
Cooking Time: 18 Mints
Ingredients:
One lime
Raw shrimp: 1 cup
Salt: 1/8 teaspoon
1 clove of garlic
Freshly ground black pepper
Directions:
In water, let wooden skewers soak for 20 minutes.
Let the Air fryer preheat to 350F. In a bowl, mix shrimp, minced garlic, lime juice, kosher salt, and pepper
Add shrimp on skewers. Place skewers in the air fryer and cook for 8 minutes. Turn halfway over. Top with cilantro and your favorite dip.
Nutrition facts: Calories: 76kcal | Carbohydrates: 4g | Protein: 13g | fat 9 g

▶Italian Veal Cutlets with Pecorino

Preparation time: 15 minutes
Cooking time: 1 hour 5 minutes
Servings: 6
6 veal cutlets
½ cup Pecorino cheese, grated
6 provolone cheese slices
Salt and black pepper, to taste
4 cups tomato sauce
A pinch of garlic salt
2 tablespoons butter
2 tablespoons coconut oil, melted
1 teaspoon Italian seasoning
Directions
Season the veal cutlets with garlic salt, black pepper, and salt. Set a pan over medium-high heat and warm oil and butter, place in the veal, and cook until browned on all sides. Spread half of the tomato sauce on the bottom of a baking dish that is coated with some cooking spray. Place in the veal cutlets then spread

with Italian seasoning and sprinkle over the remaining sauce. Set in the oven at 360ºF (182ºC), and bake for 40 minutes. Scatter with the provolone cheese, then sprinkle with Pecorino cheese, and bake for another 5 minutes until the cheese is golden and melted. Serve.
Nutrition facts (per serving)
calories: 363 | fat: 21.1g | protein: 26.1g | carbs: 8.4g | net carbs: 5.9g | fiber: 2.5g

▶Balsamic Mushroom Beef Meatloaf

Preparation time: 15 minutes
Cooking time: 1 hour 5 minutes
Servings: 12
Meatloaf:
3 pounds (1.4 kg) ground beef
½ cup chopped onions
½ cup almond flour
2 garlic cloves, minced
1 cup sliced mushrooms
3 eggs
¼ teaspoon ground black pepper
2 tablespoons chopped parsley
¼ cup chopped bell peppers
⅓ cup grated Parmesan cheese
1 teaspoon balsamic vinegar
1 teaspoon salt
Glaze:
2 cups balsamic vinegar
1 tablespoon Swerve
2 tablespoons sugar-free ketchup
Directions
Combine all meatloaf ingredients in a medium-large bowl. Press this mixture into 2 greased loaf pans. Bake at 370ºF (188ºC) for about 30 minutes. Meanwhile, make the glaze by combining all listed ingredients in a saucepan over medium heat. Simmer for 20 minutes, until the glaze is thickened. Pour ¼ cup of the glaze over the meatloaf. Save the extra for future use. Put the meatloaf back in the oven and cook for 20 more minutes.
Nutrition facts (per serving)
calories: 295 | fat: 18.9g | protein: 23.1g | carbs: 6.5g | net carbs: 6.1g | fiber: 0.4g

▶Tunisian Lamb and Pumpkin Ragout

Preparation time: 15 minutes
Cooking time: 8 hours | **Servings:** 6
Ingredients
¼ cup extra-virgin olive oil
1½ pounds (680 g) lamb shoulder, cut into 1-inch chunks
1 sweet onion, chopped
1 tablespoon minced garlic
4 cups pumpkin, cut into 1-inch pieces
2 carrots, diced
1 (14.5-ounce / 411-g) can diced tomatoes
3 cups beef broth
2 tablespoons ras el hanout
1 teaspoon hot chili powder
1 teaspoon salt
1 cup Greek yogurt

Directions

Lightly grease the slow cooker insert with 1 tablespoon olive oil. Place a large skillet over medium–high heat and add the remaining oil. Brown the lamb for 6 minutes, then add the onion and garlic. Sauté 3 minutes more, then transfer the lamb and vegetables to the insert. Add the pumpkin, carrots, tomatoes, broth, ras el hanout, chili powder, and salt to the insert and stir to combine. Cook on low cover and for about 8 hours. Serve topped with yogurt.

Nutrition facts (per serving)

calories: 450 | fat: 34.9g | protein: 22.1g | carbs: 11.9g | net carbs: 8.8g | fiber: 3.1g

›Spicy Beef Brisket Roast

Preparation time: 15 minutes
Cooking time: 60 minutes | **Servings:** 4
2 pounds (907 g) beef brisket
½ teaspoon celery salt
1 teaspoon chili powder
1 tablespoon avocado oil
1 tablespoon sweet paprika
A pinch of cayenne pepper
½ teaspoon garlic powder
½ cup beef stock
1 tablespoon garlic, minced
¼ teaspoon dry mustard

Directions

Preheat oven to 340°F (171°C). In a bowl, combine the paprika with dry mustard, chili powder, salt, garlic powder, cayenne pepper, and celery salt. Rub the meat with this mixture. Set a pan over medium-high heat and warm avocado oil, place in the beef, and sear until brown. Remove to a baking dish. Pour in the stock, add garlic and bake for 60 minutes. Set the beef to a cutting board, leave to cool before slicing and splitting in serving plates. Take the juices from the baking dish and strain, sprinkle over the meat, and enjoy.

Nutrition facts (per serving)

calories: 481 | fat: 23.6g | protein: 54.8g | carbs: 4.2g | net carbs: 3.3g | fiber: 0.9g

›Beef with Peppers

Preparation time: 15 minutes
Cooking time: 1 hour 5 minutes
Servings: 8
Ingredients
2 onions, chopped
2 tablespoons avocado oil
2 pounds (907 g) beef stew meat, cubed
2 red bell peppers, seeded and chopped
1 habanero pepper, chopped
4 green chilies, chopped
14.5 ounces (410 g) canned diced tomatoes
2 tablespoons fresh cilantro, chopped
4 garlic cloves, minced
½ cup vegetable broth
Salt and black pepper, to taste
1½ teaspoons cumin
½ cup black olives, chopped
1 teaspoon dried oregano

Directions

Set a pan over medium-high heat and warm avocado oil. Brown the beef on all sides; remove and set aside. Stir-fry in the red bell peppers, green chilies, oregano, garlic, habanero pepper, onions, and cumin, for about 5-6 minutes. Pour in the tomatoes and broth, and cook for 1 hour. Stir in the olives, adjust the seasonings and serve in bowls sprinkled with fresh cilantro.

Nutrition facts (per serving)

calories: 304 | fat: 14.1g | protein: 25.1g | carbs: 10.9g | net carbs: 7.9g | fiber: 3.0g

›Lamb Roast with Tomatoes

Preparation time: 10 minutes
Cooking time: 7 to 8 hours | **Servings:** 6
Ingredients
1 tablespoon extra-virgin olive oil
2 pounds (907 g) lamb shoulder roast
Salt, for seasoning
Freshly ground black pepper, for seasoning
1 (14.5-ounce / 411-g) can diced tomatoes
1 tablespoon cumin
2 teaspoons minced garlic
1 teaspoon paprika
1 teaspoon chili powder
1 cup sour cream
2 teaspoons chopped fresh parsley, for garnish

Directions:

Start greasing the insert of the slow cooker with the olive oil. Lightly season the lamb with salt and pepper. Place the lamb in the insert and add the tomatoes, cumin, garlic, paprika, and chili powder. Cook on low cover and for 7 to 8 hours. Stir in the sour cream. Serve topped with the parsley.

Nutrition facts (per serving)

calories: 524 | fat: 43.1g | protein: 27.9g | carbs: 5.9g | net carbs: 4.9g | fiber: 1.0g

›Pepperoni and Beef Pizza Meatloaf

Preparation time: 10 minutes
Cooking time: 60 minutes | **Servings:** 8
Ingredients
2 pounds (907 g) ground beef (80/20)
⅓ cup superfine blanched almond flour
¼ cup grated Parmesan cheese
1 tablespoon dried parsley
1 tablespoon dried onion flakes
1 teaspoon kosher salt
½ teaspoon dried oregano leaves
½ teaspoon garlic powder
½ teaspoon ground black pepper
2 large eggs
1 cup marinara sauce, store-bought or homemade, plus more for serving if desired
2 cups shredded whole-milk Mozzarella cheese
4 ounces (113 g) thinly sliced pepperoni
Chopped fresh parsley, for garnish (optional)

Directions

Preheat the oven to 370/375°F (190°C). Line a 9 by 4-inch loaf pan with foil, leaving 2 inches of foil folded over the outside edges of the pan. Place the ground beef, parsley, Parmesan cheese, almond flour, salt, onion flakes, oregano, garlic powder, pepper, and eggs in a medium-large bowl and mix well by hand until the texture is uniform. Press the meatloaf mixture into the loaf pan and flatten it out. Spoon the marinara over the top and then sprinkle with the Mozzarella. Layer the pepperoni slices on top. Bake, uncovered, until a meat thermometer in the center reads 165°F (74°C), or for 1 hour. Remove the meatloaf and let cool for about 8-10 minutes in the pan to allow it to firm up before slicing. Remove the meatloaf from the pan. Place on a cutting board and remove the foil. You can then cut it into slices and serve on individual plates, or spread some warm marinara sauce on the bottom of a serving platter, then place the loaf on top of the sauce and garnish with fresh parsley.

Nutrition facts (per serving)
calories: 440 | fat: 30.9g | protein: 32.8g | carbs: 3.4g | net carbs: 2.4g | fiber: 1.0g

›Beef Chuck Roast with Mushrooms

Preparation time: 15 minutes
Cooking time: 3 hours 10 minutes
Servings: 6
Ingredients
2 pounds (907 g) beef chuck roast, cubed
2 tablespoons olive oil
14.5 ounces (410 g) canned diced tomatoes
2 carrots, chopped
Salt and black pepper, to taste
½ pound (227 g) mushrooms, sliced
2 celery stalks, chopped
2 yellow onions, chopped
1 cup beef stock
1 tablespoon fresh thyme, chopped
½ teaspoon dry mustard
3 tablespoons almond flour
Directions
Set an ovenproof pot over medium heat, warm olive oil and brown the beef on each side for a few minutes. Stir in the tomatoes, onions, salt, pepper, mustard, carrots, mushrooms, celery, and stock. In a medium bowl, combine 1 cup water with flour. Place this to the pot, stir then set in the oven, and bake for 3 hours at 325°F (163°C) stirring at intervals of 30 minutes. Scatter the fresh thyme over and serve warm.

Nutrition facts (per serving)
calories: 326 | fat: 18.1g | protein: 28.1g | carbs: 10.4g | net carbs: 6.9g | fiber: 3.5g

›Balsamic Skirt Steak

Preparation time: 2 minutes
Cooking time: 6 minutes | **Servings:** 6
Ingredients
¼ cup balsamic vinegar (no sugar added)
2 tablespoons extra-virgin olive oil
1 tablespoon fresh chopped parsley
1 teaspoon minced garlic
1 teaspoon kosher salt
¼ teaspoon ground black pepper
2 pounds (907 g) skirt steak, trimmed of fat
Directions
In a medium-large bowl, whisk together the vinegar,

olive oil, parsley, garlic, salt, and pepper. Add the skirt steak and flip to ensure that the entire surface is covered in marinade. Cover with plastic wrap and marinate in the refrigerator for at least 2 hours, or up to 24 hours. Take the bowl out of the refrigerator and let the steak and marinade come to room temperature. Meanwhile, preheat a grill to high heat. Remove the steak from the marinade (don't forget toreserve the marinade) and place on the grill over direct high heat. Grill for about 2-3 mins per side for medium (recommended) or 5 minutes per side for well-done. Remove the steak from the grill when the desired doneness is reached and let rest for 10 minutes before slicing. Meanwhile, place the reserved marinade in the microwave and cook on high for 3 minutes, or until boiling. Stir and set aside; you will use the boiled marinade as a sauce for the steak. Slice the steak, being sure to cut against the grain for best results. Serve with the sauce.

Nutrition facts (per serving)
calories: 355 | fat: 25.1g | protein: 30.9g | carbs: 0g | net carbs: 0g | fiber: 0g

›Lamb Chops with Fennel and Zucchini

Preparation time: 10 minutes
Cooking time: 6 hours | **Servings:** 4
Ingredients
¼ cup extra-virgin olive oil, divided
1 pound (454 g) boneless lamb chops, about ½-inch thick
Salt, for seasoning
Freshly ground black pepper, for seasoning
½ sweet onion, sliced
½ fennel bulb, cut into 2-inch chunks
1 zucchini, cut into 1-inch chunks
¼ cup chicken broth
2 tablespoons chopped fresh basil, for garnish
Directions:
Start greasing the insert of the slow cooker with 1 tablespoon of the olive oil. Season the lamb with pepper and salt. In a medium bowl, toss well together the zucchini, onion, and fennel with the remaining 3 tbsps of the olive oil and then place half of the vegetables in the insert. Place the lamb on top of the vegetables, cover with the remaining vegetables, and add the broth. Cook on low and cover for 6 hours. Serve topped with the basil.

Nutrition facts (per serving)
calories: 430 | fat: 36.9g | protein: 20.9g | carbs: 5.0g | net carbs: 3.0g | fiber: 2.0g

›Beef Chuck and Pumpkin Stew

Preparation time: 15 minutes
Cooking time: 8 hours | **Servings:** 6
Ingredients
3 tablespoons extra-virgin olive oil, divided
1 (2-pound / 907-g) beef chuck roast, cut into 1-inch chunks
½ teaspoon salt
¼ teaspoon freshly ground black pepper
2 cups beef broth
1 cup diced tomatoes

¼ cup apple cider vinegar
1½ cups cubed pumpkin, cut into 1-inch chunks
½ sweet onion, chopped
2 teaspoons minced garlic
1 teaspoon dried thyme
1 tablespoon chopped fresh parsley, for garnish
Directions:
Start greasing the insert of the slow cooker with 1 tablespoon of the olive oil. Lightly season the beef chucks with salt and pepper. In a medium/large skillet over medium-high heat, heat the remaining 2 tablespoons of the olive oil. Add the beef and brown about 7 minutes, on all sides. Transfer the beef to the insert and stir in the broth, tomatoes, apple cider vinegar, pumpkin, onion, garlic, and thyme. Cook on low heat and cover for about 8 hours, until the beef is very tender. Serve topped with the parsley.
Nutrition facts (per serving)
calories: 460 | fat: 33.9g | protein: 32.0g | carbs: 10.2g | net carbs: 7.3g | fiber: 2.9g

›Hearty Beef and Pork Meatloaf

Preparation time: 15 minutes
Cooking time: 7 to 8 hours | **Servings:** 8
Ingredients
3 tablespoons extra-virgin olive oil, divided
½ sweet onion, chopped
2 teaspoons minced garlic
1 pound (454 g) ground beef
1 pound (454 g) ground pork
½ cup almond flour
½ cup heavy whipping cream
2 eggs
2 teaspoons dried oregano
1 teaspoon dried basil
¼ teaspoon salt
¼ teaspoon freshly ground black pepper
¾ cup tomato purée
1 cup goat cheese
Directions:
Start greasing the insert of the slow cooker with 1 tablespoon of the olive oil. In a medium skillet over medium-high heat, heat the remaining 2 tablespoons of the olive oil. Add the garlic and onion and sauté about 3 minutes, until the onion is softened. In a large bowl mix the onion mixture, beef, pork, almond flour, heavy cream, eggs, oregano, basil, salt, and pepper until well combined. Transfer the meat mixture to the insert and form into a loaf with about ½-inch gap on the sides. Spread the tomato purée on top of the meatloaf and sprinkle with goat cheese. Cook on low and cover for 7 to 8 hours. Serve warm.
Nutrition facts (per serving)
calories: 411 | fat: 28.9g | protein: 32.1g | carbs: 4.2g | net carbs: 1.1g | fiber: 3.1g

›Beef Chili

Preparation time: 20 minutes
Cooking time: 1 hour 20 minutes
Servings: 10
1 tablespoon olive oil
½ large onion (5.5 ounces / 156 g), chopped

8 cloves garlic, minced
2½ pounds (1.1 kg) ground beef
2 (14.5-ounce / 411-g) cans diced tomatoes, with liquid
1 (6-ounce / 170-g) can tomato paste
1 (4-ounce / 113-g) can green chiles, with liquid
¼ cup chili powder
2 tablespoons ground cumin
1 tablespoon dried oregano
2 teaspoons sea salt
1 teaspoon black pepper
1 medium bay leaf (optional)
Directions:
In a soup pot, preheat the oil over medium-high heat. Add the onion and cook for 4-7 minutes, until translucent, or longer if you like it caramelized. Add the garlic and cook for about 1-2 minutes or less, until fragrant. Add the ground beef and cook for 8 to 10 minutes, breaking apart with a spatula, until browned. Add all the remaining ingredients, except the bay leaf, and stir until combined. If desired, place the bay leaf in the middle and push down slightly. Reduce heat to low. Cook and cover for 1 hour, or until the flavors reach the desired intensity. Remove the bay leaf before serving.
Nutrition facts (per serving)
calories: 430 | fat: 26.8g | protein: 32.9g | carbs: 10.1g | net carbs: 8.0g | fiber: 2.1g

›Beef and Pimiento in Zucchini Boats

Preparation time: 10 minutes
Cooking time: 25 minutes | **Servings:** 4
Ingredients
4 zucchinis
2 tablespoons olive oil
1½ pounds (680 g) ground beef
1 medium red onion, chopped
2 tablespoons chopped pimiento
Pink salt and black pepper to taste
1 cup grated yellow Cheddar cheese
Directions
Preheat oven to 350°F (180°C). Lay the zucchinis on a flat surface, trim off the ends and cut in half lengthwise. Scoop out the pulp from each half with a spoon to make shells. Chop the pulp. Heat oil in a skillet; add the red onion, ground beef, pimiento, and zucchini pulp, and season with salt and black pepper. Cook for 6 minutes while stirring to break up lumps until beef is no longer pink. Turn the heat off. Spoon the beef into the boats and sprinkle with Cheddar cheese. Place on a greased baking sheet and cook to melt the cheese for 15 minutes until zucchini boats are tender. Take out, cool for 2 minutes, and serve warm with a mixed green salad.
Nutrition facts (per serving)
calories: 334 | fat: 24.0g | protein: 17.9g | carbs: 7.6g | net carbs: 6.9g | fiber: 0.7g

›Braised Beef Chuck Roast with Tomatoes

Preparation time: 15 minutes

Cooking time: 7 to 8 hours | **Servings:** 4
3 tablespoons extra-virgin olive oil, divided
1 pound (454 g) beef chuck roast, cut into 1-inch cubes
Salt, for seasoning
Freshly ground black pepper, for seasoning
1 (15-ounce / 425-g) can diced tomatoes
2 tablespoons tomato paste
2 teaspoons minced garlic
2 teaspoons dried basil
1 teaspoon dried oregano
½ teaspoon whole black peppercorns
1 cup shredded Mozzarella cheese, for garnish
2 tablespoons chopped parsley, for garnish

Directions:
Start greasing the insert of the slow cooker with 1 tablespoon of the olive oil. In a medium-large skillet over medium/high heat, heat the remaining 2 tablespoons of the olive oil. Season the beef with pepper and salt. Add the beef to the skillet and brown, about 7 minutes. Transfer the beef to the insert. In a medium-large bowl, stir together the tomatoes, tomato paste, garlic, basil, oregano, and peppercorns, and add the tomato mixture to the beef in the insert. Cover and cook on low for at least 7 hours. Serve topped with the cheese and parsley.

Nutrition facts (per serving)
calories: 540 | fat: 42.9g | protein: 29.8g | carbs: 6.9g | net carbs: 4.8g | fiber: 2.1g

➤Beef Chuck Chili con Carne

Preparation time: 8 minutes
Cooking time: 2 hours 15 minutes | **Servings:** 6
Ingredients
2 pounds (907 g) boneless beef chuck, trimmed and cut into 1-inch cubes
1 teaspoon kosher salt
½ teaspoon ground black pepper
2 tablespoons avocado oil or other light-tasting oil
½ cup chopped yellow onions
1 tablespoon minced garlic
3 cups beef broth, store-bought or homemade
1 tablespoon chili powder
2 teaspoons ground cumin
1 teaspoon cayenne pepper
1 teaspoon dried oregano leaves
1 teaspoon ground coriander
¼ teaspoon ground cinnamon
¼ cup canned chipotles in adobo sauce
1 tablespoon apple cider vinegar
1 tablespoon coconut flour

Directions
Season the beef with salt and pepper. Heat the oil in a large heavybottomed saucepan (make sure it has a lid) or a 4- or 6-quart Dutch oven over medium-high heat. Add the beef and brown on all sides, about 4 minutes. Remove the meat and set aside. Add in the garlic and onions to the pan and cook for 5 minutes, or until browned and translucent. Add the meat back to the pan along with the broth, spices, and chipotles. Simmer, covered, until the meat is tender, about 2 hours. Stir in the vinegar. Remove about ¼ cup of the sauce to a small bowl. Whisk the coconut flour into the

bowl of sauce, then add the sauce back to the pot and stir well.
Simmer, uncovered, for 5 more minutes, until the sauce has thickened. Taste and season with more pepper and salt, if desired.
Nutrition facts (per serving)
calories: 364 | fat: 26.9g | protein: 28.9g | carbs: 3.6g | net carbs: 2.0g | fiber: 1.6g

➤Broccoli and Beef Roast

Preparation time: 10 minutes
Cooking time: 4 hours 30 minutes | **Servings:** 2
Ingredients
1 pound (454 g) beef chuck roast
Pink Himalayan salt
Freshly ground black pepper
½ cup beef broth, plus more if needed
¼ cup soy sauce (or coconut aminos)
1 teaspoon toasted sesame oil
1 (16-ounce / 454-g) bag frozen broccoli
Directions
With the crock insert in place, preheat the slow cooker to low. On a cutting board, season the chuck roast with pink Himalayan salt and pepper, and slice the roast thin. Put the sliced beef in the slow cooker.
In a small bowl, mix together the beef broth, soy sauce, and sesame oil. Pour over the beef. Cook on low and cover for 4 hours. Add the frozen broccoli, and cook for 30 minutes more. If you need more liquid, add additional beef broth. Serve hot.
Nutrition facts (per serving)
calories: 805 | fat: 48.9g | protein: 73.8g | carbs: 18.1g | net carbs: 11.9g | fiber: 6.2g

➤Italian Sausage and Okra Stew

Preparation time: 20 minutes
Cooking time: 30 minutes | **Servings:** 6
Ingredients
1 pound (454 g) Italian sausage, sliced
1 red bell pepper, seeded and chopped
2 onions, chopped
Salt and black pepper, to taste
1 cup fresh parsley, chopped
6 green onions, chopped
¼ cup avocado oil
1 cup beef stock
4 garlic cloves
24 ounces (680 g) canned diced tomatoes
16 ounces (454 g) okra, trimmed and sliced
6 ounces (170 g) tomato sauce
2 tablespoons coconut aminos
1 tablespoon hot sauce
Directions
Set a pot over medium heat and warm oil, place in the sausages, and cook for 2 minutes. Stir in the onions, green onions, garlic, black pepper, bell pepper, and salt, and cook for 5 minutes. Add in the hot sauce, stock, tomatoes, coconut aminos, okra, and tomato sauce, bring to a simmer and cook for 15 minutes. Seasoning with black pepper and salt. Share into serving bowls and sprinkle with fresh parsley to serve.

Nutrition facts (per serving)
calories: 315 | fat: 25.1g | protein: 16.1g | carbs: 16.8g | net carbs: 6.9g | fiber: 8.9g

›Barbacoa Beef with Green Jalapeño

Preparation time: 10 minutes
Cooking time: 8 hours | **Servings:** 2
Ingredients
1 pound (454 g) beef chuck roast
Pink Himalayan salt
Freshly ground black pepper
4 chipotle peppers in adobo sauce
1 (6-ounce / 170-g) can green jalapeño chiles
2 tablespoons apple cider vinegar
½ cup beef broth
Directions
With the crock insert in place, preheat the slow cooker to low. Season the beef chuck roast on both sides with pink Himalayan salt and pepper. Put the roast in the slow cooker. In a food processor, combine the chipotle peppers and their adobo sauce, and apple cider vinegar, jalapeños, and pulse until smooth. Add the beef broth, and pulse 2 more times. Pour the chile mixture over the top of the roast. Cook on low and cover for about 7-8 hours. Transfer the beef to a cutting board, and use the forks to shred the meat. Serve.
Nutrition facts (per serving)
calories: 720 | fat: 45.8g | protein: 65.9g | carbs: 6.9g | net carbs: 2.1g | fiber: 4.8g

›Parmesan Beef Meatball alla Parmigiana

Preparation time: 10 minutes
Cooking time: 40 minutes | **Servings:** 4
Ingredients
For the Meatballs:
1 pound (454 g) ground beef (80/20)
2 tablespoons chopped fresh parsley
⅓ cup grated Parmesan cheese
¼ cup superfine blanched almond flour
1 large egg, beaten
1 teaspoon kosher salt
¼ teaspoon ground black pepper
¼ teaspoon garlic powder
¼ teaspoon onion powder
¼ teaspoon dried oregano leaves
¼ cup warm filtered water
1 cup marinara sauce, store-bought or homemade
1 cup shredded whole-milk Mozzarella cheese
Directions:
Preheat the oven to 350/355°F (185°C). Line a 15 by 10-inch sheet pan with foil or parchment paper. Put the ground beef, parsley, Parmesan, almond flour, egg, salt, pepper, garlic powder, onion powder, oregano, and water in a medium-sized bowl. Mix thoroughly by hand until fully combined. Form the meat mixture into 10-13 metballs about 1-3 inches in diameter and place them 2 inches apart on the sheet pan. Bake for 20-22 mins. Place the meatballs in a casserole dish large enough to fit all of the meatballs. Spoon the marinara evenly over the meatballs, then sprinkle the cheese over the meatballs.
Bake until the meatballs are cooked through, the sauce is bubbling, and the cheese is golden, or for 20 minutes. Garnish with chopped fresh parsley, if desired.
Nutrition facts (per serving)
calories: 431 | fat: 30.9g | protein: 32.9g | carbs: 4.8g | net carbs: 2.8g | fiber: 2.0g

›Lamb Shanks with Wild Mushrooms

Preparation time: 15 minutes
Cooking time: 7 to 8 hours | **Servings:** 6
Ingredients
3 tablespoons extra-virgin olive oil, divided
2 pounds (907 g) lamb shanks
½ pound (227 g) wild mushrooms, sliced
1 leek, thoroughly cleaned and chopped
2 celery stalks, chopped
1 carrot, diced
1 tablespoon minced garlic
1 (15-ounce / 425-g) can crushed tomatoes
½ cup beef broth
2 tablespoons apple cider vinegar
1 teaspoon dried rosemary
½ cup sour cream, for garnish
Directions:
Start greasing the insert of the slow cooker with 1 tablespoon of the olive oil. In a medium-large skillet over medium/high heat, heat the remaining 2 tablespoons of the olive oil. Add the lamb; brown for 6 minutes, turning once; and transfer to the insert. In the skillet, sauté the mushrooms, leek, celery, carrot, and garlic for 5 minutes. Transfer the vegetables to the insert along with the tomatoes, broth, apple cider vinegar, and rosemary. Cook on low and cover for 7 to 8 hours. Serve topped with the sour cream.
Nutrition facts (per serving)
calories: 474 | fat: 35.9g | protein: 30.9g | carbs: 11.1g | net carbs: 5.0g | fiber: 6.1g

›Hot Beef Tenderloin with Bell Peppers

Preparation time: 15 minutes
Cooking time: 9 to 10 hours | **Servings:** 6
Ingredients
3 tablespoons extra-virgin olive oil, divided
1 pound (454 g) beef tenderloin, cut into 1-inch chunks
½ sweet onion, chopped
2 teaspoons minced garlic
1 red bell pepper, diced
1 yellow bell pepper, diced
2 cups coconut cream
1 cup beef broth
3 tablespoons coconut aminos
1 tablespoon hot sauce
1 scallion, green and white parts, chopped, for garnish
1 tablespoon sesame seeds, for garnish
Directions:
Start greasing a bit the insert of the slow cooker with 1 tablespoon of the olive oil. In a medium-large skillet over medium/high heat, heat the remaining 2 tablespoons of the olive oil. Add the beef and brown for 6

minutes. Transfer to the insert. In the skillet, sauté the onion and garlic for 3 minutes.

Transfer the onion and garlic to the insert along with the red pepper, yellow pepper, coconut cream, broth, coconut aminos, and hot sauce. Cook on low and cover for 9 to 10 hours. Serve topped with the scallion and sesame seeds.

Nutrition facts (per serving)
calories: 442 | fat: 33.9g | protein: 24.8g | carbs: 10.9g | net carbs: 6.9g | fiber: 4.0g

›Coffee Rib-Eye Steaks

Preparation time: 5 minutes
Cooking time: 15 minutes | **Servings:** 2
Ingredients
Rub:
1 tablespoon ground coffee
1 tablespoon unsweetened cocoa powder
2 teaspoons kosher salt
¼ teaspoon cayenne pepper
2 (8-ounce / 227-g) bone-in rib-eye steaks, room temperature
Balsamic Butter:
3 tablespoons butter, softened
2 tablespoons balsamic vinegar (no sugar added)
1 teaspoon granulated erythritol
For Garnish (optional):
Chopped fresh parsley
Directions
Preheat a grill to medium heat. Combine the coffee, cocoa powder, salt, and cayenne in a small bowl. Rub the steaks generously with the coffee mixture. Grill the steaks on direct heat for 6 minutes (for medium) to 8 minutes (for medium-well) per side. Remove the steaks from the grill and let rest for about 5 minutes. Meanwhile, place the butter, balsamic vinegar, and sweetener in a small bowl and mix with a fork until blended. Serve the steaks with a generous dollop of balsamic butter. Garnish with chopped parsley, if desired.

Nutrition facts (per serving)
calories: 584 | fat: 44.9g | protein: 52.8g | carbs: 3.9g | net carbs: 2.9g | fiber: 1.0g

›Beef-Stuffed Pepper with Avocado Cream

Preparation time: 10 minutes
Cooking time: 20 minutes | **Servings:** 2
Ingredients
1 tablespoon butter
½ pound (227 g) ground beef
Pink Himalayan salt
Freshly ground black pepper
3 large bell peppers, in different colors
½ cup shredded cheese
Avocado Cream:
1 avocado
¼ cup sour cream
Directions
Preheat the oven to 390/400°F (205°C). Line a baking sheet with aluminum foil or a silicone baking mat.

In a medium-large skillet over medium-high heat, melt the butter. When the butter is hot, add the ground beef and season with pink Himalayan salt and pepper. Stir occasionally with a wooden spoon, breaking up the beef chunks. Continue cooking until the beef is done, 7 to 10 minutes. Cut off the top of each pepper, slice it in half, and pull out the seeds and ribs. Place the bell peppers on the prepared baking sheet. Spoon the ground beef into the peppers, sprinkle the cheese on top of each, and bake for 10 minutes. Meanwhile, in a medium bowl, mix the avocado and sour cream to create an avocado cream. Mix until smooth. When the peppers and beef are done baking, divide them between two plates, top each with the avocado cream, and serve.

Nutrition facts (per serving)
calories: 705 | fat: 51.9g | protein: 40.1g | carbs: 21.9g | net carbs: 12.8g | fiber: 9.1g

›Simple Pesto Beef Chuck Roast

Preparation time: 5 minutes
Cooking time: 9 to 10 hours | **Servings:** 8
Ingredients
1 tablespoon extra-virgin olive oil
2 pounds (907 g) beef chuck roast
¾ cup prepared pesto
½ cup beef broth
Directions:
Start greasing a bit the insert of the slow cooker with the olive oil. Slather the pesto all over the beef. Place the beef in the insert and pour in the broth. Cover and cook on low for 9 to 10 hours. Serve warm.

Nutrition facts (per serving)
calories: 529 | fat: 42.9g | protein: 31.9g | carbs: 1.9g | net carbs: 1.9g | fiber: 0g

›Harissa Seitan and Green Beans

Yield: 4 servings
Protein content nutrition facts (per serving): 16 g
Ingredients
1 tablespoon (15 ml) high heat neutral-flavored oil
8 ounces (227 g) Quit-the-Cluck Seitan, cut into ½-inch (1.3 cm) strips
2 handfuls green beans, trimmed, cut into bite-size pieces
½ of red bell pepper, cut into strips
1 leek, white part only, sliced into half-rounds
½ cup (80 ml) dry red wine, or vegetable broth
1½ tablespoons (24 g) harissa paste, or to taste
3 tablespoons (48 g) tomato paste
1 cup (235 ml) vegetable broth
2 cloves garlic, minced Juice from ½ lemon
Salt and pepper
Directions
Preheat the oil in a medium-large skillet over medium-high heat. Bake for 4 to 6 minutes, occasionally stirring to brown. Add the green beans and cook for at least 3 minutes until they are green. Add the pepper and the leek and cook for 2 minutes, stirring to soften but not soft. Add a glass of wine (75 ml) of wine or broth to the pan and lower each bit. Reduce heat to medium. Add harissa paste, tomato paste, broth, garlic and le-

mon juice. Stir to cover the olives and vegetables. Cook for 10 minutes, stirring occasionally. Season with salt and pepper.

►Easy Seitan for Two

Yield: 2 servings
Protein content nutrition facts (per serving): 43 g
Ingredients
½ teaspoon freshly ground black pepper
Pinch of fine sea salt
2 (each 4 ounces, or 113 g) Kind-to- Cows Seitan cutlets
1/3 cup (80 ml) vegetable broth
1 tablespoon (16 g) tomato paste
1 teaspoon balsamic vinegar
1 teaspoon Dijon mustard
1 teaspoon white miso
1 tablespoon (15 ml) high heat neutral-flavored oil
2 tablespoons (20 g) minced shallot
Directions
Rub the pepper and salt evenly into the seitan cutlets. Whisk together the broth, tomato paste, vinegar, mustard, and miso in a small bowl. Preheat the oil over medium/high heat in a medium-large skillet.
Put the cutlets into the skillet and cook for 3 to 5 minutes, until browned. Turnover and cook the second side for 3 to 4 minutes until also browned. Remove the cutlets and set aside. Reduce the heat to medium-low. Add the shallots. Cook and stir for about 2-3 mins, until softened. Be careful not to burn them. Scrape up any bits stuck to the skillet. Pour the broth mixture into the skillet. Bring to a simmer and stir for 3 to 4 minutes. Put the cutlets back into the skillet and turn to coat. Simmer for 3-4 minutes to heat the cutlets throughout. Spoon the sauce over the cutlets to serve.

►Pecan-Crusted Seitan Cutlets with Brussels Sprouts

Yield: 2 servings
Protein content nutrition facts (per serving): 51 g
Ingredients
For the cutlets:
½ cup (120 ml) unsweetened plain vegan milk
3 tablespoons (42 g) vegan mayonnaise
1 tablespoon (15 g) Dijon mustard
¼ teaspoon fine sea salt, plus a pinch
½ teaspoon ground black pepper, plus a pinch
½ cup plus 2 tablespoons (63 g) pecan halves, ground
3 tablespoons (15 g) panko crumbs
¼ teaspoons onion powder
2 (each 4 ounces, or 113 g) Kind-to* Cows Seitan cutlets
High heat neutral-flavored oil, for cooking
For the brussels sprouts:
1 tablespoon (15 ml) olive oil
12 ounces (340 g) of well- sliced Brussels sprouts
2 tablespoons (30 ml) vegetable broth
1 teaspoon Dijon mustard
3 tablespoons (21 g) grated carrots
Salt and pepper
Directions

To make the cutlets:
Whisk together the milk, mayonnaise, mustard, and a pinch each of salt and pepper in a shallow bowl. Combine the pecans, panko. Onion powder, and remaining salt and pepper on a plate. Stir to combine. Line a baking sheet with parchment paper. Cutlet in the milk mixture, then in the pecan mixture, turning to coat thoroughly. Put on the lined baking sheet and repeat with the second cutlet. Refrigerate for 15 minutes or up to 8 hours. This helps to set the coating so it will not fall off during cooking.
To cook the cutlets:
Heat a thin layer of olive oil in a medium-large heavy-bottomed skillet. Cook the cutlets for 5 to 7 minutes until browned. Turnover and cook the second side for 4 to 6 minutes until also browned.
To make the Brussels sprouts:
Heat the oil in a medium/large skillet over medium/high heat. Add the Brussels sprouts. Cook for about 6-8 minutes, stirring occasionally. The Brussels sprouts should have some dark spots and be tender. Whisk well together the broth and mustard in a small bowl. Turn the heat off. But leave the skillet on the weather. Stir in the broth mixture and the carrots. The liquid should evaporate or be absorbed — season to taste with salt and pepper. To serve, divide the Brussels sprouts between two plates and top each with a cutlet.

►Quit-the-Cluck Seitan

Yield: 6 cutlets (4 ounces, or 113 g each)
Protein content per cutlet: 41 g
For the seitan:
1¼ cups (150 g) vital wheat gluten
¼ cup (30 g) chickpea flour
3 tablespoons (22 g) nutritional yeast
1 tablespoon (7 g) onion powder
2 teaspoons dried poultry seasoning
1 teaspoon garlic powder
½ teaspoon ground white pepper
¼ cup (180 ml) vegetable broth
2 teaspoons no chicken bouillon paste
1 tablespoon (15 ml) olive oil
1 tablespoon high heat neutral-flavored oil, for cooking
For the cooking broth:
2 cups (470 ml) vegetable broth
1 tablespoon (8 g) nutritional yeast
2 teaspoons dried poultry seasoning
2 teaspoons onion powder
1 teaspoon Dijon mustard Salt and pepper
Directions
To make the seitan:
Preheat the oven to 290/300°F (150*C, or gas mark 2). Stir the dry ingredients together in a medium-size bowl. Stir the wet ingredients together in a measuring cup. Pour the wet ingredients into the dry ingredients and stir to combine. Knead with your hands until it forms a cohesive ball. Add tablespoon vital wheat gluten (9 g) or broth (15 ml), if needed, to reach the desired consistency. Divide into 6 equal portions. Sandwich a portion of dough between two pieces of parchment paper. Roll each portion into a cutlet that is no more

than 1/2 inch (1.3 cm) thick. Preheat the oil in a medium-large skillet over medium-high heat. Cook the cutlets (in batches) for 3 to 5 minutes until browned. Turnover and cook the second side for 3 minutes until browned.

To prepare the cooking broth:

Stir all the ingredients together in a 9 x 13-inch (22 x 23 cm) baking dish. Put the cutlets in the broth and cover the pan tightly with foil. Bake for 1 hour. Turn off the oven and let the seitan sit in the oven for 1 hour. Cool the seitan in the broth. Store the seitan and the broth separately in airtight containers in the refrigerator for up to three days or freeze for up to two months.

▸Best Baked Tofu and Kale

Yield: 4 servings
Protein content nutrition facts (per serving): 19 g
Ingredients
¼ cup (31 g) whole wheat pastry flour or (31 g) all-purpose flour
½ teaspoon ground white pepper
1 recipe Best Baked Tofu prepared
2 tablespoons (30 ml) high heat neutral-flavored oil
3 cloves garlic, thinly sliced
¼ cup (40 g) minced shallot
2 tablespoons (7 g) minced sun-dried tomatoes
4 cups (268 g) kale, chopped
1 can (14.5 ounces, or 412 g) diced tomatoes
½ cup (120 ml) vegetable broth
½ cup (60 ml) dry white wine
2 tablespoons (5 g) chopped fresh basil
Juice from ½ lemon
Salt and pepper
Directions
Preheat the oven to 340/350°F (180°C. or gas mark 4). Combine the pepper and flour on a plate. Coat the baked tofu slices with the mixture. Heat the oil in a medium/large skillet over medium-high heat. Cook the tofu slices (in batches) until browned, for 3 to 4 minutes. Turn over to cook the second side for about 3-4 minutes until also browned. Put the tofu in the oven to keep warm. In the same skillet, cook the garlic, shallot, and a pinch of salt over medium heat for 3 to 4 minutes, until fragrant. Add the sun-dried tomatoes, kale, tomatoes, broth, and wine (if using). Bring to a simmer, and then cook for 12 to 15 minutes until the kale is tender. Stir the basil and lemon juice and season to taste with salt and pepper. Serve the tofu slices on top of the greens.

▸Broccoli & Walnut Pesto

Yield: 4 servings
Ingredients
For the pesto:
1 head broccoli, cut into florets
75 g walnut pieces
2 cloves garlic
juice of 1 lemon
2 tbsp. olive oil
For the Pasta Alia Genovese:
500 g pasta
1 large floury potato, peeled and sliced thinly

200 g fine green beans

Directions
Boil a medium-large pot of water, then add the broccoli and cook for 5-6 minutes. Remove with a slotted spoon and place in the blender. Add the pasta and potato slices to the pot and boil again. Cook for 8 minutes, then add the green beans and cook for another 2 minutes or until the pasta is cooked. (Potato slices break while cooking, don't panic, imagine!). Meanwhile, add nuts, garlic, lemon and olive oil to the mixture with broccoli and cabbage to mix. Season generously with pepper and salt, then add a little water, cut again and continue cooking until it reaches a consistency similar to the sauce. Drain the pasta, potatoes, and beans, then return to the pot and stir through the broccoli plague. Heat the oven over low heat and stir to remove the pest. Serve immediately!

▸Broccoli, Kale, Chili & Hazelnut Pizza

Yield: 2 large pizzas
Ingredients
500 g Whole Meal Bread Mix
200 ml Passata with Garlic
1 red onion, peeled and finely sliced
6 sun-dried tomatoes, roughly chopped
75 g fresh curly kale, woody stalks removed and leaves roughly chopped
6-8 stalks purple sprouting broccoli, the lower half of stalks removed
1 red chili, finely sliced
handful hazelnuts, roughly chopped
dried oregano
black pepper
extra virgin olive oil
Directions
Pack the bread mix according to the instructions. Kneel and let it grow in a warm place for 45.45 minutes. Meanwhile, prepare the meatballs and heat the oven to 200 degrees Celsius at 400 degrees C with protein content nutrition facts (per serving) of 6 gasoline and put it in the oven if using a pizza stone. (Check if your stove has a specific pizza setting, many do, and that makes a big difference). Spread the dough on a floured surface and divide it in two. Insert each section into a ground ball and then roll with a roller in a 30 cm circle. When all the tanks are ready, and the stove is at maximum temperature, remove the pizza from the oven (or grease a baking sheet) or place the dough on the stone surface. Protein on each plate, cover with half the pasta, then the onion. Sprinkle with cabbage, broccoli, peppers, and hazelnuts, then sprinkle with mint and black pepper and sprinkle with olive oil. Repeat for the second pizza. Bake for 8-10 minutes until the slices brown and the base is well cooked.

▸Vegan Meatballs

Yield: 20 meatballs
Protein content nutrition facts (per serving) s: 14.8 g
Ingredients
For the meatballs:
110 g frozen peas

1 onion
2 tbsp. rapeseed or sunflower oil
1 tsp ready-chopped garlic Protein content nutrition facts (per serving) garlic puree
2 carrots
1 red pepper
large handful curly kale
400 g tin chickpeas
2 tbsp. olive oil
2 tbsp. nutritional yeast flakes (optional)
1 tsp vegetable stock powder
2 tbsp. gram flour
a little plain flour for dusting
For the sauce:
1 tbsp. dairy-free margarine
1 tbsp. plain flour
200 ml dairy-free milk (soy, nut or oat)
125 ml of boiling water
1 tsp vegetable stock powder
125 ml dairy-free cream (soy or oat)
2 tsp wholegrain mustard
soy sauce

Directions

Cook the peas in the microwave or a small pot for 2 minutes. Drain and set aside to cool. Peel the onion and cut it into quarters, then use a mini crusher or a food chopper (or cut it by hand). Heat the oil in a medium-large pot or large saucepan with oil and add the onions and garlic. Cook over medium heat. Peel the carrots and cut them into 4-5 slices, then finely chop the crushed protein content in each food processor and add it to the onions. Then, chop the peppers in the same way, then cook the peas and the curried cabbage. Let all the vegetables cook over medium heat. Drain and wash the chickpeas, then sprinkle with olive oil in a mini crusher or food processor in a nonstick skillet. Add to the pot, then sprinkle the yeast slices, the powdered broth, the warm flour, and a generous salt and pepper sauce. Mix all the ingredients, then remove from heat and let cool enough to cook. Sprinkle a handful of crushers and flour with a little flour, then glue a teaspoon of the mixture, wrap it tightly in a ball in your hand and place it on a crushing board. Repeat until the entire combination is used; It should have approximately 20 types of meat. Cover the bottom of a large pot with rapeseed or sunflower oil and fry the meatballs and turn until golden brown. Pour the cup into a plate covered with paper towels to drain the excess oil. To make the sauce, heat the margarine in a medium-small saucepan, stir the flour, and cook over medium heat for 2 minutes. Add non-dairy milk, water, powdered cream, and non-dairy cream and stir to mix until a thick and shiny sauce consistency is achieved. Add the mustard and stir well, then add a few drops of soy sauce at a time and try everything you want so that the condiments do not reach the right level. Serve the meatballs with the sauce on top, with mashed potatoes or French fries.

>Chipotle Black Bean Chili with Nachos

Yield: 2 servings
Ingredients

2 tbsp. rapeseed or sunflower oil
1 red onion
1 carrot
handful fresh coriander
1 tsp ready-chopped garlic Protein content nutrition facts (per serving) garlic puree
2-3 tsp chipotle paste (to your taste - 3 tsp is spicy)
1 red pepper
400 g tin black beans
400 g tin chopped tomatoes
pinch sugar
salt and black pepper

Directions

Heat the oil in a medium-large pot or a large bowl with oil. Peel the onions and carrots and remove the coriander stems from the leaves (remove them later). To chop onions, carrots, and coriander, use a mini crusher or food and then add it to the pot. Add garlic and pea paste to the pot and stir. Chop the seeds and finely chop the peppers and add them to the pan. Drain and wash the black beans and add them to the pot. Chop the tomatoes and sugar, then season with salt and black pepper. Then cover it with a lid and heat it over high heat. Cook for 8-10 minutes, stirring constantly. Adjust and adjust seasoning if necessary. Chop the coriander leaves thoroughly and chop the peppers before serving with rice, fajita or a handful of French fries. Heat the oil in a large pan. Half or a quarter of each giant mushroom and drop the smaller ones entirely and add them to the pot. Chop and chop the scallions and add to the pot with peanut nuts. Fill a pot with boiling water and add the noodles. Simmer for 5-6 minutes until freshly cooked. Drain and reserve. In a glass or small bowl, mix the pepper sauce, soy sauce, and water with the smooth saucer. When the mushrooms are cooked, and the peanuts are golden brown, pour the sauce into the pan and add the noodles when bubbling. Stir to combine, then serve immediately.

>Exotic Mushroom & Cashew Sweet Chili Noodles

Yield: 2 Servings
Ingredients
tbsp. rapeseed or sunflower oil
200 g mixed 'exotic' mushrooms
spring onions
tbsp. cashew nuts
150 g (3 nests) whole-wheat noodles
tbsp. sweet chili sauce
tbsp. soy sauce
150 ml water

Directions
Heat the oil in a medium-large pot or a large pan with oil. Peel the onions and carrots and remove the coriander stems from the leaves (remove them later). To chop onions, carrots, and coriander, use a mini crusher or food and then add it to the pot. Add garlic and pea paste to the pot and stir. Chop the seeds and finely chop the peppers and add them to the pan. Drain and wash the black beans and add them to the pot. Chop the tomatoes and sugar, then season with salt and black pepper. Then cover it with a

lid and heat it over high heat. Cook for 8-10 minutes, stirring constantly.

Adjust and adjust seasoning if necessary. Chop the coriander leaves thoroughly and chop the peppers before serving with rice, fajita or a handful of French fries.

›Easy Chicken Soup

Preparation Time: 10 minutes
Cooking Time: 1 hour
Servings: 14
Ingredients:
2 cups of Shredded chicken, cooked
1 cup of Carrots, diced
1 cup Celery, diced
1 cup of Onion, diced
10 cups of Chicken broth
1 tablespoon of Italian seasoning
1 Bay leaf
A dash of Sea salt
A dash of Black pepper
1 Spaghetti squash
Directions:
Combine all the ingredients minus the spaghetti squash in a pot over medium heat. Cook until it boils, then decrease to a simmer and cover the pot. Cook for one hour. Next, preheat the oven to about 375 degrees F, then punch holes in the spaghetti squash with a knife. Transfer to a baking sheet and bake in the oven for sixty minutes. When the spaghetti squash is cooked, cut in half and scoop out the strands using a fork. Remove the bay leaf and add in half of the spaghetti squash strands.
Nutrition facts:
Calories: 44
Carbohydrates: 4g
Protein: 5g
Fat: 1g

›Quick Healthy Avocado Tuna Salad

Preparation time: 10 minutes
Cooking Time: 0 minutes
Servings: 4
Ingredients:
2 Avocados
2 tablespoons of Lime juice
4 5-oz cans of Tuna, drained
1/4 cup of Fresh cilantro, chopped
3 tablespoons of Celery, finely chopped
3 tablespoons of red onion, minced
1 tablespoon of Jalapeños, minced
1/2 teaspoon of Sea salt
Directions:
Crush the lime juice and avocado in a bowl. Add in the sea salt and combine. Next, add in the cilantro, tuna, celery, red onion, and jalapeños. Stir to combine. Adjust seasonings as desired and serve.
Nutrition facts:
calories: 169
protein: 27g
fat: 14g
Carbohydrates: 10g

›Taco Casserole

Preparation Time: 30 minutes
Cooking Time: 1 Hour
Servings: 8
Ingredients:
1 lb. Ground Turkey
1 Cauliflower, Small & Chopped into Florets
1 Jalapeño Diced
¼ Cup Red Peppers, Diced
¼ Cup Onion, Diced
1 Teaspoon Cumin
1 Teaspoon Parsley
1 Teaspoon Garlic Minced
1 Teaspoon Turmeric
1 Teaspoon Oregano
1 ½ Cups Cheddar Cheese, Shredded
1 Cup Sour Cream
Directions:
Put your minced meat and cauliflower in a bowl before adding all your herbs and spices. Stir in your red peppers, jalapeños and onions together, mixing in a cup of your cheese. Pour into a casserole dish before topping with remaining cheese. Bake at 350 for an hour and serve with sour cream.
Nutrition facts:
Calories: 242
Protein: 18 Grams
Fat: 17 Grams
Net Carbs: 4 Grams

›Quick Blt Chicken Salad

Preparation Time: 20 minutes
Cooking Time: 0 minutes
Servings: 8
Ingredients:
1/2 cup of mayonnaise
3 to 4 tablespoons of barbecue sauce
2 tablespoons of finely chopped onion
1 tablespoon of lemon juice
1/4 teaspoon of pepper
8 cups of torn salad greens
2 tomatoes, chopped
10 strips of bacon, cooked and crumbled
2 hard-boiled eggs, sliced
1-1/2 pounds of boneless skinless chicken breasts, cooked and cubed
Directions:
Mix the first five ingredients in a bowl until combined. Cover the bowl and transfer the mixture to the refrigerator. Next, put the salad greens in a bowl. Add in the chicken, tomatoes, and bacon. Top with eggs and a drizzle of the dressing. Serve.
Nutrition facts:
Calories: 281
Protein: 23g
Fat: 19g
Carbohydrates: 5g

›Quick Roasted Tomato Soup

Preparation Time: 5 minutes
Cooking Time: 40 minutes
Servings: 6
Ingredients:
10 fresh Rome tomato, sliced into tubes
2 tablespoons of Olive oil
4 cloves of Garlic, minced
2 cup of Chicken bone broth
1 tablespoon of Herbs de Provence
1/2 teaspoon of Sea salt
1/4 teaspoon of Black pepper
1/4 cup of Heavy cream
2 tablespoons of Fresh basil
Directions:
First, preheat the oven to about 390/400 degrees F, then line a baking sheet with some foil, then grease the foil. Mix the tomato chunks with minced garlic and olive oil. Place the tomato chunks on a baking sheet. Transfer to the oven and bake until the skin wrinkles, about twentyfive minutes. Remove from the heat and put the tomato chunks into the blender and blend until smooth. Pour the tomato puree into the pot and place over medium-high heat. Add in the broth and season with sea salt, herbs de Provence, and black pepper. Boil for about fifteen minutes. Add in the basil and cream and serve.
Nutrition facts:
Calories: 95
Fat: 8g
Protein: 3g
Carbohydrates: 3g

›Delicious Low Carb Chicken Caesar Salad

Preparation Time: 10 minutes
Cooking Time: 6 minutes
Servings: 4
Ingredients:
1 cup of Parmesan crisps
1 head of Romaine lettuce, chopped
2 cup of Grape tomatoes, halved
2 grilled chicken breasts, sliced
For Keto Caesar Dressing:
1/3 cup of Caesar salad dressing
Directions:
Chill the Caesar salad dressing in the refrigerator. Combine the romaine lettuce, grape tomatoes, and cooked chicken. Break the cheese crisps into bits and sprinkle on the salad and drizzle with the dressing. Mix to combine.
Nutrition facts:
Calories: 400
Protein: 33g
Fat: 25g
Carbohydrates: 5g

›Cheesy Broccoli Soup

Preparation Time: 15 minutes
Cooking Time: 20 minutes
Servings: 8
Ingredients:

4 cups of Broccoli, chopped into florets
4 cloves of Garlic, minced
3 1/2 cups of Chicken broth
1 cup of Heavy cream
3 cups of Cheddar cheese
Directions:
Place a pot over medium-high heat, then add in the garlic and cook until fragrant. Add in the heavy cream, chopped broccoli, and chicken broth. Raise the heat and cook until it boils, then decrease heat. Cook until the broccoli is tender, about twenty minutes. Remove one third of the broccoli and keep aside. Blend the rest of the broccoli using an immersion blender. Decrease the heat to low. Add the cheddar cheese and stir well. Blend again to smooth. Remove from the heat source, then add in the reserved broccoli florets and serve.
Nutrition facts:
Calories: 292
Protein: 13g
Fat: 25g
Carbohydrates: 5g

›Low Carb Zucchini Alfredo

Preparation Time: 10 minutes
Cooking Time: 15 minutes
Servings: 4
Ingredients:
3 Zucchini
1 teaspoon of Butter
2 cloves of Garlic, minced
1/4 teaspoon of Nutmeg
1/2 cup of Unsweetened almond milk
1/3 cup of Heavy cream
3/4 cup of Grated Parmesan cheese
1 tablespoon of Arrowroot powder
A dash of Black pepper
Directions:
Prepare the zucchini noodles using a julienne peeler. Next, put butter into a skillet and place over medium-high heat. When heated, add in the garlic and cook until fragrant and soft, about a minute. Decrease the heat to low heat, then add in the heavy cream, almond milk, and nutmeg. Boil for some minutes. Combine the arrow root powder with two tablespoons of water in a bowl until dissolved, then pour into the sauce in the skillet. Add the Parmesan cheese and season with black pepper. Keep cooking while stirring frequently until the cheese melts. Transfer the sauce to a container and keep aside. Dry the zucchini using paper towels, then put in the noodles into the pan and stir fry over medium high heat. Cook until softened, about four minutes. Pour in the sauce and garnish with more Parmesan cheese and parsley. Serve.
Nutrition facts:
Servings: 1 cup
Calories: 209
Protein: 11g
Fat: 16g
Carbohydrates: 9g

➤Amazing Low Carb Shrimp Lettuce Wraps.

Preparation Time: 10 minutes
Cooking Time: 4 minutes
Servings: 4
Ingredients:
For Thai Shrimp:
1 lb of Shrimp, peeled, deveined
2 tablespoons of Coconut aminos
1/4 cup of Olive oil, divided
1/3 teaspoons of crushed red pepper flakes
1 tablespoon of Fish sauce
2 teaspoons of Lime juice
For Lettuce Wraps:
16 leaves of Bibb lettuce
1/3 fresh Cucumber, julienned
1 Avocado, diced
For Peanut Sauce:
1/4 cup of Peanut butter
1/4 cup of Coconut aminos
1 1/2 tablespoon of Lime juice
1/4 teaspoon of Sea salt
1/3 tsp of Crushed red pepper flakes
1/4 teaspoon of Garlic powder
For Garnish: Sliced green onions, lime wedges, roasted peanuts
Directions:
Combine two tablespoons of olive oil, coconut aminos, fish sauce, red peppers, and lime juice in a bowl. Add the shrimp and stir to mix. Cover the bowl and keep aside to marinate for thirty minutes. Combine the peanut sauce ingredients and keep aside. Pour two tbsps of oil into a pan and place over medium heat. Add in shrimp and cook for about six minutes, or until opaque. Share the cucumbers, shrimp, and avocados among the lettuce leaves. Add in a drizzle of peanut sauce and garnish with peanuts, green onions, and lime wedges if desired.
Nutrition facts:
Servings: 4 lettuce wraps
Calories: 470
Protein: 29g
Fat: 31g
Carbohydrates: 16g

➤Tasty Low Carb Cucumber Salad.

Preparation Time: 10 minutes
Cooking Time: 0 minutes
Servings: 6
Ingredients:
1/2 cup of Sour cream
2 tablespoons of Fresh dill, chopped
1 tablespoon of Olive oil
1 tablespoon of Lemon juice
1/2 teaspoon of Garlic powder
1/2 teaspoon of Sea salt
1/4 teaspoon of Black pepper
6 cups of Cucumber, chopped
1 Red onion, thinly sliced
Directions:
Combine the dill, sour cream, olive oil, garlic powder, and lemon juice in a bowl. Season the mixture with

black pepper and sea salt. Add in the red onions and chopped cucumbers. Serve.
Nutrition facts:
Servings: one cup
Calories: 86
Protein: 2g
Fat: 6g
Carbohydrates: 7g

➤Classic Low Carb Cobb Salad

Preparation Time: 30 minutes
Cooking Time: 10 minutes
Servings: 6
Ingredients:
1/4 cup of red wine vinegar
2 teaspoons of salt
1 teaspoon of lemon juice
1 clove of garlic, minced
3/4 teaspoon of coarsely ground pepper
3/4 teaspoon of Worcestershire sauce
1/4 teaspoon of sugar
1/4 teaspoon of ground mustard
3/4 cup of canola oil
1/4 cup of olive oil
For Salad:
6-1/2 cups of torn romaine
2-1/2 cups of torn curly endive
1 bunch of watercress, trimmed, divided
2 chicken breasts, cooked, chopped
2 tomatoes, seeded and chopped
1 ripe avocado, peeled and chopped
3 boiled large eggs, chopped
1/2 cup of crumbled blue
6 cooked bacon strips, crumbled
2 tablespoons of minced fresh chives
Directions:
Puree the first eight Ingredients in the blender, while adding in olive and canola oils until smooth. Mix the endive, romaine, and half of watercress in a bowl. Transfer to a platter, then assemble the tomatoes, chicken, eggs, avocado, bacon, and cheese on the greens. Top with chives and rest of the watercress. Drizzle one cup of dressing over the salad. serve.
Nutrition facts:
Servings: 1
Calories: 577
Protein:20g
Fat:52g
Carbohydrates: 10g

➤Yummy Mushroom Asparagus Frittata

Preparation Time: 25 minutes
Cooking Time: 20 minutes
Servings: 8
Ingredients:
8 eggs
1/2 cup of whole-milk ricotta cheese
2 tablespoons of lemon juice
1/2 teaspoon of salt
1/4 teaspoon of pepper
1 tablespoon of olive oil
1 package of frozen asparagus spears, thawed

1 onion, halved and thinly sliced
1/4 cup of baby portobello mushrooms, sliced
1/2 cup of sweet green or red pepper, finely chopped
Directions:
First, preheat the oven to about 340/350 degrees F, then whisk the ricotta cheese, eggs, pepper, lemon juice and salt in a bowl. Pour oil into a skillet and add in onion, asparagus, mushrooms, and red pepper. Cook until pepper and onions are tender, about eight minutes. Add in the egg mixture and transfer to the oven. Bake eggs about twenty-five minutes. Keep aside to cool, then cut into wedges.
Nutrition facts:
Servings: one wedge
calories: 130
protein: 9g
fat: 8g
Carbohydrates: 5g

➤Special Almond Cereal

Preparation Time: 5 minutes
Cooking Time: 5 minutes
Servings: 1
Ingredients:
2 tablespoons almonds; chopped.
1/3 cup coconut milk
1 tablespoon chia seeds
2 tablespoon pepitas; roasted
A handful blueberries
1 small banana; chopped.
1/3 cup water
Directions:
In a bowl, mix well coconut milk with chia seeds and leave aside for about 5 minutes. In your food processor, mix well half of the pepitas with almonds and pulse them well. Add this to chia seeds mix. Also add the water and stir. Top with the rest of the pepitas, blueberries and banana pieces and serve
Nutrition facts:
Calories: 200
Fat: 3
Fiber: 2
Carbs: 5
Protein: 4

➤Awesome Avocado Muffins

Preparation Time: 10 minutes
Cooking Time: 20 minutes
Servings: 12
Ingredients:
6 bacon slices; chopped.
1 yellow onion; chopped.
1/2 teaspoon baking soda
1/2 cup coconut flour
1 cup coconut milk
2 cups avocado; pitted, peeled and chopped.
4 eggs
Salt and black pepper to taste.
Directions:
Heat up a pan, add onion and bacon; stir and brown for a few minutes. In a bowl, mash avocado pieces with a fork and whisk well with the eggs. Add milk,

salt, pepper, baking soda and coconut flour and stir everything. Add bacon mix and stir again. Add coconut oil to muffin tray, divide eggs and avocado mix into the tray, heat oven at 340-350 degrees F and bake for 20 minutes. Divide muffins between plates and serve them.
Nutrition facts:
Calories: 200
Fat: 7
Fiber: 4
Carbs: 7
Protein: 5

➤WW Breakfast Cereal

Preparation Time: 10 minutes
Cooking Time: 3 minutes
Servings: 2
Ingredients:
1/2 cup coconut; shredded
1/3 cup macadamia nuts; chopped.
4 teaspoons ghee
2 cups almond milk
1 tablespoon stevia
1/3 cup walnuts; chopped.
1/3 cup flax seed
A pinch of salt
Directions:
Heat a pot of mistletoe over medium heat. Add the milk, coconut, salt, macadamia nuts, walnuts, flax seeds, and stevia and mix well. Cook for about 3 minutes. Stir again, remove from heat for about 10 minutes. Divide into 2 bowls and serve
Nutrition facts:
Calories: 140
Fat: 3
Fiber: 2
Carbs: 1. 5
Protein: 7

➤Yummy Smoked Salmon

Preparation Time: 10 minutes
Cooking Time: 10 minutes
Servings: 3
Ingredients:
4 eggs; whisked
1/2 teaspoon avocado oil
4 ounces smoked salmon; chopped.
For the sauce:
1/2 cup cashews; soaked; drained
1/4 cup green onions; chopped.
1 teaspoon garlic powder
1 cup coconut milk
1 tablespoon lemon juice
Salt and black pepper to taste.
Directions:
In your blender, mix well cashews with coconut milk, garlic powder and lemon juice and blend well. Add pepper, salt and green onions, blend again, transfer to a bowl and keep in the fridge for now. Preheat a pan with the oil over medium-low heat; add eggs, whisk a bit and cook until they are almost done Introduce in your broiler and cook until eggs set.

Divide eggs on plates, top with smoked salmon and serve with the sauce on top.

Nutrition facts:
Calories: 200
Fat: 10
Fiber: 2
Carbs: 11
Protein: 15

➤Almond Coconut Cereal

Preparation Time: 5 minutes
Cooking Time: 5 minutes
Servings: 2
Ingredients:
Water, 1/3 cup.
Coconut milk, 1/3 cup.
Roasted sunflower seeds, 2 tablespoons.
Chia seeds, 1 tablespoon.
Blueberries, ½ cup.
Chopped almonds, 2 tablespoons.
Directions:
Set a medium-large bowl in position to add coconut milk and chia seeds then reserve for five minutes. Set the blender in position to blend almond with sunflower seeds. Stir the combination to chia seeds mixture then add water to mix evenly. Serve topped with the remaining sunflower seeds and blueberries

Nutrition facts:
Calories: 181
Fat: 15.2
Fiber: 4
Carbs: 10.8
Protein: 3.7

➤Almond Porridge

Preparation Time: 10 minutes
Cooking Time: 5 minutes
Servings: 1
Ingredients:
Ground cloves, ¼ teaspoon.
Nutmeg, ¼ teaspoon.
Stevia, 1 teaspoon.
Coconut cream, ¾ cup.
Ground almonds, ½ cup.
Ground cardamom, ¼ teaspoon.
Ground cinnamon, 1 teaspoon.
Directions:
Set your pan over medium heat to cook the coconut cream for a few minutes. Stir in almonds and stevia to cook for 5 minutes. Mix in nutmeg, cardamom, and cinnamon. Enjoy while still hot

Nutrition facts:
Calories: 695
Fat: 66.7
Fiber: 11.1
Carbs: 22
Protein: 14.3

➤Asparagus Frittata Recipe

Preparation Time: 20 minutes

Cooking Time: 20 minutes
Servings: 4
Ingredients:
Bacon slices, chopped: 4
Salt and black pepper
Eggs (whisked): 8
Asparagus (trimmed and chopped): 1 bunch
Directions:
Heat a pan, add bacon, stir and cook for 5 minutes. Add salt, asparagus, and pepper, stir and cook for another 5 minutes. Add the chilled eggs, spread them in the pan, let them stand in the oven and bake for 20 minutes at 350° F. Share and divide between plates and serve for breakfast.

Nutrition facts:
Calories 251
Carbs 16
Fat 6
Fiber 8
Protein 7

➤Avocados Stuffed with Salmon

Preparation Time: 5 minutes
Cooking Time: 5 minutes
Servings: 2
Ingredients:
Avocado (pitted and halved): 1
Olive oil: 2 tablespoons
Lemon juice: 1
Smoked salmon (flaked): 2 ounces
Goat cheese (crumbled): 1 ounce
Salt and black pepper
Directions:
Combine the salmon with lemon juice, oil, cheese, salt, and pepper in your food processor and pulsate well. Divide this mixture into avocado halves and serve. Dish and Enjoy!

Nutrition facts:
Calories: 300
Fat: 15
Fiber: 5
Carbs: 8
Protein: 16

➤Bacon and Brussels Sprout Breakfast

Preparation Time: 10 minutes
Cooking Time: 15 minutes
Servings: 3
Ingredients:
Apple cider vinegar, 1½ tablespoons.
Salt
Minced shallots, 2
Minced garlic cloves, 2
Medium eggs, 3
Sliced Brussels sprouts, 12 oz.
Black pepper
Chopped bacon, 2 oz.
Melted butter, 1 tablespoon.
Directions:
Over medium heat, quick fry the bacon until crispy then reserve on a plate. Set the pan on fire again to fry garlic and shallots for 30 seconds. Stir in apple cider

vinegar, Brussels sprouts, and seasoning to cook for five minutes. Add the bacon to cook for five minutes then stir in the butter and set a hole at the center Crash the eggs to the pan and let cook fully Enjoy

Nutrition facts:
Calories: 275
Fat: 16.5
Fiber: 4.3
Carbs: 17.2
Protein: 17.4

➤Onion and Zucchini Platter

Preparation Time: 15 minutes
Cooking time: 45 minutes
Servings: 4
Ingredients:
large zucchinis, julienned
cup cherry tomatoes, halved
1/2 cup basil
red onions, thinly sliced
1/4 teaspoon salt
teaspoon cayenne pepper
tablespoons lemon juice
Directions:
Create zucchini Zoodles by using a vegetable peeler and shaving the zucchini with a peeler lengthwise, until you get to the core and seeds. Turn zucchini and repeat until you have long strips. Discard seeds. Lay strips on a cutting board and slice lengthwise to your desired thickness. Mix Zoodles in a bowl alongside onion, basil, tomatoes, and toss. Sprinkle salt and cayenne pepper on top. Drizzle lemon juice. Serve and enjoy!
Nutrition facts:
Calories: 156
Fat: 8g
Carbohydrates: 6g
Protein: 7g

➤Lemon Flavored Sprouts

Preparation Time: 10 minutes
Cooking time: 0 minutes
Servings: 4
Ingredients:
1 pound Brussel sprouts, trimmed and shredded
8 tablespoons olive oil
1 lemon, juiced and zested
Salt and pepper to taste
3/4 cup spicy almond and seed mix
Directions:
Take a bowl and mix in lemon juice, salt, pepper and olive oil. Mix well. Stir in shredded Brussel sprouts and toss. Let it sit for 10 minutes. Add nuts and toss
Nutrition facts:
Calories: 382
Fat: 36g
Carbohydrates: 9g
Protein: 7g

➤Paprika Cauliflower Steaks with Walnut Sauce

Preparation time: 5 minutes
Cooking time: 30 minutes | **Servings:** 2
Ingredients
Walnut Sauce:
½ cup raw walnut halves
2 tablespoons virgin olive oil, divided
1 clove garlic, chopped
1 small yellow onion, chopped
½ cup unsweetened almond milk
2 tablespoons fresh lemon juice
Salt and pepper, to taste
Paprika Cauliflower:
1 medium head cauliflower
1 teaspoon sweet paprika
1 teaspoon minced fresh thyme leaves
Directions
Preheat the oven to 340/350°F (180°C).
Make the walnut sauce:
Toast the walnuts in a large, ovenproof skillet over medium heat until fragrant and slightly darkened, about 5 minutes. Transfer the walnuts to a blender. Heat 2 tablespoon of olive oil in the skillet. Add the onion and garlic and sauté for about 2 minutes, or until slightly softened. Transfer the garlic and onion into the blender, along with the almond milk, lemon juice, salt, and pepper. Blend the ingredients until smooth and creamy. Keep the sauce warm while you prepare the cauliflower.
Make the paprika cauliflower:
Cut two 1-inch-thick "steaks" from the center of the cauliflower. Lightly moisten the steaks with water and season both sides with paprika, thyme, salt, and pepper. Preheat the remaining 1 tablespoon of olive oil in the skillet over medium-high heat. Add the cauliflower steaks and sear for about 3 minutes until evenly browned. Flip the cauliflower steaks and transfer the skillet to the oven. Roast in the preheated oven for about 18-20 minutes until crisp-tender. Serve the cauliflower steaks warm with the walnut sauce on the side.
Nutrition facts (per serving)
calories: 367 | fat: 27.9g | protein: 7.0g | carbs: 22.7g | fiber: 5.8g | sodium: 173mg

➤Stir-Fried Eggplant

Preparation time: 25 minutes
Cooking time: 15 minutes | **Servings:** 2
Ingredients
1 cup water, plus more as needed
½ cup chopped red onion
1 tablespoon finely chopped garlic
1 tablespoon dried Italian herb seasoning
1 teaspoon ground cumin
1 small eggplant (about 8 ounces / 227 g), peeled and cut into ½-inch cubes
1 medium carrot, sliced
2 cups green beans, cut into 1–2-inch pieces
2 ribs celery, sliced
1 cup corn kernels
2 tablespoons almond butter
2 medium tomatoes, chopped

Directions

Heat 1 tablespoon of water in a medium-large soup pot over medium-high heat until it sputters. Cook the onion for 2 minutes, adding a little more water as needed.

Add the garlic, Italian seasoning, cumin, and eggplant and stir-fry for 2 to 3 minutes, adding a little more water as needed. Add the carrot, green beans, celery, corn kernels, and ½ cup of water and stir well. Low the heat to medium, cover, and cook for 8 to 10 minutes, stirring occasionally, or until the vegetables are tender. Meanwhile, in a bowl, stir together the almond butter and ½ cup of water. Remove the vegetables from the heat and stir in the almond butter mixture and chopped tomatoes. Cool for a few minutes before serving.

Nutrition facts (per serving)

calories: 176 | fat: 5.5g | protein: 5.8g | carbs: 25.4g | fiber: 8.6g | sodium: 198mg

➤Honey-Glazed Baby Carrots

Preparation time: 5 minutes
Cooking time: 6 minutes | **Servings:** 2
Ingredients
⅔ cup water
1½ pounds (680 g) baby carrots
4 tablespoons almond butter
½ cup honey
1 teaspoon dried thyme
1½ teaspoons dried dill
Salt, to taste
Directions
Put the water into the Instant Pot and add a steamer basket. Place the baby carrots in the basket. Secure the lid. Select the Manual mode and set the cooking time for about 4 minutes at High Pressure. Once cooked, do a quick pressure release. Carefully open the lid. Transfer the carrots to a plate. Pour the water out of the Instant Pot and dry it. Press the Sauté button on the Instant Pot and heat the almond butter. Stir in the honey, thyme, and dill. Return the carrots to the Instant Pot and stir until well coated. Sauté for another 1 minute. Taste and season with salt as needed. Serve warm.

Nutrition facts (per serving)
calories: 575 | fat: 23.5g | protein: 2.8g | carbs: 90.6g | fiber: 10.3g | sodium: 547mg

➤Quick Steamed Broccoli

Preparation time: 5 minutes
Cooking time: 10 minutes | **Servings:** 2
Ingredients
¼ cup water
3 cups broccoli florets
Salt and ground black pepper, to taste
Directions
Put the water into the Instant Pot and insert a steamer basket. Place the broccoli florets in the basket. Secure the lid. Select the Manual mode and set the cooking time for 10 minutes at High Pressure. Once cooked, do a quick pressure release. Carefully open the lid. Transfer the broccoli florets to a bowl

with cold water to keep bright green color. Season the broccoli with salt and pepper to taste, then serve.

Nutrition facts (per serving)
calories: 16 | fat: 0.2g | protein: 1.9g | carbs: 1.7g | fiber: 1.6g | sodium: 292mg

➤Garlic-Butter Asparagus with Parmesan

Preparation time: 5 minutes
Cooking time: 8 minutes | **Servings:** 2
Ingredients
1 cup water
1 pound (454 g) asparagus, trimmed
2 cloves garlic, chopped
3 tablespoons almond butter
Salt and ground black pepper, to taste
3 tablespoons grated Parmesan cheese
Directions
Put the water into the Instant Pot and insert a trivet. Put the asparagus on a tin foil add the butter and garlic. Season to taste with salt and pepper. Fold over the foil and seal the asparagus inside so the foil doesn't come open. Arrange the asparagus on the trivet. Select the Manual mode and set the cooking time for 8 minutes at High Pressure. Once cooked, do a quick pressure release. Carefully open the lid. Unwrap the foil packet and serve sprinkled with the Parmesan cheese.

Nutrition facts (per serving)
calories: 243 | fat: 15.7g | protein: 12.3g | carbs: 15.3g | fiber: 7.3g | sodium: 435mg

➤Ratatouille

Preparation time: 10 minutes
Cooking time: 6 minutes | **Servings:** 4
Ingredients
2 large zucchinis, sliced
2 medium eggplants, sliced
4 medium tomatoes, sliced
2 small red onions, sliced
4 cloves garlic, chopped
2 tablespoons thyme leaves
2 teaspoons sea salt
1 teaspoon black pepper
2 tablespoons balsamic vinegar
4 tablespoons olive oil
2 cups water
Directions
Line a springform pan with foil and place the chopped garlic in the bottom. Now arrange the vegetable slices, alternately, in circles. Sprinkle the thyme, pepper and salt over the vegetables. Top with oil and vinegar. Pour a cup of water into the pot and place the trivet inside. Secure the lid and cook on Manual function for 6 minutes at High Pressure. Release the pressure naturally and remove the lid. Remove the vegetables along with the tin foil. Serve on a platter and enjoy.

Nutrition facts (per serving)
calories: 240 | fat: 14.3g | protein: 4.7g | carbs: 27.5g

| fiber: 10.8g | sodium: 1181mg

‣Mushroom and Potato Teriyaki

Preparation time: 10 minutes
Cooking time: 18 minutes | **Servings:** 4
¾ large yellow or white onion, chopped
1½ medium carrots, diced
1½ ribs celery, chopped
1 medium portabella mushroom, diced
¾ tablespoon garlic, chopped
2 cups water
1 pound (454 g) white potatoes, peeled and diced
¼ cup tomato paste
½ tablespoon sesame oil
2 teaspoons sesame seeds
½ tablespoon paprika
1 teaspoon fresh rosemary
¾ cups peas
¼ cup fresh parsley for garnishing, chopped
Directions
Add the oil, sesame seeds, and all the vegetables in the instant pot and Sauté for 5 minutes. Stir in the remaining ingredients and secure the lid. Cook on Manual function for 13 minutes at High Pressure. After the beep, natural release the pressure and remove the lid. Garnish with fresh parsley and serve hot.
Nutrition facts (per serving)
calories: 160 | fat: 3.0g | protein: 4.7g | carbs: 30.6g
| fiber: 5.5g | sodium: 52mg

‣Peanut and Coconut-Stuffed Egg-plants

Preparation time: 15 minutes
Cooking time: 9 minutes | **Servings:** 4
Ingredients
1 tablespoon coriander seeds
½ teaspoon cumin seeds
½ teaspoon mustard seeds
2 to 3 tablespoons chickpea flour
2 tablespoons chopped peanuts
2 tablespoons coconut shreds
1-inch ginger, chopped
2 cloves garlic, chopped
1 hot green chili, chopped
½ teaspoon ground cardamom
A pinch of cinnamon
⅓ to ½ teaspoon cayenne
½ teaspoon turmeric
½ teaspoon raw sugar
½ to ¾ teaspoon salt
1 teaspoon lemon juice
Water as needed
4 baby eggplants
Fresh Cilantro for garnishing
Directions
Add the coriander, mustard seeds and cumin in the instant pot. Roast on Sauté function for 2 minutes. Add the chickpea flour, nuts and coconut shred to the pot, and roast for 2 minutes. Blend this mixture in a blender, then transfer to a medium-sized bowl. Roughly blend the ginger, garlic, raw sugar, chili, and

all the spices in a blender. Add the water and lemon juice to make a paste. Combine it with the dry flour mixture. Cut the eggplants from one side and stuff with the spice mixture. Put 1 cup of water to the instant pot and place the stuffed eggplants inside. Sprinkle some salt on top and secure the lid.
Cook on Manual for 4-5 minutes at High Pressure, then quick release the steam.
Remove the lid and garnish with fresh cilantro, then serve hot.
Nutrition facts (per serving)
calories: 207 | fat: 4.9g | protein: 7.9g | carbs: 39.6g
| fiber: 18.3g | sodium: 315mg

‣Cauliflower with Sweet Potato

Preparation time: 15 minutes
Cooking time: 8 minutes | **Servings:** 8
Ingredients
1 small onion
4 tomatoes
4 garlic cloves, chopped
2-inch ginger, chopped
2 teaspoons olive oil
1 teaspoon turmeric
2 teaspoons ground cumin
Salt, to taste
1 teaspoon paprika
2 medium sweet potatoes, cubed small
2 small cauliflowers, diced
2 tablespoons fresh cilantro for topping, chopped
Directions
Blend the tomatoes, garlic, ginger and onion in a blender. Add the oil and cumin in the instant pot and Sauté for 1 minute. Stir in the blended mixture and the remaining spices. Add the sweet potatoes and cook for at least 5 minutes on Sauté. Add the cauliflower chunks and secure the lid. Cook on Manual for 2 minutes at High Pressure. Once done, release the pressure and remove the lid. Stir and serve with cilantro on top.
Nutrition facts (per serving)
calories: 76 | fat: 1.6g | protein: 2.7g | carbs: 14.4g |
fiber: 3.4g | sodium: 55mg

‣Potato Curry

Preparation time: 10 minutes
Cooking time: 30 minutes | **Servings:** 2
Ingredients
2 large potatoes, peeled and diced
1 small onion, peeled and diced
8 ounces (227 g) fresh tomatoes
1 tablespoon olive oil
2 cup water
2 tablespoons garlic cloves, grated
½ tablespoon rosemary
½ tablespoon cayenne pepper
1½ tablespoons thyme
Salt and pepper, to taste
Directions
Add 2 cup of water in the instant pot and place the steamer trivet inside. Place the potatoes and half the garlic over the trivet and sprinkle some salt and pepper on top. Secure the lid and cook on Steam fun-

ction for 20 minutes. After the beep, natural release the pressure and remove the lid. Put the potatoes to one side and empty the pot. Add the remaining ingredients to the cooker and Sauté for 10 minutes. Use an immerse blender to purée the cooked mixture. Stir in the steamed potatoes and serve hot.

Nutrition facts (per serving)
calories: 398 | fat: 7.6g | protein: 9.6g | carbs: 76.2g | fiber: 10.9g | sodium: 111mg

›Mushroom, Potato, and Green Bean Mix

Preparation time: 10 minutes
Cooking time: 18 minutes | **Servings:** 3
Ingredients
1 tablespoon olive oil
½ carrot, peeled and minced
½ celery stalk, minced
½ small onion, minced
1 garlic clove, minced
½ teaspoon dried sage, crushed
½ teaspoon dried rosemary, crushed
4 ounces (113 g) fresh Portabella mushrooms, sliced
4 ounces (113 g) fresh white mushrooms, sliced
¼ cup red wine
1 Yukon Gold potato, peeled and diced
¾ cup fresh green beans, trimmed and chopped
1 cup tomatoes, chopped
½ cup tomato paste
½ tablespoon balsamic vinegar
3 cups water
Salt and freshly ground black pepper
2 ounces (57 g) frozen peas
½ lemon juice
2 tablespoons fresh cilantro for garnishing, chopped
Directions
Put the oil, onion, tomatoes and celery into the instant pot and Sauté for 5-6 minutes. Stir well the herbs and garlic and cook for about 1 minute. Add the mushrooms and sauté for 5 minutes. Stir in the wine and cook for additional 2 minutes. Add the diced potatoes and mix. Cover the pot with a lid and let the potatoes cook for 2-3 minutes. Now add the green beans, carrots, tomato paste, peas, salt, pepper, water and vinegar. Secure the lid and cook on Manual function for 8 minutes at High Pressure with the pressure valve in the sealing position. Do a quick release and open the pot, stir the veggies and then add lemon juice and cilantro, then serve with rice or any other of your choice.
Nutrition facts (per serving)
calories: 238 | fat: 5.4g | protein: 8.3g | carbs: 42.7g | fiber: 8.5g | sodium: 113mg

›Mushroom Tacos

Preparation time: 10 minutes
Cooking time: 13 minutes | **Servings:** 3
Ingredients
4 large guajillo chilies
2 teaspoons oil
2 bay leaves
2 large onions, sliced
2 garlic cloves
2 chipotle chillies in adobo sauce
2 teaspoons ground cumin
1 teaspoon dried oregano
1 teaspoon smoked hot paprika
½ teaspoon ground cinnamon,
Salt, to taste
¾ cup vegetable broth
1 teaspoon apple cider vinegar
3 teaspoons lime juice
¼ teaspoon sugar
8 ounces (227 g) mushrooms chopped
Whole-wheat tacos, for serving
Directions
Put the oil, onion, garlic, salt and bay leaves into the instant pot and Sauté for 5 minutes. Blend the half of this mixture, in a blender, with all the spices and chillies. Add the mushrooms to the remaining onions and Sauté for 3 minutes. Pour the blended mixture into the pot and secure the lid. Cook on Manual function for 5 minutes at High Pressure. Once done, release the pressure and remove the lid. Stir well and serve with tacos.
Nutrition facts (per serving)
calories: 138 | fat: 4.1g | protein: 5.7g | carbs: 23.8g | fiber: 4.8g | sodium: 208mg

›Lentils and Eggplant Curry

Preparation time: 10 minutes
Cooking time: 22 minutes | **Servings:** 4
Ingredients
¾ cup lentils, soaked and rinsed
1 teaspoon olive oil
½ onion, chopped
4 garlic cloves, chopped
1 teaspoon ginger, chopped
1 hot green chili, chopped
¼ teaspoon turmeric
½ teaspoon ground cumin
2 tomatoes, chopped
1 cup eggplant, chopped
1 cup sweet potatoes, cubed
¾ teaspoon salt
2 cups water
1 cup baby spinach leaves
Cayenne and lemon/lime to taste
Pepper flakes (garnish)
Directions
Add the oil, garlic, ginger, chili and salt into the instant pot and Sauté for 3 minutes. Stir in the tomatoes and all the spices. Cook for 5 minutes. Add all the rest of the ingredients, except the spinach leaves and garnish. Secure the lid and cook on Manual function for 12 minutes at High Pressure. After the beep, release the pressure naturally and remove the lid. Stir in the spinach leaves and let the pot simmer for 2 minutes on Sauté. Garnish with the pepper flakes and serve warm.
Nutrition facts (per serving)
calories: 88 | fat: 1.5g | protein: 3.4g | carbs: 17.4g | fiber: 3.3g | sodium: 470mg

›Sweet Potato and Tomato Curry

Preparation time: 5 minutes

Cooking time: 8 minutes | **Servings:** 8
Ingredients
2 large brown onions, finely diced
4 tablespoons olive oil
4 teaspoons salt
4 large garlic cloves, diced
1 red chili, sliced
4 tablespoons cilantro, chopped
4 teaspoons ground cumin
2 teaspoons ground coriander
2 teaspoons paprika
2 pounds (907 g) sweet potato, diced
4 cups chopped, tinned tomatoes
2 cups water
2 cups vegetable stock
Lemon juice and cilantro (garnish)
Directions
Put the oil and onions into the instant pot and Sauté for 5 minutes. Stir in the remaining ingredients and secure the lid. Cook on Manual function for 3 minutes at High Pressure. Once done, Quick release the pressure and remove the lid. Garnish with cilantro and lemon juice. Serve.
Nutrition facts (per serving)
calories: 224 | fat: 8.0g | protein: 4.6g | carbs: 35.9g | fiber: 7.5g | sodium: 1385mg

›Veggie Chili

Preparation time: 15 minutes
Cooking time: 10 minutes | **Servings:** 3
Ingredients
½ tablespoon olive oil
1 small yellow onion, chopped
4 garlic cloves, minced
¾ (15-ounce / 425-g) can diced tomatoes
1 ounce (28 g) sugar-free tomato paste
½ (4-ounce / 113-g) can green chilies with liquid
1 tablespoon Worcestershire sauce
2 tablespoons red chili powder
½ cup carrots, diced
½ cup scallions, chopped
½ cup green bell pepper, chopped
¼ cup peas
1 tablespoon ground cumin
½ tablespoon dried oregano, crushed
Salt and freshly ground black pepper
Directions
Add the oil, garlic, and onion into the instant pot and Sauté for 5 minutes. Stir well the remaining vegetables and stir-fry for 3 min. Add the rest of the listed ingredients and secure the lid. Cook on Manual function for 2 minutes at High Pressure. After the beep, natural release the pressure and remove the lid. Stir well and serve warm.
Nutrition facts (per serving)
calories: 106 | fat: 3.9g | protein: 3.4g | carbs: 18.0g | fiber: 6.2g | sodium: 492mg

›Cabbage-Stuffed Acorn Squash

Preparation time: 15 minutes
Cooking time: 23 minutes | **Servings:** 4
Ingredients

½ tablespoon olive oil
2 medium Acorn squashes
¼ small yellow onion, chopped
1 jalapeño pepper, chopped
½ cup green onions, chopped
½ cup carrots, chopped
¼ cup cabbage, chopped
1 garlic clove, minced
½ (6-ounce / 170-g) can sugar-free tomato sauce
½ tablespoon chili powder
½ tablespoon ground cumin
Salt and freshly ground black pepper
2 cups water
¼ cup Cheddar cheese, shredded
Directions
Put the water into the instant pot and place the trivet inside. Slice the squash into 2 halves and remove the seeds. Place over the trivet, skin side down, and sprinkle some salt and pepper over it. Secure the lid and cook on Manual for 15 minutes at High Pressure. Release the pressure naturally and remove the lid. Empty the pot into a bowl. Now add the oil, onion, and garlic in the instant pot and Sauté for 5 minutes. Stir well the remaining vegetables and stir-fry for 3 minutes. Add the remaining listed ingredients and secure the lid. Cook on Manual function for 2-3 minutes at High Pressure. After the beep, natural release the pressure and remove the lid. Stuff the squashes with the prepared mixture and serve warm.
Nutrition facts (per serving)
calories: 163 | fat: 5.1g | protein: 4.8g | carbs: 28.4g | fiber: 4.9g | sodium: 146mg

›Creamy Potato Curry

Preparation time: 10 minutes
Cooking time: 18 minutes | **Servings:** 4
Ingredients
¾ large yellow or white onion, chopped
1½ ribs celery, chopped
¼ cup carrots, diced
¼ cup green onions
½ cup coconut milk
¾ tablespoon garlic, chopped
1½ cups water
1 pound (454 g) white potatoes, peeled and diced
¼ cup heavy cream
¼ teaspoon thyme
¼ teaspoon rosemary
½ tablespoon black pepper
¾ cup peas
Salt, to taste
2 tablespoons fresh cilantro for garnishing, chopped
Directions
Add the oil and all the vegetables in the instant pot and Sauté for 5 minutes. Stir in the remaining ingredients and secure the lid. Cook on Manual function for 13 minutes at High Pressure. Once it beeps, natural release the pressure and remove the lid. Garnish with fresh cilantro and serve hot.
Nutrition facts (per serving)
calories: 210 | fat: 10.1g | protein: 4.1g | carbs: 27.6g | fiber: 4.7g | sodium: 74mg

Mushroom and Spinach-Stuffed Peppers

Preparation time: 15 minutes
Cooking time: 8 minutes | **Servings:** 7
Ingredients
7 mini sweet peppers
1 cup button mushrooms, minced
5 ounces (142 g) organic baby spinach
½ teaspoon fresh garlic
½ teaspoon coarse sea salt
¼ teaspoon cracked mixed pepper
2 tablespoons water
1 tablespoon olive oil
Organic Mozzarella cheese, diced
Directions
Put the sweet peppers and water in the instant pot and Sauté for 2 minutes. Remove the peppers and put the olive oil into the pot. Stir in the mushrooms, garlic, spices and spinach. Cook on Sauté until the mixture is dry. Stuff each sweet pepper with the cheese and spinach mixture. Bake the stuffed peppers in an oven for 6 minutes at 400°F (205°C). Once done, serve hot.
Nutrition facts (per serving)
calories: 81 | fat: 2.4g | protein: 4.1g | carbs: 13.2g | fiber: 2.4g | sodium: 217mg

Black Bean and Corn Tortilla Bowls

Preparation time: 10 minutes
Cooking time: 8 minutes | **Servings:** 4
Ingredients
1½ cups vegetable broth
½ cup tomatoes, undrained diced
1 small onion, diced
2 garlic cloves, finely minced
1 teaspoon chili powder
1 teaspoon cumin
½ teaspoon paprika
½ teaspoon ground coriander
Salt and pepper to taste
½ cup carrots, diced
2 small potatoes, cubed
½ cup bell pepper, chopped
½ can black beans, drained and rinsed
1 cup frozen corn kernels
½ tablespoon lime juice
2 tablespoons cilantro for topping, chopped
Whole-wheat tortilla chips
Directions
Add the oil and all the vegetables into the instant pot and Sauté for 3 minutes. Add all the spices, corn, lime juice, and broth, along with the beans, to the pot. Seal the lid and cook on Manual setting at High Pressure for 5 minutes. Once done, natural release the pressure when the timer goes off. Remove the lid. To serve, put the prepared mixture into a bowl. Top with tortilla chips and fresh cilantro. Serve.
Nutrition facts (per serving)
calories: 183 | fat: 0.9g | protein: 7.1g | carbs: 39.8g | fiber: 8.3g | sodium: 387mg

Cauliflower and Broccoli Bowls

Preparation time: 5 minutes
Cooking time: 7 minutes | **Servings:** 3
Ingredients
½ medium onion, diced
2 teaspoons olive oil
1 garlic clove, minced
½ cup tomato paste
½ pound (227 g) frozen cauliflower
½ pound (227 g) broccoli florets
½ cup vegetable broth
½ teaspoon paprika
¼ teaspoon dried thyme
2 pinches sea salt
Directions
Add the oil, garlic and onion into the instant pot and Sauté for 2 minutes. Add the broth, tomato paste, cauliflower, broccoli, and all the spices, to the pot. Secure the lid. Cook on the Manual setting at with pressure for 5 minutes. After the beep, release the pressure and remove the lid. Stir well and serve hot.
Nutrition facts (per serving)
calories: 109 | fat: 3.8g | protein: 6.1g | carbs: 16.7g | fiber: 6.1g | sodium: 265mg

Radish and Cabbage Congee

Preparation time: 5 minutes
Cooking time: 20 minutes | **Servings:** 3
Ingredients
1 cup carrots, diced
½ cup radish, diced
6 cups vegetable broth
Salt, to taste
1½ cups short grain rice, rinsed
1 tablespoon grated fresh ginger
4 cups cabbage, shredded
Green onions for garnishing, chopped
Directions
Add all the ingredients, except the cabbage and green onions, into the instant pot. Select the Porridge function and cook on the default time and settings. After the beep, release the pressure and remove the lid. Stir in the shredded cabbage and cover with the lid. Serve after 10 minutes with chopped green onions on top.
Nutrition facts (per serving)
calories: 438 | fat: 0.8g | protein: 8.7g | carbs: 98.4g | fiber: 6.7g | sodium: 1218mg

Potato and Broccoli Medley

Preparation time: 10 minutes
Cooking time: 20 minutes | **Servings:** 3
Ingredients
1 tablespoon olive oil
½ white onion, diced
1½ cloves garlic, finely chopped
1 pound (454 g) potatoes, cut into chunks
1 pound (454 g) broccoli florets, diced
1 pound (454 g) baby carrots, cut in half
¼ cup vegetable broth
½ teaspoon Italian seasoning

½ teaspoon Spike original seasoning
Fresh parsley for garnishing
Directions
Put the oil and onion into the instant pot and Sauté for 5 minutes. Stir in the carrots, and garlic and stir-fry for 5 minutes. Add the remaining listed ingredients and secure the lid. Cook on the Manual function for 10 minutes at High Pressure. After the beep, release the pressure and remove the lid.
Stir gently and garnish with fresh parsley , then serve.
Nutrition facts (per serving)
calories: 256 | fat: 5.6g | protein: 9.1g | carbs: 46.1g | fiber: 12.2g | sodium: 274mg

➤Mushroom and Potato Oat Burgers

Preparation time: 20 minutes
Cooking time: 21 minutes | **Servings:** 5
Ingredients
½ cup minced onion
1 teaspoon grated fresh ginger
½ cup minced mushrooms
½ cup red lentils, rinsed
¾ sweet potato, peeled and diced
1 cup vegetable stock
2 tablespoons hemp seeds
2 tablespoons chopped parsley
2 tablespoons chopped cilantro
1 tablespoon curry
1 cup quick oats
Brown rice flour, optional
5 tomato slices
Lettuce leaves
5 whole-wheat buns
Directions
Add the oil, ginger, mushrooms and onion into the instant pot and Sauté for 5 minutes. Stir in the lentils, stock, and the sweet potatoes. Secure the lid and cook on the Manual function for 6 minutes at High Pressure. After the beep, natural release the pressure and remove the lid. Meanwhile, heat the oven to 370-375°F (190°C) and line a baking tray with parchment paper. Mash the prepared lentil mixture with a potato masher. Add the oats and the remaining spices. Put in some brown rice flour if the mixture is not thick enough. Wet your hands and prepare 5 patties, using the mixture, and place them on the baking tray. Bake the patties for 10 minutes in the preheated oven. Slice the buns in half and stack each with a tomato slice, a vegetable patty and lettuce leaves. Serve and enjoy.
Nutrition facts (per serving)
calories: 266 | fat: 5.3g | protein: 14.5g | carbs: 48.7g | fiber: 9.6g | sodium: 276mg

➤Potato, Corn, and Spinach Medley

Preparation time: 10 minutes
Cooking time: 10 minutes | **Servings:** 6
Ingredients
1 tablespoon olive oil
3 scallions, chopped
½ cup onion, chopped
2 large white potatoes, peeled and diced
1 tablespoon ginger, grated

3 cups frozen corn kernels
1 cup vegetable stock
1 tablespoon fish sauce
2 tablespoons light soy sauce
2 large cloves garlic, diced
⅓ teaspoon white pepper
1 teaspoon salt
3-4 handfuls baby spinach leaves
Juice of ½ lemon
Directions
Put the oil, ginger, garlic and onions in the instant pot and Sauté for 5 minutes. Add all the remaining listed ingredients except the spinach leaves and lime juice Secure the lid and cook on the Manual setting for 5 minutes at High Pressure. After the beep, release the pressure and remove the lid. Add the spinach and cook for 3 min on Sauté. Drizzle the lime juice over the dish and serve hot.
Nutrition facts (per serving)
calories: 217 | fat: 3.4g | protein: 6.5g | carbs: 44.5g | fiber: 6.3g | sodium: 892mg

➤Italian Zucchini Pomodoro

Preparation time: 10 minutes
Cooking time: 12 minutes | **Servings:** 4
Ingredients
1 tablespoon avocado oil
1 large onion, peeled and diced
3 cloves garlic, minced
1 (28-ounce / 794-g) can diced tomatoes, including juice
½ cup water
1 tablespoon Italian seasoning
1 teaspoon sea salt
½ teaspoon ground black pepper
2 medium zucchinis, spiraled
Directions
Press Sauté button on the Instant Pot. Heat avocado oil. Add onions and stir-fry for 3 to 5 minutes until translucent. Add garlic and cook for 1-2 additional minutes. Add tomatoes, water, Italian seasoning, salt, and pepper. Add zucchini and toss to combine. Lock lid. Press the Manual button and adjust time to 1 minute. When timer beeps, let pressure release naturally for 5 minutes. Quick release any additional pressure until float valve drops and then unlock lid. Transfer zucchini to four bowls. Press Sauté button, press Adjust button to change the temperature to Less, and simmer sauce in the Instant Pot unlidded for 5 minutes. Ladle over zucchini and serve immediately.
Nutrition facts (per serving)
calories: 92 | fat: 4.1g | protein: 2.5g | carbs: 13.1g | fiber: 5.1g | sodium: 980mg

➤Mackerel and Green Bean Salad

Preparation time: 10 minutes
Cooking time: 10 minutes | **Servings:** 2
Ingredients
1 cups green beans
1 tablespoon avocado oil
2 mackerel fillets
4 cups mixed salad greens

2 hard-boiled eggs, sliced
1 avocado, sliced
2 tablespoons lemon juice
2 tablespoons olive oil
1 teaspoon Dijon mustard
Salt and black pepper, to taste
Directions:
Cook the green beans in a medium-large saucepan of boiling water for about 3 minutes until crisp-tender. Drain and set aside. Melt the avocado oil in a pan over medium heat. Add the mackerel fillets and cook each side for 4 minutes. Divide the greens between two salad bowls. Top with the mackerel, sliced egg, and avocado slices. In an another bowl, whisk together the lemon juice, olive oil, mustard, salt, and pepper, and drizzle over the salad. Add the cooked green beans and toss well to combine, then serve.
Nutrition facts (per serving)
calories: 737 | fat: 57.3g | protein: 34.2g | carbs: 22.1g | fiber: 13.4g | sodium: 398mg

›Hazelnut Crusted Sea Bass

Preparation time: 10 minutes
Cooking time: 15 minutes | **Servings:** 2
Ingredients
2 tablespoons almond butter
2 sea bass fillets
⅓ cup roasted hazelnuts
A pinch of cayenne pepper
Directions:
Preheat the oven to 420/425°F (220°C). Line a baking dish with waxed paper. Brush the almond butter over the fillets. Pulse the hazelnuts and cayenne in a food processor. Coat the sea bass with the hazelnut mixture, then transfer to the baking dish. Bake in the oven for about 13-15 mins. Cool for 5 minutes before serving.
Nutrition facts (per serving)
calories: 468 | fat: 30.8g | protein: 40.0g | carbs: 8.8g | fiber: 4.1g | sodium: 90mg

›Shrimp and Pea Paella

Preparation time: 20 minutes
Cooking time: 60 minutes | **Servings:** 2
Ingredients
2 tablespoons olive oil
1 garlic clove, minced
½ large onion, minced
1 cup diced tomato
½ cup short-grain rice
½ teaspoon sweet paprika
½ cup dry white wine
1¼ cups low-sodium chicken stock
8 ounces (227 g) large raw shrimp
1 cup frozen peas
¼ cup jarred roasted red peppers
Salt, to taste
Directions:
Heat the olive oil in a skillet over medium/high heat. Add the onion and garlic and sauté for about 3 minutes, or until the onion is softened. Add in the tomato, rice, and paprika and stir for about 3 minutes to toast the rice. Add in the chicken stock and wine and stir to combine. Bring the mixture to a boil. Low the heat to medium-low and cover, and simmer for 45 minutes, or until the rice is just about tender and most of the liquid has been absorbed. Add the peas, shrimp, and red peppers. Cover and cook for an additional 5-6 min. Season with salt to taste and serve.
Nutrition facts (per serving)
calories: 646 | fat: 27.1g | protein: 42.0g | carbs: 59.7g | fiber: 7.0g | sodium: 687mg

›Garlic Shrimp with Arugula Pesto

Preparation time: 20 minutes
Cooking time: 5 minutes | **Servings:** 2
Ingredients
3 cups lightly packed arugula
½ cup lightly packed basil leaves
¼ cup walnuts
3 tablespoons olive oil
3 medium garlic cloves
2 tablespoons grated Parmesan cheese
1 tablespoon freshly squeezed lemon juice
Salt and freshly ground black pepper
1 (10-ounce / 283-g) package zucchini noodles
8 ounces (227 g) cooked, shelled shrimp
2 Roma tomatoes, diced
Directions:
Process the basil, arugula, garlic, walnuts, olive oil, Parmesan cheese and lemon juice in a food processor until smooth; add salt and pepper to taste. Heat a skillet over medium/hight heat. Add the cooked shrimp, zucchini noodles and pesto. Stir to combine the sauce over the noodles and shrimp and cook until heated through. Taste and season with more salt and pepper as needed. Serve topped with the diced tomatoes.
Nutrition facts (per serving)
calories: 435 | fat: 30.2g | protein: 33.0g | carbs: 15.1g | fiber: 5.0g | sodium: 413mg

›Baked Oysters with Vegetables

Preparation time: 30 minutes
Cooking time: 15 to 17 minutes | **Servings:** 2
Ingredients
1 dozen fresh oysters, scrubbed
¼ cup finely chopped scallions, both white and green parts
½ cup finely chopped artichoke hearts
2 cups coarse salt
¼ cup finely chopped red bell pepper
1 tablespoon almond butter
1 garlic clove, minced
1 tablespoon finely chopped fresh parsley
Zest and juice of ½ lemon
Pinch salt
Freshly ground black pepper, to taste
Directions:
Pour the salt into a baking dish and spread to evenly fill the bottom of the dish. Prepare a clean work surface to shuck the oysters. Using a knife, insert the blade at the shell joint, apply pressure to get the blade in, and work the knife around the shell to open it. Using the knife, gently loosen the oyster. Place the oysters

in their shells on the salt. Preheat the oven to 400°F (210°C). Place the almond butter in a large skillet over medium heat, add the bell bell pepper, shallot and artichoke, cooking for 5/7 min. Finally add the garlic and cook for 2 min. Remove from heat and stir in lemon juice and parsley and season to taste with pepper and salt. Bake in the preheated oven for 10/12 min, or until the vegetables are golden brown. Serve warm.

Nutrition facts (per serving)
calories: 135 | fat: 7.2g | protein: 6.0g | carbs: 10.7g | fiber: 2.0g | sodium: 280mg

›Steamed Cod

Preparation time: 15 minutes
Cooking time: 7 minutes | **Servings:** 4
Ingredients
1 pound (454 g) cherry tomatoes, halved
1 bunch fresh thyme sprigs
4 fillets cod
1 teaspoon olive oil
1 clove garlic, pressed
3 pinches salt
2 cups water
1 cup white rice
1 cup Kalamata olives
2 tablespoons pickled capers1 tablespoon olive oil
1 pinch ground black pepper
Directions:
Line a parchment paper on the basket of your instant pot. Place about half the tomatoes in a single layer on the paper. Sprinkle with thyme, reserving some for garnish. Arrange cod fillets on top. Sprinkle with a little bit of olive oil. Spread the garlic, pepper, salt, and remaining tomatoes over the fish. In the pot, mix rice and water. Lay a trivet over the rice and water. Lower steamer basket onto the trivet. Seal the lid, and cook for 7 minutes on Low Pressure. Release the pressure quickly. Remove the steamer basket and trivet from the pot. Use a fork to fluff rice. Plate the fish fillets and apply a garnish of olives, reserved thyme, pepper, remaining olive oil, and capers. Serve with rice.

Nutrition facts (per serving)
calories: 352 | fat: 9.1g | protein: 22.2g | carbs: 44.7g | fiber: 3.9g | sodium: 827mg

›Mushroom and Caramelized Onion Musakhan

Preparation time: 20 minutes
Cooking time: 1 hour 5 minutes
Servings: 4
Ingredients
2 tablespoons sumac, plus more for sprinkling
1 teaspoon ground allspice
½ teaspoon ground cardamom
3 tablespoons extra-virgin olive oil, divided
½ teaspoon ground cumin
3 medium white onions, coarsely chopped
2 pounds (907 g) portobello mushroom caps
¼ cup water
Kosher salt, to taste

1 whole-wheat Turkish flatbread
¼ cup pine nuts
1 lemon, wedged

Preheat the oven to 340/350°F (180°C). Combine 2 tablespoons of sumac, cardamom, allspice and cumin in a small bowl. Stir to mix well. Heat 2 tbsps of olive oil in an oven-proof skillet over medium-high heat until shimmering.
Add mushrooms to skillet and sauté for 8 to 10 minutes or until mushrooms are tender. Heat 2 tablespoon olive oil in the skillet over medium-high heat, add the onion and sauté for 20 minutes. Add the sumac mixture and cook for 1/2 minute. Add the water , once brought to a boil , add the salt. Place the pan in the oven and bake for 30 to 40 minutes. Remove the pan from the oven and let the mushrooms rest for 10-12 minutes. Heat the Turkish flatbread in a pan in the oven for 5 minutes and place the bread on a large plate with the mushrooms, toasted pine nuts and onions. Place the lemon wedges and sprinkle with more sumac. Serve immediately.

Nutrition facts (per serving)
calories: 335 | fat: 19.7g | protein: 11.5g | carbs: 34.3g | fiber: 6.9g | sodium: 369mg

›Red Pepper Coques with Pine Nuts

Preparation time: 1 day 45 minutes | **Cooking time: 45** minutes | **Makes** 4 coques
Ingredients
Dough:
3 cups almond flour
½ teaspoon instant or rapid-rise yeast
2 teaspoons raw honey
1⅓ cups ice water
3 tablespoons extra-virgin olive oil
1½ teaspoons sea salt
Red Pepper Topping:
2 tablespoons extra-virgin olive oil, divided
2 cups jarred roasted red peppers
2 large onions, halved and sliced thin
3 garlic cloves, minced
¼ teaspoon red pepper flakes
3 tablespoons maple syrup
1½ teaspoons sea salt
3 tablespoons red wine vinegar
For Garnish:
¼ cup pine nuts (optional)
1 tablespoon minced fresh parsley
Make the Dough
Combine the flour, honey and yeast in a food processor, gently add the water while and let the dough rest for 10/12 minutes. Stir the olive oil and salt into the dough and wrap in plastic and refrigerate for at least 24 hours.
For the topping
Heat 2 tablespoon of oil in a skillet over medium/low heat then add the onions, red peppers, garlic, red pepper flakes, bay leaves, salt and maple syrup. Sauté for 20 minutes then turn off the heat and remove the bay leaves, remove the onions from the pan and let sit for 20 minutes.
Prepare the Coques

Preheat the oven to 490/500°F (260°C). Grease two baking sheets with 3 tablespoons olive oil. Using the dough, create four balls, and place them on a baking sheet. Grease the balls with olive oil and bake for 5 to 8 minutes. Add the topping and pine nuts, then bake for another 15 to 20 minutes. Remove the coques from the oven and add the parsley. Allow to cool for 15 minutes before serving.

Nutrition facts (per serving) (1 coque)
calories: 660 | fat: 25.1g | protein: 3.4g | carbs: 112.0g | fiber: 6.2g | sodium: 1757mg

➤Ritzy Garden Burgers

Preparation time: 1 hour 30 minutes
Cooking time: 30 minutes | **Servings:** 6
Ingredients
1 tablespoon avocado oil
½ cup shredded carrots
4 garlic cloves, halved
1 yellow onion, diced
1 (15 ounces / 425 g) black beans
1 cup gluten-free rolled oats
¼ cup oil-packed sun-dried tomatoes
1 teaspoon chili powder
1 teaspoon paprika
1 teaspoon ground cumin
½ cup sunflower seeds, toasted
½ cup fresh parsley, stems removed
¼ teaspoon ground red pepper flakes
¾ teaspoon sea salt
¼ teaspoon ground black pepper
¼ cup olive oil
For Serving:
2 cup kaiware sprouts or mung bean sprouts
2 ripe avocados, sliced
6 whole-wheat buns
1 ripe tomato, sliced
Directions
Line a baking sheet with parchment paper. Heat 1 tbsp. of avocado oil in a skillet over hight heat.
Add the onion and carrots and sauté for about 10 min or until the onion is caramelized. Add the garlic and sauté for 50 seconds, place in a food processor, then add the remaining ingredients listed, except the olive oil. Divide the mixture into six patties then arrange the patties on the baking sheet and place the baking sheet in the refrigerator. Freeze for 3 hours. Remove the baking sheet from the refrigerator and let them rest at room temperature for 20 minutes. Fry the meatballs in the pan for about 15 min or until lightly browned. Assemble the buns with the patties, sprouts, avocados and tomato slices to make burgers.

Nutrition facts (per serving)
calories: 615 | fat: 23.1g | protein: 27.2g | carbs: 88.3g | fiber: 22.9g | sodium: 456mg

➤Roasted Tomato Panini

Preparation time: 18 minutes
Cooking time: 3 hours 10 minutes | **Servings:** 2
Ingredients
4 cloves garlic
2 teaspoons olive oil

4 Roma tomatoes, halved
1 tablespoon Italian seasoning
Sea salt and freshly ground pepper
4 slices whole-grain bread
4 basil leaves
2 slices fresh Mozzarella cheese
Directions
Preheat the oven to 240/250°F (121°C). Grease a baking pan with olive oil.
Place the garlic and tomatoes in the baking pan, then sprinkle salt, and ground pepper. Roast in the preheated oven for 3 and a half hours or until the tomatoes are lightly wilted. Preheat the panini press. Prepare the sandwich: Place two slices of bread on a work surface, then place them on top of the wilted tomatoes. Add the basil and mozzarella cheese. Top them with remaining two slices of bread. Cook the panini for 8 min or until lightly browned and the cheese melts. Flip the panini halfway through the cooking. Serve immediately.

Nutrition facts (per serving)
calories: 325 | fat: 13.0g | protein: 17.4g | carbs: 37.5g | fiber: 7.5g | sodium: 603mg

➤Samosas in Potatoes

Preparation time: 20 minutes
Cooking time: 30 minutes | **Makes** 8
4 small potatoes
1 teaspoon coconut oil
1 small onion, finely chopped
1 small piece ginger, minced
2 garlic cloves, minced
2 to 3 teaspoons curry powder
Sea salt and freshly ground black pepper
¼ cup frozen peas, thawed
2 carrots, grated
¼ cup chopped fresh cilantro
Directions
Preheat the oven to 340/350°F (180°C). Bake in the preheated oven for 29-30 minutes until tender. Meanwhile, heat the coconut oil in a nonstick skillet over medium-high heat until melted. Add the onion and sauté for 3-5 minutes or until translucent. Add the garlic and ginger to the skillet and sauté for about 3/5 min or until fragrant. Add the curry powder, ground black pepper and salt, then cover the onions. When the potatoes are cooked through, let them rest for 5 minutes and cut them in half. Hollow out the potatoes with a spoon, then fill the potatoes with the sautéed onion, carrots, peas and cilantro. Spoon the mixture over the tomato skins and serve immediately.

Nutrition facts (per serving) (1 samosa)
calories: 130 | fat: 13.9g | protein: 4.2g | carbs: 8.8g | fiber: 3.0g | sodium: 111mg

➤Spicy Black Bean and Poblano Dippers

Preparation time: 20 minutes
Cooking time: 21 minutes | **Servings:** 8
Ingredients
2 tbsps. avocado oil

1 poblano, deseeded and quartered
1 (12 ounces / 340 g) can black beans
1 jalapeño, halved and deseeded
½ cup fresh cilantro, leaves and tender stems
2 garlic cloves
1 yellow onion, quartered
1 teaspoon chili powder
1 teaspoon ground cumin
1 teaspoon sea salt
24 organic corn tortillas

Directions

Preheat the oven to 390/400°F (205°C). Line a baking sheet with parchment paper and grease with avocado oil. Combine all ingredients, except tortillas, well in a food processor and be sure not to puree the mixture. Warm the tortillas on the baking sheet in the preheated oven for 2/3 minutes. Add the mixture to each tortillas then fold them to one side to make rolls. Place them on a baking sheet and drizzle the tortillas with avocado oil. Bake in the oven for 25 minutes. Serve immediately.

Nutrition facts (per serving)

calories: 390 | fat: 6.5g | protein: 16.2g | carbs: 69.6g | fiber: 13.5g | sodium: 340mg

›Spicy Tofu Tacos with Cherry Tomato Sauce

Preparation time: 20 minutes
Cooking time: 11 minutes | **Makes** 4 tacos
Ingredients
Cherry Tomato Sauce:
¼ cup sliced cherry tomatoes
½ jalapeño, deseeded and sliced
Juice of 1 lime
1 garlic clove, minced
Sea salt and freshly ground black pepper
2 teaspoons extra-virgin olive oil
Spicy Tofu Taco Filling:
4 tablespoons water, divided
½ cup canned black beans, rinsed and drained
2 teaspoons fresh chopped chives, divided
¾ teaspoon ground cumin, divided
¾ teaspoon smoked paprika, divided
Dash cayenne pepper (optional)
¼ teaspoon sea salt
¼ teaspoon freshly ground black pepper
1 teaspoon extra-virgin olive oil
6 ounces (170 g) firm tofu, drained, rinsed, and pressed
4 corn tortillas
¼ avocado, sliced
¼ cup fresh cilantro

Make the Cherry Tomato Sauce

Combine the ingredients in a medium bowl. Stir to mix well. Set aside until ready to use.

Make the Spicy Tofu Taco Filling

Add 2 tablespoons of water into a saucepan, then add the black beans and sprinkle with 1 teaspoon of chives, ½ teaspoon of cumin, ¼ teaspoon of smoked paprika, and cayenne. Stir to mix well. Cook for 4/5 minutes over medium-high heat until heated through, then mash the black beans with the back of a spoon. Turn off the heat and set aside. Add remaining water

into a bowl, then add the remaining chives, cumin, and paprika. Sprinkle with cayenne, salt, and black pepper. Stir to mix well. Set aside. Preheat the olive oil in a nonstick skillet over medium-high heat until shimmering. Add the tofu and drizzle with taco sauce, then sauté for 5 minutes or until the seasoning is absorbed. Remove the tofu from the skillet and set aside. Warm the tortillas in the skillet for 1 minutes or until heated through. Transfer the tortillas onto a large plate and top with tofu, mashed black beans, avocado, cilantro, then drizzle the tomato sauce over. Serve immediately.

Nutrition facts (per serving) (1 taco)

calories: 240 | fat: 9.0g | protein: 11.6g | carbs: 31.6g | fiber: 6.7g | sodium: 195mg

›Super Cheese and Mushroom Tart

Preparation time: 30 minutes
Cooking time: 1 hour 30 minutes
Servings: 4 to 6
Ingredients
Crust:
1¾ cups almond flour
1 tablespoon raw honey
¾ teaspoon sea salt
¼ cup extra-virgin olive oil
⅓ cup water
Filling:
1 pound (454 g) white mushrooms
Sea salt, to taste
2 tablespoons extra-virgin olive oil, divided
1 garlic clove, minced
¼ cup shredded Mozzarella cheese
2 teaspoons minced fresh thyme
½ cup grated Parmesan cheese
4 ounces (113 g) part-skim ricotta cheese
Ground black pepper, to taste
2 tablespoons ground basil

Directions

Make the Crust

Preheat the oven to 340/350°F (180°C). Combine the flour, honey, salt and olive oil in a large bowl. Stir to mix well. Gently mix in the water until a smooth dough forms. Drop walnut-size clumps from the dough in the single layer on a tart pan. Press the clumps to coat the bottom of the pan. Bake the crust in the preheated oven for 50 min. Rotate the pan halfway through.

Make the Filling

While baking the crust, heat 2 tablespoon of olive oil in a nonstick skillet over medium-high heat until shimmering. Add the mushrooms and sprinkle with 1 teaspoon of salt. Sauté for 15 minutes or until tender. Add the garlic and thyme and sauté for 40 seconds or until fragrant.

Make the Tart

Meanwhile, combine the cheeses, salt, ground black pepper, and 1 tablespoon of olive. Spread the cheese mixture over the crust, then cover with the mushroom mixture. Bake in the oven for 20 min or until the cheeses are frothy and the tart is heated through. Rotate the pan halfway through the baking time. Remove the tart from the oven. Allow to cool for at least 10 minutes, then sprinkle with basil. Slice to serve.

›Turkish Eggplant and Tomatoes Pide with Mint

Preparation time: 1 day 45 min | **Cooking time:** 25 minutes | **Makes** 6 pides
Ingredients
Dough:
3 cups almond flour
2 teaspoons raw honey
½ teaspoon instant or rapid-rise yeast
1⅓ cups ice water
1½ teaspoons sea salt
1 tablespoon extra-virgin olive oil
Eggplant and Tomato Toppings:
28 ounces (794 g) whole tomatoes
5 tablespoons extra-virgin olive oil
½ red bell pepper, chopped
1 pound (454 g) eggplant
Sea salt and ground black pepper
3 garlic cloves, minced
¼ teaspoon red pepper flakes
½ teaspoon smoked paprika
5 tablespoons minced fresh mint, divided
1½ cups crumbled feta cheese
Directions
Make the Dough
Combine the flour, yeast, and honey in a food processor, pulse to combine well. Gently add water while pulsing. Let the dough sit for 15 min. Mix the olive oil and salt in the dough and knead the dough until smooth. Wrap in plastic and refrigerate for at least 1 day.
Make the Toppings
Heat 2 tbsps. of oil in a nonstick skillet over medium heat until shimmering. Add the eggplant, bell pepper and 1 teaspoon of salt. Sauté for 5 minutes or until the eggplant is lightly browned. Add the paprika ,garlic and red pepper flakes. Sauté for 2 minute or until fragrant. Pour in the puréed tomatoes. Bring to a simmer, then cook for 9/10 minutes or until the mixture is thickened into about 3½ cups. Turn off the heat and mix in 5 tablespoons of mint, salt, and ground black pepper. Set them aside until ready to use.
Make the Turkish Pide
Preheat the oven to 490/500°F (260°C). Line three baking sheets with parchment papers. On a work surface, divide and shape the dough into five ovals. Transfer the dough to the baking sheets. Brush them with 1 tablespoons of olive oil and spread the eggplant mixture and feta cheese on top. Bake in the preheated oven for 11-12 min or until golden brown. Rotate the pide halfway through the baking time. Remove the pide from the oven and spread with remaining mint and serve immediately.
Nutrition facts (per serving) (1 pide)
calories: 520 | fat: 22.1g | protein: 8.0g | carbs: 69.7g | fiber: 5.8g | sodium: 1001mg

›Veg Mix and Blackeye Pea Burritos

Preparation time: 15 minutes
Cooking time: 40 minutes | **Makes** 6 burritos
Ingredients
1 teaspoon olive oil
1 red onion, diced
2 garlic cloves, minced
1 zucchini, chopped
1 tomato, diced
1 bell pepper, deseeded and diced
1 (14-ounce / 397-g) can blackeye peas
2 teaspoons chili powder
Sea salt, to taste
6 whole-grain tortillas
Directions
Preheat the oven to 325/330°F (165°C). Heat the oil in a nonstick skillet over medium-high heat or until shimmering. Add the onion and sauté for 4-5 minutes or until translucent. Add the garlic and sauté for 40 seconds. Add the zucchini and sauté for 5 min. Add the bell pepper and tomato and sauté for 3 min. Fold in the black peas and sprinkle them with salt and chili powder. Place the tortillas on a work surface, then top them with sautéed vegetables mix. Fold one ends of tortillas over the vegetable mix, then tuck and roll them into burritos. Arrange the burritos on a plate, then pour the pan juices over the burritos. Bake in the oven for 24-25 minutes or until golden brown. Serve immediately.
Nutrition facts (per serving)
calories: 340 | fat: 18.2g | protein: 12.1g | carbs: 8.3g | fiber: 8.0g | sodium: 214mg

›Tuna and Olive Salad Sandwiches

Preparation time: 10 minutes
Cooking time: 0 minutes | **Servings:** 4
Ingredients
3 tablespoons freshly squeezed lemon juice
2 tablespoons extra-virgin olive oil
1 garlic clove, minced
2 (5-ounce / 142-g) cans tuna, drained
½ teaspoon freshly ground black pepper
1 (2.25-ounce / 64-g) can sliced olives
8 slices whole-grain crusty bread
½ cup chopped fresh fennel, including fronds

In a large bowl, whisk together the oil, lemon juice, pepper and garlic. Add the tuna, fennel and olives to the bowl. Separate the tuna into pieces and toss to incorporate all of the listed ingredients. Place the tuna salad on 4 slices of bread. Let the sandwiches sit for at least 5 min so the zesty filling can soak into the bread before serving.
Nutrition facts (per serving)
calories: 950 | fat: 18.0g | protein: 165.0g | carbs: 37.0g | fiber: 7.0g | sodium: 2572mg

›Open-Faced Margherita Sandwiches

Preparation time: 10 minutes
Cooking time: 5 minutes | **Servings:** 4
Ingredients

2 (6- to 7-inch) whole-wheat submarine
1 garlic clove, halved
1 tablespoon extra-virgin olive oil
1 large ripe tomato, cut into 8-10 slices
¼ teaspoon dried oregano
1 cup fresh Mozzarella, sliced
¼ cup lightly packed fresh basil leaves
¼ teaspoon freshly ground black pepper

Preheat the broiler to mid-High with the rack 4 inches under the heating element. Put the sliced bread on a large, rimmed baking sheet and broil for about 2 min. Remove from the oven.
Brush each piece of the toasted bread with the oil, and rub a garlic half over each piece. Put the toasted bread back on the baking sheet. Evenly divide the tomato slices on each piece. Sprinkle with the oregano and top with the cheese. Place the baking sheet under the broiler. Set the timer for 2 min, but check after 1 minute. When the cheese is melted and the edges are just starting to get dark brown, remove the sandwiches from the oven. Top each sandwich with the fresh basil and pepper before serving.

Nutrition facts (per serving)
calories: 95 | fat: 3.0g | protein: 10.0g | carbs: 8.0g | fiber: 2.0g | sodium: 313mg

›Roasted Vegetable Panini

Preparation time: 10 minutes
Cooking time: 15 minutes | **Servings:** 4
Ingredients
2 tablespoons extra-virgin olive oil, divided
1½ cups diced broccoli
1 cup diced zucchini
¼ cup diced onion
¼ teaspoon dried oregano
⅛ teaspoon kosher or sea salt
⅛ teaspoon freshly ground black pepper
1 (12-ounce / 340-g) jar roasted red peppers
2 tablespoons grated Parmesan or Asiago cheese
1 cup fresh Mozzarella (about 4 ounces / 113 g), sliced
1 (2-foot-long) whole-grain Italian loaf, cut into 4 equal lengths
Cooking spray

Place a medium-large, rimmed baking sheet in the oven. Heat the oven to 450°F (235°C) with the baking sheet inside. In a medium-large bowl, stir together 1 tablespoon of the oil, broccoli, zucchini, onion, oregano, salt and pepper. Remove the baking sheet and spritz the baking sheet with cooking spray. Spread the vegetable mixture on the baking sheet and roast for 5 minutes, stirring once halfway through cooking. Remove the baking sheet from the oven. Stir in the red peppers and Parmesan cheese. In a large skillet over medium/high heat, heat the remaining 1 tablespoon of the oil. Cut open each section of bread horizontally, but don't cut all the way through. Fill each with the vegetable mix (about ½ cup), and layer 1 ounce (28 g) of sliced Mozzarella cheese on top. Close the sandwiches, and place two of them on the skillet. Place a heavy object on top and grill for 3 minutes. Flip the sandwiches and grill for another 3 minutes. Repeat the

grilling process with the remaining two sandwiches. Serve hot.
Nutrition facts (per serving)
calories: 116 | fat: 4.0g | protein: 12.0g | carbs: 9.0g | fiber: 3.0g | sodium: 569mg

›Lemony Spelt and Avocado Bowl

Preparation time: 5 minutes
Cooking time: 25 minutes | **Servings:** 4
Ingredients
1 tbsp. plus 2 teaspoons extra-virgin olive oil, divided
½ medium onion, chopped
1 carrot, shredded
2 garlic cloves, minced
1 (6-ounce / 170-g) cup pearled spelt
2 cups low-sodium vegetable soup
2 avocados, peeled, pitted, and sliced
Zest and juice of 1 small lemon
¼ teaspoon sea salt

Heat 3 tbsp of olive oil in a saucepan over medium-high heat until shimmering. Add the onion and sauté for 3-5 min. Add the carrot and garlic and sauté for 2 min. Add the spelt and pour in the vegetable soup. Bring to a boil over high heat. Low the heat. Put the lid on and simmer for 18-20 minutes or until the spelt is al dente. Transfer the spelt in a large serving bowl, then fold in the avocado slices. Sprinkle with lemon zest and salt, then drizzle with lemon juice and 2 teaspoons of olive oil. Stir to mix well and serve immediately.
Nutrition facts (per serving)
calories: 215 | fat: 11.1g | protein: 5.2g | carbs: 27.9g | fiber: 7.0g | sodium: 152mg

›Rice and Blueberry-Stuffed Sweet Potatoes

Preparation time: 15 minutes
Cooking time: 20 minutes | **Servings:** 4
Ingredients
2 cups cooked wild rice
½ cup dried blueberries
½ cup shredded Swiss chard
½ cup chopped hazelnuts
2 scallion, white and green parts, peeled and thinly sliced
1 teaspoon chopped fresh thyme
Sea salt and freshly ground black pepper
5 sweet potatoes, baked in the skin until tender

Preheat the oven to 395°F (200°C). Mix all the ingredients, except for the sweet potatoes, in a large bowl. Stir to mix well. Cut the top third of the sweet potato off length wire, then scoop most of the sweet potato flesh out. Fill the potato with the wild rice mixture, then set the sweet potato on a greased baking sheet. Bake in the preheated oven for 20-21 minutes or until the sweet potato skin is lightly charred. Serve immediately.
Nutrition facts (per serving)
calories: 395| fat: 8.1g | protein: 10.2g | carbs: 76.9g | fiber: 10.0g | sodium: 93mg

➤Slow cooker Turkey and Brown Rice

Preparation time: 20 minutes
Cooking time: 3 hours 10 minutes
Servings: 6
Ingredients
1 tablespoon extra-virgin olive oil
1½ pounds (680 g) ground turkey
2 tablespoons chopped fresh sage, divided
2 tablespoons chopped fresh thyme, divided
1teaspoon sea salt
½ teaspoon ground black pepper
1 (14-ounce / 397-g) can stewed tomatoes
2 cups brown rice
¼ cup pitted and sliced Kalamata olives
¼ cup chopped fresh flat-leaf parsley
3 medium zucchinis, sliced thinly
1 medium yellow onion, chopped
1 tablespoon plus 1 teaspoon balsamic vinegar
2cups low-sodium chicken stock
2 garlic cloves, minced
½ cup grated Parmesan cheese, for serving

Preheat the olive oil in a nonstick skillet over medium/high heat until shimmering. Add the ground turkey and sprinkle with 1 tablespoon of sage, 1 tablespoon of thyme, salt and ground black pepper. Sauté for about 10/12 min or until the ground turkey is lightly browned. Pour them in the slow cooker, then pour in the remaining ingredients, except for the Parmesan. Stir to mix well. Put the lid on and cook on medium/high for 3 hours or until the rice and vegetables are tender. Pour them in a large serving bowl, then spread with Parmesan cheese before serving.

Nutrition facts (per serving)
calories: 500 | fat: 17.4g | protein: 32.4g | carbs: 56.5g | fiber: 4.7g | sodium: 758mg

➤Papaya, Jicama, and Peas Rice Bowl

Preparation time: 20 minutes
Cooking time: 45 minutes | **Servings:** 4
Ingredients
Sauce:
Juice of ¼ lemon
2 teaspoons chopped fresh basil
1 tablespoon raw honey
1 tablespoon extra-virgin olive oil
Sea salt, to taste
Rice:
1½ cups wild rice
1 papaya, peeled, seeded, and diced
1 jicama, peeled and shredded
1 cup snow peas, julienned
2 cups shredded cabbage
1 scallion, white and green parts, chopped

Combine well the ingredients for the sauce in a bowl. Stir to mix well. Set aside until ready to use. Pour the wild rice in a saucepan, then pour in enough water to cover. Bring to a boil. Low the heat, then simmer for 45 minutes or until the wild rice is soft and plump. Drain and transfer to a medium/large serving bowl. Top the

rice with papayas, jicama, peas, cabbage, and scallion. Pour the sauce over and stir to mix well before serving.

Nutrition facts (per serving)
calories: 446 | fat: 8.9g | protein: 13.1g | carbs: 85.8g | fiber: 16.0g | sodium: 70mg

➤Wild Rice, Celery, and Cauliflower Pilaf

Preparation time: 10 minutes
Cooking time: 45 minutes | **Servings:** 4
Ingredients
1 tbsp. olive oil
2 cups low-sodium chicken broth
1 cup wild rice
2 stalks celery, chopped
1 sweet onion, chopped
1 teaspoon minced garlic
2 carrots, peeled, halved lengthwise, and sliced
½ cauliflower head, cut into small florets
1 teaspoon chopped fresh thyme
Sea salt, to taste

Preheat the oven to 390°F (200°C). Line a baking sheet with parchment paper and grease with olive oil.
Put the wild rice in a saucepan, then pour in the chicken broth. Bring to a boil. Low the heat and simmer for 30 minutes or until the rice is plump. Meanwhile, heat the remaining olive oil in an oven-proof skillet over medium-high heat until shimmering. Add in the onion, celery, and garlic to the skillet and sauté for 3 minutes or until the onion is translucent. Add the carrots and cauliflower to the skillet and sauté for 5/7 min. Pour the cooked rice in the skillet with the vegetables. Sprinkle with thyme and salt. Set the skillet in the preheated oven and bake for 15 min. Serve immediately.

Nutrition facts (per serving)
calories: 215 | fat: 3.9g | protein: 8.2g | carbs: 37.9g | fiber: 5.0g | sodium: 122mg

➤Walnut and Ricotta Spaghetti

Preparation time: 15 minutes
Cooking time: 10 minutes | **Servings:** 6
Ingredients
1 pound (454 g) cooked whole-wheat spaghetti
2 tablespoons extra-virgin olive oil
4 cloves garlic, minced
¾ cup walnuts, toasted and finely chopped
2 tablespoons ricotta cheese
¼ cup flat-leaf parsley, chopped
½ cup grated Parmesan cheese
Sea salt and freshly ground pepper
Reserve a cup of spaghetti water while cooking the spaghetti.

Heat the olive oil in a nonstick skillet over medium-low heat or until shimmering. Add the garlic and sauté for a minute or until fragrant. Pour the spaghetti water into the skillet and cook for 8 more minutes. Turn off the heat and combine the walnuts and ricotta cheese. Put the cooked spaghetti on a large serving plate, then pour the walnut sauce over. Spread with parsley and Parmesan, then sprinkle with salt and ground pepper. Toss to serve.

Nutrition facts (per serving)
calories: 264 | fat: 16.8g | protein: 8.6g | carbs: 22.8g | fiber: 4.0g | sodium: 336mg

›Butternut Squash, Spinach, and Cheese Lasagna

Preparation time: 30 minutes
Cooking time: 3 hours 45 minutes
Servings: 4 to 6
Ingredients
2 tablespoons extra-virgin olive oil, divided
1 butternut squash, halved lengthwise and deseeded
½ teaspoon sage
½ teaspoon sea salt
¼ teaspoon ground black pepper
¼ cup grated Parmesan cheese
2 cups ricotta cheese
½ cup unsweetened almond milk
5 layers whole-wheat lasagna noodles (about 12 ounces / 340 g in total)
4 ounces (113 g) fresh spinach leaves, divided
½ cup shredded part skim Mozzarella, for garnish

Preheat the oven to 390°F (200°C). Line a baking sheet with parchment paper. Brush 1 tbsp of oil on the cut side of the butternut squash, then place the squash on the baking sheet. Bake in the preheated oven for 43-45 minutes or until the squash is tender. Allow to cool until you can handle it, then scoop the flesh out and put the flesh in a food processor to purée.
Combine the puréed butternut squash flesh with sage, salt, and ground black pepper in a large bowl. Stir to mix well. Combine the cheeses and milk in a separate bowl, then sprinkle with salt and pepper, to taste. Grease the slow cooker with 1 tablespoon of olive oil, then add a layer of lasagna noodles to coat the bottom of the slow cooker. Spread half of the squash mixture on top of the noodles, then top the squash mixture with another layer of lasagna noodles. Spread half of the spinach over the noodles, then top the spinach with half of cheese mixture. Repeat with remaining 3 layers of lasagna noodles, squash mixture, spinach, and cheese mixture. Top the cheese mixture with Mozzarella, then put the lid on and cook on low for 3 hours or until the lasagna noodles are al dente. Serve immediately.

Nutrition facts (per serving)
calories: 657 | fat: 37.1g | protein: 30.9g | carbs: 57.2g | fiber: 8.3g | sodium: 918mg

›Minestrone Chickpeas and Macaroni Casserole

Preparation time: 20 minutes
Cooking time: 7 hours 20 minutes | **Servings:** 5
Ingredients
1 (15-ounce / 425-g) can chickpeas
1 (6-ounce / 170-g) can no-salt-added tomato paste

3 medium carrots, sliced
1 (28-ounce / 794-g) can diced tomatoes
3 cloves garlic
1 cup low-sodium vegetable soup
1 medium yellow onion, chopped
½ teaspoon dried rosemary
2 teaspoons maple syrup
1 teaspoon dried oregano
½ teaspoon sea salt
½ pound (227-g) fresh green beans
1 cup macaroni pasta
¼ teaspoon ground black pepper
2 ounces (57 g) Parmesan cheese, grated

Except for the green beans, pasta, and Parmesan cheese, combine all the listed ingredients in the slow cooker and stir to mix well. Put the slow cooker lid on and cook on low for about 8 hours. Fold in the pasta and green beans. Put the lid on and cook on medium/high for 25 min. Pour them in a large serving bowl and spread with Parmesan cheese before serving.

Nutrition facts (per serving)
calories: 350 | fat: 6.7g | protein: 16.5g | carbs: 59.9g | fiber: 12.9g | sodium: 937mg

›Rich Cauliflower Alfredo

Preparation time: 35 minutes
Cooking time: 30 minutes | **Servings:** 4
Ingredients
Cauliflower Alfredo Sauce:
1 tablespoon avocado oil
½ yellow onion, diced
2 cups cauliflower florets
2 garlic cloves, minced
1½ teaspoons miso
1 teaspoon Dijon mustard
Pinch of ground nutmeg
½ cup unsweetened almond milk
1½ tablespoons fresh lemon juice
2 tablespoons nutritional yeast
Sea salt and ground black pepper
Fettuccine:
1 tablespoon avocado oil
½ yellow onion, diced
1 cup broccoli florets
1 zucchini, halved lengthwise and cut into ¼-inch-thick half-moons
Sea salt and ground black pepper
½ cup sun-dried tomatoes, drained if packed in oil
8 ounces (227 g) cooked whole-wheat fettuccine ½ cup fresh basil, cut into ribbons
Make the Sauce
Heat the avocado oil in a nonstick skillet over medium-high heat until shimmering. Add half of the onion to the skillet and sauté for 5 minutes or until translucent. Add the cauliflower and garlic to the skillet. Reduce the heat to low/medium and cook for 8 minutes or until the cauliflower is tender. Pour them in a food processor, add the remaining ingredients for the sauce and pulse to combine well. Set aside.
Make the Fettuccine
Heat the avocado oil in a nonstick skillet over me-

dium-high heat. Add the remaining half of onion and sauté for 5 minutes or until translucent. Add the broccoli and zucchini. Sprinkle with salt and ground black pepper, then sauté for 5 minutes or until tender. Add the sun-dried tomatoes, reserved sauce, and fettuccine. Sauté for 3 minutes or until well-coated and heated through. Serve the fettuccine on a large plate and spread with basil before serving.

Nutrition facts (per serving)
calories: 288 | fat: 15.9g | protein: 10.1g | carbs: 32.5g | fiber: 8.1g | sodium: 185mg

---

‣Butternut Squash and Zucchini with Penne

Preparation time: 15 minutes
Cooking time: 30 minutes | **Servings:** 6
Ingredients
1 large zucchini, diced
1 large butternut squash, peeled and diced
1 large yellow onion, chopped
2 tablespoons extra-virgin olive oil
1 teaspoon paprika
½ teaspoon garlic powder
½ teaspoon sea salt
½ teaspoon freshly ground black pepper
1 pound (454 g) whole-grain penne
½ cup dry white wine
2 tablespoons grated Parmesan cheese

Preheat the oven to 390/400°F (205°C). Line a baking sheet with aluminum foil. Combine the zucchini, butternut squash, and onion in a large bowl. Drizzle with olive oil and sprinkle with paprika, garlic powder, salt, and ground black pepper. Toss to coat well. Spread the vegetables in the single layer on the baking sheet, then roast in the preheated oven for 23-25 minutes or until the vegetables are tender. Meanwhile, bring a pot of water to a boil, then add the penne and cook for 14 minutes or until al dente. Drain the penne through a colander. Transfer ½ cup of roasted vegetables in a food processor, then pour in the dry white wine. Pulse until smooth. Pour the puréed vegetables in a nonstick skillet and cook with penne over medium-high heat for a few minutes to heat through. Transfer the penne with the purée on a large serving plate, then spread the remaining roasted vegetables and Parmesan on top before serving.

Nutrition facts (per serving)
calories: 340 | fat: 6.2g | protein: 8.0g | carbs: 66.8g | fiber: 9.1g | sodium: 297mg

---

‣Small Pasta and Beans Pot

Preparation time: 20 minutes
Cooking time: 15 minutes
Servings: 2 to 4
Ingredients
1 (14.5-ounce / 411-g) can diced tomatoes
1 (15-ounce / 425-g) can cannellini beans
2 tablespoons no-salt-added tomato paste
1 red or yellow bell pepper, chopped
1 yellow onion, chopped

1 tablespoon Italian seasoning mix
1 pound (454 g) small whole wheat pasta
3 garlic cloves, minced
¼ teaspoon crushed red pepper flakes, optional
1 tablespoon extra-virgin olive oil
5 cups water
1 bunch kale, stemmed and chopped
½ cup pitted Kalamata olives, chopped
1 cup sliced basil

Except for the kale, olives, and basil, combine all the ingredients in a pot. Stir to mix well. Bring to a boil over high heat. Stir constantly. Low the heat to medium/high and add the kale. Cook for 10 minutes or until the pasta is al dente. Stir constantly. Transfer all of them on a large plate and serve with olives and basil on top.

Nutrition facts (per serving)
calories: 360 | fat: 8.6g | protein: 18.2g | carbs: 64.5g | fiber: 10.1g | sodium: 454mg

---

‣Swoodles with Almond Butter Sauce
Preparation time: 20 minutes
Cooking time: 20 minutes | **Servings:** 4
Ingredients
Sauce:
1 garlic clove
1-inch piece fresh ginger, peeled and sliced
¼ cup chopped yellow onion
¾ cup almond butter
1 tablespoon tamari
1 tablespoon raw honey
1 teaspoon paprika
1 tablespoon fresh lemon juice
⅛ teaspoon ground red pepper
Sea salt and ground black pepper
¼ cup water
Swoodles:
1 large, sweet potato, spiralized
1 tablespoons coconut oil, melted Sea salt and ground black pepper, to taste
For Serving:
½ cup fresh parsley, chopped
½ cup thinly sliced scallions
Make the Sauce
Put the garlic, ginger, and onion in a food processor, then pulse to combine well. Add the almond butter, tamari, honey, paprika, lemon juice, ground red pepper, salt, and black pepper to the food processor. Pulse to combine well. Pour in the water during the pulsing until the mixture is thick and smooth.
Make the Swoodles:
Preheat the oven to 420/425°F (220°C). Line a baking sheet with parchment paper. Put the spiralized sweet potato in a bowl, then drizzle with olive oil. Toss to coat well. Transfer them on the baking sheet. Sprinkle with salt and pepper. Bake in the preheated oven for 20-21 minutes or until lightly browned and al dente. Check the doneness during the baking and remove any well-cooked swoodles. Transfer the swoodles on a large plate and spread with sauce, parsley, and scallions. Toss to serve.
Nutrition facts (per serving)
calories: 441 | fat: 33.6g | protein: 12.0g | carbs: 29.6g | fiber: 7.8g | sodium: 479mg

MONDAY

BREAKFAST
• **Easy Bircher:** ⅓ cup rolled oats, 1 tbs chia seeds, 1 sliced banana, ½ cup berries, 200ml milk & 2 tbs Greekstyle plain yoghurt

LUNCH
• **Cheese & hoummos wrap:** 1 tbs hommous, ½ avocado, 1 sliced tomato, ½ cup baby spinach & 20g feta in a wholegrain wrap

DINNER
Pan Fried Salmon

TUESDAY

BREAKFAST
• **Brekkie smoothie:** 200ml milk, 2 tbs Greek style plain yoghurt, 2 tbs rolled oats, ½ cup berries & 1 banana

LUNCH
• **Tuna & feta salad:** 1 cup baby spinach, 10 cherry tomatoes, ½ cucumber, ⅛ avocado, 20g feta, 95g can tuna* & balsamic dressing

DINNER
Chicken Breast Soup

WEDNESDAY

BREAKFAST
• **Almond butter toast:** 2 slices soy-linseed toast topped with 2 tbs natural almond butter & 1 sliced banana, 1 regular skim latte

LUNCH
• **Leftover Grilled salmon with 3 bean salad**

DINNER
• **Balsamic mushroom beef meatloaf**

THURSDAY

BREAKFAST
• **Easy Bircher(see Monday)**

LUNCH
• **Chicken & avo wrap:** ½ avocado, ½ cup spinach leaves, 1 sliced tomato & 60g grilled chicken* in a wholegrain wrap.

DINNER
•**Beef with Peppers**

MEAL PLAN
4 WEEKS

→ HOW TO USE THE MEAL PLAN AND LOSE WEIGHT

DAILY AVERAGE INTAKE

6000 KJ

FRIDAY

BREAKFAST
• **Almond butter toast:**(see Wednesday) 1 regular skim latte

LUNCH
•Bacon Wrapped Asparagus

DINNER
• **Easy paella**

SATURDAY

BREAKFAST
• **Eggs on toast:** 2 poached eggs, 2 slices soy-linseed toast, ¼ avocado & 1 cup baby spinach sautéed with 1 tsp olive oil

LUNCH
Low Carb Black Beans Chili Chicken

DINNER
Broccoli and Beef Roast

SUNDAY

BREAKFAST
• **Banana pancakes:** Mash 1 banana with 1 egg & 2 tbs rolled oats. Cook small pancakes & top with ½ cup Greek-style plain yoghurt, ¾ cup berries & a drizzle of maple syrup

LUNCH
• **Tuna & feta salad:** (see Tuesday)

DINNER
Simple Pesto Beef Chuck Roast

➡ **Drink 2 liters of water a day**

➡ **boost vegetables: whether it's broccolini, eggplant or cherry tomatoes, add something new to your shopping cart**

➡ **it is recommended to replace white rice with brown rice or quinoa for a protein and fiber intake that eliminates hunger.**

SHOPPING LIST

Fruit
- ■ APPLES
- ■ PEARS
- ■ BANANAS
- ■ ORANGES
- ■ BERRIES
- ■ GRAPES
- ■ MELON
- ■ LEMON
- ■ _____
- ■ _____

Dairy
- ■ MILK
- ■ BUTTER
- ■ EGGS
- ■ SOUR CREAM
- ■ CREAMER
- ■ CREAM CHEESE
- ■ YOGURT
- ■ _____
- ■ _____

Spices
- ■ SALT
- ■ PEPPER
- ■ TACO SEASONING
- ■ _____
- ■ _____
- ■ _____

Frozen food
- ■ MEALS
- ■ PIZZA
- ■ POTATOS
- ■ VEGETABLES
- ■ WAFFLES
- ■ ICE CREAM
- ■ MELON
- ■ LEMON
- ■ _____
- ■ _____
- ■ _____

Bread
- ■ SANDWICH
- ■ FRESH LOAF
- ■ BAGELS
- ■ RAZORS
- ■ MUFFINS
- ■ PITAS
- ■ TORTILLAS
- ■ CROUTONS
- ■ BUNS
- ■ _____
- ■ _____

Pasta/Rice
- ■ SPAGHETTI
- ■ MACARONI
- ■ RICE
- ■ _____
- ■ _____
- ■ _____
- ■ _____
- ■ _____
- ■ _____

Vegetables
- ■ SALAD GREENS
- ■ BROCCOLI
- ■ CARROTS
- ■ CUCUMBERS
- ■ GARLIC
- ■ GRAPES
- ■ LATTUCE
- ■ TOMATOS
- ■ MUSHROOMS
- ■ ONIONS
- ■ _____
- ■ _____
- ■ _____

Meat/Fish
- ■ BEEF
- ■ POULTRY
- ■ PORK
- ■ FISH
- ■ BACON
- ■ SAUSAGE
- ■ _____
- ■ _____
- ■ _____
- ■ _____

SHOPPING LIST

Baking

- ☐ SUGAR
- ☐ FLOUR
- ☐ PANCAKE MIX
- ☐ _____
- ☐ _____
- ☐ _____

and also...

- ☐ _____
- ☐ _____
- ☐ _____
- ☐ _____
- ☐ _____

Cereal

- ☐ HOT CEREAL
- ☐ COLD CEREAL
- ☐ _____
- ☐ _____
- ☐ _____

Beverages

- ☐ WATER
- ☐ JUICE
- ☐ SODA
- ☐ COFFEE
- ☐ TEA
- ☐ WINE
- ☐ _____
- ☐ _____
- ☐ _____
- ☐ _____
- ☐ _____
- ☐ _____
- ☐ _____

Sauces-oil

- ☐ _____
- ☐ OIL
- ☐ VINEGAR
- ☐ SALAD DRESSING
- ☐ _____
- ☐ _____
- ☐ _____

Index Recipes

D

Thank you for choosing my book!
Did you enjoy reading it?
I would love to know, if you can give
me a minute of your time write
a review about it.
Leave your feeback on amazon and
thank you very much for your
kindness.

Alicia Travis

Made in the USA
Monee, IL
25 January 2022

89826376R00155